THE OXFORD HANDBOOK OF

PHILOSOPHY OF SOCIAL SCIENCE

THE OXFORD HANDBOOK OF

PHILOSOPHY OF SOCIAL SCIENCE

Edited by

HAROLD KINCAID

OXFORD
UNIVERSITY PRESS

OXFORD
UNIVERSITY PRESS

Oxford University Press is a department of the University of Oxford.
It furthers the University's objective of excellence in research, scholarship,
and education by publishing worldwide.

Oxford   New York
Auckland   Cape Town   Dar es Salaam   Hong Kong   Karachi
Kuala Lumpur   Madrid   Melbourne   Mexico City   Nairobi
New Delhi   Shanghai   Taipei   Toronto

With offices in
Argentina   Austria   Brazil   Chile   Czech Republic   France   Greece
Guatemala   Hungary   Italy   Japan   Poland   Portugal   Singapore
South Korea   Switzerland   Thailand   Turkey   Ukraine   Vietnam

Copyright © 2012 by Oxford University Press

Published in the United States of America by
Oxford University Press
198 Madison Avenue, New York, NY 10016

www.oup.com

Oxford is a registered trade mark of Oxford University Press in the UK and certain other countries.

Library of Congress Cataloging-in-Publication Data
The Oxford handbook of philosophy of social science /edited by Harold Kincaid.
p.   cm.—(Oxford handbooks)
Includes bibliographical references.
ISBN 978-0-19-539275-3 (alk. paper)
1. Social sciences—Philosophy. 2. Social sciences—Research.
I. Kincaid, Harold, 1952-II. Title: Philosophy of social science.
H61.O95   2012
300.1—dc23   2011036789

Dedicated to the intercontinental sundowners support group:
Nelleke Bak
Robin Lessel
Don Ross

TABLE OF CONTENTS

Part II: Evidence

Part III: Norms, Culture, and the Social-Psychological

PREFACE

....

This volume results from a collaborative effort in several respects. All but two of the chapters were presented in draft form at a conference at the University of Alabama at Birmingham in 2010. The contributors made for a lively and thoughtful audience, and I am sure their comments at the conference substantially improved the chapters. After written drafts were submitted, each contributor commented on one or two other contributions in some detail. In addition, Steve Morgan, Christopher Winship, Don Ross, Gary Goertz, and Aviezer Tucker all provided useful comments on the initial proposal that led to significant improvements.

This topics represented in this handbook are shaped by several things. This volume is preceded by another: H. Kincaid and D. Ross, eds., *Oxford Handbook of the Philosophy of Economics* (Oxford: Oxford University Press, 2009). As a result, little discussion of economics has been included in this volume. The aim of the volume was to promote philosophy of science in the naturalist vein that engaged with on-going current controversies in social research (as explained and defended in the introduction), and the chapters included strongly reflect that goal.

I want to thank UAB's Center for Ethics and Values in the Sciences for support in organizing the conference for the volume, and Peter Ohlin at Oxford University Press for encouragement and advice.

CONTRIBUTORS

MARSHALL ABRAMS is assistant professor in the Department of Philosophy at the University of Alabama at Birmingham. He received his PhD from the University of Chicago and was an NSF-sponsored postdoctoral fellow at Duke University's Center for Philosophy of Biology. His philosophical research focuses on the nature and role of probability and causation in evolutionary biology and the social sciences, and on interactions between biological evolution and social processes with emphasis on modeling of cognitive coherence relations in cultural change. He is also engaged in purely scientific research on the evolution of obesity and diabetes, and is an associate editor at the journal *Frontiers in Evolutionary and Population Genetics*.

ANNA ALEXANDROVA is a philosopher of social science at Cambridge University. She has taught at University of Missouri, St. Louis, and received her PhD from the University of California, San Diego. She has written on the use of formal models for explanation and policy making in economics and history, and on the measurement of happiness in psychology. Her current work examines well-being as an object of science and a social indicator.

DAVID BYRNE is professor of sociology and social policy in the School of Applied Social Sciences, Durham University. He has worked at the interface between the academy and the application of social science throughout his career, including a period as research director of a community development project. Publications include *Beyond the Inner City* (Open University Press, 1989), *Complexity Theory and the Social Sciences* (Routledge, 1998), *Social Exclusion* (Open University Press, 2009), *Understanding the Urban* (Palgrave-Macmillan, 2001), *Interpreting Quantitative Data* (Sage, 2002), and *Applying Social Science* (Policy Press, 2011).

NANCY CARTWRIGHT is professor of philosophy at the Department of Philosophy, Logic and Scientific Method at the London School of Economics and Political Science and at the University of California, San Diego. She was president of the Philosophy of Science Association in 2010 and president of the American Philosophical Association (Pacific Division) in 2008. Her research interests include philosophy and history of science (especially physics and economics), causal inference, and objectivity and evidence, especially on evidence-based policy. Her publications include *How the Laws of Physics Lie* (Oxford University Press, 1983), *Nature's Capacities and Their Measurement* (Oxford University Press, 1989), *Otto Neurath: Philosophy between Science and Politics* (Cambridge University Press, 1995, with Jordi Cat, Lola Fleck, and Thomas E. Uebe), *The Dappled World: A Study of the*

Boundaries of Science (Cambridge University Press, 1999), and *Hunting Causes and Using Them* (Cambridge University Press, 2007).

FRED CHERNOFF is Harvey Picker Professor of International Relations and chair of the Department of Political Science at Colgate University. He holds a PhD in philosophy from Johns Hopkins University and a PhD in political science from Yale University. He has held research posts at the International Institute for Strategic Studies, the Rand Corporation, and the Norwegian Institute of International Affairs. He is author of *After Bipolarity* (University of Michigan Press, 1995), *The Power of International Theory* (Routledge, 2005) and *Theory and Metatheory in International Relations* (Palgrave-Macmillan, 2007) and has contributed to many journals of international relations and philosophy, including *International Studies Quarterly, Journal of Conflict Resolution, Millennium, International Theory, European Journal of International Relations, Philosophical Quarterly, Mind*, and *Analysis*.

ANDREW GELMAN is a professor of statistics and political science and director of the Applied Statistics Center at Columbia University. His books include *Bayesian Data Analysis* (Chapman and Hall, 2003, with John Carlin, Hal Stern, and Don Rubin), *Teaching Statistics: A Bag of Tricks* (Oxford University Press, 2002, with Deb Nolan,), *Data Analysis Using Regression and Multilevel/Hierarchical Models* (Cambridge University Press, 2006, with Jennifer Hill), and, most recently, *Red State, Blue State, Rich State, Poor State: Why Americans Vote the Way They Do* (Princeton University Press, 2009, with David Park, Boris Shor, Joe Bafumi, and Jeronimo Cortina). Andrew has done research on a wide range of topics, including why it is rational to vote, why campaign polls are so variable when elections are so predictable, why redistricting is good for democracy, reversals of death sentences, police stops in New York City, the statistical challenges of estimating small effects, the probability that your vote will be decisive, seats and votes in Congress, and social network structure.

GARY GOERTZ is professor of political science at the University of Arizona. He is the author or editor of nine books and over forty articles on issues of methodology, international institutions, and conflict studies, including *Necessary Conditions: Theory, Methodology, and Applications* (Rowman & Littlefield, 2003), *Social Science Concepts: A User's Guide* (Princeton University Press, 2006), *Explaining War and Peace: Case Studies and Necessary Condition Counterfactuals* (Routledge, 2007), *Politics, Gender, and Concepts: Theory and Methodology* (Cambridge University Press, 2008), and *A Tale of Two Cultures: Contrasting Qualitative and Quantitative Paradigms* (Princeton University Press, 2012).

FRANCESCO GUALA is associate professor of economics and philosophy at the University of Milan, Italy. His research focuses on methodological and ontological problems arising from the social sciences. He is the author of *The Methodology of Experimental Economics* (Cambridge University Press, 2005) and coeditor, with Daniel Steel, of *The Philosophy of Social Science Reader* (Routledge, 2011).

DANIEL M. HAUSMAN is the Herbert A. Simon and Hilldale Professor of Philosophy at the University of Wisconsin-Madison. His research has centered on epistemological, metaphysical, and ethical issues lying at the boundaries between economics and philosophy. His books include *The Inexact and Separate Science of Economics* (Cambridge University Press, 1992) and *Economic Analysis, Moral Philosophy, and Public Policy* (Cambridge University Press, 2006, with Michael McPherson). His most recent book, *Preferences, Value, and Choice, and Welfare*, is due out shortly from Cambridge University Press.

DAVID HENDERSON is the Robert R. Chambers Professor of Philosophy at the University of Nebraska, Lincoln. He has written on interpretation and explanation in the social sciences, with special concern for the place for finding rationality in those matters. He also writes in epistemology, where he is interested in the epistemological implications of recent work in cognitive science.

ALLAN HORWITZ is Board of Governors Professor of Sociology at Rutgers University. His most recent books are *The Loss of Sadness: How Psychiatry Transformed Normal Sorrow into Depressive Disorder* (Oxford University Press, 2007, with Jerome Wakefield), *Diagnosis, Therapy, and Evidence: Conundrums in Modern American Medicine* (Rutgers University Press, 2010, with Gerald Grob), and *All We Have to Fear: Anxiety and the Boundaries of Normality* (Oxford University Press, 2012, with Jerome Wakefield).

DANIEL KELLY is an assistant professor in the philosophy department at Purdue University. His research interests are at the intersection of the philosophy of mind, cognitive science, and moral theory. He is the author of *Yuck! The Nature and Moral Significance of Disgust* (The MIT Press, 2011), and has published papers on moral judgment, social norms, racial cognition, and cross-cultural diversity.

HAROLD KINCAID is professor in the School of Economics at the University of Cape Town, South Africa. He is the author of *Philosophical Foundations of the Social Sciences* (Cambridge University Press, 1996) and *Individualism and the Unity of Science* (Rowman & Littlefield, 2007), and coeditor of *What Is Addiction?* (The MIT Press, 2009), *The Oxford Handbook of Philosophy of Economics* (Oxford University Press, 2009), and three other volumes. He has published widely in the philosophy of the social sciences and philosophy of economics. His current research interests include causal modeling and empirical studies of addiction and time and risk attitudes in the developing world.

KEN KOLLMAN is Frederick G. L. Huetwell Professor and Professor of Political Science at the University of Michigan, Ann Arbor. His research and teaching focus on political parties, elections, lobbying, federal systems, formal modeling, and complexity theory. In addition to numerous articles, he has written *The Formation of National Party Systems: Federalism and Party Competition in Canada, Great Britain, India, and the United States* (Princeton University Press, 2004, with Pradeep Chhibber), *Outside Lobbying: Public Opinion and Interest Group Strategies* (Princeton University Press, 1998), and *The American Political System* (Norton, 2011).

TIM LEWENS is reader in philosophy of the sciences at the University of Cambridge, where he is also a fellow of Clare College. His previous publications include *Darwin*

(Routledge, 2007) and *Organisms and Artifacts: Design in Nature and Elsewhere* (The MIT Press, 2004).

RON MALLON is an associate professor of philosophy and director of the Philosophy-Neuroscience-Psychology Program at Washington University in St. Louis. His research is in social philosophy, philosophy of cognitive psychology, and moral psychology. He has authored or coauthored papers in *Cognition, Ethics, Journal of Political Philosophy, Midwest Studies in Philosophy, Mind and Language, Noûs, Philosophy and Phenomenological Research, Philosophy of Science, Social Neuroscience, Social Philosophy*, and *Social Theory and Practice*.

AMY G. MAZUR is professor of political science at Washington State University. She is coeditor of *Political Research Quarterly*. Her recent publications include *Politics, Gender and Concepts* (edited with Gary Goertz, Cambridge University Press, 2008) and *The Politics of State Feminism: Innovation in Comparative Research* (Temple University Press, 2010, with Dorothy McBride).

STEPHEN L. MORGAN is professor of sociology and the director of the Center for the Study of Inequality at Cornell University. He has a PhD in sociology from Harvard University and an MPhil in comparative social research from Oxford University. He has published two books: *On the Edge of Commitment: Educational Attainment and Race in the United States* (Stanford University Press, 2005) and, coauthored with Christopher Winship, *Counterfactuals and Causal Inference: Methods and Principles for Social Research* (Cambridge University Press, 2007).

ROBERT NORTHCOTT is currently a lecturer in philosophy at Birkbeck College in London. Before that, he was assistant professor at the University of Missouri-St. Louis. He has published widely on, among other things, causation, causal explanation, and degree of causation, including on how these notions are conceptualized and used in social science.

JULIAN REISS is associate professor in the philosophy faculty of Erasmus University Rotterdam, and specializes in philosophy of economics and general philosophy of science. Specific research interests are causal inference, measurement, models and thought experiments, and the place of values in science. Publications include *Error in Economics: Towards a More Evidence-Based Methodology* (Routledge, 2008), *Causality Between Metaphysics and Methodology* and *Philosophy of Economics* (both forthcoming with Routledge), and thirty-five papers in journals such as *Philosophy of Science, Synthese, Philosophy of the Social Sciences*, and *Theoria*.

MARK RISJORD is a professor of philosophy at Emory University. He received his PhD in philosophy from the University of North Carolina, Chapel Hill in 1990. His research interests include the epistemological foundations of the social sciences, the role of values in scientific research, and the philosophy of the health sciences.

DON ROSS is professor of economics and dean of commerce at the University of Cape Town, and a research fellow in the Center for Economic Analysis of Risk at Georgia State University. His main areas of research include the experimental economics of nonstandard consumption patterns, the philosophical foundations of economics and game theory, naturalistic philosophy of science, and trade and industry policy in Africa. He is the author of numerous articles and books, including *Economic Theory and Cognitive Science: Microexplanation* (The MIT Press, 2005) and *Every Thing Must Go: Metaphysics Naturalized* (Oxford University Press, 2007, with James Ladyman). He is coeditor (with Harold Kincaid) of *The Oxford Handbook of Philosophy of Economics* (Oxford University Press, 2009).

COSMA ROHILLA SHALIZI is an assistant professor of statistics at Carnegie Mellon University and an external professor at the Santa Fe Institute. He received his PhD in theoretical physics from the University of Wisconsin-Madison in 2001. His research focuses on time series prediction, network analysis, and inference in complex systems.

AVIEZER TUCKER is the author of *Our Knowledge of the Past: A Philosophy of Historiography* (Cambridge University Press, 2004) and the editor of *The Blackwell Companion to the Philosophy of History and Historiography* (Wiley-Blackwell, 2009). His research concentrates on the philosophy of the historical sciences, epistemology, and political philosophy. He lives in Austin, Texas. Previously he lived in New York, Prague, Canberra, and a few other places.

EMMA UPRICHARD is a senior lecturer in the Department of Sociology, Goldsmiths, University of London. She is particularly interested in the methodological challenge of applying complexity theory to the study of change and continuity in the social world. She has substantive research interests in methods and methodology, critical realism, cities, time and temporality, children and childhood, and food.

DAVID WALDNER is associate professor of politics at the University of Virginia, where he teaches courses on the political economy of developing nations and methodology. He is the author of *State Building and Late Development* (Cornell University Press, 1999) and is currently writing two books, *Democracy & Dictatorship in the Post-Colonial World* and *Causation, Explanation, and the Study of Politics*.

CHRISTOPHER WINSHIP is the Diker-Tishman Professor of Sociology at Harvard University and a member of the Harvard Kennedy School of Government's senior faculty. Prior to coming to Harvard in 1992, he was a professor in sociology, statistics, and (by courtesy) economics. At Harvard he is a member of the criminal justice program, inequality program, and the Hauser Center for the Study of Nonprofits. His research interests include models of selection bias, causality, youth violence, pragmatism, and the implications of the cognitive revolution for sociology. With Stephen Morgan, he is author of *Counterfactuals and Causal Inference* (Cambridge, 2007).

JAMES WOODWARD is distinguished professor in the Department of History and Philosophy of Science at the University of Pittsburgh. He was formerly the J. O. and Juliette Koepfli Professor of the Humanities at the California Institute of Technology. His book *Making Things Happen: A Theory of Causal Explanation* (Oxford

University Press, 2003) won the Lakatos award in 2005. He is president of the Philosophy of Science Association in 2010–12.

PETRI YLIKOSKI is currently an academy research fellow at the University of Helsinki, Finland. His research interests include theory of explanation, science studies, philosophy of the social sciences, and philosophy of biology. He is especially interested in the interfaces between the social and the biological sciences and in the idea of mechanism-based understanding in the social sciences.

THE OXFORD HANDBOOK OF

PHILOSOPHY OF SOCIAL SCIENCE

CHAPTER 1

INTRODUCTION: DOING PHILOSOPHY OF SOCIAL SCIENCE

HAROLD KINCAID

THIS volume is shaped by important developments in both the social sciences and the philosophy of the social sciences over the last several decades. In this chapter I outline these changes and argue that they have indeed been significant advances in our thinking about the social world. Rather than providing linear summaries of twenty-plus chapters, I delineate the frameworks and issues that motivate the kind of philosophy of social science and social science that is represented in this volume. Both philosophy of social science and social science itself are intermixed in the following chapters. That is because the volume is built around a guiding naturalism that denies that there is something special about the social world that makes it unamenable to scientific investigation, and also denies that there is something special about philosophy that makes it independent or prior to the sciences in general and the social sciences in particular. In the process of outlining recent developments the chapters of the handbook are related and motivated, and open unresolved issues are discussed.

1.1. DEVELOPMENTS IN PHILOSOPHY OF SCIENCE

I start with developments in the philosophy of science. Though the monikers are not entirely historically accurate, I want to contrast previous positivist philosophy of science with postpositivist views which I believe provide a much more useful framework for thinking about science and social science. Some of the key tenets of positivist philosophy of science are as follows.[1]

Theories are the central content of science. A mature science ideally produces one clearly identifiable theory that explains all the phenomena in its domain. In practice, a science may produce different theories for different subdomains, but the overarching scientific goal is to unify those theories by subsuming them under one encompassing account. Theories are composed of universal laws relating and ascribing properties to natural kinds and are best understood when they are described as formalized systems. Philosophy of science can aid in producing such formalizations by the application of formal logic.

The fundamental concepts of science should have clear definitions in terms of necessary and sufficient conditions. General philosophy of science is in large part about clarifying general scientific concepts, especially explanation and confirmation. The goal is to produce a set of necessary and sufficient conditions for application of these concepts. These definitions are largely tested against linguistic intuitions about what we would and would not count as cases of explanation and confirmation.

Explanation and confirmation have a logic—they conform to universal general principles that apply to all domains and do not rest on contingent empirical knowledge. A central goal of philosophy of science is to describe the logic of science. Explanation involves (in some sense still to be clarified) deductions from laws of the phenomena to be explained. Whether a science is well supported by evidence can be determined by asking whether the theory bears the right logical relationship to the data cited in support of it.

Independence of philosophy from science: Identifying the logic of inference and explanation and the proper definition of concepts are philosophical activities. Scientists certainly can act as philosophers, but the philosophy and the science are different enterprises with different standards. The collorary is that philosophy of science is largely done after the science is finished.

Social institutions are irrelevant. The social organization of science may be an interesting topic for sociologists, but it has little direct bearing on philosophy of science's tasks.

The criteria for explanation and confirmation allow us to properly demarcate scientific theories from pseudoscientific accounts. Pseudoscientific accounts tend to sacrifice due attention to confirmation in favor of apparent explanation, and in so doing fail to be genuinely explanatory.

It is a serious open question to what extent any of the social sciences are real sciences. This question is best explored by comparing their logical structures with those characteristic of physics and, to a lesser extent chemistry, geology, and biology. All the key characteristics described above should characterize any scientific social science and its related philosophy of science.

These positivist ideas have been replaced with a considerably more subtle and empirically motivated view of the philosophy of science in the following ways.

Theories as central: "The" theory in a given discipline is typically not a single determinate set of propositions. What we find instead are common elements that are given different interpretations according to context. For example, genes play a central role in biological explanation, but what exactly a gene is taken to be varies considerably depending on the biological phenomena being explained (Moss 2004). Often we find *no* one uniform theory in a research domain, but rather a variety of models that overlap in various ways but that are not fully intertranslatable. Cartwright (1980) gives us the example of models of quantum damping, in which physicists maintain a toolkit of six different mathematical theories. Because these aren't strictly compatible with one another, a traditional perspective in the philosophy of science would predict that physicists should be trying to eliminate all but one. However, because each theory is better than the others for governing some contexts of experimental design and interpretation, but all are reasonable in light of physicists' consensual informal conception of the basic cause of the phenomenon, they enjoy their embarrassment of riches as a practical boon. There is much more to science than theories: experimental setup and instrument calibration skills, modeling ingenuity to facilitate statistical testing, mathematical insight, experimental and data analysis paradigms and traditions, social norms and social organization, and much else—and these other elements are important to understanding the content of theories.

Theories, laws, and formalization: Laws in *some* sense play a crucial role in scientific theories. Absent any trace of what philosophers call modal structure, it is impossible to see how scientists can be said to rationally learn from induction. However, some of our best science does not emphasize laws in the philosopher's sense as elegant, context-free, universal generalizations, but instead provides accounts of temporally and spatially restricted context-sensitive causal processes as its end product. Molecular biology is a prime example in this regard, with its emphasis on the causal mechanisms behind cell functioning that form a complex patchwork of relations that cannot be aggregated into an elegant framework. Expression in a clear language—quantitative where possible—is crucial to good science, but the ideal of a full deductive system of axioms and theorems is often unattainable and not, as far as one can see, actually sought by many scientific subcommunities that are nevertheless thriving.

Conceptual analysis: Some important scientific concepts are not definable in terms of necessary and sufficient conditions but are instead much closer to the prototypes that, according to cognitive science, form the basis for our everyday concepts of kinds of entities and processes. The concept of the gene is again a good example. There is no definition of gene in terms of its essential characteristics that covers every important scientific use of the concept. Cartwright (2007) has argued recently that the same holds even for so general and philosophical an idea as *cause*: There are different senses of *cause* with different relevant formalizations and evidence conditions. Equally important, the traditional philosophical project of testing definitions against what we find it appropriate to say is of doubtful significance. Who is the relevant reference group? The intuitive judgments of philosophers, whose grasp of science is often out of date and who are frequently captured by highly specific metaphysical presuppositions, do not and should not govern scientific usage at all (Ladyman and Ross 2007, chapter 1). Questions about the usage of scientists is certainly more relevant, but this also may not be the best guide to the content of scientific results.

The logic of confirmation and explanation: Confirmation and explanation are complex practices that do not admit of a uniform, purely logical analysis. Explanations often have a contextual component set by the background knowledge of the field in question that determines the question to be answered and the kind of answer that is appropriate. Sometimes that context may invoke laws, but often it does not, at least not in any explicit way. Confirmation likewise depends strongly on domain-specific background knowledge in ways that make a purely logical and quantitatively specifiable assessment of the degree to which specified evidence supports a hypothesis unlikely. The few general things that can be said about confirmation are sufficiently abstract that they are unhelpful on their own. The statements "a hypothesis is well supported if all sources of error have been ruled out" or "a hypothesis is well supported by the evidence if it is more consistent with the evidence than any other existing hypothesis" are hard to argue with. Yet to make any use of these standards in practice requires fleshing out how error is ruled out in the specific instance or what consistency with the evidence comes to in that case. Other all-purpose criteria such as "X is confirmed if and only if X predicts novel evidence" or "X is confirmed if and only if X is the only hypothesis that has not been falsified" are subject to well-known counter examples and difficulties of interpretation.

Holism: It is a fallacy to infer from the fact that every hypothesis is tested in conjunction with background theory that evidence only bears on theories as wholes (Glymour 1980). By embedding hypotheses in differing background theoretical and experimental setups, it is possible to attribute blame and credit to individual hypotheses. Indeed, this is how the overwhelming majority of scientists view the overwhelming majority of their own research results. Judged on the basis of considerations that scientists typically introduce into actual debates about what to regard as accepted results, the relationships between theories, applications, and tests propagated by Quine, Kuhn, and Lakatos look like philosophers' fantasies. While these three philosophers were instrumental in the transition from positivist philosophy of science, their arguments and views have been superceded: Data may be theory-laden, but theory-laden comes to many things and does not mean that every piece of data is laden with whole theories, and does not prevent the kind of triangulation and piecemeal testing of specific hypotheses characteristic of good science.

Independence of philosophy from science: Philosophy of science and science are continuous in several senses. As we saw, the traditional conceptual analysis of analytic philosophy is a nonstarter and philosophical claims are subject to broad empirical standards of science. Of course, getting clear on concepts has real value. However, it is something scientists do all the time, but in ways far more sophisticated and empirically disciplined than the traditional philosophical practice of testing proposed definitions against what we would say or against intuitions (Wilson 2007). Philosophy of science is also continuous with science in that philosophy of science is not entirely or mostly something that is done after the science is settled. Instead, philosophy of science issues arise in ongoing scientific controversies and part of the process of settling those issues. Again, philosophy of science is something that scientists themselves do, and in a sense science is something that philosophers of science do. Contemporary philosophy of biology is a paradigm case in this regard. Philosophers of science publish in biology journals and biologists publish in philosophy of biology venues. The problems tackled are as much biological as philosophical or conceptual: The questions are such things as how is genetic drift to be understood or what is the evidence for group selection.

Science and pseudoscience: Several of the insights about science already discussed suggest that judging theories to be scientific or pseudoscientific is a misplaced enterprise. Scientific theories and their evidence form complexes of claims that involve diverse relations of dependence and independence and, as a result, are not subject to uniform or generic assessment. Any general criteria of scientific adequacy that might be used to distinguish science from pseudoscience are either too abstract on their own to decide what is scientific or not, or they are contentious. This is not to deny that astrology, so-called creation science, and explicitly racialist sociobiology are clearly quackery or disguised ideology; it is merely to point out that these judgments must be supported case by case, based on specific empirical knowledge.

Institutions can matter: Science has to be studied as it actually works and that requires investigating much more than a rarified logic of explanation and confirmation. Science is surely a social enterprise. It does not follow from this claim that science is a mere social construction, that evidence plays no role in science, or that science has no better epistemic status than any other institution. It is an empirical question whether the institutions, culture, power relationships, and so on of science promote or hinder the pursuit of scientific knowledge (Kitcher 1993). Social scientists, historians, and philosophers of science have indeed produced many illuminating studies of science in practice and treating science scientifically requires asking what role social processes play, but they do not support the more extreme, all-encompassing claims about mere social construction.

Scientific social science: The above discussion of science and pseudoscience should make it obvious that questions about the genuine scientific status of all—or some particular—social science are sensible only if (1) they are posed as questions about specific bodies of social research and (2) they are approached as concrete inquiries into the evidential and explanatory success of that body of work. Assessing scientific standing is continuous with the practice of science itself.

This means that providing all-purpose arguments about what the social sciences can or cannot do on broad conceptual grounds is misguided. The same holds for judging the social sciences by comparison with positivist misunderstandings of physics.

A fair amount of past philosophy of social science was this kind of unfortunate project. For example, Charles Taylor (1971) argued in a widely cited article that the "human" sciences were fundamentally different from the other sciences because explaining human behavior requires understanding meanings and therefore the human sciences cannot provide the kind of "brute" data (Taylor's word) that the natural sciences provide.

There are two clear problems with arguments like this. First, they make blanket claims about the social sciences that are implausible. Lots of social research is not about individual beliefs, interpretations, symbols, and so on. Instead it is about macrolevel or institutional processes. So organizational ecology studies the competitive environment determining the differential survival of organizations (Hannan and Freeman 1989). Individual beliefs and interpretations are not part of the story. There is an implicit individualism in arguments like Taylor's.

Secondly, Taylor's argument has an implicit positivist understanding of the natural sciences, which is ironic given that Taylor would certainly not think of himself as holding such views. Data in the natural sciences are acquired and interpreted based on a host of background assumptions and are not "brute." Understanding meanings—and this term hides a host of different things—certainly requires background knowledge, but the question for the social sciences is the same as for the natural sciences: What knowledge is assumed and what is its quality? This general point has been argued by Follesdol (1979), Kincaid (1996), and Mantzavinos (2005). In a way Daniel Dennett's entire project argues something similar. Good social science is aware of the problem that meanings bring and tries to deal with them. For example, careful experimental work in the social sciences goes to great pains to control for subjects' understanding. There are many ways such problems show up in the social sciences and no doubt some social science handles them badly. But it is a case-by-case empirical issue, not a deep conceptual truth about the nature of the human.

Views like Taylor's are a denial of an important—and correct, in my view—doctrine about the social sciences that is a form of naturalism (Kincaid 1996). Human social organization and behavior is part of the natural order and thus amenable to scientific study. No doubt human social behavior raises its own set of difficulties calling for methods not found in physics, for example. But the methods of the natural sciences differ greatly across the sciences as well. Geology, cosmology, and evolutionary biology are much less experimental than other natural sciences, but basic scientific virtues such as ruling out competing explanations are embodied in their practices. Naturalism says that those virtues are possible and necessary in the social sciences as well.

These are the guiding philosophical ideas behind the chapters in this volume. The goal has been to promote work in philosophy of social science that parallels the good work our colleagues in philosophy of biology have produced—work that engages with the science and its ongoing controversies. Plenty of philosophical issues arise but largely in the context of problems in contemporary social research. Given the latter interest, it is not surprising that contemporary developments in social science also strongly influence the chapters included. I want to next discuss some of those developments and in the process survey the issues raised by the various chapters.

1.2. OVERVIEW OF THE ISSUES

There has been a renewed interest in causality and causal complexity among social scientists that has interacted with other developments in methodology. It is arguable that much social science from the 1950s through the 1970s was suspicious of making causal claims about the social world (Hoover 2004). This suspicion goes back to Hume through Pearson, whose causal skepticism was part of the trimmings of the new statistical methods he helped develop that have been central to much social science. However, social scientists have deep interests in policy and political issues, and thinking about those things requires causal notions. So causal interest never really went away. Some social scientists—primarily economists—started trying to determine the conditions under which regressions could be interpreted causally in the 1950s, and there were further forays later. However, in the last fifteen years the tools for explicit causal modeling have expanded and increased in rigor with groundbreaking contributions from computer science (Pearl 2000) and philosophers of science (Glymour et. al 1987). Explicit causal models are now much more common in the social sciences in part due to these developments. At the same time, philosophers of science took increasing interest in nonreductive accounts of causation and the methods they entail (Cartwright 1989, 2009 and Woodward 2005).

Several other factors also contributed to renewed interest in and confidence about making causal judgments. Movements in sociology have emphasized the importance of mechanisms (Hedström and Swedberg 1998) and mechanisms are naturally explicated by causal notions. A need for such mechanisms was also motivated by the widespread expansion of rational choice game theory and then evolutionary game theory (and related modeling techniques) in social sciences outside economics. Applied game theory provides possible mechanisms for stable macropatterns, raising suspicions of macropatterns without a mechanism.

A third trend that has moved causal thinking to the fore is increasing statistical sophistication in the social sciences, made possible in part by increased computing power. Part of that sophistication appeared in the explicit causal modeling mentioned above, which moved in tandem with application of Bayesian notions in the social sciences. Another source of sophistication that led to more explicit causal thinking was the introduction of large-scale randomized trials into the social sciences and the development of statistical methods such as instrumental variables and potential outcomes analysis (Dufflo, Glennerster, and Kremer 2008, Angrist and Pischke 2008). These methods hope to indentify causes explicitly.

Parallel to increased interest in causality was an increased interest in complex causality. Complex causality is used in various ways, but some standard notions are threshholds, conjunctive causes, and necessary causes. The basic claim is that in the social world, the causes are not thought of as a set of independently acting sufficient causes that operate everywhere and are everywhere the same. These recognitions were embodied in innovative and nontraditional methods for dealing with constellations of causes, using Boolean algebra and fuzzy set theory (Ragin 1987), for example. Anthroplogists had always argued that social causality was complex and contextual, but now sociologists and political scientists were saying the same thing, using new tools to look at their subject matters.

Thus the chapters in part I take up a variety of issues about causality in the social sciences. Petri Ylikoski and I are both concerned with unpacking the claims that social science needs causal mechanisms. Ylikoski argues that on one of the best conceived pictures of mechanisms—that outlined by philosophers of biology— mechanisms in the social sciences argue against various forms of individualism. Mechanisms may certainly make heavy use of agents' perceptions, intentions, and actions. Yet nothing about a proper understanding of mechanisms makes explanations in terms of individuals the full story or the fundamental story. Rather, mechanism-based explanation is largely achieved through interfield accounts from multiple disciplines linking macro and micro in reciprocal ways. It is individual behavior acting in the preexisting institutional and social context that is important. This theme is repeated in part III, Norms, Culture, and the Social-Psychological, in the chapter by David Henderson on norms and by Don Ross on the origins of social intelligence. Both argue that such context is essential for successful explanations to take into account the institutional and cultural factors.

David Waldner continues the discussion of mechanisms by looking at the currently popular idea in the social sciences that process tracing is an important evidential and explanatory strategy, and ties it to a particular understanding of mechanisms. He notes that there is a clear distinction between wanting mechanisms for explanation as opposed to wanting them to provide evidence. Waldner argues that the most interesting understanding of process tracing comes from identifying the mechanisms that underlie established causal relations (what I call vertical mechanisms). Identifying intervening causes between established causal relations (horizontal mechanisms) has value, but it does not explain why causal relations hold. Mechanisms that do so provide explanatory added value and they are not variables as traditionally conceived (they cannot be manipulated independently of the causal relations they bring about), but are invariants—they generate the correlations and causal relations that are observed. Mechanisms in this sense can be individual actions, institutional constraints, and so on and combinations thereof.

On the evidential side, the methods associated with process tracing claim to be different than standard statistical methods. Waldner agrees. Yet he argues persuasively that these alternative methods at present are quite informal and in need of further clarification to establish their reliability. In terms of the philosophies of science sketched earlier, advocates of process tracing realize that social science evidence is not reducible to simple, more or less a priori rules. Yet that does not mean that anything goes, and defending and articulating the reasoning behind process tracing is an important and underdeveloped project essential to advancement in the social sciences.

Julian Reiss ties into Waldner's discussion of process tracing by giving clear conditions and usages for counterfactual claims in the social sciences. He points out that process tracing does not give us information about the actual difference a potential cause makes (which is Robert Northcott's main concern). Counterfactuals can help tell us about such differences. Furthermore, analyzing counterfactuals requires explicit causal models, and developing these can help avoid various biases that often operate when no such model is present (I make a parallel point).

I also point out that the notion of a mechanism can mean multiple different things, that mechanisms can be wanted for different things—for example, for confirmation of causal claims versus for providing causal claims of sufficient explanatory depth—and that the resulting variety of different claims about mechanism need not all fall or stand together. Using the directed acyclic graph (DAG) framework, I argue that there are some specific situations where mechanisms are needed to avoid bias and confounding. Standard regression analysis in the social sciences often misses these problems because they work without explicit causal models. These arguments are about mechanisms in general and give no support to the idea that the mechanisms *must* be given in terms of individuals.

The DAG framework suffers in situations where the causal effect of one factor depends on the value of another. I argue that the DAG formalism has no natural way to represent this and other complex causes such as necessary causes. In part II, Evidence, Stephen Morgan and Christopher Winship present an interesting, novel, and empirically well motivated route for handling a specific subset of interactions in DAGs motivated by the literature on education and outcomes that will be an important contribution to the literature and builds on their previous substantial work on causal modeling in the social sciences (obviously, the evidence and causation chapters overlap). Their results certainly provide another concrete sense of needing mechanisms.

The causal complexity discussed in my chapter and by Morgan and Winship refers to situations where it is unrealistic to think that a particular type of effect is caused by a list of individual causes, each having an independent measurable sufficient partial effect on the outcome. Further complications involved in this picture of social causation are investigated by Northcott and by David Byrne and Emma Uprichard. Northcott's concern is finding coherent accounts of causal effect size in the existing (mostly regression based) literature. To put the moral in brief, regression coefficients are not generally good measures of effect size or causal strength and even when they are, they depend strongly upon already having good evidence about the causal relations or structure in play, a point emphasized by Northcott as well as myself. Byrne and Uprichard discuss varieties of causal complexity—in cases where it is not realistic to think that the string of independent causes model applies—and methods for dealing with them. In particular, they focus on the qualitative comparative analysis framework of Ragin using Boolean logic and fuzzy set theory that promises to go beyond standard correlation statistics when dealing with complex causes. That framework deserves more discussion than space allowed for in this volume—it deals with complex causation in a way that philosophers would naturally understand and it has novel methodological tools that are becoming increasingly popular.

Gary Goertz picks up on the limitations of standard statistical methods for confirming causal claims. His chapter is full of rich, interesting examples of social science causal-descriptive generalizations that are well established, despite the common mantra that none such exist. He makes an important point that seems obvious once it is understood but is not widely grasped: A set-theoretical claim of all As are Bs can be consistent with zero correlation in statistical senses. In terms of the philosophy of science sketched at the beginning, statistical reasoning relies on a formal logic of inference that does not handle all relevant complexities.

A deeper, more philosophical issue lying behind work on causality in the social sciences concerns understanding the probabilities they support. While it is possible to interpret probabilities in social research as resulting from measurement imprecision or from unmeasured variables, these are not entirely satisfactory accounts. It seems that we end up with probabilistic causes even when our measurements are quite reliable. Second, why should unmeasured causes produce the kinds of stable frequencies that we see in the social realm? Marshall Abrams provided a sophisticated answer in terms of a novel account of what he calls mechanistic probability—stable frequencies produced from underlying causal processes with specific structure. Such structures exist in nature—a roulette wheel is a paradigm instance—and there is good reason to think that in the social realm there are social equivalents of roulette wheels.

Part II of the volume contains chapters about evidence. Of course, chapters in part I are also concerned with evidence, and explanation issues show up in part II. However, there is a decisive shift in emphasis in the chapters of the two parts.

Fred Chernoff surveys the history up to the present of the Duhem's underdetermination thesis. He notes that it is not nearly as radical as Quine's, which I argued earlier was excessive and ignored the variety of techniques that scientists can use to triangulate on where to place blame when hypotheses do not match the data. Duhem's concern was to deny that simply by the use of formal deductive logic, one could determine with certainty whether a hypothesis was confirmed or not. In short, he was a precursor of the postpositivist philosophy of science sketched earlier that rejects the logic of science model. Assessing the evidence depended upon the good common sense of the relevant scientific community.

Chernoff also discusses the relevance of Duhem's view that there may be multiple ways to measure or operationalize aspects of theories, and in that sense which measure is used is conventional. Duhem did not think that this made the choice arbitrary—the good common sense of the scientific community was again needed—but that adopting a common measuring procedure was crucial for scientific progress. Chernoff provides a detailed case study of two important areas in international relations—the democratic peace hypothesis and balance of power theories—showing how in the former common measures promoted significant scientific progress, and the lack of them in the latter undermines its empirical qualifications.

Andrew Gelman and Cosma Rohilla Shalizi discuss the use of Bayesian methods in social science testing based on their considerable combined experience. However, their take on Bayesian methods is quite different than the usual subjective Bayesians versus objective frequentist debate. That debate is often framed as being about which of these views is the true logic of science, and thus based on a false presupposition from the postpositivist point of view. Gelman and Shalizi don't see much value in the exercise of starting with subjective priors and updating them to a new posterior distribution. However, they argue that Bayesian methods are quite useful when it comes to model checking in the social sciences. Model checking as they mean it is a paradigm instance of the kind of piecemeal triangulation that radical holists miss.

Aviezer Tucker also uses Bayesian ideas in his discussion of the relation between the social sciences and history. He argues that history is not applied social science, and social science is generally not history. History is about inferring to common cause token events in the past using background theories of information transfer applied to currently available traces in the form of such evidence as documents. Social science is about relating types—variables—by quite different, often statistical, methods. Bayesian ideas come into play in two ways. He argues that inferring to a past token event as a common cause of multiple present information traces is a matter of the likelihood of the common cause hypothesis versus its competitor. That is not a fully Bayesian framework, because it does not involve priors. However, Tucker argues that social science results can tell historians what possible past tokens are initially plausible as common causes. Inferring who wrote the Bible can be informed by the finding that writing only arises in the presence of a centralized bureaucratic state, and thus that books of the Old Testament cannot be contemporary to the events they described. In that sense the social sciences can provide priors. However, priors in this sense are just relevant background information—in other words, good scientific common sense.

Nancy Cartwright's chapter on randomized controlled trials (RCTs) as evidence for potential policy effectiveness echoes the general theme of part II that evaluating evidence in practice is a complex and fallible affair that rules of scientific logic do not capture. RCTs are treated by the medical profession and increasingly by social scientists—they are all the rage in development economics, for example—as the gold standard. That phrase is widely used without clear explanation, but it generally means either that RCTs are thought to be near conclusive proof, the only real proof, or by far and away the best proof. In short, their logic guarantees reliable outcomes, another of the hopes for a logic of science. Cartwright argues convincingly and in detail that RCTs can be quite unreliable as guides to policy effectiveness.

Morgan and Winship take up in much greater detail the issues raised by interaction effects and heterogeneity for DAG analyses that I raise in my chapter. They provide an explicit framework for incorporating such complications into DAGs. Their basic approach to the possible errors caused by interaction and heterogeneity is to model them. Like Gelman and Shalizi, their concerns are driven by the kinds of problems they see in existing research, which in their case are the causes of educational attainment. Formal methods like DAGs are useful, but their usefulness has to be evaluated according to the kinds of causal complexity faced by practicing researchers and adapted accordingly. They note that the formalism of DAG models can be a hindrance to recognizing causal complexities.

Ken Kollman's chapter continues the emphasis on the complexities of evidence, focusing on the burgeoning field of computational models of social phenomena. In one way his topic is a classical one, especially in philosophy of economics, about the status of abstract and idealized models. Kollman notes what modelers often say in their defense—namely, that models provide insight. However, he goes a step further and realizes that appeals to insight are not enough (it could be a warm and fuzzy feeling only, though this is my formulation, not his). Kollman gives several other, more concrete reasons such models may be reasonable. It is possible to generate simulated data with computational models and then compare the patterns in the data with real empirical patterns in analogous social data. So empirical testing is possible, though Kollman cautiously notes that there are still issues about how strong the analogy is. Computational models also have explanatory virtues: They instantiate the causal mechanical ideals advocated in the chapters in part I. This means they can represent dynamics, something that rational choice game theory, for example, cannot. He also argues that they provide ways to model micro and macro social phenomena, in line with Ylikoski and Waldner's idea that mechanism-based explanation defuses individualism/holism debates.

The chapters in part III deal with an intersecting set of topics concerning culture, norms, and the explanation of sociality. Here issues of explanation (macro and micro, for example), evidence, and more philosophical issues concerning how to understand key concepts are intertwined. Most chapters ask the question: How do explanations in terms of norms, culture, and related concepts relate to psychological explanations? To what extent are the latter sufficient? Necessary? What is the basis of human sociality? Human nature or social organization or some mix of the two? And if the latter, how does that work?

Mark Risjord provides a history up to the present of the concept of culture in anthropology, where the concept is most used. That history has been a running conflict between treating culture as a trait of individuals—a form of methodological individualism—and as something superseding individuals and sometimes indeed as controlling them. The most plausible view, according to Risjord (echoing the approach emphasized by Ylikoski) is to see that debate as dissipated by a more interactive view where neither the individualist or holist view is on the table. Though that is a common theme throughout the volume, there is obviously more work to do in fleshing out that claim. My guess is that there are multiple, domain-specific ways of doing so, and I would not claim that this volume is anything like the final word on the issue.

Henderson takes on clarifying norms, a concept widespread throughout the social sciences, though it is generally not carefully explicated. Sometimes norms are only behavioral regularities. Henderson argues convincingly that in this guise they are not particularly explanatory. His main focus is on norms as knowing (and having attitudes about) a rule, following some of the most sophisticated recent analyses. Henderson argues that rules cannot be seen as entirely a psychological phenomenon, because payoffs and differences in social status and power are part of the explanation. However, there are important questions, largely unexplored in the literature, about the psychological basis and explanation of knowing rules. To what extent can cognitive science accounts be integrated with sociological, economic, and anthropological accounts? Like Ylikoski in chapter 2, Henderson thinks that an interfield account is called for.

The evolutionary program in social science is the subject of Francesco Guala's and Tim Lewens's chapters. Guala focuses particularly on the debate over whether cooperation and sociality in humans requires strong reciprocity—roughly, the willingness to perform costly sanctions to enforce norms—or can be simply explained in terms of self-interest. This empirical issue is important for policy decisions, since if humans are not generally capable of strong reciprocity, policies that assume they are will lead to bad outcomes. Lewens provides an overview of objections to theories of cultural evolution. He delineates the relation between sociobiology and other kinds of evolutionary accounts and between meme-based versions and population level learning accounts. Levens give us a balanced account that argues that not all problems raised in the literature against evolutionary models are decisive, and yet is wary of attempts to push further than we can go.

Ross looks at the interactive origins of human intelligence and sociality, specifically at the thesis that human intelligence in evolutionary history resulted from the need to meet the needs of social interactions. He surveys neurobiological and other evidence that suggests primates in general have natural dispositions to cooperate. So human intelligence seems unlikely to be the result simply of the need for social coordination. Instead, Ross suggests that that when hominid groups developed specialization and trading, greater demands arose to deal with these new forms coordination. Complex socialized selves were needed to play the more complex games that exchange and specialization involves.

Ron Mallon and Daniel Kelly examine the status of race as a social science concept. The biological notion of race seems quite unfounded, so how has it been a useful concept in the social sciences—or has it been? They deny that race is fully explained as a social role and argue that there is important empirical evidence suggesting that there are strong psychological underpinnings behind our tendencies to categorize people in terms of race. This is in keeping with the theme of many chapters that macro and micro accounts need to be involved and integrated.

The chapters in part IV focus on issues in the sociology of knowledge. Earlier chapters had already informally considered some sociological and rhetorical aspects of social science research. As argued earlier in the chapter, information about the sociological factors driving research can be useful information in assessing the scientific standing of various lines of research.

Amy Mazur discusses feminist social science research, especially feminist comparative politics (FCP), her prime area of interest. The feminist research she advocates and discusses aims to contribute to accumulation of knowledge through empirical research, and she carefully distinguishes this from extreme constructivist views about science that some feminists have espoused. The feminist research she advocates does proceed, however, with an awareness of and interest in gender issues and a recognition of how gender biases can infect standard social science research.

She details the empirical success of feminist comparative politics. Mazur describes the social organization of the FCP community and its interaction with elements of national governments that have made it a success. However, she notes that mainstream comparative politics has largely ignored these achievements and argues that gender biases continue to plague the mainstream, which is still largely comprised of male researchers.

Allan Horwitz applies the sociology of knowledge approach to mental illness. He rejects the idea that the sociology of mental illness classification and organizational embeddedness shows that mental illness is a pure social construct (just as Mazur rejects radical constructivist feminist views about science). He also thinks that saying that all mental illness is a matter of looping kinds—interaction between individual traits and the effect on the individual classified as having some mental disorder—as Hacking sometimes suggests is too crude a formulation that glosses important differences. Looping seemingly plays a much bigger role in ADHD than it does in schizophrenia. Horwitz believes that there can be neurobiologically based mental malfunctions that constitute mental illness. Looking at the social and institutional processes involved in the classification and treatment of behavior of mental disorders can be quite helpful in assessing which current practices have a grounded basis and which ones exist largely due to the sociology of the psychiatric profession and the classification process.

The final chapters of the volume comprising part V focus on normative issues that have important ties to social science research and philosophy of science issues. James Woodward uses the kind of work on reciprocity in cooperative behavior discussed by Guala and Ross to ask what implications it may have for political philosophy. Daniel Hausman discusses the difficulties in evaluating health outcomes in terms of the preferences of patients and concludes that evaluation often relies on messy ad hoc processes. Anna Alexandrova asks if social science research on well-being actually gets at well-being (something its critics wonder about). She argues that philosophical accounts of well-being are of minimal help, and in practice the different sciences that study well-being use different, local notions relevant to the context without compromising their results. This is in keeping with the postpositivist moral drawn at the beginning that science often does not work with concepts definable in terms of necessary and sufficient conditions.

NOTES

Parts of this introduction are taken from Ross, D., and Kincaid, H. "The New Philosophy of Economics," in H. Kincaid and D. Ross, eds., *Oxford Handbook of the Philosophy of Economics* (Oxford: Oxford University Press, 2009), 3–35.

   1. Another distinct difference is over the role of values. Since I have pursued this at length elsewhere (Kincaid 2007), I am not going to do so systematically here. There are many different ways values can be involved with different consequences. The short answer

is that science is a complex set of practice and that values can cause bias in some cases but not in others. For example, Mazur's chapter shows how values can both lead to better science and to bad science as does Horwitz's chapter on mental illness.

REFERENCES

Angrist, J., and J-S. Piscke. 2008. *Mostly Harmless Econometrics: An Empiricist's Companion.* Princeton, NJ: Princeton University Press.

Cartwright, N. 1980. "Causality in a World of Instrumental Laws." *PSA: Proceedings of the Biennial Meeting of the Philosophy of Science Association* 2: 38–48.

Cartwright, N. 1983. *How The Laws of Physics Lie.* Oxford: Oxford University Press.

Cartwright, N. 1989. *Nature's Capacities and Their Measurement.* Oxford: Oxford University Press.

Cartwright, N. 2007. *Hunting Causes and Using Them.* Cambridge: Cambridge University Press.

Duflo, E., R. Glennerster, and M. Kremer. 2008. "Using Randomization in Development Economics Research: A Toolkit." In *Handbook of Development Economics,* T. P. Schultz, and J. Strauss, eds., 3895–3962 Amsterdam: Elsevier.

Follesdol, D. 1979. "Hermenutics and the Hypothetical-Deductive Method." *Dialectica* 33: 319–36.

Glymour, C. 1980. *Theory and Evidence.* Princeton, NJ: Princeton University Press.

Glymour, C., R. Scheines, P. Spirtes, and K. Kelly. 1987. *Discovering Causal Structure: Artificial Intelligence, Philosophy of Science, and Statistical Modeling.* New York: Academic Press.

Hannan, M., and J. Freeman. 1989. *Organizational Ecology.* Cambridge, MA: Harvard University Press.

Hedström, P., and R. Swedberg. 1998. *Social Mechanisms: An Analytical Approach to Social Theory.* Cambridge: Cambridge University Press.

Hoover, K. 2004. "Lost Causes." *Journal of the History of Economic Thought* 26: 129–44.

Kincaid, Harold. 1996. *Philosophical Foundations of the Social Sciences.* Cambridge: Cambridge University Press.

Kitcher, P. 1993. *The Advancement of Science.* Oxford: Oxford University Press.

Ladyman and Ross. 2007. *Everything Must Go.* Oxford: Oxford University Press.

Mantzavinos, C. 2005. *Naturalistic Hermeneutics.* Cambridge: Cambridge University Press.

Moss, L. 2004. *What Genes Can't Do.* Cambridge, MA: The MIT Press.

Pearl, Judea. 2000. *Causality: Models, Reasoning, and Evidence.* Cambridge: Cambridge University Press.

Ragin, Charles. 1987. *The Comparative Method: Moving Beyond Qualitative and Quantitative Methods?* Berkeley: University of California Press.

Taylor, Charles. 1971. "Interpretation and the Sciences of Man." *Review of Metaphysics* 25: 3–51.

Wilson, M. 2007. *Wandering Significance.* Oxford: Oxford University Press.

Woodward, J. 2005. *Making Things Happen: A Theory of Causal Explanation.* Oxford: Oxford University Press.

PART I

Mechanisms,
Explanation,
and Causation

CHAPTER 2

....

MICRO, MACRO, AND MECHANISMS

....

PETRI YLIKOSKI

2.1. INTRODUCTION

....

This chapter takes a fresh look at micro-macro relations in the social sciences from the point of view of the mechanistic account of explanation. Traditionally, micro-macro issues have been assimilated to the problem of methodological individualism (Udéhn 2001, Zahle 2006). It is not my intention to resurrect this notoriously unfruitful controversy. On the contrary, the main thrust of this chapter is to show that the cul-de-sac of that debate can be avoided if we give up some of its presuppositions. The debate about methodological individualism is based on assumptions about explanation, and once we change those assumptions, the whole argumentative landscape changes.

The idea that social scientific explanations are based on causal mechanisms rather than covering laws has become increasingly popular over the last twenty years or so (Hedström and Ylikoski 2010). Interestingly, a similar mechanistic turn has occurred also in the philosophies of biology and psychology (Wright and Bechtel 2007). Until recently, the connections between these two emerging traditions for thinking about mechanisms have been rare. The aim of this chapter is to employ ideas developed by philosophers of biology to address some issues that the advocates of mechanisms in the social sciences have not yet systematically addressed. I argue that ideas about levels of explanation and reductive research strategies, which were originally developed in the context of cell biology and neuroscience, can be fruitfully adapted to the social sciences. They can both strengthen the case for mechanism-based explanations in the social sciences and bring the philosophy of social science debates closer to social scientific practice.

The chapter is structured as follows. In the first section, I will take a look at recent work on mechanism-based explanation. While I suggest that the mechanistic account of explanation presupposes some more fundamental ideas about explanatory relevance and causation, I also argue that it provides a fruitful tool for thinking about micro-macro relations in the social sciences. In the second section, I will criticize a common philosophical way of formulating the micro-macro issue and provide my own characterization that is not dependent on the assumption that there is a unique or comprehensive micro level. The third section introduces the distinction between causal and constitutive explanation, and argues that this distinction helps to make sense of the call for microfoundations in the social sciences. The final section will take on a doctrine that I call intentional fundamentalism, and it challenges the idea that intentional explanations have a privileged position in the social sciences.

2.2. Mechanism-based Explanation

The idea of mechanism-based explanation has been developed independently among social scientists (Harré 1970; Elster 1989, 2007; Little 1991; Hedström and Swedberg 1998; Hedström 2005; for a review see Hedström and Ylikoski 2010) and philosophers of biology (Bechtel 2006, 2008; Craver 2007; Darden 2006; Wimsatt 2007). In the social sciences, the idea of causal mechanism has been used mainly as a tool for methodological criticism, while in the philosophy of biology the motivation has been that of finding a descriptively adequate account of biological explanation. Despite these separate origins and motivations, both traditions are clearly building on similar ideas about scientific explanation. For example, both share the same dissatisfaction with the covering law account of explanation (Hedström 2005; Craver 2007).

There is no consensus on the right definition of a causal mechanism. Although some theorists find such a situation frustrating, I do not think this constitutes a real problem. The entities and processes studied by different sciences are quite heterogeneous, and it is probably impossible to propose a mechanism definition that would be both informative and cover all the prominent examples of mechanisms. Some disciplines, such as cell biology (Bechtel 2006) and the neurosciences (Craver 2007), study highly integrated systems, whereas others, such as evolutionary biology and the social sciences, study more dispersed phenomena (Kuorikoski 2009), so it is more plausible to think that informative characterizations of mechanisms are field specific. The task of a philosophical account is to show how these exemplars are related to general ideas about explanation, evidence, and causation, not to engage in verbal sophistry. However, it is possible to give some general characteristics of mechanisms.

First, a mechanism is always a *mechanism for something*; it is identified by the kind of effect or phenomenon it produces. Second, a mechanism is an *irreducibly causal notion.* It refers to the entities of a causal process that produces the effect of interest. Third, a mechanism has a *structure.* When a mechanism-based explanation opens the black box, it makes visible how the participating entities and their properties, activities, and relations produce the effect of interest. The focus on mechanisms breaks up the original explanation-seeking why-question into a series of smaller questions about the causal process: What are the participating entities, and what are their relevant properties? How are the interactions of these entities organized (both spatially and temporally)? What factors could prevent or modify the outcome? Finally, there is *a hierarchy of mechanisms.* While a mechanism at one level presupposes or takes for granted the existence of certain entities with characteristic properties and activities, it is expected that there are lower-level mechanisms that will explain them. In other words, the explanations employed by one field always *bottom out* somewhere. However, this fundamental status of certain entities, properties, and activities for a given mechanism is only relative, as they are legitimate targets of mechanistic explanation in another field. Of course, this chain of explanations ends somewhere—there are no mechanism-based explanations for fundamental (physical) processes (Hedström and Ylikoski 2010).

Although the mechanism-based account is often presented simply as an idea about scientific explanation, the notion of mechanism is associated with a wider set of ideas about scientific knowledge. For example, there are ideas about the justification of causal claims, the heuristics of causal discovery, the presentation of explanatory information, and the organization of scientific knowledge (Ylikoski 2011). There is no doubt that these not yet clearly articulated ideas partly explain the appeal of the approach. For example, as I will show later in this chapter, claims about the explanatory role of mechanisms are often confused with claims about their relevance to the justification of causal claims (see also Kincaid, this volume).

While I think all the above ideas are important advances in understanding explanatory reasoning in science, it is not necessary to assume that the notion of mechanism is the ultimate solution to all problems in the theory of explanation. On the contrary, the mechanistic theory presupposes accounts of explanatory relevance, causation, and the nature of generalizations that provide the basis for mechanisms. The notion of mechanism should not be treated like a black box. I have argued elsewhere (Hedström and Ylikoski 2010; Ylikoski 2011) that if the mechanistic ideas are combined with the theory of explanation developed by James Woodward (2002, 2003), we can get quite far in solving these problems. While for the present purposes we do not have to consider in detail the relation between mechanisms and generalizations, some comments on explanatory relevance are in order as later arguments depend on it.

A mechanism-based explanation describes the causal process selectively. It does not aim at an exhaustive account of all details but seeks to capture the crucial elements of the process by abstracting away the irrelevant details. The relevance of entities, their properties, and their interactions is determined by their ability to make a relevant difference to the outcome of interest. If the presence of an entity or of changes in its properties or activities truly does not make any difference to the effect to be explained, it can be ignored. This counterfactual criterion of relevance implies that mechanism-based explanations involve counterfactual reasoning about possible changes and their consequences (Ylikoski 2011). A natural way to understand these causal counterfactuals is to understand them as claims about the consequences of ideal causal interventions (Woodward 2003, 2008). The causal counterfactual tells us what would have happened to the effect if the cause had been subject to a surgical intervention that would not have affected anything else in the causal configuration. An advantage of the interventionist account of causation is that it allows talking about causal dependencies in every context where the notion of intervention makes sense. Unlike some other theories of causation, such as various process theories, it is level-blind and applicable to special sciences such as cell biology or sociology.

2.2.1. Mechanisms and Reductive Explanation

One of the distinctive features of the mechanistic approach to explanation is that it reorients the issues related to reductionism and reductive explanation. In one sense the mechanistic way of thinking is thoroughly reductionist: It attempts to explain activities of mechanisms in terms of their component parts and their activities, and then subjects the component mechanisms to the same treatment. In this sense, the reductive research strategy has probably been the single most effective research strategy in the history of modern science. However, there is another sense in which mechanism-based explanations are clearly nonreductionist: Although they do refer to the micro level, they do not replace or eliminate the higher-level facts nor the explanations citing them. Rather than serving to reduce one level to another, mechanisms bridge levels (Darden 2006; Craver 2007; Wright and Bechtel 2007; Richardson 2007; McCauley 2007; Wimsatt 2007).

The mechanistic account of reductive explanation differs significantly from the traditional philosophical accounts of intertheoretical reduction that conceive reduction as a derivation of one theory from another (Richardson 2007; McCauley 2007). The mechanical account of reductive explanation does not start with a strongly idealized picture of a discipline-wide theory that contains all knowledge about its level. Nor does it conceive reduction as a deductive relation between such theories (or their corrected versions). Rather, reductive mechanistic explanations are constructed piecemeal with a focus on particular explanatory targets. While there is an assumption that everything is mechanistically explainable and a presumption that ultimately all mechanistic accounts are mutually compatible, there is no overarching effort to combine them into one grand theory that would cover all the phenomena that the scientific field studies. Also, contrary to the traditional accounts that conceive reduction as elimination or replacement, the mechanisms are inherently multilevel. The components and their operations occur and are investigated at one level, whereas the mechanism itself and its activities occur and are investigated at a higher level. In this sense accounts of mechanisms often have the character of interfield theory (Darden 2006). This makes it difficult to characterize the reductive understanding provided by mechanical explanations as deductive relations between independent theories.

The mechanistic stance also gives reasons for rethinking the notion of levels. According to the traditional layer-cake conception, there is a neat hierarchical layering of entities into levels across phenomena, and the scientific disciplines (e.g., physics, chemistry, biology, psychology, sociology) are distinguished from each other by the level of the phenomena that they are studying (see Oppenheim and Putnam 1958). From the mechanistic point of view, this way of thinking unnecessarily drives together levels of nature and science, and misleadingly suggests that the levels are both comprehensive and the same independently of the investigative context (Craver 2007). The actual scientific disciplines do not match neatly with the metaphysical picture of levels of organization or reality. And while there are many problems in a serious characterization of the metaphysical picture of levels, there do not seem to be any particularly good reasons to accept such a metaphysical constraint for an account of scientific explanation.

The notion of the levels of mechanism plays an important role in the mechanistic account but is free from many of the traditional assumptions about levels. The levels of mechanisms are perspectival in the sense that the levels are dependent on the explanatory target. Macro-level facts are explained by appealing to micro-level processes, entities, and relations, but these items belong to the micro level just because they are required for the full explanation of the macro fact, not because they belong to some predetermined micro level. Whatever is needed for explaining the macro fact is regarded as belonging to the same level. However, there is no guarantee that these components would always be at the same level in all possible explanatory contexts. Nor it is obvious that the micro-level entities and processes that account for these components would be in any simple sense from the same level. For every hierarchy of mechanisms, there is a clear hierarchy of levels of mechanisms, but these levels are local. There is no reason to assume that separate hierarchies of mechanism levels would together produce the neatly delineated and comprehensive levels of nature assumed in the traditional layer-cake model (Craver 2007).

These views have a number of interesting consequences for traditional ways of thinking about reductive explanation and the explanatory role of microfoundations in the social sciences. For example, once we give up the outdated deductive model of theory reduction, many of the traditional fixations of the methodological individualism debate simply become meaningless. For example, there is no need to provide individualistically acceptable redefinitions of macro-social notions because the explanation of macro facts is no longer conceived as a logical derivation. Similarly, the search for any bridge laws between theories becomes pointless. This has the consequence that the key anti-reductionist argument about multiple realization loses much of its significance. From the point of view of mechanistic explanation, multiple realization is simply an interesting empirical observation that does not pose any serious threat to the possibility of explaining macro properties in terms of micro properties and relations. Just as the sciences have learned to live with the fact of alternative causes, they can learn to live with the phenomenon of multiple realization.

The advocates of the mechanism-based approach in the social sciences have noticed some of these consequences. For example, they have largely given up the old ideas about reductive explanation and have instead emphasized the importance of microfoundations (Elster 1989; Little 1991). However, I do not think that all the implications of the mechanistic perspective have been taken into account in the philosophy of social sciences. This is visible, for example, in the fact that quite often the mechanistic approach is associated with methodological individualism (Elster 1989). Similarly, much of the debate about micro-macro relations is still focused on arguments that are based on a premechanistic understanding of reductive explanation (Sawyer 2005; Zahle 2006).

The aim of this chapter is to sketch what a consistently mechanistic way to think about micro-macro relations would look like and to show that some of the key presuppositions of the traditional debate about methodological individualism should be given up. One of these is the assumption of a comprehensive, unique, and privileged individual level. The notion of *comprehensiveness* refers to the idea that there is a consistent and well-defined individual level that is sufficient to cover all social phenomena and that would serve as a reduction basis for all nonindividual social notions. *Uniqueness* refers to the assumption that in all social explanations, the micro level would always be the same level, for example, the level of intentional rational action. Finally, the notion of *privileged* refers to the presumption that explanations in terms of this special level have some special explanatory qualities that set them apart from explanations from other levels. In the following, I will challenge all three assumptions and argue that once they are given up, we can approach the micro-macro issues in the social sciences in a more clear-headed manner.

2.3. Rethinking the Macro

A popular argumentative strategy among anti-individualists has been to borrow ideas from the philosophy of mind. They are inspired by the arguments for nonreductive materialism, so they build their argument based on an analogy with the mind-brain relation. Given that these arguments are not very mind specific—it is a general practice just to talk about M- and P-predicates—their appeal is understandable. The ideas of supervenience and multiple realization seem to provide a neat way to argue against reductionism, at least if one accepts the traditional idea of derivational reduction. While there are reasons to suspect that the notion of supervenience is less illuminating than is often assumed (Horgan 1993; Kim 1993) and that the traditional view of reduction does not completely collapse under multiple realization (Kim 1998), we can set these issues aside as their relevance presupposes a premechanistic account of reductive explanation. Here I want to focus on the mind-brain analogy as I think it is misleading.

The mind-brain analogy is inappropriate because it mischaracterizes the nature of the social scientific micro-macro problem. The central problem in the philosophy of mind is to figure out how the explanations provided by psychological theories that employ mental concepts are related to the accounts of the brain's working provided by the neurosciences. The challenge is to relate two levels of description that are fundamentally talking about the same thing. The (nondualist) antireductionist position does not typically challenge the causal sufficiency of the neural-level facts. The setup is quite different in the social scientific micro-macro debates.

The problem in the social sciences is not that of bridging a comprehensive and exhaustive individual-level understanding of social processes (the analogue to the idealized knowledge of the brain) to a more social or holistic description (that would be analogue to the idealized psychological theories employing the mental vocabulary). It is typical for anti-individualists to challenge the causal sufficiency of individual facts. They often claim that the facts about individuals allowed by the individualist are either not sufficient to account for all social facts or the individualists are cheating by accepting facts that are not properly individualistic. This is because the issue is not really that of relations between two comprehensive (and potentially competing) levels of description, but that of seeing how local facts about individuals and their social interactions are related to large-scale facts about groups, organizations, and societies. So, the relation is really more like the one between the whole brain and its parts than the mind and the brain. While this contrast is useful for highlighting the inappropriateness of the mind-brain analogy, I do not want to develop it further as there are many problems with the organ-society analogy. It is better to skip all the brainy analogies and to take a fresh look at the micro-macro problem as the social scientists face it.

A useful starting point is the observation that macro social facts are typically *supra-individual*: They are attributed to groups, communities, populations, and organizations, but not to individuals. There might be some attributes that apply both to individuals and collectives, but typically macro social properties, relations, and events are such that they are not about individuals.

Another salient feature of many social micro-macro relations is the part-whole relationship. One way or another, the macro social entities *are made of* their constituting parts. Usually this relation of constitution is more than mere mereological aggregation or simple material constitution. First, many social wholes are composed of a heterogeneous set of entities; there are intentional agents, their ideas, and material artifacts. Second, in all interesting examples of social wholes, the *relations* between the components play an important role. (Similarly, often the relations between social wholes and between the social whole and its environment are also important.) However, the important thing is that the part-whole relationship makes it possible to see the micro-macro relation as a question of scale: The difference between micro and macro is the difference between small- and large-scale social phenomena.

I do not propose that we can simply define the micro-macro contrast as an issue of scale. All differences in scale do not constitute a meaningful micro-macro relation, and the heterogeneous nature of macro social facts makes it difficult to characterize the additional requirements for their defining features. However, I do want to suggest that it provides a fruitful way to think about micro-macro relations and an antidote for the tendency to see parallels in the philosophy of mind.

Thinking of the micro-macro issue as an issue of scale makes it possible to conceive of it as being without a unique micro level. Whereas the contrast between "individual" and "social" levels is categorical, the contrast between small and large is relative and allows a continuum of various sizes. Depending on the application, the micro entities could be individuals, families, firms, or groups. This flexibility is in accordance with the way social scientists think. They do not assume that micro is always about one specific set of entities.

Another consequence is that whether an attribute is a macro or micro property depends on what it is contrasted with. A friendship relationship is a macro property from the psychological point of view, but a micro property when considered from the point of view of the social networks within a community. Rather than being set a priori, the contrast between micro and macro depends on one's explanatory interests. For example, international politics and organizational sociology construct the micro-macro contrast quite differently. In the former, states and other organizations are often treated as individuals, whereas in the latter, the organizations and their properties are the macro reality to be explained. Similarly, an economist studying market processes can treat firms and households as the micro level, while for disciplines such as industrial organization and family sociology, they are the macro items that require explanation.

From the point of view of a mechanistic philosophy of science, this flexibility is not surprising. The same dependence of levels on epistemic concerns is also observable in the biological sciences. The cell biologists or neuroscientists do not think in terms of comprehensive or unique micro levels either. The levels of mechanisms found there depend on the explanatory concerns, not on a priori ontological considerations. This is not worrisome for the mechanistic point of view, as the key assumption is that whatever is found at the micro level can always be turned to a macro-level *explanandum* for another set of enquiries.

The social macro properties do not constitute a unified kind, so it makes sense to characterize them with a sample of examples rather than with a general definition. The following classification of typical sociological macro social properties is not intended to be exhaustive of sociology or the social sciences in general. There are many parts of macro social reality that fall between my four categories. However, I hope the four examples can be used to illustrate the applicability of the scale perspective.

2.3.1. Statistical Properties of a Population

A major concern for sociology is the various statistical attributes of populations. Among these are *distributions* and *frequencies*. Sociologists are interested in both distributions of attributes to various kinds of individuals and distributions of individuals with certain attributes to social positions and spatial locations. For example, when they are studying the ethnic segregation of cities, comparing societies in terms of inequality, or describing the social stratification of a society, they are attempting to account for distributions. Another relevant property of distributions are frequencies. Sociologists are interested in typical, rare, dominant, or marginal behaviors, beliefs, or attitudes within a specified population. Similarly, they are interested in ratios of attributes such as unemployment or incarceration within the population. So, when sociologists are studying changes in racial prejudices over time, comparing the level of conformism between communities or tracking the changes in the level of union memberships, they are interested in explaining frequencies.

All these statistical macro social properties are inferred (or estimated) from data about the members of a population. There is no other way to access them. However, it does not make any sense to attribute these properties to individual units. Another important thing about these macro social facts is that the units of these statistics do not have to be individuals; they can as well be families or firms. It is noticeable that statistical macro properties are in no way dependent on the members' beliefs and attitudes about them. The members of the population can have false, or even crazy, beliefs about distributions and frequencies that characterize their own society.

While the statistical properties of populations usually only serve as *explananda* in the social sciences, they do have some legitimate and nonreducible explanatory uses. For example, in the cases of frequency-dependent causation (e.g., cases in which the causal effect of an individual having a certain property depends on the frequency of that property in the population), the statistical facts are the crucial difference makers. Similarly, in many social scientific explanations, the correlations between various variables (for example, wealth, education, taste, and place of residence) play an important role in accounting for individual differences in behavior and attitudes. Both of these cases are quite easily conceived as cases of larger-scale facts influencing smaller-scale phenomena, while other ways to think about levels are not as natural.

2.3.2. Topologies of Social Networks within a Population

Sociologists are also interested in relations and interactions between individuals. When considered together, these relations constitute networks of social relations within the population. A social network can be regarded as a map of all of the relevant ties between the members of a specified population. When sociologists are studying the spread of information within an organization, comparing groups with respect to their level of network clustering or analyzing the brokering opportunities of an individual occupying a structural hole (i.e., a position between two networks that are not otherwise connected), they are examining social networks.

The importance of social networks is increasingly being recognized in the social sciences, and social network analysis is becoming increasingly popular in various social sciences. Social network analysis is based on the observation that networks have many interesting (formal) properties, such as centralization, cohesion, density, and structural cohesion (Scott 2000). While the social network is inferred from knowledge about individual relationships, the properties of the network are proto-typical macro properties. It does not make any sense to apply these attributes to individual nodes of the network. Similarly to statistical properties, the units of net-work analysis are flexible. There is no requirement that the nodes of the network (the members of the population) are persons. They can also be groups, families, organizations, or even states.

The properties of social networks serve both as the *explananda* and the *explan-antia* in sociology. As an example of the latter, consider the notion of a structural hole (Burt 1992), which is used to explain the differences in agents' ability to access information and in their opportunities to influence social processes. In these expla-nations the structure of the network plays an irreducible role, and it is quite natural to think of the social network as a large-scale social phenomenon influencing local interactions between individuals. In contrast, it is very difficult to think about them in terms of social and individual levels. As social networks are attributes of the population, it would be quite a stretch to call social networks individual properties. But if they are macro-level properties, what would be the individual-level properties that could be regarded as their bases? Collections of relevant individual relations, one might suggest, but that would be just a vague way to talk about networks. Things are simpler if one does not have to bother with such questions. A network is simply a more extensive entity that is constituted by more local relations and it can have properties that are not properties of its components.

2.3.3. Communal Properties

By communal properties I refer to social scientific notions that apply to specific communities, but not to isolated individuals. Among these notions are such things as culture, customs, social norms, and so on. For example, cultural differences are primarily between groups, not between individuals. Similarly, social norms and customs are properties of communities—attributing them to solitary individuals does not make sense. Many of these notions do not have precise definitions, and their explanatory uses are often confusing (Turner 1994; Ylikoski 2003), but they do have an important role in the social sciences.

While communal properties are attributed to groups, they are quite straightfor-wardly based on facts about individuals. Underlying these notions is the idea that the members of a group share certain beliefs, expectations, preferences, and habits. However, it is crucial that the sharing of these individual attributes is not purely accidental: The members have these individual properties because the other mem-bers of the group have them. The sharing of these properties is due to continuing interaction. For example, the existence of a social custom presupposes that the nov-ices learn specific expectations and habits when they become members and that the members of the group stick to these expectations and habits because others also do so. Underlying the (relative) unity of a culture are facts about the shared origins of the ideas, values, and practices of the members and their constant interaction with each other. Similarly, the cohesion of a culture is based on the frequency of interactions with the group and the rarity of interactions with outsiders, not on any kind of higher-level influence on individuals.

Descriptions of customs, social norms, and cultures are always based on idealization and abstraction. Members of a community never have exactly the same ideas, preferences, or routines. That would be a miracle, given what is known about human learning and communication (Sperber 2006). There is always some variation among the members, no matter how comprehensive the socialization processes are. However, these idealized descriptions are still useful. They draw attention to features of the group that are typical and salient when it is contrasted with some other group.

Although communal properties, as I have described them, are tied to a social community defined by frequent interactions, the boundaries of these communities are fluid. This makes it possible to describe culture on various scales—for example, on the levels of a village, a local area, and a nation. However, descriptions on larger scales are bound to be more abstract and less rich in detail as individual variation takes its toll. The same flexibility that characterizes statistical and network properties applies also to communal properties, which can also be attributed to nonpersonal units. For example, it is possible to describe social norms that govern interactions between organizations.

When we consider communal properties as *idealizing abstractions from shared individual properties*, there is no need to refer to them as any kind of autonomous level of reality. They just describe more extensive facts than descriptions of the individual attitudes, habits, and preferences that constitute them. The scale perspective also appears natural when the explanatory use of communal properties is considered. For example, when we are explaining the behavior of an individual by appealing to social norms, we are referring to larger-scale facts about the group members that are causally relevant to the micro-level behavior. There is no need to postulate a separate realm of norms to understand what is happening. It is just that the expectations and responses of the other group members influence the individual's judgments about appropriate behavior.

2.3.4. Organizations and Their Properties

Organizations such as states, firms, parties, churches, and sport clubs are important parts of the social reality. While the community that is the basis for communal properties is not often clearly demarcated, a clear demarcation is often the case with organizations. They usually have specified criteria for membership, at least for the operational members. They also have rules that define the rights and duties of members and the roles of various functionaries. These (written or nonwritten) rules make it possible for organizations to have stability and continuity, so that it makes sense to talk about their continuing existence when their functionaries are replaced and the members change. Furthermore, many organizations exist (and are defined) in the context of other organizations, so one has to pay special attention to context when attempting to make sense of organizations.

Organizations as entities can have many properties that are not properties of their members. They can even have goals that are not the personal goals of their members, and some organizations are treated as legal persons. This has convinced many that organizations are real entities that should be treated as a separate ontological category. I do not have strong opinions about issues of ontological bookkeeping, as it is remembered that organizations are human artifacts that are always made of persons, their ideas about the rules, and often, of material artifacts. Whatever the organization does, is done by its members in its name. It is of crucial social importance whether an action, for example, a questionable comment, was made as a representative of an organization or as a private person. But these are facts about the status attributed to the behavior, not about the two completely different entities producing the behavior.

When a person causally interacts with an organization, she interacts with other persons (although this interaction is increasingly mediated via material artifacts such as ATM machines). There is no downward causal influence from a higher level. Everything happens at the same level; it is just that the intentional attitudes and relations of a larger group of people are important to the details of the local situation. Similarly, the influence of the organization on its members happens through other members, no matter how high up some of the members are in the organizational hierarchy. While the rules (and their interpretation by others) are external to any individual person, there is no need to posit them as a separate ontological category. These observations suggest that even in the case of organizations, the layer-cake model of the social world is not very illuminating. What is interesting about organizations is the habits and mental representations of their members, the resources they control as members of the organization, and their (materially mediated) interactions, not some higher ontological level.

Again it is good to return to real social scientific questions. They concern issues such as: How do large-scale collective enterprises—for example, organizations— manage (or fail) to achieve certain things? What kinds of unintended consequences do these collective activities have? How does a membership in such collective enterprises influence the individual members? The explanatory answers to these questions often refer to organizations and their properties, but there is no problem in conceiving them as large-scale things influencing smaller-scale things or other large-scale things.

These examples of macro social facts suggest a kind of flat view of society in which the difference between micro and macro is one of scale, not of different levels. The large-scale facts about distributions, frequencies, interactions, and relations have an irreducible explanatory contribution to make, but there is nothing comparable to the mind-brain relation. As a consequence, the metaphor of levels that underlies the layer-cake model does not really help to make sense of the issues that social scientists addressing social macro facts are facing. Giving it up will have a number of beneficial consequences.

First, there are some philosophical advantages. As I will argue in the next section, once we give up the image of levels, we get rid of the problem of causal exclusion that arises from the image of causally competing levels. There is no problem of downward causation as there are only causal influences from large-scale things to small-scale things and descriptions of large-scale things at various levels of abstraction. The problem is replaced with the more down to earth problem of explanatory selection: Under which description can we formulate the most robust claims about counterfactual dependence? Secondly, we no longer have to face the problem of finding an acceptable definition of the comprehensive individual level so that we can argue for or against methodological individualism. We can start analyzing real social scientific explanations instead and focus our attention on the possible contributions that large-scale things make to those on a smaller scale and what kinds of causal mechanisms mediate these influences.

This change in framing also has some advantages when considering relations between disciplines. The division of labor between psychology and the social sciences is justified by differences in scale and the importance of large-scale relations and interactions, not in terms of independent and autonomous levels of reality. This guarantees that the social sciences will never be reduced to psychological sciences. However, thinking in terms of scale also cuts down the false aspirations of disciplinary autonomy. When the social scientists are denied their own autonomous level of reality, the ideal of completely psychology-free social science becomes less appealing. It should be an empirical matter whether the details of human cognition matter for social explanation. It might be that is some cases it makes good mechanistic sense to incorporate some processes on the sub-personal level in the explanatory theory. I will return to this possibility in the final section.

2.4. CAUSATION, CONSTITUTION, AND MICROFOUNDATIONS

One prominent idea in the recent philosophy of biology debate about mechanisms has not been employed in the philosophy of social sciences debate.[1] This is the distinction between causation and constitution. Although the difference between constitutive and causal explanation has been noted earlier (Salmon 1984; see also Cummins 1983), it has only recently become a topic of systematic study (Craver 2007).

Both causation and constitution are relations of dependence (or determination), and they are easily confused. However, there are some crucial ontological differences. Causation is a relation between events; it is about changes in properties. Causation takes time, so we talk about causal processes. Finally, causation is characterized by the asymmetry of manipulation: The effect can be manipulated by manipulating the cause, but not the other way around (Woodward 2003).

In contrast, constitution relates properties. The properties (and relations) of parts constitute the properties of the system (sometimes also the relations to the environment are important). The whole is *made of* its parts and their relations. Unlike causation, constitution does not take time, and we do not talk about the process of constitution. Furthermore, the *relata* of constitution are not "independent existences" (as Hume called them). For this reason we cannot characterize the relation of constitution with the help of the asymmetry of manipulation. For example, the molecular structure of glass constitutes its fragility: To be fragile is to have a particular molecular structure; the fragility is not a consequence of the molecular structure. However, there is another sort of asymmetry: the asymmetry of existence. The parts preexist the system in the sense that the parts can exist independently of the system, but the system cannot exist independently of its parts (although the system can exist independently of particular parts).

An interesting sort of regress characterizes both causation and constitution. In the case of causation, we talk about chains of causation. This is based on the idea that for every event that is a cause, there is another event that is its cause. A similar idea applies to constitution; we assume that all parts can be further decomposed into their parts and their organization. We could call these chains of constitution. Now a tricky question is whether there exists a first cause that is not itself caused, and a similar problem can be stated concerning the ultimate building blocks of reality, but in this context we can leave them aside. There is no danger that such ultimate things will show up in the social sciences. However, these regress properties create chains of explanations, which are relevant from the point of view of the social sciences. The crucial thing in this context is to understand that although there is always an explanation for every social scientific explanatory factor, this does not imply that their explanatory status depends on us knowing the explanation for them. Both in the case of causation and constitution, an explanation presupposes that the *explanans* facts are the case, not that we have to have an explanation for those facts. I will return to this issue in the next section.

Explanation is about tracking relations of dependence. Although metaphysically the relations of constitution and causation are quite different, in terms of explanation the basic principles are quite similar. Both explanations attempt to track networks of counterfactual dependence. A causal explanation tells us how *the antecedent events* and *their organization* (timing and location) bring about the event to be explained. In contrast, a constitutive explanation describes how *the properties of the components* and *their organization* give rise to the system's properties.

In both cases we are looking for the difference-makers: The criterion of explanatory selection is counterfactual. As the precise *explanandum* is best characterized in contrastive terms (why x is the case rather than x*), we are interested in the differences that would have made the difference we are interested in (Woodward 2003; Ylikoski 2007; Northcott this volume). In the case of causation these differences are in antecedent events; in the case of constitution these differences are in the properties of parts (or in their organization). Also in both cases it makes sense to ask a further question: Why does the counterfactual dependence hold? The answers to these questions will in both cases draw from the same body of mechanical knowledge, so it is understandable that in the philosophy of biology debates both explanations are called mechanical explanations. So, despite the important metaphysical differences, the same basic ideas about explanation can be applied to both cases.

Not only are the principles of explanatory relevance similar, so are the explanatory questions. This leads easily to confusion. Consider the question: "Why is this glass fragile?" The question is ambivalent: It could either mean "How did the glass become fragile?" or it could mean "What makes the glass fragile?" The first question is causal; the latter question constitutive. The answer to the causal question will tell us about the causal history of the glass—it will specify the crucial features of the process that led to the object being fragile rather than robust. The answer to the constitutive question will not focus on earlier events. It will detail the relevant aspects of the object's molecular structure that makes it fragile. So while the explanation-seeking questions may look the same, the request for explanatory information is quite different. Without a clear understanding of the differences between causation and constitution, some confusion is bound to occur. This is also the case in philosophy of social sciences. For example, it is quite a different thing to explain how a regime became stable than to explain what makes it stable. While some of the facts cited by both explanations might be the same, they are addressing different *explananda*: One is focused on how the causal capacity was acquired and the other on the basis of that causal capacity. A social scientist is usually interested in both questions, but she should not confuse them with each other.

For all social macro properties, one can ask both constitutive and causal why- and how-questions. (Although for some statistical properties the constitutive questions are relatively trivial.) The first sort of questions asks how the macro properties are constituted by the micro-level entities, activities, and relations. The aim is to track how the details of macro-level facts depend on the micro details. The question is often how the macro facts would have been different if some of the micro facts had been different in some specific way. These questions can also be characterized in terms of interventions: How would the macro facts change if some of the micro facts were changed? Notice that here intervention is a causal notion (all change happens in time), but the dependence of interest is constitutive.

A clear example of constitutive explanation is an explanation for the difference in the problem-solving capacities of two groups. The crucial difference might be in the properties of the members, such as their intelligence or social skills. Alternatively, the pivotal factors might be the informal social norms that characterize the interactions within the group or its formal organization. Of course, the explanation may also be found in some combination of these factors. Just like in this example, the usual *explananda* of constitutive explanations are causal capacities and dispositions of the whole. The constitutive explanation tells us what gives the whole (population, group, organization, or society) those properties, and the answer is found in the causal capacities of the parts and their organization.

The *explanantia* in constitutive explanations are always at the micro level. As the explanation attempts to capture what the whole is made of, an appeal to the properties of the whole does not really make sense. In this sense, the methodological individualists, and other reductionists, have been on the right track. On the other hand, the explanation of macro properties does not in any way diminish their reality: The wholes are as real as their parts. This implies that those methodological individualists who have suggested that a micro explanation somehow eliminates the macro properties are either metaphysically confused or just choosing their words badly. The talk about macro reducing to micro makes as little sense as the talk about reducing effects to their causes.

The causal questions about the macro social properties are concerned with their origin, persistence, and change. These explanations are tracking counterfactual dependencies between events. How would have the outcome been different if some of the causes had been different in some specified manner? What kind of difference would an intervention on some antecedent facts make? The *explanantia* in these causal explanations are always antecedent events.

This is the context in which confusion between constitution and causation can create trouble. If we are considering simple causal statements about causal dependence, individualists tend to make the claim that the causes have to be at the micro level. However, nothing in the notion of causation implies that the real causal work is always to be found at the micro level. Of course, the notion of constitution implies that every time we have a cause at a macro level, we also have micro level facts that constitute it. If we stick to the counterfactual criterion of explanatory selection, as I think we should, there is no a priori reason to privilege micro-level causes (Woodward 2003, 2008). It is sufficient that there is an appropriate counterfactual dependence between the macro variable and the *explanandum*. Of course, in many cases the justification of a claim about this causal dependence might require some knowledge of the underlying mechanisms. However, this observation about the justification of a causal claim should not be confused with the claim itself. Similarly, although adding mechanistic details to the explanation will involve references to micro-level processes, this does not imply that the macro facts will lose their explanatory relevance. They will still be possible difference-makers and legitimate explanatory factors. In other words, although the information about the relevant mechanistic details improves the explanation significantly, it does not remove the causal relevance of the initial invariance involving macro-level facts.

In the counterfactual account of causal relevance, the location of explanatory relevance at the micro or macro level is a contingent matter that depends on the *explananda* that one is addressing. There is no reason to assume that the most invariant counterfactual dependence (with respect to the contrastively specified *explanandum*) will always be found at the micro level. Similarly, one has to give up the often presented suggestion that levels of explanation should match so that macro would always explain macro and micro would always explain micro. The issues of explanatory relevance (how the explanatory factors are selected, at which level of abstraction they are described, etc.) are always determined by the facts of the case and the details of the intended *explanandum*, not by generic philosophical arguments.

2.4.1. The Proper Role of Microfoundations

Is the above argument about the legitimacy of macro-level causal facts compatible with the mechanistic call for microfoundations? I want to argue that it is fully compatible with the core ideas of mechanism-based thinking. Contrary to the common assumption, the point of mechanistic microfoundations is not that we have more real causes at the micro level, but to have a better grasp of the explanatory dependence underlying the causal relation involving macro variables. Consequently, the advocates of mechanism-based explanations should not call into question the reality of macro-level causal relations. Instead, they should emphasize the importance of microfoundations for understanding these dependencies. There are a number of reasons why microfoundations are important.

First, all causal relations involving macro properties are mechanism-mediated causal relations. Understanding how the dependence involving macro variables is constituted helps to understand why that particular dependence holds (Ylikoski 2011). It also integrates the piece of causal information contained in the macro-level generalization to other pieces of explanatory knowledge (Ylikoski and Kuorikoski 2010). This is certainly a form of explanatory understanding that we should be interested in if we take the notion of explanatory social science seriously.

However, the utility of this information is not limited to the expanded theoretical understanding. It also often tells about the conditions under which the causal dependence in question will hold. There are three dimensions to this knowledge. First, there is knowledge about the range of values of the *explanandum* variable that are possible without the dependence breaking apart. Second, there is knowledge about the sensitivity of the dependence to changes in background conditions. Finally, there is possible knowledge about alternative interventions that could bring about similar effects. Without knowledge of these issues, the explanatory use of the macro-level explanatory generalization can be very risky business. It is very difficult to extrapolate to other cases without understanding the background mechanisms (Ylikoski 2011; see also Cartwright, this volume, Kincaid, this volume).

Apart from an expanded understanding and the security of an explanatory claim, the insight into the underlying mechanisms might also help to improve the explanatory generalization. With the help of a mechanistic understanding, one might be able to make the *explanandum* more precise or to reformulate the explanatory generalization in such a manner that it allows a broader range of values of the *explanandum* variables or background conditions (Ylikoski 2011).

These considerations justify the presumption that microfoundations are important for proper explanatory understanding. However, they do not demolish the explanatory relevance of macro facts. On the contrary, they put them in the right context as the mechanisms bridge the large-scale micro facts to causal interactions between persons and to their decision-making processes. I think this is the point James Coleman (1990) attempted to make with his often misunderstood graph.

Following Hedström and Swedberg (1998, 23), I refer to the arrows in figure 2.1 as situational mechanisms (arrow 1), action-formation mechanisms (arrow 2), and

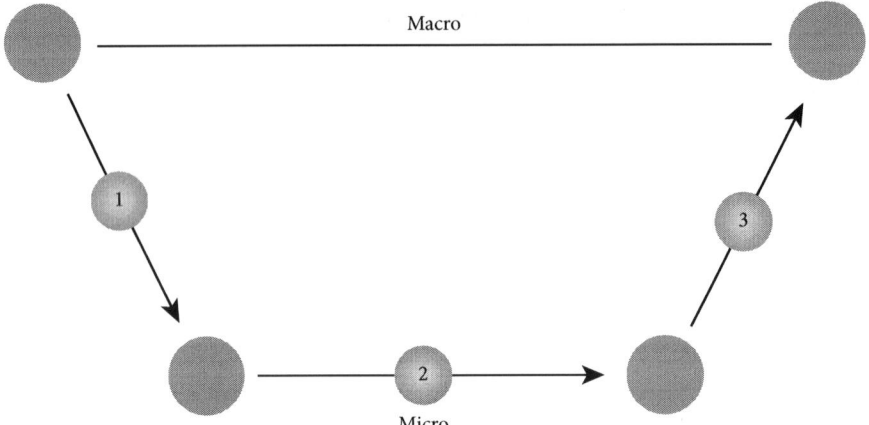

Figure 2.1 Macro-Micro Linkages

transformational mechanisms (arrow 3). The situational mechanisms describe how social structures constrain individuals' actions and cultural environments shape their desires and beliefs, the action-formation mechanisms describe how individuals choose their preferred courses of action among the feasible alternatives, and the transformational mechanisms describe how individual actions produce various intended and unintended social outcomes.

Coleman was critical of nonmechanistic explanations that remain at the level of macro regularities. However, there is no reason to assume that he was denying the causal relevance of macro social facts. Rather, his point was to make it clear that proper sociological understanding requires that we understand both the mechanisms by which large-scale social facts influence the local decision-making processes of individual agents (the situational mechanisms) and the mechanisms by which individual actions create and influence macro social facts (the transformational mechanisms). He was calling for mechanisms that bridge the levels, not just descriptions that somehow reduce the macro facts to individual level facts. Only when we understand the relevant mechanisms, do we have a satisfactory theoretical grasp of the social phenomena in question.

Coleman's criticism of Weber's (partial) explanation of the emergence of modern capitalism in Western Europe illuminates these points. Weber started with an idea that was commonplace in late nineteenth-century Germany: There is a close connection between Protestantism, entrepreneurism, and the rise of capitalism. To substantiate this vague explanatory suggestion, Weber asked what changes the emergence of Protestantism brought about in the beliefs, desires, and communal practices of individual agents. This question has both causal and constitutive dimensions that are not clear in Coleman's analysis. However, Coleman's focus is on Weber's second causal question: How did these changed life practices of individuals influence economic activities and institutions and how did these changes in turn facilitate the formation of modern capitalism? Coleman's central point was that Weber was not clear enough about this last passage of the causal chain. He was not able to give a sufficiently clear account of the transformative mechanisms that connected the Protestant ethic to the rise of modern capitalism. In other words, Weber was not able to show how the changes at the micro level (the life practices of Protestants) bought about a major macro-level outcome (the early forms of modern capitalism). As the crucial mechanism is lacking, so is the legitimacy of Weber's causal claim about history.

Here it is important to see the difference between the justificatory and explanatory roles of mechanisms. Coleman's analysis shows why it is legitimate to challenge Weber's causal claim. Knowledge of the causal mechanisms have an important role in the justification of historical causal claims, so pointing to the missing details of the causal chain constitutes a challenge to the legitimacy of the causal claim. However, this criticism of a singular causal claim does not imply that Coleman generally considers macro-level facts to be nonexplanatory or causally impotent. He is simply challenging the justification of this particular historical hypothesis.

2.5. Intentional Fundamentalism

Arguments for methodological individualism often appeal to the special explanatory status of intentional explanations. I call this position intentional fundamentalism. According to intentional fundamentalism, the proper level of explanation in the social sciences is the level of the intentional action of individual agents. The intentional fundamentalist assumes that explanations given at the level of individual action are especially satisfactory, fundamental, or even ultimate. In contrast to explanations that refer to supra-individual social structures, properties, or mechanisms, there is no need to provide microfoundations for intentional explanations. They provide rock-bottom explanations. In other words, according to intentional fundamentalism, the intentional explanations of individual actions are *privileged* explanations.

Although intentional fundamentalism can take various forms, it is often related to rational choice theory. French social theorist Raymond Boudon (1998, 177) expresses the idea clearly: "When a sociological phenomenon is made the outcome of individual reasons, one does not need to ask further questions." The idea is that in the case of supra-individual explanations there is always a black box that has to be opened before the explanation is acceptable, but in the case of intentional explanation there is no such a problem: "The explanation is final" (Boudon 1998, 172). Diego Gambetta appeals to same sort of finality (1998, 104): "Not only will a rational choice explanation be parsimonious and generalizable; it will also be the end of the story."[2]

My claim in this section is that intentional fundamentalism is not compatible with the causal mechanistic account of explanation. As intentional fundamentalism is often advocated by rational choice theorists and as many believe that rational choice explanations are the best examples of mechanical explanations in the social sciences, this incompatibility claim is of some interest. If my argument is valid, it suggests that the relation of rational choice theory and a mechanism-based philosophy of science requires some rethinking. It also implies that one common argument for methodological individualism is much less credible than is commonly assumed.

2.5.1. The Regress Argument

To make sense of intentional fundamentalism, we should start with *the explanatory regress argument for methodological individualism*. Methodological individualists often make the case that nonindividualist explanations are either explanatorily deficient or not explanatory at all. At most, they allow that explanations referring to macro social facts are placeholders for proper (individualistic) explanatory factors. In this view, the explanatory contribution of supra-individual explanations is at best derived: They are explanatory because they are (in principle) backed up by a truly explanatory story. This is the regress of explanations argument: Unless grounded at the lower level, explanations at the macro level are not acceptable. The underlying general principle is the following:

> [P] A genuine explanation requires that the *explanans* is itself explained or is self-explanatory.

In short, the explanatory buck has to stop somewhere.

The principle [P] is general, and it raises the possibility of an explanatory regress that is only halted at a fundamental (physical) level. This would be highly unintuitive, so for the intentional fundamentalist the buck stops at the level of (self-interested) rational intentional action. This level is treated as inherently understandable, as shown in the above quotations from Boudon. The inherent intelligibility of intentional action explains why the search for microfoundations should stop at the level of the individual. The special status of intentional explanation also makes the explanatory regress argument safe for the methodological individualist: He can use the argument's full force against anti-individualists who cannot make a similar claim about a privileged status, and it does not challenge the legitimacy of his favored explanatory factors.

The fundamentalist argument for individualism fails for a number of reasons. The first reason is that the principle [P] is not valid. The explanatory relation between the *explanans* and the *explanandum* is independent from the question of whether the *explanans* is itself explained. An explanation of X in terms of Y presupposes that Y is the case, but it does not presuppose that Y is itself explained. Of course, it would be great also to have an explanation for Y, but this is a separate issue from the legitimacy of the explanatory relationship between Y and X. The distinctness of these issues implies that the regress does not begin.

Why would anyone believe in [P]? One plausible suggestion is the following: The belief in [P] arises from a straightforward confusion between justification-seeking and explanation-seeking why-questions. It makes sense to ask how well justified are those things that one appeals to in justification of one's beliefs. It also makes sense to ask whether one is justified in believing the things that one appeals to in one's explanation. However, justifying one's belief in Y is not the same as explaining why Y is the case.

2.5.2. Intentional Explanations without a Special Status

Another reason for the failure of the regress argument is that intentional explanations lack the special properties assumed by the argument. If one accepts the mechanistic account of explanation, as many advocates of rational choice sociology do, such a special status does not make any sense. The assumption that human deliberation is a black box that should not be opened is more in line with nineteenth-century hermeneutic romanticism than with causally oriented social science. Of course, the chain of mechanistic explanations will end somewhere (if there is such a thing as a fundamental level), but that stopping point is not the level of individual rational action.

A mechanistic explanation appeals to micro-level processes, but nothing in the notion of mechanistic explanation implies that these micro things would always be facts about the intentional actions of individuals. Mechanisms that cite supra-individual entities or properties are certainly possible (Mayntz 2004). For example, various filtering mechanisms that are analogical to natural selection are difficult to understand other than as population-wide processes, and when the units that are selected are organizations (for example, firms), it is natural to conceive the mechanism as supra-individual. Similarly, the crucial parts of the explanatory mechanism could well be located below the level of intentional psychology. For example, various facts about human information processing—for example, implicit biases (see Kelly and Mallon, this volume)—could well be relevant for explanatory understanding of intentional action. There is no valid reason to give up mechanistic thinking in the case of intentional action.

Another reason to challenge intentional fundamentalism is the implicit realism of mechanistic thinking. For mechanists, explanation is factive. It is not enough that the explanation saves the phenomenon: It should also represent the essential features of the actual causal structure that produces the observed phenomena. So, if the explanation refers to the goals, preferences, or beliefs of agents, the agents should indeed have those mental states. Mere as-if storytelling does not suffice for a mechanistic explanation as it does not capture the relevant parts of the causal process. This realist attitude goes against the instrumentalist attitude common among many rational choice theorists. The fact that one can rationalize any behavior does not imply that those rationalizations are also the correct causal explanations for those behaviors. Similarly, the human fluency in coming up with intentional accounts for our behavior is not a reason for regarding them as superior explanations.

It is important to understand the limited nature of my argument. I am not denying that intentional explanations are, and will be, an indispensable part of the social scientific explanatory repertoire. For me, intentional explanations are legitimate causal explanations. Furthermore, the intentional attitudes of individuals play an important role in most mechanism-based explanations of social phenomena. The only thing I am challenging is the supposed special explanatory status of intentional or rational accounts of human action. In the mechanistic account of explanation, the importance of certain sorts of explanatory factors is not a basis for their privileged status.

Neither should my rejection of intentional fundamentalism be regarded as a wholesale attack on the use of rational choice theory. For many social scientific purposes, a rather simple version of intentional psychology is both preferable and sufficient. For example, when one is attempting to make sense of social complexity, it is understandable that social scientists attempt to keep the psychological assumptions of their models very simple. Such idealizations are fully legitimate if they do not lead to a gross misrepresentation of the causal mechanism under consideration. However, the practical necessity of these idealizations does not constitute a justification for accepting intentional fundamentalism.

Furthermore, my argument should not be regarded as an argument against the claim that there should exist a division of labor between the social sciences and the sciences of cognition. However, it follows from the flexibility of mechanistic levels that the boundaries of this division of labor are adjustable and not fixed. It is inherent in the idea of mechanistic explanation that all the gaps between levels of analysis are ultimately to be bridged by mechanistic interfield theories. So the challenge for the social sciences is not to define their objects of study in such a way that they are in no way touched by psychological sciences, but to look at ways in which social and cognitive mechanisms can be meaningfully combined. This is not as easy as it sounds, as recent attempts to combine neuroscience and economics show (Kuorikoski and Ylikoski 2010).

2.6. CONCLUSIONS

In this chapter, I have attempted to show what consequences the mechanism-based account of explanation would have on issues traditionally discussed under the title of methodological individualism. Borrowing some ideas developed by philosophers who have studied the mechanistic explanation in the biological sciences, I have argued that we should give up the notion of a unique, privileged, and comprehensive individual level that has been a presupposition of the individualism debates. In addition, I have argued that rather than employing metaphors borrowed from the philosophy of mind for micro-macro relations, we should pay closer attention to how real macro social facts figure in social scientific theories and explanations. There the micro-macro issue is more an issue of bridging large-scale social facts to small-scale social interactions rather than that of finding a way to see relations between autonomous levels of reality.

NOTES

....

1. There are some exceptions. For example, Wendt (1998) distinguishes between causation and constitution. However, his discussion of constitution is very confused. His notion of constitution covers not only the constitution of causal capacities, but also causal preconditions, definitions, and other conceptual relations. The standard philosophy of science notion that I am using is limited only to the constitution of causal capacities.

2. The key issue here is not whether these authors would ultimately subscribe to intentional fundamentalism. I am only claiming that in these passages they argue as if intentional fundamentalism is correct.

REFERENCES

....

Bechtel, William. 2006. *Discovering Cell Mechanisms. The Creation of Modern Cell Biology*. New York: Cambridge University Press.

Bechtel, William. 2008. *Mental Mechanism. Philosophical Perspectives on Cognitive Neuroscience*. London: Routledge.

Boudon, Raymond. 1998. "Social Mechanisms Without Black Boxes." In *Social Mechanisms: An Analytical Approach to Social Theory*, Peter Hedström and Richard Swedberg, eds., 172–203. Cambridge: Cambridge University Press.

Burt, Ronald. 1992. *Structural Holes: The Social Structure of Competition*. Cambridge, MA: Harvard University Press.

Coleman, James. 1990. *Foundations of Social Theory*. Cambridge, MA: The Belknap Press.

Craver, Carl. 2007. *Explaining the Brain: Mechanisms and the Mosaic Unity of Neuroscience*. Oxford: Clarendon Press.

Cummins, Robert. 1983. *The Nature of Psychological Explanation*. Cambridge, MA: Bradford/The MIT Press.

Darden, Lindley. 2006. *Reasoning in Biological Discoveries. Essays on Mechanisms, Interfifield Relations, and Anomaly Resolution*. Cambridge: Cambridge University Press.

Elster, Jon. 1989. *Nuts and Bolts for the Social Sciences*. Cambridge: Cambridge University Press.

Elster, Jon. 2007. *Explaining Social Behavior. More Nuts and Bolts for the Social Sciences*. Cambridge: Cambridge University Press.

Gambetta, Diego. 1998. "Concatenations of Mechanisms." In *Social Mechanisms: An Analytical Approach to Social Theory*, Peter Hedström and Richard Swedberg, eds., 102–24. Cambridge: Cambridge University Press.

Harré, Rom. 1970. *The Principles of Scientific Thinking*. London: Macmillan.

Hedström, Peter. 2005. *Dissecting the Social. On the Principles of Analytical Sociology*. Cambridge: Cambridge University Press.

Hedström, Peter, and Peter Bearman, eds. 2009. *The Oxford Handbook of Analytical Sociology*. Oxford: Oxford University Press.

Hedström, Peter, and Richard Swedberg. 1998. "Social Mechanisms: An Introductory Essay." In *Social Mechanisms: An Analytical Approach to Social Theory*, Peter Hedström and Richard Swedberg, eds., 1–31. Cambridge: Cambridge University Press.

Hedström, Peter, and Petri Ylikoski. 2010. "Causal Mechanisms in the Social Sciences." *Annual Review of Sociology* 36: 49–67.

Hempel, Carl. 1965. *Aspects of Scientific Explanation*. New York: The Free Press.

Horgan, Terence. 1993. "From Supervenience to Superduvervenience: Meeting the Demands of a Material World." *Mind* 102: 555–86.

Kim, Jaegwon. 1993. *Supervenience and Mind*. Cambridge: Cambridge University Press.

Kim, Jaegwon. 1998. *Mind in a Physical World*. Cambridge, MA: The MIT Press.

Kincaid, Harold. 1996. *Philosophical Foundations of the Social Sciences. Analyzing Controversies in Social Research*. Cambridge: Cambridge University Press.

Kuorikoski, Jaakko. 2009. "Two Concepts of Mechanism: Componential Causal System and Abstract Form of Interaction." *International Studies in the Philosophy of Science* 23 (2): 143–60.

Kuorikoski, Jaakko, and Petri Ylikoski. 2010. "Explanatory Relevance Across Disciplinary Boundaries—The Case of Neuroeconomics." *Journal of Economic Methodology* 17 (2): 219–28.

Little, Daniel. 1991. *Varieties of Social Explanation: An Introduction to the Philosophy of Social Science*. Boulder, CO: Westview Press.

Mayntz, Renate. 2004. "Mechanisms in the Analysis of Social Macro-Phenomena." *Philosophy of the Social Sciences* 34 (2): 237–59.

McCauley, Robert. 2007. "Reduction: Models of Cross-Scientific Relations and Their Implications for the Psychology-Neuroscience Interface." In *The Handbook of Philosophy of Science. Philosophy of Psychology and Cognitive Science*, Paul Thagard, ed., 105–58. Amsterdam: North Holland.

Oppenheim, Paul, and Hilary Putnam. 1958. "Unity of Science as a Working Hypothesis." In *Concepts, Theories, and the Mind—Body Problem, Minnesota Studies in the Philosophy of Science II*, Herbert Feigl, Michael Scriven, and Grover Maxwell, eds., 3–36. Minneapolis: University of Minnesota Press.

Richardson, Robert. 2007. "Reduction without the Structures." In *The Matter of the Mind. Philosophical Essays on Psychology, Neuroscience, and Reduction*, Maurice Schouten and Huib Looren de Jong, eds., 123–45. Oxford: Blackwell.

Salmon, Wesley. 1984. *Scientific Explanation and the Causal Structure of the World*. Princeton, NJ: Princeton University Press.

Sawyer, R. Keith. 2005. *Social Emergence. Societies as Complex Systems*. Cambridge: Cambridge University Press.

Scott, John. 2000. *Social Network Analysis. A Handbook*. 2nd ed. London: Sage.

Sperber, Dan. 2006. *Explaining Culture: A Naturalistic Approach*. Oxford: Blackwell.

Thagard Paul. 1999. *How Scientists Explain Disease*. Princeton, NJ: Princeton University Press.

Turner, Stephen. 1994. *The Social Theory of Practices. Tradition, Tacit Knowledge and Presupposition*. Cambridge: Polity Press.

Udéhn, Lars. 2001. *Methodological Individualism: Background, History and Meaning*. London: Routledge.

Wendt, Alexander. 1998. "On Constitution and Causation in International Relations." *Review of International Studies* 24 (5): 101–17.

Wimsatt, William. 2007. *Re-Engineering Philosophy for Limited Beings. Piecewise Approximations to Reality*. Cambridge, MA: Harvard University Press.

Woodward, James. 2002. "What Is a Mechanism? A Counterfactual Account." *Philosophy of Science* 69 (3): S366–S377.

Woodward, James. 2003. *Making Things Happen. A Theory of Causal Explanation*. Oxford: Oxford University Press.

Woodward, James. 2008. "Mental Causation and Neural Mechanisms. In Being Reduced." *Essays on Reduction, Explanation, and Causation*, eds. J. Hohwy and J. Kallestrup, 218–62. Oxford: Oxford University Press.

Wright, Cory, and William Bechtel. 2007. "Mechanisms and Psychological Explanation." In *The Handbook of Philosophy of Science. Philosophy of Psychology and Cognitive Science*, ed. Paul Thagard, 31–79. Amsterdam: North Holland.

Ylikoski, Petri. 2003. "Explaining Practices." *Protosociology* 18: 316–30.

Ylikoski, Petri. 2007. "The Idea of Contrastive Explanandum." In *Rethinking Explanation*, eds. Johannes Persson and Petri Ylikoski, 27–42. Dordrecht: Springer.

Ylikoski, Petri. 2011. "Social Mechanisms and Explanatory Relevance." In *From Social Mechanisms to Analytical Sociology*, ed. Pierre Demeulenaere, 154–72. Cambridge: Cambridge University Press.

Ylikoski, Petri, and Jaakko Kuorikoski. 2010. "Dissecting Explanatory Power." *Philosophical Studies* 148 (2): 201–19.

Zahle, Julie. 2006. "Holism and Supervenience." In *The Handbook of Philosophy of Science. Philosophy of Anthropology and Sociology*, eds. Stephen P. Turner and Mark Risjord, 311–41. Amsterdam: North Holland.

CHAPTER 3

....

MECHANISMS, CAUSAL MODELING, AND THE LIMITATIONS OF TRADITIONAL MULTIPLE REGRESSION

....

HAROLD KINCAID

My target in this chapter are three things: the idea that the social sciences need mechanisms, a standard way multiple regression is used in the social sciences to infer causality, and the usefulness of the directed acyclic graph (DAG) approaches (Sprites, Glymour, and Scheines, 2001; Pearl 2000) in understanding social causality. Philosophers of science as well as social scientists have often claimed that the social, behavioral, and biomedical sciences need mechanisms (Elster 1983; Hedström and Swedberg 1998). However, this claim is often muddled. The idea of a mechanism is often unexplained or used in different senses. The reason mechanisms given for why we need mechanism are various, often left inexplicit, and not related to the sense of mechanism at play. In this chapter I use work on causal modeling with directed acyclic graphs to show some circumstances where mechanisms are needed and not needed and to give clear reasons why that is the case. In the process I show how standard regression practices in the social sciences can go wrong and how they can be improved. I also point to some limitations of the DAG program in identifying mechanisms in the social sciences. My examples come from development economics.

3.1. A STANDARD PRACTICE AND A COMMON DEMAND

Here is a standard practice in social research:[1] An investigator is interested in some outcome variable Y. Data sets are collected or existing data sets identified which have measurements of Y and other variables $X_1 . . . X_n$ that might be associated with Y. The $X_1 . . . X_n$ variables are called the independent variables and described as the determinants of Y or as the factors associated with Y. Actual claims to causation are studiously avoided as results are reported. Multiple regressions are run on the data set, producing estimates of the coefficient sizes on the independent variables and providing statistical significance levels of those variables. The significance tests are then used as indicators of whether each independent variable is truly a determinant or factor in outcome Y. Sometimes variables are kept in the regression only if they are significant and the coefficients on the variables that remain are then re-estimated. The regression coefficients are taken to be a measure of the size of the factor or determinant. Proper caution is exercised in reporting the results by noting that correlation is not causation. However, in the closing section where the importance of the results are discussed, policy implications are noted, throwing caution to the wind for causal conclusions about what would happen if we could intervene.

This practice is widespread across the social sciences. A particularly vibrant example that I will return to later in the chapter is work in economics and development studies on growth using cross-country regressions. I have in mind, for example, Robert Barro's *The Determinants of Economic Growth* (1998). Data are collected on most countries in the world. Each country is treated as an individual data point. GDP per capita or some related variable is treated as the outcome variable. The independent variables are observations on each country concerning economic and noneconomic determinants. A regression equation of the following form is estimated:

gdp = investment + open markets + 57 other variables

The 57 other variables do not refer to Heinz, the American brand of ketchup. Rather, the total number of initial independent variables in this country regression work is generally actually 59. Some of those 59 are motivated by economic theory as investment level obviously is. However, probably the majority are variables that someone thought might somehow be relevant and variables for which we have data. So, for example, religion is always included.

Significance levels are reported, variables dropped, and regressions rerun, producing papers with titles such as "I Just Ran 2 Million Regressions" (Sala-i-Martin 1997).[2] Different studies end up with different sets of variables in the final regression. In Barro's work the final set includes common economic variables and institutional variables that fit with the Washington Consensus of the 1990s that emphasized open markets, minimal sized states, and protection of property rights among other things. Interestingly, the regressions run by Sala-i-Martin and by Hoover and Perez (2004) find the education variable to be nonsignificant. Policy recommendations are drawn based on the final surviving regression.

Cross-country growth regressions are not an outlier in social science research. The same kinds of practices are repeated again and again in the social sciences as well as in such fields as epidemiology and public health. For example, a major concern across economics and sociology is the determinants of inequality and the distribution of wealth and income across individuals. A great many studies have been published reporting regressions results using the same recipe as found in the cross-country regressions (Bowles, Gintis, and Groves 2005 is a typical example). Standard analytic epidemiological studies of disease outcomes paired with a final set of covariates or risk factors and their associated coefficients do something similar, though epidemiologists are more wary of extensive stepwise regression (Kincaid 2011a).

These standard uses of regressions to infer causes is one my concerns in this chapter.[3] Another is the demand made by both social scientists and philosophers that good social research must produce mechanisms. This idea predates the current interest in mechanisms by philosophers of science (Machamer, Darden, and Craver 2000). Elster, in *Explaining Technological Change* (1983), argued that we need mechanisms in terms of individual behavior to identify spurious correlations in the social sciences. All the authors in Hedström and Swedberg's *Social Mechanisms* argue that mechanisms should be central to social theory.

I am suspicious of any blanket claim about mechanisms in the social sciences for two reasons. First, I am suspicious of broad methodological pronouncements in science in general. In practice methodological rules require domain and context specific knowledge for their interpretation and application (Day and Kincaid 1994; Kincaid 2011b). Simplicity, for example, has a role in science, but the work that it does often comes from domain-specific instantiations that embody substantial empirical claims (Sober 1989). I would expect the same for claims about mechanisms in the social sciences. A second reason for skepticism about the demand for mechanism results from the fact that the claim can be given several different readings and motivations that are logically independent and need not stand or fall together. A framework for thinking about those differences would help clarify the issues, and I turn now to sketch out the logical space of claims.

A first question is what we want mechanisms for. As I argued some time ago (1996, 1997), we might want a mechanism for *explanatory* purposes or for providing *evidence*. These need not be the same. I may have a well-confirmed association or even a causal claim, but think it is not sufficiently deep enough to explain in some sense—that to explain I need to know how the relation obtains. On the other hand, I might want mechanisms because I doubt an association is real in the first place and believe that providing a mechanism would lend it further credibility. So explaining and confirming with mechanisms can come apart.

Though I will not emphasize it much below, the confirmation versus explanation dichotomy does not exhaust the things we might want to do with mechanisms.

If we move to a more dynamic situation where the generation of research questions and hypotheses is our interest, then mechanisms might play a role there that goes beyond confirmation or explanation. Clearly these sorts of uses are at work in the descriptive accounts of mechanisms in scientific practice from philosophers of science (Bechtel and Richardson 2010).

We can also use mechanisms to confirm two different types of causal claims: assertions that a causal relation *exists* versus assertions about the *size* of the relationship. It is one thing to know that C causes E, another to know how changes in the various values of C result in differing values of E. Mechanisms might be valuable for determining effect size but not effect or vice versa. So having a mechanism might increase my evidence that changes in the interest rate cause changes in employment or it may be needed for me to infer how much a change in interest rates increases or decreases employment.

In terms of explanation or understanding, we can likewise have distinct goals. Mechanisms might help us with the purely social scientific goal to have a *theoretical* understanding of the social phenomena. Achieving that goal does not necessarily mean we know how to *intervene* successfully to change outcomes; mechanisms might be more important in the latter case than in the former. A randomized clinical trial might show us that treatment C causes E without knowing the mechanism. But if we want to intervene, we might want to know the process whereby C causes E, for it is possible our intervention might bring about C and at the same time block the process producing the effect.

Another important difference in thinking about mechanism turns on whether we want *horizontal* or *vertical* mechanisms (see figure 3.1). Asking for horizontal mechanisms is asking for the steps that led from C to E—the intervening causes that makes for a continuous process. I label these horizontal because they are mechanisms at the same level as what the mechanisms relate. The case represented in the figure is the simplest case. In more complex cases M has itself other causal relations at the same level. I will call these more complex causal relations *causal structures*. Horizontal mechanisms are then either simply intervening variables or intervening variables plus causes they interact with over and above C and E.

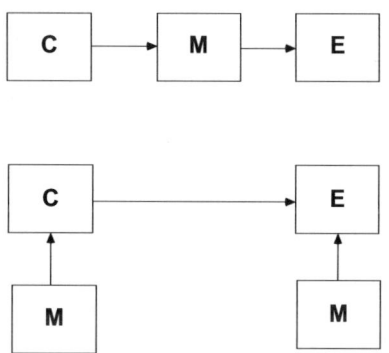

Figure 3.1 **Horizontal versus vertical mechanisms**

Table 3.1 Space of logical possibilities for different possible claims about mechanisms.

Use	Horizontal	Vertical	Effect	Size	Essential	Useful	Theory	Applied
Confirm								
Explain								
Heuristic								

In contrast, vertical mechanisms are the underlying component parts that gives C its capacities to cause E and explain the changes in E. This is what Ylikoski calls a compositional relation in chapter 1 of this volume. So if I explain how changes in the interest rate cause changes in employment by citing changes in aggregate investment, I am citing a horizontal mechanism. If I explain changes in aggregate demand that cause changes in price by citing the budget constraints and utility functions of individuals, then I am citing a vertical mechanism. Arguments for mechanisms in the social sciences are often unclear about which sort of mechanism they entail. Recent philosophical accounts of mechanisms focus on vertical mechanisms.

Orthogonal to all the above distinctions, we might think that having a mechanism is *essential* to what we want to do or we might more modestly claim that having them is helpful or *useful*. Is it the case that we cannot do without mechanisms or rather that they make things easier in scientific practice? Assertions that something is essential for good science make for much stronger demands than claims that they are of some benefit.

So the logical space of claims about mechanisms is large, as illustrated by table 3.1. As a result there are really many different things one might be claiming in asking for mechanisms and surely their plausibility has to be decided case by case and probably by domain and discipline as well. To evaluate demands for mechanisms in the social sciences we need to get specific about exactly which claim we are making among the many possibilities.

3.2. SHOWING HOW DAGS CAN HELP AND HOW STANDARD REGRESSION APPROACHES CAN FAIL

In the introduction I said that I would discuss the strengths and limitation of graphical approaches to causality in the social sciences. I turn to that topic now in order to show that there are two very clear senses, given the distinctions made above, in which mechanisms are valuable in social science research. In showing how they can help I also show how the standard use of regressions to infer causality can fail and thereby how that practice in principle can be improved.

I will argue that the two following claims about mechanisms are plausible:

a. Having a mechanism in the sense of a causal intermediary and relevant structure at the same level is useful, but not essential, in confirming causal relation

b. Having a mechanism in the sense of a causal intermediary and relevant causal structure at the same level can be essential in estimating effect sizes

In other words, horizontal mechanisms are important but not essential for showing causal relations. Horizontal mechanisms can be crucial for getting accurate estimates of how much influence one variable has on another, depending on what the actual causal structure looks like.

So using our logical space diagram, I am claiming that the assertions represented by tables 3.2 and 3.3 below are well supported.

Obviously these are just two of many possible demands for mechanisms; my project is modest. Modesty, however, in this case is a step toward progress that more aggressive and ambiguous claims about mechanisms probably thwart.

I want to support these claims by using graphical approaches to causality and causal inference. Let me provide some basics. By using DAGs it is possible to draw observational implications from different postulated causal structures. Figure 3.2 is a DAG. The lines connecting two nodes is called a path. It is directed in that the links between nodes representing variables are not symmetrical, with the arrowheads representing a postulated causal relation. The graph in figure 3.2 is acyclic in that there is no simultaneous mutual causation; it is not possible to follow a path from a node that returns to itself.[4]

Causes or nodes in the graph are categorized in several important ways. *Direct* causes are those that do not go through another node to get to their effects. The arrows coming into a node come from its *parents* and the arrows leaving go to its

Table 3.2 Horizontal mechanisms can be essential to estimating effect sizes.

Use	Horizontal	Vertical	Causal Effect	Effect Size	Possibly Essential	Useful	Theory	Applied
Confirm	T			T	T			
Explain								
Heuristic								

Table 3.3 Horizontal mechanisms are useful for establishing causal effects.

Use	Horizontal	Vertical	Causal Effect	Effect Size	Possibly Essential	Useful	Theory	Applied
Confirm	T		T			T		
Explain								
Heuristic								

ancestors. When two or more arrows come into a single node, it is called a *collider*. A *common cause* is a node with two direct descendents. So in figure 3.2, A is a parent of B and C and D are descendents of B. B is a common cause of C and D. E is a collider.

Different graphs entail different functional relations or associations that should be seen or not see in the data. Conditional associations are those seen between two variables, given or holding fixed some third variable. Marginal or unconditional associations depend on no third variable. The logic of the graph means that: (1) causes in the graph entail marginal associations, (2) conditioning on colliders create noncausal associations between variables, and (3) conditioning on intervening nodes removes associations. So the causal structure of figure 3.2 entails the dependences and independences listed in table 3.4.

This is a rich set of implications that the data might support or reject. These implications can be tested by particular uses of multiple regression and most generally approached through estimating structure equation models with maximum likelihood that test implied covariance structures.

For my current purposes, DAGs can show how mechanisms can be important or essential, depending on whether we are interested in establishing a causal relation or want to determine an effect size. To make the case that horizontal mechanisms can be quite useful in testing claims about causal relations, consider the situation in figure 3.3. Here I have some evidence for a more minimal model than

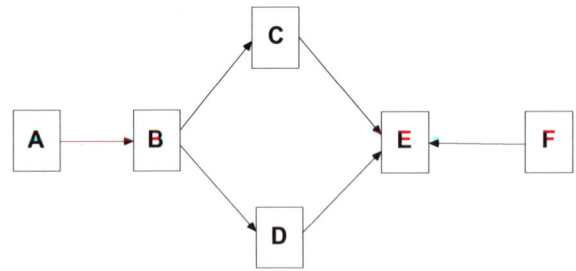

Figure 3.2 Directed Acyclic Graph

Table 3.4 Independencies and associations implied by the model of figure 3.2.

Implied Independencies	Marginal Associations	Conditional Associations
A indep C/B	A and B	C and D/E
A indep D/B	B and D	C and D/F
A indep E/CD	B and C	
A indep F	C, D, and E	
B indep E/ACD	E and F	
B indep F/A	B and E	
C indep D/B		
D indep F/B		

that in figure 3.2—I have not tested for the full causal of model of figure 3.3 with the B to C and D to E mechanism. I think there is a putative causal relation between A and E but worry that the association I am seeing between them is due to an unknown confounder U as illustrated in figure 3.4.

Suppose I next gather further data and find correlational evidence for an intervening mechanism M between A and E. Now my possible confounder has not only to explain the correlation between A and E, but also the correlation between A and M and M and E (see figure 3.5). The number of implied dependencies and independencies has grown: M should be independent of C and E given U and so on. In a structural equation model the effect of adding M is to increase the degrees of freedom and thus to make it easier to test whether the data support an unknown latent variable U.

Finally, imagine that I find correlational evidence to open the black box of M so that I now find associations consistent with our original 3.2. Now the number of implied independencies and independencies that U has to be consistent with have multiplied considerably, providing for a correspondingly more severe test. Identifying horizontal mechanisms thus allows us to provide more stringent tests and stronger evidence.

This provides the argument for my claim that horizontal mechanisms can be useful for establishing causal relations. What about the other assertion, namely, that mechanisms are not essential to establishing causal relations? Elster claimed that we

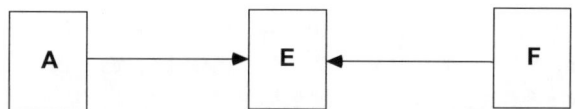

Figure 3.3 More minimal model than in figure 3.1

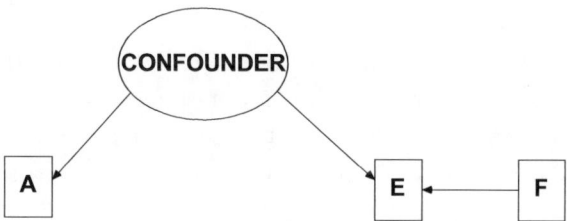

Figure 3.4 Confounder for the model in figure 3.3

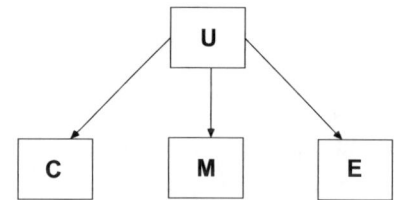

Figure 3.5 Identifying mechanism makes the confounding hypothesis have to do more work

needed individualist accounts to rule out spurious correlations in explanations invoking social entities. That is really a claim about the need for vertical, not horizontal, mechanisms and therefore not my target here. However, it is worth pointing out what is mistaken in this claim nonetheless. Elster was never clear on the horizontal versus vertical distinction in terms of mechanisms. However, providing accounts rooted in individual behavior of the capacities of social entities makes most sense as providing the processes at the individual level realizing those capacities, that is, vertical mechanisms. However, worries about confounding and spurious correlation are worries about causes at the same level as a purported and possibly confounded relation. Ruling out confounding is not helped by Elster's individualism.

Do we absolutely need intervening (i.e., horizontal) mechanisms to rule out spurious causation? No, though as I say above they can be helpful. If I think a causal relation might be confounded and can identify all the possible confounders, then controlling for all them will make the correlation I see go away if confounding is real. If the correlation does not go away, then we can rule out confounding, even though we do not have information on the intervening steps between causes and effect. Randomization in repeated trials is a pretty good way, for example, to show that a treatment has an effect by controlling for confounding causes. We know the treatment has an effect without knowing the processes whereby it does so.

As an aside, I would argue that whether a mechanism—horizontal or vertical—is important in providing evidence for a causal relation depends on the answer to three key questions:

1. How strong is the evidence for the causal connection?
2. How strongly or weakly does your causal claim presuppose specific mechanisms?
3. How strong is your understanding of possible mechanisms?

Arguably in the ideal randomized trial we are assuming nothing about how the agent has its effect either in terms of its composition—the active ingredient—or the intervening steps from administration to outcome. On the other hand, some Keynesian style macroeconomic theories may presuppose that agents are systematically stupid. In the former case the mechanism is relatively unimportant in assessing the causal claim while in the latter it is arguably quite important. Similarly, when we cannot imagine a possible mechanism we should judge differently than when we can imagine many possible mechanisms. So whether mechanisms are useful and important depends—it depends on what else we know. This is an instantiation of my earlier claim that most methodological rules are context bound.

Now I turn to argue for my second and stronger claim about mechanisms: Knowledge of horizontal mechanisms can be essential to confirming claims about *effect size*.[5] Discussions of mechanisms and causation have almost never explicitly separated the project of establishing causality from the task of determining its size. However, the distinction is crucial. Serious bias and inferential error results from assuming the wrong intervening mechanisms and causal structure when estimating how large a given cause may be.

Biases can be introduced in at least three ways:

By conditioning on a mediator—knowing whether and how M is a horizontal mediator between A and B is necessary for estimating effect size of A on B.

By conditioning on a collider—knowing that A and B collide on C is necessary for estimating true size of relation between A and B.

By conditioning on irrelevant variables—knowing which variables are not part of the mechanism is needed to calculate the true efficiency of an estimator.

All are cases where knowing mechanisms can be essential.

The third bias—inefficient estimates due to unnecessary variables—is less about causality and more about inferences from samples to populations and is correspondingly of lesser interest than the other two sources, because the other two biases are independent of sampling issues. Irrelevant variables make it more likely that size estimates of all the variables will be biased downward from the true population values. So causal effect sizes will be inaccurate. Additionally inefficient estimators make it harder to find statistical significance and so including extra variables could have been mentioned in the discussion of establishing causal relations above. So knowing about mechanisms in the sense of being clear on causal structure is important to avoid bias in statistical inference. This moral is quite at odds with the standard practice of controlling for every variable you can think of.

Colliders are important cases where understanding mechanisms in the sense of causal structure is essential to avoid bias in effect size estimates. If we condition on or control for a variable that is the joint effect of two variables whose causal relation size we want to measure, we bias the effect size upward. Conditioning on a collider creates a correlation even when variables are unrelated. So if we include B in a regression aiming to measure the size of the effect of A on C in figure 3.6, we will find a larger effect of A on C than is the case, because conditioning on B creates a correlation over and above that produced by the effect of A on C. Once again, the "throw every possible variable in" strategy will be counterproductive when the variables are colliders and we are trying to estimate effect size.

Finally, conditioning on an intermediate variable—including an intermediate variable in a multiple regression trying to estimate the effect sizes of more distal causes—produces a bias in the other direction (assuming we are dealing only with positive effects; things get more complicated if we allow for counteracting causes). Holding the intermediate variable constant removes the association—or in DAG speak, blocks the path—between the distal causes and the outcome or effect variable, thus biasing the estimate toward the null. Of course, with more complex possible causal relations and combinations of colliders and intervening variables, these

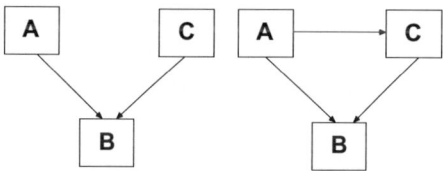

Figure 3.6 Collider bias

biases can reverberate through the results reached in univariate or multivariate regression analyses.

That concludes the destructive side of this section. However, I also promised some constructive advice about how to improve on the standard practice with multiple regression. That advice in short form is to work with an explicit causal model. There are various ways to do that. Probably the most systematic way comes from using an explicit model to identify the implied dependencies and independencies and then to test them against associations found in the data. By imposing the causal restrictions on a set of simultaneous equations representing the totality of causal relations, it is possible to use maximum likelihood estimation to estimate the jointly implied covariances that should be seen in the data if the assumed causal model is true. The differences between the implied and observed covariances will follow a chi-squared distribution. We can use it to test the fit of the model. The resulting statistic will tell us the probability of seeing discrepancies as large as those observed by chance sampling error if the assumed model were true. This reverses the usual pattern for significance tests so that a low p value means an implausible model.[6]

So practice can be improved by using such techniques to test a model. When a model fits well, the size of the coefficients on the causal variables produced by the maximum likelihood procedure will be better estimates of the size of causal effects than produced by the traditional multiple regression practice as will the significance levels on the individual variables. These results will not, however, be the final word because there may be multiple other causal models that equally fit the data. There are ways to try to rule out those possibilities (see Spirtes, Glymour, and Scheines 2001; Shipley 2002), but they involve complexities beyond the purview of this chapter.

I think that the above reasoning is compelling, but I am—and social scientists should be—wary of philosophers who make pronouncements about what scientists should do. So let me analyze an actual, frequently advocated model tested by standard practices and show how that model can be improved by exactly the approach I recommended above.

The model I have in mind is the neoclassical growth model discussed earlier and the data is that used in cross-country regression literature. Using the Sala-i-Martin data set as cleaned up by Hoover and Perez, I estimated two structural equation models, one imposing the assumptions of the Barro account and another, more complex model of my own motivated by some of the case study literature on development economics.

The Barro type model put in explicit form is described in figure 3.7.

That model makes the following assumptions:

1. All independent variables are independent of each other, regardless of any other variable held constant.
2. All independent variables are independent conditional on any other variable.
3. There is unconditional dependency between the dependent variable and each independent variable.

I tested that model by doing a maximum likelihood estimation of it against the data of Sala-i-Martin. The results are given in table 3.5.

So the Barro model does miserably. It has many degrees of freedom and thus is easily testable. The chi-squared test statistic indicates the probability of seeing the differences between the observed and predicted covariances if the Barro model were the true one. The probability that we could see such differences by chance sampling errors is zero. The Barro model is highly implausible, and any test of the preferred equation by an overall F statistic in a multiple regression as given by Barro is unbelievable.

Reality based investigations (e.g., Rodrik 2007) of development suggest that more complex stories are called for. In the Barrow model as tested by Sala-i-Martin and later by Hoover and Perez, education turns out to be insignificant.[7] That result assumes that education is a direct and independent cause of growth. One would expect, however, that the role of education should be rather more complex. Consequently I estimated the more complex model illustrated in figure 3.8 on the same data set.

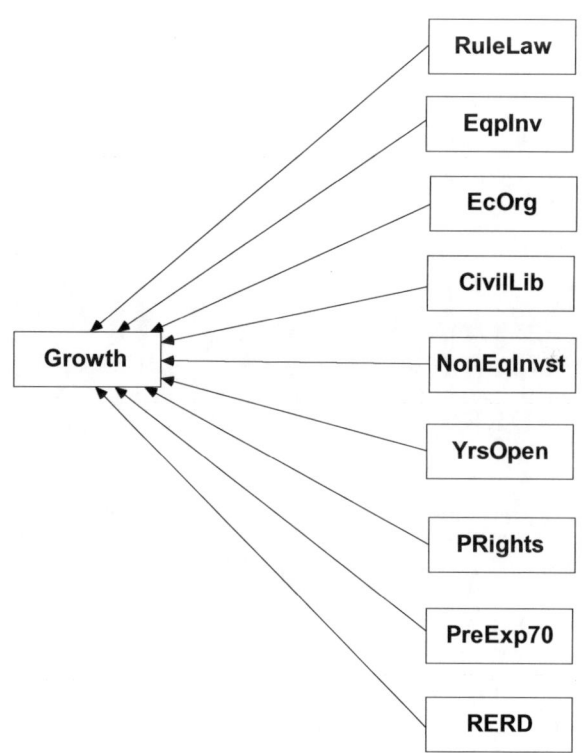

Figure 3.7 **Explicit DAG of the cross-country growth model**

Table 3.5 **Maximum likelihood estimate of the neoclassical growth causal model.**

Degrees of Freedom	36
Chi-square	657.114
Probability Level	.000

Table 3.6 Maximum likelihood estimate of more complex growth causal model.

Degrees of Freedom	2
Chi-square	2.226
Probability Level	.329

The idea is that education has indirect effects on growth, working through other variables. The maximum likelihood estimate of that model produced the results shown in table 3.6.

The model fits the data much better: The chi-square value is with a resulting probability of.329, suggesting relatively good model could not fit—that is, that the differences in the predicted and observed covariances could have happened by chance. Interestingly, the coefficient on the educational variable goes from nonsignificant in the Barro model to significant in this more complex model.

The minimal moral is that supplying an explicit causal model raises substantial doubts about the kind of causal conclusions economists have drawn from the cross-country regressions. A stronger (and thus more tentative) moral is that these results suggest that education plays a causal role in growth. I in no way claim that the model of figure 3.8 is the best model—this is meant to be an illustrative example, not a well-defended empirical conclusion. However, I do believe it is a better model than that proposed by Barro and others and I do think it suffices to make my point that explicit models and the DAG approach can improve practice.

3.3. LIMITATIONS OF DAG APPROACH FOR UNDERSTANDING MECHANISMS

So far I have argued that there are some clear, precise senses in which mechanisms play an important role in social science research and that the DAG framework shows us how that is so. Nonetheless, I think there may be important kinds of mechanisms that are not easily representable by the DAG approach. I want to sketch several circumstances where we may need something more. They all involve what we might call causal complexity. The issues here are complicated, and I do not pretend to have them completely sorted out.

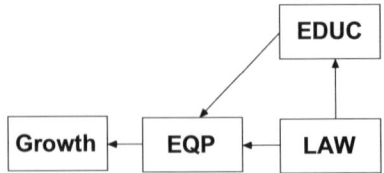

Figure 3.8 DAG for a more causally complex model tested against the Barro data

One route to causal complexity arises from necessary causes. When causes for an outcome are essential—the outcome does not happen without them—we can call them necessary causes. Contrast necessary causes with sufficient causes, where the latter have a causal effect on their own, but other factors can bring about the effect as well. Necessary causes, on the other hand, do not on their own produce the outcome in question.

Necessary causes are an obvious type of mechanism, in that they are components of a complex cause that brings about an outcome. However, the DAG framework has no obvious way to represent them.[8] In a DAG all the causes are sufficient—they all have some influence either indirect or direct that requires no other factors for their influence. Necessary causes are not like that.

Furthermore, neither regression methods nor structural equation models are set up to find necessary causes. Both methods work on using associations to provide evidence for causation. Necessary causes need not produce consistent associations. Since they work only in combination with other factors to produce an outcome, their correlation with the outcome can be tenuous. That happens when the other factors they combine with are often not present in the population sampled. In such circumstances regression coefficients or coefficients produced from a maximum likelihood estimate can be small and insignificant, despite the fact that in reality the causes are essential. This is one kind of complex causal mechanism the DAG framework does not handle. In DAG speak, necessary causes violate the causal Markov condition: The probability of an effect following from its cause is not independent when we condition on the parents of the cause and the ancestors of the effect—the probability depends on the necessary cause. The causal Markov condition is, however, a necessary assumption for determining the implied dependencies and independencies, meaning that when necessary causes are present, we will not correctly get at the evidence for causal relations.[9]

Moderating causes present similar difficulties for the DAG framework in analyzing mechanisms. A moderating cause determines the effect size of some cause on an outcome; the moderating cause has no effect on its own on that outcome.[10] (MacKinnon 2008 calls these pure moderators as opposed to quasimoderators that also have an independent causal effect.) Graphically the relation we would like to represent would look like figure 3.9.

Note that a moderating cause as I define it is not an interaction effect as traditionally conceived. Interaction effects occur when variables have separate independent

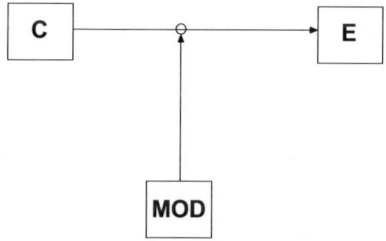

Figure 3.9 Causal moderation

effects and then in addition a joint effect. Moderating causes have no independent effect.

It is worth noting that necessary causes are actually special cases of moderating causes in the sense defined here. If we have a moderating cause such that when its value goes to zero, the effect of the relation it influences goes to zero, then that cause is a necessary one. This relation between moderating causes and necessary causes has not been noticed in the literature insofar as I know.

Why do moderating causes prove problematic for using the DAG framework for accounting for mechanisms? Moderating causes as I define them go beyond the representational power of the DAG formalism in that there is no way of explicitly noting their presence: There is no place for diagrams such as figure 3.9 where M is not a cause of any node in the graph.

It is worth noting that the traditional practice in the multiple regression framework of including product terms to measure the interaction effect of two variables does not fit in the explicitly causal approach that DAGs represent. An interaction term is a logical construct of two other variables. It is not a separate causal variable (Edwards 2009). Because of its logical, entailment relation with the two variables it combines, including an interaction variable in a DAG introduces dependencies that are noncausal and violate what is called the faithfulness condition needed to correctly infer causation from assumed graphs and covariances in the data.

What I have sketched are possibilities—conceivable kinds of causal relations that are intuitively part of horizontal mechanisms and causal structure that are not representable in the DAG framework. It is an empirical matter if and when these kinds of causes are real in the social world. Since I have already used growth and development economics as an example, let me describe some reasons to think that complex causality is real in those areas (see Goertz 2003 for a list of 150 uses of necessity claims in other parts of the social sciences).

Development and growth economics provides some suggestive examples. So let's think about education's role in development. We saw above that in the Barro model education turned out to be insignificant for growth. When I estimated a more complex model, education regained statistical significance but the size of its coefficient was small. However, it might well be that education is a necessary cause of development. Well-educated individuals living in a society that does not have the institutions and markets to put their skills to good use will find those skills wasted; they will contribute little or nothing to growth. Cuba, for example, ranks quite high in educational attainment among developing countries. Cuba's growth rate ranks notably lower. As a necessary cause, education's effect will be dependent on the presence of other causal factors. To the extent that those factors are missing, correlational methods will show low to nonexistent effects and miss its real importance.

Rodrik (2007) makes a similar claim about education vis-à-vis Brazil and El Salvador. Education levels are quite low in both countries. However, Brazil has high returns to human capital and El Salvador low. Higher education is necessary for growth in Brazil, but El Salvador shows it is not sufficient.

Rodrik makes a general case that explaining growth and development requires attention to what he calls "binding constraints"—factors that prevent growth from happening despite the presence of other components that are generally associated with growth. Other investigators point to similar phenomena under the labels of thresholds (Ghosh and Wolf 1998; McMahon and Squire 2003). It is not the presence or absence of variable that makes for a necessary cause but its value, which can of course be translated into the presence or absence of the factor above the threshold level.

These are claims about necessary causes that are a special case of (pure) moderating causes. However, there are good reasons to think that moderating causes have an important role general in explaining development and growth. Why? The growth process is apparently strongly affected by what economists call *complementarities*. Complementarities exist when the action of an agent or the existence of practice affects the marginal benefit to another agent taking an action or to the marginal benefit of another practice. Education is again a good example. A well-trained workforce promotes high value added production and the existence of the latter provides incentives for educational attainment. The influence of either on growth depends on the value of the other. Arguably, there are complementarities across the board for the factors that matter for development. Other examples besides human capital include market size and the division of labor, and financial development and investment. Complementarities create the kind of contextual effects characteristic of what I have called complex causality.

I am not claiming that using explicit DAGs and explicitly testing them in development economics or elsewhere is a bad thing; quite the opposite. It is a significant improvement over the standard practice of uninterpreted regressions. Nor am I claiming the problems I am pointing to are completely unapproachable in the causal modeling framework. For example, samples can be divided along a moderator variable and separate DAGs tested, with differences being evidence for effect modification. My concern, however, is that the DAG formalism not become a hammer where everything is a nail. Other approaches such as using Boolean logic in qualitative comparative analysis (Ragin 1987) may be better motivated when there is causal complexity, though in development economics at least they are nonexistent.

3.4. CONCLUSION

The demand for mechanisms can mean many things, not all of which are equally plausible. I have identified two specific claims that I think are plausible. Moreover, those claims point to weaknesses in standard uses of regression to infer causation, and better social science would be cognizant of those weaknesses and try to avoid them by providing explicit causal models. The DAG framework provides a way to do this, and I show how the cross-country growth models might be improved by doing so. However, social causality is complex in ways that the DAG framework cannot easily handle, and other approaches or more nuanced DAG applications are called for.

ACKNOWLEDGMENTS

Thanks to François Claveau and David Waldner for comments on this chapter.

NOTES

1. There is much social science research that goes beyond this paradigm as pointed out by Waldner in his chapter and as reflected in the chapter by Morgan and Winship. However, I think the practices I describe here are still quite standard. A look at a recent issue of *American Sociological Review, Review of Development Economics*, and *Applied Economics* on my desk revealed that the vast majority of empirical work reported there proceeds exactly as I describe

2. To be fair, Sala-i-Martin's regression numbers are so large because he is examining various robustness tests of cross-country regressions and presumably the average cross-country regression study does not run nearly this many regressions.

3. The use (and abuse) of statistic significance in these practices on my view suggests that a Bayesian framework is needed. But these inferential issues are not my target in this chapter.

4. It is possible to work with cyclic graphs in some circumstances. See Spirtes, Glymour, and Scheines (2001).

5. The "can" qualification is here because one can luck out if the world is helpful and one never has to deal with causal relations that involve colliders, for example. Further complications can arise because "knowing the mechanism" can come to multiple things as well, because the mechanism can be picked out in various ways and at various levels of detail (Kincaid 1996). So I might make a good argument that my effect size estimate is accurate by arguing that, based on background information, some variable could not be a collider and thus that conditioning on it will not produce bias. Thanks to François Claveau for making me see I needed to make this explicit.

6. It only partially represents the model's plausibility in that it tells us p (observed covariances/assumed causal model) while what rational belief requires is p (assumed model/observed covariances).

7. Others who have found education insignificant include (Benhabib and Spiegel 1994; Knowles and Owen 1995; Islam 1995; Caselli, Esquivel, and Lefort 1996; McDonald and Roberts 2002).

8. Pearl has a brief discussion of necessary causes where necessity is represented by p (effect/absence of necessary condition). However this does not so far as I can see provide a solution to epistemic issues raised here that center around the failure of the Markov condition and thus loss of information about the standard entailed dependencies and independencies.

9. It is possible to have a variable that eliminates an effect when it goes to zero but that on positive values has its own effect in addition to influencing the effect size of other variables (quasimoderators). When the causal Markov condition is applied to average values of these variables in a population, then the implied covariances can be derived from the Markov condition. Thanks to Stephen Morgan for pointing this out to me. This example also shows, I believe, that the causal Markov condition can be satisfied without an

assumption of modularity—that is, the assumption that there can be interventions that remove a variable without changing any other causal relation. This is a good reason to wonder whether the philosophical debate over modularity "is relevant to empirical social science" as Morgan puts it (personal correspondence, 2010).

10. It thus differs from Morgan and Winship's formulation (chapter 14) of contextual effects where those effects are nonetheless still direct effects of the outcome.

REFERENCES

Barro, R. 1998. *The Determinants of Growth*. Cambridge: Cambridge University Press.

Bechtel, B., and Richardson, R. 2010. *Discovering Complexity: Decomposition and Localization as Strategies in Scientific Research*. Cambridge, MA: The MIT Press.

Benhabib, J., and M. M. Spiegel. 1994. "The Role of Human Capital in Economic Development: Evidence from Aggregate Cross-Country Data." *Journal of Monetary Economics* 34: 143–73.

Bowles, S., H. Gintis, and M. Groves, eds. 2005. *Unequal Chances*. Princeton, NJ: Princeton University Press.

Caselli, F., G. Esquivel, and F. Lefort. 1996. "Reopening the Convergence Debate: A New Look at Cross-Country Empirics." *Journal of Economic Growth* 1: 363–89.

Day, T., and H. Kincaid. 1994. "Putting Inference to the Best Explanation in Its Proper Place." *Synthese* 98: 271–95.

Edwards, J. 2009. "Seven Deadly Myths of Testing Moderation in Organizational Research." 143–60. In C. Lance and R. Vanderberg, *Statistical and Methodological Myths and Urban Legends*. New York, Routledge, 143–60.

Elster, J. 1983. *Explaining Technological Change*. Cambridge: Cambridge University Press.

Ghosh, A., and H. Wolf. 1998. "Thresholds and Context Dependence in Growth." Working Paper No. 6480. Washington, DC: National Bureau of Economic Research. Issued in March 1998.

Goertz, G. 2003. "The Substantive Importance of Necessary Condition Hypotheses." In G. Goertz and H. Starr, eds. *Necessary Conditions*. Lanham, MD: Rowman & Littlefield, 65–95.

Hedström, P., and R. Swedberg. 1998. *Social Mechanisms: An Analytical Approach to Social Theory*. Cambridge: Cambridge University Press.

Hoover, K.D., and S. J. Perez. 2004. "Truth and Robustness in Cross-Country Growth Regressions." *Oxford Bulletin of Economics and Statistics* 66: 765–98.

Islam, N. 1995. "Growth Empirics: A Panel Data Approach." *Quarterly Journal of Economics* 110: 1127–70.

Kincaid, H. 1996. *Philosophical Foundations of the Social Sciences: Analyzing Controversies in Social Research*. Cambridge: Cambridge University Press.

Kincaid, H. 1997. *Individualism and the Unity of Science: Essays on Reduction, Explanation, and the Special Sciences*. Lanham, MD: Rowman & Littlefield.

Kincaid, H. 2011a. "Causal Modelling, Mechanism, and Probability in Epidemiology." *Causation in the Sciences*, P. Illari, F. Russo, and J. Williamson, eds. Oxford: Oxford University Press.

Kincaid, H. 2011b. "Naturalism and the Nature of Evidence in Economics." In U. Maki, ed., *Handbook for the Philosophy of Science: Philosophy of Economics*. Amsterdam: Elsevier.

Knowles, S., and P. D. Owen. 1995. "Health Capital and Cross-Country Variation in Income Per-Capita in the Mankiw-Romer-Weil Model." *Economic Letters* 48: 99–106.

Machamer, P., L. Darden, and C. Craver. 2000. "Thinking About Mechanism." *Philosophy of Science* 67: 1–25.

MacKinnon, D. 2008. *Introduction to Statistical Mediation Analysis*. London: Routledge.

McDonald, S., and J. Roberts. 2002."Growth and Multiple Forms of Human Capital in an Augmented Solow Model: A Panel Data Investigation." *Economic Letters* 74: 271–76.

McMahon, G., and L. Squire, eds. 2003. *Explaining Growth: A Global Research Project*. New York: Palgrave Macmillan.

Pearl, J. 2000. *Causality: Models, Reasoning, and Inference*. New York: Cambridge University Press.

Ragin, Charles C. 1987. *The Comparative Method: Moving Beyond Qualitative and Quantitative Strategies*. Berkeley: University of California Press.

Rodrik, D. 2007. *One Economics, Many Recipes: Globalization, Institutions, and Economic Growth*. Princeton, NJ: Princeton University Press.

Sala-i-Martin, Xavier, 1997. "I Just Ran Two Million Regressions." *American Economic Review* 87 (2): 178–83.

Shipley, B. 2002. *Cause and Correlation in Biology*. Cambridge: Cambridge University Press.

Sober, E. 1989. *Reconstructing the Past: Parsimony, Evolution, and Inference*. Cambridge, MA: The MIT Press.

Spirtes, P., C. Glymour, and R. Scheines. 2001. *Causation, Prediction, and Search*. Cambridge, MA: The MIT Press.

CHAPTER 4

··

PROCESS TRACING AND CAUSAL MECHANISMS

··

DAVID WALDNER

THIS chapter evaluates the utility and validity of a qualitative method called process tracing. Case-study or qualitative methods have traditionally been viewed as inferentially inferior to randomized experiments or statistical methods. Yet when leading development economists produced a collection of studies of economic growth, they justified their use of case studies instead of the more familiar econometric analysis by arguing, in the words of the volume's editor, that "any cross-national empirical regularity that cannot be meaningfully verified on the basis of country studies should be regarded as suspect" (Rodrik 2003). This endorsement of qualitative analysis is not unique; increasingly, economists, sociologists, and political scientists claim that process tracing is an invaluable tool of causal inference and explanation, as these quotes attest:

> We seek to account for outcomes by identifying and exploring the mechanisms that generate them. We seek to cut deeply into the specifics of a time and place, and to locate and trace the processes that generate the outcome of interest. (Bates et al. 1998, 12)
>
> Nevertheless, there is little doubt that causal explanations cannot be tested directly with cross-sectional studies and that it is diachronic propositions and studies of historical sequence that are needed for settling the issues of a causal interpretation of cross-sectional finding. . . . The causal forces that stand behind the relationship between development and democracy remain, in effect, a black box. (Rueschemeyer, Stephens and Stephens 1992, 29)
>
> One gain from reading these cases is a better understanding of the process leading to civil war. The cases help us understand the complex interactions among variables in the formal/quantitative model and illustrate several different ways in which the same variable can operate in different contexts. . . . Case studies

illuminate the mechanisms that underlie the Collier-Hoeffler theory but are not always distinguishable in the quantitative analysis. (Sambanis 2005, 328)

The resource dependence–civil war correlation has already been established by the large-N studies discussed above. What I wish to determine are the causal processes that link the variables together. (Ross 2004, 48)

What the authors of these quotations share is an emphasis on generative causal processes and mechanisms as crucial components of causal inference and explanation as well as skepticism that even advanced statistical methods provide sufficient information about these processes and mechanisms. Process tracing is thus viewed as a powerful solution to problems surrounding the discovery of causal relations.

There is something puzzling about this new enthusiasm for qualitative methods. Most of the core ideas of qualitative methods are not entirely new; process tracing, for example, was prefigured five decades ago by Nagel's (1961) concept of genetic explanations that identify the sequence of events through which a system is transformed. In contrast, quantitative techniques of causal inference have recently advanced far beyond the traditional model of multivariate analysis critically examined by Kincaid (this volume), as scholars root their understanding of causal inference in counterfactual models of intervention, exploit the properties of causal graphical models, and inventively refine statistical methods such as instrumental variables, regression discontinuity designs, difference-in-difference estimators, and matching algorithms (Holland 1986; Pearl 2000; Woodward 2003; Angrist and Pischke 2009). At the same time, scholars suspicious of basing causal inference on observational data have revived the use of experimental methods in the laboratory, in the field, and in so-called natural experiments (Green and Gerber 2002; Diamond and Robinson 2010). Given these new developments in statistical and experimental techniques, why has a relatively simple method like process tracing gained acceptance?

Process tracing gained acceptance based not exclusively on its methodological credentials, but because of developments in the philosophy of science, namely the critique of the deductive-nomological model of explanation and the development of new models of explanation based on causal mechanisms. Works by Elster (1989), Dessler (1991), Little (1998), and Wendt and Shapiro (1992), among others, introduced empirical social scientists to the literature about scientific realism and causal mechanisms as vital elements of causal explanation. Simultaneously, other works convincingly argued that standard statistical techniques, however elaborate, were not capable of discriminating between association and causation (McKim and Turner 1997). Process tracing benefited from this intellectual ferment; advocates of process tracing contend that this qualitative method could help bridge the gap between association and causation by identifying the intervening steps and mechanisms constituting the causal chain linking a hypothesized cause and its effect (George and Bennett 2005; Waldner 2007; Hedström 2008). Process tracing is thus firmly linked to a mechanism-based understanding of causation.

Process tracing thus promises to perform two functions that should be kept distinct. It can assist both causal inference and causal explanation. This chapter evaluates whether process tracing fulfills that dual promise. I argue that the value of process tracing is critically linked to how we conceptualize causal mechanisms. If we equate causal mechanisms to intervening variables, then process tracing can facilitate causal inference but contribute only minimally to causal explanations. If we wish to claim that process tracing produces adequate causal explanations, we must carefully distinguish mechanisms from intervening variables. Mechanisms explain, I contend, because they embody *invariant* causal properties.

The first section defines process tracing, trying to resolve some of the conceptual ambiguity surrounding it. This section emphasizes the logic of inference I call concatenation. The second section explores the concept of causal mechanisms and its relationship to process tracing. This section emphasizes the distinction between inference and explanation and between intermediary variables and mechanisms. I do not argue for a single model of explanation; rather, I argue that mechanism-based explanations provide substantial value-added relative to other valid conceptions of causal explanations. The third and final section takes a brief but critical look at the methodological foundations of process tracing. Proponents of qualitative methods draw on philosophical debates about mechanisms and causation to argue that process tracing is good; they have done much less work articulating the criteria by which we determine that a particular piece of research counts as good process tracing. Without more work to develop the methodological foundation of process tracing, its potential to provide explanatory utility will go unfulfilled.

4.1. PROCESS TRACING

Process tracing is an umbrella term encompassing a variety of approaches.[1] Definitions of process tracing pick out different features of this composite method. By some definitions, process tracing is the study of how decision-making links initial conditions to outcomes (George and McKeown 1985, 35). Hall's (2003, 393) definition emphasizes "comparing predictions about process to observations of process in the cases at hand." Another definition equates process tracing with attempts to identify the causal mechanisms linking independent and dependent variables (George and Bennett 2005, 206). Steel (2008, 187) gives a more detailed version of this definition, characterizing process tracing as "instantiating a mechanism schema by means of tracing forward or backward, where the components and interactions of one stage place restrictions on those at preceding or subsequent stages." A fourth definition highlights the nature of process-tracing evidence: "The hallmark of process tracing," Gerring (2007) writes, "is that multiple types of evidence are employed for the verification of a single inference—bits and pieces of evidence that embody different units of analysis." Process tracing evidently involves processes, mechanisms, and heterogeneous evidence. It will not be easy to subsume these considerations in a single definition.

I define process tracing as a mode of causal inference based on concatenation, not covariation. Process tracing uses a longitudinal research design whose data consist of a sequence of events (individual and collective acts or changes of a state) represented by nonstandardized observations drawn from a single unit of analysis. Contrast this research design to the more conventional statistical model analyzing a set of ordered pairs (or ordered n-tuplets) of observations of independent, dependent, and control variables, taking the form of standardized observations drawn from a cross-section of units of analysis. By relying on within-case analysis, process tracing privileges internal validity over external validity; in return for this constraint on generality, process tracing has the potential to generate relatively complete explanations.

At least since Hume, covariation has been understood as the most fundamental element of a causal relationship. To identify a causal relationship thus requires multiple observations of both cause and effect. This can be done cross-sectionally, by observing cause and effect relationship in multiple units; longitudinally using time-series data, by making repeated observations of two or more variables in one unit; or with a hybrid study, either time-series, cross-sectional (a small number of units observed repeatedly over time), or with panel data (a large number of units observed over a shorter time period). In experimental studies, the investigator generates the data, intervening to provide a treatment to only one of two groups whose potential confounding factors have been balanced by randomization; the investigator then observes whether any association between treatment and outcome exceeded what might be expected by chance variability. In observational studies without intervention, the investigator collects cross-sectional, time-series, or combined data and then determines whether an association between two or more variables exists when the effects of control variables have been taken into account. The expectation that a causal effect can only be ascertained by observing that one or more independent variables changes in tandem with variation in the dependent variable is so deeply ingrained that, according to orthodox approaches, causal inference is impossible if the dependent variable does not vary: within-case causal inference, from this perspective, is an oxymoron (King, Keohane and Verba 1994; Beck 2006).

Yet advocates of process tracing claim that causal inference can be based on a within-case, longitudinal research design without repeated measurements of causes and effect. As George and McKeown (1985, 35) remark, "case-study researchers often make causal inference without any reliance on quasi-experimental techniques or techniques inspired by a quasi-experimental logic." McKeown (2004, 146) likens process tracing to the procedures used by judges and juries to reach a verdict "based literally on a single case." If, as George and Bennett (2005, 207) state, process tracing follows a logic that is "fundamentally different from methods based on covariance," then what is the logic of process tracing?

The core idea of process tracing is concatenation. Concatenation is the state of being linked together, as in a chain or linked series. In mathematics and computer programming, it is the operation of combining vectors or strings, respectively. In process tracing, one concatenates causally relevant events by enumerating the events constituting a process, identifying the underlying causal mechanisms generating those events, and hence linking constituent events into a robust causal chain that connects one or more independent variables to the outcome in question. To claim the existence of a causal chain is to claim that given entities and mechanisms, one event constrained future events such that a subsequent event was bound to happen, or at least that an earlier event substantially shifted the probability distribution governing the subsequent event, making sequelae far more probable.

Research based on process tracing, to clarify, often contains covariational data and reasoning. Some works trace analogous processes in multiple cases, seeking correlations across space; others range in one case over extended time periods seeking correlations across time. The claim is that in principle, process tracing can be used to make causal inference in the absence of covariational data. Concatenation thus places a very heavy emphasis on claims of necessity, that a cause was necessary, sufficient, or both necessary and sufficient for an outcome to occur. These claims might be based on careful sifting of primary evidence to reconstruct the decision-making process producing a major event. They might as well be based on seemingly well-supported empirical generalizations. Finally, scholars might establish that one event was necessary or sufficient for another by using deductive theories and formal models of social processes. Typically, theories and models will be invoked to demonstrate how macrostructural conditions shape individual-level choices. Reasoning about mechanisms and seeking indirect evidence of their influence thus plays a large part in concatenation. Process tracing accounts, for this reason, tend to make deterministic causal claims that, given a set of initial and scope conditions, an outcome was bound to occur.

Process tracing thus complements the study of variables with the study of events.[2] Philosophers distinguish events, or things that happen or occur, from facts, or "states of affair that obtain." They then further distinguish "event-causation statements," in which one event causes another, from "fact-causation statements," in which one fact causes another (Bennett 1988). An election of a president is an event; the distribution of partisan loyalties in an electorate is a fact, a condition, or a variable, in social-science parlance. Process tracing involves close examination of the interplay between events and facts; it merges event-causation statements with fact-causation statements to demonstrate how initial conditions motivate action that in turn shapes social conditions. One adopts process tracing out of dissatisfaction with the explanatory adequacy of claims that associate a set of facts or variables without establishing the sequence of events, or the process, by which one fact or variable generates others.

For example, take the well-confirmed proposition that reaching a high level of wealth (a fact, or a particular value of the variable income) causes democracy (another fact, a value of the variable regime type). Process tracing responds to the perception that is very difficult to reconcile this description of the relationship between abstract, impersonal facts, with the individual and collective actors whose actions and the events they constitute are recorded in history books. Yet it is precisely through the very concrete sequence of historical events that states of affairs come into being. Process tracing thus mediates between historical events and the abstract relationship between impersonal facts conveyed by quantitative models. Process tracing merges actors and factors and thus seeks to demonstrate how one event, experiencing growing income, motivates actions that produce new events such as shifting preferences from favoring monarchy to favoring democracy, forming political parties, engaging in collective action, and bargaining with power holders. The result of the causal chain is the production of a final event, the establishment of a democratic regime.

Process tracing is most valuable when it constructs causal chains by identifying the causal mechanisms that translate states of affairs (which, as facts, lack intentionality and the capacity for action) into things that happen because the behavior of actors caused them to happen. A chain of events without causal mechanisms would be narrative history; mechanisms without events is a purely theoretical study, where the events might be formal models or informal, verbal presentations. Process tracing braids factors, events, and mechanisms. Mechanisms may be individual instances of decision-making in all its guises (under certainty or uncertainty, with or without constraints, etc.); social-choice functions that aggregate individual preferences into social outcomes; institutional constraints, cultural templates; any piece of theory that connects factors and events. Process tracing can be agnostic about the exact content of mechanisms; the point is that process tracing claims to link events and variables by identifying the underlying mechanisms generating them.

The emphasis on sequences of events and mechanism shapes the morphology of evidence. In orthodox studies, evidence takes the form of a rectangular matrix where rows index units and columns index variables. Each unit has one observation for each variable (ideally, at least: missing values are common). Variables are expected to be operationalized and explicit rules govern the assignment of a value to each variable. The data are thus standardized. The data matrix itself is subject to the basic rules of linear algebra: The rows must be linearly independent and the number of columns cannot exceed the number of rows.

Process-tracing evidence is nonstandardized. It makes no sense to speak of rows and columns in within-case analysis. In contrast to what they call "data-set observations," Brady and Collier (2004, 277) define a causal-process observation as "an insight or piece of data that provides information about context, process, or mechanism, and that contributes distinctive leverage in causal inference." In place of a regimented data set, the investigator assembles one or more observations relating to each step in the causal chain linking cause and effect. The amount of evidence is a function of the length of the causal chain and the quantity of evidence adduced in support of each its steps. The shape of the dataset depends upon the causal structure theorized in each particular case; there is no limit to the number of graphical representations of distinct processes (or, in principle, the number of rival graphical representations of a single process, as we shall see later). The evidence is nonstandardized because it is highly sensitive to the precise nature of the process being traced. Some evidence will represent a macro-structural event (evidence of growing wealth) and some evidence may represent a decision-making process (memoirs or interviews); other evidence will represent collective action (accounts of parties forming, demands being made, concessions granted). The only general properties of this data set are that it represents a sequence of events and individual pieces of evidence will be adjacent to one another. Thus, the key properties of a data set used in process tracing are length, density, and proximity; but none of these attributes can be easily subject to standardization.

Process tracing thus trades off intensive study of one case (or, less frequently, the comparative process tracing of a small number of cases) for extensive study of many cases. One implication of the trade-off between intensive and extensive study is that process tracing is better suited to achieving internal validity at the cost of external validity. One can accept this bargain because of a belief that all cases are unique and so external validity is an illusory goal. Many scholars question the assumption of causal homogeneity, the assumption that, *ceteris paribus*, equal values of the independent variable produce equal values of the dependent variable. The homogeneity assumption may be violated because of general equilibrium effects—for example, greater access to higher education might lower the returns to education—or because causal effects are highly sensitive to local, nonreproducible contexts. One might also privilege internal validity from the belief that knowledge accumulation is better served by deep causal knowledge of one or a few cases over shallow correlational knowledge of many cases.

Finally, and for similar reasons, process tracing seeks relatively complete explanations of token events.[3] One way to describe the trade-off is to distinguish effects of causes from causes of effects. In an important article that made the statistical analysis of causation respectable, Holland (1986, 945) declared that "it is my opinion that an emphasis on the effects of causes is, in itself, an important consequence of bringing statistical reasoning to bear on the analysis of causation and directly opposes more traditional analyses of causation." Defenders of qualitative methods question this emphasis. Mahoney and Goertz (2006) consider an emphasis on the causes of effects to be a defining feature of qualitative methods, process tracing included. A quantitative study of multiple cases gives us information about the expected causal effects of a variable; greater wealth, for example, might be associated with greater probability of democracy and we might feel that this represents a causal relationship between wealth and democracy. Causes of effects, on the other hand, assembles a minimal set of causes that can produce the effect and illuminates the pathways by which they do so. Process tracing, by definition, assembles this set of causes and thus has the potential to identify membership in the set of causes that, given particular contexts, were sufficient to bring about an outcome.

4.2. CAUSAL MECHANISMS

Scholars who developed methods of process tracing to determine the causal process by which a cause generates its effect rejected the claim that causality resided in constant conjunction between two variables, even after controlling for potentially confounding variables. Process tracing thus has affinity with the project of mechanism-based explanations. Mechanism-based explanations gained importance with the demise, carefully chronicled by Salmon (1989), of the deductive-nomological model of explanation. The claim that falling barometers caused storms is fully consistent with the deductive-nomological model, but everyone knows that barometers do not cause storms. Salmon, among others, has argued that scientific explanations consist of more than statistical associations; we explain by giving accounts of how causal mechanisms and processes give rise to observed associations.

The explanatory value of process tracing thus rests on the case for mechanism-based explanations. This link between method and mechanism creates two problems. First, despite widespread dissatisfaction with logical-positivist models of explanation, neither philosophers nor social scientists universally agree that causal explanations require causal mechanisms. Second, among proponents of mechanism-based explanations, there is tremendous heterogeneity in the definition of causal mechanisms. Steel (2008, 39) notes the domain-specific usage of the term "mechanism" and cautions that the term "might reflect only a superficial similarity of subject matter." Reasoning from knowledge of physical processes, Salmon defines causal mechanisms as causal interactions and processes that "are capable of transmitting energy, information, and causal influence from one part of spacetime to another" (Salmon 1998, 71). Thus, a rock striking a window but not the shadow of a passing car transmits a mark beyond the point of intersection. Biological mechanisms are defined differently; Machamer, Darden, and Craver (2000, 3) suggest that "mechanisms are entities and activities organized such that they are productive of regular changes from start or set-up to finish or termination conditions." This definition corresponds to literal systems like car engines or biological mechanisms like protein synthesis (see also Glennan 2008). A definition based on continuous spatio-temporal processes or on organized systems appears less relevant to social mechanisms that involve interacting agents but whose actions do not constitute a spatio-temporally continuous process and are not fully described by their organization (Steel 2008; Russo 2009).

Establishing the value of process tracing thus requires first giving an adequate definition of mechanisms and second establishing the explanatory value-added of mechanisms, given that nonmechanistic explanations are often considered adequate.

Among definitions of social mechanisms, there is unwelcome definitional heterogeneity. Mahoney (2001) identifies approximately two dozen definitions of causal mechanisms. To fulfill the mandate of mechanism-based explanations, definitions of mechanisms should be, using categories suggested by Hitchcock (2008), nonreductive. Reductive theories, such as regularity and probabilistic theories of causation, provide noncausal truth conditions: In this category, mechanisms are types of causal laws, including intervening variables and probabilistic laws. For example, Elster (1998, 48) distinguishes mechanisms from laws only insofar as the former imply the claim that "if $C_1, C_2, \ldots C_n$ obtain, then sometimes E." Nonreductive theories of causation, such as Salmon's ontic theory, avoid this reduction. I would contend that definitions of mechanisms that borrow from reductive theories of causation cannot provide much explanatory power; they do not add much to standard notions of statistical association. To explain associations, mechanisms should be understood in terms of their generative capacity. Little (1998, 197–98) explicitly rejects reductive notions of mechanisms, arguing that

> Causal relations are not constituted by regularities or laws connecting classes of social events or phenomena . . . Instead, social causal relations are constituted by the causal powers of various social events, conditions, structures, and the like, and the singular causal mechanisms that lead from antecedent conditions to outcomes. Accordingly, a central goal of social research is to identify the causal mechanisms that give rise to social outcomes.

George and Bennett (2005, 137) also define mechanisms nonreductively:

> We define causal mechanisms as ultimately unobservable physical, social, or psychological processes through which agents with causal capacities operate, but only in specific contexts or conditions, to transfer energy, information, or matter to other entities. In doing so, the causal agent changes the affected entities' characteristics, capacities, or propensities in ways that persist until subsequent causal mechanisms act upon it.

But many leading accounts of process tracing do not invest mechanisms with this generative capacity. Some accounts refer to causal processes without any reference to mechanisms (Hall 2003); other accounts reference mechanisms but reduce them to intervening processes. Gerring (2008, 163) defines a causal mechanism as "the causal pathway, or process or intermediate variable by which a causal factor of theoretical interest is thought to affect an outcome. Thus: $X_1 \rightarrow X_2 \rightarrow Y$, where X_1 is the exogenous cause, X_2 the pathway(s), and Y the outcome." The language of intermediate variables and pathways is difficult to reconcile with the idea of generative mechanisms, as it suggests a chain of observed associations among causes, intermediate causes, and effects.

Recent developments in causal graphical models clarify the problem with equating causal mechanisms to intervening variables or pathways. Figure 4.1 depicts a directed acyclic graph, or DAG (see Kincaid, this volume).

A graphical model is fully described by a set of vertices, ν and a set of edges, ϵ. Vertices represent random variables, edges represent relations of probabilistic dependence between adjacent nodes on a pathway. From these basic ingredients, a causal graph is constructed by representing direct causal relationships with an arrowhead, such that edges have a direction. A causal graph is acyclic if it contains no directed path that begins and ends at the same node. That the DAG depicted in figure 4.1 omits the edge $\{X_1, X_3\}$ tells us that X_3 is independent of X_1 conditional on X_2.

If we associate mechanisms with causal pathways, then we have a mechanism-based explanation when we insert the node X_2 between the root and terminal nodes, X_1 and X_3. But note that the exact same information about conditional independence

$$X_1 \rightarrow X_2 \rightarrow X_3$$

Figure 4.1 A directed acyclic graph

is conveyed by figure 4.2, called simply a graph, or an independence graph, and hence omitting arrowheads denoting direction. Figure 4.2 also tells us that X_2 screens off X_1 from X_3, making them conditionally independent. But in the independence graph, causation is not inferred from relations of probabilistic dependence.

The translation from association to causation occurs by two assumptions, the Causal Markov condition, which states that a random variable is independent of all variables other than its descendents, conditional on its parents, and the Faithfulness condition. These assumptions basically imply that the DAG is a properly specified model and there are no hidden confounders. Otherwise the two graphs convey exactly the same information. Edwards (1995, 192) thus states that "it some cases it is a matter of taste whether a given model should be thought of as directed or undirected." Pearl (2000, 21–22) prefers a pragmatic defense of the causal interpretation. But the causal interpretation is not consistent with Salmon's *ontic* notion of mechanisms. Recall that Salmon argued that demonstrating statistical relevance was only the first step in constructing an explanation; the second step involved identifying the relevant causal mechanisms and processes (Salmon 1984, 261). Mechanisms, then, should be understood as distinct from statements about conditional probabilities. DAGs convey information about probability distributions generated by mechanisms, but they give no direct information about mechanisms themselves. The causal pathway represented by X_2 does not explain the correlation between X_1 and X_3. It screens off that correlation, so that the marginal association becomes conditional independence. We are still in the world of statistical dependencies, without any clear insight into the nuts and bolts of the causal relations; any substantive causal interpretation comes from outside of the model, not from knowledge of the causal mechanisms.

To see the limitations of equating mechanisms to intermediary nodes and defining process tracing as the construction of DAGs, consider a basic causal claim. Wondering why depressing the gas pedal is correlated with the car moving faster, we use process tracing to flesh out the causal pathway: When we depress the gas pedal, the drivetrain rotates at a faster rate. The middle node screens off the root and terminal nodes: Once we know that the drivetrain is rotating faster, we know that the car must be accelerating, independent of any knowledge about the state of the gas pedal. Have we explained the relationship between the gas pedal and the rate of acceleration? Yes, in the restricted sense that we have additional information about how a car works. But no, because by adding a new variable represented by the intermediary node, we have also added a new question, represented by the new arrow: Why does depressing the gas pedal make the drivetrain rotate faster, and why does that make the car accelerate? So there appears to be a difference between adding nodes to a causal model, on the one hand, and *explaining the relationship between existing nodes*, on the other hand. Adding more nodes only increases the

$$X_1 \text{ ------- } X_2 \text{ -------} X_3$$

Figure 4.2 An independence graph

number of questions we must answer, and so has limited, but not negligible, explanatory value.

If we do not fully explain by adding more variables, how do we explain? Mechanisms explain because they embody an *invariant property*. The first mechanism, linking the gas pedal to the rotating drivetrain, is combustion: The second mechanism, linking the rotating drivetrain to acceleration, is the relationship of torque to force. Combustion is a high energy–initiated, exothermic (heat-generating) chemical reaction between a compound such as a hydrocarbon and an oxidant such as oxygen. The heat generated by combustion increases pressure in a sealed cylinder and impels a piston. A similarly brief description could be given of the relationship between torque, force, and acceleration. The key point is this: Combustion is not a variable. In the proper circumstances—the combination of specific compounds and oxidizing agents, with a high energy initiation to overcome the stability of dioxygen molecules—combustion occurs with law-like regularity. That regularity can in turn be explained by more fine-grained physical processes at the subatomic level.

By saying that a mechanism like combustion is invariant, not a variable, I am stating that it cannot be directly manipulated; one cannot intervene to turn combustion off. We can block the mechanism of combustion from working by intervening on ancestral nodes. We can remove all fuel from the car or disable the electrical system; in either case, depressing the gas pedal will not cause the car to accelerate any longer because combustion cannot take place. But if gas is present and the electrical system is functioning, we cannot intervene to set combustion to the value "off." If a fuel-air mixture is combined with a functioning ignition system, combustion occurs, and so combustion should not be represented by a node in the causal graph upon which we could intervene. Mechanisms embody invariant causal principles and, in particular instantiations, they generate observed correlations. Mechanisms are thus distinct from causal pathways; they explain the location of the directed edges (arrowheads). It is the invariant causal principle combustion that explains why (given a few more mechanical details) depressing the gas pedal makes the drivetrain rotate. Mechanisms explain the relationship between variables because they are not variables.

Let us then define a causal mechanism as an agent or entity that has the capacity to alter its environment because it possesses an invariant property that, in specific contexts, transmits either a physical force or information that influences the behavior of other agents or entities. Information might be a signal that leads a rational actor to update her beliefs, or it might be a culturally determined practice that transmits meaning to other actors. I am insisting on a distinction between causal mechanisms and a group of terms we use for intervening variables, such as causal factor, causal pathway, or causal inference and causal explanation. Causal inference is the activity by which we determine membership in the set of vertices (causal variables included in the model) and the set of edges (relations of direct causation between two variables). Causal inference is how we construct or confirm causal graphical models, determining which nodes must be included, which nodes can be excluded, and along which potential paths to place arrows. Information about causal pathways can help us decide that one of several hypothetical causal models is the correct one or that a hypothesized causal relationship is in fact spurious. Causal explanation, on the other hand, explains *why* the arrows exist on some paths but not others, and *how* probabilistic dependencies and conditional independencies are generated. It gives us causal knowledge of how things work. It does so by invoking causal mechanisms embodying invariant causal principles.

To understand the significance of the distinction between causal inference and causal explanation, consider some recent experimental work in political science that generates valid inferences without identifying causal mechanisms. Experiments are ideal interventions, represented by mutilated graphs; they control confounding variables and hence yield highly credible causal inferences. But they give little insight into underlying mechanisms and hence neglect causal explanation. For example, Hyde (2007) reports the findings of a natural experiment that randomly assigned international observers to precincts in the 2003 Armenian presidential elections. International monitors, Hyde concludes, decreased but did not eliminate electoral fraud. This credible estimation of a causal effect gives no insight into mechanisms, however; as Hyde notes,

> The precise mechanisms by which this [effect] took place are unknown, but a plausible explanation is that the presence of international observers caused polling-station officials to reduce the rate of intended election-day fraud, either because they were instructed to stop fraudulent activities in front of international observers or because they were worried about being caught.

The experiment yielded inferences but not mechanism-based explanation; the speculation about the mechanisms is certainly plausible, but is an interpretation of the experimental findings. Similarly, Wantchekon (2003) reports the findings of a natural experiment studying the effect of clientelist versus public policy mobilization strategies. But Wantchekon too is forced to use qualitative reasoning external to the experiment to speculate about plausible mechanisms. Experiments generate reliable causal inferences, but they invite explanation that must be sought from outside the experiment.

Using process tracing on intervening variables is a valuable tool of causal inference and a critical ingredient of good social science. But the identification of mechanisms has been celebrated as going one step further, as adding deep explanatory knowledge (Salmon 1998). Those who identify intervening processes but not mechanisms should take great pains to demarcate properly their explanatory accomplishments. One cannot make a generic claim about the explanatory virtues of process tracing; it must be reserved for those accounts that identify the invariant causal principles that generate observed associations between variables. One can be agnostic about the nature of those principles and the means used to identify them; one study might use formal models of decision-making to explore how policymakers update their beliefs in light of new information, while another study might use interpretive techniques to explore how expressive actors alter their behavior in light of culturally determined meanings. But to make strong explanatory claims, a process-tracing account must define mechanisms as something more than intervening processes and variables. Seeking causal explanations via process tracing is thus valid contingent on one's definition of causal mechanisms as an invariant causal principles.

Is the extra work needed to identify mechanisms worth the trouble? Kincaid (1996, 181), for example, argues that no universal claim for mechanism-based explanations is defensible, reasoning that,

> If no causal account explains without the mechanism, then almost no causal account explains. After all, we constantly give causal explanations inside science and out while never citing the relevant mechanisms . . . Do I have to cite the subatomic details to explain that the current golf ball caused the broken window?

Recent work by James Woodward (2003) associating explanation with invariant interventions also downplays the role of mechanisms. Woodward claims that his account is fully consistent with the notion of a mechanism, but his basic sketch of a causal explanation does not appear to require explicit statements of mechanisms (Woodward 2002). His position has its supporters among political scientists who discount the value of mechanisms (Sekhon 2008). If Kincaid and Woodward are correct, then identifying mechanisms via process tracing may be an explanatory luxury, not a necessity.

The term "explanation" is connotatively rich; there is surely more than one way to explain. Causal inferences that support counterfactual interventions have explanatory relevance. Put differently, it is not explanatorily irrelevant to know that depressing the gas pedal causes the car to accelerate. It is not my intent to demand a single definition of causal explanation. But it is also worth noting that causal explanations can vary in how much they explain. "We have at least the beginnings of an explanation," James Woodward (2003, 10) claims, "when we have identified factors or conditions such that manipulations or changes in those factors or conditions will produce changes in the outcome being explained." I would like to suggest that if intervention-supporting knowledge begins an explanation, mechanism-identifying knowledge completes the explanation. My proposal is that we think in terms of *explanatory value-added*.

Consider a series of explanatory propositions corresponding to major approaches to causation:

- Regularity theories of causation: Two events are causally linked if one repeatedly follows the other. Thus we explain the event "breaking of a window" by the prior event "the window's being struck with sufficient force by a baseball."
- Counterfactual theories of causation: Two events are causally linked if, were if not for the occurrence of the first, the second would not have occurred. Thus, we explain the window's breaking by claiming that had it not been struck with sufficient force by a baseball, it would not have been broken.
- Manipulation or intervention theories of causation: Two events are causally linked if properly conducted interventions on one variable change the

probability distribution of the second variable. Thus, if we intervene to cause a baseball to strike a window with sufficient force, the window will break.

- Mechanistic theories of causation: Two events are linked if a mechanism triggered by the first event propagates causal influences in a way that ultimately generates the second event. Thus, we explain the window's breaking by reference to the baseball's momentum, the effect of the force transferred to the glass, the process by which glass fractures by the stretching and breaking of the individual interatomic bonds, the weak bonds holding the glass together, and so on.

We do not need to enter into long-standing debates about causality to notice that the fourth candidate explanation, even in its obviously truncated form, provides far more information than any of its predecessors. Perhaps more importantly, it explains its predecessors: The mechanisms invoked by the fourth explanation detail why we see regular associations and why interventions work. Hence, without dogmatically claiming that propositions without mechanisms have no explanatory relevance, it is worth underscoring the tremendous value-added of mechanism-based explanations. To the extent that process tracing provides these mechanism-based explanations, they are extremely valuable tools of both inference and explanation.

4.3. Methodological Validity

The explanatory value-added of process tracing is conditional on its methodological validity. Whereas quantitative methods are anchored in well-established statistical theory that provides diagnostic tests and remedial procedures, process tracing finds justification in philosophical debates. I have provided a rationale for the belief that process tracing is good, but not yet criteria for claiming that a piece of research is good process tracing or procedures for recognizing and correcting errors in process tracing. It is not yet clear, then, that process tracing can bear the explanatory burdens this chapter places upon it.

It might appear that tracing is an unproblematic procedure. According to Merriam's dictionary, the verb *trace* has many meanings; one meaning is "to go backward over the evidence, step by step." Another meaning is "to copy (as a drawing) by following the lines or letters as seen through a transparent superimposed sheet." This connotative ambiguity perhaps creates the perception that one can easily trace causal processes and mechanisms, that carefully sifting through evidence gives transparent illumination of underlying processes and mechanisms.

There are two types of statements about the methodological goodness of process tracing. The first defends process tracing from the most frequent critique of qualitative methods: that of indeterminate research design. A standardized data set takes the form of a matrix, with rows corresponding to the number of observed units and columns corresponding to the number of variables measured. The $n \times k$ matrix represents a system of n equations in k unknowns, and is subject to the rules of linear algebra. If the number of equations is less than the number of unknowns, the system of equations has an infinite number of solutions and so it cannot be the basis for a determinate causal inference. This is known as the "small-n" problem and if the basis for the claim that a single case study is basically useless for causal inference. With only one observation on multiple variables, it is necessarily the case that $n < k$. Case studies, it follows, that are thus vulnerable to inferential errors are of very limited value for developing or testing theories.

Defenders of process tracing have available a compelling defense. The rules of matrix algebra apply to data-set observations, which consist of multiple observations of dependent and independent variables across different units or across time. Process tracing, on the other hand, analyzes causal-process observations, which rely on only one measure of X and Y along with the set of variables that connect them. The rules of matrix algebra do not apply to causal process observations: If causal inference is based on concatenation and not covariation, then we simply do not have to worry about systems of linear equations in which the number of columns exceeds the number of rows. Indeed, Hall (2003) takes the special nature of process-tracing observations to be appropriate to finding causal relations in a complex social world, aligning epistemology with our knowledge of ontology. Hall and others deny that social ontology is compatible with the assumptions of regression analysis. Qualitative researchers, with their detailed and fine-grained knowledge of individual cases, frequently invoke causal complexity, a term referring to a range of conditions that violate the assumption of causal homogeneity that linear transformations imply (Russo 2009, 85–86). Possible incarnations of causal complexity are *equifinality* or multiple causes of an outcome; temporal dependence, where the causal effect of a variable changes over time; interaction effects, where a variable causes one outcome in some cases but a very different outcome in other cases; endogeneity, where outcome variables exert feedback effects on their causes, and path dependence, where the cause of an outcome may depend on where the cause is located in a sequence that includes many other variables. But note that Hall's account of epistemology and ontology says nothing about methodology; it does not tell us which process-tracing accounts successfully navigate obstacles to causal inference amidst complexity and which accounts fail to do so. Complexity, moreover, might be more foe than friend to process tracing: Gerring (2007, 178), for example, argues that general methodological rules cannot be stated because process tracing "borders on the ineffable. Our confidence rests on specific propositions and specific observations; it is, in this sense, ad hoc." If the rules are ad hoc, then how do we evaluate individual process tracing accounts?

A second type of statement of the methodological foundations of process tracing comes closer to traditional methodological concerns about judging the validity of inferences. Lakatos (1970, 115) remarks that science involves a "three-cornered fight" between a theory, its rival, and the evidence. Bennett (2010) builds on this point, arguing that some evidence has high probative value as it disconfirms some hypotheses while simultaneously confirming others. This happy circumstance occurs when theories make certain predictions, such that they can be unequivocally rejected when the prediction is not satisfied by the evidence, and also unique predictions not made by other theories, such that they can be unequivocally accepted when the theory is supported by the evidence. Bennett (2008) argues that as probative evidence accumulates, scholars engage in Bayesian updating, such that causal inferences can be made on the basis of even a few pieces of evidence in a single case. But while Bennett defines the conditions of ideal probative evidence, his position says too little about the determination in individual cases of whether those conditions have been met. Consider an analogy to regression analysis. The Gauss-Markov theorem states the assumptions that must be fulfilled for a linear estimator to be both unbiased and efficient. Statisticians have developed diagnostic tests to evaluate whether these assumptions have been met and corrective measures when they have been violated.

Process tracing cannot yet make reference to an analogous set of diagnostic and remedial procedures. In their absence, proponents of process tracing have little choice but to agree with Collier, Mahoney, and Seawright (2004, 97) who believe that threats to the validity of a qualitative causal inference can be mitigated "if the researcher does a careful job of sifting evidence." But this seemingly reasonable claim needs to confront the philosophical literature on evidence that might puncture that sense of confidence. As Achinstein (2005, 1) summarizes,

> Scientists frequently disagree about whether, or to what extent, some set of data or observational results constitute evidence for a scientific hypothesis. Disagreements may be over empirical matters, such as whether the data or observational results are correct, or whether other relevant empirical information is being ignored. But conflicts also arise because scientists are employing incompatible concepts of evidence.

For example, some scholars might consider confirming evidence to consist of evidence about macro-structural conditions; others might insist on the inclusion of excepts from the documentary record, as in diplomatic histories; still others might contend, as does Beck (2006, 349), that accounts based on the recorded thoughts of decision makers answer the wrong question, as there is a distinction between what decision makers claim was important to them, on the one hand, and why an organization acted as it did, on the other hand. Another axis of evidentiary dispute might consist of evidence that is very general in scope—how do actors in general respond to certain generic stimuli—versus highly contextual and particularistic evidence. In addition, scholars will differ according to their tolerance for counterfactual evidence, or reasoning about what would likely have obtained had one or more causes been absent or taken on different values.

These generic problems of the relationship of theory to evidence are exacerbated in the case of process tracing. The objects being traced are extended processes or causal chains; they involve therefore multiple and independent causal inferences. It is incorrect, moreover, to refer to *the* process that connects cause and effect; processes are multiple, not singular. In fact, there are multiple *types* of processes that can play a role in generating an outcome. A quick and incomplete inventory would include processes of macrostructural change, such as demographic growth, economic development and cultural diffusion; decision-making processes, or the process, rational or impulsive, by which individuals select a course of action given beliefs, preferences, and constraints; and agent-based processes, or the observed actions, cooperative or conflictual, of individuals and groups that comprise an historical narrative. Even this abbreviated discussion implies some thorny methodological problems. First and foremost, prior to tracing a process, scholars *construct* that process by determining the exact interplay of macrostructural, decision-making, and agent-based processes constituting the causal chain. Second, two scholars working in the very same theoretical tradition can construct distinct processes linking cause and effect simply by making distinct selections from the menu of options. Third, and more unsettling, rival theoretical accounts can trace distinct processes leading to the same outcome; structuralists and methodological individualists can both consider their accounts vindicated by the empirical record. Adjudicating intra- and inter-theoretic disputes will become more difficult as proponents of each position assemble process-tracing accounts. It will no longer be a simple case of comparing the alleged predictions of a rival theory against one's own reconstruction of a process, but rather comparing actual process-tracing accounts to one another.

That process tracing works with heterogeneous extended causal chains creates an additional problem. Confronting the problem of extended causal chains and hence a large quantity of causal inferences, Gerring (2007, 182) acknowledges that "it is typical of case study research that multiple links cannot be tested in a rigorous fashion." But advocates of process tracing cannot simultaneously claim to be testing an extended causal chain and also omit multiple causal inferences out of deference to pragmatic considerations. Thus, one can agree with George and Bennett (2005, 222) who claim that "process tracing provides a strong basis for causal inference only if it can establish an uninterrupted path linking the putative causes to the observed effects, at the appropriate level(s) of analysis as specified by the theory being tested." But one can also be aware that few acts of process tracing meet this demanding standard. Claims about the accomplishments and value of process tracing should be commensurately tempered. Without the development of a set of diagnostic tests and remedial procedures, process tracing will remain vulnerable to serious methodological challenge and its promise of explanatory value added will remain unfulfilled.

ACKNOWLEDGMENTS

For helpful comments, I thank Harold Kincaid, Andrew Bennett, John Gerring, Gary Goertz, Anna Grzymala-Busse, Paul Humphreys, James Mahoney, and Daniel Steel.

NOTES

1. Terminological variety abounds: Gerring (2007, 173) reports a list of other terms including causal process observations, pattern matching, colligation, systematic process analysis, genetic explanation, narrative explanation, and sequential explanation.

2. The distinction is potentially confusing because any event can be represented as a single outcome of a random variable. The distinction is between the event "Mary's team won the coin toss" and the random variable describing the probability of obtaining heads when tossing a fair coin.

3. A collection of case studies might illustrate one general theme, such as the role of institutions in generating economic development or political order. But individual case studies explain relatively unique outcomes, such as development in a given location.

REFERENCES

Achinstein, Peter. 2005. "Introduction." In *Scientific Evidence: Philosophical Theories & Applications*, Peter Achinstein, ed. Baltimore: The Johns Hopkins University Press.

Angrist, Joshua D., and Jörn-Steffen Pischke. 2009. *Mostly Harmless Econometrics: An Empiricist's Companion*. Princeton, NJ: Princeton University Press.

Bates, Robert H., Avner Greif, Margaret Levi, Jean-Laurent Rosenthal, and Barry R.Weingast. 1998. "Introduction." In *Analytic Narratives*, Robert H. Bates, Avner Greif, Margaret Levi, Jean-Laurent Rosenthal, and Barry R. Weingast, eds. Princeton, NJ: Princeton University Press.

Beck, Nathaniel. 2006. "Is Causal-Process Observation an Oxymoron?" *Political Analysis* 14 (3): 347–52.

Bennett, Andrew. 2008. "Process Tracing: A Bayesian Perspective." In *The Oxford Handbook of Political Methodology*, Janet M. Box-Steffensmeier, Henry E. Brady, and David Collier, eds. Oxford: Oxford University Press.

Bennett, Andrew. 2010. "Process Tracing and Causal Inference." In *Rethinking Social Inquiry: Diverse Tools, Shared Standards*, Henry E. Brady and David Collier, eds. 2d ed. Lanham, MD: Rowman & Littlefield Publishers, Inc.

Bennett, Jonathan. 1988. *Events and Their Names*. Indianapolis, IN: Hackett Publishing Company.

Brady, Henry E., and David Collier, eds. 2004. *Rethinking Social Inquiry: Diverse Tools, Shared Standards*. Lanham, MD: Rowman & Littlefield Publishers, Inc.

Collier, David, James Mahoney, and Jason Seawright. 2004. "Claiming Too Much: Warnings about Selection Bias." In *Rethinking Social Inquiry: Diverse Tools, Shared Standards*, Henry E. Brady and David Collier, eds. Lanham, MD: Rowman & Littlefield Publishers, Inc.

Dessler, David. 1991. "Beyond Correlations: Toward a Causal Theory of War." *International Studies Quarterly* 35 (3): 337–55.

Diamond, Jared, and James A. Robinson. 2010. *Natural Experiments of History*. Cambridge, MA: Harvard University Press.

Edwards, David. 1995. *Introduction to Graphical Modeling*. New York: Springer-Verlag.

Elster, Jon. 1989. *Nuts and Bolts for the Social Sciences*. Cambridge: Cambridge University Press.

Elster, Jon. 1998. "A Plea for Mechanisms." In *Social Mechanisms: An Analytical Approach to Social Theory*, Peter Hedström and Richard Swedberg, eds. Cambridge: Cambridge University Press.

George, Alexander L., and Andrew Bennett. 2005. *Case Studies and Theory Development in the Social Sciences*. Cambridge, MA: The MIT Press.

George, Alexander L., and Timothy J. McKeown. 1985. "Case Studies and Theories of Organizational Decision Making." *Advances in Information Processing in Organizations* 2 : 21–58.

Gerring, John. 2007. *Case Study Research: Principles and Practices*. Cambridge: Cambridge University Press.

Gerring, John. 2008. "The Mechanismic Worldview: Thinking Inside the Box." *British Journal of Political Science* 38 (1): 161–79.

Glennan, Stuart. 2008. "Mechanisms." In *The Routledge Companion to Philosophy of Science*, Stathis Psillos and Martin Curd, eds. London: Routledge.

Green, Donald P., and Alan S. Gerber. 2002. "Reclaiming the Experimental Tradition in Political Science." In *Political Science: State of the Discipline*, Ira Katznelson and Helen V. Milner, eds. New York: Norton.

Hall, Peter A. 2003. "Aligning Ontology and Methodology in Comparative Politics." In *Comparative Historical Analysis in the Social Sciences*, James Mahoney and Dietrich Rueschemeyer, eds. Cambridge: Cambridge University Press.

Hedström, Peter. 2008. "Studying Mechanisms to Strengthen Causal Inferences in Quantitative Research." In *The Oxford Handbook of Political Methodology*, Janet M. Box-Steffensmeier, Henry E. Brady, and David Collier, eds. Oxford: Oxford University Press.

Hitchcock, Christopher. 2008. "Causation." In *The Routledge Companion to Philosophy of Science*, Stathis Psillos and Martin Curd, eds. London: Routledge.

Holland, Paul W. 1986. "Statistics and Causal Inference." *Journal of the American Statistical Association* 81 (396): 945–60.

Hyde, Susan D. 2007. "The Observer Effect in International Politics: Evidence from a Natural Experiment." *World Politics* 60 (1): 37–63.

Kincaid, Harold. 1996. *Philosophical Foundations of the Social Sciences*. Cambridge: Cambridge University Press.

King, Gary, Robert O. Keohane, and Sidney Verba. 1994. *Designing Social Inquiry: Scientific Inference in Qualitative Research*. Princeton, NJ: Princeton University Press.

Lakatos, Imre. 1970. "Falsification and the Methodology of Scientific Research Programmes." In *Criticism and the Growth of Knowledge*, Imre Lakatos and Alan Musgrave, eds. Cambridge: Cambridge University Press.

Little, Daniel. 1998. *Microfoundations, Method, and Causation*. New Brunswick, NJ: Transaction Publishers.

Machamer, Peter, Lindley Darden, and Carl F. Craver. 2000. "Thinking About Mechanisms." *Philosophy of Science* 67 (1): 1–25.

Mahoney, James. 2001. "Beyond Correlational Analysis: Recent Innovations in Theory and Method." *Sociological Forum* 16 (3): 575–93.

Mahoney, James, and Gary Goertz. 2006. "A Tale of Two Cultures: Contrasting Quantitative and Qualitative Research." *Political Analysis* 14 (3): 227–49.

McKeown, Timothy J. 2004. "Case Studies and the Limits of the Quantitative Worldview." In *Rethinking Social Inquiry: Diverse Tools, Shared Standards*, Henry E. Brady and David Collier, eds. Lanham, MD: Rowman & Littlefield Publishers, Inc.

McKim, Vaughn R., and Stephen P. Turner, eds. 1997. *Causality in Crisis? Statistical Methods and the Search for Causal Knowledge in the Social Sciences*. Notre Dame, IN: University of Notre Dame Press.

Nagel, Ernest. 1961. *The Structure of Science: Problems in the Logic of Scientific Explanation*. New York: Harcourt.

Pearl, Judea. 2000. *Causality: Models, Reasoning, and Inference*. Cambridge: Cambridge University Press.

Rodrik, Dani. 2003. "Introduction: What Do We Learn from Country Narratives?" In *In Search of Prosperity: Analytic Narratives on Economic Growth*, Dani Rodrik, ed. Princeton, NJ: Princeton University Press.

Ross, Michael L. 2004. "How Do Natural Resources Influence Civil War? Evidence from Thirteen Cases." *International Organization* 58 (1): 35–67.

Rueschemeyer, Dietrich, Evelyne Huber Stephens, and John D. Stephens. 1992. *Capitalist Development and Democracy*. Chicago: University of Chicago Press.

Russo, Federica. 2009. *Causality and Causal Modeling in the Social Sciences: Measuring Variations*. New York: Springer.

Salmon, Wesley C. 1984. *Scientific Explanation and the Causal Structure of the World*. Princeton, NJ: Princeton University Press.

Salmon, Wesley C. 1989. "Four Decades of Scientific Explanation." In *Scientific Explanation*, Philip Kitcher and Wesley C. Salmon, eds. Vol. XIII of Minnesota Studies in the Philosophy of Science. Minneapolis: University of Minnesota Press.

Salmon, Wesley C. 1998. *Causality and Explanation*. New York: Oxford University Press.

Sambanis, Nicholas. 2005. "Conclusion: Using Case Studies to Refine and Expand the Theory of Civil War." In *Understanding Civil War: Evidence and Analysis*, Vol. 1— Africa, Paul Collier and Nicholas Sambanis, eds. Washington, DC: The World Bank, 303–34.

Sekhon, Jasjeet S. 2008. "The Neyman-Rubin Model of Causal Inference and Estimation Via Matching Methods." In *The Oxford Handbook of Political Methodology*, Janet M. Box-Steffensmeier, Henry E. Brady, and David Collier, eds. Oxford: Oxford University Press, 271–99.

Steel, Daniel P. 2008. *Across the Boundaries: Extrapolation in Biology and Social Science*. New York: Oxford University Press.

Waldner, David. 2007. "Transforming Inferences into Explanations: Lessons from the Study of Mass Extinctions." In *Theory and Evidence in Comparative Politics and International Relations*, Richard New Lebow and Mark Lichbach, eds. New York: Palgrave Macmillan.

Wantchekon, Leonard. 2003. "Clientelism and Voting Behavior: Evidence from a Field Experiment in Benin." *World Politics* 55 (3): 399–422.

Wendt, Alexander, and Ian Shapiro. 1992. "The Difference Realism Makes: Social Science and the Politics of Consent." *Politics & Society* 20 (2): 197–223.

Woodward, James. 2002. "What Is a Mechanism? A Counterfactual Account." *Philosophy of Science* 69 (3): S366–S377.

Woodward, James. 2003. *Making Things Happen: A Theory of Causal Explanation*. Oxford: Oxford University Press.

CHAPTER 5

DESCRIPTIVE-CAUSAL GENERALIZATIONS: "EMPIRICAL LAWS" IN THE SOCIAL SCIENCES?

GARY GOERTZ

5.1. INTRODUCTION

A core part of the conventional wisdom states that the social sciences[1] have found or produced little or nothing in the way of strong causal or empirical regularities, not to mention empirical laws. Little expresses the standard view quite clearly: "The generalizations that are available in political science, economics, or sociology are weak and exception-laden, and they permit only tentative predictions about future developments" (Little 1993, 186; see Kincaid 1990 for a more optimistic view).

I shall argue—and show—that strong "descriptive-causal generalizations" are in fact quite common, at least common compared to the standard belief of approximately zero. I will provide quite a few examples of strong empirical generalizations throughout the chapter. In addition, we shall see that there are techniques for finding them via relatively simple database (e.g., JSTOR) and Internet searches.

The literature, in philosophy as well as social science, does not give much in the way of details about the forms that causal or empirical generalizations can take. I focus on one important kind of generalization of the form "(almost) all/none A are B." So when I claim that strong empirical and/or causal generalizations are relatively common in political science and sociology, I will be generally referring to generalizations of this form. I will briefly explore one other form that generalizations could take (meta-analytic tendency laws), but the central focus of the chapter is on generalizations of the basic "All/none *A* are *B*" type.

Causal and empirical generalizations of the All/none *A* are *B* type are of particular interest to philosophers since they connect closely with covering law philosophy of science. For example, Woodward and Hitchcock state:

> Laws have traditionally been understood as universal generalizations of the form "All A's are B's." It is our contention that such generalizations, even when they satisfy the conditions for lawhood standardly imposed by philosophers, often fail to be explanatory, or are at best very poor explainers. Discussions of the D-N model of explanation have often employed toy examples of explanations having the logical form:
>
> All A's are B's
> Object o is an A
> Therefore, o is a B
>
> These have always had an air of artificiality about them. Real scientific explanations are much more complex affairs with considerable additional structure. Philosophers of science have generally recognized this but have nonetheless assumed, no doubt under the influence of the D-N model, that [the syllogism above] is an acceptable idealization—that it captures all the essential features of genuine explanations. (Woodward and Hitchcock 2003, 18; see Cartwright 1989, 146 for a similar characterization of the D-N model).

Woodward and Hitchcock's characterization of covering laws and their skepticism about the usefulness or relevance of them seem to be widely held. Thus it is of interest to see that the social sciences have found strong generalizations that could be called covering law generalizations.

By far the most well-known generalization in the field of international relations is known as the democratic peace (e.g., for a basic initial statement see Doyle 1983a, 1983b), which is typically stated in the form: democracies do not fight wars with each other. So while democracies fight many wars (think of the United States), they do not fight wars with other democracies. So if we examine the list of *all* interstate wars (e.g., 1816–2001), *none* are between two democracies. In terms of my canonical form of generalization, *A* is dyadic democracy and *B* is interstate war.

The democratic peace is simultaneously a descriptive claim about empirical data and a causal claim about the relationship between democracy and war. It is for this reason I call generalizations of this type *descriptive-causal generalizations*. The researcher or tradition finds a strong empirical relationship between *A* and *B* and clearly ascribes a causal linkage between *A* and *B*.

Descriptive-causal generalizations can easily be converted into covering law form:

> No wars between democracies. USA and Canada are two democracies.
> *therefore*
> No war between the USA and Canada.

Since descriptive-causal generalizations rely on existing data it means the covering law is strongly confirmed by historical evidence. One can use that to make predictions about the future as well. In addition, such generalizations would support counterfactuals of the sort: If country A had been democracy then the war with country B which is a democracy would not have occurred.[2]

While it is easy—particularly for philosophers—to devise noncausal empirical generalizations (e.g., all the coins in my pocket are dimes), the job of social scientists (at least a large number of them) is to theorize about general causal relationships and try to discover them via systematic empirical analysis. If a descriptive-causal generalization makes it into print in a social science journal, it almost always means that the researchers have good theoretical reasons to believe that there is a causal relationship between A and B.

One might reasonably ask: if descriptive-causal generalizations are so common why is it that social scientists or philosophers have not really noticed them? I answer this question by focusing on the formal, mathematical, and logical nature of the All/none A are B generalization. This generalization is expressed in terms of set theory or mathematical logic. In set theoretic terms it means that A is a subset of B. In logic terms it means that A is a sufficient condition for B. Philosophers as part of their basic training learn a lot about logic; in contrast, social scientists as a rule learn almost nothing about mathematical logic. Social scientists think about generalizations in statistical terms. A really strong statistical generalization might be that A and B are almost perfectly correlated. It is certainly possible (as we shall see) that the generalization All A are B holds perfectly but there is only a modest correlation between A and B.[3] Thus the conventional wisdom which believes we have few cases where A and B are almost perfectly correlated can coexist with numerous generalizations of the form All/none A are B.

The contrast between a logic and/or set theory view of generalizations versus a statistical ones goes very deep. I will discuss a couple (there are more) of ways in which standard statistical methods have trouble "seeing" descriptive-causal generalizations and dealing with them when they see them. For example, I discuss the Paradox of the Perfect Predictor in statistical methodology. A perfect predictor is a descriptive-causal generalization of the All/none A are B form. If such a variable is inserted in standard, maximum likelihood estimation statistical procedures it produces major problems in statistical estimation. These problems are so severe that typically the descriptive-causal variable will just be removed from the analysis. In short, descriptive-causal generalizations are a *problem* for statistical methods, not a *goal* of social science.

On occasion a descriptive-causal generalization is called an *empirical law*. For example, the democratic peace has been referred to in such terms (Levy 1998, who is often cited in this context). There is a long tradition in the philosophy of science that sees scientific laws as exceptionless generalizations: "This emphasis on the role of laws naturally raises the question: 'what is a law of nature?' The standard answer is that laws are (or at least entail) exceptionless generalizations" (Woodward and Hitchcock 2003, 1).

Is there a difference between a descriptive-causal generalization and an empirical law? Our intuitions would suggest that not all of the many descriptive-causal generalizations that I can give merit this label. I argue that most social scientists have focused their attention on the criterion of *exceptionless* in making their decision. However, I think there are many reasons why too much weight is given to this criterion. In addition, there are probably other just as important criteria that are not discussed because the use of the term "law" stops the discussion at "exceptionless."

The philosophy of the special sciences has a great deal to offer to those interested in empirical laws and strong generalizations in the social sciences. Philosophers of science have long grappled with the problem that there seem to be quite successful sciences—for example biology, geology, and so on—which do not seem to conform to the covering law model. Notably, they produce strong theories and generalizations; however, they are rarely exceptionless, they often have vague scope limits, and they involve complex and problematic concepts. In short, social scientists should get their inspiration from the philosophy of biology, not the philosophy of physics.

5.2. DESCRIPTIVE-CAUSAL GENERALIZATIONS

The topic of causal generalizations and regularities has not received much attention, systematic or not, from social scientists. Often concern is expressed about the generalizability of findings either of experiments or case studies, but almost nothing has been done about the kind and nature of potential empirical and/or causal generalizations. This may be a result of the belief that there are no significant broad generalizations in the social sciences.

In contrast, philosophers, particularly those concerned with the so-called special sciences like biology and geology, have shown interest in the topic of regularities and generalizations. Here the interest seems to stem from the fact that many special sciences are quite successful, but at the same time seem to produce little in the way of covering laws.

It is quite interesting that there is little consensus on the terminology used, which suggests to me that issue is decidedly unsettled. Here is a nonexhaustive list: (1) phenomenonal regularities (Little 1993), (2) lawlike regularity (Little 1993), (3) causal regularities (Waters 1998), (4) empirical generalizations (Waters 1998), (5) explanatory generalizations (Woodward and Hitchcock 2003), (6) empirical law (Jones et al. 2009), (7) behavioral laws (Kincaid 1990 66). Philosophers have typically focused on the criteria that might separate accidental generalizations from causal ones. Social scientists who put forward such generalizations usually have good reasons—theories, causal mechanisms, etc.—for the causal relationship between *A* and *B*. The empirical generalization itself is there to support the causal claim. The key thing here is that the scholar is making a causal assertion. As such it is accurate to call these descriptive-causal generalizations since causation is being claimed.[4]

Descriptive-causal generalization can take on different forms, all variations on "(almost) all/none *A* are *B*." It is worth taking a look at some descriptive-causal claims in order to see how they get expressed in the wild. These examples are things that have come up in the natural course of my research and reading. They reflect my interest in international conflict, civil war, conflict management, democracy, comparative politics, and so on. To emphasize the (almost) all-none language of these generalizations, I have put the relevant language in boldface.

> The introduction of universal suffrage led **almost everywhere** (the United States excepted) to the development of Socialist parties. (Duverger 1954, 66)

> **No** famine in democracies. (My version of Drèze and Sen 1989)

> The final generalization is a statement of that sequence of changes in attitude which occurred in **every case** known to me in which the person came to use marihuana for pleasure. (Becker 1953, 236)

> Indeed, the effect of presidential partisanship on income inequality turns out to have been remarkably consistent since the end of World War II. The 80/20 income ratio increased under **each of the six** Republican presidents in this period. . . . In contrast, four of the five Democratic presidents—**all except** Jimmy Carter—presided over declines in income inequality. If this is a coincidence, it is a very powerful one. (Bartels 2008, cited in Tomasky 2008, 45)

> These sharp turning points in growth performance allow us to ask whether manufacturing plays a role in shaping growth performance. Johnson, Ostry, and Subramanian (2006) examined the cases of sustained growth accelerations identified by Hausmann et al. (2005) and found that **nearly all** these cases took place in the midst of a rapid increase in the share of manufactures in total exports. (Rodrik 2006, 6–7)

> **Virtually all** individuals in the top 50th percentile on the AFQT test have a high school education. (My analysis of the bell curve data in Herrnstein and Murray 1994)

> As expected, **all** binding [conflict management] attempts have been carried out by international organizations that have some degree of institutionalization. . . . The most democratic organizations in the sample almost always produce agreements, with **probability .98**. (Hansen, Mitchell, and Nemeth 2008, 307, 313)

These examples illustrate a number of characteristics of descriptive-causal generalizations in their all-none form. The first characteristic of the claim is that it usually involves central variables of the analysis. Most often one variable is a key independent variable while the second variable is a dependent variable. For example, democracy is seen as a key cause of the absence of famines.

Some of these generalizations are quite famous, such as the Duverger one, or the Drèze and Sen one. Others are given really just in passing such as in the Rodrik literature review. It is quite interesting how often scholars will report these descriptive-causal generalizations, then quickly move on, even if it concerns key variables in the analysis. Of course, if you are looking you can find them. I did some analyses of the bell curve data for a session on fuzzy logic (Ragin 2000), and it was quite easy for me to find some in the controversial bell curve data.

The list above is a heterogeneous selection from my rapidly growing collection. But in areas in which I do quite a bit of reading and research, and have PhD students, I have found it relatively easy to find them. For example, Mike Ryckman and I are quite interested in the relationship between terrorism and civil war. As such I can produce quite a few examples in these areas:

> **Every group** mounting a suicide campaign over the past two decades has had as a major objective . . . coercing a foreign state that has military forces in what the terrorists see as their homeland to take those forces out. (Pape 2005, 21)

> **Only one** of the 38 active armed conflicts in the 2001–2005 period took place in the richest quartile of the world's countries: the al-Qaeda strikes on the United States on September 11, 2001. By contrast, more than one-third (17 of 47) of the countries in the poorest quartile in the year 2000 experienced intra-state conflict within the subsequent 5 years. (Buhaung and Gleditsch 2008, 218)

> Two countries with extremely high incidence of terrorism are India and Colombia, both of which have had civil wars. In Krueger and Laitin's data, **only** 5 out of the 33 countries with civil wars had no terrorist incidents (Central African Republic, Republic of the Congo, Guinea-Bissau, Nepal, Papua New Guinea). (Sambanis 2008, 14, fn 18)

> Empirically, **all but one** of the 37 genocides and politicides that began between 1955 and 1998 occurred during or immediately after political upheavals, as determined from the State Failure's roster of ethnic and revolutionary wars and adverse regime changes. (Harff 2003, 62)

> Partition after civil war **only occurred** in cases where there was little democracy prior to the civil war; no country with preconflict democracy greater than–4 [on the polity scale of –10 to 10] was partitioned. (Chapman and Roeder 2007, 685)

> The overall findings, summarized in figure 1, are striking. Initially, we see overwhelmingly that ethnofederal states lacking a core ethnic region are very resistant to collapse—in fact, this investigation **did not reveal a single case** of collapse among thirteen such states. Conversely, **all cases** of ethnofederal state collapse have taken place in systems that featured a core ethnic region. Out of a total of fourteen core-ethnic-region cases, seven have collapsed, three involving large-scale civil war. (Hale 2004, 181)

These various examples hold to the canonical form of "almost all/none A are B." However, there are variations on this theme that can expand the population of descriptive-causal generalizations. One type can be called an asymptotic descriptive-causal generalization. This would be a generalization that gets closer and closer to the all or none point as, say, A gets larger. The Buhuang and Gleditsch example above illustrates how this could happen with GDP/capita and armed conflict. As one increases the GDP/capita level there are fewer and fewer conflicts above the threshold; eventually a point is reached where there are almost no armed conflicts above a given GDP/capita level. Another type is the temporal descriptive-causal generalization. These have the form of All/none *A* are *B* for a certain time period, but after which the generalization is no longer valid. One might have a strong generalization for the pre–World War II period but not after 1945.

In short, social scientists *do* find and make strong, and empirically supported, causal generalizations. At least in the areas in which I work—international relations, comparative politics, economic history, and related subfields of sociology—I have found a long list of them, literally dozens of similar examples. This leads me to suspect that if one hunts for descriptive-causal generalizations they are not that hard to find. I can guarantee the reader that if she is sensitive to them, she will find them in published research in her area, and likely in her own data.

5.3. KINDS OF GENERALIZATION

So if descriptive-causal generalizations are so common, why have they not appeared on the radar of social scientists, or philosophers for that matter? As a matter of scientific practice, one often does not find what one is not looking for. So if researchers are not looking for descriptive-causal generalizations, they might not find them. Another way to put this is that there are various logical or mathematical forms that generalizations can take; some might be common, some might be rare.

In this section I would like to use a famous quote by David Hume to introduce different kinds of generalizations one might make.[5] Critical in this will be a contrast between using logic to make generalizations—that is, generalizations about necessary and/or sufficient conditions versus generalizations that arise when looking at data from a statistical point of view. All/none *A* are *B* generalizations are statements of logic and set theory. They are not directly claims about correlations, average treatment effects, and the like. So the kinds of strong empirical generalizations that arise from looking at data from a statistical perspective might be rare, but empirical generalizations generated by looking at data from the perspective of logic and set theory might be common.

A famous quote from David Hume provides a useful way to introduce different ways to think about causal regularities in the social sciences:

> We may define a cause to be *an object followed by another, and where all the objects, similar to the first, are followed by objects similar to the second.* [definition 1] . . . Or, in other words, *where, if the first object had not been, the second never would have existed.* [definition 2] (David Hume in *Enquiries concerning human understanding, and concerning the principles of morals*)

As many philosophers have suggested, Hume's phrase "in other words" is misleading, if not completely incorrect. The phrase makes it appear as if definition 1 and definition 2 are equivalent, when in fact they represent quite different approaches. Lewis writes that, "Hume's 'other words'—that if the cause had not been, the effect never had existed—are no mere restatement of his first definition. They propose something altogether different: a counterfactual analysis of causation" (Lewis 1986a, 160).

Following Lewis, I shall call Hume's definition 2 the *counterfactual definition*. By contrast, I shall call definition 1 the *constant conjunction definition*, to highlight Hume's idea that causes are always followed by their effects.[6]

It bears emphasizing that I am not arguing that my interpretations should be attributed to Hume himself. Hume's views on causation have been the source of enormous debate among philosophers, and I make no claim to resolving that debate.

The question then is how could one interpret these two definitions, and what generalizations do they refer to? One might interpret definition 1 in terms of logic: if $X = 1$ then $Y = 1$, there is a constant conjunction between the cause and the effect. In other words, from the point of view of logic, definition 1 is about sufficient conditions and not particularly problematic per se. In terms of descriptive-causal generalizations it says that all $X = 1$ are $Y = 1$.

Would this be a reasonable interpretation from a statistical point of view? The answer is no. Fundamental to statistical analysis is variation, particularly on the independent variable. To get going I need to contrast $X = 1$ with $X = 0$ cases.

Much more controversially, one can see Hume's definition 2 as being about what happens for the $X = 0$ cases. One can interpret this definition 2 as being about a causal regularity when X is absent. In terms of logic this means taking the individual case counterfactual, if $\neg X_i$ then $\neg Y_i$, and making it into a causal regularity where X is a necessary condition for Y: if $\neg X$ then $\neg Y$. If this generalization is true then all cases of $X = 0$ are $Y = 0$.

This interpretation of definition 2 in terms of logic is not problematic per se. However, it is a *different* descriptive-causal generalization. One should not (however I do have examples of this happening) confuse a necessary condition with a sufficient condition generalization. It is also certainly possible for one to be completely supported by empirical data while the other is not.[7]

What about Hume's second definition from the statistical point of view? One interpretation might be the constant conjunction of $X = 0, Y = 0$. But again this is a no variance situation, with $X = 0$ instead of $X = 1$.

However, one can combine Hume's two definitions into one statistical one. A correlation of 1.00 means that there is a constant conjunction of $X = 1, Y = 1$ and $X = 0$, $Y = 0$. Definitions 1 and 2 can thus be fused together into one statistical interpretation. Definition 1 holds that when the cause is present, the outcome will be present (probabilistically). Definition 2 holds that when the cause is absent, the outcome will be absent (probabilistically). Since it makes no statistical sense to just look at cases of $X = 1$ without cases of $X = 0$ (or vice versa), the two definitions become joined as one. Neither definition can stand alone and make statistical sense. But when fused together, they offer a coherent notion about a strong generalization, that is, a correlation or R^2 of 1.00.

This is completely consistent with the main emphasis on the "average treatment effect" as the generalization looked for in the Rubin approach to causation (see Morgan and Winship 2007 for a nice treatment). Since the individual cannot receive both the treatment and control at the same time, one of the two possibilities must always remain a counterfactual. This reality leads to a fundamental problem:

> *Fundamental Problem of Causal Inference.* It is impossible to *observe* the value of
> $Y_t(i)$ [t = treatment, c = control] and $Y_c(i)$ on the same unit and, therefore, it is
> impossible to *observe* the effect of t on i. (Holland 1986, 947)

The best the statistician can do is estimate the *average causal effect*, or, to use the
more popular terminology, the average treatment effect (ATE) in the sample or
experiment.

> The important point is that the statistical solution replaces the impossible-to-
> observe causal effect of t on a specific unit with the possible-to-estimate *average*
> causal effect of t over a population of units. (Holland 1986, 947)

This is basically the average of Y_t [t = treatment] minus the average of control Y_c [c
= control], or to use my notation the average of Y for $X = 1$ minus the average of
Y for $X = 0$. If we simplify and make Y dichotomous, then a perfect relationship is
when $X = 1, Y = 1$ and $X = 0, Y = 0$.

The key thing is that we have three potential descriptive-causal generalizations:

1. if $X = 1$ then $Y = 1$ or if $Y = 0$ then $X = 0$. A generalization about sufficient
   conditions.
2. if $Y = 1$ then $X = 1$ or if $X = 0$ then $Y = 0$. A generalization about necessary
   conditions.
3. A generalization where $X = 1, Y = 1$ and $X = 0, Y = 0$. A generalization
   involving a correlation of 1.00.

It is quite possible for the statistical generalization to be only moderately supported by the empirical data, but there must be a strong and even perfect descriptive-
causal generalization of one of the first two types.

5.3.1. A Simple Example

My intuition is that necessary condition descriptive-causal generalizations are relatively common, followed at a distance by sufficient condition generalizations, and
that perfect correlations are extremely rare.

If the reader goes back to my examples of descriptive-causal generalizations
most of them have the necessary condition form. While it is obviously possible
to convert a necessary condition into a sufficient condition statement, this
involves *changing the dependent variable*. To use my favorite democratic peace
example, nondemocracy of one or both of the countries is necessary for war. This
means that joint democracy is sufficient for peace. However, if we stick with the
original dependent variable, war, we may be far from knowing the sufficient
conditions for war.

Since the descriptive-causal generalization involves two variables it is easy to
see that they are related to 2×2 tables (see Goertz, Hak, and Dul forthcoming for a
discussion of the continuous case). Often the quotes that I use arise from some
tables, but often the tables corresponding to the descriptive-causal generalization
are not explicitly given in the text.

One way to find descriptive-causal generalizations is by looking for zero cells in 2×2 or $N \times N$ tables. Table 1 gives a nice little example of this. Here the generalization is that all people admitted to the Berkeley sociology department in 2009 had over the median on the GRE quantitative test. This is the necessary condition descriptive-causal generalization.

What about a sufficient condition generalization? As seen from table 5.1 being over the median is certainly not sufficient for admission. Vaisey (2010) says that extremely high scores on the quantitative are not close to sufficient either.

Most often the search for sufficient conditions from the logic or set theory perspective involves looking not for an individual variable that is sufficient, but rather the combination of variables that is sufficient. In the social sciences Ragin's methods, based on logic, dichotomous and fuzzy, do exactly that (1987, 2000, 2008). Mackie's INUS (1980; see Baumgartner 2008, 2009 for recent treatments) provides a very familiar example of this for philosophers. In the Berkeley sociology context, it is not just high quantitative scores, but high verbal scores, high grade point average, and so on which together might be sufficient for admission. Vaisey (personal communication) states that an initial analysis of the data provided no strong consistent sets of conditions that were sufficient for admission, that is, there are no obvious descriptive-causal generalizations of the form "all $X_1 = 1 * X_2 = 1 * X_3 = 1$ are $Y = 1$."

So, in this case at least, necessary conditions for admission are relatively easy, but sufficient condition descriptive-causal generalizations are difficult.

How would statistical analysis look at this table? As we all know data can be described in many ways. Another, statistical, way to describe these data is to say that there is a correlation of .60 between admission and GRE test scores. So we see a clear connection but it is only moderately strong. The same would be true for many 2×2 tests of association, such as, χ^2.

Most measures of 2×2 association will produce significant results but are generally not very useful in picking out descriptive-causal generalizations. Almost all statistical measures of association will have trouble distinguishing between the generalization that "All A are B" and the different generalization that "All B are A," in other words they cannot distinguish between a necessary versus sufficient condition relationship. Conversely, the vast majority of significant χ^2 tables do not express a descriptive-causal generalization. In general, a significant 2×2 measure of association is not likely to be a descriptive-causal generalization, that is, it would produce massive numbers of false positives if used.

Table 5 .1 Descriptive-causal generalizations: quantitative GRE scores and admission to Berkeley sociology, 2009

	<620	>620
Admit	1	34
No Admit	98	209

Note: 620 is the median quantitative GRE score. Source: Thanks to Steve Vaisey for these data and example.

The point is that if you are defining a strong generalization to be a correlation of 1.00 (or its equivalent), then the conventional wisdom is correct: There are few strong causal generalizations to be found. However, descriptive-causal generalizations of the form all/none *A* are *B* appear on a regular basis as zero cells in *N*×*N* tables.

5.3.2. The Paradox of the Perfect Predictor

The previous subsection illustrated that statistical measures of association in 2×2 tables are not very good at capturing or evaluating All/none *A* are *B* generalizations. This is only one of the problems statistics has with these kinds of generalizations. I cannot go into all of them here (see Goertz, Hak, and Dul forthcoming for another major problem), but it is useful to look at what I call the Paradox of the Perfect Predictor.

A well-known issue in statistical methods involves the *problem* of "perfect predictors."[8] Basically, in maximum likelihood estimation if an independent variable perfectly predicts the outcome, usually a dichotomous variable, then the maximum likelihood equation cannot be estimated (see Zorn 2005 for a nice discussion). In the 1990s, probably most software (e.g., SAS version 6) ignored this problem and would produce meaningless numbers. Current software will issue warnings (e.g., SAS) or remove the variables from the model with a warning (e.g., Stata). Perhaps even worse is R, which goes ahead and estimates the model and leaves it up to the researcher to notice that standard errors are too large.

What is a perfect predictor? It is a generalization of the form all/none *A* are *B*.[9] Descriptive-causal generalizations and perfect predictors are thus in fact the same phenomenon. By definition a perfect predictor means we have a descriptive-causal generalization. Quite amazingly, these are *problems* to resolved and not goals of research.

Most scholars then follow Stata and just eliminate the variable from the model. This leads to what I call the Paradox of the Perfect Predictor:

> Paradox of the Perfect Predictor. All perfect "All/none *A* are *B*" generalizations are removed from the statistical model estimated.

So instead of being excited about finding such a strong relationship the scholar eliminates the variable and often the strongest relationship is discussed in a footnote (if at all). So not only do statistical methods have problems finding descriptive-causal generalizations, but when they do, that variable is usually discarded.

Zorn (2005) discusses several ways to get around this problem and derive "more reasonable" parameter estimates for these variables. He illustrates the classic problem of a perfect predictor:

> In an influential study, Goemans (2000) examines the fate of leaders following major international crises. . . . Goemans's fifth covariate is whether (=1) or not (=0) the leader in question faced a postwar regime change imposed by one or more foreign powers. He notes that for a host of reasons leaders who are overthrown by foreign powers are particularly likely to face punishment; in fact, all 22

of the leaders in his data subjected to such a regime change were exiled, imprisoned, or killed, while only 27 (or 14.8 percent) of the other 182 leaders in his data faced such punishment. (Zorn 2005, 166)

It is worth noting that unlike the Berkeley sociology example, here we have a sufficient condition generalization. As with 2 × 2 measures of association, logic methods cannot distinguish between necessary and sufficient condition relationships. If we converted the variable "foreign-imposed regime change" in table 5.2 into a necessary condition we would get exactly the same statistical results. This is another example where statistical analyses of data do not "see" what is obvious when thinking in terms of logic and set theory.

Zorn (2005) uses Geomans's data and analysis as one of his main examples of perfect predictors. I reproduce his reanalysis in table 5.2. The perfect predictor is "foreign-imposed regime change." Its value in the MLE is 8.4×10^9, that is, log-odds of punishment for such leaders are roughly 8,400,000,000 times greater than cases without foreign intervention.[10] In the more "realistic" model the odds ratio is only 243. In a typical model one is lucky to find an odds ratio of 5–10, here the effect is massively larger. In practice, the value on this variable completely overpowers all the other variables in the model.

This example provides another technique for finding descriptive-causal generalizations: look for variables that have been removed from statistical analysis because they are perfect predictors. These are quite regularly reported in footnotes and text, but probably there are many more where the removal is not discussed in the published findings. In fact, this technique is really a variant of the 2×2 table method described in the previous section. So not only are descriptive-causal generalizations pretty common, they are not that hard to find once one knows how to look.

Table 5.2 MLE and MPLE estimates of postwar leader punishment

Variable	MLEs		MPLEs	
	$\hat{\beta}$	Odds Ratio	$\hat{\beta}$	Odds Ratio
(Constant)	−2.955	−	−2.865	−
	(0.459)		(0.438)	
Other small loser	0.851	2.34	0.845	2.33
	(0.659)		(0.629)	
Other big loser	3.360	28.8	3.198	24.5
	(1.022)		(1.003)	
Mixed-regime small loser	2.693	14.8	2.614	13.7
	(0.622)		(0.607)	
Mixed-regime big loser	3.243	25.6	3.115	22.5
	(0.891)		(0.877)	
Foreign-imposed regime change	22.852	8.40×10^9	5.493	243.0
	(4840.2)		(1.507)	

Note. $N = 204$. Response variable is one for punished leaders, zero if not. Standard errors are in parentheses.
Source: Zorn 2005, 167.

5.4. DESCRIPTIVE-CAUSAL GENERALIZATIONS AND CONTROL OR CONFOUNDING VARIABLES

It is fair to say that much of the literature on causation both statistical and philosophical focuses on the problem of confounding variables. It is always possible that
if one includes a new control variable the key statistical relationship might disappear. A common criticism of reviewers is that the author has failed to include a key
control variable. Economists are in love with them; they include controls and fixed
effects for the cross-section, for each year, for region, and so on. As Lieberson and
Lynn say:

> There are an almost infinite number of conditions or influences on the dependent
> variable (to use the contemporary language of sociology). If a survey generates a
> complex analysis where, say, fifteen variables are taken into account, it is perfectly
> acceptable in contemporary analysis to propose that a sixteenth variable should
> also be considered. There is always the possibility that "controlling" for an
> additional attribute might completely alter the conclusions previously reached.
> (Lieberson and Lynn 2002, 8)

In general it is well known that statistical analyses are fragile: fragile in the
sense that including control variables, analyzing subsets, different indicators for
the same concept, different methods of statistical estimation, and so on can produce significant changes in the results. It is has become quite common in recent
years in political science journals for authors to devote several (precious) journal
pages to robustness analyses. These journal pages, often shadowed by significant
web sites, deal with the fragility issue by varying many of the core features of
the analysis in order to see if the main variables retain their sign and remain
statistically significant.

In philosophy of causation particular attention is typically paid to issue of control or confounding variables.[11] In many analyses of causation, particularly those
relying on statistical approaches, a requirement for X to be a cause of Y is that the
relationship is maintained when control variables are introduced or in subsets of
the population (which are effectively the same thing). Salmon (1984) made homogeneity in subpopulations a core part of his statistical relevance approach. A related
requirement is one of "invariance" (Woodward 2003) or "resilience" (Skyrms 1980).
All of this deals with the core problem of spurious correlation. Cartwright (1989)
makes controlling for spurious correlations one of her most important principles:

> The conventional solution to this problem [of spurious correlation] is to hold C
> [potential cause of the correlation between A and B] fixed: that is, to look in
> populations where C occurs in every case, or else in which it occurs in no case at
> all. . . . If *all* the other causes and preventatives of B have been held fixed as well,
> the only remaining account of the correlation is that A itself is a cause of B. . . .
> This suggests the following causal criterion:
>   CC: C causes E iff $P(E|C \pm F_1 \pm \ldots \pm F_n) > P(E|\neg C \pm F_1 \pm \ldots \pm F_n)$ where
> $\{F_1 \ldots F_n, C\}$ is a complete causal set for E. (Cartwright 1989, 55–56)

Thus to be completely certain that C is a cause of E one must control for all other causes of E, that is, F_i. Of course we typically do not know all the possible causes of E, which is exactly the point Lieberson and Lynn make above.

In contrast descriptive-causal generalizations are robust to the problem of spurious correlation. This means that in general one does not have to worry about the introduction of additional variables removing the statistical relationship:

> No control or confounding variables can defeat a descriptive-causal generalization.[12]

Unlike most statistical generalizations, descriptive-causal generalizations must be true for all subpopulations. So if all A are B for population Z, the same generalization will hold for all subpopulations of Z. Control and confounding variables look for differing relationships within subgroups. A perfect predictor in the population will always be a perfect predictor in a subpopulation.

One can see this intuitively by looking at the causal impact of the perfect predictor in table 2 above. The odds ratio is either essentially infinity or the very large 243 (a large value is typically less than 10). You can imagine adding many control variables; it is very unlikely that this causal effect will go away. In the case of actual perfect prediction the addition of variables will have no effect whatsoever. In the case of a few counterexamples (often indicated by very large standard errors), because of multicollinearity the estimated parameter is likely to decrease in size, but even here the control variables are in general not likely to have much impact.

This illustrates again the difference of looking at things via set theory or logic versus statistical models. A descriptive-causal generalization of the form All/none A are B must be true of all subsets. In contrast, a significant regression coefficient can easily disappear in analyses conducted in a subsample.

This means that descriptive-causal generalizations are thus quite robust. It will be very hard to defeat them using standard statistical strategies. Of course, this is what we would like of strong generalizations and regularities: that they be strong in the face of attempts to disprove them.[13]

5.5. Descriptive-causal Generalizations and Empirical Laws

This chapter has shown that scholars have discovered strong empirical regularities. Sometimes a descriptive-causal generalization receives the name "empirical law." Formally, they do not differ from any of the generalizations I present in this chapter. Yet something about them—and here we enter the realm of the sociology of social science—makes scholars want to use the term "law" to describe them. One of the core items on the methodological agenda for descriptive-causal generalizations is systemizing the evaluation of them. Which deserve the label "empirical law"?

The democratic peace is one of the most famous descriptive-causal generalizations in political science. Jack Levy is often quoted as saying that "this absence of war between democracies comes as close as anything we have to an empirical law in international relations" (Levy 1998, 662). It was this generalization that launched over twenty years of intensive research and theorizing into the relationship between democracy and militarized interstate conflict.

There is a tension when using the term "law," and some social scientists would avoid using that term even if they believe the generalization to be extremely firm. For example, Russett and Starr hesitate to give the democratic peace the empirical law label:

> We begin from the basic empirical observation that democracies very rarely—if at all—make war on each other. Understood as a strong probabilistic observation, rather than an absolute "law," the finding is now generally, though not universally, accepted. . . . the basic finding of a virtual absence of war between democracies emerges with every [democracy] rating scheme employed. (Russett and Starr 2000, 94)

They interpret law to mean "no exceptions," whereas "strong probabilistic observation" means that virtually all cases fit the democratic peace generalization. Russett and Starr report (2010) that they used the term "strong probabilistic observation" in order to avoid dealing with (nitpicking) critics who would use one or two counterexamples to discard the whole basic finding. When Levy says "as close to" an empirical law, he too is thinking about the few potential counterexamples (2010).

It is perhaps not an accident that important strains of philosophy of social science have moved away from the idea of universal laws for the social sciences similar to natural science laws. Much of this discussion has substituted the idea of generalization or regularity for the concept of law (e.g., Woodward and Hitchcock 2003; Waters 1998). These generalizations typically are not universal and they admit a certain number of exceptions. For example, Cooper (1998) finds various empirical regularities are core to biological thinking and research. The scope and number of counterexamples are critical in evaluating the nature and strength of these generalizations; however, these generalizations are core to many sciences outside of physics. It is exactly this sort of phenomenon that Jack Levy refers to as an empirical law in the context of the democratic peace, and which I am calling a descriptive-causal generalization.

Jones and Baumgartner's work on policy-making in general and budgets provides another illustration. Based on a view of policy-making located in the tradition of Herbert Simon and drawing heavily on complexity theory, they argue that all budgeting should fit power law distributions:

> The General Punctuation Hypothesis:
> H1: Output change distributions from human decision-making institutions dealing with complex problems will be characterized by positive kurtosis. This implies that we should **universally** observe positive kurtosis whenever we look at indicators of change in the activities of governments. (Baumgartner et al. 2009, 608–9; boldface is mine)

We have shown evidence for the first time on the generalized punctuation and the progressive friction hypotheses over 30 different government processes in three countries. Looking at dozens of processes across three nations and covering several hundred thousand observations, we have **not found a single** Normal distribution, even though the Central Limit Theorem implies that Normality would be expected in the social input series that serve as the grist for the mill of the policymaking process. (Baumgartner et al. 2009, 615; boldface is mine).

It is not surprising then that they entitle one of their recent articles "A General Empirical Law of Public Budgets" (Jones et al. 2009). They think that there are no public budget data that has a normal distribution.

In a personal conversation with Jones and Baumgartner I asked why they used the term "empirical law". They were very clear that if they had found but one counterexample to their hypothesis they would not have used that term. As we saw above, democratic peace theorists have adopted the same view of empirical law as exceptionless generalization. There seems to be a strong tendency to phrase the issue of a few counterexamples in terms of a probabilistic generalization. This is in many ways unfortunate. In practice, it appears that empirical law means a perfect generalization, while probabilistic generalization means the same generalization with few counterexamples. As such it has really nothing to do with probability but rather the meaning of empirical law.[14]

In the case of the democratic peace the few counterexamples have been examined (e.g., Ray 1993). The democratic peace is threatened if they are clear counterexamples; it is not threatened if they are "gray" cases. For example, Finland and the United Kingdom in World War II is a case of two democracies fighting. However, this conflict is very minor in the context of World War II, which itself supports the democratic peace hypothesis. In other cases (for example, the Spanish-American war), it is not clear how democratic Spain was.

These potential counterexamples show that while I have presented descriptive-causal generalizations as quite simple in the "All A are B" form, they are in practice much more complicated. Jones, Baumgartner, and their colleagues have expended tremendous effort in getting homogeneous budget categories and collecting data over time. To get a descriptive-causal generalization, particularly those we might call empirical laws, usually requires a lot of theoretical and data work.

Real life descriptive-causal generalizations involve a bunch of background conditions and conceptual issues. The democratic peace requires clarity on at least three problematic concepts: (1) war, (2) state, and (3) democracy. The state variable is the least talked about but it is just as important as the other two. The democratic peace holds for inter-*state* wars. What counts as a state is critical in the validity of the generalization. When the US government conducts wars again Indian tribes, that might be a war between two democratically run political entities but not an interstate war, because Indian tribes are not states. Covert operations against a democracy, such as the United States in Chile in 1973, are excluded for other reasons.

The key point is that one should not overemphasize the importance of counterexamples. Certainly they form a core part of the evaluation of a descriptive-causal generalization. I have many times seen hypotheses formed as descriptive-causal generalizations rejected because the critic found a counterexample. A close examination of the counterexamples can strengthen or weaken the generalization depending on whether they are gray or clear-cut counterexamples. If they are all gray, then the generalization gets stronger. If there are a fair number of clear counterexamples then the generalization is weakened. One way to think about this is via theories of falsification. Gray zone cases only weakly falsify at best the theory, whereas clear counterexamples challenge the generalization directly.

However, such analysis of counterexamples is extremely rare. Given the problematic data, concepts, measures, and so on that one uses to make descriptive-causal generalizations, it is clear that a few counterexamples might arise. In fact, it is quite surprising that given all these data, concept, and measure problems that scholars do find such strong empirical generalizations.

5.6. Meta-Analytic Tendency Laws

One key suggestion of this chapter is that there might be various types of generalizations or empirical laws. Are there other potential ways than descriptive-causal generalizations to think about empirical laws and how they might be found in social science?

Davenport (2007) is one of the few cases that I know where a scholar has made a claim about a law of human behavior. In his review of the state repression literature he arrives at "Core Finding I: The Law of Coercive Responsiveness":

> Quiescence is a major benefit to political authorities, supporting the extraction of taxes, the creation of wealth, and a major part of their legitimacy as a protector. Considering different time periods and countries, as well as a wide variety of measurements for both conflict and repression, **every statistical investigation of the subject has found a positive influence**. When challenges to the status quo take place, authorities generally employ some form of repressive action to counter or eliminate the behavioral threat; in short, there appears to be a "Law of Coercive Responsiveness." The consistency of this finding is quite astonishing in a discipline where very few relationships withstand close scrutiny. (Davenport 2007, 7; boldface is mine)

What Davenport is implicitly doing falls under the label of meta-analysis (e.g., Hunter and Schmidt 2004). He is surveying a large body of literature and finding very consistent and statistically significant relationships. Meta-analysis is quite popular in clinical sciences such as medicine and in education, but it is relatively rare in political science and sociology (see Poteete, Janssen, and Ostrom 2010 for a discussion).

Descriptive-causal generalizations of the All/none A are B will typically produce consistent findings across studies. As we have seen, they are hard to defeat by statistical means and hence are typically consistent across studies. Again, almost all studies of democracy and conflict support the democratic peace (Russett and Starr 2000). The few that do not typically have major methodological flaws (e.g., Spiro 1994).[15]

While descriptive-causal generalizations will generate consistent results across statistical studies, the converse is not necessarily the case. One could find consistently significant statistical findings across many studies without having a descriptive-causal generalization. None of these would be strong enough to be a descriptive-causal generalization, but could be candidates for an empirical law in the meta-analysis sense. For example, Jack Levy and Bill Thompson describe one potential law of international relations: "The proposition that near-hegemonic concentrations of power in the system nearly always trigger a counterbalancing coalition of the other great powers has long been regarded as an 'iron law' by balance of power theorists, who often invoke the examples of Spain under Philip II, France under Louis XIV and then under Napoleon, and Germany under the Kaiser and then under Hitler" (Levy and Thompson 2010; see also Levy and Thompson 2005). They distinguish in their analysis between different types of generalization: "These findings provide strong support for the general argument that in the last five centuries of the modern European system, great powers **tended** to balance against hegemonic threats. This argument must be qualified, however, because the evidence demonstrates that hegemonic threats are not a sufficient condition for great-power balancing . . . As we have noted, the **tendency** toward balancing reflects a probabilistic relationship rather than law-like behavior" (Levy and Thompson 2005, 28; boldface is mine).

We can combine the ideas of Davenport, Levy, and Thompson with those of Cartwright (1989) and J. S. Mill to talk what can be called *meta-analytic tendency laws*. They seem law-like in that findings are extremely consistent across empirical and statistical analyses. The variable is almost always statistically significant with the same sign. The tendency law is meta-analytic because it holds *across* studies. Because of the fragility of individual statistical or empirical analyses one might require that tendency laws be supported in a wide variety of systematic empirical analyses. The idea is that the lack of robustness in a given statistical analysis is compensated for by a consistency across studies. One might then tentatively require that meta-analytic tendency laws (1) have the same sign in almost studies and (2) almost always be statistically significant in those studies. A common theme in the discussions of tendency laws is that it might be the case that there are countervailing causes which can occur that prevent the cause from having its effect. While space considerations prevent a lengthy discussion of this point, two things can be mentioned. Unlike many discussions of tendency laws, I require such variables to have consistent and strong effects in almost all studies, hence they are meta-analytic. This means the effect does not depend that much on statistical, measurement, and other methodological details. More importantly, it implies that countervailing causes are either too weak or are not too often present.

I do not necessarily think that all the descriptive-causal generalizations presented in this chapter deserve the label of empirical law. At the same time in a formal sense they are often no different than the democratic peace, general punctuation, and coercive responsiveness empirical laws. More generally, some key research traditions have started with an implicit general empirical law observation. For example, the huge literature on wealth and democracy (e.g., Lipset 1959) started with the strong regularity that there were almost no poor countries that were democracies. While it is has not been called an empirical law, that generalization has remained basically valid for over four decades.

Much more needs to be done to think about the trade-offs involved between meta-analytic tendency laws and descriptive-causal generalizations and the relationships between them. As I have presented them, descriptive-causal generalizations might be seen as a very strong kind of tendency law. For example, the democratic peace with regard to war is a descriptive-causal generalization, but with regard to nonwar militarized conflicts it might be a meta-analytic tendency law. If given a choice would scholars prefer descriptive-causal generalizations in a smaller scope or a tendency law in a larger population?

5.7. Conclusion

In this chapter I have showed that there are many candidates for the status of empirical law in the social sciences, if law-like generalization is taken to mean—as it usually is in the philosophy of science literature—(almost) all/none A are B. Various sections of this chapter have provided simple ways for identifying these generalizations in the form of zeros in $N \times N$ tables and perfect predictors in statistical analyses. Descriptive-causal generalizations produce extremely robust findings when inserted into standard statistical models. The chapter discusses, much more briefly, another potential candidate for empirical law status, what I have called meta-analytic tendency laws. Here countervailing factors might be present and/or strong enough to prevent the cause from having its effect. However, these situations and variables are such that they almost never preclude statistically significant findings.

Focusing on descriptive-causal generalizations, we need a set of criteria for evaluating them. This would probably include, minimally: (1) number of counterexamples, (2) scope in time and space, (3) consensus on causal mechanism, (4) robustness to different measures of core concepts, and (5) theoretical and empirical implications. This chapter has briefly discussed some of these, but the term "empirical law" suggests that there are multiple dimensions that scientists use to evaluate generalizations. As the natural sciences illustrate, not all generalizations are laws; that term is reserved for the most important ones.

ACKNOWLEDGMENTS

I would like to thank participants, especially Harold Kincaid and Robert Northcutt, at the workshop on "Current Issues in the Philosophy and Methodology of the Social Sciences" at the University of Alabama, Birmingham, April 2010 for useful comments and suggestions. An earlier version was presented to the Department of Sociology at the University of Arizona, and I have benefited from numerous suggestions and comments. Robert Adcock provided useful feedback on a number of key points. Thanks also to Jim Mahoney who contributed much to the section on Hume. Bruce Russett, Jack Levy, and Harvey Starr provided much background about empirical laws and the democratic peace. Thanks also to Frank Baumgartner and Bryan Jones for discussions about the General Punctuation Law.

NOTES

1. Obviously the social sciences covers a vast terrain. I focus on political science and sociology. While I can speak with confidence about these disciplines, the extent to which my claims are defensible for other social sciences remains open.

2. There might be many problems with such counterfactuals, but standard statistical practice produces them constantly; see King and Zeng (2007) for a good critique of many of the problems associated with statistical methods of making, typically implicit, counterfactuals.

3. See Goertz, Hak, and Dul (forthcoming) for an example where a strong descriptive-causal generalization holds but where the regression line is flat.

4. A major distinction should be made between descriptive-causal and descriptive. Typically a descriptive generalization is just about A or B, e.g., the average temperature of the atmosphere is rising. This kind of generalization merits a sustained analysis in its own right (Waters 1998).

5. See Goertz and Mahoney (2012) for a longer treatment.

6. This view of causation underpins the covering law model, for example: "A [covering, scientific, Hempel (1965)] law has the form 'If conditions $C_1, C_2, \ldots, C_n$ obtain, then always E'" (Elster 1999, 5).

7. The massive philosophical literature on laws of nature almost always uses the sufficient condition generalization, that is, all X are Y and almost never the necessary condition one, that is, all Y are X.

8. In statistics this is usually called the problem of "separation," e.g., Heinze and Schemper (2002). The perfect predictor completely separates the outcome variable into zero and one groups.

9. Critical in the statistical estimation is that the fact that it is really perfect in the all or none sense. One or two counterexamples will allow the estimation of the model.

10. Another way that perfect predictors can be seen in practice is when the standard errors are massive: Notice that it is 4840 in table 2 for the offending variable.

11. Of course, there are other important issues as well, but this is certainly a central one.

12. The only exception to this is if the control variable is perfectly correlated with the generalization variable.

13. Of course, estimation of parameters in the presence of perfect predictors can be possible with other techniques than maximum likelihood. One can see this if we made the Berkeley sociology example above, table 1, a perfect predictor. We can still calculate most 2×2 measures of association, but if we put a dichotomous GRE variable in a logistic regression of admission, it would be removed from the analysis as a perfect predictor.

14. A related issue arises because hypotheses can be formulated in probabilistic terms or in terms of logic. Slantchev, Alexandrova, and Gartzke (2005) illustrate how hard it is to match mathematical logic, and descriptive-causal generalizations, with statistical/probabilistic thinking: "The problem with this reasoning is that democratic peace theories, as social scientific claims, do not typically offer hypotheses in the form of sufficient conditions. Instead, these theories make probabilistic claims . . . Theoretical models express claims about tendencies that are contributions of one or several causal factors that would prevail and produce the anticipated effect all other *things being equal*" (Slantchev, Alexandrova, and Gartzke 2005, 459–60). As it turns out social scientists frequently express their hypotheses in terms of logic and set theory (see Goertz 2003 for 150 examples).

15. Typically the main methodological problem is that the statistical tests have very low statistical power; that is, they have little chance to reject the null hypothesis. This is what the researcher wants to do in his or her attack on the democratic peace, so a low power test will do the job.

REFERENCES

Armstrong, D. 1983. *What Is a Law of Nature?* Cambridge: Cambridge University Press.

Bartels, L. 2008. *Unequal Democracy: The Political Economy of the New Gilded Age.* Princeton, NJ: Princeton University Press.

Baumgartner, F., et al. 2009. "Punctuated Equilibrium in Comparative Perspective." *American Journal of Political Science* 53 (3): 603–20.

Baumgartner, M. 2008. "Regularity Theories Reassessed." *Philosophia* 36 (3): 327–54.

Baumgartner, M. 2009. "Inferring Causal Complexity." *Sociological Methods & Research* 38 (1): 71–101.

Becker, H. 1953. "Becoming a Marihuana User." *American Journal of Sociology* 59 (3): 235–42.

Buhaung, H., and C. Gleditsch. 2008. "Contagion or Confusion? Why Conflicts Cluster in Space." *International Studies Quarterly* 52 (2): 215–33.

Cartwright, N. 1989. *Nature's Capacities and Their Measurement.* Oxford: Oxford University Press.

Chapman, T., and P. Roeder. 2007. "Partition as a Solution to Wars of Nationalism: The Importance of Institutions." *American Political Science Review* 101 (4): 677–91.

Cooper, G. 1998. "Generalization in Ecology: A Philosophical Taxonomy." *Biology and Philosophy* 13 (4): 555–86.

Davenport, C. 2007. "State Repression and Political Order." *Annual Review of Political Science* 10: 1–23.

Dion, D. 1998. "Evidence and Inference in the Comparative Case Study." *Comparative Politics* 30 (2): 127–45.

Doyle, M. 1983a. "Kant, Liberal Legacies, and Foreign Affairs, Part I." *Philosophy and Public Affairs* 12 (3): 205–35.

Doyle, M. 1983b. "Kant, Liberal Legacies, and Foreign Affairs, Part II." *Philosophy and Public Affairs* 12 (4): 323–53.

Drèze, J. and Sen, A. 1989. *Hunger and Public Action.* Oxford: Oxford University Press.

Duverger, M. 1954. *Political Parties: Their Organization and Activity in The Modern State.* London: Methuen.

Elster, J. 1999. *Strong Feelings: Emotion, Addiction, and Human Behavior.* Cambridge, MA: The MIT Press.

Goemans, H. 2000. "Fighting for Survival: The Fate of Leaders and the Duration of War." *Journal of Conflict Resolution* 44 (5): 555–79.

Goertz, G. 2003. "The Substantive Importance of Necessary Condition Hypotheses." In G. Goertz and H. Starr, eds. *Necessary Conditions: Theory, Methodology, and Applications.* Lanham, MD: Rowman & Littlefield.

Goertz, G. 2006. "Assessing the Trivialness, Relevance, and Relative Importance of Necessary or Sufficient Conditions in Social Science." *Studies in Comparative International Development* 41 (2): 88–109.

Goertz, G., and H., Starr, eds. 2003. *Necessary Conditions: Theory, Methodology, and Applications.* Lanham, MD: Rowman & Littlefield.

Goertz, G., and J. Mahoney. 2012. *A Tale of Two Cultures: Qualitative and Quantitative Research in the Social Sciences.* Princeton: Princeton University Press.

Goertz, G., T. Hak, and Dul, J. Forthcoming. Ceilings and Floors: Where are There No Observations? *Sociological Methods & Research.*

Hale, H. 2004. "Divided We Stand: Institutional Sources of Ethnofederal State Survival and Collapse." *World Politics* 56 (2): 165–93.

Hansen, H., S. Mitchell, and S. Nemeth. 2008. "IO Mediation of Interstate Conflicts: Moving Beyond the Global vs. Regional Dichotomy." *Journal of Conflict Resolution* 52 (2): 295–325.

Harff, B. 2003. "No Lessons Learned from the Holocaust? Assessing Risks of Genocide and Political Mass Murder Since 1955." *American Political Science Review* 97 (1): 57–73.

Hausmann, R., L. Pritchett, and D. Rodrik. 2005. "Growth Accelerations." *Journal of Economic Growth* 10: 303–29.

Heinze, G., and M. Schemper. 2002. "A Solution to the Problem of Separation in Logistic Regression." *Statistics in Medicine* 21 (16): 2409–19.

Hempel, C. 1965. *Aspects of Scientific Explanation.* New York: The Free Press.

Herrnstein, R., and C. Murray. 1994. *Bell Curve.* New York: The Free Press.

Holland, P. 1986. "Statistics and Causal Inference (with Discussion)." *Journal of the American Statistical Association* 81 (396): 945–60.

Honoré, T., and H.L.A. Hart. 1985. *Causation in the Law,* 2d edition. Oxford: Oxford University Press.

Hume, D. 1975 (1777). *Enquiries Concerning Human Understanding, and Concerning the Principles of Morals.* Oxford: Oxford University Press.

Hunter, J., and F. Schmidt. 2004. *Methods of Meta-Analysis: Correcting Errors and Bias in Research Findings.* Thousand Oaks, CA: Sage Publications.

Johnson, S., J. Ostry, and A. Subramanian. 2006. "Africa's Growth Prospects: Benchmarking the Constraints." IMF Working Paper. Washington, DC: International Monetary Fund.

Jones, B., et al. 2009. "A General Empirical Law of Public Budgets: A Comparative Analysis." *American Journal of Political Science* 53 (4): 855–73.

Kincaid, H. 1990. "Defending Laws in the Social Sciences." *Philosophy of the Social Sciences* 20 (1): 56–83.

King, G., and L. Zeng. 2007. "When Can History Be Our Guide? The Pitfalls of Counterfactual Inference." *International Studies Quarterly* 51 (1): 183–210.

Levy, J. 1998. "The Causes of War and Conditions of Peace." *Annual Review of Political Science*: 139–65.

Levy, J. 2010. Personal communication,

Levy, J., and W. Thompson. 2005. "Hegemonic Threats and Great Power Balancing in Europe, 1495–1999." *Security Studies* 14 (1): 1–30.

Levy, J., and W. Thompson. 2010. "Balancing at Sea: Do States Ally Against the Leading Global Power?" *International Security* 35 (1): 7–43.

Lewis, D. 1973. *Counterfactuals*. Cambridge, MA: Harvard University Press.

Lewis, D. 1986a. "Causation. Postscripts to 'Causation'." *Philosophical Papers*, vol. II. Oxford: Oxford University Press.

Lewis, D. 1986b. *Causal Explanation. Philosophical Papers*, vol. II. Oxford: Oxford University Press.

Lieberson, S., and F. Lynn. 2002. "Barking Up the Wrong Branch: Alternatives to the Current Model of Sociological Science." *Annual Review of Sociology* 28: 1–19.

Lipset, S. 1959. "Some Social Requisites of Democracy: Economic Development and Political Legitimacy." *American Political Science Review* 53 (1): 69–105.

Little, D. 1993. "On the Scope and Limits of Generalization in the Social Sciences." *Synthese* 97 (2): 183–207.

Mackie, J. 1980. *The Cement of the Universe: A Study of Causation*. Oxford: Oxford University Press.

Mahoney, J. 1999. "Nominal, Ordinal, and Narrative Appraisal in Macrocausal Analysis." *American Journal of Sociology* 104 (4): 1154–96.

Mahoney, J., and G. Goertz. 2006. "A Tale of Two Cultures: Contrasting Quantitative and Qualitative Research." *Political Analysis* 14 (3): 227–49.

Morgan, S., and C. Winship. 2007. *Counterfactuals and Causal Inference: Methods and Principles for Social Research*. Cambridge: Cambridge University Press.

Most, B., and H. Starr. 1989. *Inquiry, Logic, and International Politics*. Columbia: University of South Carolina Press.

Ostrom, E. 2005. *Understanding Institutional Diversity*. Princeton, NJ: Princeton University Press.

Pape, R. 2005. *Dying to Win: The Strategic Logic of Suicide Terrorism*. New York: Random House.

Poteete, A., M. Janssen, and E. Ostrom. 2010. *Working Together: Collective Action, the Commons, and Multiple Methods in Practice*. Princeton, NJ: Princeton University Press.

Ragin, C. 1987. *The Comparative Method: Moving Beyond Qualitative and Quantitative Strategies*. Berkeley: University of California Press.

Ragin, C. 2000. *Fuzzy-Set Social Science*. Chicago: University of Chicago Press.

Ragin, C. 2008. *Redesigning Social Inquiry: Fuzzy Sets and Beyond*. Chicago: University of Chicago Press.

Ray, J. 1993. "Wars Between Democracies: Rare or Nonexistent?" *International Interactions* 18 (3): 251–76.

Rodrik, D. 2006. *Industrial Development: Stylized Facts and Policies*. Research manuscript. Cambridge, MA: Harvard University.

Russett, B. 2010. Personal communication.

Russett, B., and H. Starr. 2000. "From Democratic Peace to Kantian Peace: Democracy and Conflict in the International System." In *Handbook of War Studies*, 2d edition, M. Midlarsky, ed. Ann Arbor: University of Michigan Press.

Ryckman, M., and G. Goertz. 2009. "Rethinking and Re-Estimating the Impact of Wealth (GDP/Capita) on Civil War Onset." Paper presented at Peace Science Society Meetings. Chapel Hill, NC.

Salmon, W. 1984. *Scientific Explanation and the Causal Structure of the World*. Princeton, NJ: Princeton University Press.

Sambanis, N. 2008. "Terrorism and Civil War." In P. Keefer and N. Loayza, eds. *Terrorism and Development*. Cambridge: Cambridge University Press.

Skryms, B. 1980. *Causal Necessity*. New Haven: Yale University Press.

Slantchev, B., A. Alexandrova, and E. Gartzke. 2005. "Probabilistic Causality, Selection Bias, and the Logic of the Democratic Peace." *American Political Science Review* 99 (3): 459–62.

Spiro, D. 1994. "The Insignificance of the Liberal Peace." *International Security* 19 (2): 50–86.

Starr, H. 2010. Personal communication.

Tomasky, M. 2008. "How Historic a Victory?" *New York Review of Books* 55 (20).

Vaisey, S. 2010. Personal communication.

Waters, C. 1998. "Causal Regularities in the Biological World of Contingent Distributions." *Biology and Philosophy* 13: 5–36.

Weber, M. 1949. *Max Weber on the Methodology of the Social Sciences*. New York: The Free Press.

Woodward, J. 2003. *Making Things Happen: A Theory of Causal Explanation*. Oxford: Oxford University Press.

Woodward, J., and C. Hitchcock. 2003. "Explanatory Generalisations, Part 1: A Counterfactual Account." *Noûs* 37 (1): 1–24.

Zorn, C. 2005. "A Solution to Separation in Binary Response Models." *Political Analysis* 13 (2): 157–70.

CHAPTER 6

....

USEFUL COMPLEX
CAUSALITY

....

DAVID BYRNE AND EMMA UPRICHARD

THE world is complex. By complex, we mean that the social emerges from multiple, multidimensional, nonlinear, networks of nested systems (Byrne 1998; Urry 2003; Kauffman 1993; Khalil and Boulding 1996; Kiel and Elliott 1996; Nicolis and Prigogine 1989). It might seem that if we attempt to understand causality in relation to the properties of such systems we are on a hiding to nothing. The argument presented in this chapter will be quite to the contrary, even though we accept that the challenge is great. We argue that we can get a grip on causality in relation to complex systems, but there are a number of necessary and intertwined epistemological and methodological specifications that need to be made about both the kind of causality we are dealing with and the ways in which we may come to know the nature of that causality. We will develop the implications of these specifications for exploring and understanding complex and contingent causality in relation to complex systems by drawing on what Reed and Harvey (1992) call "complex realism"—the synthesis of critical realism and complexity theory (see also Byrne 1998 for an introduction to this approach). More specifically, we translate this research perspective into a hypothetical description of research practice by drawing on the complexity science conceptualization of near neighbors in state space and relating this to the development of systematic classification through numerical taxonomy and systematic comparison using Ragin's (1987, 1991, 2000) and Rihoux and Ragin's (2008) qualitative comparative analysis (QCA).[1]

In short, the chapter assumes a particular methodological position discussed elsewhere (see Byrne 1998, 2007; Byrne and Ragin 2009; Byrne and Uprichard 2004). More specifically, we expand on those discussions by elaborating on three key ideas: (1) the notion of variables as variate traces; (2) the notions of difference and continuity as control parameters; and (3) the notion of effects as trajectories of complex systems over time. As will be shown, injecting these ideas into the debates about how to empirically study complex social systems problematizes debates concerned with variables and cases, similarity and "difference," as well as those of cause and effect(s), change, and "continuity." By implication, three further concerns are raised to do specifically with complex systems as cases: the classification of cases, the ontological propensity of the case, and the temporal ontology of the case.

In doing so, this chapter explicitly engages with concepts that are likely to be somewhat familiar to many readers, for example: cases and variables, cause and effect, change and continuity, time and temporality, comparison, similarity, and difference, and so on. However, and it is worth being up front about this from the outset, we deliberately twist some of these taken for granted concepts round in innovative ways, precisely because a complex realist perspective to the social necessitates a radical re-jigging of some of the key building blocks of empirical social science. Furthermore, we are aware that the language we use is taken and adapted from a relatively wide range of disciplinary fields, so some readers might understand some terms (e.g., near neighbors, state space, control parameters) with respect to their research backgrounds, which may or may not be precisely what is meant here. In part because the space of a chapter does not permit us, and also because what is being proposed is a methodological design that is genuinely transdisciplinary, we refrain from constantly defining terms of the discussion; sometimes we do specify the general disciplinary background of key terms. Where necessary, we refer readers to other sources to help with this particular issue. We also pepper our discussion with a range of different illustrative examples, often drawn from education and health, as a way of explicating our points to a diverse audience. It is worth bearing in mind, however, that despite the fact that readers might, at a first skim, only glean parts of the argument proposed here, the implications of what is discussed are arguably somewhat modest. In actual fact, the empirical practice of what is suggested is relatively straightforward; it is certainly practical, methodical, and in many ways not so novel. Rather, the novelty of what is discussed lies more in the epistemological and ontological implications of the case rather than the methodological program of how to study complex systems as cases that change over time from a complex realist perspective.

All that said, an important distinction must be made here between what, to employ Morin's (2006) terminology, we can call 'restricted complexity' and 'general complexity.' After all, while we speak of complexity and complex systems, we are very clear about the kind of complexity and complex systems we are trying to work with in terms of the social world. In the former conception of complexity, the complex emerges from the interactions among simple elements. In this frame of reference, causality is understood in terms of the rules that govern those interactions and the task of science is the discovery of those rules. Holland (1995) can stand as the exemplar of this approach. Whilst some aspects of reality can be understood in this way, our view is that most complex systems—and in particular most complex social systems and eco-social systems—do not have states which can be understood as determined by interactions among simple agents. Rather, their states at any point in time are consequent on elements within that system itself, including complex assemblages in subsystems, and the relationship of that system with other systems. This ontological specification has methodological consequences. If we are dealing with restricted complexity, then we can, subject to some truly heroic assumptions about the isomorphism of any simulation with reality, use agent based modeling as a means of establishing the rules that determine the state of a system. We cannot do this for general complex systems, and this chapter is about the actual approaches we might use when confronted with those kinds systems. It is in this respect that the emphasis on configurations (rather than correlations) matter to the extent that they do in the discussion that follows.

Note that restricted complexity regards complex states as the product of simple interactions—the basis for arguing that agent based simulations can generate causal descriptions in terms of the rules governing the interactions of the agents. However, restricted complexity is certainly not reductionist in the classical sense of attempting to define nomothetic laws with universal application. Nevertheless, it remains reductionist in its insistence on simplicity as the foundation of emergent patterns. We do not doubt or dispute that complex patterns cannot emerge from simple rules. Rather, what is problematic to us, more than the reductionist assumptions that go hand in hand with it, is the validity of the simple rules used in many agent based models in the first place. Just because macro level complex patterns emerge from rule-based interactions, this does not mean that the simplicity which is used to produce those patterns is either necessary or sufficient to explain the complex social.

Models that are deemed to be adequate with respect to representing complexity need to be reliable and valid at *multiple* micro and macro levels of observation. If they are not, then they are not representing social complex systems, but something else. That is why agent based applications have been in general trivial in relation to social systems. Kauffman (2000) makes this point very explicitly in *Investigations*—a title blatantly borrowed from Wittgenstein's own book title, *Philosophical Investigations*, because, as he explains, he is trying to say something similar about the universe as that which Wittgenstein claimed about language games. That is, Kauffman (2000, 52) follows Wittgenstein in arguing that "one cannot, in general, reduce statements at a higher level to a finitely specified set of necessary and sufficient statements at a lower level. Instead, the concepts at the higher level are codefined." It is this paradox of a system as a multidimensional entity dependent upon its constituents for its own reproduction and yet autonomous and *in*dependent to its constituents that raises particular epistemological and methodological issues which complex realist researchers need to learn to address. Rather than cleaning up or simplifying a level of abstraction, as is absolutely necessary for any simulation, we propose an alternative methodological design that seeks to not only provide a representation of the social that is arguably more valid than any simulation of it, but one that also seeks to capture real complex causation as well.

In a nutshell, we want to produce useful descriptions of the case; descriptions that are both meaningful sociologically and useful because they help us to get a grip on causality. The causal narrative that is sought is one that not only helps to explain how something came to be as it is, but also about the extent to which it is possible to produce desired future change. This may be an ambitious task, but one that is both worthwhile and possible. It is really rather important to recognize that a causal narrative is not exclusively textual in a conventional sense. Time series of numbers should be understood as narratives just as much as any textual form. However, in order to develop a useful causal narrative from a description, we need particular kinds of sociological description. Specifically, useful description for our purposes are those that help to explain why something and particularly any complex system has come to be the kind of thing it is and not something other than what it is. In other words, the descriptions achieve retroductive adequacy;[2] they act as accounts that stand up as explanations for the state of a system and are based on careful reconstructions of the history of the system—essentially on what George and Bennett (2005) call 'process tracing.'

However, we are convinced that we can go beyond the ideographic description of causality in relation to the individual case and do this through processes of systematic comparison of cases of much the same kind. In the language of complexity theory, we can explore the trajectories of ensembles of systems that in crucial respects are near neighbors. To do this, we have to have some systematic process for establishing similarity and difference, and we consider that techniques of numerical taxonomy (e.g., cluster analysis—for a description of which see Uprichard 2009) provide us with precisely this sort of classificatory process. Furthermore, our position is that establishing significant causality by comparison can potentially provide a basis for policy planning and action.

Indeed, we argue that we can move beyond retroduction to attempts at engendering change based on retrodiction. That is to say, we want to move from retroduction as "a mode of inference in which events are explained by postulating (and identifying) mechanisms which are capable of producing them" (Sayer, 1992, 107) to retrodiction as a mode of being able to understand what might happen and how to act in order to change what might happen using knowledge of how something came to be as it is. Our aim, then, is to think about modes of inquiry that not only try to explain what has happened, how any system has come to be as it is, but also through informed purposive action, how to intervene in order to produce a desired future state of a system.

A major first step of this mode of enquiry, as we have already implied, involves a particular kind of description, namely a description about the past and the present. As Abbott (1998, 176) suggests, there is a lot of merit in producing descriptions which "show various internal patterns" that "sketch the "rules of the game"; and consequently help us to "portray the limits and possibilities of action in such systems." Temporally ordered case based descriptions are fundamental to understanding complex causality and generating the kind of useful knowledge that helps to differentiate causal paths toward particular outcomes. A second key step is to work out which parts of the description of the system might be more or less open to interventions that might produce desired changes in that system. Hence, we are trying to work out how we might know about the possible "leverage points" (Meadows 1999) of a system using both retroductive and retrodictive modes of enquiry *together*. As will be shown, these two key steps also involve other meta-assumptions about cases, variables, and effects, and the chapter exposes these throughout the discussion.

Simply put, our quest for useful social causality is concerned with producing knowledge that follows Weber's approach to causality. Ringer (2002) describes this as "the kind of causal analysis that will explain why the course of historical development ultimately led to the explanandum in question, rather than to some other outcome. The projected investigation is, therefore, clearly expected to encompass both probabilistic and counterfactual reasoning, along with a dynamic vision of alternate paths of historical change." Note, though, that in much of his work, Weber sought to identify "the" single cause that generated social transformation. In relation to understanding causality in complex systems, it is important to remember that causes can be, and indeed are likely to be, multiple and complex. So while we are sympathetic to a Weberian approach to the social, we want to go much further than that, too.

More specifically, and perhaps slightly provocatively, we advance three key propositions about developing useful causality in complex systems. We acknowledge that to attempt to develop useful causality is a revolutionary claim, although of course it is fundamental to what is now a long tradition of critical realist work, including a good deal of real empirical social science as well as methodological argument. Indeed, we are emphatic as to how complex realism develops this argument. If we are dealing with causality in relation to complex systems, then *all* accounts of causality must be delimited by explicit consideration of the range in time and space of their potential applicability. We do not of course require exact specification here. The world is far too fuzzy for that. What is required is a clear recognition of limitation and some coherent effort at describing the boundaries—what Williams (2000) in his discussion of "Base and Superstructure in Marxist Cultural Theory" specifies as the useful meaning of the word *determine*—that is, not as exact specification but as the setting of limits of possibility. This of course resonates very clearly with the understanding of complex systems as having multiple but not infinite possible future states.

6.1. Proposition 1: System Traces, not Variables

In quantitative social science, the quest for causal explanations has mostly been conducted through statistical modeling. Typically, this involves having a dependent variable and explaining its variation through the use of independent variables. The dependent variable may be measured in terms of a value on a scale or it may be described in terms of a value on a nominal attribute. The radical distinction between these two is not generally considered as much as it should be. Scalar values describe differences of degree. Nominal specification describes difference of kind.[3] Usually this kind of explanation seeks to assign a discrete part of the causation to each specific variable. Complex causation is only admitted into the picture through the construction of interaction terms, conventional statistical reasoning's uneasy tribute paid to the reality of complexity in the world.

Here, we argue that the entities that matter in relation to causality are not variables but systems. Furthermore, for us, cases are also taken to be complex systems and variables are mere traces of those systems. This goes against the epistemological assumptions of almost of all statistical reasoning. Following Abbott (1998) and Byrne (2002) we assert that it is generally a fundamental ontological error to reify variables in abstraction from systems. This is such an important point to our overall argument that it is worth spelling it further with a simple illustrative example. Sometimes when something is introduced deliberately into a system—for example, in the administration of a drug or a placebo in a clinical trial—we can consider that a variable is external to the system but even here we have to consider the implications of potential interaction. So in a pedagogical trial where we might deliver, say, teaching in statistics through different statistical packages such as Minitab and SPSS, we would almost certainly find an interaction effect with the teachers delivering the method. That describes the reality that some teachers will teach better with one package than the other. In a large-scale randomized controlled trial we might average out outcomes and in effect lose that interaction effect, but that would not actually help any particular teacher to work out what package would work best for them in achieving better outcomes in terms of statistical understanding for their own classes.

To say this is not to object to measurement of variation, but rather to identify the objects of measurement in most cases as traces of systems rather than as accounts of real variable causal powers having an independent existence external to those systems. This is why we prefer to think in terms of attributes—that is, measurable properties of systems considered as cases which have no reality without the systems—and to consider change in attributes as describing traces of the systems' trajectories through time. Byrne puts it like this:

> The dynamic systems which are our cases leave traces for us, which we can pick up. We can, as it were, track them, and we can infer from the traces what is that left them. From the traces we can reconstruct a version of the real entities and of the relationships among those entities and of the emergent forms which are the product of and the producers of the relationships among those entities. We can glimpse the entities and the systemic relationships among the entities. (Byrne, 2002, 36)

This means that both epistemologically and methodologically we are doing something quite different with our data than has typically been the case across the social and natural sciences. The emphasis is placed on the case rather than the variable. We agree absolutely with Ragin when he says:

For causation, the main contrast is between the conventional view of causation as a contest between individual variables to explain variation in an outcome and the diversity-oriented view that causation is both conjunctural and multiple. In the conventional view, each single causal condition, conceived as an analytically distinct variable, has an independent impact on the outcome. In the diversity-oriented view, causes combine in different and sometimes contradictory ways to produce the same outcome, revealing different paths. (Ragin 2000, 15)

We therefore follow Ragin's QCA approach to identifying configurations of variables which give rise to particular outcomes. Fielding and Lee describe the procedure thus:

Unlike the data matrix in quantitative research, where the analytic focus is on variables displayed in the columns of the table, it is the rows which are important here. What is being examined for each row is the configuration of causes associated with the presence or absence of an outcome for the case. (Fielding and Lee, 1998, 158)

The truth table produced by QCA displays all possible and actual configurations of variables for a particular outcome. This is a flat representation of a multidimensional contingency table with one of the dimensions being the variable outcome. Each row, which represents a configuration in the truth table, describes the specific character of a single cell in that multidimensional contingency table. Thus a configuration is a description of a system, a case, in terms of attribute values. These may be expressed in dichotomous terms (as presences or absences), as multinomial terms or as discrete values when there is more than one possible state. In effect, any multinomial attribute can be considered as a summary of a set of mutually exclusive binary attributes. Each value on the multinomial is either present or absent and if present excludes all other values. We can always dichotomize a multinomial as a set of binomials.

Ragin's extension of his interpretation of set membership to "fuzzy"—that is, to partial membership—is not in our view a retreat on the notion that it is the kind of thing a system is which matters. Rather it allows for degrees of being a kind of thing—the inherent meaning of the term "fuzzy." In any event, we very much agree with Ragin's (2000) conception of causality as something that is to be understood in set-theoretic terms. He spells this out as follows: "Not only are set-theoretic relationships central to the analysis of social data, they are also central to almost all forms of social science theorizing. Most theoretical arguments . . . concern set-theoretic relationships, not linear relationships between variables."

The clear implication of this line of reasoning is that we cannot understand causation in relation to complex systems by any process of analysis because complex systems have emergent properties. What matters is the state of the system understood as an emergent property. This is by no means a new idea. It was expressed well in the nineteenth century by the polymath George Lewes:

Although each effect is the resultant of its components, we cannot always trace the steps of the process, so as to see in the product the mode of operation of each factor. In the latter case, I propose to call the emergent effect an emergent. It arises out of the combined agencies, but in a form which does not display the agents in action. The emergent is unlike its components in so far as these are incommensurable, and it cannot be reduced either to their sum or their difference. (Lewes cited in Pepper, 1926, 241)

The rejection of variable based analyses that typically seek to partial out variables is a rejection of the validity of analytical modes of causal explanation in relation to effects in complex systems. Emergent effects can be explored by examining attribute configurations. This is not merely a point to be made about methods of understanding. It is also a statement about the nature of meaningful causality in relation to complex systems. Indeed, the real crux of our project is on *explaining the difference(s) between the movement of cases between different categories over time* (see Byrne 2002; Abbott 2000). Therefore, we need to develop our argument by considering the notion of control parameters, because rethinking the ontology of cases and variables from a complex realist perspective is only part of the story. Another part is that we also need to rethink what difference and change, and conversely similarity and continuity, might mean with respect to exploring patterns of change and continuity within our data.

6.2. PROPOSITION 2: DIFFERENCE AND CONTINUITY AS CONTROL PARAMETERS

By using numerical taxonomy and QCA approaches, we can certainly establish types of cases. However, once particular kinds of cases have been examined in relation to a particular set or sets of outcomes, which can be explained in terms of particular variable configurations, then the crucial questions become: Why do certain cases have a particular set of outcomes whereas others do not? What is it about particular configurations that lead to particular sets of cases and vice versa, why do certain cases lend themselves to particular configurations and not others? These questions require us to do something quite different with respect to understanding causality. Once we shift from variables to cases, then we are doing something else with our empirical quantitative data to what tends to be customary statistical practice.

Basically, the shifting focus of attention can be thought of as a two-stage story of change in terms of the nuts and bolts of quantitative social science, that is, the focus of variables versus cases. First, there is the simple data matrix, which involves a focus on the columns (variables) and then the rows (the cases). Next, is the truth table (produced by approaches such as QCA), where the focus is first and foremost on the rows (configurations of variables) and then the columns (patterns of absence and presence of a variable). We have already proposed a methodological alternative that was precisely about rejecting the linear variable based approach in preference for a focus on the different kinds of cases journeying through different kinds of spaces over time, and vice versa, how those spaces feedback into the construction of different kinds of cases (see Byrne and Uprichard 2007). In that example, we were thinking specifically about exploring social exclusion by describing household and neighborhood-level trajectories over time. There, numerical taxonomy and QCA approaches were combined in order to map multilevel longitudinal change in a way that still allowed for both top-down and bottom-up causal dynamics.

Here, we take this further and argue that ultimately, the search to empirically describe and explore complex causality in a sociologically meaningful way is a focus on *difference*. A focus on difference is proposed by Cilliers, who has written about this at some length. He argues that a focus on difference is not only a convenience but a necessity when it comes to understanding complex systems. Moreover, re-ducing or ignoring difference "leads to error, an error which is not only technical, but also ethical" (Cilliers, 2010, 3). Indeed once we move from variables to cases, and we think about cases over time, then we are immediately forced to think about sorting out types of trajectories. We suggest doing just that, but with the deliberate intent to be able enact possible desired future change on those trajectories. And as Cilliers is quick to point out, there are clearly ethical and political issues involved in our proposed research program, but that is as it should be: We are dealing with the social and any empirical program is necessarily deeply enmeshed in ethics and pol-itics. This does not, or at least should not, detract us from our aim of producing useful complex causal narratives.

Any attempt to deal with complex causality needs to tackle *difference* head on. This is not just about differentiating types of cases, although that is certainly part of it. Rather once we move from variables to cases, then we can also move to cases over time, which in turn necessarily implies exploring trajectories. Indeed, at the heart of this second proposition is precisely a focus on difference of cases doing and be-coming different trajectories over time. This is a fundamental part of the search for useful complex causal narratives. As MacIver (1942/1964, 27–28) puts it, "the search for causes is directed to the differences between things . . . Underneath all our ques-tioning lies the implicit acceptance of the axiom that no difference exists without a cause." Difference, for both Cilliers and MacIver, then, is at the root of any causal investigation in the social world, and we follow both authors in also placing differ-ence as a core component to our methodological program.

We take MacIver's and Cillers' focus on difference even further, however, because although they are right in identifying difference as core to any causal un-derstanding of the complex social world,[4] both fail to recognize the limits of what they propose. Searching for differences alone is simply not possible; difference nec-essarily implies similarity. We propose therefore a parallel focus on—the other side of the coin, so to speak—similarity. Indeed, whereas difference to MacIver and Cil-liers is mostly related to notions of change, we suggest it is helpful to think about similarity as associated with continuity. Hence, any focus on difference and change needs to be done alongside that similarity and continuity.

Placing the onus of attention on difference and similarity of kinds over time: the different kinds of cases, kinds of variables, doing, being, and becoming different kinds of trajectories, in this way is key to beginning to explore where and how control parameters—that is, crudely speaking, the boundedness of the system's possible states that gives any complex trajectory its form—exist and how they are made to hold over time. Moreover, by exposing patterns of difference and change, alongside patterns of similarity and continuities, we argue that we can glimpse into a system's real medium-long term control parameters. The idea of control parameters is very important in relation to causality when effects are understood in terms of the trajectory of complex systems. After all, in any complex system, networked subsystems can act as control parameters to the whole system. For example, many health states are the products of multiple factors in interaction. There is good evidence that there is a genetic set that is necessary for a person to undergo schizophrenic episodes. However, many, indeed most, people with that genetic set never experience a schizophrenic episode. Rather clinical schizophrenia occurs when people who have the potential to undergo episodes are exposed to particular life stressing events, particularly during the transition from adolescence into adult life. The genetic set is a necessary but not a sufficient cause. Similar initial conditions can and do lead to different outcomes, and vice versa.

The point about similar and different initial conditions leading to similar and different outcomes derives from the significance of path dependency in social causality. This should be absolutely obvious, but the dominance of physics based understandings of cause, where in most of physics—although importantly, not in thermodynamics, cause is reversible—has meant that the importance of path dependency is not always asserted. Yet for us, path dependencies are as intrinsic to the notion of control parameters as change is. Indeed, Walby (2010) also highlights the importance of path dependency in her theorization of change and continuity, specifically in relation to social movements, gender, and modernity, as well as systems of violence and power. Ultimately, once we deal in terms of anything but single necessary and sufficient causes we are deeply enmeshed with complex causation.

The search for control parameters in the social world is of course not a straightforward one. However, we propose that clues to what these might be are not in the changes that are observed in the world, but rather in the continuities. A focus on the permanent (or the semi-permanent) "structuring structures," as Bourdieu (1990) would put it, is what we have in mind. This turns the focus on change upside down somewhat, inasmuch as it may seem paradoxical to focus on continuity when trying to understand change. But in trying to empirically to explore the control parameters that might explain (or at the very least point to) the generative mechanisms that cause difference, we might focus on phases of the system's trajectory which exhibit a *lack* of change. Note that "same" or "lack of change" does not mean exactly the same condition—that is, complete stasis. Most complex systems are robust, so most social systems stay roughly in the same state space. This is an important distinction between complex systems in general and the special category of chaotic systems. For chaotic systems small changes in control parameters can induce phase shifts and there are radical changes in system state over very short time periods. Instead, the same state over time here refers to path dependencies within a particular state space. Furthermore, this is not to say that change is unimportant. On the contrary, despite the onus on continuity, understanding why cases shift to different categories—that is, change qualitatively over time—is crucial.

The point is, to understand change we also have to understand continuity. Indeed, continuity is seen as much a part of change as transformation with respect to complex systems existing "on the edge of chaos." As Goodwin suggests, "for complex non-linear dynamic systems with rich networks of interacting elements, *there is an attractor that lies between a region of chaotic behavior and one that is 'frozen' in the ordered regime, with little spontaneous activity*" (1994,169, emphasis added). While much of the complexity literature focuses on understanding patterns of change (e.g., phase shifts, self-organization, punctuated equilibria), here patterns of continuity are also highlighted. More importantly still is the notion of "sticky trajectories"—those systems or subsystems or types of cases that do *not* change states relative to, despite, and in spite of, all other system changes going on around them. An example of a sticky trajectory might be the neighborhood which remains deprived despite decades of urban regeneration or intervention; or the school that fails to improve despite more money, better teachers, new or more students, this or that old, new, different, or same policy effort to radicalize the state of education within that particular locale, but simply fail, time after time, to have any significant impact.

Empirically, attention to contradictory configurations in a QCA derived truth table underpins what is suggested here. Like John Tukey's argument for focusing on outliers in order to provide confirmatory explanations of statistical patterns in quantitative data, here we propose a focus on difference and continuity—differences in the types of trajectories that similar cases might show as well as similar trajectories of different types of cases. The issue here for us is context. After all, no matter what system or case we are looking at, it exists within a wider historical framework. It is by examining what stays the same that key aspects of the historical nature of the context within which a system is situated are highlighted. For instance, to understand the stickiness of a failing school, the educational system needs to be closely examined. After all, as Bourdieu and Passeron (1977/2000) state and reiterated throughout Bourdieu's own work (1984; 1993; 1998), the educational system acts as a Maxwell's Demon: "it maintains the preexisting order . . . More precisely, by a series of operations, the system separates the holders of cultural capital from those who lack it" (Bourdieu 1998, 20). The notion of there being a Maxwell's Demon somehow embedded and intrinsic to particular systems is also present in many of the discussions relating to complex systems (see in particular Kauffman 2000). The point being that the state of a system is determined by a set of interactions which involve both crucial components of the system itself—subsystems which have the status of control parameters, and aspects of the environment of the system which comprise the set of intersections of any system with all other systems which are of relevance to its future trajectory. Difference and continuities help to shed light on where and what the control parameters might hinge on.

6.3. PROPOSITION 3: TRAJECTORIES AS EFFECTS

In attempting to understand causality in complex systems, we have also to define what we mean by effect in relation to complex systems. To say that the cases are complex is to say that causation will work through the interactive effects—in terms of the language of causation in the physical sciences, through the failure of super-position. This is synonymous with the statistical notion of interaction among variables—in other words, in the simplest first order case where the relationship between two variables differs according to the value of a third. This can of course be extended to multiple interactions. For us the requirement to insert interaction terms to generate a causal model is a sure indication that we are dealing with complex causation.

With causation understood in this way, we are faced with the problem of identifying the relationship between causes and their effects and that requires a specification of the pathways to outcomes. As Byrne notes:

> The implications of this proposal about the nature of effects is that we explore causality by working backwards from specific different effects—retrodiction. In other words we should engage with processes of retrodiction to explain what has happened and in terms of applied social science develop a retrodictive approach to guiding actions towards the achievement of desired outcomes. This is very much in accord with the general critical realist programme of explanation. We are dealing with effects understood as system states and understand these system states to be the product of complex *and* multiple generative mechanisms. (Byrne, 2011, 89)

By approaching effects in this way, we are adopting a critical realist understanding of causality. This implies the existence of deep generative mechanisms at the level of the real. Outcomes at the level of the actual, that is as expressed in reality, depend upon the activation of causal powers in particular contexts. Science only notices particular outcomes and this scientific knowledge can be described as constituting the level of the empirical. This form of understanding does not imply a regular conjunction of cause and effect. In other words, contingency is central to our position on causal reasoning. Sayer (2000, 14) notes that in this frame of reference describing causality relies on "identifying causal mechanisms and how they work, and discovering if they have been activated and under what conditions."

In order to describe causality in this way, just as we need to think differently about cases and variables, we need to turn the taken for granted relationship between cause and effects on its head as well. We do this by understanding effects in terms of a system's possible trajectories through time. Once we do this, effects fall into one of the following two main types. First, the system stays in roughly the same condition through time; in complexity-speak, its trajectory through state space can be described in terms of a torus attractor. Alternatively, it is possible to consider a system that stays roughly within a set of closely related multiple states. For example, we might consider "well-being" to relate to *both* a state of "health" and of "illness."

When we are healthy we do not manifest exactly the same physiological measurements at every point. These can and actually should change within a range but we remain generally healthy in social terms. By this we mean that we are able to act appropriately in relation to our social roles and are not prevented from doing so by absence of health; we are not in the sick role. However, we each see-saw in and out of both health and illness throughout our life course, even though we may stay mostly in one state more than the other. We might even consider that there are states which describe a difference between minor illnesses which only briefly interrupt our normal abilities to function and severe acute or chronic illnesses.

In contrast to the first form of effect in which continuity within state space is highlighted, the second form of effect is constituted by radical change. That is to say, in the language of complexity science, such effects are phase shifts. Note that becoming—the system emerging into reality and ending—the system ceasing to exist as a coherent entity are special cases of transformation, but they are nevertheless also considered to be phase shifts. In a phase shift the system undergoes a radical transformation, which means that it moves to a wholly new location in state space. Phase shifts are transformations of kind. And they are important because ultimately these are often the kinds of transformations that medical, policy, or other kinds of social intervention seek to implement. Transforming a failing school into a successful one is an example of an educational phases shift; preventing severe acute illnesses from killing us or moving between relatively long periods of depression to the point of being incapable of functioning and periods of normal mental health when we can function well are good examples of phase shifts in health terms.

We suggest that there are at least three important implications to considering effects as trajectories. The first issue is classification. What type of effect is the trajectory? Is it one that that lacks change or is it one in which transformation in kind is key? What, ultimately, is the case the effect belongs to? How is it defined? How is it actually measured, conceptualized, abstracted, and so on? Above all else here how is it typed, classified, described as the sort of thing it is? Ragin argues that the processes of "casing the case" are fundamental to understanding any thing as an entity. We have to first know what the thing is and then what kind of thing it is. Sometimes it seems obvious. For example, a school is a thing understood as an institution, but actually any given school will form part of a local educational ecology, which will in turn have fuzzy boundaries. In England, national government deals in schools as well as local ecologies defined as local education authorities. It also classifies on a graded scale that includes the category of "failing." Who decides what a failing school is, the measurements involved in making it, the practices involved in producing this classification, and so on (Bowker and Star, 1999)? Equally, how classifications can, do, and are made to or not made to change are similarly important issues here (see Hacking 2002, 2007). For us classification is a necessary precursor of comparison and thereby of modeling based on comparisons. And when classifying in the social world we have to be canny. Carter and Sealey identify reflexivity as the key to understanding social classifications: "In the sense that the relationship between social action and the description of that action employed by researchers is an interactive and dynamic one" (2009, 70). They do not propose an absolute distinction between classification of the physical and the social, between classification of objects which in reality are: "indifferent to their epistemological description" and others saying rather that:

> At the other end of the continuum are phenomena and processes that are so bound up with the language in which they are described, so inherently intersubjective, that they are, in a limited sense, *constituted* (original emphasis) by processes of reflexivity. At intermediate points along this continuum are other phenomena and processes that vary in the degree to which people's understanding of them influences the way they behave. (Carter and Sealey 2009,71)

This is a very useful prescription for careful consideration of just what the nature of our classifications actually is.[5] They can be products of a particular method as with cluster analysis, but they are never just that. Note that Carter and Sealey allow even at the extreme of the social construction of cases only a *limited* constitution, and the same applies to most of our social categories. Reality itself has a voice always in the nature of our scientific objects. Of course in the social world where social reality is in large part constituted by our actions, our classifications and indeed measurement devices in general become real in any event because they are real in their consequences, the position expressed about social statistics in an actor-network frame of reference by Desrosières (1998). That said, we agree with Carter and Sealey that, to put it in vernacular terms and in the words of the immortal Homer Simpson, much of reality was like this when we got here. The crucial point is that classifications precede comparisons, so we can no longer, as Rutherford put it, distinguish between science (the hunt for causes) and stamp collecting (the construction of categories). If systematic comparison is to be the basis for our hunt for complex and contingent causes, then classification is an essential preliminary part of the process.

The second issue, and one that is incredibly important to our overall argument, is relevant to a causal understanding of effects as trajectories is the ontological propensity of the case. Phase shifts, for example, necessarily imply that ontological transformation is possible; conversely effects as continuities imply that ontological transformation might be not be possible. Let us return to our school example. In order to change a failing school into a successful one, there is an important assumption being made that failing schools have indeed the propensity to both be failing schools that can also become successful schools. By "propensity" we are referring specifically to Popper's "world of propensities," in which he argues that "there exist weighted possibilities which are *more than mere possibilities*, but tendencies of propensities to become real" (1990, 18; emphasis in original). He makes the point that "propensities should not be regarded as properties *inherent in an object*, . . . but that they should be regarded as *inherent in a situation* (of which, of course, the object was a part)" (1990, 14; emphasis in original).[6]

The point is systems have a material momentum to change (or not) in particular ways. This is not a deterministic argument. But it is to say that systems have propensities to change (and not change) in particular ways, even though those possibilities to change depend on context and may vary over time and space too. Interestingly, whereas Popper uses the term "propensity," Bourdieu talks about "structuring structures" and "dispositions." Despite the differences, both authors are pointing to similar things, even though they approach their subject matter (which is also different) from different angles. Popper is trying to understand the wonders of statistical continuities, whereas Bourdieu is attempting to develop a philosophy of reproduction. They both end up turning to the language of "fields of forces" to refer to the ways in which context matters both epistemologically and ontologically, as well as suggesting that, while these fields do not determine future change, they certainly influence it in significant ways, and importantly, allow for the fields themselves to change as well. Trying to grapple with the recursive interactions between systems and their environment(s) is a key element in the work of both authors. Moreover, it is precisely at the meeting of the system and its environment that the ontological possibilities of future change are also materialized. It is at the junctions— the fuzzy boundaries, if you like—between system and context that the propensity for change changes (or does not change).

Phase shifts will occur, and it may not be possible to predict when they will occur or how they will occur. But sorting out which systems are more or less likely to change would be a very useful thing to know. Identifying which of the failing schools, for example, have the propensity to become successful ones would be a massive step forward into creating desired future change. Note that the assumption here is that not all failing schools *can* become successful schools. To reiterate the point made earlier: trajectories can get stuck—so-called sticky trajectories are in effect attractor states which are irreversible and have moved too far away in state space to be very different. Some things, including failing schools, cannot be repaired, and any change that ensues simply reinforces the relative difference(s) between them and other seemingly similar kinds of cases. Distinguishing sticky systems that have become genuinely and irreversibly stuck from those that still have the propensity to change is crucial to our argument here.

The third issue to do with effects as trajectories is time. The length of time a system takes in one state space is a consequence of the whole causal complex which derives from the internal character of the system in terms of its subsystems *and* factors in the environment which is constituted by the intersection of any given system and all others systems which are of significance for it. In addition, however, and this point is important, the possible trajectory of a system also depends on where in its temporal life course it is. This is not just about expectations of change. The same point applies of course to individuals, and indeed the manifestations of time on the body are so intrinsic to our conceptualizations of possibilities and propensities that it is easy to assume that time is only matter when it comes to body. The point is, however, the ontological temporality of the case is a key issue here. This has as much to do with the ontological properties of time as being and becoming that Prigogine refers to as the methodological and epistemological possibilities that are afforded to us in the social world. Time matters, but not just in terms of duration or events or turning points, but precisely because it is ontologically and epistemologically a material reality of being and becoming in the world. That is to say, adapting Bhaskar's (1979) approach on the possibility of naturalism for our purposes here, it is because time *is* matter (in a process of being and becoming) that it can be measured in years, the greying of hair, the creaking of joints, and so on and *not* because time can be observed in these ways that it matters (although that time can be handled this way may be a contingent necessary condition for our knowledge of time as matter). Irreversibility, probability, and the importance of scale are the hinge pins to understanding nonlinear dynamic change, but they are all embedded within in the epistemological and ontological dynamics of time *as* matter.

Note also that although the issue of space is not developed here, it is nevertheless implicit across our three propositions, and particularly in here in relation to understanding the role of time in phase shifts. Indeed, our view is that once time is considered as matter (time as ontology) and not just in terms of time points in a time series (time as epistemology), then space is necessarily brought into causality. Lynch (1972 makes this point nicely in *What Time is this place?*, where he illustrates the ways in which the materiality of time is intrinsically and necessarily related to spatial change too. When we adopt Prigogine's perspective of time as an irreversible ontological force within nonlinear dynamic systems, then we also return to appreciate the importance of materiality. We are not suggesting a positivist or anti-social constructionist approach to causality here, but rather that materiality needs to be brought back and made central in discussions about social causality. Reed and Harvey's critical complexity approach allows us to do this without diminishing the importance of meaning, culture, and history in our search for useful complex causality.

6.4. CONCLUSION

The problem of course with social systems is that the ways in which the states of the system, and indeed the materiality of those states, are constituted and classified in the practices of everyday life—or rather the *praxis* of everyday life, to use Paulo Freire's (1970) term—are themselves recursively fed back into the dynamics of the system and in turn fed back into the mechanisms that push and pull the system through its various possible states through time as well. Therefore, this recursive praxis needs to also be epistemologically embedded within the methodological repertoires designed to explore useful complex causality in order to maximize the probability that the empirical representation of that system might shed light on the various ontological layers of generative mechanisms. It is precisely for this very reason that combining retrodictive and retroductive modes of enquiry is for us such a crucial aspect to studying complex social systems in a way that also allows for agency, time, and indeed the researcher's own recursive praxis within the research design and the case based data.

Let us be clear then and return briefly to the idea of retrodictive explanation. We proposed this term based on the idea of prediction but turned backwards. It has much in common with retroductive explanation. Retroduction is often described as having explanatory capacity but without the ability to predict. This is an important point because after all an important motive in our search for causes in science is that the understanding of causality enables us to say what will happen if we do something. Given the nature of complex systems, we might, pessimistically, conclude that we can never predict. However, that is before we consider comparison in terms of comparisons made across ensembles of near neighbors. In other words, the limitations of retroduction necessarily apply if we are attempting to predict the future of a single complex system based on our exploration of the past history of that system and the establishment of what mechanisms have produced its present state. When we are comparing on the basis of difference across near neighbors then we have a much better basis for saying that having established the differences that produced different outcomes, then the application of those differences to a system might produce a different outcome. We always have to say "might," because certainty will never be possible but might still has power here.

It is worthwhile pointing out that statistical modeling based on data sets, including modeling based on longitudinal data series, is always retroductive. The model can never do more than offer a description of mechanisms that have happened in the past. In contrast both Hayles' (1999, 12–13) platonic backhand, the experiment which "works by inferring from the world's noisy multiplicity a simplified abstraction," and the platonic forehand, the simulation which "starts from simplified abstractions and . . . evolves a multiplicity sufficiently complex so that it can be seen as a world of its own," seem have predictive capacity. The abstraction in the form of law generated by experiment says this is what will happen if we do this. Of course this makes the abstraction the real—in other words the real becomes simple, as Hayles says, and messy complex reality is ignored—we might even say denied. In a very similar fashion simulations seek to develop simple rules as the driver of reality and thereby fail ever to get beyond restricted complexity. Indeed the attraction of simulation for scientistic explanation derives exactly from the way in which a rule, for example a rule in game theory, seems to have something of the same sort of general status as an abstracted scientific law.

However, both abstracted laws and the rules governing simulations[7] do seem to offer the ability to generate causal accounts that can be the basis for prediction. In many instances this works well. One of the present authors spent a good deal of his late teens working on applied mathematical problems in dynamics which would enable a gun layer to use Newton's laws of motion to drop a shell just on top of the enemy at which he (always he in those days) was aiming—with the assistance of course of the forward observer to iterate his fire in and thereby take account of contextual differences. Engineering simulations can work well. Contemporary cosmology relies to a considerable degree on simulations and has recently started to deploy statistical meta-models with a Bayesian provenance in order to reduce computational time as a basis for modeling the evolution of the universe. That said laws based on simplicity and simulations confined to representing restricted complexity never can cope with the general complexity (again after Morin) of social reality.

So far we have been primarily concerned with establishing the nature of cause and effect as these might meaningfully be understood in relation to complex systems. However, that kind of ontological specification is not much use for social science unless it is translated into a methodologically informed program of actual research practices. The foundational principles of such a program have been identified in our foregoing discussion but we can spell them out here as a basis for considering how we might actually do research which addresses social causality. First, we are concerned with trajectories, with how things stay the same or change over time. That means that we necessarily construct narratives—accounts of continuity and change through time. Note that because issues of classification matter in relation to the perceived extent to which a system has the propensity to change or not change, narratives about the possible futures of a system are as important (if not more) as narratives of the past and present trajectories of a system (Uprichard 2011). Second, our understanding of cause /effect relationships sees the former as almost always complex and contextual. Third, we work through comparison of the similar but different cases and their similar and different trajectories as the basis of our efforts at understanding causality. We really are dealing with an arrow of time in social causality. So if we are trying to understand how some system is as it is, then we need to know where it started from and examine other systems that started from the same status but are now somehow different. We need to look at the near neighbors and deploy a developed method of difference as the basis for exploring complex causation.

Our emphasis on difference and on systematic comparison as the basis for establishing significant differences means that we are making predictive claims for social science. Those claims always have to be limited and qualified but the potential of the comparative method takes us beyond the ideographic explanation of what has happened which is all that conventional retroductive method, including it must be said retroductive statistical modeling, can achieve. These approaches have considerable policy potential. This is not least because they enable us to engage with changes of kind rather than just changes of degree and that is what matters in most policy contexts. Ragin and Rihoux make this point very clearly:

> Policy researchers, especially those concerned with social as opposed to economic policy, are often more interested in different kinds of cases and their different fates than they are in the extent of the net causal effect of a variable across a large encompassing population of observations. After all, a common goal of social policy is to make decisive interventions, not to move average levels or rates up or down by some minuscule fraction. (Rihoux and Ragin 2004, 18)[8]

This does not prescribe any particular set of methods considered as ways of describing the world. Rather, it prescribes a way of interpreting the results of those investigations. It is true that qualitative comparative analysis in its various forms requires that a numerical specification be attached to attributes as a way of identifying the characteristics of the systems under consideration and this of course is a form of abstraction, but we contend that it still respects the complexity of the systems. It certainly does so to a far greater degree than any other system of exploring for causes that depends on the generation of numerical quantities. We would commend in particular a combination of numerical taxonomy to establish kinds, and QCA informed by the logic of process tracing as described by George and Bennett (2005) as a way of attempting to explain why a case falls into a kind. This seems to us to be the basis for careful historically based understanding of causality both within particular systems and across systems considered as near neighbors through the establishment of differences and similarities, and in turn enabling us to glimpse how and why patterns of change and continuity have to be the way they are and not another way. This, for us, captures the ethos behind trying to empirically capture useful complex causality from a complex realist perspective.

NOTES

1. The best general introduction to Ragin's arguments is provided by his *Redesigning Social Inquiry* (2008).

2. The critical realist position, while widely employed by social scientists in the United Kingdom and Scandinavia, is less well known elsewhere. A good introduction to essential elements in it is provided by Margaret Archer's (1998) edited collection.

3. Ordinal values on a scale can be considered either as inadequate ratio level measurements or, and more sensibly, as ranked categorical distinctions. In the latter frame the ranks reflect some aspect of system within which the systems ranked are located as with the social class of an individual that reflects hierarchy in the social system as a whole.

4. Strictly speaking, MacIver wasn't writing about complex systems, even though his book is riddled with what could well be considered complexity.

5. See chapter 23 in this volume by Horowitz for further discussion of this continuum.

6. See Abrams in chapter 9 (this volume), who seeks to explain the causal basis for such propensities.

7. Even in agent based models the agents operate according to rules. It is possible to write agents so that they have learning capacity but only in accordance with an algorithm that defines that learning capacity. That still leaves us in the realm of restricted complexity.

8. Ragin and Rihoux have noticed how policymakers work and seem aware of the actual character of applied social research. This is in marked contrast to most writers with a philosophical background who seem to have forgotten that their role is that of under laborer and rather than derive an understanding of science from scientific practice seek instead to establish principles of prescription for scientific practice.

REFERENCES

Abbott, A. 1988. "Transcending General Linear Reality." *Sociological Theory* 6: 169–86.

Abbott, A. 1998. "The Causal Devolution." *Sociological Methods and Research* 27 (2): 148–81.

Abbott, A. 2000. "Reflections on the Future of Sociology." *Contemporary Sociology* 29 (2): 296–300.

Archer, M., ed. 1998. *Critical Realism: Essential Readings*. London: Routledge.

Bhaskar, R. 1979. *The Possibility of Naturalism: A Philosophical Critique of the Contemporary Human Sciences*. Brighton: Harvester.

Bourdieu, P. 1990. *The Logic of Practice*. Palo Alto, CA: Stanford University Press.

Bourdieu, P. 1993. *The Field of Cultural Production*. Cambridge: Polity Press.

Bourdieu, P. 1998 *Practical Reason*. First published in French in 1994. Cambridge: Polity Press.

Bourdieu, P., and J.-C. Passeron. 1977/2000. *Reproduction in Education, Society and Culture*. 2nd edition. First English edition 1977. First published in French in 1970. London: Sage.

Bowker, G. C., and S. L. Star. 1999. *Sorting Things Out: classification and its consequences*. Cambridge, MA: The MIT Press.

Byrne, D. 1997. "Complexity Theory and Social Research." *Social Research Update* 18. Available at www.soc.surrey.ac.uk/sru/SRU18.html.

Byrne, D. 1998. *Complexity Theory and the Social Sciences: An Introduction*. London: Routledge.

Byrne, D. 2011. "What Is an Effect? Coming at Causality Backwards." In *The Sage Handbook of Methodological Innovations*, M. Williams and P. Vogt, eds., 80–94. London: Sage.

Byrne, D., and C. Ragin, eds. 2009. *The Sage Handbook of Case-Based Methods*. London: Sage.

Byrne, D., and E. Uprichard. 2007. "Crossing Levels: The Potential for Numerical Taxonomy and Fuzzy Set Approaches to Studying Multi-Level Longitudinal Change." *Methodological Innovations Online* 2 (2). Available at http://erdt.plymouth.ac.uk/mionline/public_html/viewarticle.php?id=42&layout=html.

Byrne, D. S. 2002. *Interpreting Quantitative Data*. London: Sage.

Carter, B., and A. Sealey. 2009. "Reflexivity, Realism and the Process of Casing." In *The Sage Handbook of Case-Based Methods*, D. Byrne, and C. Ragin, eds., 69–83. London: Sage.

Cilliers, P. 2001. "Boundaries, Hierarchies and Networks in Complex Systems." *International Journal of Innovation Management* 5 (2): 135–47.

Cilliers, P. 2010. "Difference, Identity and Complexity." In *Difference, Identity and Complexity: An Ethical Perspective*, P. Cilliers and R. Preiser, eds., 3–18. Dordrecht: Springer.

Cilliers, P., and R. Preiser. 2010. *Difference, Identity and Complexity: An Ethical Perspective*. Dordrecht: Springer.

Desrosières, A. 1998. *The Politics of Large Numbers*. Cambridge, MA: Harvard University Press.

Fielding, N. G., and R. M. Lee. 1998. *Computer Analysis and Qualitative Research*. London: Sage.

Freire, P. 1970. *Pedagogy of the Oppressed*. New York: Herder and Herder.

George, A. L., and A. Bennett. 2005. *Case Studies and Theory Development in the Social Sciences*. Cambridge, MA: The MIT Press.

Goodwin, B. 1994. *How the Leopard Changed Its Spots: The Evolution of Complexity*. London: Phoenix.

Hacking, I. 2002. *Historical Ontology*. Cambridge, MA: Harvard University Press.

Hacking, I. 2007. "Kinds of People: Moving Targets." *Proceedings of the British Academy* 151: 285–318.

Hayles, K. 1999. *How We Became Post-Human*. Chicago: University of Chicago Press.

Holland, J. 1995. *Hidden Order: How Adaptation Builds Complexity*. New York: Perseus.

Kauffman, S. 1993. *The Origins of Order: Self-Organization and Selection in Evolution*. New York: Oxford University Press.

Kauffman, S. 2000. *Investigations*. Oxford: Oxford University Press.

Khalil, E., and K. Boulding. 1996. *Evolution, Order and Complexity*. London: Routledge.

Kiel, D., and E. Elliott. 1996. *Chaos Theory in the Social Sciences.* Ann Arbor: University of Michigan Press.

Lynch, K. 1972. *What Time Is a Place?* Cambridge, MA: The MIT Press.

MacIver, R. 1942/1964. *Social Causation.* Boston: Ginn and Company.

Meadows, D. 1999. *Leverage Points: Places to Intervene in a System.* Hartland, VT: Sustainability Institute.

Morin, E. 2006. *Restricted Complexity, General Complexity.* Available at http://cogprints.org/5217/1/Morin.pdf.

Nicolis, G., and I. Prigogine. 1989. *Exploring Complexity: An Introduction.* New York: Freeman.

Pepper, M. 1926. "Emergence." *Journal of Philosophy* 23 (9): 241–45.

Popper, K. 1990. *A World of Propensities.* Bristol: Theommes.

Ragin C. 1991. *Issues and Alternatives in Comparative Social Research.* Leiden: Brill.

Ragin, C., and B. Rihoux 2004. "Qualitative Comparative Analysis (QCA): State of the Art and Prospects." *Qualitative Methods. Newsletter of the American Political Science Association Organized Section on Qualitative Methods* 2 (2): 3–13.

Ragin, C. 1987. *The Comparative Method: Moving beyond Qualitative and Quantitative Strategies.* Berkeley: University of California Press.

Ragin, C. 1994. *Constructing Social Research.* Thousand Oaks, CA: Pine Forge Press.

Ragin, C. 2000. *Fuzzy Set Social Science.* Chicago: University of Chicago Press.

Ragin, C. 2008. *Redesigning Social Inquiry.* Chicago: University of Chicago Press.

Reed, M., and D. Harvey. 1992. "The New Science and the Old: Complexity and Realism in the Social Sciences." *Journal for the Theory of Social Behaviour* 22: 356–79.

Rihoux, B., and C. Ragin, eds. 2008. *Configurational Comparative Methods: Qualitative Comparative Analysis (QCA) and Related Techniques.* London: Sage.

Ringer, F. 2002. "Max Weber on Causal Analysis, Interpretation, and Comparison." *History and Theory* 41 (2): 163–78.

Sayer, A. 1992 [1984]. *Method in Social Science: A Realist Approach.* 2d ed. London: Hutchinson.

Sayer, A. 2000. *Realism and Social Science.* London: Sage.

Uprichard, E. 2009. "Introducing Cluster Analysis: What Can It Teach us about the Case?" In *The Sage Handbook of Case-Based Methods,* D. Byrne, and C. Ragin, eds., 132–47. London: Sage.

Uprichard, E. 2011 "Narratives of the Future: Complexity, Time and Temporality." In *The Sage Handbook of Methodological Innovations,* M. Williams and P. Vogt, eds., 103–119. London: Sage.

Urry, J. 2003 *Global Complexity.* Cambridge: Polity.

Walby, S. 2010. *Globalization and Inequalities: Complexity and Contested Modernities.* London: Sage.

Williams, R. 1980. "Base and Superstructure in Marxist Cultural Theory." In *Problems in Materialism and Culture.* London: Verso.

CHAPTER 7

PARTIAL EXPLANATIONS IN SOCIAL SCIENCE

ROBERT NORTHCOTT

7.1. INTRODUCTION

How much was the increased murder rate explained by higher unemployment? What was the main cause of the American Civil War? Was it the penetrating offense or the stout defense that was most responsible for the football team's victory? It is ubiquitous in social science and indeed everyday life that the causes we have identified explain some but not all of an outcome. In such cases, the question of critical interest is to quantify each cause's contribution to the outcome. The focus is not on how general or deep or transportable a particular explanation or mechanism is, important though those concerns may also be, but rather is narrowly on how much a cause explains an effect in a particular one-off case. This is relevant historically to determine which factors explained an outcome most. It is also relevant as a guide to future intervention—which factors *would* influence an outcome most?

Comparing different causes' importance, and apportioning responsibility between them, requires making good sense of the notion of partial explanation, that is, of *degree* of explanation. This turns out to be a delicate task.[1] The vast literature on defining causation itself is of no direct help because in the cases of interest here typically all parties already agree on what causes are present. The issue at hand is, rather, degree of causation, which is clearly distinct from mere causation *simpliciter*. It turns out to be very useful to make our concepts in this area explicit. What do partial explanations amount to, and, thus, what constitutes good evidence for them? How much is degree of causation subjective, how much objective? If the causes in question are probabilistic, how much is the outcome due to them and how much to simple chance? What is the role of contrasts?

This chapter is split into four sections. Throughout, the emphasis will be primarily conceptual rather than epistemological. I begin by formulating the notion of degree of causation, or *effect size*. One particular understanding of this is standard across many sciences, and I relate it to influential recent work in the literature on causation. I use this understanding as the basis for my understanding in turn of *partial explanation*. In the second section, I examine to what extent mainstream social science methods—both quantitative and qualitative—succeed in establishing effect sizes so understood. The answer turns out to be, roughly, only to some extent. Next, the standard understanding of effect size, even though widespread, still has several underappreciated consequences. In the third section, I detail some of those. Finally, in the fourth section, I discuss the separate issue of explanandum-dependence, which is essential to assessing any cause's explanatory importance and yet which has been comparatively neglected.

7.2. Degree of causation

Let X be a cause variable and Y an effect variable. Y is a function of the state of the world, that is of X and W, where W is background conditions (i.e., formally a set of variables representing the state of the world just excluding X).[2] Let x_A denote the actual value of X, and x_C the salient counterfactual value of X. And let y_A and y_C denote the values that Y takes given x_A and x_C respectively (given actual background conditions).[3] Then define a *causal effect* (or, equivalently, the *effect size* or *strength* or *importance*) of a cause variable X with respect to an effect variable Y, to be:

$$y_A - y_C \tag{1}$$

Formula [1] is quite intuitive—in words, it is how much difference X made. Glossing over various technical details, we are interested in the quantity of effect for which x_A is responsible, and this is just the level of effect with x_A compared to the level with some alternative input x_C. For example, the causal strength (CS) of kicking a ball might be yielded by the ball's acceleration with the kick compared to its acceleration without that kick.[4] A negative CS here would correspond to accelerating the ball backward; a zero CS to leaving its acceleration unchanged. The units of a CS are whatever units are used to measure Y. At the heart of [1] is that it captures a controlled-experiment sensibility. We want to compare the level of effect with and without the cause while keeping all else equal. For instance, it would be no use comparing the acceleration of a ball with and without a kick if simultaneously a gust of wind had blown up, because obviously the calculation would then yield only the combined impact of the two changes. For this reason, in [1] the background conditions must be constant across the two terms.[5]

y_C, the right-hand term in [1], is a counterfactual—we are interested in what the level of effect *would* have been, given x_C and background conditions. How can this term be evaluated? Because, in reality, background conditions are never quite exactly the same from moment to moment, epistemologically the best we can ever do is find data from as good a re-creation of them as possible. In this respect, [1] serves as a normative ideal, guiding our treatment of actual data by telling us what hypothetical quantity is relevant to evaluating a CS. Only some actual data, namely those adequately approximating controlled constant-W conditions, will then be appropriate.[6]

Once we know a given cause's CS, we may compare it to the strengths of other causes. In this way, in principle we can compare several causes to see which of them are more responsible for a particular outcome. As is widely recognized, this notion of relative importance is choice-of-sample-specific. For example, a gas leak may be deemed a more important cause of a fire than is the presence of oxygen because of an implicit relativization to a normal population of cases. More particularly, relative to that normal population the unusual, difference-making feature is the gas leak, not the oxygen. Formula [1] (and, later, formula [3]) captures this sensitivity via its explicit relativization to choice of contrasts. Change the salient contrast situation and you change which cause is fingered as having a large CS.[7] (This reflects the highly context-sensitive nature of any CS—see section 3-1.)

Not surprisingly, [1] or something like it has a long history in several different literatures as a measure of degree of causation. In the philosophy of history, the motivation behind [1] is similar to that behind several classical views, for instance those in the nineteenth century of Yule and Weber (Turner 1986; Northcott 2008a). More recently, measures in psychology, psychiatry, epidemiology, law, and computer science are also similar. Moreover, still other measures are closely related, being again essentially comparative of an effect with and without a cause.

There are many possible formulations for [1] other than a simple difference. Why not a ratio, for instance? But [1] is more flexible than might first appear; in particular, it may be calculated anew for any choice of Y-variable. So a concern with ratios, for instance, is readily accommodated by applying [1] to the logarithms of the original Y-variable. In this way, odds ratios too, for instance, are also causal strengths in the sense of [1]. Moreover, often we are interested in the *variance* rather than level of a variable (Braumoeller 2006); after suitable re-definition of Y, again [1] applies straightforwardly.

Within analytic philosophy, [1] reflects the common emphasis on causation's difference-making aspect—a cause is something that makes a difference to its effect. Thus, naturally, the strength of a cause is how *much* difference it makes. The form of [1] can be incorporated into the contemporary Bayes net and causal modeling literatures, and arguably is endorsed by experimental practice, at least in the case of quantitative variables (Woodward 2003; Pearl 2000; Spirtes, Glymour, and Scheines 2000). More generally, it is also consistent with the mainstream literature on probabilistic causation (Hitchcock 1996). Finally, it also represents the impact of a hypothetical *intervention*, in particular one changing X from x_A to x_C, reflecting a close affinity with a manipulationist view of causation (Woodward 2003).

Both terms in [1] can be interpreted as expected values. And the Y-variable may be a probability.[8] In these ways, [1] accommodates the possibility of indeterminism. The indeterminism here is uncertainty regarding what effect results from a particular specification of cause and background conditions.[9] In practice, such indeterminism is ubiquitous in social science; its accommodation is therefore essential for any definition of CS.

There are few alternative accounts of CS with any currency. In practice, much the most widespread in science are those derived from the analysis of variance and a range of related statistical techniques. But the many critiques of these techniques as instruments for assessing causal responsibility are by now familiar. For a sampling, see Lewontin 1974; Shipley 2000; Spirtes, Glymour, and Scheines 2000; Northcott 2008b. Other alternatives will be discussed below, in particular regression coefficients and various nonprobabilistic qualitative definitions, as well as the apparent similarity between [1] and measures of average causal effect in statistics. Also, the final section below will discuss an issue—explanandum-dependence—that does suggest [1] needs to be augmented.

7.3. CAUSAL STRENGTH AND SOCIAL SCIENTIFIC PRACTICE

7.3.1. Two Traditions

Two different methodological traditions have arisen within political science, which Mahoney and Goertz (2006) label "two cultures." Analogous traditions exist in other social sciences too. These traditions are:

1. *Qualitative.* This typically examines the causal structure behind only a small number of events, via detailed historical investigation. The structure is taken to apply to every event in the sample, thus allowing qualitative comparative analysis (QCA). (Ragin 1987 is an especially influential advocate.) For example, what explains social revolution in agrarian-bureaucratic states that were not formally colonized (Skocpol 1979)? At the time of Skocpol's work, this analysis applied to only three examples, namely the revolutions in France, Russia, and China. In Mahoney and Goertz's phrase, the focus is on "causes of effects"—what is the detailed causal structure behind these particular events?

2. *Quantitative.* This typically analyzes conditioned statistical associations over large samples, often by running regression analyses. For example, what is the influence of earnings and education on political participation? The focus is now on "effects of causes"—what is the average level of effect when a cause is present compared to when it is absent? King, Keohane, and Verba (1994) are especially influential advocates of the quantitative approach.

I will focus on the specific issue of how each tradition furnishes us with partial explanations. That is, do their methods successfully yield us causal strengths?

7.3.2. The Qualitative Approach

A theory in the QCA tradition may be summed up by a simple Boolean formula. Take, for instance, Moore's (1966) theory of the development of early modern democracies. Expressed in Boolean terms:

$$Y = X \& (A \vee B)$$

where Y = democracy, X = a strong bourgeoisie, A = alliance between bourgeoisie and aristocracy, B = weak aristocracy. In other words, what was necessary for the development of democracy was a strong bourgeoisie, together with an aristocracy neutered either by its own weakness or by alliance with the bourgeoisie.

There are several characteristic features to note:

1. The theory offers a causal *structure*, not just a singular causal explanation, typically with *multiple pathways* to the same outcome.
2. It is meant to apply to *several* cases.
3. It is *deterministic*, couched in terms of necessary and sufficient conditions.

These features lead in turn to two noteworthy consequences: First, causal explanations are provided of singular instances. The Boolean formula, assuming it is correct, provides in particular instances an appropriate *invariance relation* (Woodward 2003)—that is, it licenses answers to the what-if-things-had-been-different questions characteristic of causal explanations. For example, given that there was a weak aristocracy, then the bourgeoisie being strong rather than weak explains why there was democracy rather than no democracy.

Second, however, it only enables us to calculate causal strengths, and thus partial explanations, that are trivially all-or-nothing. For example, a strong bourgeoisie receives 100 percent credit because it is a necessary condition. According to formula [1], nontrivial causal strengths are possible in such cases only if the analysis is probabilistic. But the qualitative approach, at least in its QCA version, is characteristically and explicitly nonprobabilistic.[10] This unfortunately renders it inapplicable to the many explananda for which we do not have full explanations—that is, for which the causes we identify account for only some rather than all of the effect.

Aware of this limitation, several ingenious recent papers attempt to evade the second conclusion, and to define nontrivial causal strengths even within a framework of deterministic necessary and sufficient conditions. I applaud this recognition of the problem. Although there is no space here to discuss them fully, I will very briefly outline some of these recent proposals before indicating why I think they are unsatisfactory substitutes for [1].

Mahoney, Kimball, and Koivu (2009) present a definition based partly on set theory and partly on sequence analysis. If X is necessary for Y, then on a Venn diagram Y is a subset of X, and vice versa if X is sufficient. Matters of degree may then be incorporated via an implicit metric over the Venn diagram space. For instance, if X is a sufficient condition for Y, it may be more or less important depending on how much of set Y is filled by set X, that is, depending on the size of $(Y - X)$ relative to X. Sequence analysis, roughly speaking, then traces the impact on such set-theoretic calculations of adding in new entries to the chain of causes leading up to the effect. In this way, a qualitative importance ranking can be defined over the different causes in the chain.

Despite its ingenuity, the Mahoney, Kimball, and Koivu proposal has some weaknesses. Perhaps the most striking are two of scope. First, the authors themselves note that their scheme is able only to compare different causes on the same chain. It is therefore inapplicable to causes that are not themselves causally linked, that is, not to multiple independent or simultaneous causes. Second, there is a further serious restriction of scope, namely inapplicability to quantitative explananda. By the latter, I do not mean here the large-sample regression analyses mentioned already. Rather, I have in mind singular cases where the effect of interest is not a simple all-or-nothing event, such as a revolution, but rather a quantitative variable. For instance, what explains the rise in average global temperature over the last few decades? This effect is a sample of one, but we will typically be interested in the quantitative contribution to it of various factors—how much did deforestation contribute, how much did air travel, how much did volcanoes? Similar remarks apply to many other effects of interest, such as crime rates, voting shares, or economic growth indices.

In addition to these restrictions of scope, there are significant conceptual worries. Mahoney, Kimball, and Koivu's scheme requires a metric over Venn-diagram space, but is not clear either how to motivate such a metric or about the source of the particular universe of possibilities over which the sets range. Yet these issues are crucial to their scheme. Ultimately, they relate to choice of comparison population or, in the terms of [1], to choice of contrasts, and should be addressed explicitly. Finally, whereas [1] is easily interpreted as representing the result of an intervention, results from Mahoney, Kimball, and Koivu's scheme—because framed set-theoretically— can only be interpreted as degrees of necessity or sufficiency. It thus cannot inform us precisely about the impact of a future or past hypothetical intervention. (This shortfall is related to the inapplicability to quantitative explananda.)

A second ingenious nonprobabilistic definition of CS for singular cases is due to Braham and Van Hees (2009). Much of their focus is on the relation between causal and moral/legal responsibility, but their measure is intended to apply to the former. They import tools from game theory and voting theory to define a cause's strength to be, roughly speaking, the proportion of possible routes to the effect that include that particular cause. Unlike Mahoney et al.'s this new measure certainly can be applied to multiple independent causes. On the other hand, this gain is offset by its now no longer being clear that it can be applied to different causes on a single chain. ([1] can be applied in both circumstances.) More fundamentally, Braham and Van Hees's approach suffers from the same shortfall as Mahoney et al.'s namely in being inapplicable to quantitative effects.[11] It also is subject to an analogous worry as before regarding interpretation of their results.

Ragin (2006) and Goertz (2006) present a third approach, framed in terms of fuzzy sets—that is, sets whose membership can be a matter of degree. For instance, a state might be deemed a democracy to degree 0.6. Naturally, this makes it much easier to define a nontrivial measure of CS even for the qualitative case, and moreover a measure that is applicable to multiple independent causes. On the other hand, the particular measures endorsed by Ragin and Goertz seek to define one summary CS score for a whole population (see below for why this is problematic).

Goertz (2006) also analyzes CS in terms of actual frequencies. In particular, when considering the CS for a necessary condition in a particular one-off case, he appeals to a wider sample of analogous cases. For instance, suppose state breakdown is necessary for social revolution but only actually leads to it on 3 of 16 relevant occasions (Goertz 2006, 92). Then, roughly speaking, it is assigned a CS of 3/16. Formula [1] appeals to probabilities; if those probabilities are interpreted as actual frequencies rather than single-case chances, then (assuming agreement on the relevant sample) it would yield the same result as Goertz's scheme (bracketing for now issues about background conditions). On the other hand, three worries: First, the actual-frequency approach leaves us vulnerable to actual samples that do not happen to proxy satisfactorily the counterfactuals relevant to CS. Second, Goertz's scheme again seeks to define a single score for CS across a whole population of cases. And third, it seeks to combine into a single measure not only CS as understood in this chapter but also what Goertz calls "trivialness"—by the latter Goertz has in mind something like gravity, which may be a necessary condition for revolution but, since it occurs in all relevant cases of nonrevolution too, is of only trivial interest and thus should have its CS downgraded. But, in line with philosophical consensus, my view is that such trivialness should lead merely to our pragmatic neglect of gravity rather than to a denial of its causal strength (see the references in note 7 for discussion).

Finally, none of these proposals speaks to the range of issues that [1] does. In particular, they address either incompletely or not at all the matters to be discussed in sections 7.4 and 7.5 below.

7.3.3. The Quantitative Approach

I will focus on the relation between causal strength and regression coefficients. To keep the conceptual issues clear I will consider just the simplest case, that is, a regression equation of the form:

$$Y = a + bX + e$$

where Y is the dependent variable, X the independent variable, a and b are constants, and e is an error term. For instance, perhaps Y = political participation and X = earnings. The relevant population will typically be large, for example, every adult citizen.

The regression coefficient b is usually taken to represent the influence of X on Y. The central question is: Does it represent X's causal strength?[12] Start with the simple binary case where X only takes two values, as when a population is split into treatment and control groups. The coefficient b is then a measure of X's causal effect, namely:

$$Y(X = 1) - Y(X = 0) \qquad\qquad [2]$$

where 1 and 0 are conventional values for treatment X being present or absent, and where the values for Y are averages across all the data points in the sample. Thus the quantitative tradition's conception of causal effect, [2], is obviously analogous to the CS of [1], albeit now applying to particular populations of individuals rather than to those individuals themselves (on which more shortly).[13]

However, there is also one obvious and significant disanalogy between formulas [1] and [2], namely the issue of *confounders*. In particular, the right-hand term Y(X = 0) in the quantitative formula is derived from actual data. The hope is that these data serve as satisfactory proxies for the counterfactuals deemed relevant by [1], but there is no guarantee of that. In particular, they will not do so if there is too much causal heterogeneity within the population. For instance, suppose lack of education causes people both to be low earners and also not to participate in politics. Then there will be a correlation between the latter two variables, reflected in a positive score in [2], even if there is no causal relation between them because the real work is all being done by lack of education. Formally, the background conditions are inconstant in such a way that the actual data from the X = 0 (control) group are not a good proxy for the counterfactual of what would have happened to the X = 1 (treatment) group *if* the latter's members had not received the treatment.

The problem of confounders is avoided by [1] because the right-hand term is a counterfactual relativized to constant W, precisely so as to avoid spurious correlations and thus spurious CS scores. The problem is also addressed in the paradigm case of a randomized controlled trial, where all confounders are (at least on average) equally distributed between the treatment and control groups. But most regressions are run on observational rather than experimental data. Accordingly, in those cases there is no guarantee that [2] captures the size of a genuinely *causal* effect.

Of course, social scientists are long familiar with this issue and a huge literature has built up around how best to test for and avoid such confounding. (Morgan and Winship 2007 and Pearl 2000 are notable recent contributions.) Much boils down to sufficient knowledge of the underlying causal structure that is generating the data, as this in turn enables us to ensure there are no significant omitted variables, that the causal relations between the modeled variables are specified correctly, and so on. (Ultimately, there's an analogous requirement in the qualitative case too.) In practice, much of the hard work in social science lies precisely in establishing this requisite knowledge. However, I will pass over the many details of that work here in order to focus instead on a separate question: If good circumstances do prevail— that is, if the regression equation is indeed a correct causal specification—are regression coefficients good proxies for CS even then? For it turns out that even in such good cases, difficulties still remain.

First, a regression can only estimate a CS whose inputs the regression's particular sample happens to proxy. For example, what if we wanted to know the CS of the actual treatment compared to a dosage outside the actual range? No data from the actual sample would proxy the relevant counterfactual; neither would the actual data alone license any extrapolation of the regression result to a new range of data.[14] (Remember, most analyses are of observational, not experimental, data.)

Second, return temporarily to the case where X is binary, that is, where it only takes two values in the population. For $Y = a + bX + e$, the coefficient b may then be interpreted in either of two different ways:

1. As a fixed constant, giving the CS that applies to the two values of X for every member of the population.
2. As some average of the varied CS scores that apply to each individual member of the population.

These two options are often not distinguished but their implications are significantly different. In particular, in the case of 2, the value of b does not directly bear on individual cases at all. Rather, it gives a CS only at the population level.

(In passing, a note on levels: In accordance with difference-making views of causation generally, formula [1] is not reductionist. That is, [1] may apply to X and Y variables at any level. In particular, X and Y may be population-level variables in which case a positive CS indicates a population-level cause, specific to the particular population sampled (and salient counterfactual population). Where there can be a problem is if background theory yields the causal structure only at the individual level, because then aggregation issues mean it may not be straightforward to infer the relevant causal structure at the population level—and without the latter, it is not possible to identify population-level causal strengths reliably. For instance, it is one thing to have in mind a mechanism for why an individual's education might increase his or her level of political participation. But at the population level, what matters is how *rates* of education affect *rates* of political participation. Perhaps, for instance, after a while ever-higher rates of education no longer much increase rates of political participation because of some macro-threshold effect. The point is that such a population-level mechanism could be invisible to the postulated individual-level mechanism, meaning that we did not have the population-level causal structure right, meaning in turn that we were unable to evaluate the counterfactuals necessary to any calculation of CS. In this chapter, though, I will again focus on conceptual rather than such epistemological issues.)

Third, what if, as in the general case, the X-variable is interval-valued rather than binary? Then X may take any of a range of values, and the use of regression coefficients to estimate causal strengths becomes considerably more complicated. For such a population will contain within it many different causal strengths, corresponding to different pairs of values of X. For instance, the data could be used to estimate the CS of X = 2 rather than 1, or of 5 rather than 2, or of some mixture of 3 and 1 rather than some mixture of 2 and 1 . . . and so on. Any regression coefficient gives just a single value for the population and so could only be a mèlange of these various possibilities.[15,16]

However, a regression equation can still be useful for calculating causal strengths sometimes. For in good cases it will represent accurately the underlying causal structure, and estimation of its coefficients will then enable particular causal strengths to be inferred, much as they can be inferred in physics if we know the relevant law. This may occasionally be especially straightforward. In particular, in the linear case, when X is a cause of Y, and when background conditions were not causally heterogeneous, the value of a regression coefficient will equal the average value of a "unit CS" in that population.[17]

Finally, there are several parallels with the qualitative case. In both traditions, causal strengths can be calculated only if the correct underlying causal structure has been identified. In the one case, this is done via detailed historical investigation, in the other via a mix of this or more abstract theory (in order to motivate the initial regression equation) combined with statistical analysis. Moreover if, against QCA practice, we interpreted qualitative analyses probabilistically, the resultant uncertainty would be analogous to the error term in a regression equation.[18]

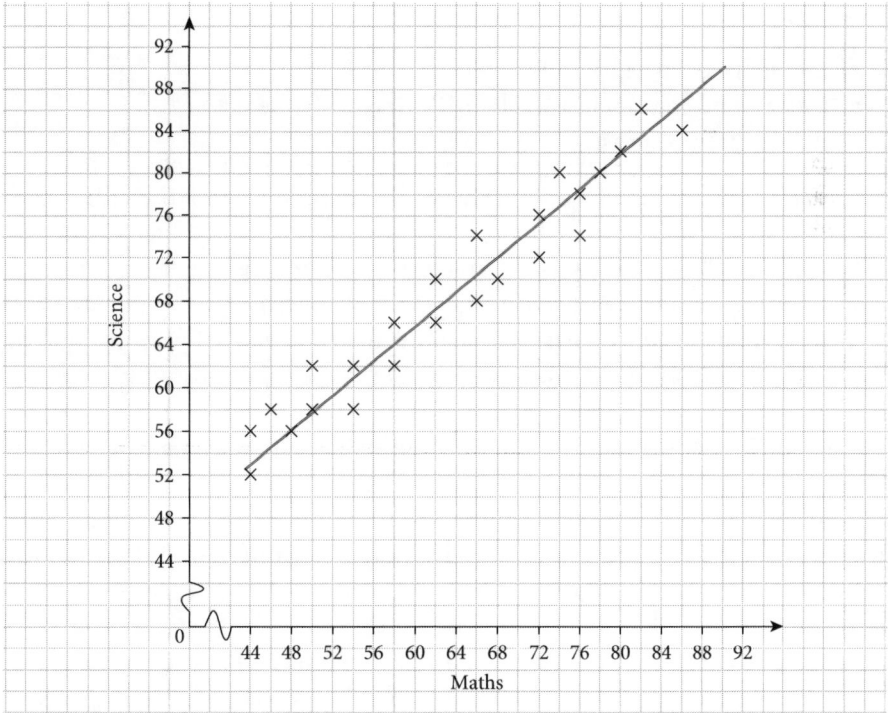

Figure 7.1 A line of best fit. Comparing any two data points generates a new CS each time. Many different causal strengths may thus be found within the same population.

7.3.4. Recap

Qualitative analysis is certainly capable of delivering CS scores, assuming that the causal structure has been identified correctly. However, QCA's deterministic emphasis purely on necessary and sufficient conditions means that these CS scores will only ever be trivially all-or-nothing.

In favorable circumstances, quantitative analysis too can estimate the correct causal structure, from which, in principle at least, nontrivial CS scores of interest can then be inferred. On the other hand, even in these favorable circumstances, the value of the regression coefficient itself will only rarely equal that of the CS of interest. Moreover, the CS estimates will only ever be at the population level; it is then a substantive further issue whether they apply also at the individual level.

7.4. FEATURES OF CAUSAL STRENGTH

7.4.1. Context-specificity

Although, as noted, formula [1] is ubiquitous across many sciences, nevertheless several of its implications are often unappreciated. Begin with a quick theoretical detour. According to [1], any CS value for a cause X is relativized to three things:

1. the choice of effect variable Y
2. background conditions (reflecting the levels of other causes of Y)
3. the choice of contrast x_C

Regarding (1), for instance, kicking a ball may be a strong cause of the ball's acceleration but a weak cause of its changing color. Regarding (2), striking a match is a strong cause of light if background conditions include sufficient oxygen in the atmosphere, but not otherwise. Regarding (3), how much difference a cause makes depends on what we are comparing it to. The difference made by a substitute in a sports team, for instance, depends critically not just on the substitute but also on which player they are replacing.

Combining (2) and (3) above, for any given cause-effect type pair there will therefore be many associated token causal strengths—a new one for every change of background conditions or x_C. In a phrase, any CS is *context-specific*. No cause has a univocal strength *simpliciter*. Rather, as background conditions or choice of x_C vary, the very same cause X may have a different strength even with respect to the same effect Y.

Stated baldly like this, the context-specificity thesis perhaps seems so obvious as to be uninteresting. Yet this feature of CS turns out to have several significant implications. One, for instance, is the familiar problem of extrapolation between populations. Any population-level CS is relativized to a particular population (formally, to a particular x_A, x_C and value of W), so there is no guarantee that the same CS will be true also of some new population. Knowledge of the underlying causal structure will, of course, be relevant to determining whether the CS value can indeed be so extrapolated.

Other implications of context-specificity seem to be less widely recognized. I survey several of these now. (Northcott 2008a covers some of the same ground in more detail.)

7.4.2. Nonadditive Causal Interaction

Consider a fictional example, simplified for illustration. Suppose that, statistically, graduating from college has a certain impact on earnings for whites—say, it increases it by four units (in comparison to finishing education before college). For blacks, on the other hand, college raises earnings by only one unit. In other words, race and education interact nonadditively, as summarized below:

	No college	College
Black	2	3
White	3	7

What is the CS of college education here? *There is no univocal answer.* It is four units for whites, one unit for blacks, and presumably some weighted average of those two numbers for the population as a whole (assuming both that there are no other races in the population, and that the figures in the table are good proxies for the counterfactuals relevant to CS calculations). Moreover, the same is true for the CS of race, which may be either one unit or four. That is, being white rather than black increases earnings by a different amount, depending on whether one has a college education. This lack of univocality follows directly from the context-specificity of any CS—in general, there is a different CS for every change in background conditions.[19]

Notice an important feature here. Consider the income of a college-educated white. The CS of their college-rather-than-no-college education is four units; that of their being white rather than black is also four units. These two causal strengths therefore add up to *more* than their total actual earnings of seven units. But there is no contradiction here. Neither individual CS is more than the total actual effect. Arguably, the adding up to more than the total is just what we should expect—that is the very meaning of nonadditivity. It is a mistake to think of a fixed pie of causal credit waiting to be divided up between the causes. Rather, it may be that many causes simultaneously have a large CS, or that none does. As it were, the total amount of pie can vary.[20]

How does current social scientific practice handle interactive effects? Begin with qualitative approaches. First, Braham and Van Hees's (2009) scheme to define nontrivial causal strengths in a deterministic setting is committed to a fixed-pie view of causal credit, which is problematic in nonadditive situations, for the reasons just noted. (Mahoney, Kimball, and Koivu's (2009) scheme, recall, is not applicable to multiple independent causes in the first place.) By contrast, and for all its other difficulties, the traditional QCA apparatus of necessary and sufficient conditions does take on board nonadditive interaction appropriately. For instance, two independently necessary conditions—which is formally a case of positive interaction—will both be assigned full causal importance by it.[21]

What of regressions? Often, one of the independent variables in a regression equation is an interaction term, precisely in response to the possibility that two other independent variables interact nonadditively. As noted earlier, sometimes regression estimation can help establish the causal structure from which a CS of interest may then be inferred even though the regression coefficients themselves typically do not correspond to CS values. The same applies now in the nonadditive case. In general, the size of an interactive effect between two causes is the CS of both causes together, minus the causal strengths of each cause individually (hence is of size three units in our example above, as per note 20). There is no reason to suppose the regression coefficient for an interactive term will track this quantity, and besides there will in any case be many different values for such an interactive effect within a population just as there are many different values for a CS. For the purpose of elucidating causal strengths, therefore, inclusion of an interaction term is of dubious relevance.

7.4.3. Small Causes Can Be Important

At Waterloo, the British fought Napoleon to a standstill; the arrival of the Prussians was merely the straw that broke the camel's back. Is it true that the British contribution was therefore more causally important? Measurably asymmetric contributions, the reasoning runs, imply asymmetric causal importance. But it turns out that this is not true in general—even if we do measure the British and Prussian contributions in an identical currency of number of soldiers and even if, further, the British number was indeed the greater.

To see this, for simplicity assume determinism here. Label: x_A = the fighting of the British soldiers, as measured by their number; z_A = the fighting of the Prussian soldiers, as measured by their number. Let the salient contrasts in both cases be zero soldiers. Denote Napoleon's actual defeat by $Y = 1$, his nondefeat by $Y = 0$. Finally, in line with historical consensus, assume that neither the British nor the Prussians could have won the battle alone.

Then, applying formula [1]:

1. CS of the British = the outcome with the British compared to that without them = (Y given x_A and z_A – Y given x_C and z_A) = $1 - 0 = 1$
2. CS of the Prussians = the outcome with the Prussians compared to that without them = (Y given z_A and x_A – Y given z_C and x_A) = $1 - 0 = 1$

That is, the British and Prussians are awarded equal causal strengths with respect to winning the battle. This is true regardless of the exact number of soldiers each contributed—the calculation would have been unchanged even if the British had ten times as many men as the Prussians. The result follows (in this deterministic case) simply from x_A and z_A's individual insufficiency and joint sufficiency.

With respect to many *other* effects, of course, the British would have had far greater causal importance because of their far superior numbers. Probably too our moral intuitions may be sensitive to such "type" considerations. But with respect to this particular effect in these particular circumstances, we have no justification for awarding the British any more causal credit than the Prussians. Besides, with respect to some other effects, say the army's German-language competence, it is the Prussians that would be more important. Any CS is a token, sensitive to every change in effect variable as well as background conditions.[22]

One source of confusion is the easy *commensurability* of the number of British and Prussian soldiers. This fools us into thinking that the British must therefore somehow have greater CS here. But such commensurability is a red herring: Commensurable or not, the British and Prussian forces were nonetheless equally and symmetrically necessary to the defeat of Napoleon at Waterloo. More generally, commensurability can be shown to be neither necessary nor sufficient for asymmetric attributions of CS (Northcott 2005a).

The take-home message is that even so-called small causes, such as the Prussian army at Waterloo, can have big causal strengths. Indeed, more fundamentally, it seems to me that what it even means for a cause to be large or small can only be a large or small CS. It follows that a cause's size can only be defined relative to a choice of *effect* variable, not by considering the cause variable in isolation from any explanatory context.

7.4.4. Limits versus Selections

In the next two subsections, there is space briefly to flag two other common confusions. (See Northcott 2008a for further discussion.) First, a claim often heard, from Marxists and others, is that the deep structural factors underpinning history are the only truly important ones. For example, Przeworski and Wallerstein (1988) argue that the threat available to capitalists of an investment strike, a threat that in the past has often been exercised, has constrained the politically possible range of government policy throughout postwar Latin America. This underlying structural constraint, the thought runs, is thus what really determines policy, not the mere surface matter of whichever choice some government then makes from the limited range of options still open to it. The background limits are what matter, not the subsequent restricted selections.

But it is a mistake to privilege the deep structural factors as necessarily more important (again understanding causal importance, here as elsewhere, to be CS as defined by [1]). Imagine that there are 30 different policies available—5 radical ones and 25 more conventional ones. Suppose that the capitalist threat structure limits those available to just the latter 25. Then it seems that a government official's particular selection, narrowing the field from 25 to 1, can be more important than the threat structure, which narrowed the field merely from 30 to 25.

All turns on the precise explanandum of interest. Suppose the actual policy is a conventional one. Then it may well be that without the threat structure there would have been a radical policy, whereas swapping ministers would have changed nothing. Thus it is the threat structure—not the particular choice of minister—that explains why we have the actual policy rather than a *radical* one. But at the same time, it may well be the particular choice of minister—and not the threat structure—that explains why we have the actual policy rather than an *alternative conventional* one. (Northcott 2008a explicates this rather intuitive line of reasoning more formally. See also Sober, Wright, and Levine 1992, from which the example is adapted.) I discuss the issue—crucial in this example— of explanandum-dependence in section 7.5 below. The point here is that there is no general, explanandum-independent sense in which limits are more causally important than selections.

7.4.5. Underlying versus Proximate Causes

The second common confusion concerns the relative strengths of underlying and proximate causes. In particular, there is no general reason to think the former more important. Intuitively, merely being an earlier link on a causal chain does not imply also being a more important one (Sober, Wright, and Levine 1992). For example, suppose the first link in a chain raises the probability of an effect from 0.1 to 0.2, whereas a later link raises it from 0.2 to 0.7. The second cause is clearly the more important, as [1] reflects. It is also evident the situation could be reversed just as easily. Position on the chain in itself implies nothing.

There is one clear objective asymmetry though: An earlier link on a chain is a cause of a later link, but not vice versa. Does this asymmetry imply greater CS for the earlier link? The inference is not uncommon. The famous Roman historian A.H.M. Jones, for instance, argued in favor of the primacy of barbarian invasions as a cause of Rome's fall by noting that the chief rival suspect—internal decay—was itself in part an *effect* of those invasions (Martin 1989, 65). But this is a red herring. Formally, the asymmetry is already reflected by the earlier cause (or rather, its consequences) forming part of the background conditions in the later cause's CS calculation, whereas the later cause is completely absent from the earlier cause's CS calculation. But that asymmetry does nothing to negate the central fact that what actually matters for CS is only how much a cause raises an effect's probability at the time of that cause's own occurrence.

Often, a preference for the greater importance of underlying causes reflects a focus on a particular kind of explanandum. In particular, if we are interested in longer-term or broader-scale effects, then with respect to them indeed an underlying cause will often have a higher CS than a shallow proximate one. Perhaps these kinds of explananda are more often of theoretical significance, but ultimately this is still all interest-relative. For example, if we are interested instead in the precise time at which a war broke out, then the war's short-run proximate triggers may well now have a much higher CS than its deeper underlying causes.

7.5. EXPLANANDUM-DEPENDENCE

Despite its importance, evident in both the preceding subsections, providing a formal account of explanandum-dependence is a notable lacuna in the philosophical literature. Among the few even to emphasize it in this context are Sober, Wright, and Levine (1992), Martin (1989), and Miller (1987). Rectifying this lacuna turns out to have significant consequences for our understanding of what a cause's explanatory importance amounts to. I turn to the issue now.

7.5.1. Roots in the Literature

As noted, formula [1] or something like it has a long history in several different literatures. Yet, notwithstanding this ubiquity, it cannot yet be a complete account of degree of causal *explanation*. The reason is that, at least according to contemporary theory, causal explanation is contrastive with respect to both cause *and* effect. On this view, explanation takes the general form:

x_A-rather-than-x_C explains y_A-rather-than-y_C

where y_A and y_C are respectively the actual and contrast values of the effect variable Y. The contrastive view dates from Dretske (1972). Notable developments of it include Van Fraassen (1980), Garfinkel (1981), Achinstein (1983), Hitchcock (1996), and—most influential recently—Woodward (2003). A major advantage of it is that its sensitivity to y_C enables us, as we will see, to capture explanandum-dependence.

The problem—for everyone—is that formula [1] is insensitive to y_C. To be sure, y_C appears in [1], but there it is by definition the value that Y would have obtained given x_C. The y_C that is relevant here, as we will see, is that prespecified by an explanandum quite independently of any x_C. To avoid confusion, I will denote explananda by y_A^*-rather-than-y_C^*. Thus, in the asterisk notation, the real issue is [1]'s insensitivity to y_C^*. Rather, [1] incorporates choice of contrast only on the cause side (i.e., x_C), which is fine for an analysis of causal strength but not for one of *explanatory* strength (ES).[23] No one (to my knowledge) has ever adapted the full contrastive machinery to the issue of *degree* of explanation. To be clear: y_C^*-dependence is already standard in theories of causal explanation; the problem is its absence from the standard definition of degree of causation/explanation.

Consider a tragic example: the first dropping of an atomic bomb in war. What explains the timing of this event—that is, of the bomb at Hiroshima? Consider two causes: the fine weather that day and Japan's reluctance to surrender. In accordance with contrastive theory, we must also specify respective salient contrasts: bad weather that day and Japan amenable to surrender. Here's the point: *Both* these causes can be argued greatly to have increased the bombing's probability:

1. If the weather had been bad instead of good, the bombing would have been postponed.[24]

2. If Japan had been willing to surrender, Truman would likely have thought the bombing unnecessary.

But the two causes increase the probability of, so to speak, different aspects of the bombing:

1. The weather impacted its precise timing.
2. The Japanese attitude impacted only its rough timing (or, for those optimists who believe that there might otherwise never have been such an event, whether a first atomic bombing occurred at all).

Thus the weather is highly explanatory only of the short-term explanandum—why the first bombing occurred on August 6, 1945 rather than the subsequent few days. Japan's attitude, by contrast, is highly explanatory only of a longer-term explanandum—why the first bombing occurred in 1945 rather than some subsequent year. Unfortunately, the simple formula [1] is unable to capture this crucial distinction. Both the weather and the Japanese attitude made a big difference to whether the bomb was dropped, and for this reason both factors score well on [1]. It is impossible to represent in [1] the crucial distinction between the long-run and short-run explananda, because just specifying the bomb-drop alone (i.e., just y_A^* alone) still leaves unclear which aspect of it is explanatorily relevant.[25] We need a successor to [1] that is y_C^*-sensitive.[26]

Neither is this need of merely theoretical interest. The Hiroshima example illustrates its pertinence, as do the issues discussed earlier of underlying versus proximate causes and limits versus selections. More widely, the worry is that disputes ostensibly about substance often turn out to be cases merely of people talking past each other; or, more precisely, cases of people addressing different explananda and thus not really being in conflict. Sober, Wright, and Levine (1992, 134) comment in this regard: "A problem that constantly befuddles debates about the importance of different causes . . . is the correct designation of the object of explanation (the explanandum)." The point is that these episodes could be avoided by an explicit specification of the explanandum of interest—that is, in our terminology, by a specification of y_C^* as well as of y_A^*.

7.5.2. A Definition of Explanatory Strength

Generally, providing a formal analysis of ES proves an intricate business. There are several categories of cases and many nuances, but there is space here only to give a bare-bones account of one kind of case, namely where the effect is a qualitative variable with no quantitative nuance. (See Northcott 2011a for more, including the relation between what previous accounts do exist and the one advanced in this chapter.)

To begin, any ES will be a relation between an explanandum and an explanans. The sequence of analysis is then as follows:

1. Define a target explanandum y_A^*-rather-than-y_C^*, this being specified independently of any cause variable X.

2. Consider a particular explanans x_A-rather-than-x_C, i.e., an actual level of cause x_A and a contrast level of cause x_C.
3. Define what it means for the change from x_C to x_A to fully explain that from y_C^* to y_A^*, then assess to what extent this actually occurs.

Regarding (3), the phrase "fully explain" deserves explication. So, to be clear: The sense of "fully explanatory" I will have in mind is when a cause makes all (rather than only some of) the difference with respect to an effect. This is the sense that is of critical interest when considering interventions. Moreover, any difference-making view of causal explanation naturally lends support to describing as "fully" explanatory any cause that makes all the difference; what else, on a difference-making view, could full explanation be?[27]

More formally then, in the sense just specified, x_A-rather-than-x_C *fully explains* y_A^*-rather-than-y_C^* if and only if the following two conditions are both satisfied:

1. $\mathrm{pr}(y_A^* / x_A \& W) = 1$, (i.e. y_A^*) occurs when x_A occurs
2. $\mathrm{pr}(y_C^* / x_C \& W) = 1$, (i.e. y_C^*) *would* have occurred had x_C occurred[28]

Our true goal, however, is a measure of *partial* explanation. We may now define this as the degree to which the conditions for full explanation are satisfied. Formally, the ES of an explanans x_A-rather-than-x_C with respect to an explanandum y_A^*-rather-than-y_C^* is:

$$\mathrm{pr}(y_A^* / x_A \& W) + \mathrm{pr}(y_C^* / x_C \& W)$$

The higher the score the better the explanation, and a maximum score of 2 indicates full or perfect explanation. Often, an ES score of 1 is the neutral one indicating no explanation at all.[29]

Like [1] earlier, formula [3] is rather more adaptable than might first appear. In particular, it is readily extended to cases where the contrast of interest is a *range* of values. For instance, "why was the budget as much as $2m?" can be represented by y_C^* = the event of a budget under $2m. Other forms of explananda can be accommodated similarly, such as a concern only with ordinal outcomes (y_C^* = the budget was less than the y_A^* value). Analogous remarks apply also to y_A^*. That is, the same actual event may be described in many ways, possibly impacting the ES score. In this sense, ES is description-dependent. Fundamentally, formula [3] is only defined once given a prior choice of explanandum, that is, of y_A^* and y_C^*. One result of this is the flexibility to encompass many different explanatory concerns about the same actual event.

The relation between ES and the more commonly cited CS is illuminated by considering interventions. The CS definition [1], recall, directly tracks the impact of these. In particular, it tracks the impact on Y of a change from x_C to x_A. Things are not quite the same with ES. Rather, we can think of ES instead in terms of the desired *result* of an intervention. In particular, ES tracks how well a change from x_C to x_A will yield the desired change from y_C^* to y_A^*. That is, CS tracks the impact of an intervention; ES tracks to what extent this impact is the one we want.

We may illustrate the ES formula [3] by applying it to the Hiroshima example. Let:

$y_A^* =$ the actual dropping of the Hiroshima bomb

$x_A =$ (the occurrence of) fine weather that day, $x_C =$ bad weather that day

$z_A =$ Japanese reluctance to surrender, $z_C =$ Japanese willingness to surrender

Recall the short-term explanandum—that is, why the bomb was dropped exactly when it was. This is represented by $y_C^* =$ the bomb was dropped in the few days after August 6, 1945. Intuitively, recall, the fine weather is highly explanatory of this whereas the Japanese reluctance to surrender is not. For brevity, simplify here by assuming $pr(y_A^* / x_A \& W) = 1$. Then, applying [3]:

1. Good weather's ES $= pr(y_A^* / x_A \& W) + pr(y_C^* / x_C \& W) = 1 + pr$(given bad weather on 6th August 1945, the bomb would have been dropped in the few days after) $= (1 + $ quite high$) = (1 + 0.9,$ say$) = \underline{1.9}$.

2. Japanese attitude's ES $= pr(y_A^* / x_A \& W) + pr(y_C^* / z_C \& W) = 1 + pr$(given Japanese willingness to surrender, the bomb would have been dropped in the few days after) $= (1 + $ quite low$) = (1 + 0.1,$ say$) = \underline{1.1}$.[30]

Thus, as desired, the weather but not the Japanese attitude is endorsed as highly explanatory.

As is easily shown, the results are reversed for the long-term explanandum: For a new $y_C^* = $ a bomb was first dropped only in subsequent years. Then it is the Japanese attitude, but not the weather, that comes out highly explanatory. Of course, what matters here is not the exact figures but rather only the general point they illustrate—namely that [3] successfully tracks those factors that determine ES.

Overall, although of course there may be ways of formalizing explanandum-dependence other than by [3], nothing (to my knowledge) so explicit or quantitative has yet appeared in the literature. Meanwhile, being so explicit carries significant benefits: It helps prevent pseudo-disputes in which the participants are unwittingly talking past one another. It makes clear the connection to the general philosophical literature on causation and explanation. It makes clear the precise roles here of chance,[31] counterfactuals, and contrasts. And it also makes clear which aspects of ES are subjective or interest-relative (i.e., choice of contrasts and initial choice of effect variable), and which are objective (i.e., background conditions and the value of ES once given Y, y_C^*, and x_C). It reveals a range of often overlooked features, namely those discussed with reference to CS in section 7.4. Further benefits, discussed in Northcott (2011a), include: clarity regarding the relation between qualitative and quantitative cases; a general account of explanatory relevance; and, depending on one's wider metaphysical commitments, also some light shed on the relation between causation and causal explanation.

7.6. CONCLUSION

Formula [1], I have argued, represents our philosophically best-supported measure of degree of causation, one accepted and adopted, implicitly or explicitly, across many sciences. Yet methods widespread in social science conform with it only very imperfectly. In particular, except in unusually favorable circumstances, regression coefficients do *not* track meaningful CS scores, *even when* the regression equation represents the causal structure truly. Current qualitative methods are also ill suited to estimating CS scores in all but deterministic cases. Moreover, if our focus is on degree of explanation rather than degree of causal effect, then we must also take into account the exact specification of the explanandum, yet no current formal technique does so.

On a more positive note, we can do our best to establish the information that [1] tells us is necessary for estimating any CS score. In particular, we need a good estimate of the relevant counterfactual term, which in turn requires a specification of the relevant cause-contrast and background conditions. Sometimes, as noted in section 7.3, estimating regression equations may be indirectly useful for this purpose. Meanwhile, if we are interested further in degree of explanation then, as formulated by [3] for instance, we need in addition to be explicit about the target explanandum too.

NOTES

1. Notable pioneers in the field include: Good (1961), Holland (1986), Miller (1987), Sober (1988), Martin (1989), Sober, Wright, and Levine (1992), Strevens (2000), Pearl (2000), Spirtes, Glymour, and Scheines (2000), and Hitchcock and Woodward (2003). See also Northcott (2005a, 2005b, 2006, 2008a, 2008b).

2. In causal graph terms, there are arrows into Y from both X and W.

3. For ease of exposition, as well as using y_A, x_C etc., to denote particular values of a variable, throughout I will also use them to denote particular events that instantiate those values.

4. Often, as with temperature or price level, the absence of a cause may make little sense. Rather, in such cases we are interested in the impact of a cause relative to some specific alternative. Thus in its right-hand term, [1] cites the general formulation x_C rather than absence of X or some such.

5. Strictly speaking, in fact the background conditions *do* vary across the formula because as well as impacting Y, in general a change from x_C to x_A will also impact W too. But for our purposes we may ignore that wrinkle, so long as any change in W is only a consequence of the change in X. The point is that conditioning on W eliminates spurious correlations.

6. If the relevant counterfactuals are vague or indeterminate, then so too will be the corresponding CS. Generally, I do not endorse any particular semantics for counterfactuals here, as the salient locus of philosophical dispute lies elsewhere. See Reiss, Chapter 8, for further discussion of counterfactuals.

7. Much recent philosophical and psychological work has focused on the related issues of why we tend to pick out one or other counterfactual dependency among several as marking "the" cause (Hitchcock and Knobe 2009), or more broadly on why some dependencies tend to be judged "causal" more easily than are others (Woodward 2006).

8. I take the probabilities here to be objective single-case chances (and the relevant expected values to be derived from the distributions of such chances). See note 28 below for further discussion.

9. I express no opinion on the further metaphysical issue of whether that uncertainty in turn results merely from the coarse-grainedness of such specifications, or in addition from the world itself ultimately being indeterministic all the way down.

10. QCA is not the only possible qualitative approach, however. The alternatives need not be committed to the same deterministic framing, and accordingly may furnish nontrivial causal strengths. I have in mind detailed narrative or historical investigations of single cases, including process tracing. See also the mention of fuzzy sets below.

11. Tellingly, the only quantitative examples considered in their paper feature critical thresholds, so that an effect only ever occurs all-or-nothing, that is, without any possibility of quantitative nuance.

12. Because my focus is on conceptual rather than inferential issues, I pass over here consideration of the error term or of how well b might have been estimated. (I also do not consider here the important question of how X and Y might best be defined and measured in the first place.) Instead, the issue will be: Assuming b has been estimated correctly, would it then give the value of X's causal strength?

13. I am glossing over various technical estimation issues here. Several different formulations of [2] are possible, although all share the same basic difference-making idea (Morgan and Winship 2007, 42–50).

14. An analogous problem afflicts the use of analysis of variance here (Lewontin 1974, Northcott 2008b).

15. In principle, stratification techniques could yield a separate regression coefficient for each pair of X values. But in practice, this is rarely done—or even feasible if, for instance, X is continuous. Moreover, in general there will be many different data points for any given X value, rendering even the fine-grained CS an average over many cases.

16. A separate issue concerns the appropriate counterfactual term in each CS calculation. For instance, if $x_C = 1$, should we assess the value of Y using the actual data point for X = 1, or the value of Y calculated from the underlying function, i.e., now ignoring the error term component to the actual value of Y? I do not address that choice here, but the latter option would mean that a regression coefficient might after all capture a univocal CS, as per the next paragraph in the text.

17. Although even this rosy scenario requires in addition that the X-variable is such that one unit of it makes sense. For example, if X represents discrete political parties or policy options, then a one-unit change in X will have no meaning.

18. One disanalogy between the two traditions is that the distinction between individual- and population-level causal strengths is not important in the qualitative case. As noted, the goal in the latter is to outline a causal structure that applies only to (every member of) a particular prespecified small-N population.

19. Notice, therefore, that the presence of nonadditive interaction in no way renders causal strengths somehow incalculable or ill defined. Rather, it simply emphasizes that the same cause-effect pair can have a different CS for every change in W.

20. Neither is it feasible to define each individual cause's credit minimally, allocating the rest of the credit to a joint interactive effect. (In the example in the text, for instance, that would imply giving race and education one unit of credit each for the college-educated white's income, and a joint interactive effect the credit for the remaining three units [above the baseline outcome of two].) There is no space here for a full discussion of why not but, briefly, it turns out that the amount allocated to interactive effects would then depend unacceptably on the arbitrary choice of which causes are foregrounded for our attention

(Northcott 2011b). Further, in effect the approach commits itself to the untenable position that each individual cause has a unique context-independent CS.

21. Note though a further implication of [1], which is that merely being necessary is *not* sufficient for full CS, contrary not just to QCA but also to several suggestions in the philosophy of history literature (Northcott 2008a). For instance, a cause might raise an effect's probability from 0 to 0.1, thereby making it necessary, but nevertheless of much less importance than a second cause that although unnecessary raises the effect's probability from 0.1 to 0.9.

22. Braham and van Hees (2009) endorse asymmetric causal strengths in some voting games analogous to the Waterloo example. But I see their reasoning as involving unwarranted appeal to various type considerations.

23. Explanatory strength, or near-synonyms such as explanatory power, has also been used to refer to many other things, such as an explanation's range, robustness, or degree of integration with wider theory. Ylikoski and Kuorikoski (2010) provide a useful taxonomy, although they discuss CS only very briefly. They do also mention the issue of explanandum-dependence but give no analysis of it.

24. In fact, bad weather at Hiroshima would likely have led to the mission being diverted to a target where the weather was better. So we must interpret bad weather here to cover, say, every other sizeable Japanese city too.

25. Neither, it turns out, can this problem be overcome simply by judicious choice of Y-variable (Northcott 2011a).

26. In general, it also proves problematic that [1] is defined in terms of y_A rather than y_A^* (Northcott 2011a).

27. Therefore I am not concerned here with explanations that are partial in the sense of specifying only one cause out of the many that determine any given event. On this latter view, full explanation would apply only when we had an accurate description of *all* an event's causes. But this seems pointlessly to insist on an unattainable perfection and in practice would render no explanation anything other than partial. For instance, that a match was struck seems fully explanatory of that match being alight, without also insisting on the details of the friction between match-head and surface, or of why I chose to strike the match, or of every necessary background condition such as oxygen in the atmosphere, the match not being wet, and so forth.

28. "pr()" here denotes probability. As noted in note 8, these probabilities are to be conceived as objective single-case chances. Such chances are, of course, philosophically controversial, and taking them to be the effect variables deviates from usual practice in the causal modeling literature. In defense: In practice, they are invoked ubiquitously in many sciences but it does not seem common that actual disputes turn on disputes about partic-ular evaluations of them. Besides, of course, other accounts of the metaphysics of proba-bility have their own difficulties too. At any rate, such chances seem to be a presupposition of many claims of CS and ES. If their value really is crucially unclear in any particular case, then so will be the associated CS or ES.

I do not endorse here any particular account of objective chance. The goal is only to explicate ES once *given* the probabilities in an explanandum and explanans, not to explicate those probabilities' underlying metaphysics. See Abrams (chapter 9 in this volume) for an account of objective chance applied to the social sciences.

29. An example may help intuition: Suppose we want to explain y_A^* = the water in a cup is liquid, rather than y_C^* = it is not liquid. Consider an obviously irrelevant explanans, say x_A = I won a game of tennis this morning, rather than x_C = I lost it. Then ES = $pr(y_A^* / x_A$ & W) + $pr(y_C^* / x_C$ & W) = 1 + 0 = 1. In other words, 1 is exactly that ES score achieved by the irrelevant explanans, and thus is the "neutral" score. (See Northcott 2011a for fuller discussion.)

30. Strictly, the composition of W is not constant here across each term, as sometimes it will incorporate the value of X and sometimes that of Z instead. But the main point goes through regardless.

31. For more on [3]'s treatment of indeterminism, see Northcott 2011a.

REFERENCES

Achinstein, P. 1983. *The Nature of Explanation.* Oxford: Oxford University Press.

Braham, M., and M. Van Hees 2009. "Degrees of Causation." *Erkenntnis* 71: 323–44.

Braumoeller, B. 2006. "Explaining Variance; Or, Stuck in a Moment We Can't Get Out Of." *Political Analysis* 14: 268–90.

Dretske, F. 1972. "Contrastive Statements." *Philosophical Review* 81 (4): 411–37.

Garfinkel, A. 1981. *Forms of Explanation.* New Haven: Yale University Press.

Goertz, G. 2006. "Assessing the Trivialness, Relevance, and Relative Importance of Necessary or Sufficient Conditions in Social Science." *Studies in Comparative International Development* 41: 88–109.

Good, I. J. 1961. "A Causal Calculus Parts I and II." *British Journal for the Philosophy of Science* 11: 305–18 and 12: 43–51.

Hitchcock, C. 1996. "The Role of Contrast in Causal and Explanatory Claims." *Synthese* 107: 395–419.

Hitchcock, C., and J. Woodward. 2003. "Explanatory Generalizations, Part II: Plumbing Explanatory Depth." *Noûs* 37 (2): 181–99.

Hitchcock, C., and J. Knobe. 2009. "Cause and Norm." *Journal of Philosophy* 106: 587–612.

Holland, P. 1986. "Statistics and Causal Inference." *Journal of the American Statistical Association* 81 (396): 945–60.

King, G., R. Keohane, and S. Verba. 1994. *Designing Social Inquiry.* Princeton, NJ: Princeton University Press.

Lewontin, R. 1974. "Analysis of Variance and Analysis of Causes." *American Journal of Human Genetics* 26: 400–11.

Mahoney, J., and G. Goertz. 2006. "A Tale of Two Cultures: Contrasting Quantitative and Qualitative Research." *Political Analysis* 14 (3): 227–49.

Mahoney, J., E. Kimball, and K. Koivu. 2009. "The Logic of Historical Explanation in the Social Sciences." *Comparative Political Studies* 42: 114–46.

Martin, R. 1989. *The Past Within Us*, Princeton, NJ: Princeton University Press.

Miller, R. 1987. *Fact and Method.* Princeton, NJ: Princeton University Press.

Moore, B. 1966. *Social Origins of Dictatorship and Democracy.* Boston: Beacon Press.

Morgan, S., and C. Winship. 2007. *Counterfactuals and Causal Inference.* New York: Cambridge University Press.

Northcott, R. 2005a. "Comparing Apples with Oranges." *Analysis* 65 (1): 12–18.

Northcott, R. 2005b. "Pearson's Wrong Turning: Against Statistical Measures of Causal Efficacy." *Philosophy of Science* 72 (5): 900–12.

Northcott, R. 2006. "Causal Efficacy and the Analysis of Variance." *Biology and Philosophy* 21 (2): 253–76.

Northcott, R. 2008a. "Weighted Explanations in History." *Philosophy of the Social Sciences* 3 (1): 76–96.

Northcott, R. 2008b. "Can ANOVA Measure Causal Strength?" *Quarterly Review of Biology* 83: 47–55.

Northcott, R. 2011a. "Partial Explanations." Unpublished manuscript.

Northcott, R. 2011b. "Causal Interaction and Symmetric Overdetermination." Unpublished manuscript.

Pearl, J. 2000. *Causality*. New York: Cambridge University Press.

Przeworski, A., and M. Wallerstein. 1988. "Structural Dependence of the State on Capital." *American Political Science Review* 82 (1): 11–29.

Ragin, C. 1987. *The Comparative Method*. Berkeley: University of California Press.

Ragin, C. 2006. "Set Relations in Social Research: Evaluating Their Consistency and Coverage." *Political Analysis* 14: 291–310.

Shipley, B. 2000. *Cause and Correlation in Biology*. Cambridge: Cambridge University Press.

Skocpol, T. 1979. *States and Social Revolutions*. Cambridge: Cambridge University Press.

Sober, E. 1988. "Apportioning Causal Responsibility." *Journal of Philosophy* 85: 303–18.

Sober, E., E. O. Wright, and A. Levine. 1992. "Causal Asymmetries." In *Reconstructing Marxism*, 129–75. London: New York: Verso.

Spirtes, P., C. Glymour, and R. Scheines. 2000. *Causation, Prediction, and Search*, 2d ed. Cambridge, MA: The MIT Press.

Strevens, M. 2000. "Do Large Probabilities Explain Better?" *Philosophy of Science* 67: 366–90.

Turner, S. 1986. *The Search for a Methodology of Social Science*. Dordrecht: Reidel.

Van Fraassen, B. 1980. *The Scientific Image*. Oxford: Oxford University Press.

Woodward, J. 2003. *Making Things Happen: A Theory of Causal Explanation*. New York: Oxford University Press.

Woodward, J. 2006. "Sensitive and Insensitive Causation." *Philosophical Review* 115: 1–50.

Ylikoski, P., and J. Kuorikoski. 2010. "Dissecting Explanatory Power." *Philosophical Studies* 148: 201–19.

CHAPTER 8

....

COUNTERFACTUALS

....

JULIAN REISS

8.1. Introduction: Varieties of Counterfactuals in the Social Sciences

Counterfactuals are conditional or "if-then" statements that describe what *would* follow if something *were* the case. Using A for its antecedent, C for its consequent, and > for the counterfactual conditional, a counterfactual statement has the general form "A > C" or "Had A been, C would have been."

Statements of that form are used in various functions throughout the social sciences. Consider the following quotations:

> The judgment that, if a single historical fact is conceived of as absent from or modified in a complex of historical conditions, it *would* condition a course of historical events in a way which would be different in certain *historically important* respects, seems to be of considerable value for the determination of the "historical significance" of those facts. (Weber 1949 [1905], 166; emphasis original)
>
> The counterfactual approach to causal analysis for this problem focuses on the collection of potential responses $Y := (Y_i(u): i \in T, u \in U)$, where $Y_i(u)$ is intended to denote "the response that would be observed if treatment i were assigned to unit u." (Dawid 2000, 409)
>
> In the field of evaluation, Mohr (1995) points out that the use of the counterfactual is essential in impact evaluation, as it provides the alternative against which the program's impact can be measured. In its broadest sense, the counterfactual is an estimate (either quantitatively or qualitatively) of the circumstances that would have prevailed had a policy or program not been introduced. (Cummings 2006)
>
> But what if we envision, as we have done, a world without medicine? There would be no primary care, nor would there be surgery, nor other specialties, nor pharmaceuticals. The medical model as well would disappear. At first glance, the effect would seem to be devastating. Surely more people would die and die before their time. Our thought experiment reveals a different picture. (Markle and McCrea 2008, 129–30)

One implication of this analysis is that the value of the NAIRU concept depends on the monetary regime. If we lived in a world where inflation was close to white noise, rather than highly persistent, then adaptive expectations would be a bad approximation to optimal behavior. (Ball and Mankiw 2002, 115–136)

In the first three quotations, the counterfactuals are intimately linked with causality. The first is an example of a long tradition of establishing actual causation by means of the so-called but-for test, which is prominent in history and the law. According to this tradition the legal scholar can test whether some action was a cause of harm by asking whether the harm occurred but for the action or "would the harm have occurred if the action hadn't?". Similarly, a historian can determine if a decision of a historical actor was a cause of an outcome of interest by asking "did the outcome occur but for the decision?".

The second quotation is a description of the potential-outcomes framework in statistics. Its core quantity is the so-called individual causal effect (ICE), defined as:

$$\mathrm{ICE}(u) = Y_t(u) - Y_c(u),$$

which is the difference between the outcome that would have obtained had the unit been treated (i.e., in the treatment group t) and the outcome that would have obtained had the unit not been treated (i.e., in the control group c). The approach originated in statistics (e.g., Rubin 1974, 1977; Holland 1986) but is now widely applied throughout the social sciences (Morgan and Winship 2007; Morton and Williams 2010; Heckman 2005).

The third case is closely related. Here counterfactual worlds are constructed in order to evaluate the impact of policies. Questions are asked such as "What would the outcome be if our policy had been implemented?" or "What if it had not been implemented?" (For a discussion, see Reiss and Cartwright 2004; Cartwright 2007.)

The fourth quotation stems from a book written by two medical sociologists who imagine a world without medicine. Such counterfactual speculations are done for a variety of cognitive purposes—that is, not only to estimate causal effects—and can be found in many disciplines inside and outside of science. In world history the genre of "virtual history" has become popular in recent years (Ferguson 1997; Tetlock and Belkin 1996; Tetlock et al. 2006; Hawthorn 1991). The related genre of "alternate history" is a popular branch of fiction (see, for instance, Hellekson 2001).

Finally, the fifth quote contains in fact two counterfactuals. The explicit counterfactual ("if inflation was white noise, adaptive expectations would not be a good approximation to optimal behavior") concerns the justification of an assumption of an economic model. Such model-based counterfactual reasoning is ubiquitous in branches of the social sciences that are heavily mathematized such as theoretical economics and political science. The implicit counterfactual is part of the concept of a NAIRU or non-accelerating inflation rate of unemployment. This is the rate of unemployment that *would* obtain *were* inflation non-accelerating. Counterfactually defined concepts are frequent in economics.

In this chapter I will only be concerned with counterfactuals insofar as they relate to causal inference about singular events; that is, with the first type and type three to the extent that causal inference is the purpose of the counterfactual speculation. As mentioned above, this type of counterfactual is specifically relevant to causal analysis in the historical sciences and in the law.

8.2. STARTING POINTS

Counterfactual speculation has not always had a good press. In the words of Marxist historian Edward Carr, it is a mere parlor game, and he recommends: "Let us get rid of this red herring once and for all" (Carr 1961: 91f.; but see also Fischer 1970; Thompson 1978). To some extent, this critical attitude has to be understood as being a product of positivism. If, as positivists held, only that which is observable is meaningful, then counterfactuals should have no place in science or indeed anywhere in human reasoning. But counterfactuals have stood the test of time with more success than positivism, and a world without at least some speculation about what would, could, or might have been would be utterly impoverished. Indeed, many cognitive psychologists today believe counterfactual speculation is at the heart of learning about the world (Gopnik 2009; Sloman 2005).

In many cases, we assert counterfactuals with as much confidence as factual claims. Had I just dropped my coffee mug, it would have fallen to the ground. If I hadn't written this chapter, you would not read it now. In other cases, it is similarly clear that a counterfactual is *not* assertable: "Had I rolled a die, it would have landed on 6 (or on any other specific number)." Or suppose that Jones is an average golf player. On this occasion he slices the ball but, as it happens, it hits a tree, which deflects the ball straight into the hole. In this case, we would not be justified in asserting that had Jones not sliced the ball, he would still have made a hole-in-one. But to assert the opposite would be wrong too. We just don't know.

Arguably, many historical counterfactuals are more of the latter type than of the former. Had the 2008 financial crisis occurred if the US government had not allowed Lehman Brothers to fail? Would European values be as dominant in the world as they are had Themistocles lost the battle at Salamis in 480 BC? Counterfactuals such as these are thorny.

A presupposition I make in this chapter is that counterfactual speculation is not idle, at least not always. That is, at least sometimes, the relevant counterfactuals are of the former, evaluable, and not of the latter, inscrutable, type. In other cases we may learn something useful while trying to establish a specific counterfactual even if it turns out that we cannot know its truth value with a reasonable degree of confidence.

As mentioned in the introduction, this chapter focuses on counterfactuals that are closely related to claims about actual causation. Some philosophers, most notably David Lewis, have maintained that counterfactual dependence is all there is to actual causation, and that actual causation, in turn, just *is* causation.

I deny both of these ideas. That there is more to actual causation than counterfactual dependence is evident when one considers cases of so-called redundant causation where two or more causes compete in their bringing about an effect. To give an example, suppose that two campers in different parts of the woods leave their campfires unattended. A forest fire results, but with or without either campfire (though not without both). As regards the law, both campers' actions are equally causes of the fire, even though the fire counterfactually depends on neither.

Moreover, actual causation does not exhaust the kinds of causal relations that exist and that social scientists are interested in. Factors can be causally relevant to an outcome or a type of outcome without being the actual cause of it. In particular, social scientists are often interested in generative causal mechanisms, which often do not stand in relations of actual causation to their effects (see, for instance, Goldthorpe 2001; for a critical discussion, see Reiss 2007).

Nevertheless, claims about actual causation are important in the social sciences and the counterfactual approach to actual causation is a significant one, even if it is not universally valid. Therefore, rather than dismissing any attempt at developing a counterfactual account of actual causation upfront, I will here take it seriously and address some more specific questions such as:

- How precisely do counterfactuals and causation relate?
- How can we use knowledge about counterfactual dependencies for causal inference?
- How do we support claims about counterfactual dependence with evidence?

In what follows I will first introduce a philosopher's answer to the first question and examine whether that account doubles up as an answer to the second. After pointing out severe difficulties with both, I will move on to a group of social scientists who have developed an account to address the second and third issues. It will also turn out to be flawed. I will then introduce and discuss a third approach regarding the relationship between counterfactuals and causation, argue that it is the most convincing but point out that eventually it shows that this way of thinking about the relationship between counterfactuals and causation implies that the second and third are hard nuts to crack indeed.

8.3. THE PHILOSOPHERS' APPROACH

A brief quotation from David Hume's *Enquiry Concerning Human Understanding* nicely summarizes two ideas concerning causation that have dominated the philosophical debate in the twentieth century (Hume 1777 [1902], section 7; emphasis original):

we may define a cause to be an object followed by another, and were all the objects,
similar to the first, are followed by objects similar to the second. Or, in other words,
where, if the first object had not been, the second never had existed.

These two definitions of cause, though equivalent to Hume, refer to the regularity
and the counterfactual accounts, respectively. The regularity account, dominant in
analytical philosophy through the 1960s, asserts that causation is a form of constant
conjunction: For a factor to cause another means to be universally associated with
it, among other things.[1]

David Lewis's account of causation, which has been hugely influential after the
demise of the regularity theory, builds on Hume's second definition. Specifically, it
lays out two sufficient conditions for causation:

C causes E if:

- C, E are actual, distinct events; and
- $\neg C > \neg E$.

The first condition is to rule out certain counterexamples that arise from logical,
conceptual, and other connections that induce counterfactual dependence for noncausal reasons. Thus, the appearance of the evening star counterfactually depends
on the appearance of the morning star but the former event is not a cause of the
latter. The second condition is the but-for test for causality: We judge an event to be
the cause of another if the second would not have occurred but for the first.

To evaluate the counterfactual $\neg C > \neg E$ Lewis invokes possible-worlds semantics. He first stipulates that all possible worlds can be (weakly) ordered in terms of
distance to the actual world. For him, one world is closer to the actual world than
another if the first is more similar overall to the actual world than the second. Lewis
therefore assumes that different aspects of similarity trade off against each other:
When Jill is more similar than Beth to Mary in terms of height and Beth is more
similar than Jill in terms of weight, there is a sense in which Jill is more similar to
Mary than Beth overall (for instance, because height counts more for overall similarity than weight).

Second, Lewis defines the counterfactual $\neg C > \neg E$ to be non-vacuously[2] true if
and only if some $\neg C$-world in which $\neg E$ holds is closer to the actual world than any
$\neg C$-world in which E holds. In other words, in order to evaluate whether an actual
event C causes another, distinct event E, we have to ask whether there is any possible
world in which E obtains even though C does not that is more similar to the actual
world than the most similar world in which neither C nor E obtain; if such a world
exists, C does not cause E but if it does not exist, C causes E.

In response to counterexamples (e.g., Fine 1975) Lewis later revised his theory,
rendering it more precise thereby. In particular, he proposed the following system
of weights or priorities for judging similarity (Lewis 1986, 47):

1. It is of the first importance to avoid big, widespread, diverse violations of law.
2. It is of the second importance to maximize the spatio-temporal region
   throughout which perfect match of particular fact prevails.

3. It is of the third importance to avoid even small, localized, simple violations of law.

4. It is of little or no importance to secure approximate similarity of particular fact, even in matters that concern us greatly.

There remain some counterexamples but we can ignore these here.[3] Assume therefore for the sake of the argument that Lewis's theory perfectly tracks our ordinary concept of counterfactual dependence. My question here is whether we can employ his ideas about counterfactual dependence for causal inference in the social sciences.

From the point of view of the social scientist, the problems with Lewis's account are twofold. There is, first, a semantic problem. In Lewis's semantics a putative cause is removed from world history by inserting a miracle—a violation of a natural law—just before the cause occurs. The departure from actuality is minimal in *one* sense: A minimal number of natural laws is to be violated (relative to actuality) in order to realize the counterfactual antecedent. But it is not minimal in a different sense: It contradicts a law claim we hold to be true of the world. Many social scientists prefer to evaluate counterfactuals in a way that does not contradict firm beliefs they hold about the world. Consider the following criticism of the so-called early-warning counterfactual concerning the Cuba missile crisis made by political scientists Richard Ned Lebow and Janice Gross Stein. The early-warning counterfactual asserts that if only Kennedy had issued a timely warning in the spring of 1962, Khrushchev would not have sent missiles to Cuba.[4] Lebow and Stein argue (Lebow and Stein 1996, 129):

> In April, before the conventionals buildup began, Kennedy had no reason to suspect a missile deployment, and months away from an election campaign, had no strong political incentive to issue a warning. To sustain the early-warning counterfactual, other counterfactuals would have to be introduced to provide foreign or domestic motives for warnings in April.

Under a Lewisian reading of counterfactuals, such a criticism would be beside the point. In the deterministic world Lewis conceives *any* counterfactual antecedent has to be brought about by miracle, by violation of natural law. Fewer, more localized violations of law constitute a smaller departure from actuality to be sure but in principle there are no differences among the laws. By contrast, many social scientists make such distinctions. Certain events seem more haphazard than others and can therefore more confidently be removed from the course of history. The assassination of Archduke Franz Ferdinand is often considered such a haphazard event (Lebow 2010, 44):

> I use realistic here in a more subjective and psychological sense of not violating our understanding of what was technologically, culturally, temporally, or otherwise possible. In chapter 3, I imagine a world in which Archduke Franz Ferdinand and his wife, Countess Sophie, returned alive from their visit to Sarajevo. This counterfactual is eminently plausible because their assassination was such a near thing, and never would have happened if the archduke and those responsible for his security had acted sensibly either before the first, unsuccessful attempt on his life or in its immediate aftermath.

That Kennedy did not issue an early warning is less of an accident of history. Many things would have to have been different for Kennedy to have issued an early warning: He would have to have had better intelligence, which would have required institutional differences. Or he would have to have stood in the need of a national political success, which also would have required a different institutional setting.[5]

Not all Lewisian counterfactuals are therefore regarded as admissible by social scientists. As we will see, there is a further difference that requires a more radical departure from Lewis's semantics.

The second problem is epistemic. Lewis parted with the Humean tradition in important ways. Hume sought to reduce the concept of cause to constant conjunction because, being an empiricist, he thought that causation is suspicious qua not being observable. We can observe one billiard ball moving towards another and, upon impact, the second ball moving, but we cannot observe the "push," the causal power of the first ball to move the second. Regularities are, however, straightforwardly observable and therefore an analysis of cause in terms of regularity makes sense from an epistemic point of view: An epistemically inaccessible (because unobservable) concept has been analyzed in terms of an epistemically accessible (because observable) one.

This is not so on the Lewisian analysis. Possible worlds, laws, and miracles are certainly no more and quite possibly much less epistemically accessible than the concept of cause we are analyzing. But then trying to use the account for causal inference would be futile.

This is easy to see. In Lewis's account the notion of natural law plays a crucial role. But laws—in the sense of strict regularities—are few and far between in the social world. Few events, even those we believe to have explained causally, will fall under a natural law. At any rate, such laws, to the extent that they exist, are not known by social scientists and can therefore not be used for causal inference via counterfactuals.

8.4. The Social Scientists' Approach

Social scientists working in the counterfactual tradition tend not to develop semantics for counterfactuals as such but rather a list of desiderata counterfactuals should realize in order to be regarded as admissible or "good." The following is a typical list.

8.4.1. Specificity

In Lewis's examples and those of his followers, there is usually a reasonably unambiguous way to remove the putative cause-event from the course of history.[6] Billy's not throwing rocks at a bottle (that would have shattered it) means that Billy is standing still rather than throwing a hand grenade (the example is due to Lewis

2000). The dog's not biting off the assassin's right forefinger (who subsequently has to use his left forefinger to detonate the bomb) means that the dog is doing nothing to the assassin rather than biting in his throat and thereby killing him (the example is due to McDermott 1995). Usually, it is therefore unnecessary to say more about the counterfactual antecedent apart from it being the proposition that some actual event did not happen.[7] Social scientists have to provide considerably more detail. According to Lebow and Stein the antecedent of the Cuba crisis counterfactual "Had the United States attacked the missile bases, the Soviet Union would have responded to an attack on Cuba with military action of its own" is too unspecific to entail an unambiguous counterfactual consequent: The Soviet response would presumably have depended on whether the attack had been a surgical air strike or an invasion that would have toppled the Castro government (Lebow and Stein 1996, 139). On the other hand, the antecedent should not be overdescribed because outcomes are usually not dependent on other events in all their historical detail. Thus, while the Soviet response depends on whether the US attack would have been an air strike or an invasion, it does not depend on the exact timing of the attack, on precisely how many planes or ships would have been involved, and on who is commanding them.[8]

8.4.2. Cotenability

Intuitively, the cotenability desideratum says whatever else we assume in order to make the counterfactual true should not be undermined by the counterfactual antecedent.[9] That is, it should not be the case that the researcher assumes some statement B to be true in order to make the judgment regarding C but if the counterfactual antecedent A were true, B would be false. To give a classical philosopher's example—because it nicely exhibits the difference between the philosophers' and the social scientists' approach—consider the following (Lewis 1986, 33):

> Jim and Jack quarreled yesterday, and Jack is still hopping mad. We conclude that if Jim asked Jack for help today, Jack would not help him.

In this case, A is "Jim asks Jack for help today," B is "Jim and Jack quarrelled yesterday," C is "Jack does not help Jim." In order to derive the consequent from the antecedent, use of the additional clause B is made. The next two sentences show that A and B are not cotenable (Lewis 1986, 33):

> But wait: Jim is a prideful fellow. He never would ask for help after such a quarrel; [. . .]

Thus, if it were the case that Jim asked Jack for help today, it would have to have been that Jim and Jack did not quarrel. The passage continues (Lewis 1986, 33):

> In that case Jack would be his usual generous self. So if Jim asked Jack for help today, Jack would help him after all.

If it is known that Jim is a prideful fellow, A and B are not cotenable: A counterfactually entails the negation of B. Therefore, B cannot be used in deriving the consequent "Jack does not help Jim."

Jon Elster criticizes Robert Fogel's work on the American railroads (Fogel 1964) on these grounds (Elster 1978). In Fogel's counterfactual the antecedent *A* is "America has no railroad," the auxiliary *B* is "the combustion engine is invented earlier," and the consequent *C*, "the US social product is about the same as the actual." Elster effectively argues that *A* and *B* are not cotenable because under any theory of technological innovation, if there had been no railroad, there would have been no combustion engine either. The theory of technological innovation thus plays the same role as Jim's character trait "being a prideful fellow": Given this principle, *A* counterfactually entails the negation of *B*.

Lewis, by contrast, goes on to argue that the counterfactual "Had Jim asked Jack for help today, Jack would not help him" is true after all. This is because, Lewis argues, (a) counterfactuals are vague and (b) we ordinarily resolve the vagueness in such a way that counterfactual dependence is asymmetric: The future counterfactually depends on the present and past but not vice versa (ibid., 34). Accordingly, the counterfactual "If Jim had asked Jack for a favor today, there would have to have been no quarrel yesterday" is false under the "ordinary resolution of vagueness." Lewis does not require cotenability because antecedents, implemented by miracle, are cotenable with any other truth. This way Lewis avoids backtracking counterfactuals. In the present case *A* and *B* are cotenable because even if there was a quarrel yesterday Jim would have asked Jack for a favor today because in Lewis's semantics the law that says that prideful fellows do not ask for favors a day after a quarrel is broken. Hence it does *not* follow that if there had been a quarrel, Jim would not have asked Jack for a favor.

Social scientists, by contrast, aim to keep as much as possible about historical actors' situations and dispositions intact (see section 8.4.3). In order to achieve cotenability, then, counterfactuals will sometimes have to backtrack. Whether they do so would depend on the nature of the involved events and generalizations as well as the strength of the evidence in their favor. In our case the relevant events and generalizations are: "There was a quarrel between Jim and Jack yesterday," "Jim is a prideful fellow," and "prideful fellows do not ask for favors a day after a quarrel." If the quarrel had been accidental and unimportant—Jim and Jack are good friends; they both have amiable characters; nothing important for understanding their lives happened to caused the quarrel; what was responsible was an accidental splashing of Jack by a careless driver and Jack's resulting foul mood—and at the same time there is good reason to believe that Jim is a prideful fellow and that prideful fellows don't ask for favors a day after a quarrel, in order to implement the antecedent, one would have to remove the quarrel and consequently judge the counterfactual "Had Jim asked Jack for a favor today, Jack would oblige" to be true. This is a backtracking counterfactual as "Had Jim asked Jack for a favor today, there would have to have been no quarrel" would also be true.

If, by contrast, the quarrel was a major event in their lives and nonaccidental— for instance, caused by grievances both friends have accumulated over the years— then the antecedent could only be true if Jim isn't (believed to be) such a prideful fellow after all or the generalization about prideful fellows is (believed to be) unreliable. In this case, the counterfactual "If Jim had asked Jack for a favor today, Jack would not oblige (because he is still hopping mad)" would be judged to be true. If both (a) the quarrel was important and (b) belief in Jim's character and the generalization is strong, the antecedent would not be cotenable with auxiliary beliefs.

In the already mentioned paper on the Cuba crisis by Lebow and Stein one finds an example for background information that is not cotenable with a proposed antecedent. Lebow and Stein argue that the counterfactual "Had President Kennedy issued a timely warning in the spring of 1962, Khrushchev might not have sent missiles to Cuba" does not satisfy the cotenability desideratum because for Kennedy to issue a warning there would have to have been an election campaign or different intelligence. Those in turn would require further changes in the past of the antecedent event. It would have been very unlikely that these changes would or could have happened. Therefore, the only way to make the antecedent cotenable with certain background beliefs much history would have to be rewritten. But doing so is proscribed by the following desideratum.

8.4.3. Historical Consistency

This is an interesting desideratum because it sounds similar to one of Lewis's criteria (see above: "(2) maximize the spatio-temporal region throughout which perfect match of particular fact prevails") but is in fact different in crucial ways.[10] Tetlock and Belkin explain that the substance of this desideratum is that possible worlds should (Tetlock and Belkin 1996, 23):

> (a) start with the real world as it was otherwise known before asserting the counterfactual; (b) not require us to unwind the past and rewrite long stretches of history; (c) not unduly disturb what we otherwise know about the original actors and their beliefs and goals.

(a) looks like the requirement that the *closest* possible world is the relevant one, (b) looks like the prohibition of backtracking counterfactuals, and (c) looks like the requirement to avoid big, widespread violations of laws. But the interpretations of (b) and (c) are in fact quite different.

I already discussed that social science counterfactuals sometimes involve backtracking. Here is an example of how aiming to satisfy the desideratum of historical consistency can lead to a backtracking counterfactual. Yuen Foong Khong 1996 asks if World War II could have been avoided if the UK foreign policy had been more confrontational. A Lewis counterfactual would make the antecedent true by miracle: by a surgical intervention that changes nothing but the UK foreign policy. In that possible world the UK would still be led by Neville Chamberlain and his cabinet, only their policies would be different. But this would violate what we know about the UK leaders at the time and therefore the desideratum of historical consistency. We know that Chamberlain was averse to policies that would have risked war because the horrors of the World War I were still in his memory and that of the British public, because he felt that Britain was militarily ill prepared, and because he had a firm belief in himself, his diplomacy, and Hitler (Khong 1996, 100–1). A confrontational Britain with Chamberlain's cabinet in the saddle is therefore historically inconsistent. However, backtracking ever so slightly allows us to implement the antecedent after all. Because more confrontational potential prime ministers (in particular Winston Churchill, Anthony Eden, and Duff Cooper) were at the top of British politics at the time and they could have been prime ministers given the UK electoral system, a world with a UK that rejects appeasement because a different prime minister heads the government is conceivable.

Hence, there may be a trade-off between Tetlock and Belkin's desiderata (b) and (c). Unless an event is a particularly close call—such as the failed assassination of Ronald Reagan or the successful assassination of Archduke Franz Ferdinand—undoing it will either involve more than one counterfactual (say, Britain takes a more confrontational stance in 1938 *and* Chamberlain has different political convictions) or require backtracking. The main difference to the philosophers' semantics is therefore that the proscription of backtracking is not absolute. Backtracking is to be avoided but not at the cost of falsifying what we otherwise know about historical contexts and actors' motivations and beliefs.

There is another, related difference. As mentioned above, in Lewis's semantics every violation of a natural law is on par. Therefore, in order to measure the distance between possible worlds we merely have to count the number of violations. For social scientists, "the *nature* of the changes made by the experiment are [*sic*] nevertheless more important than the *number* of changes" (Lebow 2010, 55; emphasis in original). In a deterministic world, there is no difference between moving Hinckley's bullet from Reagan's lungs to his heart and changing one of Kennedy's decisions in the Cuba crisis. Both require a violation of laws. But from a historian or social scientist's point of view, there are massive differences. That Hinckley's bullet punctured Reagan's lung but not his heart was an accident, and a failure from the point of view of Hinckley's intentions. Kennedy's decisions were not accidents, or at least are not regarded as such, but rather the outcome of deliberative processes that make use of Kennedy's beliefs and motives and those of his aides. It requires a small miracle to change the trajectory of Hinckley's bullet. But it requires a far larger miracle to make Kennedy show greater resolve given he had neither domestic nor foreign reasons to do so.

Norms, not natural laws, play a role in determining the importance of changes (cf. Hitchcock and Knobe 2009). In the case of Franz Ferdinand's assassination, for example, it was only the violation of norms that enabled the attack: He had been warned of possible assassination attempts and could easily have returned to Belgrade immediately; security was unusually bad; his touring car took a wrong turn; a failed assassination attempt preceded the successful one and could have made the archduke more cautious. We make the counterfactual true by imagining that Franz Ferdinand complied with behavioral norms and norms of prudence. By contrast, in order to make the Kennedy counterfactual true, we would have to imagine Kennedy to violate norms (such as the norm that a US president should not issue a warning unless he has good reason to do so). It is therefore that the latter counterfactual requires more rewriting than the former.

8.4.4. Consistency with Well-established Theoretical Statistical Generalizations

Some social scientists think there are no accepted theories in (some of) the social sciences at all.[11] Others, most notably rational-choice theorists, structural realists,[12] and others of nomothetic bent, think that all social events fall under a theory. But whatever our take on that issue, counterfactual speculation is impossible without generalizations of one sort or another. That Reagan would have died had Hinckley's bullet taken a minimally different trajectory is only true only to the extent that humans normally die when their heart is punctured and they can't be given immediate surgery. Even particularists such as Lebow and Stein make generalizations of that kind. In their book on the cold war (Lebow and Stein 1996), for instance, they draw on a psychological theory of decision-making under stress to derive the consequent that if Kennedy had shown greater resolve, Khrushchev would still have deployed missiles.

Importantly, no matter how much we are inclined to think that theories have limited and local validity at best, they must satisfy minimal projectability requirements. Insofar as our counterfactuals are to be based on evidence, the theory has to cover at least two cases: that for which we have direct evidence and from which we are projecting and the counterfactual case we are projecting on.

To give assertability conditions analogously to Lewis's semantics one could proceed as follows (cf. Reiss 2008). Let H be a historian or social scientist with background beliefs about relevant evidence and causal generalizations B, and X a historical context such that $\neg A$. Then, relative to B, the counterfactual $\neg A > \neg C$ is assertable iff

    a. A, C actually obtained;
    b. $\neg A$ is historically consistent and specific enough to allow H to make a judgement regarding $\neg C$;
    c. $\neg A$, $\neg C$ are cotenable and consistent with well-established theoretical and statistical generalizations;
    d. H judges $\neg C$ to obtain in X.

The social science desiderata are very plausible and useful but hardly rigorous. The first desideratum does not tell us precisely how specific the counterfactual antecedent is to be described. The third uses vague terms such as "long" stretches of history and "unduly" disturb what we know, but how long is long and when do we unduly disturb what we know about history? Moreover, if I am right in saying that there is sometimes a trade-off between avoiding falsifying our historical knowledge and avoiding backtracking, how are we to trade off these desiderata? The fourth may be too weak or too strong, depending on the reading of "consistency," and it is vague and ambiguous. If by consistency logical consistency is meant, it is very weak, especially if there are few well-established generalizations. Suppose Lebow and Stein are right in denying that there are any well-established social science theories. If so, nearly every counterfactual will be true as long as it does not contradict the laws of physics or other natural sciences. On the stronger and more plausible (albeit literally incorrect) reading, the desideratum demands that the counterfactual follow deductively from the conjunction of antecedent, auxiliary assumptions and the generalizations. In this case, d) of the above assertability conditions above would be superfluous because ¬C would already be entailed by c). However, very few counterfactuals will be true if there are only few social science generalizations. Further, "well-established" is a vague and ambiguous term. Economists will regard rational-choice theory as well-established but many other social scientists think it is false. Established according to whose criteria? How much evidence do we need in order to regard it as well-established?

In order to avoid problems such as these, in the following section I will introduce a (philosophical) theory of counterfactuals that makes use of causal modeling tools. As we will see, the theory preserves the main intuitions of the social scientists' approach and it has the additional advantage of being more precise. At the same time, it makes counterfactuals true relative to a model so that many of the above-mentioned worries regarding the vagueness and ambiguity of the criteria are relegated to assessing whether any given model is one that is good or adequate. Nevertheless, the tool of causal modeling provides a neat language within which one can address these problems.

8.5. Causal Theories of Counterfactuals

Much of the philosophical tradition regards counterfactuals as being analytically more basic than causation and thus aims to provide a counterfactual analysis of causation. But there are good reasons to think that the relationship goes the other way. We judge counterfactuals on the basis of our causal background knowledge. The conviction that my headache would have gone by now if only I had taken an aspirin stems from my knowledge of the causal power of aspirins to relieve headaches (in conjunction perhaps with the more specific causal facts that I am not allergic to aspirin and that they have been effective in me before). This point is stressed by Jon Elster when he charges David Lewis's theory with circularity (Elster 1978, 218):

> My objections to Lewis's theory have been of two kinds. In the first place I have argued, quite generally and without reference to historical counterfactuals, that to explain causality by counterfactuals and counterfactuals by similarity is a circular procedure, as causal importance is an element in our intuitive notions about similarity.

According to Elster, Lewis's theory is circular because judgments of similarity rely on causal judgments (whereas it's not necessarily the case that all causal judgments rely on judgments about counterfactuals or similarity among possible worlds).

The second reason is epistemic. It is controversial whether or not causation is observable. Humeans believe that we can observe only the manifestations of causation in the resulting changes but not the causal *oomph* itself. Others think that causal relations can be observable under certain conditions, and indeed there is some evidence that small children form causal concepts before concepts even of persisting objects (Gopnik et al. 2004). Without taking a stance in this debate, let me make two uncontroversial points. First, counterfactuals are uncontroversially unobservable. Whatever facts there are in the world, there are only facts. A counterfactual refers to a possible but not actual state of affairs and is therefore by its very nature unobservable. Second, there are very reliable, and well understood, methods of causal inference. For many causal claims, we know how to test them. Counterfactuals, by contrast, first have to be translated into a different kind of claim (for instance one regarding laws, similarity among possible worlds, and, indeed, causation) and these then may or may not be testable. Lewis's similarity metric, at any rate, has no empirical counterpart.

There are now various causal accounts of counterfactuals (an early theory is Jackson 1977; more recent accounts include Pearl 2000; Reiss and Cartwright 2004; Maudlin 2007). Here I will introduce and discuss an account by Eric Hiddleston (Hiddleston 2005) because it is both rigorous and has the right semantics for social science applications.

In Hiddleston's theory, a causal model is a triplet $<G, E, A>$. G is a directed acyclic graph, which consists of a set of variables and arrows or *edges* indicating direct causal relations between some of them. The graph is *directed* in that it does not contain any undirected edges (indicating a correlation or the existence of a common cause). The graph is *acyclic* in that it does not contain any cycles such as $X \rightarrow Y \rightarrow Z \rightarrow X$. E is a set of structural equations relating the (probabilities of values) of each variable X in G to the values of its direct causes or *parents* pa(X) in G. They represent the causal principles assumed to be true of the modelled scenario. The equations have the general forms:

$$(Y_1 = y_1 \& \ldots \& Y_n = y_n) \Rightarrow X = x,$$

$$(Y_1 = y_1 \& \ldots \& Y_n = y_n) \Rightarrow p(X = x) = z,$$

for the deterministic and the indeterministic case, respectively, where the Y's are X's parents, the y's their specific values and z is the probability that X has the value x. "$\Rightarrow$" reads "causes." Thus, the entire equations read, "Y_1's having value y_1 in conjunction with . . . and Y_n's having the value y_n causes (the probability of) X to have/having the value x (to be z)".

A is an assignment of values to the variables in G which is possible given E so that no variable X has a value A(X) which the equations say has probability 0 given the values A assigns to X's parents: For any X, $p(A(X) \mid pa(A(X))) > 0$.

I will use the appeasement counterfactual as the main example throughout. I will start with an extremely simplified model, which is made more realistic as we go on. Suppose for now that there are only three variables BFP (for British foreign policy), PM (for prime minister) and Cab (for other members of the cabinet). BFP has the two values A(BFP) = {dove, hawk}, where "dove" means appeasement and "hawk" confrontation, PM has the four values A(PM) = {Chamberlain, Churchill, Cooper, Eden} and Cab has the two values A(Cab) = {dove, hawk}, where the values mean that the majority of other cabinet members prefer appeasement or a confrontational policy, respectively. The actual values are listed first. The equation describing the causal relations among these variables is simply:

PM = Chamberlain & Cab = dove => BFP = dove (BFP = hawk otherwise).

That is, in this model British foreign policy is appeasing if both the prime minister is Chamberlain and the majority of other cabinet members are also doves (and confrontational otherwise).[13] The corresponding graph is described in figure 8.1.

We now need to characterize the concepts of *direct positive influence, positive parents*, and *causal break* (Hiddleston 2005, 640–1). Suppose X is a parent of Y in a model M, X = x, Y = y, Y's other parents are Z, and these parents have the values **z**.

Direct positive influence. X = x has direct positive influence on Y = y in M iff

$$p(Y = y \mid X = x \,\&\, Z = z) > p(Y = y \mid X \neq x \,\&\, Z = z).$$

Y's positive parents in M are $\mathbf{ppa}(Y)_M$ = {X: X = x has direct positive influence on Y = y in M}.

That is, holding fixed Y's other parents, X = x has direct positive influence on Y = y if and only if X's having value x raises the probability of Y's having value y. The positive parents of a variable in a model are all those parents that have a direct positive influence. Both parents in our example are also positive parents.

Causal break. A causal break in model M_i from M is a variable Y such that $A_i(Y)$ ≠ A(Y), and for each X ∈ $\mathbf{ppa}(Y)_M$, $A_i(X) = A(X)$.

Break(M_i, M) = {Y: Y is a causal break in M_i from M}.
Intact(M_i, M) = {Y: $A_i(Y)$ = A(Y) and for each X ∈ $\mathbf{ppa}(Y)_M$, $A_i(X) = A(X)$}.

A causal break is thus simply a variable that takes a nonactual value in M_i while all of Y's positive parents have their actual values. **Break** is the set of breaks in M_i from M and **Intact** the set of variables for which M_i gives actual values both to Y and its parents. In our example, we can consider a model M_i in which Churchill is prime minister in 1938 instead of Chamberlain. In that model, PM is a causal break, **Break**(M_i, M) = {PM}, **Intact**(M_i, M) = {Cab} and BFP = hawk.

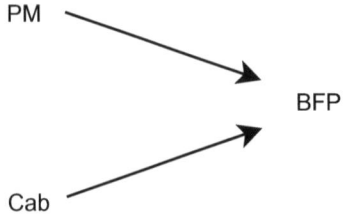

Figure 8.1 Causes of BFP

Two further definitions have to be made. The first one concerns the notion of a minimally altered model. Call a model in which some proposition ϕ is true a ϕ-model. The variable set **Break**(M_i, M) is minimal among ϕ-models if and only if there is no ϕ-model M_k such that **Break**$(M_i, M) \supset$ **Break**(M_k, M): **Break**(M_i, M) is minimal iff no other ϕ-model has a set of causal breaks that is included in the one of M_i. Similarly, **Intact**(M_i, M) is maximal among ϕ-models iff there is no ϕ-model M_k such that **Intact**$(M_i, M) \subset$ **Intact**(M_k, M). ϕ is an "atomic" proposition $X = x$. Thus:

> ϕ-*Minimal Model.* Model M_i and **Break**(M_i, M) are ϕ-minimal relative to M iff
>
> a. M_i is a ϕ-model;
> b. for **Z**, the set of variables in G that are not descendants of ϕ, **Intact**(M_i, M) $\cap$ **Z** is maximal among ϕ-models;
> c. **Break**(M_i, M) is minimal among ϕ-models.

Clauses (b) and (c) are a formalization of the idea that the counterfactual world should constitute a minimal departure from actuality as regards the noneffects of the counterfactual antecedent and that the changes introduced to make the antecedent true should be minimal: as minor and as late as possible, given the causal laws. Finally (cf. Hiddleston 2005, 643):

> TCM (Theory of Counterfactuals in a Model).
> $(\phi > \psi)$ is true in a model M and a context C iff ψ is true in every model M_i 1) that is ϕ-minimal relative to M and 2) for which **Break**(M_i, M) is relevant in C.

TCM roughly says that the counterfactual "Had ϕ been the case, ψ would have been the case" is true iff ψ follows, according to M's causal principles, from (a) ϕ itself, (b) events causally unrelated to ϕ and (c) actual causal relations ϕ does not prevent from obtaining. Context C determines what set of causal breaks is relevant to evaluate the counterfactual.

This theory of counterfactuals differs in important aspects from Lewis's and most other philosophers. Here I want to discuss two differences, both of which demonstrate that TCM is more useful for applications in the social sciences than that of the philosophers' tradition. First, counterfactual antecedents are implemented not by miracle—by breaking a law—but by *changing the value of a variable from actual to nonactual within the assumed system of causal principles.*

In the causal modeling literature that follows Lewis in this respect (e.g., Pearl 2000), a counterfactual antecedent is implemented by *changing* the laws. In particular, to evaluate whether a variable Y counterfactually depends on another variable X, all causal principles that have X as an effect are eliminated and replaced by the constant X = x. Doing so assumes that it is always possible to change causal principles one by one. In the semantics outlined here, causal principles remain the same.

As a consequence, second, counterfactuals will often backtrack. To see this, consider a slightly modified version of our example in which we now include a causal arrow from BFP to War, a binary variable describing whether or not the

Second World War happened. Let us suppose that BFP has indeed an influence on War so that:

$$(BFP = dove) \Rightarrow p(War = 1) = .75$$

$$(BFP = hawk) \Rightarrow p(War = 1) = .25.$$

Now, in order to evaluate the counterfactual "Had Britain taken a more confrontational stance in 1938, the likelihood of war would have been lower," we have to find a set of minimal causal breaks that make the antecedent true. There are four such sets: PM = {Churchill}, PM = {Eden}, PM = {Cooper}, and Cab = {hawk}. We cannot change BFP without changing either of its causes because the assumed causal principles do not allow such a change: In order for BFP to be different, either of its causes (or both) must be changed.

Therefore, the social scientists' criterion of historical consistency has a clear counterpart in this theory, but it is rendered more precise. Within the system of causal principles, a minimal change should make the antecedent, and "minimal" has a very precise meaning. Causal principles are not to be disturbed at all.

The remaining criteria can be accommodated within this theory. One can make a model more specific, for instance, by including more detail in the description of values for variables. Whether or not a given counterfactual is true is always determinate within a model. Cotenability is given by the causal principles. Moreover, depending on his or her orientation, a social scientist can demand that the causal principles follow from a theory or refuse to do so.

8.6. FOUR PROBLEMS FOR THE CAUSAL THEORY OF COUNTERFACTUALS

In this section I will discuss four problems that trouble the theory of counterfactuals that I have presented in the last section: the problem of circularity, the problem of backtracking, the problem of actual causation, and the problem of indeterminacy.

8.6.1. Circularity

Causal inference is not the only purpose of evaluating historical counterfactuals but it is an important one. The most obvious potential problem for the theory presented here is its circularity. If one needs a causal model in order to evaluate the counterfactual, doesn't one presuppose that the answer to the causal question is already known? This is certainly the case in above simplified example: BFP = hawk was *assumed* to have a direct causal influence on War = 1. It is therefore useless for causal inference.

However, the example was overly simplified. Adding slightly more structure shows that causal questions can have nontrivial answers, even if a lot of causal knowledge is presupposed. According to Khong, a confrontational British foreign policy would have influenced the occurrence of the Second World War through three separate routes (Khong 1996, 114–17). First, deterrence could have been successful, with Hitler backing down. Second, if unsuccessful, Hitler would have started a war but that would have triggered a coup d'état in turn, and the new German leaders would have sued for peace immediately. Third, Hitler would have jumped at the chance of war by invading Czechoslovakia, which would have started an earlier European war.

To model this scenario, we keep BFP for British foreign policy, distinguish two binary war variables, War_{38} for the war starting in 1938 and $War_{39\text{-}45}$ for the Second World War, and introduce two new binary variables, Det for whether or not deterrence was successful and CDE for whether or not a coup d'état was staged. The causal graph is illustrated in figure 8.2.

In this structure, it is not at all clear whether BFP makes a difference to $War_{39\text{-}45}$. This depends on the precise formulation of the causal principles, which, as mentioned above, may be indeterministic. Suppose the following principles are true:

$(BFP = hawk) \Rightarrow p(Det=1) = .5;$

$(BFP = dove) \Rightarrow p(Det = 1) = 0;$

$(Det = 1) \Rightarrow p(War_{38} = 1) = p(War_{39\text{-}45} = 1) = 0; ["Hitler backing down"]$

$(Det = 0) \& (BFP = hawk) \Rightarrow p(War_{38} = 1) = 1;$

$(Det = 0) \& (BFP=dove) \Rightarrow p(War_{38} = 1) = 0;$

$(War_{38} = 1) \Rightarrow p(CDE = 1)=.7$

$(CDE = 1) \Rightarrow p(War_{39\text{-}45} = 1) = 0; ["Coup"]$

$(CDE = 0) \& (War_{38} = 1) \Rightarrow p(War_{39\text{-}45} = 1) = .7; ["Hitler jumping at war"]$

$(Det = 0) \& (War_{38} = 0) \Rightarrow p(War_{39\text{-}45} = 1) = .7.$

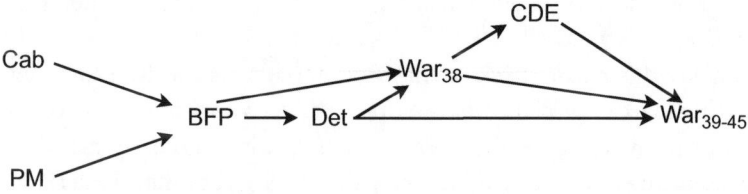

Figure 8.2 Many routes between BFP and $War_{39\text{-}45}$

Here I assume that the probability of a war starting in 1938 because of a confrontational British foreign policy but otherwise no different from World War II (i.e., $War_{38} = 1$ & $War_{39-45} = 1$) to be the same as the probability of the war as it happened (BFP = dove & $War_{39-45} = 1$) to represent the judgment that the "worst outcome [of confrontation] would have been 'no worse than the course of 1939.'" (Khong 1996, 117). For simplicity, other relations are deterministic except that confrontation may or may not have deterred Hitler, and that the coup d'état may or may not have happened given an earlier war.

In this model, with a confrontational course, the probability of war would have been .12, which is considerably lower than the .7 of appeasement. But this of course depends on the numbers. If we believe instead that an earlier war without a coup d'état would have made the Second World War *more* likely (.9), a coup d'état would have been overwhelmingly *un*likely (.1) and so was Hitler's backing down (.1), then a confrontational course would have increased the chances of war (from .7 to .729). The point is that these are not results that are directly built into the model or always obvious. The more complex the model, the more calculation one will need to reach conclusions.

8.6.2. Backtracking

I mentioned above that these semantics can force backtracking counterfactuals if causal principles of a certain kind are in place. Specifically, if the probability of a nonactual value of the variable that makes the counterfactual antecedent true, given its parents, is zero, only changing values for its parents can make the antecedent true (if anything). This may or may not lead to problems if causal inference is the purpose of evaluating the counterfactual.

The reason for Lewis and others to insist counterfactuals be nonbacktracking is that backtracking counterfactuals can lead to mistaken causal judgments. A stock philosopher's example will illustrate. Suppose you look at the barometer in your vestibule, see that its dials point to *very low*, and exclaim, "If only the hands were on *high*, there wouldn't have been a storm and I could have gone for my picnic!" In this context there is nothing wrong with this mode of counterfactual reasoning. What is required here is that the barometer provide evidence of the weather conditions, no matter for what reason. The reason that (a properly functioning) barometer is a reliable predictor of the weather conditions is that atmospheric pressure is a common cause of both the barometer reading and the weather conditions. Implicitly, the reasoning is therefore: If the dials were on high, atmospheric pressure would have been high, and therefore the weather would have been fair.

For exactly this reason backtracking counterfactuals can lead to counterexamples, if evaluating causal claims is the purpose. If, say, a child wanted to find out whether the barometer causes the storm (because she has observed that whenever the barometer said *low*, a storm would follow), it won't do to ask the counterfactual question "What would the weather conditions have been if the barometer reading had been different?" and to evaluate the counterfactual by backtracking. Counterfactual dependence is not a reliable indicator of causal connections when the counterfactual backtracks. To find out about the causation, the child would have to tinker with the barometer, change its reading in a way that breaks the causal connection with atmospheric pressure, observe whether the correlation persists, and only then make the causal judgment.

In the cases we focus on here, we are in a less fortuitous situation because we cannot tinker with the systems at hand. We resort to counterfactual speculation for precisely that reason. But if that is so, using backtracking counterfactuals as evidence for causal connections can lead to counterexamples. We can see that this is not a mere theoretical problem by adding yet another (plausible) causal pathway to our model: If Chamberlain had not been prime minister, Britain would have rearmed earlier.[14] The resulting causal graph is pictured in figure 8.3, where Arm is a binary variable indicating sufficient rearmament by 1938. In this structure, there can be counterfactual dependence of $War_{39\text{-}45}$ on BFP even though the likelihood of the former is unaffected by the latter (again, depending on the numbers of course).

The counterfactual thought experimenter who is interested in causal inference therefore seems to be in a dilemma: He either uses Lewis-style semantics but then winds up constructing historically inconsistent counterfactuals (in which, for example, Chamberlain confronted Germany after all), or he maintains historically consistent counterfactuals at the expense of incorrect causal judgments.

Either alternative is highly undesirable. Historical consistency isn't a mere academic prerequisite. In the tradition that goes back to Max Weber historical consistency is demanded in part for epistemic reasons: "Max Weber insisted that plausible counterfactuals should make as few historical changes as possible on the grounds that the more we disturb the values, goals, and contexts in which actors operate, the less predictable their behavior becomes" (Lebow 2010, 55). Thus, we seem to face the choice between an unreliable method for evaluating counterfactual dependence, which, if correct, reliably indicates causation, and a reliable method for evaluating counterfactual dependence, which is unreliable as an indicator of causation.

One way out of this dilemma consists in exploiting causal background knowledge—which is required to evaluate the counterfactual anyway. The definition TCM above mentions a context that determines what variables $\mathbf{Break}(M, M_i)$ are relevant, and so far I have not said more about what this context is and how it determines the

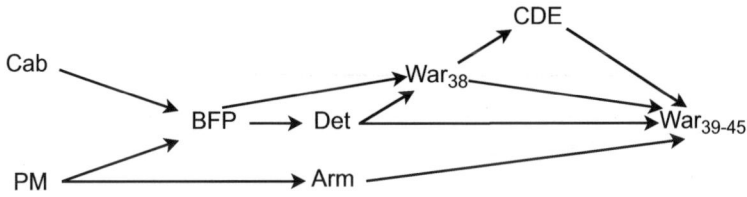

Figure 8.3 PM influences $War_{39\text{-}45}$ via a route that does not go through BFP

relevant causal breaks. Lewis mentions context dependence of counterfactuals in a passage that discusses backtracking (Lewis 1986, 34):

> (1) Counterfactuals are infected with vagueness, as everyone agrees. Different ways of (partly) resolving the vagueness are appropriate in different contexts. Remember the case of Caesar in Korea: had he been in command, would he have used the atom bomb? Or would he have used catapults? It is right to say either, though not to say both together. Each is true under a resolution of vagueness appropriate to some contexts. (2) We ordinarily resolve vagueness . . . in such a way that counterfactual dependence is asymmetric . . . Under this standard resolution, back-tracking arguments are mistaken . . . (3) Some special contexts favor a different resolution of vagueness, one under which the past depends counterfactually on the present and some back-tracking arguments are correct.

Lewis is mistaken to call the nonbacktracking resolution of vagueness ordinary or standard; it is just one resolution among others. In fact, there are good reasons to believe that ordinary language counterfactuals standardly backtrack. I gave the pressure-barometer-storm example above. Examples like this can be multiplied easily. They are particularly conspicuous in criminal investigations (which are, of course, not entirely unrelated to the historical counterfactuals we have been discussing). Here is a case that has the opposite structure of the barometer case. It is known that it was raining in the morning of the day of the crime. The detective sends forensic experts to look for tire marks near the crime scene. He reasons thusly: If there were tire marks, then if the suspect's car had been near crime scene, it would have to have stopped raining (as the car wouldn't have left marks if it hadn't stopped). Therefore, the car would have been at the crime scene in the afternoon.[15] The structure of this and the barometer case are as depicted in figure 8.4.

Here, then, are two contexts in which backtracking counterfactuals are permissible. Both are instances of evidential reasoning: We take the low (high) barometer reading as evidence for an oncoming storm (fair weather) just as we take, given the tire marks, the suspect's car being at the crime scene as evidence for the rain having stopped.

As is well known, causal reasoning differs from evidential reasoning. No one would take the evidential connection between the barometer reading and the storm or between the suspect's car being at the crime scene and the rain having stopped, given the tire marks, as indicating a causal connection. Causal analysis therefore differs from these contexts.

I propose to amend TCM as follows. In the context of causal analysis, **Break**(M, M$_i$) may only contain variables that are connected to the putative effect variable, if

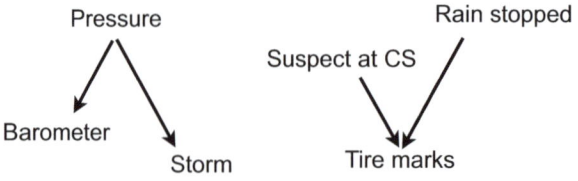

Figure 8.4 Backtracking counterfactuals

at all, only through directed paths that include the putative cause variable.[16] By a directed path I mean an ordered sequence of variables A, D_1, D_2, ..., D_n, C such that an arrow goes from A to D_1, from D_1 to D_2 and so on to C. In our example, there is a directed path from PM to War_{39-45} via BFP and Det, one via BFP, Det and War_{38} and so on, and, importantly, one via Arm. BFP is the putative cause variable and War_{39-45} the putative effect variable. Therefore, there is one path, PM → Arm → War_{39-45}, that does not include the putative cause variable. In the context of causal analysis, this is an inadmissible counterfactual.

However, there is another variable, Cab, that is connected to War_{39-45} only through directed paths that contain BFP. Khong includes this alternative way to make the antecedent true because he is not so sure about whether it is indeed the case that someone other than Chamberlain could have been prime minister; that is, he is uncertain as to whether nonactual values of the variable PM have a positive probability.[17] Khong wants to be on the safe side of historical consistency. I have argued that the existence of this additional cause is fortuitous from a methodological point of view: Without it, counterfactual dependence of the Second World War on British foreign policy would not be a good indicator of a causal dependence. It is evident, however, that nothing guarantees that such a variable will always be available.

8.6.3. Actual Cause

As mentioned in section 8.2, the counterfactual theory of causation is plagued by counterexamples that involve cases of redundant causation in which two or more causes compete in their bringing about an effect. Billy and Suzy throw rocks at a bottle. As it happens, Suzy's rock hits the bottle first, shattering it into 1,000 pieces. But there is no counterfactual dependence: Had Suzy not thrown her rock (or had it not hit the bottle first), Billy's rock would have shattered the bottle anyway. Saying that the shattering caused by Suzy's rock is a different event from the shattering that would have been caused by Billy's rock may help in this case (though I doubt it) but describing an event in more detail as a strategy does not work in general (see section 8.4.1).[18]

In Reiss 2009 I argued that social scientists, by and large, are not interested in causes that do not make a difference. Suppose that appeasement was indeed an actual cause of the Second World War: Hitler perceived the UK leaders as weak and took their weakness as reason to occupy the remainder of Czechoslovakia after annexing the Sudetenland and eventually to attack Poland. But suppose too that there was a second psychological mechanism waiting in the offing that would have caused him to order the occupation of Czechoslovakia *despite* Britain's threat ("now more than ever!"). In this hypothetical scenario, appeasement was the actual cause of war but it wasn't a cause that made a difference.

One purpose of evaluating counterfactuals is to provide insight into policy choices (Reiss and Cartwright 2004). To the extent that policy analysis is the goal of the investigation, finding factors that do not make a difference to the outcome of interest is not very useful. Thus, while the counterfactual approach can and will lead to misjudgments about *actual* causes, this problem is benign from a policy point of view. Historians and social scientists look for *causes that make a difference*, not for actual causes.

8.6.4. Indeterminacy

The fourth and final problem is the most serious of the four. In fact, as far as I can see there is no solution to it within the present framework. Social scientists and historians often use qualifiers such as "likely," "probably," "the chance that," and so on. In TCM, such uncertainty can be modeled by assigning probabilities to outcomes that lie strictly between zero and one. But if even one link on the route from antecedent to consequent is indeterministic, the probability of the consequent will be strictly between zero and one. That, in turn, makes all "would" counterfactuals false.

Consider the example discussed in section 8.6.1. Here the probability of the Second World War is .12, given BFP = hawk. However, in this scenario the counterfactual "Had Britain confronted Germany, the Second World War would have been avoided" is obviously false. By contrast, the counterfactual "Had Britain confronted Germany in 1938, the Second World War *might* have been avoided" is true. But this is not very informative, especially given the probability of war given appeasement was also below unity (that is, the counterfactual "Had Britain tried to appease Germany in 1938, the Second World War might have been avoided" is also true).

We could say that the model sustains the counterfactual "Had Britain confronted Germany in 1938, the Second World War would *probably* have been avoided." But then we would encounter a threshold problem: How small does the probability of an outcome have to be in order for an outcome being "probable not to have happened" (and vice versa for high probabilities)? A possible threshold is .5: Outcomes with a probability below .5 are probable not to have happened, above .5 they are probable to have happened. What about .5 itself? Should we say that the event is both probable to have happened *and* probable not to have happened? This is obviously awkward, but arbitrarily deciding either way is just as awkward. Similarly awkward choices have to be made for any threshold level.

Moreover, even if one could settle the threshold question, the "probably" counterfactual would still not be very informative. Suppose the counterfactual "Had Britain confronted Germany in 1938, the Second World War would *probably* have been avoided" was evaluated by TCM and is indeed true. To learn this claim is only useful to the extent that the alternative policy made the Second World War very likely. We are interested in whether or not Britain's foreign policy *made a difference* to the likelihood of war, not in the likelihood of war per se.

We are now moving close to a probabilistic theory of causation. We could for example define:

> PTM (Probabilistic Theory of Causation in a Model)
> $X = x$ rather than $X = x'$ causes $Y = y$ iff $P(Y = y \mid X = x) > P(Y = y \mid X = x')$ in an $(X = x)$-minimal model.

It is beyond the scope of this chapter to discuss the probabilistic theory. Suffice it to say that variables that *lower* the probability of an outcome can be its causes. This can happen whenever an outcome occurs *despite* the existence of a preventer. Suppose that Britain did indeed confront Germany in 1938. Hitler could not be deterred and the war breaks out early. A coup d'état is staged but it fails. The Second World War happens almost as it did except for an earlier beginning. In this scenario confrontation lowers the probability of War$_{39-45}$ (using the figure from section 8.6.1) but it is among the causes of the war.

8.7. IMPLICATIONS: COUNTERFACTUALS AND PURPOSE

Whether or not counterfactual speculation is a worthwhile activity depends on the purpose and the specific facts of the case being speculated about. This chapter has concentrated on one salient purpose, causal inference. I have argued that there are four major problems in the way of using the counterfactual account for causal inference. Of the four, I argued that the fourth—the problem of indeterminacy—is likely to be the most damaging: To the extent that some of the causal principles that connect counterfactual antecedent and consequent are genuinely indeterministic, the counterfactual will be of the "might have been" and not the "would have been" kind. I want to finish with some observations regarding these might have been counterfactuals.

Jon Elster made a very perceptive remark in his *Logic and Society* (Elster 1978, 184–5):

> One crucial aspect is that the theory T emerges as something more than just an instrument that permits us to conclude from the hypothetical antecedent to the hypothetical consequent: it also serves as a filter for the acceptance or the rejection of the antecedent itself. Thus for a successful counterfactual analysis a delicate balance must be struck: the theory must be weak enough to admit the counterfactual assumption, and also strong enough to permit a clear-cut conclusion.

Here I have focused on parts of the social science with few accepted theories such as history and international relations but a similar observation holds: The causal principles describing a situation of interest must be weak enough—that is, contain genuinely indeterministic relations so that the counterfactual antecedent can be implemented. If there was no hawk in British politics in 1938, Britain could never have confronted Germany. At the same time, the principles must be strong enough—that is, contain enough deterministic relations so that the consequent follows from the antecedent together with the principles. Using the semantics of section 8.5, we can thus make Elster's observation more precise: What is required is enough indeterministic causal relations so that the antecedent can be implemented and enough deterministic relations so that the consequent (or its negation) follows.

Evidently, this is a tall order: Why would deterministic and indeterministic causal principles be distributed in just this way? Wouldn't it seem likely that to the extent we are willing to believe that the antecedent event was contingent, we are also willing to believe that the outcome remained contingent given the antecedent event? Contrapositively, wouldn't it seem likely that to the extent we are willing to believe that a consequent had to follow given the antecedent, we also believe that the antecedent was necessary to begin with?

Despite this in my view very serious problem of the counterfactual account, counterfactual speculation nevertheless has some virtue. First, if it is conducted in accordance with strict rules such as those described in section 8.5, a lot can be learned in the process of building a causal model. The causal principles necessary to implement the antecedent and evaluate the consequent cannot be read off standard historical accounts of a given situation. Judgments concerning causal relations among events of interest and their probabilities given the causal parents must be supplied with evidence. One of the advantages of the formal apparatus introduced here is that the apparatus provides definite guidelines regarding the required information for evaluating a counterfactual. Another advantage is that once a model has been built disagreements can be made explicit and specific. One might disagree with the counterfactual "Had Britain confronted Germany in 1938, the Second World War would have been no worse and most likely would have been less detrimental than it was" because one denies that Britain could have confronted Germany, or because one denies that the three routes through which Britain's policy affected the war existed. If one denies that Britain could have confronted Germany, one would have to supply an argument to the effect that a confrontational politician such as Churchill could not have been prime minister at the time. One would have to supply an alternative model in which Churchill's preferred course of action was inevitable, and one would have to establish that this is the better model of the situation.

Second, counterfactuals are useful for purposes other than causal inference. One such purpose is the reduction of cognitive bias. Social scientists tend to regard the future as open and contingent but the past as inevitable: "Work on hindsight bias shows that as soon as observers learn the outcome of an historical process they begin to reorganize their understanding of the causal forces at work so that the outcome appears more retrospectively foreseeable than it was prospectively" (Tetlock and Parker 2006, 25). Having to build an explicit causal model for a situation will force commentators to make explicit judgments about the probabilities of events given outcomes and it is likely that even someone who will initially regard the First or Second World War as inevitable will not judge all causal principles to be deterministic. By that means, perceptions of outcomes as being inevitable will be reduced and hindsight bias decreased.

A final argument in favor of counterfactuals even in the context of establishing causation is that there are no alternatives that are unequivocally superior. The main alternative to the counterfactual account is process tracing. But process tracing is itself not without problems. One issue is conceptual: Process tracing establishes whether a factor is causally connected to an outcome but this may not at all be what we want to know. As argued above, social scientists tend to be interested in causes that actually made a difference, and a factor's being causally connected to the outcome does not entail that it made a difference to it. For instance, a factor might be causally connected to an outcome through various routes, some of which promoted the outcome, some prevented it, and knowing just about the links does not tell us whether the overall contribution was positive, negative, or nil. The second issue is epistemic. Process tracing works best at the individual level and requires a great deal of knowledge about actors' motivations, goals, and deliberations, which cannot always be had. Even if, for instance, there are records of members of staff reporting that some decision was made for such-and-such a reason, the politician in question may just have said so because that was the politically acceptable, but not necessarily actual, reason. For all its difficulties, counterfactual speculation may sometimes be the only way to make causal inferences about singular events.

ACKNOWLEDGMENTS

I would like to thank the participants of the the Philosophy and Methodology of the Social Sciences held at the University of Alabama Birmingham in April 2010 for valuable comments, and especially Harold Kincaid for putting the conference together and his comments on this paper. I would also like to thank audiences at the Philosophy of Social Science Roundtable (Paris, March 2011), at a workshop on causation held in Dijon in June 2010, and students at Erasmus University Rotterdam for their comments and suggestions. Financial support from the Spanish government (research projects FFI2008-01580 and CONSOLIDER INGENIO CSD2009-0056) is gratefully acknowledged.

NOTES

1. Much more detail needs to be added to make the account plausible even on the surface. These details do not matter, however, to the present discussion.

2. It is vacuously true iff there are no ¬C-possible worlds.

3. Most counterexamples involve statistical mechanical or other indeterministic scenarios, see Jackson 1977; Elga 2000; Schaffer 2004; Hawthorne 2005; Noordhof 2005.

4. In fact, it reads "Had President Kennedy issued a timely warning in the spring of 1962, Khrushchev *might* not have sent missiles to Cuba" (Lebow and Stein 1996, 124; emphasis added). I will discuss the difference between "would" and "might" counterfactuals below, and will not complicate the discussion unnecessarily here.

5. Elster 1978 criticizes Robert Fogel and other so-called new economic historians partly on similar grounds. Fogel 1964, for instance, evaluates the social savings the

United States made relative to a no-railway economy without asking whether such an economy could have existed in the late nineteenth century. See the more detailed discussion below.

6. Cf. Lebow 2010, 54; Tetlock and Belkin 1998, 19.

7. In some recent work on the counterfactual account (e.g., Schaffer 2005; North-cott 2008; Reiss 2011) causation is made explicitly contrastive; that is, causal relations are three or four place and of the form "C rather than C^* causes E" or "... E rather than E^*". Thus, Susan's *stealing* the bike (rather than buying it) caused her to be arrested; but Susan's stealing *the bike* (rather than the skis) did *not* cause her to be arrested. The problem of clarity reappears when contrast events are described. Perhaps had Susan bought the bike using counterfeit money or a stolen credit card, she would have been arrested anyway.

8. This problem is recognized among philosophers, who discuss it in connection with the nature of eventhood. They call an event "fragile" to the extent that small differences in time, place, or manner of occurrence make for a numerically different event and realize that events must be understood as having the appropriate degree of fragility in order to avoid counterexamples. Collins, Hall, and Paul (2004, 44) therefore rightly argue that "the theory of events thus counts as a subtheory of a complete theory of causation." There is nevertheless a difference between the philosophers' and the social scientists' treatment of this question. Whereas philosophers tend to presume that there is one correct theory of eventhood that covers all cases, social scientists merely demand that the details of cause and effect be specific enough to get the particular case right.

9. Cf. Tetlock and Belkin 1996, 21; Lebow 2010, 55.

10. Cf. Tetlock and Belkin 1996, 23; Lebow 2010, 55; Weber 1949 [1905]; Hawthorn 1991, 158.

11. Cf. Tetlock and Belkin 1996, 25–30; Lebow 2010, 56. Also cf. for instance: "there are no 'law-like' and few well-established statistical generalizations in the field of international relations" (Lebow and Stein 1996, 127; see also Lebow 2010, 56).

12. By that of course I mean the structural realists in international relations, not those in the philosophy of science.

13. The influence of the cabinet on foreign policy I take from the following passage: "My argument does not depend on one of them being prime minister in 1938. Had two or more of the Churchill-Eden-Cooper trio been members of the Chamberlain cabinet in September 1938, the chances of Britain's confronting Hitler would have greatly increased" (Khong 1996, 113–14).

14. "Perceived military weakness in 1938 definitely stayed Chamberlain's hand, but Chamberlain's handiwork—both as chancellor of the exchequer and as prime minister—was also responsible for Britain's military underpreparedness" (Khong 1996, 101).

15. The variable Tire Marks is what in the causal modeling literature is called a "collider." It is well known that conditioning on a collider creates dependencies among its parents.

16. Such a variable is akin to an instrumental variable in econometrics. See, for instance, Reiss 2008, chapter 7.

17. "For those dubious about whether any one of the trio could have been prime minister, in 1938, this respecification of just having two or more of them as cabinet ministers in 1938 might be closer than the original specification of one of them as prime minister to the counterfactual world in which a confrontational Britain challenges Germany" (Khong 1996, 114).

18. This problem is recognized in the law; see, for instance, Fumerton and Kress 2001.

REFERENCES

Ball, L., and G. Mankiw. 2002. "The NAIRU in Theory and Practice." NBER Working Paper 8940. Cambridge, MA: National Bureau of Economic Research.

Carr, E. 1986 [1961]. *What Is History?* 2d ed. Houndmills: Macmillan.

Cartwright, N. 2007. "Counterfactuals in Economics: A Commentary." In *Hunting Causes and Using Them*, 236–61. Cambridge: Cambridge University Press.

Collins, J., N. Hall, and L. Paul. 2004. *Causation and Counterfactuals*. Cambridge, MA; The MIT Press.

Cummings, R. 2006. " 'What if': The Counterfactual in Program Evaluation." *Evaluation Journal of Australasia* 6 (2): 6–15.

Dawid, P. 2000. "Causal Inference Without Counterfactuals." *Journal of the American Statistical Association* 95 (45): 407–27.

Elga, A. 2000. "Statistical Mechanics and the Asymmetry of Counterfactual Dependence." *Philosophy of Science* 68 (Supplement): 313–24.

Elster, J. 1978. *Logic and Society: Contradictions and Possible Worlds*. Chichester: John Wiley.

Ferguson, N. 1997. *Virtual History: Alternatives and Counterfactuals*. New York: Basic Books.

Fine, K. 1975. "Critical Notice: David Lewis' Counterfactuals." *Mind* 84 (1): 451–58.

Fischer, D. H. 1970. *Historians' Fallacies: Toward a Logic of Historical Thought*. New York: Harper and Row.

Fogel, R. 1964. *Railroads and American Economic Growth*. Baltimore: Johns Hopkins University Press.

Fumerton, R., and K. Kress. 2001. "Causation and the Law: Preemption, Lawful Sufficiency, and Causal Sufficiency." *Law and Contemporary Problems* 64 (4): 83–105.

Goldthorpe, J. 2001. "Causation, Statistics, and Sociology." *European Sociological Review* 17 (1): 1–20.

Gopnik, A. 2009. *The Philosophical Baby*. London: Bodley Head.

Gopnik, A., C. Glymour, D. Sobel, L. Schulz, and T. Kushnir. 2004. "A Theory of Causal Learning in Children: Causal Maps and Bayes Nets." *Psychological Review* 111 (1): 3–32.

Hawthorn, G. 1991. *Plausible Worlds: Possibility and Understanding in History and the Social Sciences*. Cambridge: Cambridge University Press.

Hawthorne, J. 2005. "Chance and Counterfactuals." *Philosophy and Phenomenological Research* 70 (2): 396–405.

Heckman, J. 2005. "The Scientific Model of Causality." *Sociological Methodology* 35 (1): 1–97.

Hellekson, K. 2001. "The Alternate History: Refiguring Historical Time." Kent, OH: Kent State University Press.

Hiddleston, E. 2005. "A Causal Theory of Counterfactuals." *Noûs* 39 (4): 632–57.

Hitchcock, C., and J. Knobe. 2009. "Cause and Norm." *Journal of Philosophy* 106 (11): 587–612.

Holland, P. 1986. "Statistics and Causal Inference." *Journal of the American Statistical Association* 81 (396): 945–60.

Hume, D. 1777 [1902]. *Enquiry Concerning Human Understanding*. L. A. Selby-Bigge, ed. Oxford: Clarendon Press.

Jackson, F. 1977. "A Causal Theory of Counterfactuals." *Australasian Journal of Philosophy* 55 (1): 3–21.

Khong, Y. F. 1996. "Confronting Hitler and Its Consequences." In *Counterfactual Thought Experiments in World Politics*, P. Tetlock and A. Belkin, eds., 95–118. Princeton, NJ: Princeton University Press.

Lebow, R. N. 2010. *Forbidden Fruit: Counterfactuals and International Relations*. Princeton, NJ: Princeton University Press.

Lebow, R. N., and J. G. Stein. 1996. "Back to the Past: Counterfactuals and the Cuban Missile Crisis." In *Counterfactual Thought Experiments in World Politics*, P. Tetlock and A. Belkin, eds., 119–48. Princeton, NJ: Princeton University Press.

Lewis, D. 1986. "Counterfactual Dependence and Time's Arrow." In *Philosophical Papers*, vol. II, 32–51. Oxford: Oxford University Press.

Lewis, D. 2000. "Causation As Influence." *Journal of Philosophy* 97 (4): 182–97.

Markle, G., and F. McCrea. 2008. *What If Medicine Disappeared?* Albany: State University of New York Press.

Maudlin, T. 2007. *The Metaphysics Within Physics*. Oxford: Oxford University Press.

McDermott, M. 1995. "Redundant Causation." *British Journal for the Philosophy of Science* 46 (4): 523–44.

Mohr, L. 1995. *Impact Analysis for Program Evaluation*. Thousand Oaks, CA: Sage.

Morgan, S., and C. Winship. 2007. *Counterfactuals and Causal Inference: Methods and Principles for Social Research*. Cambridge: Cambridge University Press.

Morton, R., and K. Williams. 2010. *Experimental Political Science and the Study of Causality*. Cambridge: Cambridge University Press.

Noordhof, P. 2005. "Morgenbesser's Coin, Counterfactuals and Independence." *Analysis* 65 (3): 261–63.

Northcott, R. 2008. "Causation and Contrast Classes." *Philosophical Studies* 139 (1): 111–23.

Pearl, J. 2000. *Causation: Models, Reasoning and Inference*. Cambridge: Cambridge University Press.

Reiss, J. 2007. "Do We Need Mechanisms in the Social Sciences?" *Philosophy of the Social Sciences* 37 (2): 163–84.

Reiss, J. 2008. *Error in Economics: Towards a More Evidence-Based Methodology*. London: Routledge.

Reiss, J. 2009. "Counterfactuals, Thought Experiments and Singular Causal Analysis in History." *Philosophy of Science* 76 (5): 712–23.

Reiss, J. 2012. "Causation Isn't Contrastive, It's Contextual." *Philosophy Compass*. Forthcoming.

Reiss, J., and N. Cartwright. 2004. "Uncertainty in Econometrics: Evaluating Policy Counterfactuals." In *Economic Policy Under Uncertainty: The Role of Truth and Accountability in Policy Advice*, P. Mooslechner, H. Schuberth, and M. Schürz, eds., 204–32. Cheltenham: Edward Elgar.

Rubin, D. 1974. "Estimating the Causal Effects of Treatments in Randomized and Nonrandomized Studies." *Journal of Educational Psychology* 66 (5): 688–701.

Rubin, D. 1977. "Assignment to Treatment Group on the Basis of a Covariate." *Journal of Educational Statistics* 2 (1): 1–26.

Schaffer, J. 2004. "Counterfactuals, Causal Independence and Conceptual Circularity." *Analysis* 64 (4): 299–309.

Schaffer, J. 2005. "Contrastive Causation." *Philosophical Review* 114 (3): 327–58.

Sloman, S. 2005. *Causal Models: How People Think About the World and Its Alternatives*. Oxford: Oxford University Press.

Tetlock, P., and A. Belkin, eds. 1996. *Counterfactual Thought Experiments in World Politics: Logical, Methodological and Psychological Perspectives*. Princeton, NJ: Princeton University Press.

Tetlock, P., and G. Parker. 2006. "Counterfactual Thought Experiments: Why We Can't Live Without Them & How We Must Learn to Live With Them." In *Unmaking the West:*

"What-If" Scenarios that Rewrite World History, P. Tetlock, R. N. Lebow, and G. Parker, eds., 14–44. Ann Arbor: University of Michigan Press.

Tetlock, P., R. N. Lebow, and G. Parker. 2006. *Unmaking the West: "What-If" Scenarios that Rewrite World History.* Ann Arbor: University of Michigan Press.

Thompson, E. 1978. "The Poverty of Theory: or an Orrery of Errors." In *The Poverty of Theory and Other Essays,* 193–398. London: Merlin.

Weber, M. 1949 [1905]. *Objective Possibility and Adequate Causation in Historical Explanation. The Methodology of the Social Sciences,* M. Weber, E. Shils, and H. Finch, eds., 164–88. New York: The Free Press.

CHAPTER 9

MECHANISTIC SOCIAL PROBABILITY: HOW INDIVIDUAL CHOICES AND VARYING CIRCUMSTANCES PRODUCE STABLE SOCIAL PATTERNS

MARSHALL ABRAMS

THIS chapter explores a philosophical hypothesis about the nature of (some) probabilities encountered in social sciences. It should be of interest to those with philosophical concerns about the foundations of probability, and to social scientists and philosophers of science who are somewhat puzzled by the nature of probability in social domains. As will become clear below, the chapter is not intended as a contribution to an empirical methodology such as a particular way of applying statistics.

9.1. INTRODUCTION

A relative of mine tells this story: While pulling on his overcoat after a day of interviews at an academic conference, a stranger walking past, noticing the name badge on his jacket, said, "We've been looking for you!" The stranger and his colleagues asked my relative to interview immediately, as they were to fly out in the morning. The relative eventually got the job and moved to a new city, remaining at the same university for over fifty years. Apparently, the subsequent course of his life depended in part on his pace and the speed with which he put on his coat in that moment. I'll give reasons that cases like this, with sensitive dependence of individual outcomes on vagaries of individual circumstances, are the rule rather than the exception. I'll also argue that even though such idiosyncratic sequences of events appear peripheral to much work in the social sciences, their commonality is in fact what allows that work to proceed as it does. More specifically, sensitive dependence of *individual* outcomes on circumstances helps produce enough stability in *social* phenomena that they can be studied at all, allowing claims about probabilities of social phenomena to succeed. In the next sections I'll provide further details about the questions this chapter is intended to address.

9.1.1. Social Probabilities

Social science research routinely makes claims about probabilities. These may be explicit claims that such and such outcome has a given probability, or may be represented by error terms or other terms, or may simply be implicit in assumptions. My interest here is in claims that one or another social outcome has (at least roughly) a certain probability. For example, consider the claim that among a group of ten- to twelve-year-olds living in a single-parent household in Seattle, there is a 25 percent probability of becoming a gang member by age 18 (cf. Hill et al. 1999). This is a claim about a relationship between two properties: living in a single-parent home during one period and being a gang member during a later period. What is that relationship? It is certainly mathematical, but it's not merely mathematical, for social scientists use such probabilities to predict, explain, or otherwise make sense of social phenomena. Further, social scientists seem to believe that this sort of probabilistic relationship can sometimes be manipulated. For example, it's often thought that policy interventions and broad economic changes have the potential to alter such probabilistic relationships between antecedent conditions and outcomes; if successful, such manipulations can affect overall patterns of outcomes in a society. If social scientists did not think that probabilities of outcomes could be affected by policy, there could be no reasonable debate, for example, about whether the drop in crime in New York City during the 1990s was due to government crime-prevention policies or the healthy US economy during that period. Whether one thinks this question has been resolved or not, few would argue that such debates are senseless.

If the probabilities mentioned by social scientists are not merely mathematical, what is their nature? This a version of a longstanding question in the philosophy of science: What is an appropriate *interpretation of probability*—in this case, for certain probabilities in social sciences? Note that claims about probability in social sciences are often closely connected to claims about frequencies of outcomes, usually in populations of people. Indeed, it's often claimed that the probabilities mentioned by social scientists just are frequencies. This is to adopt a *frequency* interpretation of probability for some contexts.[1] Although I'll give some of the (many) reasons that probabilities in social sciences should not be understood as frequencies, it's clear that an interpretation of probability for some central cases in social sciences should have a close connection to frequencies. In particular, I'll argue that social scientists frequently assume that frequencies of certain properties in populations are *stable*, which is to say that frequencies don't fluctuate wildly, but remain roughly the same over moderately short periods, and change only gradually over long periods. I think social scientists are often right to assume this, for the data often supports such assumptions. Why, though, should frequencies of outcomes for members of various social categories be stable? What explains that fact?

9.1.2. Individualism and Social Structure

Jencks et al. (1973) argue that factors they measured—family background, occupational status, educational background, and cognitive skill—played only a small role in determining income. Income inequality among randomly chosen men was just 12–15 percent greater than inequality between any of the categories studied. Jencks et al. suggest this result is not just due to the effects of unmeasured differences in ability:

> Income also depends on luck: chance acquaintances who steer you to one line of work rather than another, the range of jobs that happen to be available in a particular community when you are job hunting, the amount of overtime work in your particular plant, whether bad weather destroys your strawberry crop, whether the new superhighway has an exit near your restaurant, and a hundred other unpredictable accidents. (Jencks et al. 1973, 227)

Consider, on the other hand, the view that certain factors themselves guarantee particular outcomes for people of particular types. Garfinkel (1981) describes a view inspired by Adam Smith, according to which those with given resources and ability who make certain choices will be rewarded by the free market in a way appropriate to those factors. The market guarantees this outcome. This view assumes that there is no luck so bad, or so good, that it can prevent a person from achieving his or her appropriate end.[2] Now, Garfinkel (1981) argues against the view that such individualistic properties are typically relevant to the kinds of outcomes studied by social scientists.[3] Instead, structural factors such as the distribution of available jobs provide more appropriate explanations of social outcomes. Garfinkel nevertheless seems to suggest that given a set of structural factors, what happens to individuals sharing a set of relevant properties (e.g., educational background) is guaranteed.[4] The view is not that other factors make no difference to a person's life, but that those within a relevant social category will, one way or another, end up with a particular outcome. Again, this view assumes that there is no luck so good or so bad that an individual will not experience the outcome determined for her kind by prevailing structural conditions. It is implausible, however, that either a simple individual property or membership in a certain social category by itself guarantees an outcome. At the very least, some participants in state lotteries will find their income bracket changed, but the phenomenon is more general: As the example of my job-seeking relative and the discussion of Jencks et al. above illustrate, much of what happens in an individual life, including events with major consequences, can depend on idiosyncratic vagaries. I'll argue for this point further below.[5]

Now, it may be that for any given person in her particular, detailed circumstances, there is no other way that things could turn out than how they do. Nevertheless, in the aggregate, outcomes for people in different categories seem to occur with certain frequencies. Even if the world is fundamentally indeterministic, this indeterminism seems usually to average out to something like determinism in the gross physical and physiological processes that underlie social interactions. Why, then, do outcomes for members of different social categories often fall into certain frequencies in the aggregate? This question has no simple answer, but I will nevertheless offer what I think is a plausible answer.

9.1.3. Summary

We can summarize points of the preceding discussion as follows:

- Membership in few if any categories used in social sciences guarantees any interesting outcome.
- Much, perhaps almost all of what happens to each particular individual is plausibly determined by the details of his/her circumstances in a roughly deterministic manner.
- Much of what happens to individuals is such that minor variations in circumstances could have given rise to other outcomes.

I'll provide further support for these points below. If they are correct, how can it be that, for many categories used in social sciences, there are stable frequencies of outcomes? And what is the nature of probabilities in claims about the world in the social sciences?

The goal of this chapter is to suggest an answer to these questions for some central sorts of cases, by explaining how to apply a new interpretation of probability, far flung frequency (FFF) mechanistic probability (Abrams, forthcoming), to central cases in social sciences.[6] (In what follows I'll often abbreviate "FFF mechanistic probability" by dropping "FFF." Context will make it clear when I intend "mechanistic probability" in a more general sense.) More specifically, my goals are to:

1. Further explain and motivate the need for an interpretation of probability appropriate for some social science contexts (§<1>9.2).
2. Summarize the core ideas of mechanistic probability, which depends in part on sensitive dependence of outcomes to initial conditions. (§<1>9.3).

3. Explain how FFF mechanistic probability could apply in some social science contexts, and argue that it's plausible that it does so, in part because individual outcomes do exhibit the requisite sort of sensitive dependence (§<1>9.4).

4. Connect my proposal to some related ideas and describe areas for further research (§<1>9.5).

Note that (2) and (3) together constitute a fairly modest goal: To make plausible a hypothesis that has potential to resolve what seem to be difficult philosophical puzzles about probability and frequencies in social sciences. However, part of task (1) will involve arguing that no alternative hypothesis is even on the horizon.[7] Given the lack of alternatives, it will be significant if the hypothesis of social mechanistic probability can be made reasonably plausible.

9.2. Puzzles about Probability

9.2.1. Social Probability and Methodological Probability

I call probabilities such as those mentioned in the claim above about gang membership *social probabilities*, and distinguish them from another use of probability which I'll label *methodological probability*; this distinction will be important here, even if it's not one that social scientists routinely make explicit. Social probabilities relate social conditions to social outcomes. They are part of what social scientists seek to discover, understand, provide evidence for, and so on. Methodological probabilities, on the other hand, arise from sources other than facts about social systems. For example, when a random-number generating algorithm is used to help sample members of a population, the probability of an individual being selected reflects, in part, the probability of the algorithm generating a number of a certain kind. The latter is a methodological probability. Similarly, when a Monte Carlo simulation is used to learn about a social system, the random numbers used to determine parameters on different simulation runs reflect methodological probabilities set by the researcher.[8] Note that sampling and Monte Carlo methods are used to make inferences about the world, and conclusions which these methods help to justify may often concern social probabilities.[9]

Probabilities in error terms can reflect both methodological and social probabilities. For example, one kind of error is due to the fact that a sample might not accurately represent a population. Some of this error has to do with the fact that the random numbers used to generate the sample need not be distributed precisely according to an algorithm's underlying probability distribution (just as flipping a fair coin ten times need not produce five heads and five tails). However, the error might also reflect idiosyncrasies in the sample, as when it happens that there are correlations between relevant properties of sampled individuals, which differ from correlations between the same properties in the population. The correlation in the sample then reflects probabilities in the population, as well as those generating the random choices of individuals. Although the distinction between social and methodological probabilities raises subtle issues deserving of further discussion, I don't need to address these issues here, as long as it is clear that some claims about social phenomena concern probabilities that are purely social. For example, my earlier claim about the probability of gang membership has nothing to do with random-number generators or any other nonsocial source of probabilities, even if the evidence for it might depend partly on methodological probabilities. In the rest of the chapter my focus will be on social probabilities.

9.2.2. The Need for an Interpretation of Probability

First note that from the point of view of mathematics, a probability is any function $P()$ which satisfies these axioms concerning subsets of a set Ω:[10]

1. Probabilities range from 0 to 1: $0 \leq P(A) \leq 1$, for any subset A of Ω.
2. An outcome which is certain to occur has probability 1: $P(\Omega) = 1$.
3. The probability of either A or B occurring, where A and B are mutually exclusive, is the sum of A's and B's probabilities: $P(A \cup B) = P(A) + P(B)$ for any two subsets A and B which have no elements in common.

A function satisfying these requirements is a *probability measure*, and the number it assigns to a set is the set's *measure*.[11] (This use of "measure" carries no implication that empirical measurement is involved.)

Now consider the question "What is the probability of the portion of the page above this printed sentence?" This is a perfectly reasonable question from the point of view of mathematics: If we divide the page up into a finite number of basic subsets, proportion of area of the page satisfies the preceding axioms, and thus counts as probability in the mathematical sense. The question will no doubt sound odd to most readers, however, because the sense of probability used in science (and everyday life) typically goes beyond what mathematics requires. Exactly how it does so depends, somewhat, on context. At the very least, probability in this sense:

1. Concerns situations, events, states, and so on that might occur in the world.
2. Satisfies mathematical axioms of probability.
3. Satisfies other criteria that capture roles of probability in scientific contexts.

There is disagreement about what this last item should include. However, probability plays different roles in different contexts, so it seems implausible that a single set of criteria will be universally appropriate. At the very least, we can distinguish probabilities that in some sense capture facts about degrees of confidence and probabilities that capture facts about relationships in the world. The former are called *subjective* or *epistemic* probabilities, the latter *objective probabilities*. I'll argue that an objective interpretation of probability is needed to make sense of claims about social probabilities. In addition to satisfying probability axioms, I claim that the following somewhat loose criteria are important for many (objective) probabilities in social sciences.[12]

1. Ascertainability: It should be possible, in principle, to determine the numerical values of probabilities.
2. Objectivity: Probabilities should be constituted only by facts about states of the world; epistemic factors such as belief or justification are not involved.
3. Explanation of frequencies: That an outcome A has the probability it does should help explain why frequencies of A are what they are.
4. Distinguishability of nomic regularities: Closely related to the preceding is that an interpretation of probability should be able to make at least a rough distinction between instances of nomic regularities, that is, cases in which frequencies are what they are for some systematic reason, and instances of accidental regularities, in which frequencies just happen to turn out the way they do for no particular reason (Strevens, 2011).

The importance of ascertainability should be obvious. A simple example will clarify the general ideas behind the other three criteria.

Consider these two procedures for generating a set of heads and tails from a coin dropped on a table 1,000 times.

1. I toss an evenly weighted coin 1,000 times in the usual way; it comes up heads on 493 tosses.
2. I decide to stop strangers on the street, and get three people to give me a number between 0 and 9. This will produce a 3-digit number. I'll then drop a coin from a small height onto a table 1000 times, doing so carefully in order make the number of heads equal whatever 3-digit number resulted from my street interviews. I follow the plan: The strangers give me the numbers 4, 9, and 3, in that order, so I drop the coin 1000 times from a centimeter above the table, producing exactly 493 heads.

It's clear that the explanation of the frequency of .493 must be different in the two scenarios. The frequency of .493 fits a systematic pattern in the first instance in a way that it doesn't in the second: There is something about the coin and the standard coin-tossing strategy that explains the fact that the frequency of heads is near .5 in the first scenario. In the second scenario, it's not clear that there is any systematic explanation of the frequency of .493. At the very least, there doesn't seem to be any particular reason that the frequency is near .5. Note that in either case, what explains the frequency concerns objective factors in the world, rather than facts about my subjective or epistemic state.[13]

Here I'll briefly mention some well-known interpretations of probability. My goal is not to do justice to them, but merely to use some of their most obvious drawbacks as a way to clarify the motivation for mechanistic probability.[14] Note that my discussion in this section is largely independent of debates about Bayesian versus frequentist statistics. Though these two schools of statistical methodology do draw their initial motivation from Bayesian and frequency interpretations of probability, in practice their use is not firmly tied to either interpretation.

First consider a simple *finite frequency* interpretation of probability, according to which probabilities in science are identified with frequencies of outcomes—for example, gang membership—in an actual set[15] of occurrences—for example, the set of actual teenagers in Seattle during the 1990s. However, this interpretation implies that *improbable* combinations of outcomes cannot come to have a high frequency by chance—if they did, they would by definition not be improbable (Hájek, 1996). That is, finite frequency doesn't distinguish nomic from accidental regularities, since whatever outcomes occur, for whatever reason, are treated identically. For example, there is no difference between the two coin tossing scenarios above from the point of view of a simple finite frequency theory.

Long-run frequency interpretations define probability as frequency in large, counterfactual sets of events, or as the limit of frequencies in a counterfactual infinite sequence. However, in addition to deep problems that I will pass over (Hájek, 1996, 2009a), neither long-run frequency nor finite frequency interpretations can explain frequencies in actual events, since the sets of events whose frequencies these interpretations trade on merely contain the actual events to which probabilities are attributed. In the case of a simple finite frequency theory, a probability simply is the frequency in an actual set of events; it therefore can't explain that same frequency in that same set of events. In the case of a long-run frequency theory, a set of actual events is supposed to be a subset of the full counterfactual sequence of events that define a probability. Putting aside problems about the explanatory power of such counterfactual frequencies, a frequency in a set or sequence of events will not explain a frequency in a proper subset of those events, without additional substantive assumptions—for example, assumptions about processes which sample from the larger set/sequence. Such assumptions would be difficult to justify in the general case, and are not usually part of a long-run frequency interpretation of probability.[16]

Best System Analysis *chance* interpretations of probability (Lewis, 1980, 1994; Loewer, 2001, 2004; Hoefer, 2007) have some popularity among philosophers currently because they do a good job of addressing certain philosophical problems. These theories are too elaborate to summarize quickly. One core idea is, very roughly, that an objective chance exists whenever assuming its existence plays a simplifying role in an ideal, ultimate set of scientific theories—which are those that succeed well in summarizing all actual events in the universe, past, present, and future. What Best System theories don't do well is allow probabilities to explain frequencies, for Best System chance probabilities are defined in terms of whatever states the actual world has. We then again end up explaining frequencies in terms of themselves.[17]

Bayesian interpretations define probabilities as degrees of belief or epistemic relations. Apart from the fact that these interpretations don't satisfy *objectivity*, Bayesian probabilities can only reflect and track frequencies in the world; they don't explain them. A researcher's degree of confidence in an outcome for Seattle children will not explain that outcome, in general.

Propensities are postulated indeterministic dispositions, modeled on determin-istic dispositions.[18] According to some common philosophical theories concerning causal properties, a lump of salt sitting in a salt shaker has deterministic *disposition* to dissolve when placed in water at room temperature, even if it is never placed in water. Propensity is a proposed extension of this notion of disposition. For example, some authors claim that an evenly weighted coin has an indeterministic disposition of strength 1/2 to produce the outcome heads when tossed in the usual way. Note that since propensities are supposed to be dispositions, and dispositions are sup-posed to involve causal properties, propensities would have potential to provide causal explanations of outcomes and frequencies. However, because there's not much more to propensity theories than what I have just said, many philosophers argue that propensity theories are too vague and unmotivated to have explanatory force. There are other objections to propensity theories as well (Eagle 2004). My view is that at the very least, attempting to give propensities a legitimate role outside of fundamental physical contexts requires an incoherent conception of causation, tantamount to allowing a single token event to simultaneously cause and fail to cause an effect (see Abrams, 2007, forthcoming).

9.2.3. Why Are Social Frequencies Stable?

Social scientists often assume that although social conditions change, frequencies don't usually fluctuate wildly. Sometimes there is evidence for such stability. For example, although per capita welfare caseloads in the United States between 1970 and 2005 have fluctuated from year to year, with a precipitous drop between 1995 and 2002, a graph of caseloads from year to year appears roughly continuous (figure 9.1). There are no years in which the caseload shows a large drop or jump, and where there are large changes, they are usually followed or preceded by changes in the same direction. Even without data to prove that patterns at the level of populations don't fluctuate wildly, social scientists regularly assume such stability, even if tacitly. For example, Hill et al. (1999) found correlational patterns between characteristics or circumstances of juveniles aged ten to twelve, and prevalence of gang member-ship in the same cohort a few years later. The authors suggest possible interventions to reduce gang membership. It would make no sense, though, to consider interven-tions on a system unless data collected earlier were likely to be somewhat represen-tative of patterns at later periods of time. For that matter, it seems unlikely that most social science research on groups of individuals would have any interest at all, if we didn't think that conclusions were in most cases roughly projectable into the past and the future. Further, when there are radical changes in frequencies from one time period to another, the response thought appropriate is usually to look for an explanation of the change, whether in social conditions, the physical environment (e.g., an earthquake), or in research methodology. The default assumption of rela-tive stability is simply a precondition for much work in social sciences. It is an as-sumption, moreover, which plausibly has borne fruit; to the extent that social science research has been successful, the stability assumption is empirically justified.

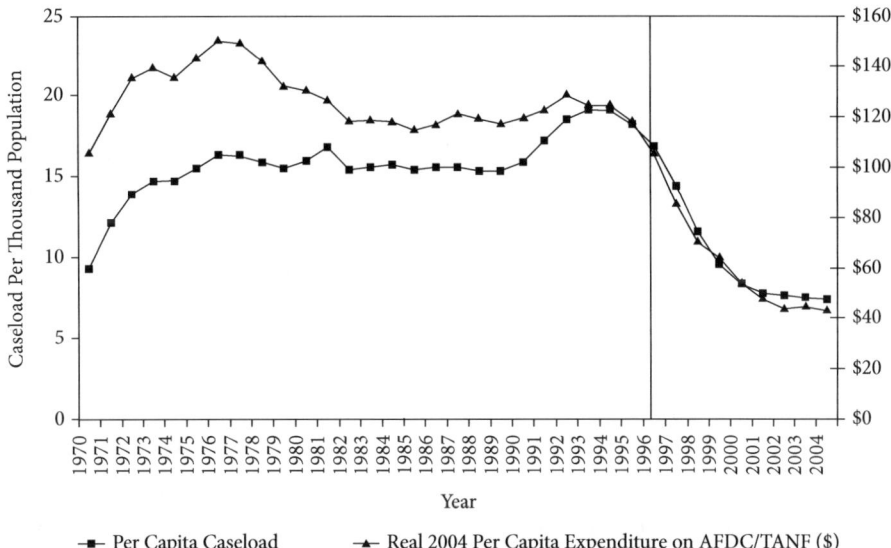

Figure 9.1 **Per capita AFDC-TANF caseload and expenditure 1970–2004.** Sources: U.S. Department of Health and Human Services, "Indicators of Welfare Dependence," *Annual Report to Congress*, Appendix A, Table TANF4, Washington, D.C.: Office of the Assistant Secretary for Planning and Evaluation, 2006; and U.S. Department of Commerce, *Statistical Abstract of the United States*, U.S. Census Bureau, Washington, DC, 2006, Table 2, Population. (From Moffitt 2008)

That frequencies are stable is such a pervasive background assumption that it may seem that no explanation of stability is needed. But patterns in populations such as the one that Hill et al. studied are the result of numerous decisions by people with different characters, in circumstances that differ both in large and small ways. Notwithstanding common intuitions, there's no obvious, good reason that this should result in stable frequencies rather than wild, chaotic fluctuations. When pushed, I think the first explanation of stability that comes to mind, for many, is something like this:

(1) Some children and other people act in one manner, others act in another. At some level of description, there are no particular patterns to what people do or don't do. As long as you aggregate a sufficient number of individuals, the average behaviors will remain stable over time, producing stable frequencies concerning gang membership.

This argument is incomplete at best. Why do the underlying behavioral causes of measured outcomes comport themselves so as to maintain stable frequencies? That there is no particular pattern does not imply that the underlying behavioral causes should manage to sort out, year after year, so as to keep frequencies of outcomes from changing radically. It would be different if there were a reason to think that there were stable patterns in the underlying behaviors producing the observable frequencies. For example, if there were objective probabilities that the underlying behaviors tended to follow for some principled reason, and the distribution was such that the effects of these behaviors would be stable, such probabilities could explain stable frequencies.[19] But the mere assumption that there are no particular patterns to the underlying behaviors doesn't justify the claim that there are probabilities governing those behaviors. "No particular pattern" is consistent with frequencies following an unsystematic chaotic pattern, or being stable, or anything in between.

This suggests another possible answer to the question of why social frequencies are often stable:

(2) Twelve-year-olds are like quantum phenomena: Each child in the same economic class is fundamentally indeterministic, and has exactly the same tendency to join a gang as any other member of the class—independent of any of his/her characteristics or any circumstances encountered. (If quantum mechanical probabilities are propensities, then the claim is that there is a determinate propensity for gang membership given being in a certain economic class.) That would be why the frequency of gang membership within each class is stable over time. On this view, once we determine the child's economic class, there is nothing else to be learned which might be relevant to gang membership.

If this were true, economic class would be the *only* factor determining whether a child joined a gang or not. There would no point in investigating other factors such as race, number of parents, availability of drugs, quality of teachers, and so on. Nor could it be relevant to investigate the effects of early childhood trauma, fetal environment, brain chemistry, or genetic influences. Individual circumstances would be irrelevant to individual outcomes as well. It could not make a difference, for example, whether an existing gang member moved in next door, or whether a child was traumatized when an inadequately maintained bridge collapsed. Thus the present view, according to which a particular social category gives rise to probabilities of outcomes all by itself, precludes any further scientific research of any kind, social or otherwise.

Consider, finally, this explanation of stable frequencies:

(3) The relationship between properties of children and later gang membership is deterministic, or effectively deterministic (i.e., fundamental indeterminism has almost no noticeable effect on outcomes). In principle, if we could learn enough about a given child, her genes, and the history of her interactions with the world, gang membership would be determined, or would at least have an irreducible probability very near 0 or 1. However, at some point in the past, initial conditions were such as to produce frequencies like those we see today, and the entire social system is such as to roughly reproduce frequencies from year to year. That is, society has a causal structure that makes it carry forward frequencies from the recent past (cf. Millikan, 2000). Stable social frequencies are thus analogous to a distribution of rock sizes over a hillside during a landslide: The distribution of rock sizes across the hill at one level is roughly the same as that at a slightly higher level a moment earlier because the interaction with gravity and the underlying shape of the hillside preserves, roughly, the ordering of rocks across the hillside. (This might not be true for balls dumped into the top of a pinball machine.)

I don't have a general theory about what kind of causal structures might have this property of carrying forward frequencies, and even if we did have such a theory for social systems, a mystery would remain: Why should the determinants of so many properties of so many social systems have this kind of special, frequency-preserving causal structure? I'll argue instead that social systems in effect repeatedly *recreate* similar frequencies (except for important special cases, section 9.5.2).

Although I will assume below that social systems are effectively deterministic, I'll argue that for the most part social frequencies are stable because social systems have a special causal structure, "bubbliness," which I'll describe below.[20] This "bubbly" causal structure helps generate frequencies in a way that's largely insensitive to variations in recent conditions. That is, rather than stable frequencies being the result of a system that reproduces frequencies from the recent past, I'll argue that many social systems have a causal structure which makes it difficult for any but a narrow range of frequencies to be produced over a wide range of initial conditions. It is this causal structure that is at the core of the notion of FFF mechanistic probability (Abrams, forthcoming), and I'll argue that FFF mechanistic probability is an appropriate interpretation of probability for many contexts in the social sciences. As some propensity interpretations are supposed to do, FFF mechanistic probability is defined in terms objective aspects of the world and helps explain stable frequencies. FFF mechanistic probability is one of three closely related objective interpretations of probability that have recently been proposed, as mentioned above, including also Streven's "microconstant probability" (Strevens, 2011) and Rosenthal's "natural range" conception of probability (Rosenthal, 2010). I call all of these interpretations "mechanistic probability" interpretations, because they depend on the same causal structure, but there is no established term for such interpretations at present.[21]

9.3. Mechanistic Probability

In this section I'll sketch the core concepts of mechanistic probability using the idea of a wheel of fortune. In the next major section I'll explain how to apply mechanistic probability in common social science contexts.

9.3.1. Why Wheels of Fortune Generate Stable Frequencies

Consider a wheel of fortune, a simplified roulette wheel in which the outcome is indicated by the wedge nearest to a fixed pointer when the wheel stops. No ball is involved. If such a wheel is repeatedly given a fairly fast spin, the frequency of an outcome in a set of such spins will usually be close to the outcome's proportion of the circumference of the wheel. This is so in general, no matter who the croupier is. Casinos depend for their livelihood on such facts. It's natural to think there is in some sense an objective probability of an outcome equal to its proportion of the circumference—even in unusual cases in which a run of good or bad "luck" produces a frequency that departs significantly from that probability. I want to explain why the wheel of fortune exhibits stable frequencies, and lay the groundwork for defining an interpretation of probability that will apply to the wheel of fortune and other systems.

The wheel of fortune is what I call a *causal map device*, an effectively deterministic device which, given an initial condition, produces an outcome. A croupier gives the wheel a spin—imparts an angular velocity to it—and Newtonian physical processes take over. The wheel then produces a particular outcome, red or black, depending on which wedge is nearest to the pointer when the wheel stops. Figures 9.2(a) and (b) will help clarify what it means to say that the wheel of fortune is a causal map device.

Note that we can divide the set of initial conditions, consisting of angular velocities possible for human croupiers, into those regions which lead to the red outcome, and those which lead to the black outcome; Figure 9.2(a) provides a schematic representation of this point. Velocities are represented on the horizontal axis, increasing as we move from left to right. The velocities are divided into regions of velocities leading to red or to black (marked by "red" and "black" above the line); lines rise from the borders between regions, or intervals. For example, the leftmost interval marked on the horizontal axis represents a set of similar velocities, from lowest to highest. These are velocities that would cause the wheel to stop with the pointer indicating the red wedge near the top of the wheel (between 11:00 and 12:00). The fact that the curved lines lead to the uppermost red wedge is intended to convey this relationship. Similarly, the endpoints of the next velocity interval to the right are starting points for curved lines that rise to the black wedge that's adjacent and the left of the red wedge just mentioned (i.e., the black wedge between 9:00 and 11:00). The idea is that initial velocities in this black region would cause the wheel to spin a little bit longer, so that the pointer will end up pointing at the next wedge after the uppermost red wedge, that is, at the black wedge next to it. This pattern continues as velocities increase along the horizontal axis. Velocities in the rightmost interval marked on the diagram cause the wheel to spin a full revolution further than do velocities in the leftmost interval, so that these greater velocities also produce a red outcome by causing the pointer to indicate the red wedge between 11:00 and 12:00. Thus the curved lines from both the leftmost and rightmost velocity intervals lead to the edges of this same wedge.

Figure 9.2(b) is a general representation of the abstract structure of a causal map device. The oval on the right represents a space of possible output effects from a causal map device; these outputs are divided into three outcomes, *A*, *B*, and *C*. (For the wheel of fortune, particular locations on the wheel when it stops count as outputs, which are divided into only two outcomes, red and black.) On the left side of the diagram, a space of initial conditions is divided up into three sets A^{-1}, B^{-1}, and C^{-1}, which are the sets of initial conditions which would cause outputs in *A*, *B*, and *C*, respectively.[22] Recall that in the case of the wheel of fortune, different velocities

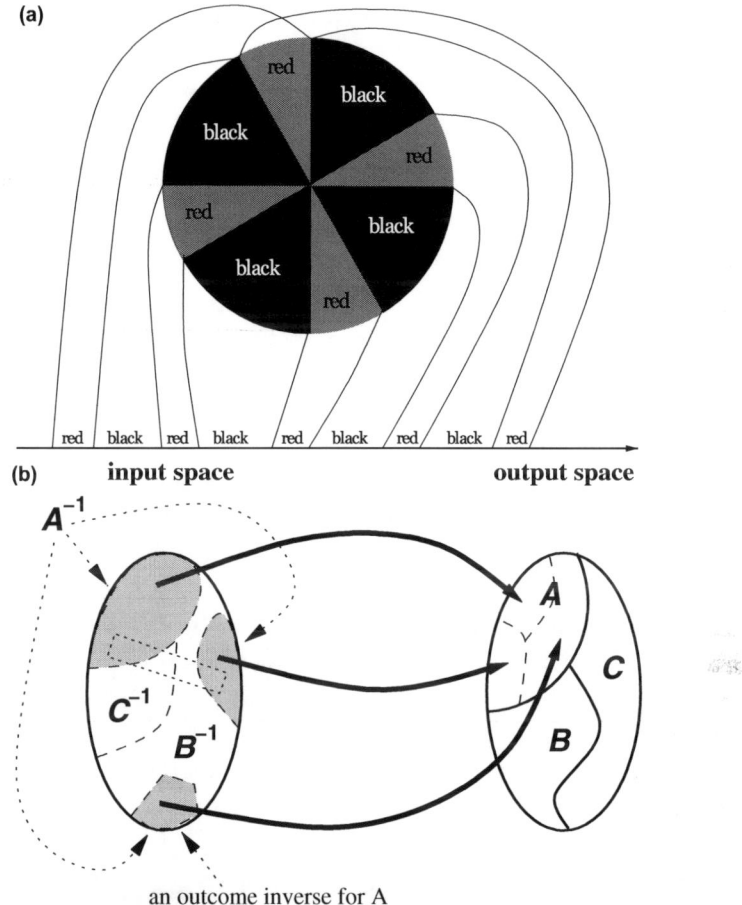

Figures 9.2 (a): Wheel of fortune: velocity-outcome mapping; (b): Causal map device: abstract structure

all produced the red outcome. Further, velocities in disjoint subsets—different intervals—caused outputs corresponding to points in distinct subsets of those outputs that counted as red outcomes; there the subsets were distinct red wedges. In the same way, figure 9.2(b) shows that initial conditions in different parts of A^{-1} (the three gray areas) produce outputs in different parts of the A outcome region. This is indicated by dark arrows leading from the three parts of A^{-1} to subsets of A divided by dashed lines.

The wheel of fortune is a "bubbly" causal map device: Its input space can be divided into many "bubbles", small regions containing initial conditions leading to all outcomes—in this case, red and black.[23] More specifically, consider any adjacent pair of intervals, one containing velocities leading only to red and one containing velocities leading only to black. The union of those two intervals counts as a bubble, because it contains initial conditions, or inputs, leading to each outcome.[24] For example, the two leftmost intervals along the horizontal axis in figure 9.2(a) constitute a bubble. Intuitively, in a normal wheel of fortune, such a bubble is small, in that the distance between its smallest and largest velocity is a small fraction of the distance from one end of the input space to the other. (This remark is only intended to be suggestive, though. I'll give a fuller characterization of bubble size shortly. At this point an informal presentation with a few slightly inaccurate remarks will make it easier to follow the more systematic description of mechanistic probability below.)

For a given croupier, we can graph the number of spins she imparts at any given velocity. Figure 9.3(a) illustrates this idea for a croupier who spins the wheel many, many times, but who tends to give the wheel faster spins more often than slower ones. The height of the curve at each point reflects the number of spins the croupier gives at the velocity represented by that point on the horizontal axis. This curve is called a density curve, since it represents the "density" of spins at each velocity. (On the other hand, the graph in figure 9.3(a) represents the croupier as generating spins at *every* velocity possible for human croupiers; this is of course unrealistic. I'll come back to this shortly.)

To summarize what's to come: Very roughly, it can be proven that if bubbles are small and if the slope of a croupier's density curve over inputs is not extremely steep in any region, the frequency of red will be close to the proportion of the input space occupied by points leading to red (Strevens, 2003; Abrams, forthcoming). The same claim holds for the black outcome. In other words—again very roughly—if the red and black intervals can be paired so that each pair (bubble) is small compared to the entire range of possible spin velocities, and if the height of the croupier's density curve is roughly the same in both parts of each bubble, then the relative frequencies of outcomes will be close to the relative sizes of red and black wedges. The relevant proofs provide at least a partial explanation of what it is about the wheel of fortune

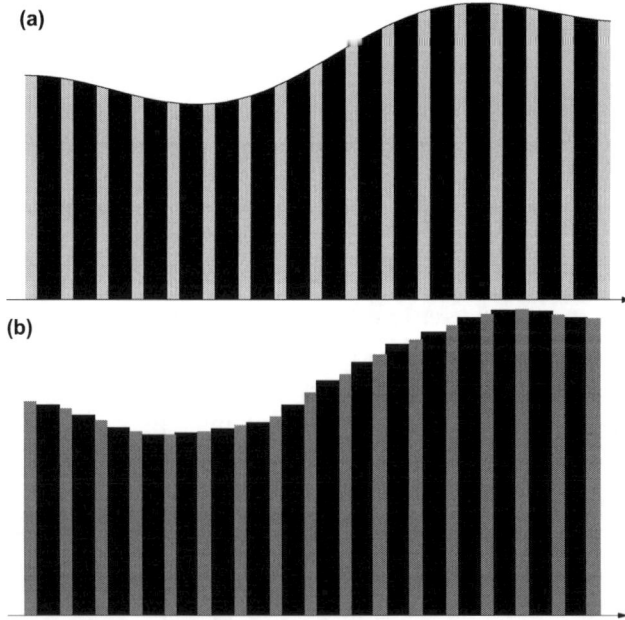

Figures 9.3 (a): Hypothetical velocity distribution for a croupier (continuous); (b): Hypothetical velocity distribution for a croupier (discontinuous)

that gives rise to the phenomenon of stable frequencies matching proportions of the input velocity space.

An understanding of the general idea of the proofs can be gotten from figure 9.3(a). Notice that since the height of the curve at a particular velocity represents the number of spins at that velocity, we can think of the area of the region under the curve and above a particular interval as representing the total number of spins in that region of velocities, with larger areas containing more spins. Roughly, we multiply the width of a region by the average height of the curve over it to get the approximate number of spins at velocities in the region. (I'll give a more careful account of this idea shortly.) Since in each pair of contiguous red and black regions, heights don't differ much, the ratio between the number of spins in the two corresponding velocity ranges is then close to the ratio between the widths of the two ranges. As this is true for each such pair—each bubble—the ratio between number of red and black outcomes will also be close to the ratio between the summed velocity intervals leading to red and the summed intervals leading to black. In this case, that ratio is close to the ratios between sizes of red and black wedges. It can be argued that this sort of pattern is a large part of what explains the stable frequencies found in many mechanical casino games.[25]

9.3.2. Mechanistic Probability: Preliminaries

Of course, no real croupier will ever spin a wheel of fortune at every point in a continuous interval of velocities. It makes more sense to replace figure 9.3(a) with a step-shaped curve, as in figure 9.3(b). Here the area of each rectangular region represents the number of spins in the velocity interval, which is represented as the lower edge of the rectangle. A more abstract version of this idea will be part of the characterization of FFF mechanistic probability, and will help illuminate the reasons that wheels of fortune—and social systems, I'll argue—exhibit stable outcomes frequencies. Let me first provide some background.

Recall that a mathematical probability measure is nothing more than a function which assigns numbers between 0 and 1 (inclusive) to sets in such a way that axioms like those given above are satisfied. This idea plays an essential role in the account of mechanistic probability, so a concrete illustration may be useful: One possible probability measure on the input space of the wheel of fortune uses the fact that velocities are represented by real numbers. Let's call the minimum and maximum velocities possible for a human being v_0 and v_1. Suppose that our probability function P assigns 1 to the set containing all of the velocities possible for a human croupier ($P([v_0, v_1]) = 1$). More generally, consider any interval containing all velocities lying between two real numbers, v_i and v_j, which lie between the minimum v_0 and maximum v_1, where v_j is larger than v_i. One way to assign a probability to an interval of velocities is to take its probability to be the ratio between the interval's length and the length of the set of humanly possible velocities. In other worlds, let the probability of any interval within the range bounded by the minimum velocity v_0 and the maximum v_1, be the difference between the interval's largest and smallest velocities, divided by the difference between the largest and smallest velocities which are humanly possible:

$$P([v_i, v_j]) = \frac{v_j - v_i}{v_1 - v_0}$$

This is the core idea of what's called a "normalized Lebesgue measure" for the wheel's input space.[26] It corresponds to the intuitively natural way that we measured "widths" of velocity intervals above.

Although normalized Lebesgue measure is in some sense a natural way of thinking about probabilities for sets of initial velocities, I intend it mainly to illustrate the application of a mathematical probability measure to an input space. Many such mathematical probability measures could be assigned to the input space of a wheel of fortune. We might, for example, give higher probabilities to regions containing large velocities, or regions that happen to lead to black outcomes. These are only some of the simplest examples. Whether any of these mathematical probability measures correspond to a probability measure in an objective sense—whether a particular mathematical function captures mathematical aspects of an objective probability function that satisfies the desiderata above—is a further question. Note, however, if a given mathematical probability measure *did* correspond to probabilities of inputs to the wheel of fortune in some objective sense, it might be appropriate to define the probability of an *outcome* as the probability of those inputs which can produce it. Thus, suppose, for example, that a normalized Lebesgue measure on the wheel of fortune's input space captured mathematical aspects of an objective probability measure concerning sets of possible initial conditions. Then there would be an objective probability of red equal to the total probability of the velocity intervals whose points could produce the red outcome.[27] In figures 9.3(a) and (b) this probability would be proportional to the summed widths of the velocity intervals with red (i.e., gray) rectangles over them.

For now, let us assume—pretend, if you like—that we are given a mathematical probability measure P on the input space of initial conditions, for a causal map device such as a wheel of fortune. This assumption will help us get clear on ideas, though in the end I'll dispense with it, and it doesn't matter at this point which function the probability measure is. It might be normalized Lebesgue measure, or it might be some other mathematical probability measure. Note that whether or not there is an objective correlate to a given mathematical input probability measure, we can nevertheless define a derived mathematical probability measure on outcomes as we did in the preceding paragraph: That is, we can define the mathematical probability of an outcome as the probability of those inputs which can lead to it. The fact that this relationship mirrors a causal relationship between inputs and outcomes will be significant below, but at this stage the point is just that it provides a way of defining a *mathematically* legitimate probability measure over outcomes. (Shortly, I'll explain how we can *choose* an appropriate input probability measure so that outcome probabilities will usually correspond to stable frequencies.)

Now, assuming a given probability measure on the input space, the microconstancy inequality theorem (see appendix to this chapter) says that for a given distribution of initial conditions, the difference between the relative frequency of outcome A and the input measure of initial conditions which lead to A is constrained by *bubble-deviations* and bubble measures. I'll explain what a bubble-deviation is in a moment, but first let me give the context in which they appear: What the theorem says, roughly, is that when bubble-deviations and bubble measures are small, outcome frequencies will usually be close to outcome probabilities which have been defined by an input measure in the way just considered. (That is, an outcome probability is the probability of inputs that could cause it.) This will mean that any input measure that can make bubble-deviations and bubble measures small for most real distributions of inputs will also make outcome frequencies close to outcome probabilities defined in terms of that input measure. I'll present these points in more detail below.

The notion of a bubble-deviation is a little bit abstract, but it can be viewed as an analogue of slope for a distribution of initial conditions. Bubble-deviation is defined in terms of an input measure of a bubble and a distribution of inputs—for example, of spins of a wheel at the possible velocities. Unlike slope, bubble-deviation doesn't depend on using a real-numbered scale. (Velocities fall on a real-numbered scale, and we can use that fact to define probability measures such as Lebesgue measure, but bubble-deviation doesn't depend on this fact.)

To understand the idea of a bubble-deviation, look at figure 9.4(a), which here represents part of a distribution over initial spin velocities for one particular croupier. More specifically, 9.4(a) displays, in schematic form, one pair of black/red bars from figure 9.3(b). The bottom edges of the boxes represent two velocity intervals, making up one bubble. The bottom edge of the right-hand rectangle then represents a set a in the input space—a set of inputs that all would lead to one outcome, red. Thus a could be, for example, the rightmost interval along the horizontal axis in figure 9.2(a). The bottom edge of the left-hand rectangle (here $\bar{a}$) would then correspond to the next interval to the left in 9.2(a).

In figure 9.4(a), width represents input measure, and the right-hand rectangle represents the croupier's total number of inputs in a. The rectangle's height represents the average number E_a of inputs in a, where this average is computed using the input measure p_a; in other words, E_a = *(number of inputs in a)/p_a*. Note this means that the average number of inputs in a, E_a, depends on a's input measure: Given a fixed number of spins in the region a, if p_a were greater, E_a would be smaller. (This is illustrated by comparison with 4(b), described below.) We can also consider a croupier's average number of inputs for the entire bubble, again defined as the number of inputs divided by the bubble's measure: E_b = *(number of inputs in bubble b)/p_b*.[28] A bubble-deviation for red over the red-black pair of velocity intervals in figure 9.4(a) is then the absolute difference between the height of the right-hand rectangle (the average number of inputs in the corresponding input region) and the average height over the entire bubble (the average number of inputs over the entire bubble) divided by the input probability of the bubble. Specifically, the bubble-deviation for red in a bubble b is defined, relative to an input probability measure, as the absolute

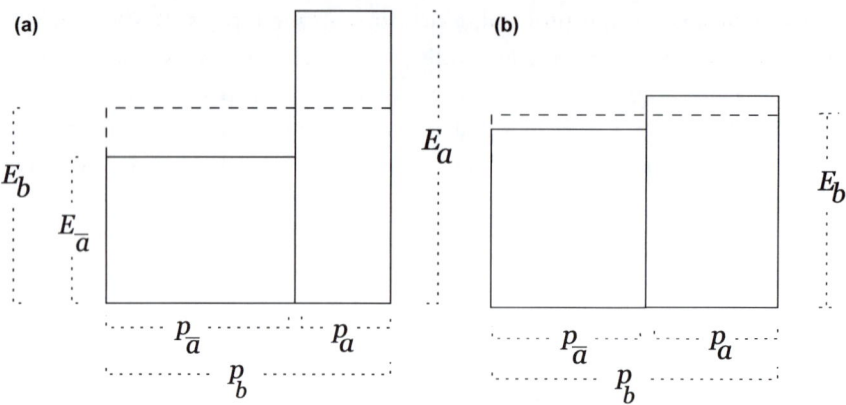

Figure 9.4 Initial condition distribution within a bubble. Width represents measure. (a): First input measure; (b): Second input measure

value of the difference between the expectation E_b of the number of inputs conditional on b and the expectation E_a of the number of inputs conditional on a, divided by b's measure. The bubble-deviation is equal to: $\left|\dfrac{E_b - E_a}{p_b}\right|$.

Figures 9.4(a) and (b) together illustrate how bubble-deviation depends on input measure. Both diagrams represent one croupier's distribution of spins over the same bubble: Numbers of spins in each region are the same: The area of the right-hand rectangle in (a) is equal to the area of the right-hand rectangle in (b), and similarly for the left-hand rectangles. However, because of the difference in input measures assigned to a (width in the two diagrams), (b) shows a smaller bubble-deviation than does (a): The difference between the height of the right-hand rectangle, and the height of the dashed line representing average number of inputs in the bubble is smaller in (b).

As mentioned above, according to the microconstancy inequality theorem, the smaller bubbles' measures are, and the smaller the bubble-deviations of a distribution are, the closer frequencies will be to the probabilities of outcomes defined by input probabilities. Figure (b) illustrates part of the idea: When an input measure sets probabilities so that it makes the (probability-weighted) average number of inputs in special subsets of bubbles close to the average number of inputs for the entire bubble (it makes bubble deviation small), the step-shaped curve of average numbers of inputs in a bubble will be close to flat. That means that the frequencies of outcomes in the subsets will be close to the sets' measures according to the given probability measure.

9.3.3. Mechanistic Probability

In order to describe mechanistic probability, it will help to extend the notation from the previous section slightly. Let A represent an outcome (e.g., red), and let a represent the set of initial conditions which can lead to A. Let b be a bubble in the input space—that is, a set containing possible inputs leading to both A and its negation (or complement), $\bar{A}$. Then $P(a|b)$ is the probability of an input leading to A given that it occurs in bubble b. This probability is equal to $\dfrac{P(a\,\&\,b)}{P(b)}$, the probability that an input in bubble b would lead to outcome A divided by the probability that an input would fall in b.

So far we've simply assumed the existence of a probability measure that assigns values to subsets of the input space. Now we can work toward a way of defining an appropriate input measure. The following relationship will play a central role below. Given a set of collections of inputs to a bubbly device (e.g., a set of collections of spins by different croupiers), *if* there's an input measure that

1. Makes maximum bubble size small, and
2. Makes bubble-deviations small for all (most) of the collections of inputs (i.e., makes the collections "macroperiodic" [Strevens, 2003]), and
3. Makes probability $P(a|b)$ of A's causes conditional on coming from b the same for all bubbles b (i.e., P is "microconstant" [Strevens, 2003]),

then the microconstancy inequality theorem implies that frequencies will be near probabilities in all (most) of the collections of inputs. The strategy for defining FFF mechanistic probability is to define an input measure which best satisfies conditions (1–3) relative to a special set of collections of actual initial conditions. If (1)–(3) are satisfied well enough by the resulting input measure—in the sense that bubble sizes (1) and bubble-deviations (2) are small for most collections of initial conditions, and (3) is true, then mechanistic probability will be well-defined and will exist—for example, for a particular actual wheel of fortune. The special set of collections of initial conditions is specified in the next few paragraphs (for other details see the appendix to this chapter and Abrams, forthcoming).

In the case of some causal map devices, such as a particular wheel of fortune, it happens that there is a large set of actual collections of inputs to similar devices, where each collection is produced by a single device—a croupier, in this case—over a single interval of time. More specifically, there is a large set of actual collections of inputs to causal map devices whose input spaces are similar to that of the wheel of fortune in question (figure 9.5). Some of these collections contain spins of a particular wheel of fortune by a particular croupier. Some contain spins of a roulette wheel by a croupier. Some of the collections may contain spins of old mechanical one-armed bandit slot machines, in which vertical wheels were caused to turn by the pull of a lever. Note that in each case, what matters is that there is a set of inputs to a device whose input space is similar to that of the particular wheel of fortune of interest to us. In the case of the roulette wheels, we can ignore the tossed balls, since there is nevertheless a spin of the wheel each time. Similarly, the fact that the wheels in the one-armed bandits are vertical doesn't change the fact that these wheels realize a type of causal map device whose input space consists of angular velocities within a certain general range. (For that matter, there are both vertically and horizontally mounted wheels of fortune.) Determining what all of these distributions are is impractical, though possible in principle.

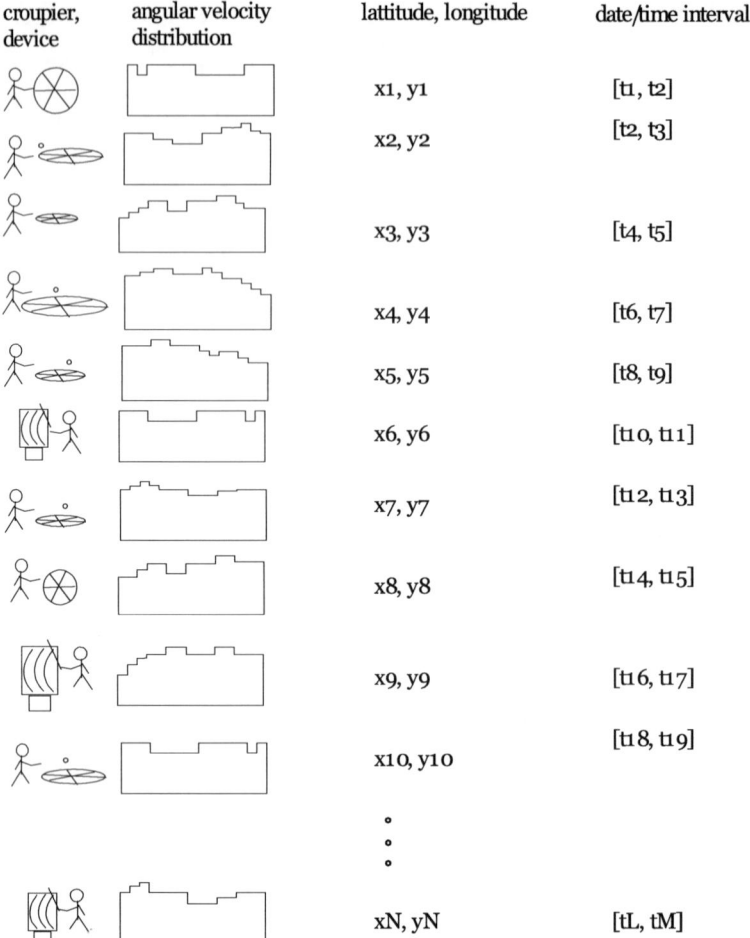

Figure 9.5 Distributions in a set of natural collections of inputs for one wheel of fortune, including spins of this wheel of fortune and others, roulette wheels, and mechanical slot machines

We can then define an input measure for a particular, concrete causal map device D (e.g., a wheel of fortune) relative to a large set of such "natural collections," each containing a large number of inputs. These are those inputs to D and to other actual causal map devices D', which (a) exist in a large region of space and time around D, and (b) are similar to D in having roughly the same input space.[29] In addition, (c) a natural collection must consist of events that are all and only those produced by a single concrete device (e.g., a croupier) in a single interval of time. (This rules out gerrymandered collections containing only red spins, for example, and some other problematic cases; see Abrams, forthcoming.)

The FFF mechanistic probability of an outcome (e.g., red) from a particular causal map device (e.g., an actual wheel of fortune) is then equal to the input probability of initial conditions which can lead to that outcome, where the input probability measure is one which:

- Makes the probability of the outcome (red) the same conditional on each member of a partition of inputs into bubbles ($P(A|b_i) = P(A|b_j)$ for all bubbles b_i and b_j), and
- Minimizes bubble sizes and bubble-deviations relative to all members of the natural collections of inputs.

FFF mechanistic probability then exists if those bubble sizes and bubble-deviations are sufficiently small.[30] Of course, since it's impractical to determine what all of these natural collections might be, it's impractical to completely verify that FFF mechanistic probability exists in a given case. Nevertheless, it's possible to get evidence for the existence of FFF mechanistic probability, and it's often reasonable to assume its existence. The dearth of adequate alternative explanations of stable frequencies in cases such as the wheel of fortune provides one reason for taking the postulation of FFF mechanistic probability to be reasonable. (See Abrams, forthcoming for further discussion.)

The definition of FFF mechanistic probability and the microconstancy inequality theorem have the following implications. (See [Abrams, forthcoming] for further discussion and defense of these points.)

- Frequencies in large sequences of trials will usually be close to mechanistic probabilities, because by definition, mechanistic probabilities are close to frequencies in most natural collections.
- Stable relative frequencies are explained by mechanistic probability. Bubbliness as it were compresses the diversity of frequencies in collections of initial conditions into the regularity of outcome frequencies.
- Bubbliness buffers against certain kinds of counterfactual variation in natural collections: Nearby worlds in which natural collections differ in small ways are ones in which frequencies of outcomes will generally be similar to what they are in the actual world. (Truthmakers for mechanistic probability are in the actual world, however.)
- Since the same set of natural collections should apply to just about any causal map device with the same input space, probabilities of outcomes for causal map devices with the same input space and the same outcomes will differ in outcome probabilities primarily because of differences in their internal causal structure, as in the case of two wheels of fortune with different red and black wedge size ratios.
- A related point is that we can manipulate frequencies by modifying the structure of the device so that larger or smaller sets of initial conditions are mapped to outcomes—by changing sizes of wedges on a wheel of fortune, for example. Thus mechanistic probability at least causally influences frequencies.

The last two points will be particularly important in the application of mechanistic probability to social contexts.

9.3.4. Causal Map Condition Categories

The following tale will help illustrate concepts which will be important for the application of mechanistic probability in social sciences.

> *At the end of a dirt road in a remote area there is an old, run-down casino, Casino Ruota, in which several wheels of fortune are often visible. Though the ratio between red and black wedge sizes is uniform within each wheel, the ratio is not the same for all wheels, which are otherwise identical. Thus red has a different probability on different wheels. Sal, the only croupier, races from one wheel to the next, spinning the wheel and quickly collecting and paying out at each wheel. She must be quick, because by magic that only Sal understands, each wheel comes into existence when it is spun, disappearing soon after it stops. (Sal also believes she is able to change the percentage of wheels favoring red and black using esoteric procedures she calls "policy interventions.")*

The fantasy that wheels magically come in and out of existence will help convey the point that the concepts described next don't depend on properties such as wheels' physical persistence. Since such properties will usually have no analogs in social science applications of mechanistic probability, it's important to see that they're inessential to the strategy for applying FFF mechanistic probability explored in the rest of the chapter.

The properties of wheels of fortune in a collection such as Sal's can be classified into four *causal map device condition categories* (cf. Abrams, 2009, section 3.3.2):

1. The wheels have a set of mutually exclusive *outcomes*, in this case, red and black.
2. All wheels in the set share *common structuring conditions*: for example, having a certain diameter.
3. Wheels differ in which of several mutually exclusive *alternative structuring conditions* they involve. For example, for wheels in which the common structuring conditions require only two colors, red and black, with uniformly sized wedges for each color on an evenly weighted wheel, the alternative structuring conditions are different possible ratios between wedge sizes.
4. The wheels have a set of *circumstances of functioning*—conditions which change from trial to trial and change during the course of a trial: These include initial conditions (velocities), aspects of the process of spinning and slowing down, relation between the pointer and the wedge it points to, and so on.

Each trial—each spin—corresponds to a realization of the common structuring conditions, one consistent configuration from the set of alternative structuring conditions, and a configuration of initial conditions, which then cause the other circumstances of functioning to unfold until an outcome is produced. Call causal map devices that share common structuring conditions and outcomes but have different alternative structuring conditions *alternative causal map devices* (relative to a specification of such common and possible alternative structuring conditions). Classifying a set of similar causal map devices in this way is useful when we want to compare the effects of different alternative structuring conditions on probabilities of outcomes, given an assumption that the other aspects of the devices will be held fixed. As I'll explain below, this scheme will be useful in understanding the application of mechanistic probability in social science contexts.

9.4. APPLICATION IN SOCIAL SCIENCES

In this section I'll outline a way in which the preceding interpretation of probability can be applied in some social science contexts. I'll make repeated reference to the following illustration.

Hill et al. (1999) studied a sample of about eight hundred ten- to twelve-year-olds in Seattle during the 1990s. They identified several factors which seemed to affect frequency of an individual joining a gang between the ages of thirteen and eighteen. For example, the frequency of gang membership (0.233) among those whose families had household income in the lowest quartile was about twice as large (vs. 0.127) as for those with incomes in the highest quartile.

Family income itself of course does not guarantee any outcome, and following arguments in Section 9.2, I'll assume that lives of individuals in their physical and social context are deterministic. Thus, given all of the details of an individual's circumstances, probabilities for events in a particular individual's life will be very close to 0 or 1. The relevant variables are too numerous and too fine-grained to measure in practice, but what happens to an individual is plausibly affected by details of her psychology, physiology, interactions with others (and their psychology and physiology), media broadcasts, weather, and much more. From this point of view, a portion of the world containing an individual has a certain very complex initial state at a time t_0 (e.g., tenth birthday), and then everything just unfolds—the machine runs. Along the way, certain identifiable outcomes (e.g., joining a gang) are realized: A state which incorporates those outcomes—those properties—becomes actual.

9.4.1. Some Say the Heart Is Just Like a Wheel

Casino Sociale takes up large parts of the city of Seattle (and aspects of the rest of the planet). The gambling devices are both overlapping and ephemeral. They are realized by aspects of the city and its surroundings, each device focused on the life of a particular individual. No gamblers come from outside to play the games of chance, yet, routinely, a very complex "spin"—i.e., a configuration of initial conditions—is fed into the machine. A life unfolds; outcomes determined by that "spin" eventually occur or fail to do so. As before, the croupier is the same for each gambling device. However, here the croupier is realized by the same system that realizes the devices.

The heart isn't like a wheel of fortune; however, a heart along with the context in which it's embedded is.[31] In the system studied by Hill et al. (1999), we can think of the life of a child, beginning from a specified time, as the focal element of a trial analogous to a spin of a wheel of fortune. However, since an outcome (e.g., gang membership by eighteen) is determined by the child's interactions with the world around him/her, the relevant causal map device includes much of what goes on in the child's nervous system and body, his/her neighborhood, the surrounding city, and to a lesser extent, events elsewhere on the planet. Call such a causal map device a "person-focused causal map device," or more briefly, a "personal causal map device." Not everything in the universe plays a role in such a device: Minute shifts in the molecular structure of a rock in Iowa usually won't affect children's lives, nor do subtle fluctuations in light reaching the earth from a distant pulsar. What does and does not count as part of the causal map device depends on the causal structure of the large system realizing it. (Note that "personal" is not meant to suggest that a personal causal map device belongs to or is associated with a particular individual; a personal causal map device is simply a device in which outcomes concern properties of the kind that persons realize individually.)

Different children are focal elements of different realizations of personal causal map devices. As with the ephemeral wheels of fortune in Casino Ruota, each trial—each course of operation of a device embedded in Seattle and its broader context—is a trial of a physically distinct device. Realizations of causal map devices relevant to Hill et al.'s (1999) study can be classified in terms of the four causal map device condition categories mentioned above. These devices have:

1. *Outcomes*: Properties such as joining or not joining a gang by a given age. (These are analogous to red and black outcomes for the wheel of fortune.)

2. A set of *common structuring conditions* shared by trials of the causal map devices, such as general properties of a person at age ten, general relations shared by virtue of living in Seattle, living in the United States in 1990. (These are analogous to the fact that it's a wheel of a certain diameter and mass which is spun, with given friction coefficients, and so on.)

3. A set of mutually exclusive *alternative structuring conditions*. Each personal causal map device realizes exactly one of these conditions. A set of mutually exclusive ranges of family income levels is one possible set of alternative structuring conditions. Racial and ethnic categories present a different set of alternative conditions. Conditions can be conjoined/intersected to produce a more fine-grained set of alternative conditions, such as these, for example: African American and high income, African American and low income, white and high income, white and low income.[32] (The difference between income levels or racial categories corresponds to the difference between wheels of fortune with wedges of different sizes. For example, if we treat the red outcome as analogous to eventually joining a gang, then a wheel with large red wedges corresponds to living in a low-income family, while a wheel with smaller red wedges corresponds to living in a higher-income family.)

4. There are also *circumstances of functioning*, including a set of possible initial conditions at the beginning of a trial, along with everything else that varies in a child's life, family, neighborhood, the city, and so on—until, say, the child reaches the age of eighteen, at which point one of the gang member/ not gang member outcomes has been realized. (Circumstances of functioning in the case of a wheel of fortune are simpler, including, primarily, only the initial angular velocity and the position of the wheel at each moment until it stops.)

Such conditions define a personal causal map type. A trial or realization of such a causal map type occurs whenever a set of common structuring conditions and one member of the set of alternative structuring conditions is realized, along with a specific set of initial conditions. All other properties involved in the realization of a personal causal map type count as circumstances of functioning, beginning from initial conditions. These include states of the focal person other than those included in the structuring conditions, states of other people in his/her community, physical configurations of the person's surroundings, and so on. Such trials take place repeatedly in Seattle and its broader context, just in Sal's Casino Ruota.[33]

By deciding which conditions to study and estimate, a researcher implicitly selects a set of causal map types defined by conditions of the four kinds described above. For example, the researcher takes for granted certain background conditions, such as the fact that the only people being studied are those living in Seattle in the 1990s who are of a certain age. These are part of what define the common structuring conditions. The researcher also selects independent variables, which define alternative structuring conditions, and dependent variables, which define outcomes. Most circumstances of functioning usually go unmeasured, as they would be difficult to study in any detail.

However, the fact that researchers choose which aspects of a society to study doesn't imply that the causal relations connecting those aspects are themselves constituted by researchers' choices. Two researchers interested in different properties might (implicitly) select different sets of causal map types, which nevertheless might be realized by exactly the same persons in their physical and social contexts. What is a common structuring condition for one researcher (e.g., living in Seattle) might be an alternative structuring condition for another. (Suppose that city of residence is treated as an independent variable.) Moreover, what is a structuring condition for one researcher might be part of the circumstances of functioning for the other. (Suppose that individuals who relocate between cities during the period of study continue to be tracked. Note though that most circumstances of functioning will remain unmeasured by any researcher.[34]) The two researchers *may* simply be asking about causal and probabilistic relationships between different properties that happen to be coinstantiated by the same system at the same time. On the other hand, suppose that two researchers choose to focus on the same outcomes and common structuring conditions, but on different sets of alternative structuring conditions. One researcher might focus on income while the other focuses on race.

These researchers are asking different questions: One asks about probabilities given various income properties, the other about probabilities given racial properties. Nothing I've said so far implies whether these questions have equally good answers, or whether one study might identify factors which are causally primary. Similarly, if one researcher takes for granted residence in Seattle and another doesn't, the first may miss interesting relationships between living in Seattle and the outcomes that interest her.

So far, I've explained how to see alternative personal causal map devices, analogous to wheels of fortune with different wedge sizes, within parts of a social system. However, I haven't yet argued that other conditions required for the existence of mechanistic probability are satisfied by such causal map devices. In the next two sections I'll argue that it's plausible that many personal causal map devices are bubbly in a sense needed for mechanistic probability (in section 9.4.2) and that it's reasonable to see actual initial conditions which are inputs to personal causal map devices as forming natural collections of inputs in the way needed for mechanistic probability (in section 9.4.3).

9.4.2. Life Is Like a Box of Chocolates

My momma always said, "Life was like a box of chocolates. You never know what you're gonna get."—Forrest Gump[35]

Individuals don't know what they're going to get, I'll argue, in this sense: For the kinds of outcomes which social scientists study—such as achievement of various kinds, well-being, drug use, voting behavior, participation in various groups—the complexity of the processes which actually govern a particular individual's life usually generates sensitive dependence of outcomes on initial conditions: Trivial differences in circumstances at one time routinely produce large differences in outcomes. Despite the fact that membership in a social category can make certain outcomes commonplace, it rarely guarantees any narrow set of outcomes. This point may seem obvious, but it is important to be clear about its implications here.

More importantly, I'll argue that it's plausible that the causal map devices realized by individuals in their social circumstances are typically bubbly: It's possible to partition the input space for a personal causal map device into many sets of similar circumstances, so that each set contains initial conditions leading to every outcome defined for the device. That is, it is possible to partition the input space into bubbles.[36] A bubble of this kind will be a set of possible circumstances in individuals' lives—circumstances which probably all seem trivially similar to us—among which are variations, of an even more trivial character, which would lead to distinct social outcomes were they realized. (All of this is constrained by a choice of structuring conditions—see section 9.4.1.) Individuals don't know what they're going to get, then, because they don't know into which portion of some bubble the initial conditions for their life fall. Causal paths between initial conditions and outcomes giving rise to the bubble structure are simply more complex than anyone can understand in practice.

Since rigorous demonstration of these claims would require impractically detailed empirical studies, my goal in this section is to give informal arguments to make it plausible that personal causal map devices are bubbly—that is, that bubbles of certain kinds exist—even if, as a practical matter, we can't usually identify particular bubbles. (As I noted at the end of section 9.1, the main goal of the chapter is to make a certain hypothesis reasonably plausible. This is the claim that many probabilities of social outcomes are mechanistic probabilities. Given arguments in sections 9.1 and 9.2 that there is a need for such a hypothesis, and that no alternative seems to be in the offing, merely making mechanistic probability plausible for social science contexts is significant.)

At various points in the chapter I've suggested that the complexity of human lives makes it plausible that there is sensitive dependence of outcomes on details of circumstances at every stage of life. The story of the importance of my relative's pace and speed in putting on his coat (section 9.1) provided one illustration, and most people know of someone who got a job, chose their career path, or met a romantic partner as a result of what seemed to be a chance meeting between two people. Such events typically have other ramifications, both important and trivial. More prosaically, a delay in rounding a corner can lead to an encounter with a troubling or enlightening individual who would otherwise have been missed, which may in turn lead to missing a bus, being late for work, and so on. Or a slight puff of air in a small room can lead to an infection being transmitted. In a footnote to section 9.4.1, I mentioned that the circumstances of functioning for a causal map device can include circumstances such as who is in the same line in a shop, when a stoplight changes, when a car turns into the street in front of a person, whether a new sidewalk fracture creates a puddle to be avoided, whether a strong wind slows one down, whether one is the target of a robbery which is or is not successful, whether a subtle insult is given at a moment when it is able to hit its target, vagaries of disease transmission and food nutrition, and so on. (Fiction sometimes uses small coincidences engineered by authors; that such events often seem uncontrived is some evidence of the ubiquity of small coincidences in real lives.[37]) My claim here is that the complexity of social, biological, and physical interactions involved in human life means that even minor variations in factors like those just mentioned can ramify to produce divergent outcomes. The claim is not that human lives exhibit no robustness to minor variation in circumstances; I suspect that not all variations in circumstances would make a difference to outcomes studied by social scientists (cf. section 9.5.1). (On the other hand, since a bubble is any small set containing inputs leading to every outcome, if all minute variations in circumstances *did* make a difference to outcomes, and we knew it, justifying claims about mechanistic probability would be, if anything, easier, since very small sets would count as bubbles.) What I want to make plausible is only that in general, among sets of very similar circumstances, there are variations that would, if realized, produce each member of a wide range of outcomes that might be chosen for study within the social sciences. (Note that the very ubiquity of such sensitive dependence makes it hard to notice except in special cases. Part of the reason for this is that the dependence on minor variation in circumstances in human lives is so common, and the ramifications of such variations so complex, that it would be impossible to trace the consequences of all such minor variations in practice.) If I'm right that in every small region of initial conditions for lives—that is, for a personal causal map device—there are small variations which lead to divergent outcomes, then person-focused social causal map devices are bubbly. That is, it would be possible to partition the input space of such a device into many sets, each containing some paths that lead to each outcome defined for the device.

A detailed, concrete illustration of the bubbliness of a personal causal map device would be helpful but impractical, requiring description in minute detail of numerous possible lives. Figure 9.6 provides a schematic representation, analogous to Figures 9.2(a) and (b), of a division of the input space of a personal causal map device into initial conditions leading to two outcomes: Gang membership (light gray) and lack thereof (dark gray). Similarity of conditions is represented by distance, probability is represented by area, and gang membership is less probable. Descriptions of what might ensue from two individual points in the input space are attached to the diagram. Though the stories in figure 9.6 are made up, they should not sound implausible. That they lack sufficient detail to predict the sequence of events conveys the extent to which further details of circumstances might have led to different outcomes than those in each story. Notice that the input space in figure 9.6 is represented in such a way that it's easy to divide it into many subsets of similar conditions containing initial conditions leading to both outcomes. That is, it's easy to show that this causal map device is bubbly. Of course I've designed this schematic illustration that way. One should imagine a much more fine-grained division with many more dimensions, however. The fact that points leading to gang membership or lack of gang membership are clustered in discernible regions is not essential to the diagram.[38]

9.4.3. The Input Measure

In the last two sections I argued that we can view lives of persons in context as realizations of causal map devices (section 9.4.1), and that these causal map devices are usually bubbly (section 9.4.2). In this section I'll argue that it's reasonable to think that an input measure of the kind required by FFF mechanistic probability exists for these devices. That is, I'll argue that for many personal causal map devices, the social world distributes initial conditions across bubbles of the kind just described in a more or less even way. In particular, bubble-deviations will generally be very small relative to an input measure defined with respect to natural collections of those initial conditions. If this is correct, then the requirements for mechanistic probability would plausibly be met for many personal causal map devices.

First, as the story about Casino Sociale loosely suggests, the croupier for a social causal map device, for example, one focused on a child in Seattle, is the whole system in which that device is embedded. That is, different person-focused causal map devices, defined by different alternative structuring conditions (but identical

Child's mother struggles on and off with depression but works during some periods. Father has been around during some periods. Beginning at age 10, child and two younger siblings live with grandmother, who provides a friendly household with fairly strict rules. Child internalizes goal of doing well in school, and has some academic success while also doing regular babysitting work. Several childhood friends from immediate neighborhood have older siblings who join local gang, and those friends do so as well. Child remains committed to staying out of gangs, while also spending some time with friends who are gang members. However, child, along with friends, is mistreated in a few encounters with a local police officer, and child does poorly during one school year partly as a result of dealing with mother, who has been around but has been depressed. Father tries to spend more time with child in order to provide support but ends up leaving town for a job opportunity. Somewhat demoralized, child starts spending more time with gang friends, and ultimately joins gang after being beat up by members of a rival gang.

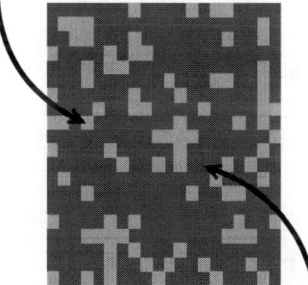

Focal child is from working-class, divorced family. Child sees both parents regularly. Parent in home is generally supportive but sometimes distracted by relationship issues. Some children harass child at school. This increases after child develops temporary limp due to playground fall, increasing tendency toward insecurity. Other parent is occasionally verbally abusive but also warm toward child. Close friend of child gradually increases use of marijuana over several years. Child sometimes threatened and robbed by a child who transfers to school. Some local police treat marijuana-using friend in heavy-handed way. Hangs out more with other drug-using friends who buy from gang members. Other gang members threaten child and friends are encouraged to join gang by peers; thinks about joining gang, but ends up encountering gang members less often after a close friend is expelled from school, and child gets more interested in basketball when another friend helps child improve skills, while one parent gets a less stressful job and then devotes more attention to child.

Figure 9.6 Schematic diagram of input space for personal causal map device for which gang membership (light gray) is less likely than avoiding it (dark gray). Events resulting from two points in input space are partially described. Distance represents similarity of initial conditions, and probability is represented by area.

input spaces, outcomes, and common structuring conditions) are realized within a larger device, the city of Seattle, or North America, and so on. This larger deterministic system is what chooses initial conditions to feed into each person-focused causal map device. (For example, these initial conditions might include the state of a child at age ten as well as her circumstances.) It may seem odd that the very

devices whose outcomes will end up having mechanistic probabilities, are themselves a part of the device that produces the inputs to each of these more limited
devices. However, nothing in the logic of mechanistic probability rules out such a
relationship between causal map devices and the devices that generate initial conditions to them. In this case there is a single, large natural collection of inputs, each
fed into a different realization of a causal map device, and all produced by the single
concrete device that is the larger system.

Second, note that the larger system which is the social croupier has been and
will be spinning the wheels of many personal causal map devices, one for each individual in Seattle over a substantial period of time, at least.[39] The extremely large
sequence of initial conditions fed into these devices can be divided into a large
number of large subsequences—that is, a large of set collections of inputs, as
required by the definition of FFF mechanistic probability.

Finally, it seems plausible that the croupier—society, Seattle, and so on—
tends to distribute initial conditions in such a way that there are no *particular,
narrow* sets of conditions which are significantly more prevalent. It's implausible
that the idiosyncratic, detailed circumstances that vary from individual trial to
individual trial would do so in any systematic way that would produce large concentrations of inputs in small regions of the initial condition space. That is, initial
conditions should be *very roughly* evenly distributed across bubbles and across
subsets of bubbles leading to different outcomes. (A very roughly even distribution
is all that's needed for FFF mechanistic probability—bubbliness then compresses
the variation in the distribution of initial conditions into stable frequencies; cf.
section 9.3.3.) Moreover, it's reasonable to think that all of this would hold for
most subsequences of the very large sequences of initial conditions produced by
Seattle the croupier.

Thus, for personal causal maps such as those implicit in Hill et al.'s study (1999),
it seems plausible that there is a bubble-partition and an input measure that:

1. Makes the maximum input probability measure of all bubbles small (as
   described in section 9.4.2).
2. Makes the most of the natural collection of inputs macroperiodic, that is,
   such that bubble-deviations are small: Changes in input-probability-
   weighted average frequencies for gang membership, for example, and its
   complement within each bubble are small.
3. Makes the input probability measure P microconstant, that is, $P(a|b)$ of A's
   causes conditional on b is the same for all bubbles b. (This requires adjusting the weights on portions of bubbles so that 1 and 2 aren't violated.)

Note that the set of actual initial conditions that defines the input measure for any
one of the alternative personal causal map devices is the set of actual inputs to all of
them, and the probability measure defined in terms of these inputs is the same for
each alternative causal map device. The probabilities of outcomes for these devices
differ only because of differences in their internal causal structures, defined by the
different social conditions that they reflect.

As with the sensitive dependence of personal causal map devices, described above, illustrating the way in which initial conditions are distributed among bubbles for such devices would be difficult in practice, since it would require describing many actual situations in great detail. However, the more fine-grained the sensitive dependence is in a personal causal map device, the less plausible it seems that actual initial conditions would distribute themselves so as to favor any very small region in the input space containing outcomes leading to a single outcome, or that actual initial conditions would consistently favor one outcome over another across disparate portions of the input space. For example, it's implausible that initial conditions would consistently produce one of the precise scenarios described in figure 9.6 rather than others.

Thus it's reasonable to think that social outcomes defined for person-focused causal map devices such as those implicit in Hill et al.'s (1999) study have mechanistic probabilities: There is, plausibly, a bubble-partition and a probability measure over initial conditions to alternative causal map devices centered on ten-year-old Seattle residents (defined, e.g., by alternative parental income levels), such that the probability of gang membership conditional on each bubble is the same, such that every bubble's input measure is small, and such that the maximum bubble-deviation for the set of actual initial conditions over a long period of time is small.

If this is correct, then according to the microconstancy inequality theorem, when a particular causal map device, satisfying requirements for mechanistic probability, is repeatedly realized, frequencies of outcomes will usually be close to their mechanistic probabilities. These probabilities, I suggest, are often the probabilities, determined by the causal structure of social systems, that social scientists are in fact measuring, modeling, and estimating. (For example, on the present view, the frequency of joining a gang among children whose parents are in the lowest income quartile will probably be close to the mechanistic probability of gang membership for that condition.) More generally, I suggest that the reason that it can be useful to make predictions and develop policies based on social science research is that the system being studied is, underneath, a causal map device satisfying the requirements for FFF mechanistic probability.[40]

I have argued only that all of the parts of this story about social probabilities are plausible, at the same time pointing out the severe practical difficulties of rigorously supporting the proposal. On the other hand, there does not seem to be any other account of social probabilities that can explain stable social frequencies. That does not make FFF mechanistic probability a purely theoretical postulate, however.[41] Rather, FFF mechanistic probability is a complex explanatory hypothesis with plausibility, and moreover, the only one available. It may be that some future mechanistic probability interpretation other than FFF mechanistic probability—perhaps deriving from Strevens's (2011) or Rosenthal's (2010) work—will turn out to have more plausibility for social sciences. However, I'm unaware of any alternatives to mechanistic probability interpretations that could satisfy the desiderata specified above.[42]

9.5. Discussion

9.5.1. Independent Social Variables: Comparisons and Analogies

According to the present picture, the difference between values of independent variables—alternative structuring conditions such as high versus low family income—is like the difference between different wedge sizes for wheels of fortune: Differences in family income bias the frequencies produced (relative to a common input probability measure) by these alternative causal map devices. James Garbarino makes a related point about psychological factors which could be viewed as defining a set of alternative structuring conditions:

> Most children are like dandelions; they thrive if given half a chance. Some are more like orchids. They do fine while young enough to be nurtured by loving parents, but wilt as adolescents subjected to peer competition, bullying and rejection, particularly in big high schools. (Garbarino, 1999, 51)

I would put the point this way: A personal causal map type defined by a more resilient, dandelion character biases probabilities—and frequencies—of better outcomes, compared to that defined by an orchid character. Some events that would send an orchid individual into a path that would (probably) lead to a bad outcome, would (probably) lead to good outcomes in many circumstances when a dandelion is the focal individual. (The instances of "probably" concern mechanistic probability.[43]) In other words, compared to an orchid, a dandelion has larger—more probable, that is—neutral spaces (Wagner, 2005) leading to positive outcomes, where neutral spaces are regions of the input space in which outcomes are robust to possible small modifications of a path through life.[44] Similar points can be made about the effects of racial or economic differences and other factors on individual outcomes. (It's plausible, however, that when there's an alternative causal map device with larger neutral spaces for a given outcome, the neutral spaces are not so large as to destroy bubbliness. Otherwise there would be large regions of the initial condition space in which no variation, no coincidences, could lead to an outcome other than the one which is probable in that region.)

Note that despite the effects of alternative structuring conditions on aggregate effects, the outcome for any given individual is determined once the causal map device begins its operation, according to the present view. This point may be made clearer by considering an analogy with the motion of particles of dust in a liquid as they are affected by both Brownian motion and the underlying flow of the liquid. Although quantum mechanical indeterminism presumably affects these processes in real liquids, similar processes would occur with deterministic molecular interactions, and simple models of Brownian motion reflect this assumption. On this view, a dust particle moves erratically because of variation in the numbers and forces of individual molecules impinging on it deterministically. As a result, some dust particles may move against the flow for some time, but the average effect of the molecules buffeting dust particles will be such that average movement of particles is in the direction of the liquid's flow. The path of each dust particle is nevertheless completely determined by the particular impacts on it. On the present picture of social phenomena, even individuals who realize social conditions that generate an average "flow" toward outcomes with high mechanistic probability may be those buffeted by life's deterministic "molecular" impacts so as to be pushed toward outcomes with low mechanistic probability.[45]

9.5.2. Correlations in Initial Conditions

In the United States, race is correlated with income. This is probably due in part to the structure of causal map devices with different racial categories as alternative structuring conditions. For example, if a significant proportion of employers are more willing to hire people perceived as white than people perceived as black, FFF mechanistic probabilities of various incomes will be different for personal causal map devices corresponding to white as opposed to black focal individuals.

The correlation between race and income could also be due in part to correlations among initial conditions. For example, consider personal causal map devices whose input spaces consist of circumstances at the time of an individual's birth. If there is a correlation between race and income among parents—a correlation in initial conditions for children—and if there's a correlation between parents' income and the educational opportunities of children, the observed correlation between race and income may be partly the result of patterns in initial conditions, rather than the causal structure of personal causal map devices alone. Obviously, this correlation between race and parental income may be due to the causal structure of personal causal map devices focused on individuals in the parents' generation. Thus discrimination in one generation can cause a correlation between race and income among parents of individuals in the next generation, which affects the pattern of initial conditions for the following generation. This correlation in initial conditions can contribute to a similar race-income correlation in this second generation. Thus it could well be that to some extent, the race/income correlation is not merely regenerated by discrimination in every generation, but persists because the structure of current personal causal map devices as it were passes on race/income correlations from one generation to the next. This is in contrast to the picture painted above, in which alternative causal map devices generate different mechanistic probabilities solely due to their internal differences of causal structure *from the same input probability measure*, and frequencies are supposed to differ for the same reason. That is, the picture given above assumed that alternative causal map devices were in effect subject to the same overall patterns of inputs, and as a result could be treated as having the same input measure. In the race/income scenario just described, though, frequencies differ in part because of differences in the ways in which initial conditions are distributed to causal map devices corresponding to black versus white children. It appears that personal causal maps for white children and for black children should be given different input measures. Mechanistic probabilities in this case should reflect these different input measures as well as differences in the internal causal structure of the alternative causal maps due, for example, to discrimination. Of course, the historical root of the correlation in initial conditions many generations ago undoubtedly has to do with discrimination as well, but the framework I've set up in this chapter doesn't have a clear role for the effects of discrimination which took place many generations ago.

Note, however, that if instead we define a set of alternative causal map devices in terms of race, parental income, and perhaps some other factors all at once, it can turn out that there are no remaining correlations in initial conditions that affect frequencies of outcomes differently in different alternative causal map devices. There may be more realizations of white plus high-income-parent causal map devices than black plus high-income-parent devices, at present, but that doesn't affect frequencies conditional on each device. I believe that with the right set of alternative structuring conditions, FFF mechanistic probability will apply in spite of correlations in initial conditions for less specific causal map devices.

9.6. CONCLUSION

Probabilities in social sciences might have all been artifacts of models, or might have literally referred to population frequencies. When frequencies are stable, however, there would seem to be something systematic about the underlying social system that produces that stability. Since such systematic facts would generate stable frequencies, it's reasonable to view them as playing a role in constituting objective probabilities inhering in the social system. Since we are interested not just in whatever frequencies in social systems happen to be, but also in manipulating these frequencies, it appears as if we do think that there are such probabilities. However, we have not had a good account of what it is about social systems that could count as this kind of probability; we have not had an interpretation of probability that can play the role of explaining stable frequencies. FFF mechanistic probability can play this role. The evidence for FFF mechanistic probability in social contexts is not as strong as one would like, however. I can only argue that it's plausible that certain conditions for the existence of FFF mechanistic probability are satisfied in social systems. However, given that there does not seem to be a good alternative, FFF mechanistic probability should be taken seriously as an account of the kind of probability to which many claims in social sciences implicitly refer.

APPENDIX: MECHANISTIC PROBABILITY: TECHNICAL ASPECTS

As mentioned above, the bubble-deviation of a bubble b is defined relative to an input probability measure as the absolute value of the difference between the expectation E_b of the number of inputs conditional on b and the expected number E_a of inputs conditional on the set of inputs leading to A (i.e. A^{-1}) within b, divided by b's measure: $\left| \dfrac{E_b - E_a}{p_b} \right|$ [See figure 9.4(a).] The microconstancy inequality theorem A^{-1} (Abrams, forthcoming) says that the difference between the relative frequency of outcome A and the input measure of A^{-1} (the set of initial conditions which lead to A) is constrained by bubble-deviations and bubble measures:

Theorem 1 *The difference between the relative frequency R(A) of A outcomes and the probability P(A) of A is less than the product of the maximum bubble-deviation S, the square of the maximum bubble size π, and the number of bubbles n:*

$$nS\pi^2 \geq |P(A) - R(A)|$$

(Abrams, forthcoming)
Mechanistic probability exists if and only if (Abrams, forthcoming):

1. There's a large set of natural collections (all inputs produced by single process in single interval of time) of inputs—a set containing all and only those collections of inputs to actual devices D^* such that:
   a. The inputs are all and only those produced by a single physical device;
   b. D^* has approximately the same input space as D;
   c. D^* occurs somewhere in a large spatiotemporal region around the location and time of D;
2. a. D is bubbly: There is a bubble partition for D with a large number of bubbles, and this bubble partition is such that:
   b. A microconstant input measure (i.e., such that within-bubble outcome probabilities are uniform across bubbles), constructed through minimization of the sum of squares of bubble-deviations for all members of the set of natural collections, makes most of the collections macroperiodic relative to this input space and the device's bubble partition. (Or: Most collections generate a small maximum bubble-deviation.)
   c. Moderately expanding or contracting the spatial or temporal range across which natural collections are defined doesn't affect whether condition 2b is satisfied for outcome probabilities.

See (Abrams, forthcoming) for clarification and discussion of details.

ACKNOWLEDGMENTS

I'm grateful for Harold Kincaid's feedback, especially his help clarifying the presentation. (He's not responsible for the remaining unclarities.) Brenda Smith provided valuable discussion and suggestions concerning useful source material. I'm also grateful for helpful interactions with Aidan Lyon, David Teira, Don Ross, Erik Angner, Fred Chernoff, Jim Woodward, Julian Reiss, Ken Kollman, Lois Barnett, Mark Risjord, Norman Abrams, Philippe Huneman, Robert Northcott, Ron Mallon, Ted Benditt, as well as others who participated in workshops at which these ideas were presented: the conference on Current Issues in the Philosophy and Methodology of the Social Sciences, and the International Network for Economic Method Conference, both at the University of Alabama at Birmingham in 2010, and a presentation at the Université de Paris I in 2011. Finally, since this chapter grows directly out of the research which led to (Abrams, forthcoming), those acknowledged there are here, implicitly, as well. No one mentioned should be assumed to be in agreement with or even sympathetic to the ideas presented above.

NOTES

1. Frequency interpretations are widely taken to be the foundation of so-called frequentist statistical methods, but what these methods actually require is just an interpretation of probability that satisfies the assumptions of the methods. My view is that FFF mechanistic probability, described in this chapter, roughly satisfies those assumptions, and that it can be modeled by mathematical probabilities that precisely satisfy them.

2. Compare the popular advice to "follow your dreams, no matter what, and you will succeed."

3. Garfinkel (1981, 91ff) comments directly on the previously quoted passage from Jencks et al. 1973.

4. Garfinkel (1981) repeatedly compares social processes to his view that a rabbit about to be eaten by a fox would nevertheless still have been eaten, had circumstances been slightly different. He takes this illustration as a good analogy for the correct way to think about many explanations in social sciences. I'll note that I think the story about the fox and the rabbit is implausible, especially if we consider subtle alterations in circumstances leading up to the moment of predation. Natural selection usually pushes organisms to the limits of their capabilities in one dimension or another; otherwise, there is room for selection to improve until some such limits are reached. Prey are often difficult to catch, and no doubt some prey are only just barely caught. In the usual highly complex environments, circumstances that can make a difference to outcomes are likely to be subtle, a point I will discuss elsewhere.

5. Garfinkel (1981) eventually seems to argue (in his chapter 6) that social science (and science in general) *can't* proceed where there is sensitive dependence of outcomes on subtle variations in initial conditions. What Garfinkel fails to emphasize is the extent to which social science only makes probabilistic claims about aggregate outcomes, which often do not exhibit pernicious sensitive dependence.

6. FFF mechanistic probability is closely related to other recently proposed interpretations of probability (Strevens 2011; Rosenthal 2010; Myrvold 2012) but I believe it is more appropriate for understanding probabilities in social sciences.

7. Except, possibly, proposals similar to the one I describe here, as remarks I make below about Strevens's and Rosenthal's interpretations of probability suggest.

8. Sometimes methodological probabilities are alluded to without being explicitly described, as in "a total of 10,000 individuals were drawn from the national population database in a random procedure which was stratified by age, gender, and county of residence" (Wenzel, Øren, and Bakken 2008).

9. Bayesian statistical methods require that researchers choose a prior probability distribution or a class of such distributions. Is this an instance of social probability or methodological probability? I suggest the following: If the prior distribution is chosen arbitrarily, because it will wash out—because the choice of prior distribution has little influence on the inferences made in the end—then the priors are methodological probabilities. If, on the other hand, a prior distribution is tailored to facts about social systems, it may be that it is, at least in part, an estimate of a social probability.

10. The set of subsets must be closed under finite unions.

11. (3) is often replaced with a stronger requirement which generalizes it to infinite sums: $P\left(\bigcup_j^\infty A_j\right) = \sum_j^\infty P(A_j)$. if distinct A_j's can have no members in common. This is usually paired with a requirement that the set of subsets is closed under infinite unions. Mechanistic probability will only satisfy the finite additivity requirement in (3) rather than this stronger requirement of countable additivity. It can nevertheless be mathematically convenient to model mechanistic probabilities with countably additive probabilities. Most mathematical treatments of probability as a measure require countable additivity, though if Ω is given only a finite number of subsets, finite additivity implies countable additivity.

12. See, e.g., Hájek 2009b and Williamson 2010 for other sets of criteria and further discussion.

13. There are ways to argue, concerning either scenario, that a rational subjective or epistemic probability assignment would make a frequency near .5 probable in this sense. However, common notions of subjective or epistemic probability won't capture the difference between these scenarios.

14. See, e.g., Gillies 2000 and Hájek 2009b for more thorough surveys of interpretations of probability and their advantages and disadvantages.

15. Known as a "reference class"—a class with reference to which frequencies are to be calculated.

16. Nor could frequencies in one set of events explain frequencies in another set of events without additional, substantive assumptions (for example, that there are causal connections between the two sets of events).

17. This is true of Hoefer's (2007) theory despite his emphasis on what he calls statistical nomological machines (SNMs), such as the wheel of fortunes I describe below. The problem is that Hoefer also defines chances in term of frequencies alone when no such SNMs exist.

18. The notion of a propensity was originally proposed by Popper (1957). This notion is not related to propensity scores or any other statistical or methodological principles involving the same term.

19. The assumption that underlying causes are governed by probabilities is part of what's needed, for example, to justify a claim that errors in observation of a single physical state will have a Gaussian distribution.

20. It isn't difficult to modify this picture if some causes of behavior are indeterministic (cf. Strevens 2003, chapter 2).

21. I believe that it's clearer how to apply FFF mechanistic probability in social sciences than it is to apply the other two interpretations, in part because FFF mechanistic probability was originally developed with the special sciences in mind, while Strevens's and

Rosenthal's interpretations apply more naturally in physical sciences. However, ideas developed in Strevens (2003, 2005) might be used to apply Strevens's or Rosenthal's interpretations in social sciences. I discuss the relationship between an aspect of Strevens's interpretation and mine in Abrams (forthcoming).

22. The $^{-1}$ notation for the set of elements that is mapped to a given set is common in mathematics. The set A^{-1} is the result of the inverse of the function from inputs to outputs, somewhat in the way that applying $^{-1}$ to a number x produces, x^{-1} the inverse of x.

23. "Bubble" was suggested by the fact that a soap bubble reflects its surroundings in miniature; similarly, an input space bubble reflects the outcome space "in miniature."

24. In figure 9.2(b) the small rectangle in the input space is a bubble, in this case for a causal map device with three outcomes.

25. In addition to Strevens (2003), cf. Poincaré (1912, 1952 [1903], 1952 [1908]) and works by other authors on the method of arbitrary functions cited in von Plato (1994), as well as more recent work by Keller (1986) and Engel (1992).

26. Lebesgue measure generalizes summed lengths, areas, or volumes to an arbitrary number of dimensions, while avoiding some technical problems using mathematical refinements that won't concern us here.

27. Recall that one of the axioms says that the probability of the union of two nonintersecting sets is the sum of their individual probabilities.

28. It makes sense to use average numbers of inputs, e.g., in the set a, rather than counting the croupier's numbers of inputs at each velocity in the input space, since it's likely that there is no more than one spin at any *particular* velocity, with no spins at all at most velocities. Tracking numbers of spins at particular velocities would make it difficult to see an overall pattern to a croupier's spins such as that illustrated in figure 9.3(b). It's such patterns that are the key to understanding mechanistic probability. Averaging over the input measure of a set in this way allows mechanistic probability to use an input measure that has been adjusted to reflect evidence of general tendencies to produce certain stable frequencies.

29. Other criteria might be required; see later discussion of this point for social science contexts.

30. See the appendix to this chapter and Abrams (forthcoming) for discussion of the appropriate sense of minimization and what "sufficiently small" means. Abrams (forthcoming) discusses what is important concerning the number and size of the natural collections.

31. The title of this section is from Anna McGarrigle's song "Heart Like a Wheel" (McGarrigle 2010).

32. Neither alternative structuring conditions nor common structuring conditions need correspond to what social scientists call "structural conditions."

33. Abrams (2009) fleshes out some aspects of this picture in a biological context, using what I call "organism-environment history spaces." The framework described there is applicable to many social contexts with minimal modification.

34. These circumstances of functioning include, at various moments in time, e.g., who is in the same line in a shop, when a stoplight changes, when a car turns into the street in front of a person, whether a new sidewalk fracture creates a puddle to be avoided, whether a strong wind slows one down, whether one is the target of a robbery which is or is not successful, whether a subtle insult is given at a moment when it is able to hit its target, vagaries of disease transmission and food nutrition, etc.

35. From the movie *Forrest Gump* (1994) directed by Robert Zemeckis, and written by Winston Groom and Eric Roth.

36. Technically, bubbliness is not independent of other requirements for mechanistic probability: The partition into bubbles must be one that allows satisfaction of the other conditions required for mechanistic probability. A consequence of this fact is that my use of "similar" in this paragraph is inessential, though useful for conveying the idea I have in mind. See appendix to this chapter and Abrams (forthcoming).

37. My favorite illustration is the 1998 film *Run, Lola, Run* by Tom Tykwer, in which differences between three counterfactual scenarios seem to depend in large part on small differences in timing in an initial sequence of events common to all three scenarios.

38. A similar diagram with intermixed gray and black dots would illustrate the idea just as well, if not better, but would make it difficult to see which outcome had greater probability.

39. A question remains about whether circumstances of ten-year-olds in other cities also should be viewed as helping to determine the input probability measure causal map devices relevant for Hill et al.'s study (1999). It may be that inputs to personal causal map devices for children in other cities, where the devices have the same input and output spaces, are relevant whenever patterns of correlations in initial conditions are similar to those in Seattle.

40. In some situations we are not only interested in probabilities and frequencies for trials of a given kind—e.g., of a given wheel of fortune or lives of children—but also in whether individual trials are probabilistically independent. Some statistical methods depend on such independence assumptions. To ask whether two trials or realizations of a single causal map device are independent is to ask a question about a complex device defined by two distinct trials of a simpler device. Thus, the wheel of fortune device discussed above is defined by an input space of angular velocities and an outcome space of red and black. We can also define a causal map device in which the input space consists of pairs of angular velocities for successive spins, and whose outcomes are pairs of red/black outcomes. In a more complex device such as this one, we can ask whether the outcome A-on-trial-one is independent of A-on-trial-two. Similarly, a question about independence of outcomes of two realizations of a given personal causal map device is really a question about a causal map device composed of two such devices. (In order to represent the outcomes of two trials together, we need to consider an outcome space that can represent both trials' outcomes. We are able to make claims about probabilities of such joint outcomes only using probabilities of outcomes on one trial given the outcome of the other trial. This is exactly what an assumption of probabilistic independence of trials gives us, for example: We assume that the probability of A on one trial is equal to A probability on that trial given the outcome of the other. However, the outcome space of a simple causal map device doesn't include joint outcomes. For example, the outcome space of a wheel of fortune device consists only of red and black, and FFF mechanistic probabilities for that device concern only those outcomes. Since mechanistic probabilities are defined only relative to a particular kind of causal map device, we have to consider a device whose outcome space includes joint outcomes of distinct trials in order to have mechanistic probabilities which give probabilities of one kind of outcome conditional on the other.) Questions about independence in a multitrial causal map device in social contexts can be less clear than in the case of a wheel of fortune: Some realizations of the same personal causal map device may even involve direct interactions between the focal individuals. (Consider realizations corresponding to two children in the same family.) Nevertheless, there are reasons to think that bubbliness can often allow probabilistic independence even when there are causal interactions between realizations of different simple causal map devices. Strevens (2003, chapter 3) argues for this point.

41. An example of the latter would be Sober's (2005) "no-theory" theory of probability, which claims that objective probabilities are purely theoretical postulations; their theoretical role in particular sciences is all there is to no-theory probabilities.

42. Explaining why I think that Strevens's (2011) and Rosenthal's (2010) interpretations are unsuitable for probabilities in social sciences would require a long digression, but I'll mention that their interpretations depend on an input measure defined in terms of purely physical properties, which—I would argue—would usually be unsuitable as a basis for probabilities in social sciences. (Abrams [forthcoming, section 4.1] includes one general criticism of Strevens's [2011] way of defining an input measure.)

43. More specifically, I view the probabilities underlying the two instances of "probably" in this sentence as mechanistic probabilities conditional on a particular event type (e.g., on being an act of rejection), occurring during the functioning of possible realizations of a causal map type. See Abrams (2009) for a conception of an organism (e.g., person) in its environment consistent with the present conception of mechanistic probability, which allows a clear way of understanding such conditional probabilities.

44. See Wimsatt (2007) for related discussions of robustness in a variety of contexts.

45. William Upski Wimsatt (1994) wrote that life as a white American is like riding a bicycle with the wind at one's back: It helps one along but its effects are typically unnoticed. The effects of the wind are harder to miss when one has to ride into it. My metaphor would fit Wimsatt's if air molecules were very large.

REFERENCES

Abrams, Marshall. 2007. "Fitness and Propensity's Annulment?" *Biology and Philosophy* 22(1): 115–30.

Abrams, Marshall. 2009. "Fitness 'Kinematics': Altruism, Biological Function, and Organism-Environment Histories." *Biology & Philosophy* 24 (4): 487–504.

Abrams, Marshall. "Mechanistic Probability." In *Synthese*. Forthcoming.

Eagle, Antony. 2004. "Twenty-One Arguments Against Propensity Analyses of Probability." *Erkenntnis* 60 (3): 371–416.

Engel, Eduardo M. R. A. 1992. *A Road to Randomness in Physical Systems*. Berlin: Springer-Verlag.

Garbarino, James. 1999. "Some Kids Are Orchids." *Time Magazine* 154 (25): 51.

Garfinkel, Alan. 1981. *Forms of Explanation: Rethinking Questions in Social Theory*. New Haven: Yale University Press.

Gillies, Donald A. 2000. *Philosophical Theories of Probability*. New York: Routledge.

Hájek, Alan. 1996. "'Mises Redux'-Redux: Fifteen Arguments Against Finite Frequentism." *Erkenntnis* 45 (2–3): 209–27.

Hájek, Alan. 2009a. "Fifteen Arguments Against Hypothetical Frequentism." *Erkenntnis* 70 (2): 211–35.

Hájek, Alan. 2009b. "Interpretations of Probability." In *The Stanford Encyclopedia of Philosophy*, ed., Edward N. Zalta, ed. Available at http://plato.stanford.edu/archives/spr2009/entries/probability-interpret/.

Hill, Karl G., C. Howell James, J. David Hawkins, and Sara R. Battin-Pearson. 1999. "Childhood Risk Factors for Adolescent Gang Membership: Results from the Seattle Social Development Project." *Journal of Research on Crime and Delinquency* 36 (3): 300–22.

Hoefer, Carl. 2007. "The Third Way on Objective Probability: A Sceptic's Guide to Objective Chance." *Mind* 116 (463): 449–596.

Jencks, C., M. Smith, H. Acland, M. J. Bane, D. Cohen, H. Gintis, B. Heyns, and S. Michelson. [1972]. *Inequality: A Reassessment of the Effect of Family and Schooling in America.* New York: Harper Colophon.

Keller, Joseph B. 1986. "The Probability of Heads." *The American Mathematical Monthly* 93 (3): 191–97.

Lewis, David. 1980. "A Subjectivist's Guide to Objective Chance." In *Studies in Inductive Logic and Probability*, vol. II, Richard C. Jeffrey, ed. Berkeley: University of California Press. Reprinted in Lewis, 1986.

Lewis, David. 1986. *Philosophical Papers*, volume II. Oxford: Oxford University Press.

Lewis, David. 1994. "Humean Supervenience Debugged." *Mind* 103 (412): 473–90.

Loewer, Barry. 2001. "Determinism and Chance." *Studies in the History and Philosophy of Modern Physics* 32B (4): 609–20.

Loewer, Barry. 2004. "David Lewis's Humean Theory of Objective Chance." *Philosophy of Science* 71 (5): 1115–125.

McGarrigle, Anna. 2010. "Heart Like a Wheel." Lyrics of the song "Heart Like a Wheel," published by Garden Court Music (ASCAP). www.mcgarrigles.com/music/kate-and-anna-mcgarrigle/heart-like-a-wheel.

Millikan, Ruth Garrett. 2000. "What Has Natural Information to Do with Intentional Representation?" In *On Clear and Confused Ideas*, 217–37. Cambridge: Cambridge University Press.

Mofitt, Robert. 2008. "A Primer on U.S. Welfare Reform." *Focus* 26 (1): 15–25.

Myrvold, Wayne C. 2012. "Deterministic Laws and Epistemic Chances." In *Probability in Physics*, Meir Hemmo and Yemima ben Menahem, eds. Berlin: Springer-Verlag.

Poincaré, Henri. 1912 [1896]. *Calcul des Probabilités*, 2d ed. Paris: Gauthier-Villars.

Poincaré, Henri. 1952 [1903]. "The Calculus of Probabilities." Chapter XI in *Science and Hypothesis*. In Poincaré 2001.

Poincaré, Henri. 1952 [1908]. "Chance." Chapter 4, Part I in *Science and Method*. In Poincaré 2001.

Poincaré, Henri. 2001. *The Value of Science*. New York: The Modern Library.

Popper, Karl R. 1957. "The Propensity Interpretation of the Calculus of Probability, and the Quantum Theory." In *Observation and Interpretation*, S. Körner, ed., 65–70. London: Academic Press.

Rosenthal, Jacob. 2010. "The Natural-Range Conception of Probability." In *Time, Chance, and Reduction: Philosophical Aspects of Statistical Mechanics*, Gerhard Ernst and Andreas Hüttemann, eds., 71–90. Cambridge: Cambridge University Press.

Sober, Elliott. 2005. "Evolutionary Theory and the Reality of Macro Probabilities." In *The Place of Probability in Science*, Ellery Eells and James Fetzer, eds., 133–61. Berlin: Springer.

Strevens, Michael. 2003. *Bigger Than Chaos: Understanding Complexity through Probability*. Cambridge, MA: Harvard University Press.

Strevens, Michael. 2005. "How Are the Sciences of Complex Systems Possible?" *Philosophy of Science* 72 (4): 531–56.

Strevens, Michael. 2011. "Probability Out of Determinism." In *Probabilities in Physics*, Claus Beisbart and Stephann Hartmann, eds., pp. 339–64. Oxford: Oxford University Press.

Von Plato, Jan. 1994. *Creating Modern Probability*. Cambridge: Cambridge University Press.

Wagner, Andreas. 2005. *Robustness and Evolvability in Living Systems*. Princeton, NJ: Princeton University Press.

Wenzel, Hanne Gro, Anita Øren, and Inger Johanne Bakken. 2008. "Gambling Problems in
    the Family—A Stratified Probability Sample Study of Prevalence and Reported
    Consequences." BMC Public Health 8(412). Available at http://www.biomedcentral.
    com/1471-2458/8/412, doi:10.1186/1471-2458-8-412.
Williamson, Jon. 2010. *In Defence of Objective Bayesianism*. Oxford: Oxford University
    Press.
Wimsatt, William C. 2007. *Re-Engineering Philosophy for Limited Beings: Piecewise Approxi-
    mations to Reality*. Cambridge, MA: Harvard University Press.
Wimsatt, William Upski. 1994. *Bomb the Suburbs*, 2d ed. New York: Subway and Elevated
    Press.

PART II

Evidence

CHAPTER 10

THE IMPACT OF DUHEMIAN PRINCIPLES ON SOCIAL SCIENCE TESTING AND PROGRESS

FRED CHERNOFF

INTRODUCTION

The goal of this chapter is to draw on several elements of Pierre Duhem's account of science to illuminate issues of the cumulation of knowledge and scientific progress in the social sciences. The chapter focuses on Duhem's principle of underdetermination of theory by evidence, his holist account of the growth of scientific knowledge, and his conventionalist view of theories.

Section 10.1 shows the value of a focus on Duhem and notes several assumptions the chapter makes. Section 10.2 outlines the debate over the underdetermination thesis and argues that there are Duhemian-style conventionalist limitations on (objective) knowledge in theoretically driven, empirical disciplines. Section 10.3 presents two case studies from the field of international politics, "democratic peace studies" and the "balance of power," that have exhibited very different levels of scientific progress in two of the major theoretical debates in the field—differences that may be explained by reference to the notion of measure-stipulation in Duhem's conventionalist account of science. Section 10.4 offers conclusions.

10.1. GOALS AND ASSUMPTIONS

Philosophers of science as diverse as Quine, Gillies, and Harding have described Duhem as one of the major thinkers of the twentieth century. Harding, for example, has said that Duhem's underdetermination thesis "may well take its place in the history of ideas as signaling a radical change in our understanding of the nature of both human knowledge and human knowers" (1976, xxi).[1] Duhem's major work, *The Aim and Structure of Physical Theory*, contains far-reaching principles that fundamentally challenged the orthodoxy of the nineteenth and early twentieth centuries and shaped key debates for decades to come. Even the transformative physical theory of Einstein was, at least in Karl Popper's view (1965), heavily influenced by Duhem's *Aim and Structure* (cf. Howard 1990). Debate was energized in the 1950s, first by Quine, who derived sweeping consequences from Duhem in his influential 1951 paper "Two Dogmas of Empiricism," and again by the English translation in 1954 of Duhem's *Aim and Structure*.

In view of the importance of Duhem in the philosophy of science and the tendency of philosophers of social science to draw on concepts and models of science developed by philosophers of natural science (either positively or negatively), it is astonishing that there are so few social science references to Duhem. Social science disciplines that make extensive use of hypothesis testing and have lively methodological debates—such as sociology, political science, and psychology—contain virtually no mention of Duhem whatsoever. Only in economics, which sees itself as especially close to the natural sciences, does one find any references to Duhem in methodology texts, and at least a minor debate in journals over Duhem's underdetermination thesis.[2] This lacuna is unfortunate, as many of Duhem's views of theoretical enquiry and scientific knowledge have important consequences for the social sciences.

Due to space limitations, this chapter assumes, rather than defends, several propositions. The assumptions are that some, but not all, questions and areas of enquiry in the social sciences may reasonably be modeled on the methods of the natural sciences; that the natural sciences constitute the best available example of a systematic, reliable, and useful body of empirical knowledge; and, building on the second, that, unless otherwise demonstrated, the social sciences are not exempt from limitations that affect the natural sciences (i.e., it is not reasonable to expect other areas of enquiry to transcend the limitations established on the natural sciences).[3]

10.2. Duhem's Principles of Underdetermination, Holism, and Conventionalism

10.2.1. Underdetermination

Standard approaches to research design in the social sciences build on the idea that when investigators seek to determine which of two or more competing hypotheses is true, they should create conditions, or find historical examples of such conditions, in which each hypothesis, if true, predicts a distinct outcome. This is akin to the so-called crucial experiment in the natural sciences. Duhem argued a century ago that such experiments are not truly crucial, since logical reasoning does not permit investigators to conclude in such cases that one hypothesis or theory is true and the others are false. Duhem provided two major paths to the conclusion that such a procedure is impossible: the theory we think we have proved true may be false because of fallibilism, and the rival theory we think we have proved false may be true because of holism.

Fallibilism

With respect to the first path, fallibilism, someone who affirms the possibility of crucial experiments might do so by claiming that the investigator can enumerate all of the possible explanations for an observed phenomenon, consider the conditions under which the different principles or the various explanations would predict distinct outcomes, create those conditions, and then observe the results. Such an experiment will reveal the truth of one explanatory theory to the exclusion of the others. Duhem denies the possibility of such a procedure by pointing out that, unlike in mathematics where it is typically possible to specify the features of all of the cases, in physical theory there will be an indefinitely large number of possible explanatory theories that are compatible with any finite set of available observations. It is always possible that some day someone will devise another explanatory theory that is consistent with all known observations, including the recent crucial experiment. This form of fallibilism has sometimes been labeled "contrastive" underdetermination.

Duhem adds that it is possible that future observations will conflict with the current theory, but those theories will be consistent with the future as-yet-unknown alternative. That is, whichever theory survives the current test may yet run afoul of future observations and prove to be inferior to some new theory. Duhem concluded that at any given time, the finite evidence scientists have available to them is not sufficient to determine with certainty which theory or hypothesis should be accepted as true.

Holism

The second path that led Duhem to reject crucial experiments starts from his holist view of scientific enquiry and theory-testing. Duhem maintains that the theory scientists presume to have refuted may not in fact be false: The appearance of falsifying evidence does not warrant conclusive rejection of a theory. The test of any theory or hypothesis requires acceptance of many auxiliary hypotheses, assumptions, and background beliefs—for example, regarding the accuracy of measuring instruments that allow the investigator to connect abstract theoretical principles. For this reason the only conclusion that scientists may validly infer from the inconsistent observation is that there is a falsehood somewhere in their corpus of accepted beliefs that include the background beliefs, auxiliary hypotheses, and so on.[4] The falsehoods in the conjunction may well be found among the background beliefs and/or auxiliary hypotheses. Duhem argued that an area of scientific theorizing constitutes an integrated, unified whole. It is thus impossible to treat a single hypothesis in isolation from the totality of principles, auxiliary hypotheses, assumptions, and background beliefs.

Duhem held that the relationship of evidence to hypothesis is a comparison "between the whole of the theory and the whole of the experimental facts" (1954, 208). Moreover, we can never be sure either that future observations will not conflict with our current theory or that an as-yet-unknown theory may come to light that explains all current observations as well as the new anomalies. When scientists believe they have refuted a theory, it is possible that further investigation will prove the theory to be correct and prove that the falsifying observation was a result of the acceptance of one or more faulty auxiliary hypotheses. This form of the thesis has been called "holist" underdetermination.

To cite an example, if one seeks to test Newton's law of gravity, it is necessary to accept all of Newton's laws of motion, since the law of gravity cannot be tested without assumptions about acceleration and so on which are derived from Newton's other laws of motion. A negative result of the test would not logically justify the conclusion that the law of gravity is false, since there is no way at that point to eliminate the possibility that the law of gravity is true and the falsehood lies elsewhere among Newton's laws of motion or among the auxiliary assumptions. All that would have been logically shown is that there is a false conjunct in the larger conjunction, but that false conjunct could be the law of gravity just as it could be any of the laws of motion, or any of the other auxiliary hypotheses, or an element of background beliefs about measuring instruments.

Consider Foucault's experiment concerning the nature of light—one of the most famous crucial experiments in the history of science. Supporters of the wave hypothesis had long battled supporters of the corpuscular hypothesis. The experiment was designed to show which group was right. Light, if it were composed of waves, would travel through water more slowly than through a vacuum and, if composed of particles, would travel more rapidly. The experiment was ultimately understood by proponents of both hypotheses as showing the superiority of the wave hypothesis. But Duhem argued that both sides were wrong insofar as they regarded the experiment as definitive in itself. The experiment required a chain of inferences from the observations to the conclusion, and that chain included a very substantial store of auxiliary hypotheses. Duhem concluded that the experiment was not decisive as regards the choice between the two hypotheses about the nature of light but rather forced a choice between two entire systems of optics. As Duhem puts it, "for it is not between two hypotheses, the emission and the wave hypotheses, that Foucault's experiment judges trenchantly; it decides rather between two sets of theories, either of which has to be taken as a whole, that is, between two entire systems, Newton's optics and Huygens's optics" (Duhem 1954,189).

Quine's Underdetermination Principle

Many authors use the term "Duhem-Quine thesis." However, the view of underdetermination that Duhem advanced is quite different from that of Quine, and the difference stems in part from the distinct kinds of holism each endorses.[5] As just noted, Duhem's holism entailed that experiments in physics "can never condemn an isolated hypothesis but only a whole theoretical group" (1954, 183). Scientific observation is capable of falsifying a finite group of propositions, which include theoretical laws, scientific hypotheses, auxiliary hypotheses, and background knowledge. What is subject to falsification is this entire conjunction of propositions.

Quine's version is holism on a still larger scale than Duhem's. The difference between the two forms of the doctrine gives rise to what Lakatos calls a "strong" and a "weak" form of the underdetermination thesis. As Lakatos puts it, the weak interpretation of underdetermination, which he claims Duhem holds, "only asserts the impossibility of a direct experimental hit on a narrowly specified theoretical target and the logical possibility of shaping science in indefinitely many different ways" (Lakatos 1978, 96–97). The strong interpretation, which he attributes to Quine, "excludes the possibility of any *rational* selection rule among the alternatives" (1978, 97; emphasis in original). Duhem holds that falsification shows an error in a whole theoretical group, something like what Kuhn later called a paradigm. Quine's holism, in contrast, is epistemically global; what is subject to empirical falsification is one's entire corpus of beliefs. For Quine, the unit of significance is not a single statement but rather "the whole of science" (1951, 39).

While Duhem believed that an anomalous result requires revision somewhere in the concatenation of hypothesis, theory, auxiliary hypotheses, and background beliefs, for Quine, the revision may be anywhere in the set of accepted beliefs. According to Quine, "any statement can be held true, come what may, if we make drastic enough revisions elsewhere in the system [of accepted scientific beliefs] . . . Conversely, no statement is immune to revision" (1951, 40). As a result, Quine's version of underdetermination (which is sometimes referred to as "radical underdetermination") permits adjustments to be made anywhere in the corpus of accepted beliefs, including the recalcitrant observation itself, or the laws of logic. The latter is possible, since Quine uses this argument to reject the idea that analytic statements are exempt from revision. Despite his rejection of the analytic/synthetic distinction, Quine's position, especially his extreme form of holism, is incompatible with falsificationism. As he famously said, "our statements about the external world face the tribunal of sense experience not individually but only as a corporate body" (1951, 38). So there is no basis for optimism that experiments can show that some specific theory or hypothesis can be falsified.

There is an extensive philosophical debate on the Duhem thesis, which is only touched upon here. There have been vigorous critiques and intense scrutiny of Duhem's philosophical position because the implications of his work undercut so many widely held views. Indeed, Duhem's principles (underdetermination, holism, and conventionalism) appear to jeopardize the whole classical inductivist view of science, familiar from the works of Bacon, Newton, Mill, and Whewell and Popper's twentieth-century deductivist-falsificationism. Although inductivism was already under assault prior to the publication of *Aim and Structure* in 1905, many have regarded Duhem's arguments as a decisive blow.[6]

Some of the more prominent attacks on Duhem's position have come from Popper (1959, 1965), Lakatos (1978), and Grünbaum (1960, 1966). Debate continues today in the philosophy of science over the implications of the underdetermination thesis for scientific progress and method. Lakatos (1978, 21–22) sees Duhem and Popper as reacting to the same set of problems posed by the physicist Henri Poincaré (1952)—problems that could lead to a view that permits the ossification of scientific theory. On this view, scientists see theories that have stood the test of time as decreasingly subject to refutation. He says, "as science grows, the power of empirical evidence diminishes" (Lakatos 1978, 21). Lakatos regards the positions of both Duhem and Popper as forms of "revolutionary conventionalism"; Duhem's version was "methodological justificationism," while Popper's was "methodological falsificationism" (Lakatos 1978, 22). Popper was of course concerned about the implications for the certainty and solidity of scientific knowledge posed by Hume's critique of induction. This concern led Popper to his deductivist account of scientific knowledge, according to which scientists make bold conjectures and subject those conjectures to vigorous falsification tests. If it is not possible to apply modus tollens inference from recalcitrant observations to the rejection of scientific hypotheses or theories, then Popper's method of conjectures and refutations becomes suspect.

With regard to deductivist-falsification, Popper argues that any theory T has various observable consequences, such as $O_1, O_2 \ldots O_n$, such that $T \to O_1, O_2 \ldots O_n$. If an experiment contradicts any of the consequences, for example, if an experiment yields the observation $\sim O_i$, by modus tollens we may reject T. [That is, $(T \to O_i); \sim O_i, \therefore \sim T$.] Duhem argued that this is not the case. Background beliefs and auxiliary hypotheses are necessary to derive any of the consequences $O_1 \ldots O_n$ from T, where T is the sort of theory physicists develop. Thus, Duhem concluded that the experimental result $\sim O_i$ falsifies not the theory T, but the conjunction $(T \& B_1 \ldots B_n \& A_1 \ldots A_n)$. The single falsifying observation does not, in fact, lead scientists to abandon their theories; rather, scientists abandon theories as they encounter more and more anomalies which, over time, render the theory increasingly vulnerable.[7]

Recent Debate

Because of its profound consequence for scientific methodology, the debate over the Duhem thesis has continued up to the present. Many have questioned the success of the various attempts, including Popper's, to save science from underdetermination. Van Fraassen (1980), for example, offers several arguments, one of which outlines an algorithm that, given theory T, will generate other theories, such as T_1, T_2, T_i, all of which are "empirically adequate," that is, are such that all available observations will be the same for T and T_i. Earman (1993) also argues that some form of underdetermination is unavoidable, which he uses to highlight problems of inductive inference needed to support theoretical conclusions.

Other authors, however, continue to seek ways to combat, or at least limit, the effects of the underdetermination thesis. For example, Laudan (1990) presents a major effort in limiting the effects of underdetermination by arguing that supporters of the thesis have overreached. He distinguishes a range of possible underdetermination claims and argues various philosophers have defended some of the more minimal (and defensible) forms but have drawn conclusions for science as if they had shown the stronger and more sweeping forms. Laudan's argument is an important one, and has force against some of the skeptical sociological and feminist accounts of science according to which science is fundamentally beyond logical and rational theory choice and is driven ultimately by political relationships of power. But Laudan's argument has less effect against more moderated underdetermination views like Duhem's, which do not assert that theory choice is devoid of a rational basis. Laudan and Leplin (1991) try to limit the implications of underdetermination by arguing that we cannot really know if two apparently empirically equivalent theories will remain so, as future evidence against which to test them accumulates. Kitcher (1993) tries to limit the effects of underdetermination on scientific practice by arguing that unless we are aware of the empirically equivalent alternative theories, there is no reason to resist accepting the one available theory supported by the evidence.

Sklar (1975, 1981) seeks a way to save theory choice from underdetermination by means of the idea of "transient" underdetermination, according to which rival theories to our accepted theory will keep changing over time as new evidence mounts. But if it is the case that there will always be such alternatives, then the practical problem of theory choice for scientists is essentially the same as with the more global form of underdetermination. Stanford (2003) argues that as long as there is a continual process of transient underdetermination—and he argues on inductive grounds that there will be—then the effect on the practice of scientific theory choice is essentially the same. More recently Magnus (2005a, 2005b) offers an attack on the underdetermination thesis by developing a concept of "total science."

The fact that the main journals in the philosophy of science currently publish works directly focused on the Duhem underdetermination thesis is a strong indication that there has thus far been no widely accepted satisfactory response.

10.2.2. Conventionalism

The conventionalism of Poincaré, Duhem, and their followers was stimulated by problems in the philosophy of geometry. Geometers in the nineteenth century repeatedly attempted, and failed, to use Euclid's axioms to derive the parallel postulate. The failures eventually led geometers to recognize the independence of the parallel postulate, which opened the way to the non-Euclidean geometries of Bolyai, Lobachevsky, and Reimann. Euclidean geometry had been accepted for 2,200 years as the true geometry of space, and its truth was regarded as beyond doubt—especially in light of the apparent reconfirmation in the seventeenth century by the astonishing success of Euclidean-based Newtonian mechanics. Philosophers and mathematicians gained even greater confidence in Euclid in the eighteenth century, when Kant presented his highly influential argument conferring synthetic a priori status on Euclid's principles.

Poincaré regarded the relationship between various competing sets of physical laws as comparable to the relationship between different sets of geometric axioms—analytically and definitionally true and incapable of being falsified by experience. He said that Newton's "principles of dynamics appeared to us first as experimental truths but we have been compelled to use them as definitions" (1952, 104). Experiments "will never invalidate" the principles of mechanics (1952, 105). He also declared that "principles are conventions and definitions in disguise. They are, however, deduced from experimental laws, and these laws have, so to speak, been erected into principles to which our mind attributes an absolute value" (1952, 138).

Poincaré offered an intriguing parable, though he and Duhem drew different conclusions from it. Poincaré imagines that we travel to a distant, spherical universe in which objects are apparently subject to forces that systematically shrink (or expand) them as they are moved away from the center of the universe. In this universe there is an aether of variable index of refraction affecting the visual appearance of the objects as they move through it, to resemble the way they would appear if space were curvilinear. Physicists who have observed and measured objects might then ask, "Do the objects change length because of the forces exerted on them, or is space curved?" An investigator might take a rigid measuring rod to check whether the objects change size as they are moved. But if there are such forces, then they will also act to shrink or expand the measuring rod. Of course, it will do no good to get a second measuring rod to check the first. Poincaré argued that there is no way to prove whether the objects change size when moved or, alternatively, whether space is curvilinear. Poincaré said that the Euclidean physicist traveling there from our world would likely conclude that space is Euclidean and that there are forces acting on the objects. However, a physicist from that world would be more likely to infer that space is curvilinear and that there are no such postulated forces. Since there is in principle no way to answer the question of the true geometry of space on purely logical grounds, physicists resolve the matter by resorting to an arbitrary convention. Physicists will have to accept—by convention—one of the two extra-theoretical "measure-stipulations," namely, that the measuring rod is rigid (and space is curvilinear), or that the objects and measuring rods are subject to forces that change their length as they are moved (and space is Euclidean).

Duhem agreed with Poincaré that there is no purely logical and objective way to choose the measure-stipulation; different scientific communities may draw different conclusions about physical theory. But Duhem differed from Poincaré on several fundamental points. First, Poincaré held that physical laws are chosen in isolation from a system of geometry while Duhem saw them as *parts of a unified system* that have to be compared to other whole systems. Second, Poincaré held that the choice of a measure-stipulation is both conventional and arbitrary, while Duhem argued that the choice is conventional but held that there are nonarbitrary, rational grounds for the conventions and, consequently, that there are rational grounds for theory choice. Third, Poincaré held that scientific laws are analytically true within the definitional framework of the theory in which they are embedded, and thus are immune to falsification, while Duhem held that laws, or at least the larger theoretical structures of which they are a part (see note 12), are *falsifiable*. And fourth, Duhem held that a form of *scientific good sense* affects scientific theory choice.

With regard to the first difference, Duhem did not think that the choice of a set of physical laws and its geometric axiom system could be made in isolation from one another. Physical scientists must approach the subject matter holistically, which means the criteria of theory choice are applied holistically to the entire set of physical principles and geometric axioms. With regard to their views of geometry, Poincaré added that Euclidean geometry will always be preferred because of its advantage of simplicity. Duhem agreed that scientists will accept the simpler theory, but as a holist he argued that greater simplicity would have to be judged by the entire system of physical laws plus geometric axioms, and so on. Thus Duhem left open the possibility that scientists might accept a non-Euclidean world.[8]

With regard to the second difference, Poincaré held that the decision of which measure-stipulations to accept was arbitrary. Duhem disagreed and argued that one's choice of which geometric or which physical theory to accept is not based merely on convenience. The choice is subject to debate and is the product of reasoned conclusions. And even though these conclusions do not follow strictly from observation and the application of formal logic, there are rational, philosophical arguments that support a preference for theories that are simpler or have more utility than their rivals. Such grounds for choice do not follow purely deductively, yet they are far from arbitrary. On the third point, Duhem denies Poincaré's claim that general physical principles cannot be shown to be false. Duhem maintained that falsifying evidence is always a possibility. It must be remembered, though, because of Duhem's holism, that when falsifying evidence arises, what is falsified is the holistic conjunction of hypothesis, theory, background assumptions, and methodology. Nevertheless, for Duhem theoretical principles are not analytically true; hence empirical observation can affect theory.

Finally, Duhem held that good sense is an ingredient in scientific theory choice. Duhem's holism led him to argue, as noted above, that when a theoretical hypothesis appears to be disproved, what has been falsified is only the larger conjunction. Since theories and theoretically based hypotheses cannot be tested without reliance on a range of background assumptions and beliefs and auxiliary testing hypotheses, one may ask: How do we decide whether the fault resides with the test hypothesis, one of the auxiliary hypotheses, one of the substantive background beliefs, or some other proposition? Duhem held that there is no logical or formal method capable of producing certainty. Nevertheless, for Duhem, conventionalism does not entail that the choice of which set of laws to accept is ultimately arbitrary. Guidance about which set to accept is possible, and the choice involves recourse to *le bon sens* of the scientific community. While falsifying observations may allow scientists to adjust auxiliary hypotheses in ways that allow them to save the theory, it is not scientifically (as opposed to logically) possible to do so indefinitely.[9] Duhem maintains that when the negative tests pile up, good scientific practice will compel scientists eventually to reject the test hypothesis and the theoretical system from which it derives. That is, enough counterevidence will bring down the system "under the weight of the contradictions inflicted by reality on the consequences of this system taken as a whole" (1954, 216). In the controversy over the nature of light, the corpuscular school could have continued to alter auxiliary hypotheses and patch up the underlying theory indefinitely. But the good sense of the scientific community prevented that. Thus while science is, in an important sense, conventional for Duhem, the grounds for theory choice are not arbitrary.[10] Since science is not arbitrary, it is necessary to find clear, rationally based criteria of theory choice.[11]

The philosophical resort to scientific *le bon sens* may strike many philosophers of science as imputing to science an unjustifiable and fundamental subjectivity, which reduces the epistemic value of the enterprise of science. However, it can be argued that Duhem's conventionalism does not introduce anything that weakens standard views of science but is rather consistent with what most philosophers of science recognize in one form or another. Consider the debate over the question of how theories are chosen. Duhem's underdetermination thesis assures us that there will always be more than one possible "empirically adequate" theory. Whether one is an instrumentalist or a scientific realist, and so on, one must choose among the available theories. There are many more or less universally agreed-upon criteria of theory choice (internal consistency, parsimony, etc.) and others that are widely but less universally accepted (falsifiability, methodological conservatism, and so on).

The criteria of theory choice will often come into conflict with one another, as one empirically adequate theory may be simpler, but another may account for a greater range of phenomena. With this in mind, we note that science has over the centuries scored many successes (however one chooses to define that term), during which time the philosophical and scientific merits of different criteria have been debated. Science has managed as well as it has thus far by a process of reasoned, rational debate—very often leading to agreement—on questions of when one particular criterion should dominate another criterion and when not. These questions cannot be decided on purely logical grounds (or else debate would long since have ended), but are subject to rational judgment. Duhem's appeal to *le bon sens* does not introduce any damaging subjectivity into an account of science beyond what most philosophers of science recognize. This is clear given that by the very fact they are philosophers of science, they regard as legitimate philosophical (nonlogical) debate over methodological rules of scientific theory choice. Such a notion or something similar would seem to be already present once we begin to think about actual theory choices made by scientists—even by those who otherwise have no affinity for conventionalism.

10.3. Implications for the Social Sciences: Conventional Measure-Stipulation and the Explanation of Social Science Progress

How far can the preceding account of natural science be extended into the social sciences? Although this Handbook (see Kincaid, in the introduction to this volume) and this chapter (see section 10.1) both assume it is reasonable to accept some form of naturalism (i.e., a strong but not absolute parallel between the natural and social sciences), there is still the question of how applicable Duhem's particular view of science—underdetermination, fallibilism, holism, and conventionalism—may be applied to the social sciences.[12]

10.3.1. Conventionalism, Scientific Progress, and the Democratic Peace Debate

Many social science domains have been justly criticized for failing to demonstrate progress over the decades. The lack of progress in so many areas prompts the question whether the social sciences, especially those other than economics, are inherently incapable of progress. An answer could come from the discovery of areas of bone fide scientific progress. Political science offers one likely candidate in the debate over whether democracies are somehow more peaceful than nondemocracies. Progress in this debate can be understood by considering Duhem's account of science.

The claim that democratic states are different in their external behavior is usually traced back to Kant's 1795 essay "Perpetual Peace." Kant argued that tyrannical states are more likely to enter into wars because leaders' potential gains of victory are not checked by the costs of defeat, since those costs, in terms of taxes and lives surrendered, are directly borne by other individuals. Nearly two centuries later several authors published works briefly dealing with this question (Babst 1964, 1972; Small and Singer 1976; and, more extensively, Rummel 1979). The debate began to take center stage in international relations (IR) in the 1980s, especially after the publication of Michael Doyle's works in *Philosophy and Public Affairs* (1983a, 1983b) and the *American Political Science Review* (1986). Soon there were quantitative tests of several hypotheses. The two principle hypotheses under consideration came to be known as the *monadic hypothesis*, which asserts that democracies are less war-prone than nondemocracies, and the *dyadic hypothesis*, which asserts that democracies fight wars against other democracies (democracy versus democracy) less frequently than any other sorts of dyads or pairs of states (e.g., democracy versus nondemocracy or nondemocracy versus nondemocracy).

The democratic peace (DP) debate had vast implications for both foreign policy and IR theory. The policy implications were significant because, in the late 1980s and early 1990s, the Cold War was ending and the world saw the rise of many new states (as the USSR, Yugoslavia, and Czechoslovakia splintered) and new regimes (as existing states abruptly discarded Soviet-imposed socialism). Western states, inclined to support liberal democracies on grounds of trade, would have an incentive to invest even more heavily in promoting democracy, if they believed that doing so would also help to create a peaceful international system.

For academic political science, the consequences of the DP debate cannot be overstated: The results could radically undercut one of the two main theoretical traditions in IR, liberalism or political realism, in their long-running debate. Liberals believe that individuals, international organizations, and ideology can make a difference in how states behave not only internally but also externally; they can affect levels of cooperation and, ultimately, war and peace. In their view the proper sorts of states could create a better and more peaceful world. Thus liberals initially believed both the monadic and dyadic hypotheses.

Political realists, in contrast, hold that history is a series of cycles of war and peace; major powers compete for hegemony in a system permanently without any hierarchy of legitimate authority. Members of this theoretical school, who have dominated academic debate for centuries, maintain that states are the most important international actors, far more so than international organizations, nongovernmental organizations, individual personalities, religions, ideological groups, and so on. They believe that all states—regardless of domestic political system—seek power and pursue rational policies to secure territory and influence in the ways that appear most effective given available information. Since all states pursue power, sooner or later violent conflict will erupt. External policies will have to take into account power structures: States must adapt to the existing international power structure (since systems of two great powers have different characteristics than systems of three or more great powers), and to their position in that power structure (e.g., Napoleon had more options in 1800 than a leader such as Francis II of Bohemia had at that time). Since political realists say that the type of political regime governing the domestic affairs of a state makes no difference for its foreign policy, they deny both the monadic and dyadic hypotheses. Clearly a resolution of the DP debate would greatly impact the core debate in IR between liberals and realists.

Five years after Doyle's initial DP publications, Jack Levy endorsed the dyadic hypothesis, with an oft-quoted comment: "Absence of war between democracies comes as close as anything we have to an empirical law of international relations" (1988, 662; cf. also Levy 1989, 209). Soon thereafter Bruce Russett's first volume on the subject appeared, *Controlling the Sword: The Democratic Governance of National Security* (1990), followed by his *Grasping the Democratic Peace* (1993). Bold claims like Levy's and statistical supporting arguments like Russett's brought out legions of critics. The result was a flood of scholarship on the question, with many of the most methodologically sophisticated realists and liberals entering the fray. Realists launched vigorous attacks on the research designs, statistical techniques, and data choices that liberals used to support DP claims. Many of the supporters of DP claims followed with detailed replies to these criticisms.

One of the most widely cited articles in the field is Maoz and Russett's (1993) *American Political Science Review* paper, which treated the behavioral claims of the monadic and dyadic hypotheses as already settled—negatively for the monadic and positively for the dyadic. These seemingly paradoxical results called for more complex explanations; why are democracies peaceful toward one another but not overall? Maoz and Russett described and tested two prominent explanatory models, one based on democratic norms and the other based on distinctively democratic decision-making structures, which could handle both the affirmation of the dyadic hypothesis and negation of the monadic hypothesis.

There were many challenges to DP claims through the 1990s. To mention a few of the most prominent ones, Layne (1994) argued that in near-miss cases (where two democracies came close to going to war with one another but did not), documents and process-tracing arguments show that the reasons war did not occur had nothing to do with democratic norms or decision-making structures. Spiro (1994) argued that Russett used a flawed method for counting cases or data points, which overstated the number of democracies living peacefully together and which in turn overstated the statistical significance of the dyadic hypothesis tests. And Farber and Gowa (1995, 1997) argued that so many of the world's democracies came about after World War II that statistical tests cannot parse out the effects of the bipolar structure of the Cold War political system. Criticisms of DP claims focusing on substance and conceptualization were offered by Kegley and Hermann (1995, 1997) and Oren (1995); criticisms focusing on research design and statistical testing were presented by Beck, Katz, and Tucker (1998) and Gartzke (1998), Green, Kim, and Yoon (2001), and Henderson (2002); and criticisms focusing on the direction of causality were presented by Midlarsky (1995) and Thompson (1996).[13]

Skeptics doubt political science's status as a science and its capacity to achieve scientific progress; they believe that in the social sciences it is always possible to hold onto one's theory because each opposing school of thought tends to argue past the other without engaging its key claims and evidence. Such skeptics expect that neither side will ever gain ground on the other because so many political scientists on both sides have so much to lose if proved wrong. But this is not what happened. Instead, defenders of the dyadic hypothesis (especially Russett and his coauthors, principally John Oneal) took opponents' arguments seriously; they reran tests using more complete data and restructured research designs to take into account the critical arguments. Both sides accepted the same methodology, the same statistical norms of inference, and, significantly, the same measure-stipulation.

While there are numerous examples of how the critics' objections were incorporated into new rounds of analysis by DP proponents, two should give a flavor for the nature of the dialogue. Farber and Gowa (1995, 1997), as noted above, argued that because so many of history's democracies came about only after World War II, tests using all democracies would be skewed toward that brief and unique period. They claimed that statistical tests (e.g., by Russett 1993, Maoz and Russett 1993, and others) are unable to discriminate the effects of democracy from the effects of the Cold War alliances, bipolarity, and other properties of the 1945–1990 international system. Oneal and Russett re-designed their study to separate the pre-1945 period from the post-1945 period and compared the results. They found that new tests "reveal no statistically significant differences between the pacific benefits of democracy and interdependence before and after World War II" (Oneal and Russett 2001, 476; see also Oneal and Russett 1999). Second, Mansfield and Snyder (1995) have argued that new democracies are more war-prone than other sorts of regime types. This is not only a denial of the monadic hypothesis but something of a reversal of it. They claim that their finding, while inconsistent with the monadic hypothesis, is consistent with the dyadic hypothesis. Maoz (1998) criticized Mansfield and Snyder by arguing that they did not consider the various possible causes of war and that they studied time periods too lengthy to permit inferences about causal effects from start to finish. Rather than responding by attempting to discount or attack Maoz's objections, in a later paper Mansfield and Snyder (2002) instead acknowledged the force of the criticisms and carried out new analyses with a "refined research design" (2002, 298) which showed similar effects for transitional democracies.[14]

Key Variables and the Measure-Stipulation

The DP debate in some ways came about at a propitious time in the development of academic IR, since the field had recently come to accept numerous measure-stipulation conventions thanks to the ambitious, long-range correlates of war (COW) project (Singer and Small 1972). The COW project, begun in the 1960s, sought to identify scores of variables that IR scholars employed in order to determine how to define and measure those variables. The project then oversaw the coding of those variables for all cases over a period of centuries. This of course included a definition for and measure of war, the dependent variable of DP studies. Because this well-known database had been developing for over twenty years and was an accepted part of the background against which IR debates were prosecuted by the 1980s, it was difficult for scholars to define or code variables in biased and self-serving ways that would best support their preferred statistical conclusions.

Prior to the COW project scholars had debated how to define peace. Different definitions were based on ideas such as long-term stability, the absence of both violence and threats of violence, and so on. The COW founders chose to define peace in the most directly observable (and least subjective) fashion, namely, as the absence of war, and defined war in terms of the number of battle deaths in inter-state conflict. The threshold they chose was 1,000 battle deaths. This is a convention, but not a purely arbitrary one. For example, one would not regard a violent interaction between states that resulted in ten deaths as what we mean by war. On the other hand, no one would doubt that a violent interaction between states that resulted in 100,000 deaths as a war; however, that number is not a reasonable minimum, since a violent dispute with a tenth as many deaths would obviously fit our concept of war. The question Small and Singer faced is, where should the cutoff point be set? The number they chose, 1,000, is arbitrary to a degree, since one could make as good an argument for placing the cutoff point at 900 or 1,100. But it is not entirely arbitrary in that a cutoff of ten or 100,000, and so on, can be reasonably eliminated as candidates. The norm of using the COW measure of war was significantly reinforced by the fact that the first data-based study of DP was by Small and Singer (1976), two of the founders of the COW.

With regard to the variable called democracy, we note that there has been a wide array of definitions. Throughout history there have been many different kinds of regimes and with many sorts of characteristics. Thus in developing a notion of democracy for DP studies one would presumably focus on what aspects of liberal democratic states, if any, could plausibly be thought to generate an impetus for peace.[15] Is it a separation of powers, accountability of the government to voters, broad franchise, protection of the rights of minorities, and so on? As Owen (1994) notes, some states are liberal but not democratic (Britain before 1832), whereas others are democratic but not liberal (the Confederate States of America). And, as with the dependent variable, DP researchers must decide if they require a quantitative or qualitative measure.[16] Statistical results will differ depending on what particular regime characteristics are chosen to test against war.

Depending on the specific question posed by a study, there may be good reasons to use a different indicator—for example, to study only great power wars or conflict in which there is an exchange of threats but no violence. In such cases different indicators will be used. But a norm has developed in IR according to which authors who choose measures and coding other than those of COW (Singer 1972), Polity (Eckstein and Gurr 1975), or Freedom House (Freedom House 1973) bear the burden of providing good reasons for their alternatives. Without some compelling reason, scholars are expected to make use of these standard databases.

There was somewhat more difficulty in developing a measure-stipulation for the independent variable democracy. Still, the timing was fortunate. Different DP studies have indeed used different measures. When Small and Singer published their early critique of the DP hypotheses, they said, "There is no generally accepted typology of national regimes or governmental types" (1976, 53). But just at that time the first publications of two databases defining "democracy" appeared, which, in the years since, have come to be widely used. Like the COW database, both the Polity and Freedom House databases were developed for purposes other than testing DP hypotheses, which added to the legitimacy of their definitions and measures. The Polity database, now in its fourth iteration, is more complex, as it conceptualizes (and measures) democracy and autocracy as distinct dimensions, not simply as opposites.

Progress and the Current Debate

There is a good deal of continuing DP debate, primarily in the form of attempts to derive corollaries and draw further implications from the two core hypotheses. Those two claims have generally held sway among political scientists for twenty years, though works occasionally appear that question them. One can identify the current near-consensus by noting that most of the authors who initially disagreed with these two results no longer publish on the subject, and a few have even explicitly acknowledged that they were wrong. On balance it has been a victory for liberal IR theory, since acceptance of the dyadic hypothesis shows that a core tenet of realism is mistaken, namely that domestic politics, ideology, norms, and/or regime type do make a difference in foreign policy behavior.

The ongoing DP debate is now focused primarily on claims other than the monadic and dyadic hypotheses. A range of corollaries and extensions of the basic hypotheses have been advanced. Russett and Oneal (2001) have taken Kant's view that peace arises in a system that has democratic states, free trade, and properly formed international organizations to formulate what they call a "Kantian tripod" theory of international cooperation and peace. Others have looked at how democracy and peace relate to territorial disputes (Huth and Allee 2003), interventions and extra-systemic wars (Kegley and Hermann 1997; Hermann and Kegley 2001), war initiation (Small and Singer 1976; Reiter and Stam 1998, 2002), geography (Gleditsch 1995; Gleditsch and Ward 1997), crisis escalation (Hewitt and Wilkenfeld 1996; Senese 1997), and third party mediation (Dixon 1993; Raymond 1994). These claims form part of what Lakatos (1978) calls the auxiliary hypotheses of a research program (see also Ray 2003). A wide range of these propositions are combined by Bueno de Mesquita et al. (1997). And there remains a search for better explanations for the combination of the dyadic hypothesis and the negation of the monadic hypotheses.

The Duhemian Measure-Stipulation

The Duhemian measure-stipulation convention helps explain both how so many authors managed to argue at cross-purposes for many years and how they were, at a particular point, able to begin to move toward agreement on the two core hypotheses. A Duhemian would expect progress to occur when a common measure-stipulation is chosen in the discipline. And this is what happened in the DP debate, as most authors on both sides of the theoretical divide accepted the same conventional measure-stipulations for peace and democracy. The conventionalist account suggests that DP research has been able to exhibit cumulation and approach-to-consensus in a way that approximates what one finds in the natural sciences. But not all social science debates have followed this trajectory.

10.3.2. Balance of Power and Its Critics

One of the few areas in which authors have claimed to have found a law of international relations, other than democratic peace, is the balance of power. While there are many variations on the balancing notion, the core claim attached to this law can be summarized in the principle

> BP *states act in such a way so as to prevent any other state from becoming powerful enough to attain the status of hegemon and as such become capable of dominating the system.*

Proponents of BP infer from this principle the following three propositions:

BPa) *that balanced systems are more stable than unbalanced,*
BPb) *that systems are usually balanced, i.e., hegemons rarely arise,* and
BPc) *that states (as long as they cannot be a hegemon) prefer balanced, nonhegemonic systems.*[17]

The phrase "balance of power" has been used for centuries and has acquired many meanings. Some authors use the term to mean that in any system there will be an automatic mechanism that leads states to act in ways that produces balances, whether they intend balances or not, and some use the term to mean that in any system there will be one particular state that plays the role of balancer. Both are compatible with BP. Some authors use the term in very different ways, for example, to refer to a normative guide for foreign policymaking, namely, that states should balance because balances are stable, and some use it normatively to mean much the opposite, namely, that states should not choose alliance partners based on balancing because major decisions should be based on what is right rather than on amoral balance of power calculations.

The automatic mechanism notion of balancing is common among structural realist supporters of BP. The picture resembles that of supply and demand in classical economics, where the so-called invisible hand of the market is cited to evoke this particular self-regulation concept. No individual unit need consciously seek a balance. But as each agent acts to maximize profitability, balances emerge. Similarly, with the balance of international political power, each state seeks to maximize power by trying to minimize the relative advantages of a rising hegemon. Blunting those advantages leads each state to form coalitions to limit the potential hegemon's range of action and ability to threaten.

Some scholars have argued that the plethora of uses of balance of power has robbed the term of meaning. Haas laments that in the academic world the term suffers from "philological, semantic, and theoretical confusion." Cobden has called the term an "undescribed, indescribable, incomprehensible nothing." Holsti says there are so many theories of the balance of power that the term "ends up essentially meaningless."[18]

But a dismissal of balancing theories on the grounds of their number would be unjustified, since some specific examples might individually be defensible. A fair assessment requires a look at one or more specific principles. The following discussion examines the most widely held such principle, namely BP and the most prominent supporters. Because it is less problematic to identify divergence in measures than it is to show convergence, if there is divergence and an absence of a conventional measure-stipulation, a brief survey of major theorists suffices.

The long-standing opposition to the law of balancing has recently received prima facie support in view of post–Cold War developments. With the demise of the Soviet Union in 1991, the United States became a system-wide hegemon. Yet it has not been opposed by any formal, counterbalancing alliance. Some authors have sought to defend BP from this counterexample by arguing that balancing is indeed inevitable but simply has not begun yet, while some have introduced a notion of "soft balancing" (informal coalition formation) to salvage BP (Paul 2005, 3).[19]

In recent decades four families of theory have arisen that reject balancing by opposing some or all of BP's implications (BPa, BPb, and BPc). They are theories of hegemonic stability, bandwagoning/buck-passing, power transition, and long cycles. Hegemonic stability theory rejects both BPa and BPb by arguing that systems are most stable when there is a hegemonic power able to create stable regimes (see Kindleberger 1973, Krasner 1976, and Keohane 1984). They reject BPc by claiming that international systems often have hegemonic leaders. Bandwagoning/buck-passing theories argue that states sometimes balance but often do not. Sometimes they bandwagon—that is, form coalitions with the hegemon—reasoning that it is better to be on the side with the rising power than against it. For example, Mussolini joined with Germany, continental Europe's most powerful state. Bandwagoning implies that states do not always prefer to avoid hegemony (thus rejecting BPc). And sometimes states buck-pass, that is, do nothing to oppose a rising hegemon, hoping that others who see the same threat will be forced to act (and incur attendant costs). Britain is interpreted as having done this in the 1930s, believing that France would have to confront the threat of rising German power (Schweller 1994).

Power transition theories hold that systems are most stable under hegemony and least stable when a balance is nearing equality, that is, when a second-rank state increases its power to the point that it approaches the power of the hegemon. Great power war is most likely in such periods (see Organski 1958; Organski and Kugler 1980; Gilpin 1981). Power transition theories also reject BPc, claiming that systems have hegemonic leaders most of the time. Long cycle theories hold that systems are usually dominated by a hegemon, whose military force allows it to control the international economy (Modelski 1978; Thompson 1986; Rasler and Thompson 1983). Because of space limitations, the discussion will focus on power transition and long cycle theories. But an analysis of the other two bodies of theory would reveal the same result.

The Concept of Power and the Measure-Stipulation

The discussion above of democratic peace showed how critics attacked the arguments of supporters and how supporters took those criticisms into account and built upon them in revising and extending their research designs. The process yielded a substantial degree of consensus and progress stemming from conventional agreement on both sides about the measure-stipulations for democracy and peace.

Although the balance of power debate has been going on for much longer, it has not shown any comparable progress. With the democratic peace experience in mind, it would seem worthwhile to look for measure-stipulations in connection with the central concepts of principle BP, especially power, preponderant power or hegemony, and stability. Again, because of space limitations, this chapter will look only at power and hegemony.[20]

Balance of Power Measures of Power and Hegemony

Even the balance of power supporters do not entirely agree on measures of key terms like power and hegemony. But they do overlap substantially on some points. One is that balance of power realists all see power in IR as a single, unified thing. In contrast, many liberals hold that power has different dimensions; in other words, a state may have power only within specified issue-areas. Japan is powerful in the trade issue-area, Saudi Arabia is powerful in the international energy issue-area, but in international politico-military relations neither is a major player alongside the United States, Russia, and China. Each issue-area has its own distribution of power. But realists, whether or not they endorse balance of power theory, hold that power in international relations is one thing that is fungible across different issue-areas (Keohane and Nye 1977). Secondly, balance of power theorists all focus on "hard power," which is the ability to influence by coercion and is constituted by military, political, and economic components. This contrasts with a state's "soft power," the ability to influence by attractive forces rather than coercive forces (Nye 1990). Balance of power theorists claim that this coercive capability can be applied in any issue-area.

If there is any agreement on a conventional measure-stipulation, the terms "power" and "preponderant power" or "hegemony" would be the key terms. Let us then consider the definitions of the leading balance of power realists, Morgenthau, Claude, Waltz, and Mearsheimer. Morgenthau defines power as control over others, and state power as one state's control over others: "Power may comprise anything that establishes and maintains the control of man over man. Thus power covers all social relationships which serve that end, from physical violence to the most subtle psychological ties by which one mind controls another" (1954, 8). Morgenthau here includes both brute material force and psychological methods of control as elements of political power.

Claude's definition of state power emphasizes a state's ability to coerce others to comply with its wishes. He says, "I use the term power to denote what is essentially military capability—the elements which contribute directly or indirectly to the capacity to coerce, kill, and destroy" (1962, 6). He concurs with recent BP supporters by thus excluding the psychological element of Morgenthau's definition. Claude adds that "the capacity to do physical violence is the central factor in this study" (1962, 6).

Waltz not only offers a different definition, he specifically observes that "power does not bring control" (1979, 192–93). Waltz famously ranks the leading powers based on a very materialistic measure of capabilities. There are at most a few states that count as great powers—that is, as achieving top rank status. For any state, its "rank depends on how they score on all of the following items: size of population and territory, resource endowment, economic capability, military strength, political stability and competence" (1979, 131). The power of a state is measured by its score on this list.

Mearsheimer defines power very much in the mold of Waltz. He says that "the balance of power is largely synonymous with the balance of military power. I define power largely in military terms because offensive realism emphasizes that force is the *ultima ratio* of international politics" (2001, 56). He adds, "military power is based largely on the size and strength of a state's army and its supporting air and naval forces. Even in a nuclear world, armies are the core ingredient of military power" (2001, 56). According to Mearsheimer's use of the term, "a hegemon is a state that is so powerful that it dominates all the other states in the system. No other state has the military wherewithal to put up a fight against it. In essence, a hegemon is the only great power in the system" (2001, 40).

Thus far we see major differences between the ways power is defined and measured by the most influential balance of power supporters. Morgenthau defines power as control, including psychological control, while Claude emphasizes military forces. Waltz refers to material capabilities broadly and avoids using the term "control" as part of the definition. He goes so far as to say that control is not even a consequence of power. So we cannot expect these theorists to agree on preponderance or hegemony. We will see further differences with the opponents of balancing.

Power Transition and Long Cycles

Two related views reject BP, and in particular BPa, that balances are stable. One is power transition theory, most closely associated with A.K.F. Organski, and a variation developed by Robert Gilpin. The second is long cycle theory, inspired by economists' work on business cycles and now associated with political scientists such as George Modelski and William Thompson.

Organski defines power as "the ability to influence the behavior of others in accordance with one's own ends" (1958, 96; see also Organski and Kugler 1980, 5). Power may be exercised by means of persuasion, rewards, punishments, or the use of force. The various determinants may be classified as either natural (such as geography, resources, and population), social (such as economic development, political structure, diplomatic skill, and national morale), and intangible (such as propaganda, ideals, and good will) (1958, 99). The three most important determinants of national power, according to Organski, are wealth, population, and government efficiency. Thus the best available single index of power is national income, since it accounts for two of the three major determinants, population and economic development, as well as other, lesser factors.

Gilpin, as a supporter of structural realism, agrees with Waltz in many ways about how to analyze world politics. However, he sees international politics as manifesting cycles of hegemony rather than recurrent balances. Gilpin uses both an idealized individualist rational choice analysis and a systemic sociological analysis to produce his explanation. He offers an abstract characterization of the international system according to which (a) the system is in stable equilibrium in that no major power sees the costs of change as worth the benefits; the continual process of differential power growth of states leads eventually to (b) a redistribution of power in the system, which in some cases will constitute (c) a state of disequilibrium of power; in those cases there will be (d) a resolution of the systemic crisis typically by means of war, which will result in (a), thus completing the cycle. Gilpin distinguishes "power" from "prestige." He says, "In this book, power refers simply to the military, economic, and technological capabilities of states. This definition obviously leaves out important and intangible elements that affect the outcomes of political actions, such as public morale, qualities of leadership, and situational factors" (1981, 13–14).

Proponents of long cycles, like George Modelski, argue that the world system began with the rise of sea power five hundred years ago, and each century has been influenced by the leadership of one particular state that was both innovative and able to control sea lanes. During that time there have been major wars occurring in hundred-year cycles: the Italian and Indian Ocean Wars, 1494–1516; the Dutch-Spanish Wars, 1580–1608; the Wars of Louis XIV, 1688–1713; the Napoleonic Wars, 1792–1815; and the World Wars, 1914–1945. As a result of these wars and other factors, the past five centuries were lead, respectively, by Portugal, Holland, England, England again, and the United States.

While balance of power theorists tend to identify hegemony as reliant entirely on control of resources, Modelski credits the material capabilities, including technology and innovation, as constituting only one side of leadership, namely the supply side. He argues that there is also a demand side. The other states in the system (the principles challenger, other major powers, and minor powers) have variable needs for a leader as the system evolves. The need is greatest in periods of high conflict and war. The effects of leadership vary over time, and are greater in times of crisis and war because of the greater demand (1987, 13–14).

Rasler and Thompson (1983) note that scholars have debated "the possibility that periods of warfare between major powers are traceable to shifts in the underlying distribution of economic resources . . . We may state that rising economic powers challenge declining economic powers for a greater share of the benefits of predominance in the world economic order" (1983, 489). It is clear then that if there is balancing along the lines of what BP asserts, then states should form coalitions to limit a potential hegemon's ability to dominate the system's economy.

Sharp Opposition of Measures

Mearsheimer and Modelski are perhaps the leading exponents today of balance of power and long cycles, respectively, and it is clear how different are their measures of hegemony. Mearsheimer says explicitly that a hegemon must have no rival great powers—a condition nineteenth-century Britain did not satisfy. He says that "a state that is substantially more powerful than the other great powers in the system is not a hegemon, because it faces, by definition, other great powers. The United Kingdom in the mid-nineteenth century, for example, is sometimes called a hegemon. But it was not a hegemon, because there were four other great powers in Europe at the time . . . In fact, the United Kingdom considered France to be a serious threat to the balance of power. Europe in the nineteenth century was not unipolar" (2001, 40). In vivid contrast, Modelski argues that nineteenth-century Britain was a hegemon. He says that "entities uniquely dominant in the global system will be called world powers. An example of a historical world power is Britain: In the nineteenth century Britain maintained a structure of world order that at the end of that period came to be called Pax Britannica. More technically we might define world powers as those units monopolizing (that is, controlling more than one half of) the market for (or the supply of) order-keeping in the global layer of interdependence. In the case of Britain, this would refer to the command of the sea and a related capacity to shape global affairs" (Modelski 1978, 216).

Modelski says, "In the modern world system a useful indicator of capacity for . . . global power status, has been the distribution of naval forces . . . Naval operation on the so-called world ocean is a phenomenon of the past half-millennium and has been engaged in by all powers competing in the global leadership stakes. Sea power has also been a stabilizer of the modern status quo. No state could overthrow the prevailing world order without first establishing command over the oceans" (1987, 9–10). In terms of measuring this capability, Modelski says, "'naval concentration ratios' are good operational indices for the position of global powers" (1987, 10). In contrast, Mearsheimer emphasizes ground forces, as noted above. Air and naval power are of secondary importance. Mearsheimer says, "Even in a nuclear world, armies are the core ingredient of military power. Independent naval forces and strategic air forces are not suited for conquering territory, nor are they much good by themselves at coercing other states into making territorial concessions" (2001, 56).

In sum, it is clear that no measure-stipulation has been accepted by contemporary authors on all sides of the balance of power debate, as evidenced by the writings of supporters of balancing (Morgenthau, Claude, Waltz, Mearsheimer) and their opponents who advocate for power transition theory (Organski, Gilpin) and long-cycle theory (Modelski, Thompson). The inability to agree on what constitutes and how to measure power and hegemony is likely related to the disputants' inability to agree on whether (and why) states in fact balance against hegemons.[21]

Space limitations led to a focus only on power transition and long cycle opponents of BP (excluding hegemonic stability and buck-passing/bandwagoning) and to a focus on power and hegemony (excluding a parallel analysis of stability). However, this did not affect the conclusion. Since the argument here is that there is an absence of conventional measure-stipulations across the debate, it suffices to show that some theories diverge on some of the essential measure-terms.

The fact that there has thus far been no progress on the balancing debate that mirrors the progress in the democratic peace debate in no way implies that such progress is impossible. Progress may commence if, among other conditions, scholars come to accept common measure-stipulations for power, hegemony, and stability. But at this stage in the major theoretical debates in international relations, the presence or absence of Duhemian conventional measure-stipulations can help explain why substantial approach-to-consensus has occurred on the democratic peace debate and has not occurred in the balances of power debate.

10.4. CONCLUSION

This chapter has outlined Duhem's principles of holism, conventionalism, and underdetermination of theory by data and has shown their implications for the methodology of the social sciences. The social science meta-theory literature is replete with defenses of, and calls for, methodological pluralism. There are many avenues from which to approach it. There are some limits, as various pseudo-academic approaches lack legitimacy and philosophical grounding. Still, many approaches are possible—quantitative, qualitative, social scientific, humanistic, interpretive, moral, legal, and others. The social world is complex and multifaceted and, appropriately, Duhemian conventionalism allows for a good deal of pluralism.

The chapter has attempted to show that, given the need for conventional choice in the natural sciences (from the final assumption stated in section 10.1), it should not be surprising that international relations scholars, especially those engaging in quantitative studies, cannot get by without measure-stipulation conventions. The examination of the DP debate reveals how authors came to adopt conventions for the measure-stipulations; both liberals and realists have largely accepted the same methods of measurement for the same variable concepts. And with the conventional acceptance of measure-stipulations in DP studies, there has been at least some progress and cumulation of knowledge. Realists and liberals have each given up at least part of their initial positions, and recent authors use the results of previous studies to generate and test new ideas and hypotheses that derive from the core notions of democracies' pacific treatment of one another.

The chapter has also sought to show that many elements of Duhem's account of physical science can help illuminate methodological issues in the social sciences. The chapter has shown that the concept of the measure-stipulation, which is a matter of convention, can explain the progress or absence of progress of debates in social science just as well as those in the natural sciences. The presence of a well-articulated measure-stipulation for key terms has helped to facilitate progress on one central question of international politics, while its absence has been an obstacle in generating progress over another otherwise similar question.

NOTES

1. As Redman puts it, "the significance of the Duhem thesis is one of the central themes in the modern philosophy of science" (1993, 38).

2. A search of the Web of Science and the Philosopher's Index for journal articles citing Duhem in the social sciences yields single-digit results, almost exclusively in economics. To cite another example, there is no mention of Duhem in any of the

twenty-two essays, covering six hundred pages, of Kincaid and Ross, eds., *The Oxford Handbook of Philosophy of Economics*. Debate in economics on Duhem is found, for example, in works like Boylan and O'Gorman (2003), Cross (1982), Guala (2005), Hahn (1996), Hausman (1992), Kuenne (1986), Sawyer, Beed, and Sankey (1997), and Shearmur (1991).

3. This assumption is not held universally. Shearmur (1991, 65) notes that some hold that the social scientists have an advantage over natural scientists, since the former study human phenomena which allows investigators the opportunity to gain knowledge of the actors from the inside of those phenomena.

4. In a different context, Leibniz made essentially the same point. He says, "I have noticed that the reason why we make mistakes so easily outside of Mathematics (where Geometers are so felicitous in their reasonings), is only because in Geometry and the other parts of abstract Mathematics, we can continually submit to trials or tests not only the conclusion but also, at any moment, each step made from the premises, by reducing the whole to numbers. But in physics after many inferences are made experiment often refutes the conclusion and yet does not rectify the reasoning and does not indicate the place where we went wrong" (Leibniz 1951, 51).

5. Gillies (1993) and Harding (1976) also provide clear explanations of the differences. Lakatos described the versions of underdetermination and holism as "very different" from one another (1978, 96).

6. As with any major historical figure, there is philosophical debate concerning Duhem's principles, even though his prose and arguments were unusually clear and lucid. Hence, at least in comparison to debates over other philosophers' views, the debate here is stimulated more because of the far-reaching implications of his position.

7. See Magnus (2005a), who defends a concept of "total science" that allows some arguments of underdetermination and who argues against standard interpretations of Duhem. The principle area of Duhem's philosophy of science applied in this chapter for understanding social science progress is the measure-stipulation, which gains some force from the doctrine of underdetermination, but is logically independent of it.

8. Interestingly, Duhem's meta-theory clearly allows for the rejection of Newton and its replacement by a radically different, non-Euclidean system of physical principles-plus-geometric axioms, while Poincaré's does not. Yet it was Poincaré who came to adopt Einstein's theory and Duhem who did not.

9. This connects to what Lakatos more formally described as a degenerating research program, and may have prompted Lakatos to develop important aspects of his theory of science (see note 15).

10. One philosopher of science has argued that Duhem should not even be classified as a conventionalist, but rather as a particular form of falsificationist (Gillies 1993, 104, 223).

11. The case for Duhem's account for good sense can be strengthened by comparing two very important advances in physical science and how falsifying observations were handled in the nineteenth century. The Foucault experiment in the mid-nineteenth century, discussed above, after a time led to agreement between those who had accepted the corpuscular hypothesis and those who accepted the wave hypothesis. The former gave up a basic theoretical principle "under the weight of the contradictions inflicted by reality" (1954, 216) However, consider the contrast to the falsifying observations about the orbit of Uranus. The Newtonian view could be salvaged by discarding one of the auxiliary hypotheses, that is, that Uranus was the farthest planet. Adams and Le Verrier

postulated the existence of an additional planet that could account for the observations, and indeed the body was later observed (Gillies 1993, 99–102). See also Koertge's discussion (1978, 256–57) of a case in which a single scientist, Mendeleev, treated two sets of recalcitrant observations in diverse ways with respect to the significance of the periodic table.

12. Both Poincaré and Duhem advanced conventionalism within the realm of physical theory but not as universal as Quine has. Duhem said that some sciences, for example, physiology, do not have "the same logical simplicity" as physics (1954, 180). Gillies agrees that there are important differences regarding possible "crucial experiments" in various scientific areas, but he believes that the distinctions cut across scientific disciplines; that is, even physics has both unfalsifiable laws as well as falsifiable laws, such as Snell's law of refraction applied to glass (1993, 110).

13. Some critics of the dyadic hypothesis claim that there have been wars between democracies. The most oft-cited conflicts are the War of 1812, the American civil war, the Spanish-American War, and Finland's alliance with Nazi Germany against the Soviet Union. The first three are suspect as legitimate cases of democracy-versus-democracy wars because at least one belligerent was not very democratic. And tiny Finland faced the two most powerful European states, Stalin's Soviet Union and Hitler's Germany; both were totalitarian and led opposing alliances. But the former had invaded Finland. In any event, legitimate democracy-versus-democracy wars are rare enough not to disrupt the standard probabilistic formulations of the dyadic hypothesis.

14. Additional examples of the criticisms, and replies by way of adjustments, are provided in Chernoff (2004), which also offers several definitions of scientific progress provided by nineteenth- and twentieth-century philosophers of science. For further applications, see also Chernoff (2005).

15. Rummel (1983) focuses on "libertarianism," defined as a combination of political and economic freedoms.

16. Elkins (2000, 299) argues for quantitative tests as more valid because "measures of democracy which provide for gradations best fit the behavior that theoretical work on democracy would predict."

17. Authors usually intend to refer only to major powers when they talk of states, since small powers, microstates, etc., cannot have any effect on blunting the advance of a rising hegemon.

18. Haas (1953, 442); Cobden (1878, 111–14), cited by Haas (1953, 443); Holsti (2004, 26) cited by Little (2007, 10).

19. During the Cold War, Waltz (1979, 121) emphasized that BP qualifications were unnecessary, as balancing occurs universally whenever two minimal conditions are met: The system is anarchical (as all international systems are) and states wish to survive. Tetlock (2005) brilliantly examines how authors avoid acknowledging that their theories have been falsified.

20. An investigation of measurements of stability would show divergence, as well, since it is variously defined as absence of war, the absence of major-power war, the absence of the decrease in the total number of major powers, and the absence of the loss of any specific major powers from the system.

21. Levy (2003) offers an interesting argument according to which land powers are more threatening than maritime hegemons to most states, which leads to balancing coalitions against the former but not the latter.

REFERENCES

Babst, Dean. 1964. "Elective Governments: A Force for Peace." *Wisconsin Sociologist* 3 (1): 9–14.

Babst, Dean. 1972. "A Force for Peace." *Industrial Research* 14: 55–58.

Beck, Nathaniel, Jonathan N. Katz, and Richard Tucker. 1998. "Taking Time Seriously: Time-Series-Cross-Section Analysis with a Binary Dependent Variable." *American Journal of Political Science* 42 (4): 1260–88.

Boylan, Thomas A., and Paschal F. O'Gorman. 2003. "Foundations of Science, Pragmatism in Economic Methodology: The Duhem-Quine Thesis Revisited." *Foundations of Science* 8 (March): 3–21.

Bueno de Mesquita, Bruce, James D. Morrow, Randolph M. Siverson, and Alastair Smith. 1997. "An Institutional Explanation of the Democratic Peace." *American Political Science Review* 93 (December): 541–68.

Chernoff, Fred. 2004. "The Study of Democratic Peace and Progress in International Relations." *International Studies Review* 6 (April): 49–77.

Chernoff, Fred. 2005. *The Power of International Theory*. London: Routledge.

Claude, Inis. 1962. *Power in International Relations*. New York: Random House.

Cobden, Richard. 1878. *Political Writings of Richard Cobden, with an Introductory Essay by Sir Louis Mallet*. London: W. Ridgeway.

Cross, Rod. 1982. "The Duhem-Quine Thesis, Lakatos and the Appraisal of Theories in Macroeconomics." *The Economic Journal* 93 (June): 320–40.

Dixon, William J. 1993. "Democracy and the Management of International Conflict." *Journal of Conflict Resolution* 37 (1): 42–68.

Doyle, Michael W. 1983a. "Kant, Liberal Legacies, and Foreign Affairs." *Philosophy and Public Affairs* 12 (Summer): 205–35.

Doyle, Michael W. 1983b. "Kant, Liberal Legacies, and Foreign Affairs, Part 2." *Philosophy and Public Affairs* 12 (Autumn): 323–53.

Doyle, Michael W. 1986. "Liberalism and World Politics." *American Political Science Review* 80 (December): 1151–69.

Duhem, Pierre. 1954. *The Aim and Structure of Physical Theory*, Philip P. Weiner, trans. Princeton, NJ: Princeton University Press.

Earman, John. 1993. "Underdetermination, Realism and Reason." *Midwest Studies in Philosophy* 18 (1): 19–39.

Eckstein, Harry, and Ted Robert Gurr. 1975. *Patterns of Authority: A Structural Basis for Political Inquiry*. New York: Wiley.

Elkins, Zachary. 2000. "Gradations of Democracy? Empirical Tests of Alternative Conceptualizations." *American Journal of Political Science* 44 (2): 293–300.

Farber, Henry, and Joanne Gowa. 1995. "Polities and Peace." *International Security* 20 (2): 123–46.

Farber, Henry, and Joanne Gowa. 1997. "Common Interests or Common Politics?" *Journal of Politics* 59 (2): 393–417.

Freedom House. 1973. Comparative Study of Freedom. *Freedom at Issue* 17 (Jan/Feb): 2–24.

Gartzke, Erik. 1998. "Kant We All Just Get Along? Opportunity, Willingness and the Origins of the Democratic Peace." *American Journal of Political Science* 42 (1): 1–27.

Gillies, Donald. 1993. *The Philosophy of Science in the Twentieth Century: Four Central Themes*. Oxford: Blackwell.

Gilpin, Robert. 1981. *War and Change in World Politics*. Cambridge: Cambridge University Press.

Gleditsch, Kristian, and Michael D. Ward. 1997. "War and Peace in Space and Time: The Role of Democratization." *International Studies Quarterly* 44 (1): 1–29.

Gleditsch, Nils Peter. 1995. "Geography, Democracy, and Peace." *International Interactions* 20 (4): 297–323.

Green, Donald, Soo Yeon Kim, and David Yoon. 2001. "Dirty Pool." *International Organization* 55 (2): 441–68.

Grünbaum, Adolf. 1960. "The Duhemian Argument." *Philosophy of Science* 27 (January): 75–87.

Grünbaum, Adolf. 1966. "The Falsifiability of a Component of a Theoretical System." In *Mind, Matter, and Method*, Paul K. Feyerabend and Grover Maxwell, eds., 273–305. Minneapolis: University of Minnesota Press.

Grünbaum, Adolf. 1976. "Is It Never Possible to Falsify a Hypothesis Irrevocably?" In *Can Theories Be Refuted? Essays on the Duhem-Quine Thesis*, Sandra G. Harding, ed., 260–88. Dordrecht: D. Reidel Publishing.

Guala, Francesco. 2005. *The Methodology of Experimental Economics*. Cambridge: Cambridge University Press.

Haas, Ernst B. 1953. "The Balance of Power: Prescription, Concept, or Propaganda." *World Politics* 5 (July): 442–77.

Hahn, Frank H. 1996. "Rerum Cognoscere Causus." *Economics and Philosophy* 12 (2): 183–95.

Harding, Sandra G. 1976. "Introduction." In *Can Theories be Refuted? Essays on the Duhem-Quine Thesis*, Sandra G. Harding, ed., ix–xxi. Dordrecht: D. Reidel Publishing.

Howard, Don. 1990. "Einstein and Duhem." *Synthèse* 83 (3): 363–84.

Hausman, Daniel M. 1992. *The Inexact and Separate Science of Economics*. Cambridge: Cambridge University Press.

Henderson, Errol R. 2002. *Democracy at War: The End of an Illusion?* Boulder, CO: Lynne Reinner.

Hermann, Margaret G., and Charles W. Kegley, Jr. 2001. "Democracies and Intervention: Is There a Danger Zone in the Democratic Peace?" *Journal of Peace Research* 38 (2): 237–45.

Hewitt, J. Joseph, and Jonathan Wilkenfield. 1996. "Democracies in International Crisis." *International Interactions* 22 (1): 123–42.

Holsti, K. J. 2004. *Taming the Sovereigns: Institutional Change and International Politics*. Cambridge: Cambridge University Press.

Huth, Paul K., and Todd L. Allee. 2003. *Democratic Peace and Territorial Conflict in the Twentieth Century*. Cambridge: Cambridge University Press.

Kegley, Charles W., Jr., and Margaret G. Hermann. 1995. "Military Intervention and the Democratic Peace.: *International Interactions* 21 (1): 1–21.

Kegley, Charles W., Jr., and Margaret G. Hermann. 1997. "Putting Military Intervention into the Democratic Peace." *Comparative Political Studies* 30 (1): 78–107.

Kegley, Charles W., Jr., and Margaret G. Hermann. 2001. "Democracies and Intervention: Is There a Danger Zone in the Democratic Peace?" *Journal of Peace Research* 38 (March): 237–45.

Keohane, Robert O. 1984. *After Hegemony*. Princeton, NJ: Princeton University Press.

Keohane, Robert O., and Joseph Nye. 1977. *Power and Interdependence*. Boston: Little Brown.

Kincaid, Harold, and Don Ross. 2009. *The Oxford Handbook of Philosophy of Economics*. New York: Oxford University Press.

Kindleberger, Charles P. 1973. *The World in Depression 1929–1939*. Berkeley: University of California Press.

Kitcher, Philip. 1993. *The Advancement of Science*. New York: Oxford University Press.

Koertge, Noretta. 1978. "Towards a New Theory of Scientific Inquiry." In *Progress and Rationality in Science*, G. Radnitzsky, ed., 253–78. Dordrecht: D. Reidel Publishing.

Krasner, Stephen D. 1976. "State Power and the Structure of International Trade." *World Politics* 28 (April): 317–47.

Kuenne, Robert E. 1986. *Rivalrous Consonance: A Theory of General Oligopolistic Equilibrium*. Amsterdam: North Holland.

Lakatos, Imre. 1978. "Falsification and the Methodology of Scientific Research Programmes." In *The Methodology of Scientific Research Programmes*, John Worrall and Gregory Currie, eds., 6–101. Cambridge: Cambridge University Press.

Laudan, Larry. 1990. "Demystifying Underdetermination." In *Scientific Theories Minnesota Studies in the Philosophy of Science Volume 14*, C. Wade Savage, ed., 267–97. Minneapolis: University of Minnesota Press.

Laudan, Larry, and Jerrod Leplin. 1991. "Empirical Equivalence and Underdetermination." *Journal of Philosophy* 88: 449–72.

Layne, Christopher. 1994. "Kant or Cant? The Myth of Democratic Peace." *International Security* 18 (1): 5–49.

Leibniz, G.W.F. 1951. "The Art of Discovery (1685)." In *Leibniz Selections*, Philip P. Weiner, ed., 50–58. New York: Scribner's.

Levy, Jack. 1988. "Domestic Politics and War." *Journal of Interdisciplinary History* 18 (4): 653–73.

Levy, Jack. 1989. "The Causes of War: A Review of Theories and Evidence." In *Behavior, Society, and Nuclear War*, Philip E. Tetlock, Jo L. Husbands, Robert Jervis, Paul S. Stern, and Charles Tilly, eds., 209–333. New York: Oxford University Press.

Levy, Jack. 2003. "Balances and Balancing: Concepts, Propositions, and Research Design." In *Realism and the Balancing of Power: A New Debate*, John A. Vasquez and Colin Elman, eds., 128–53. Upper Saddle River, NJ: Pearson.

Little, Richard. 2007. *The Balance of Power in International Relations*. Cambridge: Cambridge University Press.

Magnus, P. D. 2005a. "Background Theories and Total Science." *Philosophy of Science* 72 (December): 1064–75.

Magnus, P. D. 2005b. "Peirce: Underdetermination, Agnosticism, and Related Mistakes." *Inquiry* 48 (1): 26–37.

Mansfield, Edward D., and Jack Snyder. 2002. "Democratic Transitions, Institutional Strength, and War." *International Organization* 56 (2): 297–337.

Mansfield, Edward D., and Jack Snyder. 1995. "Democratization and the Danger of War." *International Security* 20 (1): 5–38.

Maoz, Zeev. 1998. "Realist and Cultural Critiques of Democratic Peace: A Theoretical and Empirical Re-assessment." *International Interaction* 24 (1): 3–89.

Maoz, Zeev, and Bruce M. Russett. 1993. "Normative and Structural Causes of Democratic Peace 1946–1986." *American Political Science Review* 87 (September): 624–38.

Mearsheimer, John J. 2001. *The Tragedy of Great Power Politics*. New York: Norton.

Midlarsky, Manus I. 1995. "Environmental Influences on Democracy: Aridity, Warfare, and a Reversal of the Causal Arrow." *Journal of Conflict Resolution* 39 (2): 224–62.

Modelski, George. 1978. "The Long Cycle of Global Politics and the Nation-state." *Comparative Studies in Society and History* 20 (April): 214–35.

Modelski, George. 1987. *Long Cycles in World Politics*. Seattle: University of Washington Press.

Morgenthau, Hans J. 1954. *Politics Among Nations*. 2d ed. New York: Knopf.

Nye, Joseph. 1990. *Bound to Lead: The Changing Nature of American Power*. New York: Basic.

Nye, Joseph. 1999. "The Kantian Peace: The Pacific Benefits of Democracy, Interdependence, and International Organizations, 1885–1992." *World Politics* 52 (1): 1–37.

Oneal, John R., and Bruce Russett. 1999. "Is the Liberal Peace Just an Artifact of Cold War Interests? Assessing Recent Critiques." *International Interactions* 25 (1): 1–29.

Oneal, John R., and Bruce Russett. 2001. "Clear and Clean: The Fixed Effects of Democracy and Economic Interdependence." *International Organization* 55 (2): 469–85.

Oren, Ido. 1995. "The Subjectivity of the 'Democratic Peace.'" *International Security* 20 (2): 147–84.

Organski, A.F.K. 1958. *World Politics*. New York: Knopf.

Organski, A.F.K., and Jacek Kugler. 1980. *The War Ledger*. Chicago: University of Chicago Press.

Owen, John M. 1994. "How Liberalism Produces Democratic Peace." *International Security* 19 (Autumn): 87–125.

Paul, T.V. 2005. "Soft Balancing in the Age of U.S. Primacy." *International Security* 30 (Summer): 46–71.

Poincaré, Henri. 1952. *Science and Hypothesis with a preface by J. Larmor*. New York: Dover.

Popper, Karl. 1959. *The Logic of Scientific Discovery*, Karl Popper, Julius Freed, and Lan Freed, trans. London: Hutchinson.

Popper, Karl. 1965. *Conjectures and Refutations: The Growth of Scientific Knowledge*. London: Routledge & Kegan Paul.

Quine, Willard Van Ormand. 1951. "Two Dogmas of Empiricism." *Philosophical Review* 60 (January): 20–43.

Rasler, Karen, and William Thompson. 1983. "Global Wars, Public Debts, and the Long Cycle." *World Politics* 35 (July): 489–516.

Ray, James Lee. 2003. "A Lakatosian View of the Democratic Peace Research Programme: Does It Falsify Realism (or Neorealism?)" In *Progress in International Relations Theory: Appraising the Field*, Colin Elman and Miriam Fendius Elman, eds., 205–44. Cambridge, MA: The MIT Press.

Raymond, Gregory A. 1994. "Democracy, Disputes, and Third Party Intermediaries." *Journal of Conflict Resolution* 38 (1): 24–42.

Redman, Deborah. 1993. *Economics and the Philosophy of Science*. New York: Oxford University Press.

Reiter, Dan, and Allan C. Stam III. 1998. "Democracy, War Initiation, and Victory." *American Political Science Review* 92 (2): 377–89.

Reiter, Dan, and Allan C. Stam III. 2002. *Democracies at War*. Princeton, NJ: Princeton University Press.

Rule, James B. 1997. *Theory and Progress in Social Science*. Cambridge: Cambridge University Press.

Rummel, R. J. 1979. *Understanding Conflict and War. Vol. 4 War, Power, Peace*. Thousand Oaks, CA: Sage.

Rummel, R. J. 1983. "Libertarianism and International Violence." *Journal of Conflict Resolution* 27 (1): 27–71.

Russett, Bruce. 1990. *Controlling the Sword: The Democratic Governance of National Security*. Cambridge, MA: Harvard University Press.

Russett, Bruce. 1993. *Grasping the Democratic Peace: Principles for a Post–Cold War World*. Princeton, NJ: Princeton University Press.

Russett, Bruce, and John R. Oneal. 2001. *Triangulating Peace: Democracy, Trade, and International Organizations*. New York: Norton.

Sawyer, K. R., Clive Beed, and H. Sankey. 1997. "Underdetermination in Economics: The Duhem-Quine Thesis." *Economics and Philosophy* 13 (April): 1–23.

Schweller, Randolph. 1994. "Bandwagoning for Profit: Bringing the Revisionist State Back In." *International Security* 19 (Summer): 72–107.

Senese, Paul D. 1997. "Between Dispute and War: The Effect of Joint Democracy on Interstate Conflict Escalation." *Journal of Politics* 59 (1): 1–27.

Shearmur, J. 1991. "Common-Sense and the Foundations of Economic-Theory—Duhem versus Robbins." *Philosophy of the Social Sciences* 21 (March): 64–71.

Singer, J. David 1972. "The Correlates of War Project: An Interim Report and Rationale." *World Politics* 24 (2): 243–70.

Singer, J. David, and Melvin Small. 1972. "The Correlates of War Project: An Interim Report and Rationale." *World Politics* 24 (January): 243–70.

Sklar, Lawrence. 1975. "Methodological Conservatism." *Philosophical Review* 84 (3): 384–400.

Sklar, Lawrence. 1981. "Do Unborn Hypotheses Have Rights?" *Pacific Philosophical Quarterly* 62 (1): 17–29.

Small, Melvin, and J. David Singer. 1976. "The War-Proneness of Democratic Regimes." *Jerusalem Journal of International Relations* 1 (1): 50–69.

Spiro, David E. 1994. "The Insignificance of the Liberal Peace." *International Security* 19 (Autumn): 50–86.

Stanford, P. Kyle. 2003. "No Refuge for Realism." *Philosophy of Science* 70 (December): 913–925.

Tetlock, Philip. 2005. *Expert Political Judgment.* Princeton, NJ: Princeton University Press.

Thompson, William R. 1986. "Polarity, the Long Cycle, and Global Power Warfare." *Journal of Conflict Resolution* 30 (December): 587–615.

Thompson, William R. 1996. "Democracy and Peace: Putting the Cart before the Horse?" *International Organization* 50 (1): 141–74.

Van Fraassen, Bas C. 1980. *The Scientific Image.* Oxford: Oxford University Press.

Waltz, Kenneth N. 1979. *Theory of International Politics.* New York: McGraw-Hill.

CHAPTER 11

PHILOSOPHY AND THE
PRACTICE OF BAYESIAN
STATISTICS IN THE SOCIAL
SCIENCES

ANDREW GELMAN AND
COSMA ROHILLA SHALIZI

This chapter presents our own perspective on the philosophy of Bayesian statistics, based on our idiosyncratic readings of the philosophical literature and, more importantly, our experiences doing applied statistics in the social sciences and elsewhere. Think of this as two statistical practitioners' perspective on philosophical and foundational concerns. What we bring to the table are our substantive claims about actual social science research, and we attempt to explain those practices here.

We are motivated to write this chapter out of dissatisfaction with what we perceive as the standard view of the philosophical foundations of Bayesian statistics. Here's what we take as the standard view:

- Bayesian inference—"inverse probability"—is subjective and inductive, learning about the general from the particular. The expression $p(H|y)$ says it all: The Bayesian learns the probability that a hypothesis H is true, given data. In the conventional view, this is completely different from classical frequentist statistics which is based on null hypothesis testing, that is, falsification.[1]

- The paradigmatic setting of Bayesian inference is the computation of the posterior probability of hypotheses, with scientific progress represented by the updating of these probabilities.

To give a quick sense of our position, we agree essentially entirely with Greenland (1998), who attributes to Karl Popper the following attitude toward inductive inference: "We never use any argument based on observed repetition of instances that does not *also* involve a hypothesis that predicts both those repetitions and the unobserved instances of interest." To put it another way, statistical models are a tool that allow us to do inductive reasoning in a deductive framework.

In taking a broadly Popperian perspective, we are not committing to many of Popper's specific ideas such as the existence of a logical criterion for demarcating science from conscience or that there is something called collaboration of a theory which is central to science but provides no evidence for the truth of a theory. Rather, what we view as central is the scientific—and statistical—ideal of building serious models that make strong predictions, leaving themselves wide open to being falsified by data. This is "severe testing" in the terminology of Mayo (1996), who works in a frequentist framework but whose ideas, we believe, are equally applicable to modern Bayesian data analysis.

What is salient about our social science research experiences is that the models are all wrong. As we like to say, our models are not merely falsifiable, they are also false! To put it another way, we are confident that, by gathering a moderate amount of data, we could reject any model we have ever fit to data.

11.1. FROM NULL HYPOTHESIS TESTING TO MODEL CHECKING

We write that, in our applied work, we fit complex models and check them with data, and we characterize model checking as central to statistical learning. This perspective differs in both philosophy and practice from the two dominant conceptions of the philosophy of statistics:

1. Classical frequentist inference is centered upon null hypothesis testing, with the goal often being to reject the null, for example demonstrating that two distributions are not in fact identical or that a particular parameter is not exactly zero. In contrast, our models are not null hypotheses but rather complex structures within which one can learn about parameters of interest.

2. The dominant strain of Bayesian philosophy, as presented by Savage (1954) and others, subsumes inference within decision theory and treats all probabilities as subjective. In contrast, we agree that probabilities are model-dependent, but we treat statistical models as testable and thus as potentially objective as any other scientific measurements.

We are not claiming that our approach to applied statistics is optimal or even, in many cases, qualitatively different from other methodologies. For example, there is a well-developed classical framework of estimation, prediction, and multiple comparisons that can handle complex models without recourse to the Bayesian formalism.

What we are claiming is Bayes need not be associated with subjectivity and inductive reasoning. It is possible to work within a model-checking, error-statistical framework without being tied to classical null hypotheses. And, conversely, one can use Bayesian methods without being required to perform the typically meaningless task of evaluating the posterior probability of models.

11.2. THE USUAL STORY

Is statistical inference inductive or deductive reasoning? What is the connection between statistics and the philosophy of science? Why do we care?

Schools of statistical inference are sometimes linked to philosophical approaches. "Classical" statistics—as exemplified by Fisher's p-values and Neyman's hypothesis tests—is associated with a deductive, Popperian, or error-statistical view of science: A hypothesis is made and then it is tested. It can never be accepted, but it can be rejected (that is, falsified). In the language of Mayo (1996), statistics and science interact via the design and analysis of experiments that yield severe tests of models.

Bayesian statistics—starting with a prior distribution, getting data, and moving to the posterior distribution—is associated with a formal inductive approach in which new information is smoothly integrated into scientific understanding via the updating of posterior probabilities of competing hypotheses, paradigms, or statistical models.

Our disagreement with the usual philosophical understanding of statistics can be conveniently expressed with reference to the following passage from the Wikipedia[2] entry on Bayesian statistics:

> Bayesian inference uses aspects of the scientific method, which involves collecting evidence that is meant to be consistent or inconsistent with a given hypothesis. As evidence accumulates, the degree of belief in a hypothesis ought to change. With enough evidence, it should become very high or very low. . . . Bayesian inference uses a numerical estimate of the degree of belief in a hypothesis before evidence has been observed and calculates a numerical estimate of the degree of belief in the hypothesis after evidence has been observed. . . . Bayesian inference usually relies on degrees of belief, or subjective probabilities, in the induction process and does not necessarily claim to provide an objective method of induction. Nonetheless, some Bayesian statisticians believe probabilities can have an objective value and therefore Bayesian inference can provide an objective method of induction.

This story does not fit applied Bayesian statistics as we have experienced it. Except in some very narrowly construed problems, we do not view "the degree of belief in a hypothesis" as a meaningful scientific statement, we do not consider probabilities to be subjective (or, at least, no more subjective than any other aspects of scientific modeling), nor do we believe Bayesian inference to provide a method of induction, if that is meant to imply a direct mapping from data to posterior probabilities of hypotheses. We elaborate on these points below.

11.3. OUR ALTERNATIVE STORY

We have no quarrel with the general idea that scientific knowledge builds upon the past, or that we can learn inductively from the particular to the general. As has been long realized, induction is most effective within the context of a good model.

Our key departure from the usually expressed Bayesian philosophy is that we have experienced two kinds of learning: Inference about parameters within a model and decisive rejections of models that have forced us to improve or simply replace earlier paradigms. In our applied work, we have *not* found ourselves making gradual conceptual transitions based on evaluations of posterior probabilities of models.

Our progress in applied modeling has fit the hypothetico-deductive pattern pretty well: We build a model out of available parts and drive it as far as it can take us, and then a little farther. When the model breaks down, we take it apart, figure out what went wrong, and tinker with it, or else try a radically new design. In either case, we are using deductive reasoning as a tool to get the most out of a model, and we test the model—it is falsifiable, and when it is falsified, we alter or abandon it. To give this story a little Kuhnian flavor, we are doing normal science when we apply the deductive reasoning and learn from a model, or when we tinker with it to get it to fit the data, and occasionally enough problems build up that a new paradigm is helpful.

Okay, all fine. But the twist is that we are using Bayesian methods, not classical hypothesis testing. We do not think of a Bayesian prior distribution as a personal belief; rather, it is part of a hypothesized model, which we posit as potentially useful and abandon to the extent that it is falsified.

Subjective Bayesian theory has no place for falsification of a prior distribution, except to the extent that it can be placed within a larger model in competition with other candidate prior distributions. But if we think of the model just as a set of assumptions, they can be falsified if their predictions—our deductive inferences—do not fit the data.

Here's an example of what we consider to be a flaw of the standard view of Bayesian learning about models. In the 1800s, physicists believed that Newton's laws were true, an attitude potentially expressible as Pr (Newton | information available as of 1890) = 0.99. But after Einstein's theory came out and was tested by experiment, the evidence moved to Pr (Einstein | information available as of 1920) = 0.999 and Pr (Newton | information available as of 1920) = 0.001, or something of the sort.

We see two big problems with this standard approach. First, a lot of data and analysis showed critical problems with Newton's laws—even if the relativistic alternative had not been proposed. Quantum states, the black body paradox, the stability of the atom, and all the rest. We would like our philosophical model to be able to reject Newton's model—to reveal serious problems with it—without the need for an alternative that beats it under a likelihood ratio criterion or any other.[3]

The second problem with this framing is that physicists do not think Einstein's theory, as stated, is true either. Relativity has problems too, and researchers have been working for decades to come up with possible alternatives. In this search for new models, the various falsifications of classical relativity theory have been crucial. What is important is not that Einstein's theory has been rejected, but rather the particular ways that it does not correspond to reality.[4]

11.4. WHY DOES THIS MATTER?

Philosophy matters, even to practitioners, because philosophy is used as a guide to practice. We believe that the idea of Bayesian inference as inductive, culminating in the computation of the posterior probability of scientific hypotheses, has had malign effects on statistical practice. At best, the inductivist view has encouraged researchers to fit and compare models without checking them; at worst, theorists have actively discouraged practitioners from performing model checking because it does not fit into their conventional framework.

In contrast, a philosophy of deductive reasoning, accompanied by falsifiability, gives us a lot of flexibility in modeling. We do not have to worry about making our prior distributions match our subjective knowledge, or about our model containing all possible truths. Instead we make some assumptions, state them clearly, and see what they imply. Then we try to falsify the model—that is, we perform posterior predictive checks, creating simulations of the data and comparing them to the actual data. The comparison can often be done visually; see chapter 6 of *Bayesian Data Analysis* (Gelman et al., 2003) for lots of examples.

We associate this objective Bayes approach—making strong assumptions and then testing model fit—with the work of the philosophically minded physicist E. T. Jaynes. As he has illustrated (Jaynes 1983, 1996), the biggest learning experience can occur when we find that our model does not fit the data—that is, when it is falsified—because then we have found a problem with our underlying assumptions.

Conversely, a problem with the inductive philosophy of Bayesian statistics—in which science learns by updating the probabilities that various competing models are true—is that it assumes that the true model is one of the possibilities being considered. This does not fit our own experiences of learning by finding that a model doesn't fit and needing to expand beyond the existing class of models to fix the problem.[5]

We fear that a philosophy of Bayesian statistics as subjective, inductive inference can encourage a complacency about picking or averaging over existing models rather than trying to falsify and go further. Likelihood and Bayesian inference are powerful, and with great power comes great responsibility. Complex models can and should be checked and falsified.

11.5. EXAMPLE: ESTIMATING VOTING PATTERNS IN SUBSETS OF THE POPULATION

In recent years, political scientists have been increasingly interested in the connections between politics and income inequality (see, for example, McCarty, Poole, and Rosenthal 2006). In our own contribution to this literature, we estimated the attitudes of rich, middle-income, and poor voters in each of the fifty states (Gelman, Park, et al. 2008). As we described in our article on the topic (Gelman, Shor, et al. 2008), we began by fitting a varying-intercept logistic regression: modeling votes (coded as y = 1 for votes for the Republican presidential candidate or y = 0 for Democratic votes) given family income (coded in five categories from low to high as -2, -1, 0, 1, 2), using a model of the form, logit $\Pr(y = 1) = a_s + bx$, where s indexes state of residence—the model is fit to survey responses—and the varying intercepts a_s correspond to some states being more Republican-leaning than others. Thus, for example, a_s has a positive value in a conservative state such as Utah and a negative value in a liberal state such as California. The coefficient b represents the slope of income, and its positive value indicates that, within any state, richer voters are more likely to vote Republican.

It turned out that this varying-intercept model did not fit our data, as we learned by making graphs of the average survey response and fitted curves for the different income categories within each state. We had to expand to a varying-intercept, varying-slope model: logit $\Pr(y = 1) = a_s + b_s x$, in which the slopes b_s varied by state as well. This model expansion led to a corresponding expansion in our understanding: We learned that the gap in voting between rich and poor is much greater in poor states such as Mississippi than in rich states such as Connecticut. Thus, the polarization between rich and poor voters varied in important ways geographically.

We found this not through any process of Bayesian induction as usually defined (via the computation of the posterior probabilities of competing hypotheses, paradigms, or scientific models) but rather through model checking. Bayesian inference was crucial, not for computing the posterior probability that any particular model was true—we did not do that—but in allowing us to fit rich enough models in the first place that we could study state-to-state variation, incorporating in our analysis relatively small states such as Mississippi and Connecticut that did not have large samples in our survey.

Life continues, though, and so do our statistical struggles. After the 2008 election, we wanted to make similar plots, but this time we found that even our more complicated logistic regression model did not fit the data—especially when we wanted to expand our model to estimate voting patterns for different ethnic groups. Comparison of data to fit led to further model expansions, leading to our current specification, which uses a varying-intercept, varying-slope logistic regression as a baseline but allows for nonlinear and even nonmonotonic patterns on top of that. Figure 11.1 shows some of our inferences in map form, and figure 11.2 shows some of the data and model fit.

Again, the power of Bayesian inference is deductive: Given the data and some model assumptions, it allows us to make lots of inferences, many of which can be checked and potentially falsified. For example, look at New York State (in the bottom row of figure 11.2): Apparently, voters in the second income category supported John McCain much more than did voters in neighboring income groups in that state. This pattern is possible but it arouses suspicion. A careful look at the graph reveals that this is a pattern in the raw data that was moderated but not entirely smoothed away by our model. The natural next step could be to examine data from other surveys. We may have exhausted what we can learn from this particular dataset, and Bayesian inference was a key tool in allowing us to do so.

11.6. INDUCTIVE INFERENCE AND THE KUHNIAN PARADIGM

We see Bayesian data analysis—or, really, applied statistical analysis in general—as fitting well into the falsificationist approach, as long as we recognize that data analysis includes model checking (as in chapter 6 of Gelman et al. 2003) as well as inference (which, as far as we can see, is purely deductive—proceeding from assumptions to conclusions). Yes, we learn, in a short-term sense, from Bayesian inference—updating the prior to get the posterior—but this is more along the lines of what a Kuhnian might call "normal science." The real learning comes in the model-checking stage, when we can reject a model and move forward. The inference is a necessary stage in this process, however, as it creates the strong conclusions that are falsifiable.

We don't see Bayesian statistics as subjective (any more than any science is subjective in the choice of problems to study and data to focus on). We see a Bayesian model as a clear set of assumptions, whose implications are then deductively evaluated. The assumptions can be subjective but they need not be—except to the extent that all statistical procedures are subjective in requiring some choice of what to do.

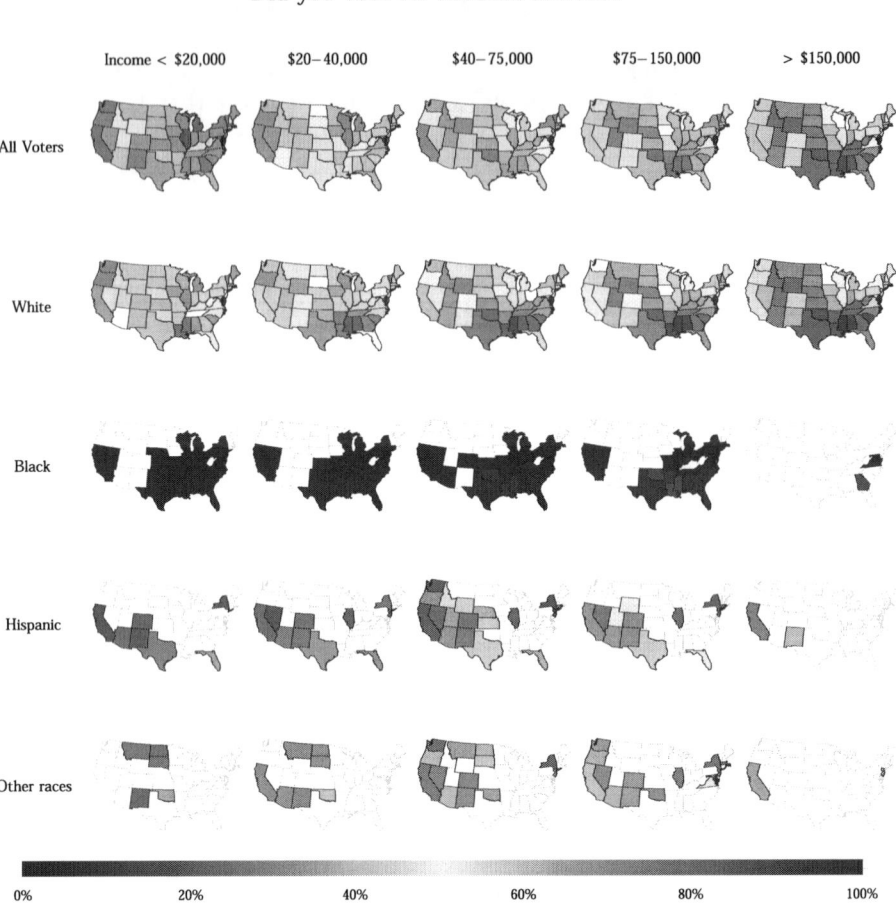

Did you vote for McCain in 2008?

When a category represents less than 1% of the voters in a state, the state is left blank

Figure 11.1 Based on a model fit to survey data: states won by John McCain and Barack Obama among different categories of income and ethnicity (Gelman, Lee, and Ghitza, 2010). States colored deep red and deep blue indicate clear McCain and Obama wins; pink and light blue represent wins by narrower margins, with a continuous range of shades going to pure white for states estimated at exactly 50/50.

In our view, a key part of model-based data analysis is model checking. This is where we see the link to falsification. To take the most famous example, Newton's laws of motion really have been falsified. And we really can use methods such as chi-squared tests to falsify little models in statistics. Now, once we've falsified, we have to decide what to do next, and that isn't obvious. A falsified model can still be useful in many domains (once again, Newton's laws are the famous example). But we like to know that it's falsified.

2008 election: McCain share of the two-party vote in each income category
within each state among all voters (black) and non-Hispanic whites (gray)

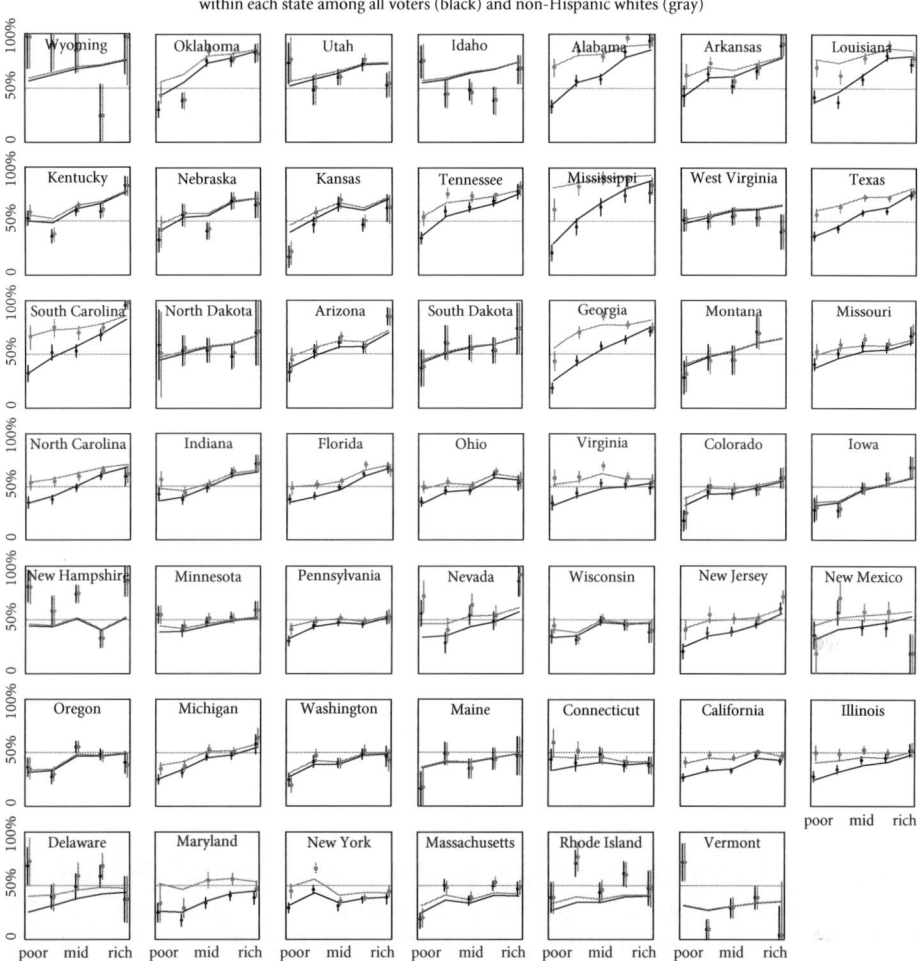

Figure 11.2 Data and fitted model used to make the maps shown in figure 11.1. Dots are
weighted averages from pooled June-November Pew surveys; error bars show +/-1
standard error bounds. Curves are estimated using multilevel models and have a
standard error of about 3 percent at each point. States are ordered in decreasing order
of McCain vote (Alaska, Hawaii, and D.C. excluded). We fit a series of models to these
data; only this last model fit the data well enough that we were satisfied. In working
with larger datasets and studying more complex questions, we encounter increasing
opportunities to check model fit and thus falsify in a way that is helpful for our
research goals.

In our own philosophy of statistics (derived, in part, from our own readings,
interpretations, and extrapolations of Jaynes, Popper, and Lakatos), the point of
falsifying a model is not to learn that the model is false—certainly, all models
that we've ever considered are false, which is why the chi-squared test is sometimes described as a measure of sample size—but rather to learn the ways in

which a model is false. Just as with exploratory data analysis, the goal is to learn about aspects of reality not captured by the model (see Gelman 2003 for more on this).

So, yes, the goal of falsification (as we see it), is not to demonstrate falsity but rather to learn particular aspects of falsity. We are interested in learning about flaws in a model without needing a new model to compare it to.

A standard view of Bayesian model comparison is that you just throw a new model into your class of explanations, and see what comes out having the best posterior odds. This doesn't really work for us, at least not in the problems we've worked on.

11.7. EXAMPLE: ESTIMATING THE EFFECTS OF LEGISLATIVE REDISTRICTING

Our stories of model rejection and new models are more on the lines of: We fitted a model comparing treated and control units (in the particular example that comes to mind, these are state legislatures, immediately after redistrictings or not), and assumed a constant treatment effect (in this case, parallel regression lines in after versus before plots, with the treatment effect representing the difference between the lines). We made some graphs and realized that this model made no sense. The control units had a much steeper slope than the treated units. We fit a new model, and it had a completely different story about what the treatment effects meant. The graph falsified the first model and motivated us to think of something better. The graph for the new model with interactions is shown in figure 11.3. For us, falsification is about plots and predictive checks, not about Bayes factors or posterior probabilities of candidate models.

11.8. CONNECTIONS TO POPPER'S FALSIFICATIONISM

To get back to the philosophers: We suspect that our Popperianism follows the ideas of an idealized Popper (following Lakatos 1978, who introduced the concepts of $Popper_0$, $Popper_1$, and $Popper_2$ to capture different extrapolations of his mentor's ideas).

Apparently the actual Popper didn't want to recognize probabilistic falsification. When one of us read (or attempted to read) *The Logic of Scientific Discovery*

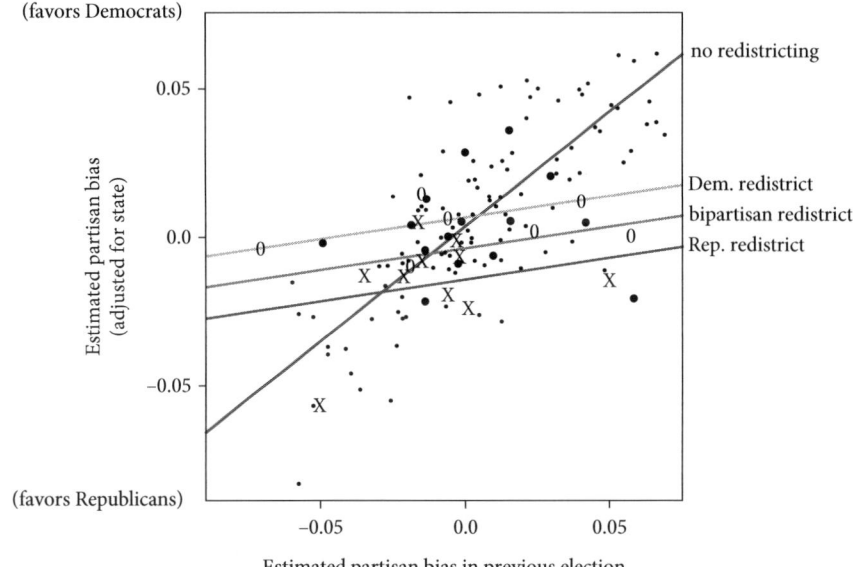

Estimated partisan bias in previous election

Figure 11.3 Effect of redistricting on partisan bias. Each symbol represents a state
election year, with dots indicating controls (years with no redistricting) and the other
symbols corresponding to different types of redistricting. As indicated by the fitted lines,
the "before" value is much more predictive of the "after" value for the control cases than
for the treated (redistricting) cases. The dominant effect of the treatment is to bring the
expected value of partisan bias toward 0, and this effect would not be discovered with
the usual approach, which is to fit a model assuming parallel regression lines for treated
and control cases.

The relevance of this example to the philosophy of statistics is that we began by
fitting the usual regression model with no interactions. Only after visually checking
the model fit—and thus falsifying it in a useful way without the specification of any
alternative—did we take the crucial next step of including an interaction, which
changed the whole direction of our research. The paradigm shift was induced by a
falsification—a bit of deductive inference from the data and the earlier version of
our model.

twenty years or so ago, we skipped over the probability parts because they seemed
full of utopian and probably unrealizable ideas such as philosophical definitions of
randomness. But the idea of falsification—and the dismissal of inductive
inference—well, that part resonated. We're on Popper's side in not believing in
induction as a mode of inference. We don't mind induction in the sense of prediction and minimum-description-length (with more data in a time series, we should
be able to better form an accurate prediction rule using fewer bits to describe the
rule), but induction doesn't fit our understanding of scientific (or social-scientific)
inference.

The main point where we disagree with many Bayesians is that we do *not*
think that Bayesian methods are generally useful for giving the posterior

probability that a model is true, or the probability for preferring model A over model B, or whatever. Bayesian inference is good for deductive inference within a model, but for evaluating a model, we prefer to compare it to data (what Cox and Hinkley 1974 call "pure significance testing") without requiring that a new model be there to beat it.

11.9. The fractal Nature of Scientific Revolutions

With all this discussion of Kuhn and scientific revolutions, we have been thinking of the applicability of these ideas to our own research experiences.

At the risk of being trendy, we would characterize scientific progress as self-similar (that is, fractal). Each level of abstraction, from local problem solving to big-picture science, features progress of the normal science type, punctuated by occasional revolutions. The revolutions themselves have a fractal time scale, with small revolutions occurring fairly frequently (every few minutes for an exam-type problem up to every few years or decades for a major scientific consensus). This is related to but somewhat different from the fractality-in-subject-matter discussed by Abbott (2001).

At the largest level, human inquiry has perhaps moved from a magical to a scientific paradigm. Within science, the dominant paradigm has moved from Newtonian billiard balls, to Einsteinian physics, to biology and neuroscience, and perhaps to developments such as nanotechnology. Within, say, psychology, the paradigm has moved from behaviorism to cognitive psychology. But even on smaller scales, we see paradigm shifts. For example, in working on an applied research or consulting problem, we typically will start in a certain direction, then suddenly realize we were thinking about it wrong, then move forward, and so forth. In a consulting setting, this reevaluation can happen several times in a couple of hours. At a slightly longer time scale, we commonly reassess our approach to an applied problem after a few months, realizing there was some key feature we were misunderstanding.

Thus, we see this normal-science and revolution pattern as fundamental. Which, we think, ties nicely into our perspective of deductive inference (Bayesian or otherwise) as normal science and model checking as potentially revolutionary.

In conclusion, we emphasize that this chapter is our attempt to connect modern Bayesian statistical practice with falsificationist philosophy of science, and does not represent anything like a comprehensive overview of the philosophy-of-science literature. Because we feel the status quo perception of Bayesian philosophy is wrong, we thought it more helpful to present our own perspective forcefully, with the understanding that this is only part of the larger philosophical picture.

ACKNOWLEDGMENTS

We thank Igor Carron, Deborah Mayo, and Harold Kincaid for helpful discussions and the National Science Foundation for grants SES-1023176, ATM-0934516, and SES-1023189, the Institute of Education Sciences for grant ED-GRANTS-032309-005, the Department of Energy for grant DE-SC0002099, and the National Security Agency for grant 523876.

NOTES

1. The so-called Bayesian hypothesis test, in which a null hypothesis H_0 and an alternative hypothesis H_1 are created, and then one computed their relative posterior probabilities, $p(H_0|y)/p(H_1|y)$, is an attempt to reproduce the aims of hypothesis testing in an inductive framework that is not based on falsification. For reasons we discuss in the present article, we do not think the Bayesian hypothesis test as described here makes much sense—it turns out to be completely sensitive to aspects of the model that are untestable from data and are in practice typically set based on conventional rules—but at this point all that is relevant is that, in the standard view, Bayesian inference is based on updating the probability that hypotheses are true, *not* on setting models up for potential falsification.

2. We are citing Wikipedia not as an authoritative source on philosophy or statistics (let alone the combination of the two) but rather as a handy indicator of current consensus.

3. One might think it possible to simply include an alternative, "not-Newton," whose probability would gradually rise toward 1 as new evidence arises to contradict Newton's theory. But this would not work, for two reasons: First, to apply the Bayesian formulation, one would need to specify a specific model for not-Newton, and this would be nothing so simple as merely taking a parameter in the model and allowing it to vary. Our whole point in this example is that Newton's model was falsified in decisive and interesting ways *before* any coherent alternative had been specified. The second reason why the not-Newton gambit would not work, at least nowadays, is that in the modern era we recognize that all scientific models have holes in them. Einstein's relativity has not yet been integrated with quantum mechanics; the familiar probability calculations of genetics are, given the complexities of live cells, only approximations; the laws governing chemical interactions need modification under extreme conditions; and so on. Social science models tend to be even more contingent and full of holes—consider, for example, supply and demand curves, spatial models of voting, and probability distributions for social networks—and the not-Newton alternative in any of these fields, were it even possible to express such a thing, could safely be assigned the probability of 1 without the need to gather any data at all.

Our point here is not that it is impossible to compare models but merely that, under the traditional Bayesian paradigm in which one evaluates the posterior probability of models, it is not possible to reject a model without comparing it to a specific alternative. We find this aspect of the theory unfortunate, given that in our applied research we routinely reject models by themselves. In fact, it is often the information gained in a falsification that gives us direction in searching for a reasonable improvement to the model. Flexible, open-ended model checking is well known in statistical graphics (see, for example, Tukey 1977) but has no formal place in the traditional Bayesian philosophy of statistics. See Gelman (2003) for further discussion of this issue.

4. As Sober (1991) notes, concepts such as simplicity of a model are domain specific and cannot merely be expressed in terms of mathematical structure. This relates to our point that a model check necessarily relates to some aspect of interest of observable reality; even a so-called omnibus test of a model represents some projection in a high-dimensional space. Similarly, Day and Kincaid (1994) argue that the choice of best explanation in any field is domain specific, which is consistent with the statistical idea that model choice must be based on utilities rather than posterior probabilities alone.

5. See the earlier footnote for an explanation why one cannot simply augment Bayesian inference with a catchall hypothesis that represents the space of possible alternatives to the models being studied. In short, there is generally no way to set up such a catchall as a probability model; and if it were possible to formulate a catchall hypothesis, it would (in all the applications we have ever worked on) have a probability of 1: All the models we have ever used have been wrong.

REFERENCES

Abbott, A. 2001. *Chaos of Disciplines*. Chicago: University of Chicago Press.

Beller, M. 2000. *Quantum Dialogue*. Oxford: Oxford University Press.

Cox, D. R., and D. V. Hinkley. 1974. *Theoretical Statistics*. New York: Chapman and Hall.

Dawid, A. P. 2004. "Probability, Causality and the Empirical World: A Bayes-de Finetti-Popper-Borel Synthesis." *Statistical Science* 19: 44–57.

Day, T., and H. Kincaid. 1994. "Putting Inference to the Best Explanation in Its Place." *Synthese* 98: 271–95

Gelman, A. 2003. "A Bayesian Formulation of Exploratory Data Analysis and Goodness-of-Fit Testing." *International Statistical Review* 2: 369–82.

Gelman, A. 2008. "Objection to Bayesian Statistics (with Discussion)." *Bayesian Analysis* 3: 445–78.

Gelman, A., J. B. Carlin, H. S. Stern, and D. B. Rubin. 2003. *Bayesian Data Analysis*. 2d ed. London: CRC Press.

Gelman, A., and G. King. 1994. "Enhancing Democracy Through Legislative Redistricting." *American Political Science Review* 88: 541–59.

Gelman, A., D. Lee, and Y. Ghitza. 2010. "A Snapshot of the 2008 Election." *Statistics, Politics, and Policy*.

Gelman, D. Park, B. Shor, J. Bafumi, and J. Cortina. 2008. *Red State, Blue State, Rich State, Poor State: Why Americans Vote the Way They Do*. Princeton, NJ: Princeton University Press.

Gelman, B. Shor, D. Park, and J. Bafumi. 2008. "Rich State, Poor State, Red State, Blue State: What's the Matter with Connecticut?" *Quarterly Journal of Political Science* 2: 345–67.

Greenland, S. 1998. "Induction Versus Popper: Substance Versus Semantics." *International Journal of Epidemiology* 27: 543–48.

Jaynes, E. T. 1983. *Papers on Probability, Statistics, and Statistical Physics*, R. D. Rosenkrantz, ed. Dordrecht, Netherlands: Reidel.

Jaynes, E. T. 1996. *Probability Theory: The Logic of Science*. Cambridge: Cambridge University Press.

Kuhn, T. S. 1970. *The Structure of Scientific Revolutions*, 2d edition. Chicago: University of Chicago Press.

Mayo, D. G. 1996. *Error and the Growth of Experimental Knowledge*. Chicago: University of
    Chicago Press.
Lakatos, I. 1978. *The Methodology of Scientific Research Programmes*. Cambridge: Cam-
    bridge University Press.
McCarty, N., K. T. Poole, and H. Rosenthal. 2006. *Polarized America: The Dance of Ideology
    and Unequal Riches*. Cambridge, MA: The MIT Press.
Popper, K. R. 1959. *The Logic of Scientific Discovery*. New York: Basic Books.
Savage, L. J. 1954. *The Foundations of Statistics*. New York: Wiley.
Sober, E. 1991. *Reconstructing the Past*. Cambrige, MA: The MIT Press.
Tarantola, A. 2006. "Popper, Bayes and the Inverse Problem." *Nature Physics* 2: 492–94.
Tukey, J. W. 1977. *Exploratory Data Analysis*. Reading, MA: Addison-Wesley.
Wikipedia. 2009. "Bayesian Inference." Available at http://en.wikipedia.org/wiki/Bayesian_
    Inference. Accessed June 9, 2010.

CHAPTER 12

SCIENCES OF HISTORICAL TOKENS AND THEORETICAL TYPES: HISTORY AND THE SOCIAL SCIENCES

AVIEZER TUCKER

PHILOSOPHERS have attempted to distinguish history from the social sciences at least since the neo-Kantians. The criteria they proposed for this distinction are related to larger issues in epistemology (Do history and the social sciences offer different kinds of knowledge? Do they support each other's claims for knowledge, and if so, how?), metaphysics and ontology (do the types of objects history and the social sciences attempt to study, represent, describe, or explain differ, and if so, how does it affect their methodologies?), and the philosophy of science (what is science and how do the social sciences and history relate to it, are they sciences, semi-sciences, or something else?).

Answers to these philosophical questions had practical social implications in affecting the institutional structure of the university. Windelband's 1894 (1980) proposal in his rectorial address outlined the philosophical foundations for the modern distinction between the faculty of humanities (in continental Europe the faculty of philosophy) and the faculties of the sciences, including later the social sciences.[1] Debates within disciplines about interdisciplinary intellectual ventures like historical sociology, social science history, and political history have also revolved around the proper relations between historiography and the social sciences.

In this chapter I first examine critically and dismiss some popular philosophical proposals for distinguishing between historiography and the social sciences. Then

I propose that the distinction between them is between a science that infers *common cause tokens* and sciences that infer *common cause types*. Historiography infers common cause tokens from their information preserving effects. The social sciences infer causal relations between types using statistical methods. I explain why historiography and the social sciences are less relevant for each other than many have assumed. Finally, I argue that the distinction between historiography and the social sciences is a particular case of a more general distinction between the *historical sciences* and the *theoretical sciences*.

A few words about terminology before I continue: Since *history* is ambiguous in ordinary language, I divide its common meanings into three and use two different words to convey those meanings. *Historiography* means here the scientific study of the past, its methodologies and practices. *Historiography* also means the representation of history (the past) that historians infer. *History* means the past. Most of this chapter is about historiography and how it differs from the social sciences, like political science, sociology, and economics.

12.1. CLEARING THE DECK

I do not attempt to present a historical survey of philosophical distinctions between the social sciences and historiography. Still, it is necessary to clear the deck of the clutter of old philosophical theories that have survived in the popular imagination far longer than other philosophic approaches of similar vintage. I speculated elsewhere (Tucker 2010) that the accumulation of philosophies of historiography with little apparent communication among them or resulting progress in the form of intellectual creative destruction is the result of the absence of institutional basis for a community of philosophers of historiography who would use the same language to debate shared problems. I should start then with a bit of much needed creative destruction.

The oldest distinctions between disciplines were founded on the domains of reality they represented. Allegedly, the human subject matter defies scientific methods and rigor and therefore requires different methods of investigation in fields like psychology, the social sciences, and historiography. Since Hegel, the mandarin of the University of Berlin, adhered to this dogma while he was alive, there could be no psychology department at the University of Berlin. Once Hegel died, the apparent dialectical contradiction between science and humanity was resolved (Köhnke 1991). Since then, undeniably scientific methods have been applied successfully to all human and social subject matters (Kincaid 1996). At the same time, the diversity of methods within the sciences has increased exponentially. Today, the methodological or epistemological gap between physics and geology is not narrower than between physics and political science (Miller 1987). Most significantly, even if there had been a yawning epistemic and methodological abyss between the natural and human sciences, it would not help in resolving the relations between historiography and the social sciences since their subject matters are equally human. It could be argued that the old nineteenth-century political historiography was about events, whereas the social sciences are about processes, or that historiography is about the past whereas social science is about the present. But at best, these distinctions are outdated. It is impossible to distinguish historiography from the social sciences on the basis of correspondence with different realm of nature.

The neo-Kantians distinguished among the sciences according to the *purposes* of inquiry and the methodologies appropriate for their achievement. Windelband (1980) proposed that the *nomothetic* sciences aim at the inference of laws whereas the *ideographic* sciences aim at a comprehensive description of events. Ideographic description is the conceptual ancestor of Geertz's (1973) more contemporarily popular "thick" description. Both nomothetic and ideographic sciences may refer to the same realm of nature, the same entities or events. Windelband went as far as asserting that any event can be the subject of both ideographic and nomothetic studies. Windelband overstated his case. Theoretically defined concepts like the electron and events like the degrading of a uranium atom are entirely theory laden; they cannot receive ideographic descriptions. Vice versa, unique events (in some appropriate sense of uniqueness) may necessarily underdetermine all laws that attempt to regulate them and so cannot be the subject of nomothetic science (Tucker 1998). The ideographic ideal is impossible because there is no exhaustive description of anything. Philosophers usually debate explanations of events under descriptions, which are usually theory laden. The nomothetic characterization of science may not fit all or even any of the sciences. Some philosophers of science have argued that when scientists talk of laws of nature they mean symmetry and invariance, rather than the universal laws philosophers have constructed (Van Fraassen 1989).

Windelband's successor, Rickert (1962), attempted to develop the neo-Kantian tradition while interfacing with the positivism of Comte. Comte wanted to construct a science of society in the mold of what he perceived as Newtonian science, made of laws of stability and change. Rickert reinterpreted Comte's distinction in Windelband's terms, associating *stability* with *nomothetic* science and *change* with *ideographic* science. The social sciences would be then nomothetic sciences of stability, whereas historiography would be an ideographic science of change. The origin of this association was Comte's consideration of a contingent element of Newtonian physics, the depiction of stable systems at equilibrium between opposing forces like the solar system, as essential. But there is no correspondence between contemporary social science and stability (*pace* functionalism in sociology), nor does historiography study exclusively change. The social sciences are interested in social change (for example, revolutions), while historiography can study long periods of stability, during what Braudel (1972) called the long duration.

Hempel's (1965) often sited logical-positivist account of explanation in historiography was a "diet" version of the neo-Kantian proposals of Windelband and Rickert, a curious continuity of one philosophical tradition in the guise of another that has usually been overlooked. Like Windelband, Hempel thought that historiographic explanations have a deductive structure. The social sciences would provide many of the major premises and historiography the minor ones. Hempel dropped Windelband's ideographic characterization of historiographic descriptions. Historiography, according to Hempel, is mostly applied social science since most of the covering laws and other generalizations would come from the social sciences (other laws and generalization could come from other sciences or be trivial). The distinctive task of historiography then is to infer descriptions of initial conditions that can be plugged into covering law models. Hempel did not consider how historians infer such historiographic descriptions in the first place.

Humanist foes of Hempel's model argued for limitations on the extent to which historiography can be an applied social science because of the uniqueness or complexity of historical events. They hoped that within such constraints, historiography could carve for itself some autonomy from the social sciences (Dray 1957). The uniqueness of historical events (in some appropriate sense) could prohibit connecting them with universal statements. The complexity of historical events may prevent testing multivariable hypotheses, ascertain causal relations between variables, or determine covering laws.

Both sides to this classical debate assumed that historiography is made of atomic observation-like sentences of the past that are epistemically immediate and unproblematic. In an early Wittgensteinian fashion, the philosophical debate was about how historians string together these atomic beads using conditionals or causal links and explanatory deductive or inductive structures and how they justify these constructs. However, since history was in the past (that is, a tautology), it cannot be perceived, and so there are no observation sentences of history, none at all. The only exception is in cosmology where since it takes time for light to travel from distant space, it is possible to literally observe the cosmic past.[2] It is possible, of course, to observe evidence for the past in the present, but that evidence is not the past itself. Kosso (2001) is the only philosopher I know of to have argued that it is actually possible to observe the past. To make this claim, he had to broaden the concept of observation beyond any other philosophy I know of, to include indirect inferences through evidence. The concept was subjected then to deflation by overinflation, and it became so broad that it failed to make a useful distinction, for example, between observable evidence in the present and the representations that are inferred from it (cf. Ankersmit 2001).

If everything in historiography is inferred rather than observed, including representations of past states of affairs, descriptions, explanations, assertions of causal relations, absolutely everything, there must be a theoretical background for these inferences from the present to the past. If there are no observations of history (with the exception of cosmology), historiography is already theory laden before it could possibly be fitted (or not) into a social science covering law model. Historiography is not applied social science because it has its own theories that infer historiography from evidence. These theories may be able to infer causal relations in the past without resorting to the social sciences. I will argue that these theories are about the transmission of information in time, information theories for short.

Another group of Central European immigrants like Hempel were the Austrian economists. Like Hempel and Popper, they too were immersed in the neo-Kantian philosophy that dominated German-speaking universities until the First World War. Their neo-Kantian allegiances were more explicit: Hayek wrote the introduction to the English language translation of Rickert (1962). But while Windelband and Rickert accepted the existence of psychology and other sciences with a human subject matter and based their distinction of the nomothetic from the ideographic on the purpose of inquiry, Ludwig von Mises retreated into the earlier association of ontological realms of nature with purpose and methodology. Mises associated inanimate nature with search for laws, determinism, and materialism, and the "historical sciences of human action" with the individual characteristics of events (he did not use the term "ideographic") (Mises 2005, 60). This move forced him not just to deny the existence of psychology (Mises 2005, 176–180), but also to deny the possibility of social science that is not derived from action theory and historical sciences whose subject matter is not human—for example, natural history. Obviously he was out of step with the stochastic sciences.

Mises's misconception of historiography is nowhere more apparent than in the statement "the ultimate data of history beyond which no historical research can go are human ideas and actions" (Mises 2005, 106, cf. 123–124). Mises's idealism led him to believe, like Hegel and Croce, that historians can be acquainted directly with ideas and actions as data. Still, there is nothing ultimate about ideas floating in an ephemeral universe outside of space and time. Everything historians learn of historical ideas and actions is inferred through the evidence, typically documents in archives which are the so-called ultimate data of history if any. If so, historiography is not going to be derived from an a priori theory of action, praxeology, but from information theories, about the transmission of information in time from the past to the evidence in the present. Mises (2005, 133–137) dismissed the study of historical evidence as part of what he called historicism—a derogatory conflation of political, methodological, and ontological positions that he linked by association though they had little or nothing to do with each other in the history of ideas.[3]

A final strategy of philosophic defeat may be to conduct anthropological studies of academic departments and examine how the practices and cultures of social science departments differ from those of history departments. But many different things go on in academic departments and they are in constant flux not just because methods improve, but also as the result of random fashions that create intellectual processes akin to genetic drift when some character trait comes to dominate a population not because it endows its bearers with superior survival and reproduction skills, but because of drift (Klein and Stern 2009). From epistemic and methodological perspectives, it is difficult to find much in common within the academic social sciences; some of them are not even scientific (Kincaid 2009). The evolutionary historical process that resulted in the present academic divisions and compositions of departments has been contingent on its origins and sometimes influenced by pragmatic or vocational as distinct from epistemic and methodological considerations. Path dependency is particularly important for eclectic "magpie" social sciences like political science that have amalgamated aspects, theories, and methodologies from law, historiography, economics, game theory, philosophy, and so on. Anthropology is not going to be the salvation of philosophy here.

12.2. TYPES AND TOKENS

I argue here for a simple succinct thesis: Historiography is distinctly interested in inferring common cause *tokens*. The social sciences, by contrast, are distinctly interested in inferring common cause *types*. I show how these mutually exclusive though not exhaustive goals necessitate entirely different methodologies. My thesis is continuous with the neo-Kantian tradition in arguing that the distinction between historiography and the social sciences lies in different goals of inquiry that necessitate different methodologies. I disagree with the neo-Kantians about what these different aims are. Instead of ideographic descriptions and universal laws, I propose the inferences of common cause tokens and types. The methodologies that I propose are appropriate for these two distinct inferences bear no likeness to what the neo-Kantians imagined.

Pierce's type-token distinction has been useful for the analysis of myriad philosophical problems in metaphysics and the philosophies of mind, language and science, ethics and aesthetics (Wetzel 2009, 1–2). For current purposes, it is sufficient to make the fairly uncontroversial claim that as particulars, tokens necessarily occupy a unique spatial-temporal location, whereas types as abstracts do not: "A token event is unique and unrepeatable; a type event may have zero, one or many instances" (Sober 1988, 78). For example, revolution is a type. The French Revolution or the Russian Revolution were tokens of this type. Revolution as a type does not exist in space and time. The French or Russian revolutions had a beginning, middle, and an end and they happened in particular geographical locations.

The French Revolution is the common cause of millions of documents, material remains, and other forms of evidence like paintings. Historians attempt to infer representations of, or claims about, the French Revolution from its contemporary information preserving effects. By contrast, social scientists attempt to generate theories about the causes and effects of revolution as a type. Since types and tokens do not have to share properties (Wetzel 2009, 118–119), social science theories about types like revolution do not have to be about their tokens like the French Revolution. Vice versa, tokens like the French Revolution can illustrate discussions of their types like revolution, but cannot confirm or refute theories whose building blocks are types.

There is a high correlation between the goals, methods, practices, and paradigmatic success stories of historiography and the social sciences, and respectively, the inferences of common cause tokens and types. The evidence for common cause tokens is made of other tokens, documents, material remains, and so on, all existing in space-time. The theories that connect the evidence with the inferred representations of common cause tokens are information theories about the transmission of information in time. By contrast, the social sciences infer common *types* of causes from *types* of effects. The theoretical background for this inference is often from statistics. Often these common cause types are hidden or are not obvious. Their inference is therefore a discovery. Common cause types can be theoretical entities such as nationalism, risk aversion, or social function. Nationalism is a type of mental state whose tokens cannot be observed directly. Various types of effects like wars, artistic expressions, and state formations are explained as the effects of this common cause type. As types, neither the cause nor its effects have specific space or time.

Philosophers who worked on the problem of the inference of common cause have only rarely noted the distinction between the inference of common cause types and tokens. Arntzenius (1992, 230–1) stressed correctly the frequent confusion between types and tokens in philosophic discussions of the inference of common cause. Reichenbach's (1956) examples for inferences of common causes are all of tokens. But his characterization of correlations between effects of common causes as correlations between statistical frequencies is of types. He may have confusedly thought it possible to infer common cause tokens from types of effects. Reichenbach's seminal influence on the philosophic discussion of the problem of inference of common cause and his formulation of the influential "principle of the common cause" that conflated types with token have led to a great deal of confusion in subsequent discussions (Tucker 2007). Within the context of inferences of common cause tokens in phylogeny, Sober (1988; 2001, 339) cleared some of the mess by clearly stating that he was discussing the inference of common cause tokens. I argue too that distinguishing historiography from the social sciences requires the presentation of a clear distinction between the inference of common cause tokens from tokens of effects, and common cause types from types of effects.

12.3. Historical Science

Historians look first for properties that tend *to preserve information* about their origins as evidence for inferring their common causes. The extent to which certain properties of events tend to preserve more information than others is an empirical question that should be examined by what we can call information science that studies the transmissions of types of information via types of media in time and forms and examines theories about them. Some processes tend to preserve in their end states information from their initial state more than others. Processes have varying levels of information preservation, varying levels of *fidelity*, a term used by textual critics to evaluate the reliability of texts (Maas 1958), or *reliability*, the same concept as used in probability theory, or *credibility*, the same concept as used in jurisprudence (Friedman 1987). Information theories also assist in extracting nested information from evidence: Some information is *nested*, and can be inferred only with the aid of theories that link properties explicit in the information signal with information that is nested in it (Dretske 1981, 71–80). For example, historians and detectives use information theories to infer token events from what is *missing* from the evidence: the dog that did not bark in the night. In addition to general theories about the fidelities of certain processes, the evaluation of the reliability of evidence may involve the examination of evidence for the causal chains that purportedly transmitted information from a common cause to the evidence. When authors who report about historical events were separated by time or space from those events, historians look for evidence for the causal chains that may have connected the events with them and estimate their reliabilities. The selection of historical evidence according to its information preserving qualities is theory laden and is bootstrapped by historiographic knowledge of the chains that transmit information in time.

Evidence in historiography always includes correlations or similarities between reliable documents, testimonies, languages, material remains, and so on. I argue that the first stage in the inference of common cause tokens is the comparison of the likelihoods of the similar, information preserving properties of the evidence given *a common cause token* and given *separate causes*: *The common cause hypothesis* asserts that the information preserving properties of the evidence preserve information about some common cause or causes *without specifying the properties of that common cause*. For the common cause hypotheses to be accepted, the likelihood of the evidence given some common cause must be higher than its likelihood given separate causes. Usually, the properties of the separate causes are specified in the hypothesis, unlike the properties of the common cause. For example, suppose that the evidence consists of a set of testimonies that share telling that a certain king murdered his father to inherit the throne. The common cause hypothesis would simply claim that the testimonies share preserving information transmitted from a common cause without specifying its properties—maybe the king indeed murdered his father or maybe a group of false witnesses colluded to frame the orphan, or maybe some other common cause was at work. The separate causes hypothesis would usually specify the separate causes: that one witness hated the king, for example, while another was loyal to the next in line for the throne, a third had an interest in discrediting the dynasty, and a fourth lost his job as a result of the succession.

It is often difficult but also unnecessary to assign *precise* quantitative likelihoods because historians do not prove the high likelihood of the evidence given the hypothesis they favor as much as prove its negligible likelihood given the alternative hypothesis. Since the common cause and separate causes hypotheses are exhaustive and mutually exclusive, proving that one of the hypotheses is improbable implies that the other must be the case.

Formally, if E_1 & E_2 & ... E_n are units of evidence that share certain properties and C is some common cause, the likelihood of the evidence given the common cause hypothesis is:

$$\Pr(E_1 \& E_2 \& ...E_n|C) = \Pr(E_1|C) \times \Pr(E_2|C). \; ... \times \Pr(E_n|C)$$

Reichenbach mentioned the same formal equation (1956, 157–167). However, the meaning of C in my equation is of *some token common cause* without specifying its properties, whereas Reichenbach's concept of the common cause was ambiguous not to say confused about whether it is a type or a token and whether or not its properties are specified. Formally, assessing the likelihood of the evidence given separate causes $(S_1, S_2, \ldots S_n)$, background knowledge B, and their respective prior probabilities can be expressed by the following equation:

$$Pr(E_1 \& E_2 \ldots \& E_n | S_1 \& S_2 \ldots \& S_n)$$
$$= [Pr(S_1|B) \times Pr(E_1|S_1)] \times [Pr(S_2|B) \times Pr(E_2|S_2)] \ldots \times [Pr(S_n|B) \times Pr(E_n|S_n)]$$

In assessing the priors of the common cause and separate causes hypotheses, historians examine whether causal chains that extend backward from the units of the evidence could or could not have intersected and converged.

The likelihood of the evidence given separate causes reflects the functions of the shared properties of the evidence. Sometimes, the shared properties of the evidence have the same *type* of function and the same *type* of cause. For example, if in a culture such as the Roman one, the worst insult to a man would be to claim that he married a prostitute and then committed incest with their children, testimonies that share the desire to insult the man or defame his memory will say so about him. The causes for these shared properties of the testimonies are tokens of the same *type*, the desire to smear somebody's reputation in a common cultural context. These testimonies do not preserve information about any token event.

Evidence whose shared information preserving properties have no conceivable functional value or even confer a disadvantage on their bearers—such as testimonies that present the witnesses in a negative light or run counter to their interests or political or ideological commitments—usually radically decrease the likelihood of the evidence given separate causes. The likelihood of any single such testimony given separate causes is low, the likelihood of several identical ones given separate causes is vanishing. When the likelihood of each unit of evidence given separate causes is low, the effect of multiple members, such as similar testimonies, is to decrease exponentially this likelihood. Therefore, historians devote great efforts for the discovery of multiple testimonies and other units of evidence.

Multiple units of evidence such as testimonies often achieve a significant gap between the roughly estimated likelihoods of the evidence given these two hypotheses. Formally, the ratio of likelihoods of similar evidence given common cause to separate causes hypotheses is:

$$\{[Pr(E_1|C) \times Pr(C|B)] \times [Pr(E_2|C) \times Pr(C|B)] \times \ldots \times [Pr(E_n|C) \times Pr(C|B)]\}$$

$$\{[Pr(E_1|S_1) \times Pr(S_1|B)] \times [Pr(E_2|S_2) \times Pr(S_2|B)] \times \ldots \times [Pr(E_n|S_n) \times Pr(S_n|B)]\}$$

$E_1, E_2, \ldots E_n$ stand for units of evidence; C stands for the hypothetical common cause; $S_1, S_2 \ldots S_n$ stand for separate causes, and B stands for background knowledge.

The upper part represents the likelihood of the evidence, given the common cause hypothesis; the lower its likelihood, given separate causes.

If the likelihood of the evidence given some common cause is significantly higher than that of separate causes, historians attempt to determine a causal-informational map that connects all the units of evidence, such as testimonies with some common cause. Five alternative types of causal nets are possible:

(1) *A single historical event is the common cause of all the units of evidence*: The modeling of the history of the transmission of information would be tree-like and composed of Y- or V-like intersections. They were all caused by this single event.

(2) *Multiple ancestral common causes:* All the units of evidence are the effects of the same set of common causes. For example, suppose there are two sources of evidence today for an event in ancient history. Both were written hundreds of years after the event by historians who had access to the same two primary sources that had since been lost. The modeling of the history of the transmission of information would be bush-like with W-like intersections.

(3) *The common cause may be one of the units of evidence.* For example, historians may have three sources for an ancient event. But two of the sources may have simply copied the third one. The model of the history of the transmission of information would contain <-like intersections.

(4) All the units of the evidence may have affected each other, for example, if several witnesses discussed what they saw after the event or if editors compared several versions of a text to unify them. The model of the history of the transmission of information would look like a web composed of H-like intersections where information is transmitted between all the units.

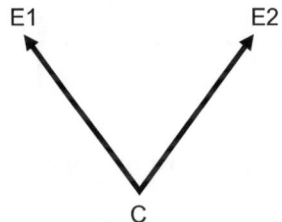

Figure 12.1 Causal-Information Net 1

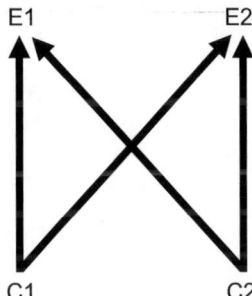

Figure 12.2 Causal-Information Net 2

(5) *Complex combinations of types 1 or 2, with types 3 or 4.* The evidence had one or more common sources and later there were interaction between the various units of evidence. For example, several ancient oral traditions were combined together to create a unified text. The editors sought not just to preserve the ancient sources, but also to create a coherent text that may also have fitted their political interests. The model of historical information transmission would include A-like (or upside-down A-like) or X-like intersections.

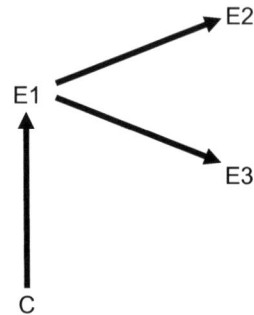

Figure 12.3 Causal-Information Net 3

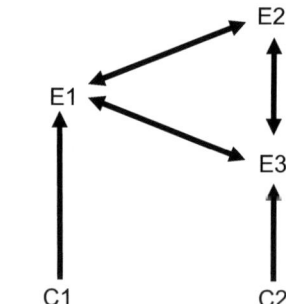

Figure 12.4 Causal-Information Net 4

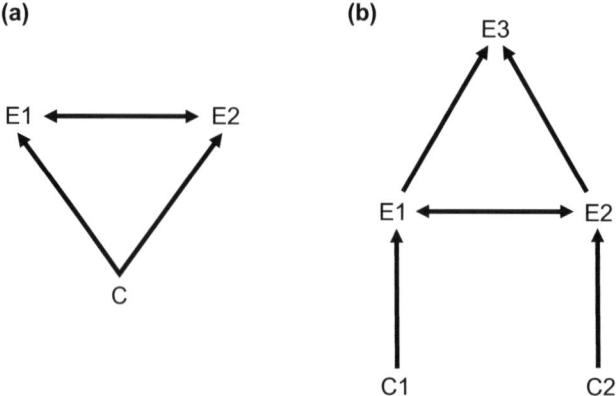

Figure 12.5 Causal-Information Net 5

Another way of saying that the evidence has common cause or causes but no mutual causal influences, corresponding exclusively with the first V or second W models of information transmission above, is by describing its members as *independent. Independence of evidence is the absence of intersection between the causal-information chains that connect the units of evidence with their common cause or causes.* If the evidence is not independent, the historian needs to distinguish the properties of the evidence that preserve information about an original common cause or causes from those that preserve information about later stages in information transmission between the units of evidence.

When evidence for the information transmission is scarce, more than one of the five possible common cause hypotheses may confer equal likelihoods on the evidence. For example, though it is highly more probable that the Indo-European languages had common rather than separate causes, the evidence underdetermines whether it was a single language, proto-Indo-European, or whether several geographically proximate languages mutually influenced each other until they became very similar, before spreading tree-like around the globe through the Latin, Germanic, and Slavic language families while continuing to influence each other, as in the wave theory of language.

Historians are able in many cases to infer which of the five possible common cause hypotheses is most probable. For example, textual critics were able to prove that the various exemplars of the Bible and Homer's epics had initially multiple common causes and then they influenced each other in the process of editing (the A-like model 5). There is independent evidence in many cases for links on the causal information chains that connect events with evidence for the presence of a single or multiple common causes. Composite documents may preserve linguistic differences that indicate multiple common causes. Historians and textual critics look for discontinuities in style, conceptual framework, and implicit values, as well as internal contradictions, gaps in the narrative if there is one, and parts that are inconsistent with the alleged identity of the author. Frequently, the theories that assist in the assessment of the fidelity of evidence and the competitiveness of the common cause hypothesis also assist in proving whether there was a single or multiple common causes. For example, assuming the theory that the mutation rate of the names of God is lower than those of other words, that the fidelity of the names of God is higher than that of other parts of edited documents, it is possible to analyze parts of the Bible into its constituent parts, as the first biblical critics did, according to the different names of God used in the text.

When one of the possible five common cause hypotheses clearly increases the likelihood of the evidence more than its alternatives, scientists may attempt to infer the properties of the common causes. The evidence may not suffice for determining the properties of the common causes. For example, from the references in the Bible to two lost older books, the *Book of the Wars of Jehovah* and the *Book of Righteousness*, it is possible to infer that some of the materials in the Bible were caused by these books, but there is not much that can be known about them. Likewise, humans and apes had a single most recent common ancestor about six million years ago, but many of the character traits of that ancestor are unknown.

When there is sufficient evidence, historians compare the likelihoods of the evidence given competing representations of history. Historians evaluate the prior probabilities of these competing specific common cause hypotheses according to whether the hypotheses are coherent with established historiography and internally coherent (cf. Kosso 2001, 106–108).

The prior probabilities of common cause hypotheses, C_1, C_2, ... C_n, given background information B can then be multiplied by the likelihoods of the evidence, E_1, E_2, ... E_n, given these common cause hypotheses:

$$Pr(E_1 \& E_2, \ldots \& E_n | C_1)$$
$$= [Pr(C_1|B) \times Pr(E_1|C_1)] \times [Pr(C_1|B) \times Pr(E_2|C_1)] \times \ldots \times [Pr(C_1|B) \times Pr(E_n|C_1)]$$

The comparison of competing common cause hypotheses is then simply

$$Pr(E_1 \& E_2 | C_1) : Pr(E_1 \& E_2 | C_2)$$

12.4. THE INFERENCE OF COMMON CAUSE TYPES IN THE SOCIAL SCIENCES

The most prominent character of the social sciences over the last hundred years has been an increasing concentration on the inference of causes (Box-Steffensmeier et al. 2010). Some institutionally recognized social scientists use the methodologies of the historical sciences to infer common cause tokens, for example in case studies and process tracing (George and Bennett 2005; Bennett 2010). The inference of causal models connecting types of common cause with types of effects through the application of statistical methods such as the Neyman-Rubin model of causal inference is not exclusively distinct from the social sciences. The social subject matter distinguishes the social sciences from sciences that use similar statistical methods to infer common cause types like medicine or agronomy (Morgan and Winship 2007; Brady 2010; Sekhon 2010).

The social sciences begin with hypotheses that connect types of causes with correlated types of effects. The transition from tokens to types of causal relations is achieved via the averaging of causal effects. For example, the correlation between higher than average income, interest in classical music, and the number of books purchased annually may be the result of higher education. Social scientists would measure the average effect of higher education, not its effect on this or that individual. The inference of common cause types proceeds in two stages:

In the first stage, social scientists need to prove that the correlations between the types of effects (income, music, and books in my contrived example) are more likely given the common cause type (higher education) than given separate types of causes. Social scientists specify the properties of the common cause type they propose, but do not specify the properties of the alternative types of separate causes (confounders whose properties are specified are alternative common causes). The method for achieving a significant gap between the likelihoods of the correlations given the common cause type and the unspecified separate causes that may be many, varied and unknown, is the random assignment of members to two populations to make them nearly identical in sharing the same types of (unknown or unspecified) variables with the exception of the common cause type (sometimes called the treatment) that all the members of one group share and none of the members of the other (control) group are affected by. Significant differences between the two populations are likely then to be the result of that common cause type. For example, social scientists may choose a random sample of persons representing a population and divide the random sample into two randomly assigned equal and sufficiently large groups, whose only difference is the presence or absence of the hypothetical common cause type (higher education in our example). Then, social scientists would measure the difference in the putative effects between the two populations (e.g., annual income, hours per week spent listening to classical music, and number of books purchased annually) and see if there is a significant gap between the two groups. If so, the correlation between the types of effects is more likely given the common cause type than given unspecified separate types of causes.

Social scientists may test simpler hypotheses that relate just one type of effect with one type of cause, say, the effect of higher education just on the level of income. Proving that the cause (the "treatment") increases the likelihood of the effect, rather than another hidden cause or causes, follows the same procedure: the comparison of two randomly assigned populations, one with and the other without the treatment. Such simple cause-effect hypotheses are not very common, even in medicine, where hypotheses deal more often with the effect of a treatment on symptoms rather than on a single type of illness. Since types of causes usually have multiple types of effects, scientists are usually, though not universally, interested in studying multiple types of effects of a common cause type.

Let me emphasize the differences between historiography and the social sciences. Their goals and methods are the mirror image of each other. Historiography is interested in inferring common cause tokens. The social sciences infer common cause types. Historiography compares in the first stage the likelihoods of information preserving evidence given a *common cause token whose character traits are unknown*, and separate *cause tokens whose character traits are known and are often separate tokens of the same type* like the will to defame somebody in a cultural context. In the social sciences the character traits of the proposed common cause type are specified. But the character traits of the alternative separate causes are not specified. A comparison with any separate causes hypothesis that specifies their properties would not yield the increase in likelihood of the effects given the common cause type that social scientists (and medical and crop scientists) are interested in. The potential number of separate causes types is infinite. No single model can evaluate the effects of specific types of separate causes on types of effects.

Historians try to prove that the evidence is more likely given a common cause token than separate causes *using information theories*. By contrast, social scientists use statistical randomization techniques to prove the causal relevance of common cause types. Types of effects in the social sciences need not preserve information about their causes.[4]

Historically, the methods of historiography and the social sciences were borrowed from other disciplines with different subject matters. Historiography adopted the methods of turn of the nineteenth century textual criticism and philology (Tucker 2004, 46–85). The social sciences borrowed their methodologies in the early twentieth century from the statistical observation data analysis methods that had been developed for the analysis of crop yields and for clinical trials of medicines (Morgan and Winship 2007, 6–13). Both history and the social sciences have increased the sophistication and expanded the methodological tool kit they received. But their Lakatosian theoretical core has not been replaced since the early nineteenth and early twentieth centuries, respectively.

Once the social sciences establish that the evidence is more likely given the specified common cause type than given separate causes, social scientists attempt to find the exact causal relations, which may be complex. One or more of the effect types may affect the others requiring the construction of multicollinear, interactive, and so on models. Some social scientists demand further the discovery of mechanisms as necessary conditions for the inference of causal relations in the social sciences. It is not necessary to take sides in these debates here (see chapter 2 and 3 in this volume), since I attempt to do a descriptive rather than normative philosophy of the social sciences. Suffice it to say that in this second stage social scientists attempt to use a variety of tools to infer increasingly precise causal nets. For example, high income may grant its beneficiaries the free time to listen to classical music and read books and the money to buy books and CDs. Perhaps reading books improves income through acquisition of knowledge and cognitive skills. Additionally, social scientists need to control for hidden variables types that may cause both the common cause type and its effects. For example, family wealth may affect both the level of educational attainment, the level of income, and leisure time for cultivating one's taste in music and reading.

In the experimental sciences, including experimental social science, experimental designs control types of variables to isolate their effects. When such experiments are impossible, as is the case with most of the theories and hypotheses of the social sciences, they resort to statistical observational data analysis. If successful, using a variety of statistical control techniques to hold different variables constant while measuring others, social scientists conduct multivariate regression analyses that generate equations and multi-equation models, and causal maps that measure levels of causal influence that each variable exerts on the others on a scale from 0 to 1. The posterior probabilities of causal hypotheses need not be affected by the means by which the researcher infers them, whether control of types of causes is achieved in the laboratory by design and intention, or through other "natural" undersigned experimental methods, or by using statistical analysis of observational data.

Historians operate entirely differently. If they wish to examine a token of the relation between education and income, say in the biography of a person, they will collect evidence and infer from it representations of the events or process that took place. They will find out that the philosopher Charles Sanders Peirce's very high education did not do much for his income. By contrast, Irving Berlin's lack of education did not stop him from becoming wealthy. Historians can follow exactly why Peirce's education was of no financial advantage to him (his unconventional morals in the context of puritanical America acted as an intervening variable to prevent him from gaining an academic position; and his writings and other skills were not in demand) and why Irving Berlin did not need formal education to become a successful composer of popular music.

It is possible to conduct a regression analysis for a sample drawn from a spatio-temporally defined population. It may be possible, for example, to draw a causal map that connects higher education, income, and so on, say, in the United States before and after 1945 tracing the effects of the GI Bill. However, I would argue that this kind of research infers common cause types and not tokens, and so is part of the social sciences or social science history. The variables studied—higher education, income, and so on—are abstract objects that may have instances: They are types. The income of no single individual after 1945 had the kind of regression analysis that the social scientist would discover any more than any family has ever had 2.3 children. Historians by contrast would find out how the GI Bill affected individuals and then amalgamate. They would not randomize or conduct regression analysis.

Let me be clear: There is nothing wrong with using social science methodologies on historical data. Some people who are institutionally identified as historians do it; that is fine and their results are interesting. However, when they infer common cause types, abstract object that do not correspond with any historical event, they do so as social scientists and not historians. Theoretical science can but does not have to be universal. Vice versa, there are scholars who make a living as social scientists by doing qualitative analysis and trace path dependencies and processes (George and Bennett 2005). There is nothing wrong with what they do and their results are interesting. But what they actually do is historical science, not social science. They trace common cause tokens and not types.[5]

12.5. Interactions between Historiography and the Social Sciences

Single tokens are not useful for the evaluation of theories made of types. An unemployed PhD does not disprove the causal relation between higher education and higher income. The British-American war of 1812 or the British-Finnish conflict within the Second World War or any of thirty possible exceptions do not disprove that democracy favors peace among democratic nations according to the democratic peace theory (George and Bennett 2005, 37–59). Many variables affect income or war and peace. If democracy is one factor that encourages peace among democratic states (as discussed by Chernoff in chapter 10 in this volume), the theory does not deny that other variables are at play in history and may overwhelm the effects of democracy, just as other factors may overwhelm the effects of higher education on income, as in the case of poor Peirce.

It is possible to characterize a type as having a certain property even if not all its tokens have the property. Though many tokens (for example, of letters and words) resemble each other and share properties, not all do: "The analogy to zoology is helpful . . . Not every so-called black bear is black; not every grizzly is four-legged, brown or has a hump . . . It may be permissible to characterize the species in terms of such properties anyway . . . In many cases, one extrapolates from properties of the tokens, individually or collectively, to properties of the type. However, . . . even if the overwhelming majority of the tokens have a property it does not entail that the type has it" (Wetzel 2009, 119, 120). A type may also have a property that most of its tokens do not share. For example, most of the tokens of a word type may be spelled differently than the type. Some properties of a type are not shared by any of its tokens; for example, "the grizzly bear is endangered" (Wetzel 2009, 120). The relations between social science types and historiographic tokens are not closer.

Historiography and the social sciences typically resort to each other when their usual evidence and methods of inference are insufficient for inferring respectively common cause tokens or types. Such underdetermination is manifested often as multiple different or even mutually inconsistent competing underdetermined hypotheses and theories. While the social sciences and historiography can and do help each other in reducing underdetermination, the scope of this mutual assistance is limited. The challenge is to connect the right types with the right tokens, so they are mutually relevant.

Social science theories may participate in the token inferring process as *information transmission theories*. Historians possess a toolkit of information theories. Some theories originated in historiography itself or in adjacent fields like jurisprudence or philology, for example, that eyewitness reports written immediately after the events are more reliable than memoirs written years later or that reports written by people with an interest in the effects of the reports are less reliable than reports written by people without such interests (for example, diaries or deathbed confessions). From a contemporary anachronistic perspective these information theories may appear to be commonsense psychology, but their historically recent origins demonstrate that they are neither commonsensical nor trivial. There is no evidence for communities that shared these theories prior to the eighteenth century, only for isolated individuals who developed some such theories without measurable effect on the history of ideas. Social science theories can help in extracting nested information from the evidence, or direct historians to examine new sources of evidence containing nested information. For example, theories of inflation from economics interpret ancient "shaved" metal coins that debased the coinage as a form of devaluation of the currency in relation to a gold (or other metal) standard. They extract the nested information about a rate of inflation embedded in the coins according to the percentage of the metal lost in the debasing (De Cecco 1985).

Social science theories may also assist in all three stages of historiographic inference by helping to assess priors. For example, historians attempt to find when, where, and who wrote the Bible. The social science theory that connects the introduction of writing to the establishment of strong bureaucratic central government that develops or adopts writing to keep track of the taxes it collects would decrease the prior probability that the texts that became the Bible could have been written before the establishment of a strong monarchy. Therefore, the Pentateuch and the books of Joshua and Judges could have been written only centuries after the events they describe were supposed to have happened.

Archaeology uses the methodologies of the social sciences and of historiography. Archaeological social science theories assist in evaluating the prior probabilities of historical archaeological hypotheses that explain archaeological evidence, usually material remains (Salmon 1982, 42–49).

Historiography can provide social science with data that may participate in the process of inferring types of causes. Selected, abstracted, and conceptually homogenized through averaging to fit a theory that makes correlations between types apparent, historiography can provide raw evidence for the inference of common cause types. However, since history and therefore historiography are usually complex, it is difficult for social scientists to isolate appropriate multiple tokens of type-type causal relations. It is difficult to distinguish which tokens of types of causes were responsible for which tokens of types of effects. If a social science theory claims that cause of type A has an effect of type B, if a token of B does not follow a token of A in a historical case, it does not imply that the theory is false. The theory may be flawed, but its scope may be limited, or it may require auxiliary hypotheses to deal with intervening variables (George and Bennet 2005, 115–117). Vice versa, if token A is indeed followed by token B, B could be the result of a token of another type of cause or causes. B may be overdetermined by different processes, what social scientists call equifinality (George and Bennett 2005, 161–162).

12.6. THE COSTS OF BRIDGING THE GAP

The social sciences and historiography can coexist harmoniously without disturbing each other. However, when social science theories are pressured to explain history or fit historiography, social science theories may attempt to bridge the gap between what they say about types and historical tokens that appear not to fit the theory in four ways:

First, the theories can become vague, so they can be interpreted in different and even inconsistent ways and remain vaguely intact. For example, the democratic peace theory can be vague in its characterization of democracy and peace, so apparent counterexamples could be dismissed as wars between at least one not-truly-democratic state or as not really wars but lesser conflicts. Marxist theories are notoriously vague in the same way about class, the bourgeoisie, and so on. Another more polite way of putting it is to suggest one should "make assumptions of unit homogeneity or similarity of cases that may not be justified . . . to redefine and broaden the research problem to make it possible to identity a large enough number of cases to permit statistical analysis" (George and Bennett 2005, 164).

Second, social science theories can become complex and ad hoc; add many ad hoc hypotheses and mini-theories to account for all the apparent historical anomalies. For example, Skocpol's theory of social revolution had to add many ad hoc hypotheses and become very complex to fit all the differences between the three cases she compared and the theory of revolutions she developed (Tucker 2004, 151–160).

Third, social science theory may fit perfectly one and only one historical case. It may turn descriptions of tokens into descriptions of types merely by dropping their specific space-time coordinates, keeping all their other complex properties. Such a social science theory would have no anomalies or exceptions. But it would have the underdetermining scope of a single historical case.

Fourth, all three methods can combine into one when a theory that is vague or complex is fragmented into ad hoc theories each of which fits one and only one historical case perfectly. The ad hoc theories are loosely linked with each other as different interpretations of the same vague or complex theory. They would mention the same vague concepts and theories but use them to convey different and mutually inconsistent meanings. Fragments of complex theories use different corners of the complex theory. But if it were attempted to put all these fragments together, reassemble the jigsaw puzzle, they would not fit together. Alternatively, it is possible to interpret vague theories clearly and consistently, but then add numerous ad hoc hypotheses to explain away all the anomalies. The result is a theory that is clear and of a wide scope, but also cumbersomely complex with ad hoc hypotheses heaped on top of each other to explain the anomalies. This is the basic problem of all attempts to create a synthesis between the social sciences and historiography: historical sociology, historical economics, social science history, Marxist historiography, structuralist historiography, and so on. They have to face trade-offs between scope and accuracy, complexity and incoherence. Schematically the forced moves of historical social science look like figure 12.6.

A vague theory can have a broad scope but no accuracy. If it attempts to become more accurate, it must do so at the cost either of becoming cumbersomely complex with numerous ad hoc hypotheses, or fragment into mutually incoherent small theories.

Consequently, the views that historiography is applied social science and the social sciences provide the laws or general principles for historiographic explanations, or that history is the subject matter of the social sciences do not reflect reality. The actual interaction between historiography and the social sciences is limited. The social sciences may lend historiography some of their theories as applied information

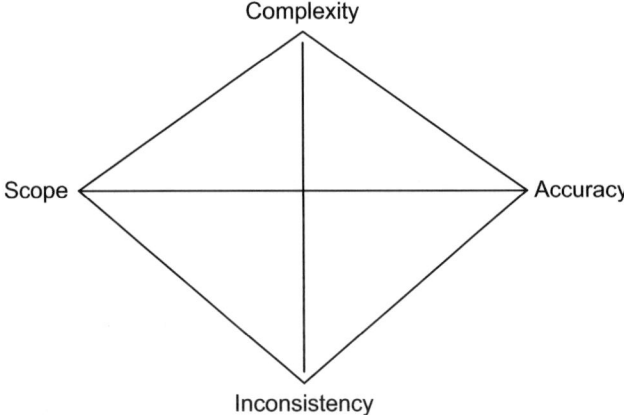

Figure 12.6 **Forced moves in social science history**

theories. They may also affect the evaluation of the priors of historiographic hypo-theses. The conclusions of historiographic research may *illustrate* rather than confirm or refute the results of social science research (cf. George and Bennett 2005, 57). It may also inspire the development of theory, especially when a historical case seems to deviate from what a social science theory would lead the researcher to expect. Ad hoc explanations invoking new hidden variables may explain the deviation and evolve into a new theory (George and Bennett 2005, 111–115). That is about it.

12.7. CONCLUSION: OVERCOMING THE POSITIVIST AND HUMANIST DOGMAS

The argument I have been presenting here entails the sacrifice of two philosophic holy cows, or dogmas, associated respectively with the humanist and the positivist schools. Both are deeply rooted in the intellectual world of the first half of the nine-teenth century in Europe, yet they proved incredibly resilient for two centuries. They keep echoing through the chambers of philosophy like ghosts that haunt the divided house of philosophy long after they died of natural causes.

Despite the establishment of psychology in the nineteenth century, humanists have continued to claim that there is a crucial epistemic and methodological dis-tinction between the sciences that have human and those that have nonhuman subjects. Instead, we saw that the epistemically and methodologically relevant distinction is between the historical and theoretical sciences of tokens and types. Historiography has more in common with geology, phylogeny, and historical lin-guistics than with the social sciences. To quote Bennett: "All attempts to diagnose or explain individual or historical cases involve process tracing. This is true not only of social events like the Fashoda crisis, the end of the First World War, and the end of the cold war, but of historical events in the hard sciences, like the origins of a particular rock formation (geology), the extinction of the dinosaurs (evolutionary biology), or the origins of the universe (cosmology)" (Bennett 2010, 705). Epistemically and methodologically, the social sciences have more in common with agronomy and epidemiology than with historiography.

Another tradition started with Hume, continued with Comte and Mill, and culminated in a somewhat more modest form with the neo-Kantians and Hempel. It has considered history to be an applied science. For Hume and Mill the relevant science was of human nature. Comte called it sociology. Far from it: We saw that currently there is no such science and there has never been such a science. Attempts to apply social science theories to history as represented by historiography usually stumble against the gap between types and tokens and the complexity of the subject matter and have to resort to vagueness or ad hoc complexity or fragment into incoherent mini-theories.

The difference between historiography and the social sciences is a particular case of the difference between the historical and theoretical sciences of tokens and types. Several historical sciences are concerned with inferring token common causes or origins: phylogeny and evolutionary biology infer the origins of species from information preserving similarities between species, DNAs, and fossils; comparative historical linguistics infers the origins of languages from information preserving aspects of existing languages and theories about the mutation and preservation of languages in time; archaeology infers the common causes of present material remains; and cosmology infers the origins of the universe. These are the historical sciences, sciences that attempt to infer rigorously descriptions of past events, processes, and their causal relations from their information preserving effects. The theoretical sciences are not interested in any particular *token* event, but in *types* of events: Physics is interested in the atom, not in this or that atom at a particular space and time; biology is interested in the cell, or in types of cells, not in this or that token cell; economics is interested in modeling recessions, not in this recession; and generative linguistics studies language generally and not any particular language that existed in a particular time and was spoken by a particular group of people. The theoretical sciences are interested in regularities between types. The distinctions between realms of nature and academic disciplines are epistemically and methodologically arbitrary.

Since from an epistemic and methodological perspective, historiography has more in common with geology, and the social sciences with agronomy, than with each other, one implication of this chapter is the elimination of a special place for human beings, their societies and histories in epistemology. Following the Galilean and Darwinian revolutions, it is time to release ourselves from yet another narcissistic belief in our uniqueness, this time our alleged epistemic uniqueness. Epistemically, understanding our past is like understanding rocks and stones and understanding our society is like understanding wheat and weeds.

The positivist dream of a science of theoretical historiography has led to a further fantasy of applied human engineering that could then use this theoretical knowledge to control history often through central planning and the state. As I noted above, the main mutual relevance of the social sciences and historiography is limited, partly because of the complexity of history. Well-confirmed social science theories cannot be applied to historical cases while maintaining their accuracy, scope, simplicity, and internal coherence. When social engineers attempt to apply theoretically based models to brute reality, unpredictable anomalies, unintended consequences, and so on always creep, emerge, and then accumulate. This does not imply that there is anything wrong with social science theories. True, sometimes the model is wrong because it contains false assumptions—by assuming that the prices of real estate never go down, for example—but most of the time, what is wrong with social engineering is not its models, but the expectation that historical reality will conform to them.

NOTES

1. The traditional philosophically founded structure of the university, introduced by Windelband at the University of Strasburg, is still the dominant one in most European and many American universities. The main competing model, of schools, larger than departments but smaller than faculties, was introduced more recently in the United Kingdom. The reasons for this competing model are not philosophical or epistemic, but managerial, the alleged efficiency of sharing the secretarial pool. Intellectually, the admirable ideal was to foster interdisciplinary research and education in a unit larger than a department but smaller than a faculty to facilitate interactions between researchers. However, in practice, like other state-sponsored top-down coercive projects of social engineering, this one backfired as well. Since the amalgamation of academic units is often intellectually arbitrary, there is no organic growth of interdisciplinary cooperation, but a coerced simulation of it to the exclusion of interdisciplinary cooperation with competing schools. A British joke foresees the amalgamation of the Faculty of Engineering with the Department of Comparative Literature in the School of Construction and Deconstruction (cf. Tucker 2012).

2. In principle, if some alien thousands of light years away from earth directed a cosmic magnifying mirror toward earth and then broadcast the images back to earth, it could be possible to observe the past. But this is a science fiction scenario.

3. Popper in his *Poverty of Historicism* also used *historicism* as a derogatory term, conflating many different positions he despised (Passmore 1975). Still, as broad and confused as Popper's concept of historicism is, Mises used *historicism* in an even broader and more confused fashion.

4. "Classical" social and political theories, e.g., the works of Max Weber, Karl Marx, and Émile Durkheim, classical economics in the tradition of Adam Smith, and contemporary rational choice, game theoretical, and other formal models are just as theoretical, composed entirely of types and their relations. They differ from contemporary social science in attempting to justify their theories often deductively, without resorting to the statistical methods or empirical data that dominate much of contemporary social science.

5. Be that as it may, in the Darwinian jungle of academic departmental politics some will always object to somebody's interesting and rigorously derived results because they are "really" this rather than that, and so should not be employed "here."

REFERENCES

Ankersmit, F. R. 2001. *Historical Representation*. Stanford, CA: Stanford University Press.

Arntzenius, Frank. 1992. "The Common Cause Principle." *PSA: Proceedings of the Biennial Meeting of the Philosophy of Science Association* 1992, Vol. II: 227–337.

Bennett, Andrew. 2010. "Process Tracing: A Bayesian Perspective." In *The Oxford Handbook of Political Methodology*, Janet M. Box-Steffensmeier, Henry E. Brady, and David Collier, eds., 702–21. Oxford: Oxford University Press.

Box-Steffensmeier, Janet M., Henry E. Brady, and David Collier. 2010. "Political Science Methodology." In *The Oxford Handbook of Political Methodology*, Janet M. Box-Steffensmeier, Henry E. Brady, and David Collier, eds., 3–31. Oxford: Oxford University Press.

Brady, Henry E. 2010. "Causation and Explanation in Social Science." In *The Oxford Handbook of Political Methodology*, Janet M. Box-Steffensmeier, Henry E. Brady, and David Collier, eds., 217–70. Oxford: Oxford University Press.

Braudel, Fernand. 1972. *The Mediterranean and the Mediterranean World in the Age of Philip II*, Siân Reynolds, trans. New York: Harper and Row.

De Cecco, Marcello. 1985. "Monetary Theory and Roman History." *The Journal of Economic History* 45: 809–22.

Dray, William. 1957. *Laws and Explanation in History*. Oxford: Oxford University Press.

Dretske, Fred I. 1981. *Knowledge and the Flow of Information*. Cambridge, MA: The MIT Press.

Friedman, Richard. 1987. "Route Analysis of Credibility and Hearsay." *Yale Law Journal* 96: 667–742.

Geertz, Clifford. 1973. *The Interpretation of Cultures: Selected Essays*. New York: Basic Books.

George Alexander L., and Andrew Bennett. 2005. *Case Studies and Theory Development in the Social Sciences*. Cambridge, MA: The MIT Press.

Hempel C. G. 1965. *Aspects of Scientific Explanation*. New York: The Free Press.

Kincaid, Harold. 1996. *Philosophical Foundations of the Social Sciences: Analyzing Controversies in Social Research*. Cambridge: Cambridge University Press.

Kincaid, Harold. 2009. "Philosophies of Historiography and the Social Sciences." In *A Companion to the Philosophy of History and Historiography*, Aviezer Tucker, ed., 297–306. Malden, MA: Wiley-Blackwell.

Klein Daniel B., and Charlotta Stern. 2009. "Groupthink in Academia: Majoritarian Departmental Politics and the Professional Pyramid." *The Independent Review* 13 (4): 585–600.

Köhnke, R. C. 1991. *The Rise of Neo-Kantianism: German Academic Philosophy between Idealism and Positivism*, R. G. Hollingdale, trans. Cambridge: Cambridge University Press.

Kosso, Peter. 2001. *Knowing the Past: Philosophical Issues of History and Archeology*, Amherst, NY: Humanity Books.

Maas, Paul. 1958. *Textual Criticism*, Barbara Flower, trans. Oxford: Clarendon Press.

Miller, Richard W. 1987. *Fact and Method: Explanation, Confirmation and Reality in the Natural and Social Sciences*. Princeton, NJ: Princeton University Press.

Mises, Ludwig von. 2005. *Theory and History: An Interpretation of Social and Economic Evolution*, Bettina Bien Greaves, ed. Indianapolis: Liberty Fund.

Morgan, Stephen L., and Christopher Winship. 2007. *Counterfactuals and Causal Inference: Methods and Principles for Social Research*. Cambridge: Cambridge University Press.

Passmore, John. 1975. "The Poverty of Historicism Revisited." *History and Theory* 14 (4): 30–47.

Reichenbach, Hans. 1956. *The Direction of Time*. Berkeley: University of California Press.

Rickert, Heinrich. 1962. *Science and History: A Critique of Positivist Epistemology*, George Reisman, trans. Princeton, NJ: D. Van Norstrand Company.

Salmon, Merrillee H. 1982. *Philosophy and Archaeology*. New York: Academic Press.

Sekhon, Jasjeet S. 2010. "The Neyman-Rubin Model of Causal Inference and Estimation via Matching Methods." In *The Oxford Handbook of Political Methodology*, Janet M. Box-Steffensmeier, Henry E. Brady, and David Collier, eds., 271–99. Oxford: Oxford University Press.

Sober, Elliott. 1988. *Reconstructing the Past: Parsimony, Evolution, and Inference*. Cambridge, MA: The MIT Press.

Sober, Elliott. 1999. "Modus Darwin." *Biology and Philosophy* 14: 253–78.

Sober, Elliott. 2001. "Venetitian Sea Levels, British Bread Prices, and the Principle of the Common Cause." *British Journal for the Philosophy of Science* 52: 331–46.

Tucker, Aviezer. 1998. "Unique Events: The Underdetermination of Explanation." *Erkenntnis* 48 (1): 59–80.

Tucker, Aviezer. 2004. *Our Knowledge of the Past: A Philosophy of Historiography*. New York: Cambridge University Press.

Tucker, Aviezer. 2007. "The Inference of Common Cause Naturalized." In *Causality and Probability in the Sciences*, Jon Williamson and Federica Russo, eds., 439–66. London: College Press.

Tucker, Aviezer. 2010. "Where Do We Go from Here: A Jubilee Report on History and Theory." *History and Theory* theme issue No. 49 (December 2010): 64–84.

Tucker, Aviezer. 2012. "Bully-U: Higher Education and Central Planning." *The Independent Review*. Forthcoming.

Van Fraassen, Bas. 1989. *Laws and Symmetry*. Oxford: Oxford University Press.

Wetzel, Linda. 2009. *Types and Tokens: On Abstract Objects*. Cambridge, MA: The MIT Press.

Windelband, Wilhelm. 1980. "Rectorial Address, Strasbourg, 1894." Guy Oakes, trans., *History and Theory* 19: 169–85. (Translation of "Geschichte und Naturwissenschaften," in Praludien Vol. II, Verlag von J.G.B. Mohr, Tübingen, 136–60.)

CHAPTER 13

RCTS, EVIDENCE, AND PREDICTING POLICY EFFECTIVENESS

NANCY CARTWRIGHT

13.1. INTRODUCTION

"To Test Housing Program, Some Are Denied Aid," declared a headline in the *New York Times* published on December 8, 2010. Why were they denied aid? Because they were in the control wing of a randomized controlled experiment (RCT) to determine for a New York City Homeless Services program called Homebase, "whether the $23 million program . . . helped the people for whom it was intended."

Apparently New York City has bought into a standard claim in the movement for evidence-based policy and practice (EBPP): that RCTs are the gold standard for establishing "what works." So too it seems has the Greater London Authority, whose Project Oracle "aims to establish a coordinated London wide way of understanding and sharing what really works." That's according to the Authority's *Standards of Evidence* document, which later explains that "the Standards value evaluations that use a comparison or control group . . . If the children going into the comparison or control group are assigned at random, so much the better as far as confidence in the results is concerned."

And according to the same *New York Times* article so too does the US federal Department of Housing and Urban Development, which is also doing a RCT on families in homeless shelters. The article also reports on the very vigorous movement to introduce RCTs widely in development economics, spearheaded by a group of MIT economists.

Such trials, while not new, are becoming especially popular in developing countries: "It's a very effective way to find out what works and what doesn't," said Esther Duflo, an economist at the Massachusetts Institute of Technology who has advanced the testing of social programs in the third world. "Everybody, every country, has a limited budget and wants to find out what programs are effective" (Buckley 2010).

I urge we resist this movement. RCTs, if done very well, can indeed establish something about a program—that it worked in the studied situation. Just that, according to the *New York Times*, is what the Department of Housing and Urban Development is trying to do: "The goal, a HUD spokesman, Brian Sullivan, said, is to find out which approach most effectively ushered people into permanent homes." Pay careful attention to the form of the verbs. To show that a program usher*ed* people into homes—that is, that the program work*ed* for the population studied—is a long way from establishing that it *will work* in a particular target, let alone that it *works* in general. I will here show just how long—and tortuous—this way is. That however is not the impression you get from the Duflo quote nor from the GLA document, which propose to use RCTs to find out what *works*.

I have for a while been urging that we need a theory of evidence in terms of which we can evaluate strong claims like these for RCTs (Cartwright 2009; Cartwright and Stegenga 2009, 2011). Here I shall provide such a theory, a simple straightforward theory that allows us to see just what must be in place for RCT evidence to be relevant to predicting that a program or treatment will work in a target setting. Often the claim that a program worked in a studied population is called an *efficacy* claim, and the prediction that it will work in a target, an *effectiveness* claim. It is widely acknowledged that the two are not the same. But little is said about how to get from one to the other and often it seems to be implied that the fallback position is that it is a reasonable bet that a program that was efficacious somewhere will be effective in any other situation unless we have specific reason to think it won't work in that other situation, especially if the two have superficial similarities that are salient in the discipline proposing the inference (e.g., demographic features like urban versus rural, physiological features like gender or age, or socioeconomic ones like class, wealth, or religion). On the contrary, I shall argue, the demands that must be met for efficacy to count as evidence for effectiveness at all, let alone sufficient evidence, are high and need good reasons in their favor if this bet is to be reasonable.

Before turning to the theory of evidence for effectiveness claims, I shall first explain what RCTs can show, and why.

13.2. RCTs and What Can Be Inferred from Them

I shall describe here an ideal RCT. Randomization of subjects to treatment and control groups, blinding and large study populations are supposed to provide warrant for the assumption that a real RCT approaches the ideal—or near enough. This assumption is controversial (Worrall 2002, 2007). But I should like to sidestep this controversy and consider what can be inferred from a positive RCT result if we are willing to take it as well established.

An ideal RCT for cause X and outcome Y randomly assigns individual participants in the study, $\{u_i\}$, into two groups where $X = x$ for some value x universally in one group (the treatment group) and $X = x' \neq x$ universally in the other (the control group). No differences are to obtain in the two groups other than X and its downstream effects.

The standard result measures the so-called *treatment effect, T*, across the units participating in the study (letting $<\theta>$ represent the expectation of θ):

$$T = df < Y(u)/X(u) = x) > - < Y(u)/X(u) = x' >$$

Of what interest is this strange statistic about randomized units in a study group—and familiarity should not make you forget that it is strange? There are two standard answers. One relies on the counterfactual analysis of Paul Holland and Donald Rubin (Holland and Rubin 1988). This is, for instance, the method of analysis adopted by James Heckman, who won the Nobel Prize for his work evaluating social programs, especially on selection bias and particularly with respect to labor markets (Heckman 2001, 2005).[1] Let

$Y_x(u) = df$ the value u would have for Y if X were set at x by a David Lewis–type miracle (which changes only X and its downstream effects).

Now consider the expectations for the difference in counterfactual values of Y across units in the study. That is, the difference in Y each individual would experience were they treated with x' versus with x, and take the average. So:

$$< CD > : < Y_x(u) - Y_{x'}(u) > = < Y_x(u) > - < Y_{x'}(u) > .$$

Notice that this is not the same as T since we can't observe $<Y_x(u)>$ across all the units in the experiment but only $<Y_x(u)/X(u) = x>$ or the same for $X = x'$. But we may suppose that randomization—in the ideal at least—guarantees that for u's in the study the value u would have for Y if u received the treatment or control is (probabilistically) independent of whether u gets the treatment or control. Then

$$< Y_x(u) > - < Y_{x'}(u) > = < Y(u)/X(u) = x) - Y(u)/X(u) = x' >$$

Or

$$T = < CD > : \text{the observed treatment effect}$$

$$= \text{the expectation of the counterfactual difference.}$$

What use is the treatment effect under this interpretation, that is, where it is taken to be the expectation of the counterfactual difference? It's surely good for post hoc assignment of responsibility. It tells us that X definitely contributed to the Y values of some individuals in the study and further tells us the average contribution. For these individuals, X is definitely to blame—or praise—for part of their Y values. This is *attribution* or *evaluation*—which is what, according to the *Times* article, the HUD spokesman said their RCT was aimed at. RCTs can be very good for that. But beyond that?

We can look for so-called *external validity*. Where else does the same result hold?

Range of external validity = those situations where the same result holds.

But with the assumptions so far, I see no way to begin to answer this question. Here the canonical trade-off between internal validity and external looms large. The study is perfectly geared to yield the average counterfactual difference. But without a lot more assumptions—both substantive and metaphysical—there's no place to go with it.

Notice that the counterfactual interpretation makes no mention of causal principles. The other common analysis of RCTs postulates that Y values for the units in the study (or their probabilities) are determined by a causal principle. The RCT can tell us something about the role of X, if any, in this principle.

Suppose then that Y in the study population of individuals is determined by the causal principle L:

$$L : Y(u)c = \alpha(u) + \beta(u)X(u) + W(u)^2$$

where W represents the net contribution of causes that act additively in addition to X, and X may not play a role in the equation at all if $\beta = 0$. The formula makes clear that β not only determines whether X contributes to Y at all but it also controls how much a given value of X will contribute to Y.

From L and the definition of T it follows that

$$T =_{df} < Y(u)/X(u) = x > - < Y(u)/X(u) = x' >$$

$$= < a(u)/X(u) = x > - < \alpha(u)/X(u) = x' > +$$

$$< \beta(u)/X(u) = x > x - < \beta/X(u) = x' > x' +$$

$$< W(u)/X(u) = x > - < W(u)/X(u) = x' > .$$

If we are prepared to suppose that the random assignment of units to x and x' assures that for units in the study, X is probabilistically independent of a,β,W, then

$$T = < \beta(u) > (x - x').$$

If T is positive then β is too. So X genuinely appears as a cause for Y in the law L for the study population. If $\beta = 0$ for all units, then X does not appear in L. So under L, X makes no contribution to Y outcomes; these are produced entirely by the quantities represented in the variable W.

Note that the effect size of X with respect to Y does not tell the actual value of Y that occurs, nor its mean; rather it tells only the *contribution* of X. What actually happens, or happens on average, depends on W as well. And this can be a problem. Sometimes things are getting worse naturally (due to the action of factors in W); then the net results after the policy may be worse than before even though the policy improved matters over what they otherwise would have been. Sometimes we make matters worse ourselves in implementing the policy, as in the California class-size reduction program, where class sizes were reduced but so too, due to the sudden need for many more teachers, was teacher quality (Bohrnstedt and Stecher 2002). So what's in W matters to forecasting actual results. Here though I shall lay aside consideration of factors in W in order to concentrate on the effect size and what can be learned from it.

13.3. What We Want for Predicting Effectiveness and What's On Offer

For evidence-based policy we want to predict with reasonable confidence[3] that the proposed policy will contribute positively to targeted outcomes in our situation as the policy would in fact be implemented there. What characterizes a body of evidence that can do this for us? I propose a broad swipe at a straightforward answer, an answer that works for any empirical hypothesis H. This proposal is clearly very crude but it will suffice for moving the discussion along:

> H is well supported by a set S of empirical facts if
> > The facts (fact claims) in S are true.
> > The facts in S are relevant to the truth of H.
> > "All" or "enough" of the true relevant facts are in S.
> > All told, these speak for the truth of H.

There is currently no dearth of what turn out to be very similar guides that tell you how to evaluate effectiveness claims. Here is a sample:

> IARC: International Agency for Research on Cancer
> > SIGN: Scottish Intercollegiate Guidelines Network
> > US Department of Education What Works Clearinghouse
> > USEPA: US Environmental Protection Agency
> > CEPA: Canadian Environmental Protection Act
> > Cochrane Collaboration

Oxford Centre for Evidence-Based Medicine
Daubert decision (US Supreme Court).

How do these guides help with A.–D.? First they make a bad presupposition about relevance (B): The only kind of fact seriously relevant to predicting that a policy will work for you is that the policy worked in some studied situation. Then they focus on A., the *quality* of proffered facts of this kind—how likely are they to be true? And they take an odd view about that. Only comparison studies are allowed to count as good evidence that the policy worked in a studied situation, with RCTs as the best among comparison studies. Econometric models, for instance, which can under specifiable circumstances produce good support for causal claims, are not even considered; nor is derivation from well-established theory (Cartwright 2007; Reiss 2005; Fennell 2007a, 2007b). Then the advice given explicitly about B is generally of little practical use. They most often ignore C. And they are very weak on D.

Here, for instance, is the quality grading scale from SIGN, which is used by NICE (the National Institute for Clinical Excellence) to set best health practice in the UK:

Notice that, as I remarked, what are ranked are study designs for establishing claims about the efficacy of a policy or treatment in a studied population, and they are all, bar the strange last entry, comparative studies.

The marks from 1++ to 4 are then to be used to help grade policy predictions, presumably to grade them according to how likely they are to be true (or perhaps to be "likely, failing good reason to the contrary"). The grades are assigned thus (Scottish Intercollegiate Guidelines Network 2008):

So a really good RCT testing the policy on a study population can be enough to warrant confidence that the policy will work for you—at least it can, on this grading

Table 13.1 Levels of Evidence

1++	High quality meta-analyses, systematic reviews of RCTs, or RCTs with a very low risk of bias
1+	Well conducted meta-analyses, systematic reviews, or RCTs with a low risk of bias
1-	Meta-analyses, systematic reviews, or RCTs with a high risk of bias
2++	High quality systematic reviews of case control or cohort studies
	High quality case control or cohort studies with a very low risk of confounding or bias and a high probability that the relationship is causal
2+	Well conducted case control or cohort studies with a low risk of confounding or bias and a moderate probability that the relationship is causal
2-	Case control or cohort studies with a high risk of confounding or bias and a significant risk that the relationship is not causal
3	Nonanalytic studies, e.g., case reports, case series
4	Expert opinion

Table 13.2 Grades of Recommendation

A	At least one meta-analysis, systematic review, or RCT rated as 1++, and directly applicable to the target population; or
	A body of evidence consisting principally of studies rated as 1+, directly applicable to the target population, and demonstrating overall consistency of results
B	A body of evidence including studies rated as 2++, directly applicable to the target population, and demonstrating overall consistency of results; or extrapolated evidence from studies rated as 1++ or 1+
C	A body of evidence including studies rated as 2+, directly applicable to the target population and demonstrating overall consistency of results; or extrapolated evidence from studies rated as 2++
D	Evidence level 3 or 4; or extrapolated evidence from studies rated as 2+

scale, if that RCT is "directly applicable" to your population. That is, it is *relevant* to your population. But when is a well-established claim that the policy worked somewhere—in some study population—relevant to your prediction that it will work for you? The US Department of Education is equally vague. They tell you that strong evidence for your policy is two or more high quality RCTs in "settings similar to that of your schools/classrooms ."[4] The only elaboration later adds four lines— trials on white suburban populations do not constitute strong evidence for large inner city schools serving primarily minority students.

These two grading schemes address C. and D. together in one fell swoop. The advice is to take the best. If you have two good RCTs, that's enough to go with the policy; you don't need to look at the rest of the evidence. It looks then as if this is advice to reject C. and do D. an easy way. Other guides take C. more seriously and suggest a judicious consideration of "lower grade" evidence as well, allowing that sometimes lower grade evidence that the policy failed in some study populations should dilute your confidence that the policy will work for you (e.g., the Grading of Recommendations Assessment n.d.). But how do you "weigh it all up together?" And isn't weighing already perhaps a misleading way to put the problem? On this issue I think no one offers very good, practicable advice, and I'm afraid I can't either.[5]

What justifies these answers? There is little grounded discussion. Most of what there is focuses on the grading schemes, in defense of putting RCTS way out ahead. Only these, we are told, control for unknown confounders. But how did unknown confounders enter? This is clearly a remark somewhere very deep in the middle of an argument. I propose to start back at the beginning of the argument, to offer a theory of what counts as evidence from which we can construct answers. The simple theory I propose does not help much with C. and D. But it has immediate conse- quences for B., *relevance*, and this is where I shall concentrate. Already, just looking at relevance we will get a very different account of the role of RCTs in warranting effectiveness predictions than we see in these guides and that is suggested by the remarks of Duflo and the GLA document cited in section 13.1.

13.4. A Simple Theory of Relevance for Predicting Effectiveness

This theory has two straightforward claims. The first theory claim is

TEE 1. X as implemented will contribute positively to the production of Y in situation S iff

TEE 1.1. There is a causal principle that holds in S from implementation till time of outcome in which X figures as a cause of Y,
and
TEE 2.1. All the factors that are required in that principle for X to contribute to Y obtain in S at the required times.
TEE 1. is based on two presuppositions:
Law-governedness: If X is to contribute to the production of Y it must do so under the governance of a causal principle.
Analyticity: Causal principles generally allow different kinds of contributions to the same effect from different distinguishable sources, some positive, some negative.

The first presupposition supports theory claim TEE1.1. Causings don't happen by accident, by mere hap, but in accord with causal principles at work in the situation. These need not be deterministic. They could, for instance, be probabilistic causal principles or expressions of causal powers, which may not have probabilities attached. For simplicity though I will use deterministic principles here to keep formal complications to a minimum.

I do not want to endorse the claims that causings happen under principles as a universal truth and, personally, I do not think it is true. But I take it that I am in the minority. More importantly, it is happening under a principle that ensures that a causing can be relied on to happen. It is this that makes effects predictable; and for policy, it is predictability that matters.

Analyticity supports theory claim TEE 1.2. As with law-governedness, I do not take analyticity to be a universal truth and again I personally have argued that sometimes a kind of causal holism that counters it is true. But analyticity is at the base of much scientific method, and it is the standard assumption in physics and economics and in large swathes of biology. It may not be so reasonable to assume in social contexts but in that case again policy prediction will be exceedingly difficult, as indeed the Historical School scholars who favored holism argued. So as with law-governedness, I shall take analyticity to be true for the kinds of policy causes that we can sensibly make predictions about. In that case we can suppose that the kind of causal principles that will produce predictable policy outcomes can be represented like this:

$$Y c = C_1 + \ldots + C_n - P_1 . - P_m.$$

where the C's and P's are complex combinations of empirical factors and the meaning of "+" can vary. (For instance, when it comes to forces "+" will represent vector not scalar addition.[6])

Principle L from section 13.2 is just a shortened form of this that focuses on terms that show X as a cause of Y with all the remaining terms gathered together in W.

To complete my simple theory we need only add the second theory claim:

TEE 2: The facts relevant for predicting 'X as implemented will contribute positively to the production of Y in S' are those that must obtain in S if that claim is to be true.

So we are warranted in predicting that X will make a positive contribution in S to the extent that we are warranted in assuming:

Rel 1. There is a causal principle that holds in S from implementation till time of outcome in which X figures as a cause of Y,
and
Rel 2. All the factors that are required in that principle for X to contribute to Y obtain in S and at the right times.

These are the two kinds of facts that are *directly relevant* to predicting a positive contribution from X. Other facts can be relevant—indirectly—by speaking for the truth of either of these.[7]

13.5. RCTs and Relevance 2

Let us start with Rel 2., since that is easiest and my remarks here are probably familiar. As earlier I shall suppose that laws of form L govern the production of Y for individuals u in the situations of interest, represented by S:

$$L : Y(u)c = \alpha(u) + \beta(u)X(u) + W(u).$$

Causes are INUS conditions. From that it follows that two kinds of facts are directly evidentially relevant to predicting "X will contribute positively to the production of Y in S":

Rel 2.1. Facts about which *are* the factors that regulate whether X contributes to Y in S, and by how much, under a law that governs the production of Y in S,
and
Rel 2.2. Facts about *which of those will be present* in S and at the right times were the policy to be implemented as envisaged.

When laws are expressed in the familiar form of L, facts that are mentioned in Rel 2.1. are represented, in one fell swoop, in β. It is important not to be misled by β's simple form into taking it as a constant or as a simple random variable. β will generally represent a complex function of further factors that together fix whether and how much X contributes to Y. Also keep in mind that there might well be different sets of complexly interacting factors, any one of which allows X to contribute to Y. So β looks like this: $\beta = f_1(z_{11}, \ldots, z_{1n}) + \ldots + f_m(z_{m1}, \ldots, z_{mp})$.

The quantities represented by z's are sometimes called *confounding factors*. That term though is often applied to the quantities represented in W as well. I suggest instead calling the z's that must act in tandem with X to produce a contribution to Y the *support factors* for X with respect to outcome Y. To make good predictions about the effects of X on Y in S you need first to identify what these are in laws that obtain in S and then to ascertain which of these will in fact obtain in S were the policy to be implemented. The usual advice you receive does not mention the support factors explicitly. But there is an assumption about β built into it. Look back to section 3 and the advice there from SIGN or the US Department of Education. You can expect the same contribution in your situation as in an RCT if your situation is "similar to" that in the RCT or the RCT is "directly applicable" to your situation.

So, similar in what respects? Or when is a result "directly applicable?" That is not hard to answer, though the guides don't write it out for you. Looking at formula 2.3. for the treatment effect, it is clear that you will get the same treatment effect in S as in an RCT only if your situation and that in the RCT share a law in which the same support factors figure for X with respect to Y and the two situations have the same mean value for these. Otherwise it is an accident. And having the same mean is pretty much an accident unless the two share the same distribution of the different values of β, which represent different combinations of values for support factors.

How are you to make any kind of reasoned judgment about whether the two have the same mean or same distribution of combinations of support factors if you have no idea what these factors are and what range of values they might take in your situation and with what probability? If you adopt the policy you will be betting that your situation has enough of the right combinations of support factors to ensure a positive contribution overall. But you are seldom urged to consider these and standard guides give little or no advice about how to evaluate the evidential weight of claims offered in support of proposals about them. Edward Leamer, famous for his paper "Let's Take the Con out of Econometrics" (Leamer 1983), in discussing RCTs expresses the same worry about this that I have: "If little thought has gone into identifying these possible confounders, it seems probable that little thought will be given to the limited applicability of the results in other settings" (Leamer 2010).

What if some thought has gone into it and you have reason to believe you have identified a number of the necessary support factors for X to contribute to Y–the Z's? Then the advice in the guides is poor advice. For you do not really want your situation to reproduce the same distribution across β as in the RCT. Rather, you want a distribution that is heavy on the combinations of values of Z's that boosts the input of the value of X you propose to implement and is light on the values in which that X value contributes little or nothing, or worse, is harmful.

Where does this leave us with respect to the relevance of RCTs to our policy predictions? Look at Rel 2.1. RCT results will be indirectly evidentially relevant if they help support claims about what the requisite supporting factors are in our situation. And this they can do. Suppose we hypothesize that Z is a support factor and that $Z = z_g$ is a good value for us—that is, it boosts the contribution of the X value (say x) we propose to implement, and we hypothesize that $Z = z_b$ is a bad value. If we can find an RCT situation that we have good reason to believe shares laws for the role of X in the production of Y with our own, then we can use an RCT to test this hypothesis, by setting the treatment as $X = x$ and $Z = z_g$ and the control as $X = x$ and $Z = z_b$. It is important to note, however, that this test is only relevant for us if we have reason to believe that this RCT situation has the same laws for the production of Y from X as does ours—and that needs warranting.

As to Rel 2.2., RCT results are clearly no help in telling whether various factors that have been identified as support factors for us will obtain in our situation. For that we need local information. Sometimes we can tell by looking; sometimes it can require careful measurement; often—as I will discuss in the next section—it will require careful interpretation of what exactly those factors amount to on-the-ground, in-the-concrete in our situation.

13.6. RCTs and Relevance 1

If we assume law-governedness, as I did in my second treatment of RCTs in section 2, then a successful well-conducted RCT provides good evidence in favor of the claim that a causal principle like L in which X figures as a cause of Y held in the study situation. This provides no evidence that X will produce a positive difference in the target unless the target and the study share L. L must be, at least to that extent, a general causal principle. I take it this is what is supposed to be expressed in the claim "X works." But the stretch of L is certainly not addressed in the RCT and for the most part generality cannot be taken for granted. That's because the kinds of causal principles that govern policy effectiveness are both local and fragile.

These principles are local because they depend on the mechanism or the social organization—what I have called the *socioeconomic machine*—that gives rise to them. I have developed this claim for locality at length in many places (Cartwright 1999, 2007). Let me give one vivid example here, far removed from our topic of social science and evidence: the case of a Rube Goldberg machine, like this one in the figure below.

We can fly the kites repeatedly and in different conditions to determine the exact form of the equation by which flying kites lift the small door. The equation may look like this:

Size of door opening $c = \beta$ (height of kite) $+ W$.

Pencil Sharpener

The Professor gets his think-tank working and evolves the simplified pencil sharpener.

Open window (A) and fly kite (B). String (C) lifts small door (D), allowing moths (E) to escape and eat red flannel shirt (F). As weight of shirt becomes less, shoe (G) steps on switch (H) which heats electric iron (I) and burns hole in pants (J).

Smoke (K) enters hole in tree (L), smoking out opossum (M) which jumps into basket (N), pulling rope (O) and lifting cage (P), allowing woodpecker (Q) to chew wood from pencil (R), exposing lead. Emergency knife (S) is always handy in case opossum or the woodpecker gets sick and can't work.

Figure 13.1

But we cannot take this principle very far. Kites do not very generally open doors. This causal principle is true but local. This, as I said, is an old theme of mine I have returned to in recent work because of its central importance for successful prediction about policy interventions.

Some economists are very clear about locality. The Chicago School notoriously used it as an argument against government intervention: The causal principles that governments have to hand to predict the effects of their interventions are not universal. They arise from an underlying arrangement of individual preferences, habits, and technology and are tied to these arrangements. Worse, according to the Chicago School, these principles are *fragile*. When governments try to manipulate the causes in them to bring about desired effects, they are likely to alter the underlying arrangements responsible for those principles, so the principles no longer obtain (Lucas 1981).

Or, British econometrician Sir David Hendry (Clements and Hendry 2008; Hendry 2006) urges the use of simple "quick catch-up" models for forecasting rather than more realistic causal models, because the world Hendry lives in is so fluid that yesterday's accurate causal model will almost certainly not be true today. John Stuart Mill had similar views (Mill 1967 [1836], 1973 [1843]). Economics cannot be an inductive science, he argued, because underlying arrangements are too shaky; there's little reason to expect that a principle that has held over some period or in some place will hold at a different period or in a different place.

For purposes of policy we want to predict the truth of a singular counterfactual: "This program would work for us, given where and how we would implement it." Nature fixes the outcomes of our policy interventions by working through her own casual principles for the situation. We can try to follow her lead, but we will need causal principles *appropriate to our situation*. Our situation will almost certainly have a different complex of causal factors present than any study populations. And implementation generally produces even more differences. We seldom manage to introduce the intended intervention by itself; we usually end up changing lots of other causally relevant factors as well. (Recall the brief discussion of the importance of factors in W in section 13.2.) Even more fundamentally, our situation may well have a different underlying structure than the study situations and thus be subject to *different causal principles*; and even if the structure wasn't different to begin with, our actions can alter it, as the Chicago School warns.

Because causal principles are local you can't just take a causal principle that applies here, no matter how sure you are of it, and suppose it will apply there. Perhaps you think—as many other economists and medical RCT advocates seem to— that the different populations you study, here and there, are more likely to share causal structure than not. That's fine. But to be licensed in that assumption you need good evidence and generally varied in form: evidence about the nature and stability of the structures involved and evidence about the nature and stability of the causal principles they give rise to.

This is a quarrel I have with Judea Pearl (Pearl 2000), who has done such marvelous work on causal inference. I worry about the comprehensiveness of his methods, not their validity. Pearl offers a complete methodology from hunting to using causes. First he provides a general way to represent causal principles; I believe he maintains that his representations are general enough to treat any kinds of causal principles we are familiar with. I don't quarrel with this here. Second he offers a detailed semantics for inferring singular counterfactuals from causal models of this form. Nor do I quarrel with this. Third he points to reliable methods like causal Bayes-nets and RCTs for inferring causal principles from probabilities. Though we probably disagree about how widely the assumptions hold that are necessary for these methods to be valid, I agree that the methods are both powerful and often reliable. The scheme is ideal. We have trustworthy methods for going from data to model and from model to prediction. So the predictions are well supported by the empirical evidence.

The problem is in the joining-up. We need reasons to suppose that the causal principles that produced the data in the studied situation are the same as those that will produce the outcomes we want to predict in the target situation. But we seldom have such guarantees. The probabilistic methods that Pearl and others endorse for discovering causes can provide good descriptive accounts of the network of causal relations that obtain in various populations. These can be a part of the evidence base for the more basic science that allows us to predict what the causal principles might be in new situations.

But simple induction, even if the models are for what is supposed to be the "same" population, is seldom a good tool of inference—and to be warranted in using it, we need good reasons to believe we are studying an entrenched structure. Otherwise for new situations we need to predict new principles and we can't do this by collecting statistics on populations in the not-yet-existing situations. We can though sometimes do so with an understanding of underlying mechanisms and how they interact to generate new causal principles. But for this we need theory, not necessarily grand sweeping theory but theory nonetheless, and in consequence we need the large and tangled confluence of evidence and hypotheses that go into building up and supporting reasonably reliable theory. Of course theory is hard—and unreliable. Simple induction is far easier. But it requires stability and stability is hard to come by. Without at least enough theory to understand the conditions for stability, induction is entirely hit or miss.

Here are the remarks of a pair of other economists who like me stress the importance of finding shared laws if study results on a policy or program are to serve as evidence that the policy will be effective in a target setting:

> Structural analysis gives us a way to relate observations of responses to changes in the past to predict the responses to *different* changes in the future.
>
> It does so in two basic steps: First, it matches observed past behavior with a theoretical model to recover fundamental parameters such as preferences and technology. Then, the theoretical model is used to predict the responses to possible environmental changes, including those that have never happened before, under the assumption that the parameters are unchanged (Nevo and Michael 2010).
>
> To find shared laws I do not think we always have to go all the back to first principles, as the talk of "fundamental parameters' and 'theoretical models" suggests. But if we are to use results from a study situation as evidence for predictions about a target, we had better have reason to believe the study results depend on a law that is at least wide enough to cover both.

One way to find shared principles can be to "climb up the ladder of abstraction"— to provide more abstract descriptions of the cause and effect factors at work in the study. This is a good idea, because usually laws that hold relatively widely involve abstract features. So there is a very rough correlation. The higher the level of abstraction of the features in a principle the wider is its range of applicability. For example, the sun causes the earth to move around it in an the orbit we observe yearly; a large mass causes smaller ones to move around it in elliptical orbits; a mass of size M causes objects at separation r from it to accelerate at GM/r^2. Each of these principles is true, and each is true of the earth, which is the original object of focus. But each involves more abstract features than the one before. And each has a wider domain of application than the one before.

These layers of principles can all be true at once, and all apply at once to the earth, because of a simple fact about the abstract and the concrete. Abstract features are always instantiated in more concrete ones. Fables and morals often relate in just this way. Consider a favorite of mine by the German Enlightenment thinker and playwright, G. E. Lessing (Lessing 1967 [1759]):

A marten eats the grouse.
A fox throttles the marten; the tooth of the wolf, the fox.
Moral: The weaker are always prey to the stronger.

The moral of the fable teaches a lesson in the abstract, the fable shows what it amounts to in one or more concrete cases.

The same is very often the case in the social sciences. Economic agents do not always act so as to maximize their income, or their leisure, or their consumption, or the educational levels of their children, or anything else in the concrete. But perhaps for the most part economic agents act so as to maximize their expected utilities and when we see them acting for income or leisure this is what, on that occasion, constitutes their utility.

It is just this assumption that underwrites a good many social science experiments. Consider economics. We engineer situations to ensure as much as possible that for the nonce, at least, the only source of utility is, say, money to be won in the experimental game. Then we look to see whether, if the monetary rewards are structured like those in a prisoner's dilemma game, agents play the antisocial equilibrium solution predicted from the principle that agents act to maximize their expected utility. If they do, the experimental results are not only an instance of the principle "In a prisoner's dilemma game, agents both defect," but also "Agents act to maximize their expected utility." Conversely, if agents in the experiment cooperate it is not just a challenge to the principle about what should happen in a prisoner's dilemma game, but a challenge to the fundamental principle of utility maximization as well.

To get a shared lesson from a study like an RCT it is often best then to couch that lesson in far more abstract terms than those in which it is carried out. But there is a problem. How do you know when you have made the right associations between the abstract and the concrete?

Sometimes the identification can be easy. Here's a case I discuss in more detail elsewhere (Cartwright, forthcoming). There was good evidence that a nutritional counseling program for mothers in the Indian state Tamil Nadu improved the nutrition of their young children. Yet a similar program did not succeed in Bangladesh. The principle "nutritional counseling in mothers improves their young children's nutrition" was too local to cover Bangladesh as well. The after-the-fact evaluation of the Bangladesh program indicated that a good part of the reason the program didn't work there was that often mothers neither did the shopping (the men did it) nor controlled food distribution in the family (their mother-in-law did that). Let's take this account for granted for purposes of illustration.

The information from the evaluation plus the background knowledge that prompted the nutrition program in the first place[8] make it a good hypothesis that there is a more abstract principle that holds in both Tamil Nadu and Bangladesh: Nutritional counseling for those who procure the family food, control its distribution in the family, and reflect concern for a child's nutritional welfare in doing these improves the child's nutrition. In India mothers satisfied the complex description in this (hypothetically) shared principle, though not in Bangladesh. And in this case it would not be hard to verify that in Bangladesh the "mothers" do not do so—just go to the market and notice that all the food shoppers are male.

Other cases will be more problematic. The prisoner's dilemma experiment is designed to make easy the identification of money won in the game with utility, but what tells us what is to count as utility in most naturally occurring situations? I take it that sometimes we will be in a position to make and defend identifications and sometimes not; it will depend on our background knowledge, both local and general. It is important to stress that this is not the kind of knowledge that RCTs are good at securing. It requires a different kind of scientific backup and exactly what kind—or better, *kinds*—is required can differ from case to case.

This points out a great shortfall in helpful advice. In general evidence hierarchies like those mentioned in section 13.3 only rank methods for producing evidence that a program works somewhere, with no advice at all about how to judge when evidence proffered for identifying features across levels of abstraction is likely to be sound and strong.

Let us return finally explicitly to the lessons about where RCTs are relevant. RCT results are relevant only to situations where the effect is produced under a principle shared with the study situation. The very methodology of the RCT tends to restrict its range of relevance. In order to ensure that all members of the treatment group receive the same treatment it is important for a proper RCT that the program under test—the treatment protocol—be very precisely specified. This means describing the treatment in very concrete terms and the very concrete features picked out by the protocols are likely to figure only in very local principles. Yet the very same RCT results can at the same time be evidence for a principle connecting more abstract features that has far wider coverage—if only we can import the web of background knowledge that it takes to recognize those features and support the breadth of the more abstract principle. The point is that sometimes we have such knowledge, or at least a body of evidence that provides reasonable support for it.

Many RCT advocates, however, urge trusting to nothing but what can be established by an RCT. The irony is that this advice undermines the usefulness of RCT results and it is at any rate impossible to follow. To present results some choice must always be made about what the relevant treatment and effect features are. That is a choice that cannot be underwritten by RCTs. Rather, it depends on the complicated kind of consilience of theory and empirical studies that is always necessary to grasp what features, among the panoply on offer, are linked in the kinds of regular ways we describe in our causal principles.

Perhaps we get carried away by drug trials, where we suppose a vast amount of biochemistry and knowledge of human physiology picks out what are the widely applicable relevant treatment features, background knowledge that we take to be so secure that we can ignore its role in warranting our choice of features to figure in the causal principles that we take the RCT to test. Whether this is true about drugs and certain other medical treatments, it is surely very doubtful about social interventions.

It is almost a truism in social science that one and the same thing, concretely described, can have very different meanings in different social, cultural, and economic settings, and hence have very different effects.[9]

What, then, of advice that urges that exactly the same protocol as in the RCT should be satisfied if one is to expect the same kinds of results in a new setting as in the RCT? For instance, the Greater London Authority Standards of Evidence document claims that "it is now established that programs that are delivered with what is called 'fidelity'—meaning they are implemented as intended by the program designers—achieve the best results"(Greater London Authority, n.d.).

On the one hand, this can be good advice. Policymakers quite reasonably often try to cherry-pick through the features of a program to implement only ones that are cheaper, or more feasible, or more politically/culturally acceptable in hopes that they will still get reasonably close results to those in the RCTs. This can be a very bad idea for often program features are interactive and program designers have been at pains to include enough of the right combination to ensure that the program, taken as a whole, will generate positive contributions, but if factors are omitted, a positive contribution is unlikely—that is, they have worked to ensure that many of the main members of what I have called the requisite *support team* is built into the program design.

An example might be the Nurse-Family Partnership (Olds 2006; Olds et al. 2003) that has been used in a number of US cities and is now being introduced into the United Kingdom to improve pregnancy outcomes, child health and development, and parents' economic self-sufficiency. It involves a heavy program of prenatal and infant home visiting and is thus costly—though, as designers claim, not relative to the costs saved from many of the later problems averted by the program, let alone the suffering averted. The designers will not sell the license for this program unless it is to be taken up in its entirety—though they are concerned to pursue ways to adapt the program to make it more suitable to, for instance, use in Birmingham, which is where it is first being tried in Britain.

So it can be a good idea to stick to the RCT protocol. On the other hand, it can be a very bad idea for the reasons I've rehearsed: It's not the protocol that matters more widely but rather something more abstract that the protocol instantiates in the RCT situation.

How do you judge when it is good advice and when bad? As I said, that takes a good network of theoretical and empirical knowledge. A policy that worked somewhere will not work for you unless there's a shared principle that governs the results in both the study situation and your own. If you don't have good reason to believe there is one, and that you have correctly identified what the appropriate concrete form of the treatment is under that principle in your situation, then you are betting when you set out on a policy course and probably betting at unknown odds. Sometimes you need to do this. But it's best to acknowledge it and manage the uncertainty best as possible, not act as if you have warrant that you lack.

13.7. SUMMARY

There are two kinds of facts directly relevant to predicting "X will contribute to Y in S": The facts that

> Rel 1. The production of Y in S is governed by a law L in which X appears as a cause of Y.
>
> Rel 2. All the factors necessary under L to support X in producing a contribution to Y obtain in S.

Other facts are relevant—indirectly—if they are relevant to establishing either of these facts. This includes the kind of fact that an RCT can lend support to—that X caused Y in a study situation, or that the effect difference for X with respect to Y was positive in a study situation.

What then in more detail of the evidential relevance of RCT results to effectiveness predictions? A positive effect size for treatment X and outcome Y in an RCT in situation R is directly evidentially relevant to "R is governed by a law, say L, in which X causes Y." The positive effect size can be indirectly relevant to facts about the laws in another situation S—"S is governed by a law in which X causes Y"—but its relevance is conditional on the fact that R and S share L. That is, a positive effect size in R is relevant to whether X figures as a cause of Y in S if, but only if, R and S share L. For evidence-based policy we should have good reason before we assume this. And RCTs will be hard pressed to provide that reason. Even if the RCT were conducted on a sample of the target population, samples can be misleading. Equally important, one must suppose that the causal structure does not change from the time of study till the time the policy begins to work its effects. That is, an empirical hypothesis that may or may not be true and that should not simply be assumed without reflection and without reason to back it up.

Not only do RCTs not tell us that two situations share a causal structure. They also fail to tell us what the operative factors in the causal principles are. S may share with the study situation R a general causal principle under which the results in the study are produced, but the causes in the shared principle need not be the ones described in the protocol of the study. The protocol may pick out causes at too low a level of abstraction for sharing and the very same protocol carried out in S may not constitute the same cause that it constitutes in Y. Again, the RCT can be indirectly relevant, but only conditionally, in this case conditional on the fact that the protocol in the study and the proposed policy both instantiate the causes in a shared causal principle.

As to Relevance 2, RCTs are not relevant to "All the supporting factors required by L for T to contribute to O obtain in S." That requires different kinds of evidence, more local and different in kind. It requires studies aimed at establishing what features are there in S, not ones geared to establishing causal connections. RCTs can be relevant to identifying what the supporting factors are. But again, only conditionally: If—but only if—the study and target situations share the relevant causal structure. And again, for evidence-based policy this should not be assumed without reflection and without reason.

Overall, the lesson is simple. It is a long road from an RCT that evidences the fact that a policy works somewhere to the prediction that the policy will work for us. A lot of different kinds of facts requiring evidence of different kinds to support them must be in place before the road is secure, or secure enough for us to bet on it given the costs and benefits of success and failure. That makes policy predictions dicey—but then that is something to expect. Many of the facts we need to establish are sometimes within our grasp or can become so with reasonable effort. Sometimes they aren't and we need to hedge our bets as best we can. But in any case, the more of the road we support, the more likely it is that our inferences will go through.

NOTES

1. See also my discussion of Heckman in Cartwright 2007.
2. The symbol "c = " implies that the left- and right-hand side are equal and that the factors on the right-hand side are causes of the one on the left.
3. I don't imagine that we will generally be able to assign numerical probabilities to these hypotheses in any reasonable way; but we can certainly often make sound judgments about when a hypothesis is fairly well supported given the current state of knowledge and when badly supported. For policy prediction I would expect that most often the support that we can muster is weak. If so, we should acknowledge that and manage the uncertainty in sensible ways, not pretend we have assurances we lack.
4. USDE (2003).
5. For a survey of problems on evidence amalgamation see Stegenga 2009, forthcoming.
6. For examples of other methods of combination see Cartwright 1999, 54.
7. We may not be interested just in whether X would contribute positively but in how much contribution we would get from inputting a given value of X. In this case we are not just concerned with whether positive β values obtain in our population (or whether enough positive ones obtain to outweigh the effects of those producing negative contributions) but also with what the mix of values of β is for us.
8. This might include, for instance, well-evidenced claims that in both places mothers believed in eating down during pregnancy or conventional child rearing habits forbade certain nourishing food to children, like fish.
9. For another example involving child welfare practices, see Cartwright (forthcoming b).

REFERENCES

Bohrnstedt, G. W., and B. M. Stecher, eds. 2002. *What We Have Learned About Class Size Reduction in California*. Sacramento, CA: California Department of Education.
Buckley, Cara. 2010. "To Test Housing Program, Some Are Denied Aid." *The New York Times*, December 8. Available at www.nytimes.com/2010/12/09/nyregion/09placebo.

html?scp=1&;sq=To%20Test%20Housing%20Program,%20Some%20Are%20
Denied%20Aid&st=cse (accessed December 26, 2010).

Cartwright, Nancy. 1999. *The Dappled World: A Study of the Boundaries of Science*. Cambridge: Cambridge University Press.

Cartwright, Nancy. 2007. *Hunting Causes and Using Them*. Cambridge: Cambridge University Press.

Cartwright, Nancy. 2009. "Evidence-Based Policy: What's to Be Done About Relevance, Models, Methods, and Evidence." Proceedings of the 38th Oberlin Colloquium in Philosophy, M.T.-J., ed. *Philosophical Studies* 144 (1): 127–36.

Cartwright, Nancy. 2011. "Evidence, External Validity and Explanatory Relevance." In *The Philosophy of Science Matters: The Philosophy of Peter Achinstein*, G. J. Morgan, ed. Oxford: Oxford University Press.

Cartwright, Nancy. "Will This Policy Work for You? Predicting Effectiveness Better: How Philosophy Helps." *Philosophy of Science*. Forthcoming.

Cartwright, Nancy, and Jacob Stegenga. 2009. "Towards a Theory of Evidence for Effectiveness for Evidence-Based Policy." In NRC Conference on Evidence-Based Policy: International Experiences. Paris. Available at www.oecd.org/dataoecd/36/62/42382313.pdf, accessed December 30, 2010.

Cartwright, Nancy, and Jacob Stegenga. 2011. "A Theory of Evidence for Evidence Based Policy." In *Evidence, Inference and Enquiry*, Philip Dawid, William Twining, and Mimi Vasilaki, eds. London: British Academy Publication.

Clements, Michael P., and David.F. Hendry. 2008. "Economic Forecasting in a Changing World." *Capitalism and Society* 3 (2): 1–18.

Fennell, Damien. 2007a. "Why and When Should We Trust Our Methods of Causal Inference? Lessons from James Heckman on RCTs and Structural Models." *Contingency and Dissent in Science Technical Report 06/07*. London: London School of Economics, Centre for Philosophy of Natural and Social Science.

Fennell, Damien. 2007b. "Why Functional Form Matters in Structural Models in Econometrics." *Philosophy of Science* 74 (5): 1033–45.

Greater London Authority. n.d. Available at www.london.gov.uk/priorities/crime-community-safety/time-action/project-oracle/about-oracle, accessed December 30, 2010.

Heckman, James J. 2001. *Econometrics, Counterfactuals and Causal Models*. Keynote Address at the 53rd World Statistics Congresses for the International Statistical Institute. August 27. Seoul, South Korea.

Heckman, James J. 2005. "The Scientific Model of Causality." *Sociological Methodology* 35 (1): 1–97.

Hendry, David F. 2006. "Robustifying Forecasts from Equilibrium-Correction Systems." *Journal of Econometrics* 135 (1–2): 399–426.

Holland, Paul W., and Donald B. Rubin. 1988. "Causal Inference in Retrospective Studies." *Evaluation Review* 12 (3): 203–31.

Leamer, Edward E. 1983. "Let's Take the Con Out of Econometrics." *American Economics Review* 73 (1): 31–43.

Leamer, Edward E. 2010. "Tantalus on the Road to Asymptopia." *Journal of Economic Perspectives* 24 (2): 31–46.

Lessing, Gotthold Ephraim. 1967 [1759]. *Abhandlungen uber die Fable*. Stuttgart: Philipp Reclam.

Lucas, Robert E. 1981. "Economic Policy Evaluation: A Critique." In *Studies in Business Cycle Theory*, R. Lucas, ed. Oxford: Basil Blackwell

Mill, John Stuart. 1967 [1836]. "On the Definition of Political Economy and on the Method of Philosophical Investigation in That Science." In *Collected Works of John Stuart Mill.* Toronto: University of Toronto Press.

Mill, John Stuart. 1973 [1843]. "On the Logic of Moral Sciences." In *Collected Works of John Stuart Mill.* Toronto: University of Toronto Press.

Nevo, Aviv, and Whinston Michael. 2010. "Taking the Dogma Out of Econometrics: Structural Modeling and Credible Inference." *Journal of Economic Perspectives* 24 (2): 69–82.

Olds, David L. 2006. "The Nurse-Family Partnership: An Evidence-Based Preventive Intervention." *Infant Mental Health Journal* 27 (1): 5–25.

Olds, David L., Peggy Hill, Ruth O'Brien, David Racine, and Pat Moritz. 2003. "Taking Preventive Intervention to Scale: The Nurse-Family Partnership." *Cognitive and Behavioral Practice* 10 (4): 278–90.

Pearl, Judea. 2000. *Causality: Models, Reasoning, and Inference.* Cambridge: Cambridge University Press.

Reiss, Julian 2005. "Causal Instrumental Variables and Interventions." *Philosophy of Science* 72 (5): 964–76.

Scottish Intercollegiate Guidelines Network. 2008. *SIGN 50 A Guideline Developer's Handbook, Annex B: Key to Evidence Statements and Grades of Recommendations.* Available at www.sign.ac.uk/pdf/sign50.pdf, accessed December 10, 2010.

Stegenga, Jacob. 2009. "Robustness, Discordance, and Relevance." *Philosophy of Science* 76 (5): 650–61.

Stegenga, Jacob. 2011. "Is Meta-Analysis the Platinum Standard of Evidence?" *Studies in History and Philosophy of Biological and Biomedical Sciences* 42 (4): 497–507.

The Grading of Recommendations Assessment, Development and Evaluation Working Group. n.d. Available at www.gradeworkinggroup.org/.

US Department of Education (USDE). 2003. *Identifying and Implementing Educational Practices Supported by Rigorous Evidence: A User Friendly Guide.* Washington, DC: Coalition for Evidence-Based Policy. Available at http://www2.ed.gov/rschstat/research/pubs/rigorousevid/index.html.

Worrall, John. 2002. "What Evidence in Evidence-Based Medicine?" *Philosophy of Science* 69 (S3): S316–S330.

Worrall, John. 2007. "Why There's No Cause to Randomize." *The British Journal for the Philosophy of Science* 58 (3): 451–88.

CHAPTER 14

BRINGING CONTEXT AND VARIABILITY BACK INTO CAUSAL ANALYSIS

STEPHEN L. MORGAN AND CHRISTOPHER WINSHIP

THE methodology of causal analysis in the social sciences is often divided into two ideal type research scenarios: experimental social science and observational social science. For experimental social science, the researcher can manipulate the cause of interest. The most common research design is one where the analyst assigns values of the cause according to a randomization scheme and then calculates post-treatment differences in outcomes across levels of the assigned cause. Typically, the researcher gives little or no attention to individual-specific differences in the inferred causal effects or to the context in which the experiment is conducted.[1]

For observational social science, the analyst cannot manipulate the cause through intervention because some process outside of the analyst's control determines the pattern of causal exposure. To develop causal assertions, the analyst must adopt a model of causal exposure based on assumptions about how the cause is distributed in the population. Most commonly, a model is adopted that warrants causal inference from differences in outcomes calculated within sets of observed individuals who are exposed to alternative values of the cause but who are deemed otherwise comparable by the maintained model of causal exposure. Individual-level variation in causal effects is then presumed to exist within and across comparison sets, often arising from interactions between individuals' characteristics and the contexts within which they are exposed to the cause.

In this chapter, we will discuss methods for modeling causal effects in observational social science, giving particular attention to the capacity of new graphical methods to represent and then motivate models that can effectively deliver estimates of underlying heterogeneity of causal effects. We have several related goals that we will pursue in the following order: (1) explain why quantitatively oriented social science that adopted path modeling methodology became a target of critiques that it had ignored variability and context, (2) demonstrate how such effects can be expressed within a more recent methodology of causal graphs, (3) consider feasible empirical strategies to identify these effects, and (4) explain why causal graphs pose a risk of obscuring patterns of heterogeneity that deserve full scrutiny.

To set the stage for our explanations, consider some classic examples from sociology that have sought to model explicitly the effects of individual-level heterogeneity of causal effects as they interact with consequential social contexts. At least since the 1980s, sociologists have investigated the effects of neighborhoods on educational outcomes, deviance, and the transition to adulthood (for insightful reviews, see Jencks and Mayer 1990 and Harding et al. 2011). Because neighborhoods have many characteristics, and individuals living within them can be influenced to varying degrees by circumstances only partly under their own control, the effects of neighborhoods have proven persistently difficult to estimate. These debates have not been settled by first-rate observational data analysis or by large-scale experimentation (see Sampson 2008).

Alongside this work on neighborhoods, sociologists of education have studied the variable effects of schooling on the academic achievement of students. These studies include attempts to estimate the differential effects of public schooling on learning for students from different socioeconomic strata. For example, Downey, von Hippel, and Broh (2004) show that schools help to narrow differences in learning that would result only from differences attributable to baseline family background differences. A complementary stream of literature has shown that Catholic schooling may generate even larger "common school effects" (see Hoffer, Greeley, and Coleman 1985; Bryk, Lee, and Holland 1993), though this pattern may instead reflect differential self-selection on the causal effect itself (see Morgan and Todd 2008).

Sociologists have also considered the differential consequences of labor market conditions and training opportunities for young adults. For example, Mare and Winship (1984) studied the extent to which changes in the unemployment rate for black youths can be considered differential responses to labor market conditions across youths who have differential propensities to enter the military or postsecondary schooling. More recently, Brand and Xie (2010) have studied the differential payoff of college across different types of students, challenging the position implicitly maintained by many economists that college provides the greatest benefits to those most likely to enter college.

Our focal example in this chapter will be the contentious research on charter schooling in the United States that has been the subject of substantial and recent public debate. In an excellent book on these debates, Henig (2008, 2) introduces and defines charter schools in the following way:

> Just a little more than fifteen years since the first charter school opened in Minnesota, there are now nearly 4,000 nationwide, serving an estimated 1.1 million students. . . . The laws governing charter schools differ—sometimes substantially—from state to state, of course, but some general characteristics have emerged. Charter schools receive public funding on a per-student basis, are often responsible for achieving educational outcomes defined by their government chartering entity, and are subject to at least nominal public oversight. They typically are barred from charging tuition on top of the public per-pupil allocation, but are free to pursue other forms of supplementary support from donors, foundations, or corporate sponsors. Although they must observe certain baseline regulations, such as prohibitions on discrimination and the provision of safe environments, they are exempt from many of the rules and regulations that bind regular public schools to specific standards and procedures. This hybrid status . . . has made charter schools a special focus of attention and helped draw them into ideological whirlpools that raise the stakes surrounding the research into their actual form and consequences.

At their core, the central research questions in the debate are simple: Do students who attend charter schools perform better on standardized tests than they would have performed if they had instead attended regular public schools? Would students who attend regular public schools perform better on standardized tests if they had instead attended charter schools?

The contentious research that has addressed these questions is distinguished in many respects. Not only are some of its combatants leading researchers at the nation's top universities, many of these researchers are unusually ideological (as Henig shows brilliantly in his book). This scholarly energy is amplified by the public attention that has been paid to charter schools by the national press, which is related to the support that charter schools have received from celebrity donors and from presidential aspirants. At the same time, the research that informs the debate is cutting edge in the best sense. Careful attention is paid to details of measurement, and the research designs that have been adopted are a healthy mixture of basic comparisons of achievement levels as well as daring attempts to leverage quasi-experimental variation from the ways in which charter school programs are administered.[2]

What makes pursuing these questions complex is the underlying heterogeneity of the real world. The process by which some students become enrolled in charter schools is only partly observed. It is likely that some students in charter schools are much more likely to benefit from them than others, and it is even more difficult to assess how students who never contemplated entering charter schools might fare if given the opportunity to attend them. At the same time, charter schools differ greatly from each other, such that the effect of charter schooling must surely vary because of quality differences, as well as the match between each student and the unique features of each charter school.

In the next section, we provide necessary background for our subsequent presentation of the new methodology of causal graphs by first offering a presentation of the charter school effect from a path-modeling perspective. We also use this material to explain how quantitatively oriented sociology opened itself up to the critique that variability and context were too frequently ignored in attempts to estimate causal effects.[3]

14.1. AN EMERGENT VULNERABILITY TO CRITIQUE

In the 1980s and early 1990s, a robust critique of dominant forms of quantitative research arose in sociology (see Abbott 1988, 2001; Lieberson 1985; Lieberson and Lynn 2002; Ragin 1987). This literature objected to the overly strong causal assertions in the published literature in many areas of sociology, which these authors claimed were based on misplaced faith in the capacity of linear regression results to generate warranted causal conclusions from the analysis of survey data. A great deal of this critique of research practice was on target, and it arose in response to the naivete of what we labeled elsewhere "the age of regression" (see Morgan and Winship 2007).

We will not review these critiques in this chapter, but for this section we will use the models at the heart of these critiques—simple path diagrams and their underlying linear regression equations—as a point of departure. In the remainder of the chapter that follows this section, we will explain why we feel that this robust critique of quantitatively oriented causal analysis has now been weakened by improved practice that draws on a virtuous combination of causal graphs with nonparametric foundations and causal effects with potential outcome definitions.

To understand the graphical appeal of traditional path models, consider the path diagram presented in figure 14.1, and suppose that we have data on all sixth graders in a large metropolitan school district. For this path diagram, Y is a standardized test taken at the end of the sixth grade, and C indicates whether or not a student attended a charter school for the past year. The variable P represents an omnibus parental background measure that captures differences in economic standing and other basic dimensions of resources that predict school performance. The variable N is neighborhood of residence, and we assume that there are meaningful differences in the extent to which neighborhood environments are conducive to engagement with schooling. Thus, C is the cause of primary interest, P is a baseline confounder that represents individual determinants of C that also have direct causes on the outcome Y, and N is a measure of the social context in which the effect of C on Y occurs.

The structure of the path diagram in figure 14.1 implies that the proper regression specification for Y is

$$Y = a_Y + b_{C \to Y}C + b_{P \to Y}P + b_{N \to Y}N + e_Y, \tag{1}$$

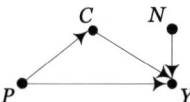

Figure 14.1 A traditional linear additive path diagram for the effects of parental background (*P*), charter schools (*C*), and neighborhoods (*N*) on test scores (*Y*).

where e_Y is a regression representation of all omitted factors that determine *Y*. The final e_Y term in Equation 1 is suppressed in figure 14.1 because it is assumed to be independent of *C*, *P*, and *N*. (Similarly, as we will discuss later, no other analogous error terms are depicted in figure 14.1, such as e_C, e_P, or e_N.)

In the literature on path models that swept through the social sciences in the 1960s and 1970s, the effects $b_{C \rightarrow Y}$, $b_{P \rightarrow Y}$, and $b_{N \rightarrow Y}$ were presumed to be linear and constant across individuals. Accordingly, the directed arrows in figure 14.1 were interpreted as linear additive effects. With the example just specified, this assumption then requires that there are separable and linear additive effects of families, schools, and neighborhoods on student achievement, and furthermore, that these effects apply with equal force to all sixth graders in the school district.[4]

How would such a path diagram have been presented and then discussed in a typical research methods class in the 1970s (assuming that the charter school research question was on the table)? Following an introduction to graphical representations of causal relationships via path models, at least one student would invariably ask the instructor:

> Can the effect of *C* on *Y* vary across *P*? That seems reasonable, since it would seem that the effect of a charter school would depend on family background. Parents with college degrees probably help their kids get more out of school. Actually, now that I think about it, since *N* captures neighborhood characteristics, don't we think that there are better schools in some neighborhoods? In fact, charter schools are more likely to be established in areas with troubled neighborhood-based schools. And neighborhoods with weaker schools also tend to have stronger deviant subcultures with gangs and such. So the effect of charter schooling probably also depends on the neighborhood in which one lives. How do we represent such variation in effects in the path model?[5]

In response, an instructor would typically explain that one can think of such effects as supplemental arrows from a variable to an arrow in the path diagram, such that the variable itself modifies the arrow. Yet since these sorts of arrows are not formally justified in traditional path diagrams, the instructor would almost surely have then recommended a shift toward a more complex regression specification, such as

$$Y = a_Y + b_{C \rightarrow Y}C + b_{P \rightarrow Y}P + b_{CP \rightarrow Y}(C \times P) + b_{N \rightarrow Y}N + b_{CN \rightarrow Y}(C \times N) + e_Y. \tag{2}$$

In this case, the path diagram ceases to represent an underlying set of structural causal relationships and is instead best interpreted as only a simplified reflection of a more specific regression model. After all, the interaction between the effects of *C* and *P* on *Y* (as well as the interaction between the effects of *C* and *N* on *Y*) can be estimated with little trouble. One need only calculate effects of interest, for example, by plugging in values for $\breve{b}_{C \to Y}C + \breve{b}_{P \to Y}P + \breve{b}_{CP \to Y}(C \times P)$ after producing standard regression output from estimation of Equation 2. The differences then produced can be imbued with causal interpretations, assuming no other variables that are common causes of P, C, N, or Y have been mistakenly omitted from Equation 2.

We see two related outcomes of the rise and then demise of linear path models. First, when it became clear that there was no agreed upon way to represent variability and context within path diagrams, they came to seem much less useful. Researchers interested in such variability and context may have continued to draw path diagrams on yellow pads in their offices, but rarely did their drawings turn up in published articles. Path diagrams were thereby relegated to heuristic devices for laying out possible causal relationships of interest to researchers. Estimation and reporting became a word and number affair, often with too much of each.

Second, and far more troubling, many scholars apparently chose to retain a linear additive orientation, even while no longer using path diagrams. For some, empirical research could be fruitfully advanced by ignoring the genuine interactive nonlinearity of the real world, in pursuit of a "first approximation" pragmatism. This might have been an acceptable form of pragmatism if the approximation spirit had carried over to model interpretation. Too frequently it did not, and many causal assertions can be found in the literature based on linear additive models that are overly reductionist. This incautious literature then opened up quantitative research to the claims of critics that too many practitioners had fallen prey to the belief that linear regression modeling reveals strong causal laws in which variability and context play minor roles. The most cogent presentation of this criticism is Abbott's oft-cited "Transcending General Linear Reality" (see Abbott 1988). Although its straw-man style is irksome to methodologists who knew of these problems all along and who urged better practice, it was a reasonable critique of much practice at the time. In the next section, we explain how the literature has since advanced by scaling back the ambitiousness of the regression enterprise, while at the same time adopting a dedicated set of notation to define causal effects that had no necessary connection to regression methodology.

14.2. Moving Beyond Path Diagrams and Simplistic Linear Regression Models

Consider the general multiple regression model of the form

$$Y = a + b_1 X_1 + b_2 X_2 + \ldots + b_k X_k + e_Y, \tag{3}$$

where Y is an interval-scaled outcome variable and X_1 through X_k are predictor variables. Estimation of the slope parameters b_1 through b_k can be motivated as a descriptive data reduction exercise where the goal is to obtain a best-fitting linear approximation to the population-level relationship between Y and X_1 through X_k. Alternatively, and more ambitiously, the model can be estimated as a full causal model where the interest is in identifying the expected shifts in Y that would result from what-if interventions on all possible values of the variables X_1 through X_k. The path model tradition embraced the second and more ambitious of these two approaches.

The more recent literature that we will consider in this chapter has examined an intermediate case. For this model, the variable X_1 in Equation 3 is an indicator variable C, as in

$$Y = a_Y + b_C C + b_2 X_2 + \ldots + b_k X_k + e_Y,$$ (4)

and the goal of the analysis is to estimate the causal effect on Y under what-if shifts of C from 0 to 1. In this case, the variables X_2 through X_k are considered adjustment variables that are entered into the regression equation solely to aid in the effective estimation of the causal effect b_C. Accordingly, estimates of b_2 through b_k are of secondary interest and are not necessarily given a causal interpretation.

Most importantly, under this motivation it is generally presumed that individual-level causal effects may vary, such that the effect on Y of shifting C from 0 to 1 is not the same for all individuals. For our focal charter school example, suppose that the population of interest is again sixth graders in a large metropolitan school district, and the outcome is performance on a standardized test. The variable C is again an indicator variable for whether a student attended a charter school in the past year, and the causal effect of charter schooling, b_C, is presumed to vary across students, either because of their own characteristics, those of their schools, or even those of the neighborhoods in which they live.

The first step in moving toward models that give substantial attention to heterogeneous effects was the introduction of interaction-based multilevel modeling. One way to introduce heterogeneity of this form into Equation 4 is to define b_C as a random coefficient and then to model it as a function of other variables. A simple version of this strategy was already introduced in the last section, where such variability would have been estimated by forming cross-product interactions between C and other variables within X_2 through X_k, which were variables such as P and N for parental background and neighborhoods (see Equation 2). A more general approach was then developed in a new multilevel modeling tradition, in which any variable could be seen as a predictor of the variability of b_C, especially higher-level predictors in nested social structures. Although technically these variables were specified as additional variables within X_2 through X_k, the multilevel modeling framework offered considerable conceptual appeal as well as some elegant methods for modeling variance components (see Raudenbush and Bryk 2002 and Gelman and Hill 2007).

At the same time that this multilevel modeling literature was reaching maturity, and its power for modeling heterogeneity came to be utilized in practice, a potential outcomes model of causality, which had been in development since at least the early 1970s, took center stage in observational data analysis from the 1990s onward. The most important foundational work on this potential outcomes framework was completed in statistics and econometrics (see the citations offered in Heckman 2000, Manski 1995, Rosenbaum 2002, and Rubin 2005, 2006 to their own work and that of their respective predecessors).

Consider the focal charter schools example again. The outcome of interest Y remains a standardized test score for sixth graders. Within the potential outcome framework, the outcome variable Y is given a definition that is based on potential outcomes associated with the causal effect of interest. Accordingly, y_i^1 is the potential outcome in the treatment state (a charter school) for individual i, and y_i^0 is the potential outcome in the control state (a regular public school) for individual i. The individual-level causal effect of the treatment is then defined as

$$\delta_i = y_i^1 - y_i^0,\tag{5}$$

which is the causal effect of charter schooling instead of regular public schooling for each individual i.

The variables Y^1 and Y^0 are then population-level potential outcome random variables, and the average treatment effect (ATE) in the population is

$$E[\delta] = E[Y^1 - Y^0],\tag{6}$$

where $E[.]$ is the expectation operator from probability theory. The observed outcome variable Y is defined as

$$Y = CY^1 + (1-C)Y^0.\tag{7}$$

Thus, the observed values for the variable Y are $y_i = y_i^1$ for individuals with $c_i = 1$ and $y_i = y_i^0$ for individuals with $c_i = 0$.

Although quite simple, this notational shift changed perspectives and allowed for the development of new techniques, as we will discuss later. It also made clear (to social scientists who may have forgotten) that causal effects exist independent of regression models and can be expressed without relying on regression-based language. With this notation, causal effects could be defined over any subset of the population. Two particular average causal effects of interest became common to investigate. The average treatment effect for the treated (ATT) is

$$E[\delta \mid C = 1] = E[Y^1 - Y^0 \mid C = 1]\tag{8}$$

while the average treatment effect for the controls (ATC) is

$$E[\delta|C=0] = E[Y^1 - Y^0|C=0].\tag{9}$$

For the charter school example, these are, respectively, the average effect of charter schooling for those who attend charter schools and for those who attend regular public schools. If there is reason to expect that these average causal effects do not equal each other, then this is sufficient a priori grounds to expect meaningful heterogeneity of individual-level causal effects. In this case, a simple regression model, as in Equation 4, that attempts to develop an estimate of a single charter school effect would be misleading, since it would mask the difference in the expected effect for those who typically do and do not attend charter schools.

More generally, individual-level heterogeneity exists if $\delta_i \neq E[\delta]$ for all individuals i. Variability of δ_i across individuals could be produced by an observed variable or by an unobserved variable, and such variability is particularly consequential when the other variables that produce it are not independent of the cause. Heterogeneity of this type, for example, is present if the average causal effects in Equations 8 and 9 do not equal each other. Many other forms of heterogeneity are of interest as well and can be masked by standard forms of data analysis (see Angrist and Pischke 2009, Elwert and Winship 2010, and Morgan and Winship 2007, esp. chapter 5).

The third major advancement that has allowed scholarship to move beyond simple regression models is the elaboration of a new form of graph-based causal modeling. Here, the contribution is in enabling new methodological insight and in providing new levels of clarity to researchers. Since this perspective is less familiar to social scientists, and often both misunderstood and underappreciated, we present it in considerable detail in the next section.

14.3. A New Methodology of Causal Graphs

Since the 1990s, the rationale for graphical depictions of causal relationships has been strengthened by scholars working at the margins of the social sciences. Judea Pearl's 2000 book *Causality: Models, Reasoning, and Inference* has been the most important contribution, although much of the work within it was developed in collaboration with others in the prior decade (see Pearl 2000, 2009). Morgan and Winship (2007, chapter 3) provide an introduction to the directed acyclic graphs (DAGs) that Pearl and his colleagues are credited with developing, and we will present here only the essential points necessary to demonstrate how variability and context can be incorporated into current graphical methods for causal analysis.[6]

The causal graph in figure 14.1 is not only a traditional linear additive path model; it can also be understood as a fully nonparametric causal graph. Moreover, it also has a foundation in structural equations, though these are written in quite different form than in the older path model tradition. For the two endogenous variables C and Y in figure 14.1, the path model's structural equations would have been

$$C = a_C + b_{P \to C}P + e_C,$$ (10)

$$Y = a_Y + b_{C \to Y}C + b_{P \to Y}P + b_{N \to Y}N + e_Y.$$ (11)

When seen as a causal graph as developed in the more recent literature, the structural equations for figure 14.1 would have a more flexible form. They would be written for all variables in the graph and in unrestricted (possibly nonlinear and interactive) form as

$$P = f_P(e_P),$$ (12)

$$C = f_C(P, e_C),$$ (13)

$$N = f_N(e_N),$$ (14)

$$Y = f_Y(P, C, N, e_Y).$$ (15)

Reading from left to right in the causal graph in figure 14.1 and top to bottom in these equations, P is defined as an unspecified function, $f_P(.)$, with e_P as its sole argument. The function $f_P(.)$ is often labeled a "kernel" (which can be confusing because the word *kernel* is also used in other ways in statistics and mathematics). For our purposes, the input e_P represents all causes of P that are external to the causal model in the sense that they are completely independent of C, N, and Y.[7] This idiosyncratic determinant of P is suppressed in the causal graph for simplicity, since it could be included by simply adding the causal relationship $e_P \to P$ (as would have been common in the path model tradition). The next three equations then represent analogous unrestricted functions with inputs that represent all causes of the variables on the left-hand sides of the equations. The last is the most elaborate, in that Y is a function of three observed variables P, C, and N, as well as e_Y, all of which transmit their effects on Y via the function $f_Y(.)$.

In this tradition, causal identification can be considered (and, indeed, is often best understood) without introducing any functional form for $f_P(.)$, $f_C(.)$, $f_N(.)$, or $f_Y(.)$. A value is produced for the outcome variable of each equation for every combination of the values in the corresponding function on the right-hand sides of these equations. For example, Y takes on a distinct value for each combination of values for $P = p$, $C = c$, and $N = n$ (typically then with the assumption that values of e_Y are drawn at random from some common distribution that is presumed to have finite moments; see Freedman [2010, chapter 15] for discussion of alternative approaches).

An implication of this flexibility deserves particular emphasis, and preexisting knowledge of path models can hinder full recognition of its importance. *All* interactions between the effects of P, C, and N on Y are implicitly permitted by the lack of restrictions placed on $f_Y(.)$. Most importantly, this also means that the causal graph in figure 14.1 is consistent with all such interactions, since the arrows merely signal which causes of Y in the graph belong in the function $f_Y(.)$. Thus, no new arrows are needed to represent interactions for more specific parameterizations where, for example, the effect of C on Y varies with the level of P or N.

As a result, even though it may feel natural to want to "see" a specific arrow present in the causal graph to represent an interaction effect that corresponds to a cross-product term in a regression equation, one must learn to suppress such a desire. The key point, in considering an analysis that utilizes causal graphs, is to drop regression models from one's mind when thinking about identification issues. Instead, if one must use a data analytic machine to conceptualize how to perform an appropriate empirical analysis of the puzzle under consideration, one should default to simple tabular stratification. In this case, one should think of a sufficiently large sample, such that one could, for example, estimate with great precision the value of Y for every conceivable combination of values for $P = p$, $C = c$, and $N = n$. Average causal effects can then be calculated by appropriately weighting differences calculated within such a stratification of the data.

14.4. Representing Variability and Contextual Effects in Causal Graphs

Although there are tremendous advantages that accrue from the general non-parametric structure of causal graphs, it can still be hard to encode heterogeneity in causal graphs in transparent ways for social scientists. Moreover, many scholars who work with causal graphs but who are not social scientists (including those who have developed the case for their general applicability to all causal analysis) do not fully understand how social scientists think about heterogeneity, especially when produced by an interaction with an unobserved variable. To promote understanding by making the key conceptual linkages, we start with a model that is simpler even than the one in figure 14.1. We will then add complexity to build an explicit model for a full pattern of heterogeneity that represents variability of effects that emerge in consequential contexts, using the focal charter schools example.

14.4.1 Two Separate Causal Graphs for Two Latent Classes

Consider the two causal graphs in figure 14.2, and suppose that the population is partitioned into two latent classes, each of which has its own graph in panel (a) or panel (b). Suppose again that P is a family's parental background, C is charter school

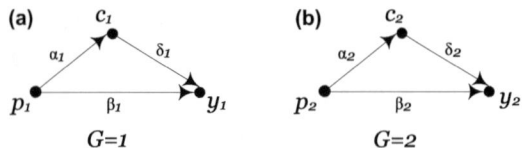

Figure 14.2 Separate causal graphs for two groups of individuals ($G = 1$ and $G = 2$) where the effects of parental background (P) and charter schools (C) on test scores (Y) may differ for the two groups.

attendance, and Y is a standardized test for all sixth graders in a large metropolitan school district. For these two graphs, the subscripts refer to the latent classes, which are also indicated by a latent class membership variable G that takes on values of 1 and 2.[8]

Although surely a gross oversimplification, suppose nonetheless that the population is composed of sixth graders who have been raised in two types of families. Families with $G = 1$ choose schools predominantly for lifestyle reasons, such as proximity to their extended families and tastes for particular school cultures, assuming that all schools are similar in instructional impact because achievement is largely a function of individual effort. Families with $G = 2$ choose elementary schools for their children by selecting the school, subject to constraints, that they feel will maximize the achievement of their children, assuming that schools differ in quality and that their children may learn more in some schools than in others. Accordingly, they are attentive to the national press on educational policy, in which both the Bush and Obama administrations argued for increasing the number of charter schools in the country because some researchers had argued that charter schools are more effective. As a consequence, the second group of families is more likely to send their children to charter schools, such that the mean of C is higher for those families with $G = 2$ than $G = 1$.

Finally, suppose that parents with college degrees are more likely to value distinctive forms of education, and as a result are more likely to send their children to charter schools (independent of whether or not highly educated parents are more likely to be found in the latent class for whom $G = 2$, which we will discuss later). They are also more likely to be able to support children in completing homework and otherwise making the most of the educational opportunities that are offered to their children. Accordingly, suppose that in both groups the causal effects $P \to C$ and $P \to Y$ are positive and substantial (i.e., that α_1, β_1, α_2, and β_2 in figure 14.2 are all positive and substantial).

The question for investigation is whether the effect of C on Y is positive for both groups, and if so, whether it is the same size for both groups. If we are willing to assume, as some of the literature suggests, that the second group of families is correct in the sense that school quality does matter for student learning, and further that charter schools are higher quality (as authors of this chapter, we neither agree nor disagree with this position; see Henig 2008), then we should expect that both δ_1

and δ_2 are more likely positive than not. And if we believe that parents with $G = 2$ have some sense that this is correct, then not only will more of them send their children to charter schools, they will also sort their children more effectively into charter and noncharter schools. In other words, they will also be more likely to continue to enroll their children in regular public schools if they feel that their children will not benefit from the distinctive characteristics of available charter schools (e.g., if the charter schools that have openings have instructional themes that their children find distasteful). Because both of these self-selection effects are reinforcing, it is likely that $\delta_2 > \delta_1$.[9]

If this plausible scenario is true in reality, what would happen if a researcher ignored the latent classes (either by mistake or, more realistically, because the membership variable G is unobserved) and simply assumed that a single DAG prevailed? In this case, a researcher might estimate the effect of C on Y for each value of P and then average these effects over the distribution of P, yielding a population-level estimate δ. At best, this estimate would be uninformative about the underlying pattern of heterogeneity that suggests that $\delta_2 > \delta_1$. At worst, this estimate would be completely wrong as an estimate of the average causal effect of C on Y. For example, if P predicts latent class membership G, and G predicts the size of the effect of C on Y, then P-stratum-specific effects mix together individual-level causal effects that vary with the conditional distribution of G within the strata of P. Combining P-stratum-specific effects by calculating an average effect across only the distribution of P does not properly weight the G-stratum-specific effects that are embedded in differential patterns within the strata of P.

In order to consider these possibilities, we need to have a model of selection into C that is informed by a model of the traits of individuals that would cause them to be found in underlying latent classes. It is most natural to pursue such a model in a single causal graph that explicitly represents the latent classes by including the variable G as a node within it.

14.4.2 A Single Causal Graph for Two Latent Classes

Consider figure 14.3, which contains a standard triangular system where C has an effect on Y and where both C and Y share a common cause P. To this standard triangle, the latent class membership variable G is introduced as an explicit cause of C.[10] The variable G is given a hollow node, o, to indicate that it is unobserved. The arrow from G to C is present because there are alternative groups of families, coded by the alternative values of the unobserved variable G, that approach differently the decision of whether to send their children to charter schools. As a result, G predicts charter school attendance, C.[11]

The corresponding structural equations for the causal graph in figure 14.3 are then

$$P = f_P(e_P) \tag{16}$$

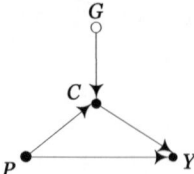

Figure 14.3 A causal graph where groups are represented by an unobserved latent class variable (*G*) in a single causal graph.

$$G = f_G(e_G) \tag{17}$$

$$C = f_C(P, G, e_C) \tag{18}$$

$$Y = f_Y(P, C, e_Y) \tag{19}$$

The latent class membership variable *G* only enters these structural equations in two places, on its own in Equation 17 and then as an input to $f_C(.)$ in Equation 18.

To accept figure 14.3 as a full representation of the true causal model that relates *G* to *P*, *C*, and *Y*, we must be able to assume that *G* shares no common causes with *P*, *C*, or *Y* that have been mistakenly suppressed. For our focal example, the necessary assumptions are that students who have parents with high levels of education are no more likely to know of the educational policy dialogue that claims that charter schools have advantages and also are no more likely to think that school quality has any effects on achievement when student effort and skill are held constant. We must also be willing to assume that, within values of *P* and *C*, *G* has no causal effect on *Y*, which with our example is tantamount to assuming that those who attempt to maximize the learning of their children by selecting optimal schools (a) do not manage to do so well enough so that the obtained effect is any larger on average, conditional on other factors, for their own children than for those who do not attempt to select on the causal effect of schooling and (b) do not do anything else that helps their children to benefit from the learning opportunities provided to them in school or in the home that is not already captured by the direct effect $P \rightarrow Y$. This would require that the impulse to select into charter schools based on beliefs about the size of the charter school effect for one's own child is a completely ignorable process, since it does not result in any actual selection on the variation in the causal effect nor generate any reinforcing behavior that might complement the charter school effect. For the charter school effect, there is no literature to support such a dismissal of the power of self-selection.

Accordingly, for figures 14.4(a) and (b), we add an arrow from *G* to *Y* to the graph presented earlier in figure 14.3, which brings these two new graphs into alignment with the discussion earlier of the heterogeneity in the causal graphs in figure 14.2. For figure 14.4(a), which includes only this one additional arrow, the structural equations are then

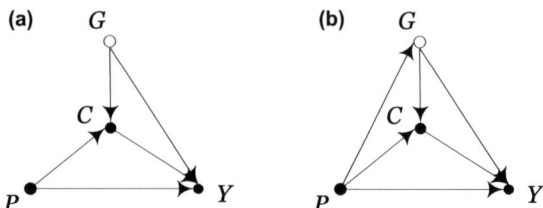

Figure 14.4 Two causal graphs where selection into charter schools (C) is determined by group (G) and where selection renders the effect of C on Y unidentified as long as G remains unobserved.

$$P = f_P(e_P), \tag{20}$$

$$G = f_G(e_G), \tag{21}$$

$$C = f_C(P, G, e_C), \tag{22}$$

$$Y = f_Y(P, C, G, e_Y). \tag{23}$$

For figure 14.4(b), we drop the assumption that G is independent of P. This elaborated graph now includes an arrow from P to G. As a result, $f_G(e_G)$ is no longer the appropriate function for G. Equation 21 must be replaced by

$$G = f_G(P, e_G) \tag{24}$$

so that family background is an explicit cause of latent class membership. It is likely that parents with high socioeconomic status are more likely to select on the possible causal effect of charter schooling, which is how the latent classes were discussed for figure 14.2. Still, how these latent classes emerge is not sufficiently transparent in figure 14.4. A more explicit causal model that gives structure to the causal pathway from P to G may help to clarify the self-selection dynamic, as we show next.

14.4.3 Self-Selection into the Latent Classes

Suppose that latent class membership G is determined by a variable that measures a family's subjective expectation of their child's likely benefit from attending a charter school instead of a regular public school. Although we could enter this variable into a causal graph with a single letter, such as S or E, for figure 14.5 we use a full mnemonic representation as a variable labeled $\text{Exp}(C \rightarrow Y)$. For figure 14.5(a), which is a direct analog to figure 14.4(a), this subjective expectation is the sole determinant of G. The structural equations are then

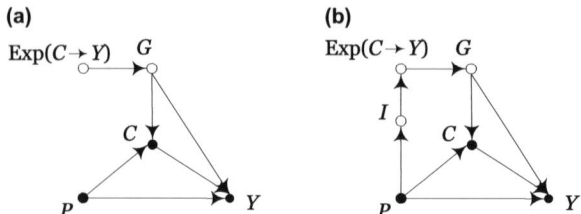

Figure 14.5 Two causal graphs where selection on the unobservables is given an explicit representation as self-selection on subjective expectations of variation in the causal effect of C on Y. For panel b, these expectations are determined by information (I) that is only available to families with particular parental backgrounds (P).

$$P = f_P(e_P), \tag{25}$$

$$\text{Exp}(C \to Y) = f_{\text{Exp}}(e_{\text{Exp}}), \tag{26}$$

$$G = f_G[\text{Exp}(C \to Y), e_G], \tag{27}$$

$$C = f_C(P, G, e_C), \tag{28}$$

$$Y = f_Y(P, C, G, e_Y). \tag{29}$$

Note that $\text{Exp}(C \to Y)$ is determined solely by e_{Exp} in Equation 26. Thus, figure 14.5(a) would be an accurate representation of the system of causal relationships if subjective expectations were either completely random or instead based solely on characteristics of families that are independent of the family background variables in P.

Given what we have written in the last section about the likelihood that families with different patterns of P will end up in different latent classes represented by G, it seems clear that figure 14.5(a) is not the proper representation for the research scenario we have already specified. Accordingly, in figure 14.5(b), e_{Exp} is joined by an unspecified additional input I into the subjective expectation of the child-specific causal effect of C on Y, which is then presumed to be caused, in part, by family background. As a result, there is now a path from P to G through I and $\text{Exp}(C \to Y)$. The structural equations are now augmented as

$$P = f_P(e_P), \tag{30}$$

$$I = f_I(P, e_I), \tag{31}$$

$$\text{Exp}(C \to Y) = f_{\text{Exp}}(I, e_{\text{Exp}}), \tag{32}$$

$$G = f_G[\text{Exp}(C \to Y), e_G], \tag{33}$$

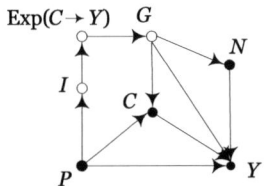

Figure 14.6 A causal graph where self-selection on the causal effect of charter schooling also triggers self-selection into consequential and interactive neighborhood contexts (*N*).

$$C = f_C(P, G, e_C),\tag{34}$$

$$Y = f_Y(P, C, G, e_Y),\tag{35}$$

In sociology, the causal effect of *P* on Exp(*C* → *Y*) via *I* follows from the position that privileged positions in social structure are occupied by advantaged families. From these positions, individuals acquire information *I* that allows them to recognize benefits that are available to them.[12]

By elaborating the causal graph progressively from figure 14.3 through figure 14.5(b), we have explicitly elaborated what is often presumed in models that incorporate self-selection. Background variables in *P* are related to the cause *C* by way of a set of latent classes in *G* that encode subjective evaluations of the individual-specific causal effect of *C* on *Y*. These expectations are functions of characteristics in *P* by way of the information *I* that is differentially available to families that differ on *P*. Yet, even though we now have an elaborate representation of self-selection, we still have not brought contextual effects into the model.

14.4.4 Self-Selection into the Treatment and a Complementary Context

How hard is the task of allowing for contextual effects? With causal graphs, it is considerably easier than one might expect. Consider figure 14.6, which incorporates a contextual variable *N* into the causal graph in figure 14.5(b). The variable *N* represents all causes of student achievement that can be conceptualized as either features of a student's residential neighborhood or features of a charter school's surrounding neighborhood. The component variables in *N* might be access to resources not measured by *P* or specific local cultures that may or may not promote student achievement.[13] With the addition of *N*, the function for *Y* is now $f_Y(P, C, G, N, e_Y)$. Recall, again, that *N* is not restricted by any functional form assumption for $f_Y(.)$. As a result, the causal effect of *N* can modify or interact with the partial effects of *G*, *C*, and *P* on *Y*.[14]

Figure 14.6 also allows for even more powerful effects of self-selection. Suppose that self-selection into the latent classes in *G* is associated with self-selection into *N* as well. We see two separate and countervailing tendencies. Parents attuned to the potential benefits of charter schooling are also more likely to choose neighborhood contexts that best allow them to encourage their children to study hard in school. At the same time, after obtaining an attendance offer from a charter school, a family may also decide to move to an alternative neighborhood in the catchment area of a suboptimal regular public school, since attendance at such a school may no longer be a consideration in the family's residential decision. If either effect is present, then the function for N is equal to $f_N(G, e_N)$, and we then have seven structural equations as

$$P = f_P(e_P), \tag{36}$$

$$I = f_I(P, e_I) \tag{37}$$

$$\text{Exp}(C \rightarrow Y) = f_{\text{Exp}}(I, e_{\text{Exp}}), \tag{38}$$

$$G = f_G[\text{Exp}(C \rightarrow Y), e_G], \tag{39}$$

$$C = f_C(P, G, e_C), \tag{40}$$

$$N = f_N(G, e_N), \tag{41}$$

$$Y = f_Y(P, C, G, N, e_Y). \tag{42}$$

With this set of structural equations, the nonparametric nature of the kernels allows for fully interactive effects. Again, the function for Y, $f_Y(P, C, G, N, e_Y)$, allows for the effects of C and N to vary within each distinct combination of values between them, as would be the case if the charter school effect varied based on the neighborhood within which students lived.[15]

14.5. EMPIRICAL STRATEGIES FOR MODELING VARIABILITY AND CONTEXT IN CAUSAL ANALYSIS

There are two basic goals of writing down a causal graph: (1) to represent the set of causal relationships implied by the available state of knowledge, (2) to assess the feasibility of alternative estimation strategies. Figure 14.6 represents a causal graph that is a reasonable representation of the causal structure that generates the charter school effect. This is a matter of judgment, and one might contend, for example, that the claim that self-selection on the charter school effect generates movement between neighborhoods is overly complex. If so, then $G \to N$ could be removed from the graph, which would simplify the function in Equation 41 to $f_N(e_N)$ and the estimation procedures required.

Suppose that one has access to observational data, such as the National Assessment of Education Progress (NAEP) data analyzed by Lubienski and Lubienski (2003), that provide data on standardized test scores, school type, and some family background characteristics. For the sake of our exposition, suppose further that these NAEP data had even better measures of family background and neighborhood characteristics, so that we could conclude that high-quality data are available for all of the variables in figure 14.6 with solid nodes: Y, C, N, and P. Yet, no data are available for the variables with hollow nodes: I, $\text{Exp}(C \to Y)$, and G. The primary goal of analysis is to estimate the average causal effect of C on Y, as this effect interacts with the complementary causal effect of N on Y. Can one adjust for confounding in order to estimate these effects?

We answer this question by drawing on the identification rule developed by Pearl (2000, 2009), which he labels the "back-door criterion." Many explications of the back-door criterion are available, and we draw directly from our own presentation in Morgan and Winship (2007, section 3.1.3), which contains additional explanation beyond what we have space to offer here.

For Pearl, a back-door path is any sequence of arrows between a causal variable and an outcome variable that includes an arrow that points to the causal variable. Pearl's back-door criterion states that if one or more back-door paths connects the causal variable to the outcome variable, the causal effect is identified by conditioning on a set of variables W if all back-door paths between the causal variable and the outcome variable are blocked after conditioning on W. Pearl proves that all back-door paths are blocked by W if each back-door path:

1. contains a chain of mediation $A \to M \to B$ where the middle variable M is in W, or
2. contains a fork of mutual dependence $A \leftarrow M \to B$ where the middle variable M is in W, or
3. contains an inverted fork of mutual causation $A \to M \leftarrow B$ where the middle variable M and all of M's descendants are *not* in W.[16]

Consider now how this back-door criterion applies to the causal graph in figure 14.6. The relevant back-door paths are

For C:

1. $C \leftarrow P \to Y$,
2. $C \leftarrow P \to I \to \text{Exp}(C \to Y) \to G \to Y$
3. $C \leftarrow P \to I \to \text{Exp}(C \to Y) \to G \to N \to Y$,
4. $C \leftarrow G \to N \to Y$,
5. $C \leftarrow G \to Y$.

and

For N:

6. $N \leftarrow G \rightarrow Y$,
7. $N \leftarrow G \rightarrow C \rightarrow Y$,
8. $N \leftarrow G \leftarrow \mathrm{Exp}(C \rightarrow Y) \leftarrow I \leftarrow P \rightarrow Y$,
9. $N \leftarrow G \leftarrow \mathrm{Exp}(C \rightarrow Y) \leftarrow I \leftarrow P \rightarrow C \rightarrow Y$,
10. $N \leftarrow G \leftarrow \mathrm{Exp}(C \rightarrow Y) \leftarrow I \leftarrow P \rightarrow C \leftarrow G \rightarrow Y$.

How many of these paths can be blocked by conditioning on the observed data? For models that estimate the effect of C on Y, the paths 1 through 4 can be blocked by conditioning on P and N. However, path 5 remains unblocked. Likewise, the paths 7 through 10 can be blocked by conditioning on P and C, but path 6 remains unblocked.

For the two unblocked paths, the same problematic arrow is present $G \rightarrow Y$, which carries forward exogenous causal determinants of I, $\mathrm{Exp}(C \rightarrow Y)$, and G (i.e., e_I, e_{Exp}, and e_G) and which are not fully blocked by conditioning on P and N. Thus, if there is selection on the causal effect itself, independent of family background, then it enters the model through G and confounds the conditional association between C and Y. As a result, effective estimation of the effects of C and N on Y is impossible given the available data. Selection into charter schools and neighborhoods is partly on an unobserved variable (the concatenation of $I \rightarrow \mathrm{Exp}(C \rightarrow Y) \rightarrow G$), and this confounding cannot be eliminated by conditioning on the observed data.[17]

How can analysis proceed under these circumstances? There are two main choices. First, the analyst can concede that self-selection on the causal effect is present, which may even generate neighborhood-based selection as a by-product. In these circumstances, the presence of the causal relationship $G \rightarrow Y$ renders estimates of C and N on Y unidentified, either in interactive fashion or when averaging one over the other. In this case, analysis must then be scaled back, and we would recommend that set identification results be pursued (see Manski 1995, 2003). The new goal would be to estimate an interval within which the average causal effect must fall.

In the actual empirical literature on the charter school effect, this humble option has not been pursued by any of the main combatants in the debates. The desire to provide point estimates of causal effects has been too strong, even though it would seem clear to many outside readers that the debate persists simply because the point-estimate of the average causal effect is unidentified.

Instead, researchers have used the lottery nature of charter school enrollments in order to define the charter school effect in a different way: the effect of charter schooling among those who would self-select into it. This is a type of bounded analysis, and it is entirely appropriate. The problem is that these same scholars too quickly forget the bounded nature of their conclusions, issuing overly broad claims. For example, in their study of charter schools in New York City, Hoxby, Murarka, and Kang (2009, vii) introduce their results in their executive summary with three bullet points:

- Lottery-based analysis of charter schools' effects on achievement is, by far, the most reliable method of evaluation. It is the only method that reliably eliminates selection biases which occur if students who apply to charter schools are more disadvantaged, more motivated, or different in any other way than students who do not apply.
- On average, a student who attended a charter school for all of grades kindergarten through eight would close about 86 percent of the Scarsdale-Harlem achievement gap in math and 66 percent of the achievement gap in English. A student who attended fewer grades would improve by a commensurately smaller amount.
- On average, a lotteried-out student who stayed in the traditional public schools for all of grades kindergarten through eight would stay on grade level but would not close the Scarsdale-Harlem achievement gap by much. However, the lotteried-out students' performance does improve and is better than the norm in the U.S. where, as a rule, disadvantaged students fall further behind as they age.

Nowhere in their executive summary is it stated that these comparisons across lotteried-in and lotteried-out students are only informative about those who self-select into charter schools. It is not conceded that the results are uninformative about the first order question: What is the expected charter school effect for a randomly chosen student from New York City?

How else can analysis proceed even though back-door conditioning is infeasible? The second choice is simply to assume away the unblocked paths that include $G \rightarrow Y$, which is tantamount to assuming that self-selection does not exist. The study by the Center for Research on Education Outcomes (CREDO, 2009) is closer to this position, and they offer a complex set of conclusions based on national results where charter school students are matched to students from traditional public schools:

> In our nationally pooled sample, two subgroups fare better in charters than in the traditional system: students in poverty and ELL [English Language Learner] students. . . . These findings are particularly heartening for the charter advocates who target the most challenging educational populations or strive to improve education options in the most difficult communities. Charter schools that are organized around a mission to teach the most economically disadvantaged students in particular seem to have developed expertise in serving these communities. . . . The flip-side of this insight should not be ignored either. Students not in poverty and students who are not English language learners on average do notably worse than the same students who remain in the traditional public school system. Additional work is needed to determine the reasons underlying this phenomenon. Perhaps these students are "off-mission" in the schools they attend. (CREDO 2009, 7)

These conclusions are offered based on models that match students on observable characteristics, leaving unobserved selection on the causal effect unaccounted for. In fact, past research on private school effects on achievement suggests that self-selection may be able to account for the pattern of findings reported in the CREDO study. It is possible that students from families who are living in poverty but who make their way into charter schools are fleeing poor alternatives in their own neighborhood schools and, furthermore, have extra amounts of motivation to succeed in school. At the same time, it is likely that students from more advantaged families are more likely to be attending charter schools solely for lifestyle reasons. In fact, they may be trading off academic opportunities high-quality quality schools that they have found distasteful for medium-quality charter schools with peer cultures that are more appealing.

When back-door conditioning does not identify the causal effect, there is one final possibility for analysis. One can attempt to eliminate the self-selection bias problem by locating a natural experiment. This research design has not been utilized in the charter schools debate to attempt to estimate the unconditional average causal effect (i.e., Equation 6), and we offer a cautionary assessment on its prospects in an appendix to this chapter. However, as we explain in the appendix, instrumental variables that encode natural experiments have strong potential to illuminate some aspects of the estimation challenge, even though they cannot be considered a general solution for estimating all average causal effects of interest.

14.6. Important Caveats on the Utility of Causal Graphs

In the last section, we argued that one of the primary benefits of Pearl's causal graphs is that they are nonparametric. As such, they implicitly incorporate nonlinearities and interactions among the variables that are causes of any outcome. In many circumstances, this feature is an enormous advantage because one can state the causal relationships among variables without having to worry about the specification of the functional relationships among the variables. In this way, causal graphs allow for a careful consideration of identification challenges without also requiring that an analyst simultaneously grapple with specification issues.[18]

In this section, we want to temper our enthusiasm for this property of graphs, embedded within a more general discussion of types of heterogeneity. The main message is the following: Precisely because of their flexibility, causal graphs can obscure important distinctions. In some circumstances, whether a relationship is nonlinear and/or a set of variables interact in their effects on an outcome is of considerable theoretical and substantive interest.

We have already discussed a variety of models in which it has been critical to explicitly model the effects of heterogeneity in order to understand how family background and neighborhood characteristics might interact with the effect of enrolling in a charter school. In situations such as these, the fact that it is possible to bury nonlinearities and interactions in a causal graph can become a disadvantage, especially if the science of the problem demands that the particular nature of the heterogeneity be emphasized. For many applications, it would be unwise to move quickly from model identification to estimation without giving due consideration to how one should represent heterogeneity in the model specification that is selected.

In order to make some of these issues explicit, in this section we consider three different types of heterogeneity, which we label compositional heterogeneity, specification-dependent heterogeneity, and fundamental heterogeneity.[19] Each of these types of heterogeneity can be obscured by a causal graph, if such a graph and the estimation strategy that it suggests are not handled with due care.

14.6.1 Compositional Heterogeneity

In our presentation of the charter school example, we did not give any attention to an important source of heterogeneity: Charter schools themselves are heterogeneous in the programs they offer to students. Indeed, charter schools are established precisely to cultivate distinctive identities, and there seems to be widespread recognition among all researchers engaged in this area that these differences matter.

In this sense, the two-category variable C in the causal graphs presented earlier is reductive. Research on charter schools must assiduously attend to variation across charter schools, as well as regular public schools that serve as comparative cases, in order to generate sufficiently meaningful results. Causal graphs are powerful precisely because they are compact representations of underlying structural equations, but they pose a danger in suppressing too much detail. If subdividing a causal variable into meaningfully different groups then yields alternative causal effects that depend on the contrast that is selected, then compositional heterogeneity exists and is obscured by the original causal graph.[20]

14.6.2 Specification-Dependent Heterogeneity

In many situations, a "natural" metric for a variable may not be clear. An obvious example is the relationship between education and income. Should we think about earnings in dollars or in the logarithm of dollars? It would make sense to think about earnings in dollars if we thought that an additional year of education increased one's earnings by the same amount independent of one's current education (or income). In fact, a vast literature primarily from economics has argued that an increase in education by one year increases one's earnings by differing amounts depending on one's education, but, roughly at least, increases earnings by the same percentage amount for individuals with differing years of education.[21]

To understand when specification-dependent heterogeneity can arise, and then how it can be eliminated by model respecification, suppose that we have a fully specified causal structural model, including parameter values for all causal variables, that is the same for everyone in the population under consideration. In this situation, there are no fundamental differences in the way that the causal process operates because the same causal model applies to all individuals.

In this case, apparent individual differences may emerge in the effect of a particular causal variable if differences between individuals in the true model are not reflected in a constrained specification chosen by an analyst. This would occur, for example, when (1) a cross-product interaction between two variables appears to fit the data, (2) the true functional relationship between the outcome variable and one of the variables in the cross-product interaction is quadratic, and (3) this variable in the cross-product interaction term was mistakenly parameterized only with a single linear term for its main effect when the empirical specification was submitted for estimation.

Moving away from this abstract description of specification-dependent heterogeneity, consider the charter school example when both compositional and specification-dependent heterogeneity are likely present together. Suppose that for an estimated model the effect of C on Y appears to differ by a student's race, where the effect of C on Y is larger for black and Hispanic students than for white and Asian students. Suppose that this pattern revealed itself during empirical analysis after interactions between C and dummy variables for race were added to the model. This result does not necessarily imply that black and Hispanic students experience their charter schools in any fundamentally different way. Instead, it may be the case that (1) on average the regular schools that black and Hispanic students would have attended are worse than those that white and Asian students would have attended and/or (2) a crucial variable with a nonlinear effect on achievement and with a distribution that differs by race, such as family income, is given only a linear parameterization in the model. Compositional heterogeneity would arise because of the former while specification-dependent heterogeneity would arise because of the latter. If either (1) or (2) were present, the estimates would suggest incorrectly that the charter school experience is more effective for black and Hispanic students.

14.6.3 Fundamental Heterogeneity

Suppose now that we have a causal graph and its associated structural equations, but suppose that the parameter values attached to the variables vary across individuals. Suppose further that no unappreciated compositional or specification-dependent heterogeneity is present.

Why would the parameter values differ across individuals? We will argue in this section that this can only happen if the causal processes differ fundamentally across individuals, such that the mechanism by which the cause generates its effect differs across individuals.

Suppose again that the effect of charter schools is thought to be larger for black and Hispanic students than for white and Asian students. Suppose that this is still thought to be the case, even though compositional and specification-dependent heterogeneity have been explained away because the model now properly adjusts for quality differences across schools that students of different races would typically attend and all adjustment variables are given sufficiently flexible parameterizations.

Fundamental heterogeneity would be present across race if the mechanism that generates the charter school effect differs in meaningful ways across racial groups.

A prominent strand of literature in education research suggests that stereotypes of inherent intellectual inferiority plague black and Hispanic students in regular public schools. It may be that some charter schools are effective at mitigating the effects of these stereotypes for black and Hispanic students, either by directly confronting the stereotypes as completely unfounded or instead by making students feel that they are attending unique schools that shield them from the effects of stereotypes that exist in the broader culture. As a result, for black and Hispanic students, the charter school effect emerges from two sources: (1) the mitigation of stereotype effects and (2) quality differences in instruction. For white and Asian students, the same stereotypes are irrelevant, and they therefore benefit only from the same higher-quality instruction that is offered to all students. We would regard any such difference in the causal process as a form of fundamental heterogeneity, since part of the causal mechanism is distinct for subgroups of the population.

One might counter this presentation of fundamental heterogeneity with the argument that it is simply a more virulent form of specification-dependent heterogeneity. The argument would run as follows: A more complete causal graph can be written down, with its structural equations including structural zeros, such that subgroup-distinct portions of the mechanism switch off and on depending on the individuals' characteristics at the time they are exposed to the cause. For the example just given, stereotype effects would exist nominally for white and Asian students in the causal graph, but the joint distribution of the variables in the mechanism would give them no weight in the production of the charter school effect for white and Asian students.

Technically, this argument is sound. However, much is lost, in our view, when such fundamental differences in the causal processes within a population are explained away so artificially. We would argue that separate causal graphs should be specified instead.[22]

14.7. Conclusion

In this chapter, we have explained how a new methodology of causal graphs can be used to represent variability and context in causal analysis in the social sciences. In developing this explanation, we have also provided a brief analysis of why the practice of quantitatively oriented sociology between the 1960s and the 1980s opened itself up to the critique that its methods could not represent such features of causal systems. We have also discussed some alternative empirical strategies for estimating these effects, demonstrating the limited power that backdoor conditioning offers when heterogeneity due to unobserved variables is present. Finally, we have concluded with a cautionary perspective on causal graphs,

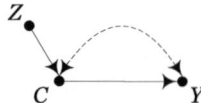

**Figure 14.A1 Instrumental variable identification of the causal effect of charter schools
(*C*) on test scores (*Y*), where *Z* is the instrument.**

noting that their simplifying power has the potential to obscure the heterogeneity that they so easily accommodate. Still, we would maintain that their flexibility enables careful and precise consideration of the challenges of causal effect identification, separated in helpful ways from many specification issues that are less fundamental.

APPENDIX: THE ALTERNATIVE NATURAL EXPERIMENT APPROACH

Because the natural experiment perspective may be unfamiliar to readers when expressed with the econometric language of instrumental variables, we will build toward the charter schools example from a more basic set of causal graphs. Figure 14.A1 presents a standard causal graph where identification is achieved through an instrumental variable. For simplicity, assume that no data are available for confounders such as *P*, and thus the analyst is left with no feasible way to even begin to enact a back-door conditioning strategy for the effect of charter schools *C* on achievement *Y*. In this situation, a double-headed, dashed, and curved arrow can be used to signify the existence of common unobserved variables that cause both *C* and *Y*.

Suppose, however, that a variable *Z* is observed that is a cause of *C* and that has no effect on *Y* except through its causal effect on *C*. This variable *Z* is an instrumental variable, and it can be thought of as a shock to *C* that is independent of the confounders represented by the double-headed arrow that connects *C* and *Y*. If such an instrumental variable exists, the classical econometric literature demonstrates that an estimate of the causal effect of *C* on *Y* can be obtained by first calculating the association between *Z* and *Y* and then dividing by the association between *Z* and *C*.

Are there any plausible instrumental variables for charter school attendance? A typical candidate, as one might find in the economics literature, would be the distance between the treatment site and an individual's residence. The justification would be that the location of the treatment site is arbitrary but has an effect on enrollment propensity because of the implicit costs of traveling to the site. For the charter school example, it is unclear whether such an instrument would have any chance of satisfying the relevant assumptions, and it would depend crucially on the extent to which charter schools are located in arbitrary places. One would tend to assume, in fact, that they are located nearer to students more likely to benefit from charter schooling, both because many have missions to serve disadvantaged students who are thought to benefit most from having a charter school opportunity and because families may then move to neighborhoods that are closer to the charter schools that they elect to attend. It is possible that these problems could be mitigated by conditioning out some other determinants of the location of charter schools within the district and also obtaining family residence data before students entered charter schools.

For the sake of methodological clarity in our presentation, we will use as our example a more convincing but unlikely instrumental variable (in the sense that it has never yet become available and is unlikely to become available). Suppose that in New York City conditional cash transfers are offered to families that send their children to charter schools. Suppose that this program is modeled on New York City's recent Opportunity NYC program, which was justified by the position that families should be given incentives to make decisions that promote their children's futures. Suppose that for the new hypothetical program $2,500 in cash is offered each year to families for each child that they enroll in a charter school. Since charter schools do not charge tuition, families can spend the $2,500 per child however they see fit.

Suppose further that, because of a budget constraint, cash transfers cannot be extended to all eligible families. For fairness, it is decided that families should be drawn at random from among all families resident in New York City with school-age children. Accordingly, a fixed number of letters is sent out notifying a set of winning families.

It is later determined that 10 percent of students in charter schools received cash transfers. A dataset is then compiled with performance data on all students in the school district, and the cash transfer offer is coded as a variable Z, which is equal to 1 for those who were offered a cash transfer and 0 for those who were not.

A quick analysis of the data shows that many families who received offers of cash transfers turned them down and chose to send their children to regular public schools. Moreover, it is then assumed that at least some of the charter school students who received cash transfers would have attended charter schools anyway, and they were simply lucky to have also received a cash transfer.

Relying on the classical literature in econometrics, this variable Z would typically be considered a valid instrumental variable. It is randomly assigned in the population, and it has a direct causal effect on C because it is an effective incentive for charter school attendance (recall that we have assumed that the data show that Z predicts C). The crucial assumption is then that the entire association between Z and Y is attributable solely to the causal pathway through C.

As we will further discuss in the conclusion to this appendix, this assumption is debatable because the subsidy is cash and, without further restrictions, could be used by families to purchase other goods that have effects on Y. Any such alternative uses of the cash transfer would open up additional causal pathways from Z to Y that are not intercepted by C. For now, however, we will provisionally accept the identification assumptions. In this case, an IV estimator would deliver an estimate of the causal effect of C on Y that would be considered valid by the standards articulated in the classical literature in econometrics.

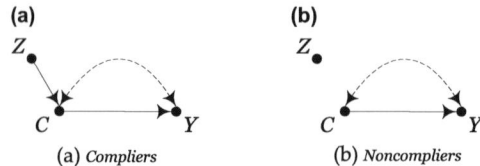

Figure 14.A2 Instrumental variable identification of the causal effect of charter schools (C) on test scores (Y), where the average effect for compliers is identified in (a) but the average effect for noncompliers is not identified in (b).

Would this causal effect then apply to everyone in the population? A more recent literature has provided an answer to this question: No, unless one is willing to make the artificial assumption that the causal effect is constant in the population.[23] Instead, in this case Z will be interpretable as the average effect of charter schooling among those who enter charter schools in response to the cash transfer.[24] This effect is known as the local average treatment effect (LATE), or sometimes the complier average causal effect. Figure 14.A2 explains how to interpret estimators of this form.

Suppose that the population can be partitioned into two mutually exclusive groups, compliers and noncompliers. Compliers are those who, in theory, would send their children to charter schools if they received the cash transfer but would not send their children to charter schools if they did not receive the cash transfer. Noncompliers include two other groups, "always takers" and "never takers."[25] The former enter charter schools regardless of whether they receive the cash transfer, and the latter do not enter charter schools regardless of whether they receive the cash transfer. Figure 14.A2(a) is the causal graph for compliers, and it is isomorphic with the causal graph in figure 14.A1 based on the classical instrumental variable literature. Figure 14.A2(b), however, applies only to noncompliers, and here the graph is different because Z does not cause C for noncompliers. Thus, it should be clear from figure 14.A2 that the estimate for the effect of C on Y that is enabled by Z cannot apply to noncompliers without the introduction of additional assumptions that allow for extrapolation from compliers to noncompliers. The standard assumption in the classical literature is that the causal effect is constant in the population. Under this assumption, the effect is fixed, such that obtaining an estimate for any subset of the population is sufficient to identify the fixed parameter in the population. The more recent literature has demonstrated how unreasonable such assumptions are in real-world contexts, and in this case it would seem self-evident that the charter school effect cannot be assumed to be a constant fixed effect in the population. Certainly none of the literature that has evaluated the charter school effect is consistent with this position.

Thus, our overall conclusion is that LATEs, generated by IVs, can be very illuminating. But they are limited causal parameters because they apply only to subsets of individuals who are exposed to the treatment of interest. Moreover, one cannot even observe who is a complier, since they are a theoretically defined group. All one can

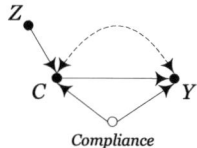

Figure 14.A3 A combined causal graph for panels (a) and (b) from figure 14.A2, where Z is the instrument and compliance is represented as an unobserved latent class variable *(Compliance)*.

recover from the data is the proportion of the population that is composed of compliers.[26] Nonetheless, knowing the size of the LATE and the percentage of the population that it applies to does then allow for some policy guidance, such as offering a lower bound on the total expected benefit for the entire population of introducing the cash transfer program.

Given that a central theme of this chapter is the power of causal graphs to represent complex patterns of heterogeneity, we will conclude by addressing a final question: Can the clarity of figure 14.A2 be represented in a single causal graph, akin to the move from figure 14.2 to figure 14.3 in the main body of the chapter? Yes, but readers may not agree that the clarity is preserved. This may be another situation in which separate causal graphs should be maintained.

Figure 14.A3 is a combined representation of figure 14.A2, which now applies to the full population. The representation of compliance-based heterogeneity is accomplished by augmenting the graph with a latent class dummy variable, *Compliance*, which signifies whether an individual is a complier.[27] *Compliance* interacts with Z in determining C, and *Compliance* also may have its own nonzero effect on Y (if compliers have average causal effects that differ from others).

Now, to make the connection to the fully elaborated figure 14.6 presented earlier, consider figure 14.A4, which includes all of the relevant back-door paths between C and Y that are packed into the double-headed arrow that connects C and Y in figure 14.A3. Note that for simplicity we have replaced the path $I \to \text{Exp}(C \to Y) \to G$ from figure 14.6 with the single variable V. This simplification is permissible under the assumption that an implicit error term e_V contains all of the information in the error terms e_I, e_{Exp}, and e_G in the causal graph in figure 14.6. The cash transfer instrumental variable is then represented as a variable Z, which has a sole causal effect in the graph on C because we have assumed that the cash transfer does not have other effects on Y. We then add in the additional back-door path from C to Y through their new common cause *Compliance*.

With the addition of $C \leftarrow Compliance \to Y$ to the graph, two sources of confusion may arise for some readers. First, it remains true that we cannot use back-door conditioning to estimate the effect of C on Y because of the unblockable back-door path through $C \leftarrow V \to Y$ (which includes implicitly the unobserved latent class variable G). However, it is important to remember that the similarly structured back-door path $C \leftarrow Compliance \to Y$ does not present any problems for an IV estimator because this back-door path does not generate an unblockable

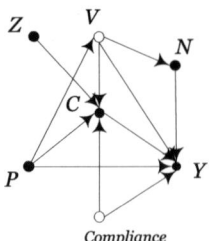

Figure 14.A4 Identification of the local average treatment effect using an instrument (Z) for the charter school causal graph presented earlier in Figure 6. The unobserved variable V is a composite for the causal chain that generates self-selection in figure 14.6 through information access and selection on the subjective evaluation of the individual-level causal effect.

path from Z to Y. It only represents an additional unblocked back-door path from C to Y, which is yet another path that IV estimation proceeds in spite of. Second, nothing in the causal graph itself explains why a resulting IV estimator delivers an average causal effect that applies only to compliers. To understand this point, it is more helpful to deconstruct the graph into two separate causal graphs as in figure 14.A2. The single causal graph conceals the fact that there is an implicit interaction between Z and *Compliance*. The instrument Z does not cause C for non-compliers, and *Compliance* does not cause C for those who do not receive the offer a cash transfer. Only the co-occurrence of Z and *Compliance* switches members of the population from $C = 0$ to $C = 1$. That the single causal graph does not reveal this point clearly might be regarded as a weakness of causal graph representations of underlying structural equations in this context.

Now, to conclude the discussion of the estimation of the charter school effect, consider two final points. It is likely that figure 14.A4 improperly omits a likely causal effect $P \rightarrow Compliance$. The parental background variable P implicitly includes within it a variable for family income. Students from families with high incomes should be less likely to switch from regular public schools to charter schools because of a $2500 incentive offered to their parents. Adding such a path, however, would not harm the feasibility of the IV estimator, since it does not generate an unblockable path from Z to Y. In fact, it helps to explain who compliers likely are, since it suggests that they are more likely to be lower income families. In this sense, recognizing the likely presence of that path helps to interpret the LATE that the IV identifies.

But, of course, not all additional causal effects will help to clarify the IV estimator. Suppose, for example, that Z generates an effect on N because the cash transfer is used to pay higher rent in another neighborhood for some families. As a result, a direct path from Z to N is opened up. Conditioning on the observed variable N will block the new problematic pathway $Z \rightarrow N \rightarrow Y$. But because N is a collider on another pathway, $Z \rightarrow N \leftarrow V \rightarrow Y$, conditioning on N opens up this pathway by inducing a relationship between Z and V. Thus, conditioning away self-selection into neighborhoods then allows self-selection on the causal effect of charter schooling to confound the IV estimate of the LATE.

ACKNOWLEDGMENTS

Address all correspondence to Stephen L. Morgan, Department of Sociology, 358 Uris Hall, Cornell University, Ithaca, NY 14853 (morgan@cornell.edu) or Christopher Winship (cwinship@wjh.harvard.edu), Department of Sociology, 620 William James Hall, Harvard University, Cambridge, MA 02138. We thank Richard Berk, David Bills, Jennie Brand, Nancy Cartwright, Felix Elwert, David Harding, Harold Kincaid, Emily Levitan, Judea Pearl, Herb Smith, Michael Spiller, Jennifer Todd, Tyler VanderWeele, Kim Weeden, and seminar participants at Duke University for helpful comments on an earlier version of this chapter.

NOTES

1. This does not mean that the results imply that individual-level differences do not exist. All such differences are, by construction, balanced in expectation across arms of the randomization scheme. Moreover, for the many experiments that are performed on convenience-based collections of individuals willing to participate (e.g., college students), this balancing often does not even generate the average causal effect in a target population of fundamental interest.

2. For very high-quality examples of this research, see Abdulkadiroglu et al. (2009), Angrist et al. (2010), Center for Research on Educational Outcomes (2009), and Hoxby, Murarka, and Kang (2009).

3. Before carrying on, we should note that our title "Bringing Context and Variability Back into Causal Analysis" is slightly misleading, since we will explain how context and variability have been brought back into causal analysis in the past fifteen years in ways that provide a solid foundation for future research. Thus, the tone of our chapter is optimistic and forward looking, not an indictment of current practice (which is often how the phrase "Bringing _____ Back In" has been used in the long series of critical papers in sociology that followed from Homans's classic manifesto on methodological individualism, delivered as "Bringing Men Back In" in his 1964 presidential address to the American Sociological Association).

4. Such assumptions are entirely implausible, of course, and one doubts that any researchers would ever have endorsed them had they been asked to do so. Rather, such assumptions would have been implicitly maintained, in part because the methodological literature had not yet shown how restrictive such assumptions can be nor offered alternative models to relax them in productive ways.

5. Were this exchange occurring in the substance of the day, a path model from the status attainment tradition would represent the substance of the exchange. The outcome variable Y would be career success and C would be college education. All of the same interactions noted for the charter school case would then apply in this case, though based on different narratives of causation.

6. We will not discuss the new literature in epidemiology on the distinction between an interaction and an effect modification (see VanderWeele 2009 and VanderWeele and Robins 2007). This literature uses casual graphs and associated structural equations to clarify many subtle points, which we will note briefly later when discussing contextual effects.

7. There is considerable debate over how to interpret these external causes. Their existence implies to some scholars that causality is fundamentally probabilistic. However, Pearl (2009) would maintain that the variables embedded in e_p are simply implicit causes of P. Under this interpretation, causality can still be considered a structural, deterministic relation. Freedman (2010, esp. chapter 15) discusses some of the drawbacks for statistical inference of assuming determinism of this form. Although convincing in some sense, his critique does not alter the utility of these sorts of causal graphs for clarifying when causal effects are identified.

8. The lowercase values x, d, and y for the two causal graphs are meant to connote that these are realized values of X, D, and Y that may differ in their distributions across the two latent classes.

9. These target parameters, δ_2 and δ_1, are defined implicitly as the average effect of charter schooling for all students from families with $G = 2$ and $G = 1$, respectively.

10. See Elwert and Winship (2010) for a related usage of a latent class variable G to represent effect heterogeneity.

11. Although we will continue to write as if G only takes on two values that identify two latent classes, this restriction is no longer necessary. G may take on as many values as there are alternative groups of families who approach differently the decision of whether to send their children to a charter school.

12. In addition, it may be that there are also additional common causes of P and I, which would then require that a double-headed arrow between P and I be added to the graph. This would be reasonable if informational advantages that structure expectations for optimal school choices are determined by deeper structural factors that also confer socioeconomic advantages on parents before they arrive at the decision point of whether or not to send their children to charter schools.

13. If the latter are only diffuse cultural understandings that only weakly shape local norms about the appropriateness of enacting the role of achievement-oriented student, then such variables may be difficult to observe. In this case, N might then be coded as a series of neighborhood dummy identifier variables. Analysis of these effects would then only be possible if there were sufficient numbers of students to analyze from within each neighborhood studied. Without such variation, the potential effects of N could not be separated from individual characteristics of students and their families. And, if modeled in this way, only the total effects of N would be identified, since the dummy variables for N would not contain any information on the underlying explanatory factors that structure the neighborhood effects that they identify.

14. See VanderWeele (2009) for an incisive analysis of the difference between an interaction and an effect modification. Our interest, conceptually at least, is in instances of genuine causal interaction, although much of what we write would hold under simpler structures of only effect modification.

15. We should also note that we could enrich the causal model further by drawing from the literature that posits deeper causal narratives for the joint determination of P and N, as well as other causal pathway that link P to N. This additional detail would not change the analysis of the conditioning strategies that follows in the next section.

16. Pearl (2000, 2009) expresses his back-door criterion in a more extended way, using the concept of D-separation. This more elaborate explanation allows for the development of additional specificity that can be important. For example, the variables in the permissible conditioning set W cannot include any variables that are affected by the cause of primary interest (i.e., "descendants of C"). This point is irrelevant to our discussion here, since the only variable that descends from C in our graphs is the outcome variable Y.

In other scenarios, where multiple outcomes of the cause are included in the graph, this additional restriction on the permissible set of conditioning variables in W can become very important. For a full discussion of the back-door criterion, we recommend a careful reading of Pearl (2009).

17. This conclusion is hardly revelatory for readers who already know the literature on self-selection bias. Nonetheless, we would argue that there is substantial didactic and communicative value in seeing this result expressed with a causal graph to which the back-door criterion is then applied.

18. For example, a researcher can first determine whether a conditioning strategy can identify relevant causal effects by examining a causal graph. If the effects of interest are identified, then the researcher can proceed to consider the alternative specifications that might be used to estimate the effects from the data, considering whether interactions between causes should be explicitly modeled or instead averaged in some meaningful way. If, however, it is clear from the causal graph that the effects of interest cannot be identified, then the issue of how to specify any subsequent empirical models would be far different, since the goal of the analysis would then be to understand in a provisional way how the unidentified causal effects may appear in masked form under alternative fallible models. The goal would be to represent the contingencies in the data, not offer up estimates that warrant causal conclusions.

19. These are our own labels. Other scholars have offered their own categorizations of types of heterogeneity, but we have not found a typology that matches our own explanatory goals for this section of the chapter.

20. In the philosophy of the social sciences, compositional heterogeneity exists when token-level differences exist within a type-level causal analysis. If it is the case that token-level causal accounts are to be privileged, then compositional heterogeneity is easy to solve. One must simply define causal states carefully so that their instantiations are sufficiently homogeneous.

21. And a more recent literature has suggested that these effects vary substantially between adjacent years. As such, there is no general functional relationship between earnings and years of education, and only piecewise year-by-year comparisons make sense to consider.

22. This position is consistent with (1) arguments from philosophy that mechanistic explanations should "bottom out" at a level that is appropriate to practitioners in a field (see Machamer, Darden, and Craver 2000) and (2) Cartwright's perspective that alternative nomological machines should be used to define distinct causal relations (see Cartwright 1999, chapter 3).

23. This clarity has been provided by Angrist, Imbens, and Rubin (1996), Heckman and Vytlacil (2005), and Manski (2003), both in these pieces and in their prior work. An explanation of this literature, written for noneconomists, can be found in Morgan and Winship (2007, chapter 7).

24. To warrant this interpretation, one additional assumption is required, which is that Z has a monotonic effect on C. In this case, the assumption is likely satisfied, since cash transfers would not create a disincentive to enter charter schools. For the alternative IV that we discussed—distance from the charter school—monotonicity would probably also hold, though its tenability would be less transparent.

25. This partition holds only under the assumption (see last note) that monotonicity applies so that there are no "defiers." If monotonicity does not hold, then defiers exist, and the IV no longer identifies the LATE.

26. See Morgan and Winship (2007, equation 7.26), which explains for a similar example that the proportion of compliers in the population would be (1-the proportion of

cash transfer winners in traditional public schools—the proportion of cash transfer losers in charter schools).

27. An alternative and more compact graph could be used for figure 14.A3 (as well as figure 14.A4 introduced later). Since *Compliance* is unobserved, one could simply declare that it is a member of the set of variables that generate the double-headed arrow in figure 14.A3 (or as a member of the set of variables in *V* that will be introduced later for figure 14.A4). We give *Compliance* its own pair of explicit causal effects on *C* and *Y* for clarity, even though it makes the graph more complex than it needs to be.

REFERENCES

Abbott, Andrew D. 1988. "Transcending General Linear Reality." *Sociological Theory* 6: 169–86.

Abbott, Andrew D. 2001. *Time Matters: On Theory and Method*. Chicago: University of Chicago Press.

Abdulkadiroglu, Atila, Joshua D. Angrist, Susan M. Dynarski, Thomas J. Kane, and Parag Pathak. 2009. "Accountability and Flexibility in Public Schools: Evidence from Boston's Charters and Pilots." Working Paper w15549. Cambridge, MA: National Bureau of Economic Research.

Angrist, Joshua D., Susan M. Dynarski, Thomas J. Kane, Parag A. Pathak, and Christopher R. Walters. 2010. "Inputs and Impacts in Charter Schools: KIPP Lynn." *American Economic Review: Papers & Proceedings* 100: 1–5.

Angrist, Joshua D., Guido W. Imbens, and Donald B. Rubin. 1996. "Identification of Causal Effects Using Instrumental Variables." *Journal of the American Statistical Association* 87: 328–36.

Angrist, Joshua David, and Jörn-Steffen Pischke. 2009. *Mostly Harmless Econometrics: An Empiricist's Companion*. Princeton, NJ: Princeton University Press.

Brand, Jennie E., and Yu Xie. 2010. "Who Benefits Most from College? Evidence for Negative Selection in Heterogeneous Economic Returns to Higher Education." *American Sociological Review* 75: 273–302.

Bryk, Anthony S., Valerie E. Lee, and Peter B. Holland. 1993. *Catholic Schools and the Common Good*. Cambridge, MA: Harvard University Press.

Cartwright, Nancy. 1999. *The Dappled World: A Study of the Boundaries of Science*. New York: Cambridge University Press.

Center for Research on Education Outcomes (CREDO). 2009. "Multiple Choice: Charter School Performance in 16 States." Stanford, CA: Center for Research on Education Outcomes, Stanford University.

Downey, Douglas B., Paul T. von Hippel, and Beckett A. Broh. 2004. "Are Schools the Great Equalizer? Cognitive Inequality During the Summer Months and the School Year." *American Sociological Review* 69: 613–35.

Elwert, Felix, and Christopher Winship. 2010. "Effect Heterogeneity and Bias in Main-Effects-Only Regression Models." In *Heuristics, Probability and Causality: A Tribute to Judea Pearl*, R. Dechter, H. Geffner, and J. Y. Halpern, eds., 327–36. London: College Publications.

Freedman, David. 2010. *Statistical Models and Causal Inference: A Dialogue with the Social Sciences*. New York: Cambridge University Press.

Gelman, Andrew, and Jennifer Hill. 2007. *Applied Regression and Multilevel/Hierarchical Models*. Cambridge: Cambridge University Press.

Harding, David J., Lisa Gennetian, Christopher Winship, Lisa Sanbonmatsu, and Jeffrey
    Kling. 2011. "Unpacking Neighborhood Influences on Education Outcomes: Setting
    the Stage for Future Research." In *Social Inequality and Educational Disadvantage*,
    G. Duncan and R. Murnane, eds., 277–96. New York: Russell Sage.
Heckman, James J. 2000. "Causal Parameters and Policy Analysis in Economics: A
    Twentieth Century Retrospective." *The Quarterly Journal of Economics* 115: 45–97.
Heckman, James J., and Edward Vytlacil. 2005. "Structural Equations, Treatment Effects,
    and Econometric Policy Evaluation." *Econometrica* 73: 33–9.
Henig, Jeffrey R. 2008. *Spin Cycle: How Research Is Used in Policy Debates: The Case of
    Charter Schools*. New York: Russell Sage.
Hoffer, Thomas, Andrew M. Greeley, and James S. Coleman. 1985. "Achievement Growth in
    Public and Catholic Schools." *Sociology of Education* 58: 74–97.
Homans, George C. 1964. "Bringing Men Back In." *American Sociological Review* 29: 809–18.
Hoxby, Caroline M., Sonali Murarka, and Jenny Kang. 2009. "How New York City's
    Charter Schools Affect Achievement." Cambridge, MA: National Bureau of Economic
    Research.
Jencks, Christopher S., and Susan E. Mayer. 1990. "The Social Consequences of Growing
    up in a Poor Neighborhood." In *Inner-City Poverty in the United States*, L. E. Lynn and
    M.G.H. McGeary, eds., 111–86. Washington, DC: National Academy Press.
Lieberson, Stanley. 1985. *Making It Count: The Improvement of Social Research and Theory*.
    Berkeley: University of California Press.
Lieberson, Stanley, and Freda B. Lynn. 2002. "Barking up the Wrong Branch: Scientific
    Alternatives to the Current Model of Sociological Science." *Annual Review of Sociology*
    28: 1–19.
Lubienski, Sarah T., and Christopher Lubienski. 2003. "School Sector and Academic
    Achievement: A Multilevel Analysis of NAEP Mathematics Data." *American Educational
    Research Journal* 43: 651–98.
Machamer, Peter, Lindley Darden, and Carl F. Craver. 2000. "Thinking About Mechanisms."
    Philosophy of Science 67: 1–25.
Manski, Charles F. 1995. *Identification Problems in the Social Sciences*. Cambridge, MA:
    Harvard University Press.
Manski, Charles F. 2003. *Partial Identification of Probability Distributions*. New York: Springer.
Mare, Robert D., and Christopher Winship. 1984. "The Paradox of Lessening Racial
    Inequality and Joblessness among Black Youth: Enrollment, Enlistment, and Employment,
    1964–1981." *American Sociological Review* 49: 39–55.
Morgan, Stephen L., and Jennifer J. Todd. 2008. "A Diagnostic Routine for the Detection of
    Consequential Heterogeneity of Causal Effects." *Sociological Methodology* 38: 231–81.
Morgan, Stephen L., and Christopher Winship. 2007. *Counterfactuals and Causal Inference:
    Methods and Principles for Social Research*. Cambridge: Cambridge University Press.
Pearl, Judea. 2000. *Causality: Models, Reasoning, and Inference*. 1st ed. Cambridge:
    Cambridge University Press.
Pearl, Judea. 2009. *Causality: Models, Reasoning, and Inference*. 2d ed. Cambridge: Cambridge
    University Press.
Ragin, Charles C. 1987. *The Comparative Method: Moving Beyond Qualitative and Quantitative
    Strategies*. Berkeley: University of California Press.
Raudenbush, Stephen W., and Anthony S. Bryk. 2002. *Hierarchical Linear Models: Applications
    and Data Analysis Methods*. Thousand Oaks, CA: Sage.
Rosenbaum, Paul R. 2002. *Observational Studies*. New York: Springer.
Rubin, Donald B. 2005. "Causal Inference Using Potential Outcomes: Design, Modeling,
    Decisions." *Journal of the American Statistical Association* 100: 322–31.

Rubin, Donald B. 2006. *Matched Sampling for Causal Effects.* New York: Cambridge University Press.

Sampson, Robert J. 2008. "Moving to Inequality: Neighborhood Effects and Experiments Meet Social Structure." *American Journal of Sociology* 114: 189–231.

VanderWeele, Tyler J. 2009. "On the Distinction between Interaction and Effect Modification." *Epidemiology* 20: 863–71.

VanderWeele, Tyler J., and James M. Robins. 2007. "Four Types of Effect Modification: A Classification Based on Directed Acyclic Graphs." *Epidemiology* 18: 561–68.

CHAPTER 15

THE POTENTIAL VALUE OF COMPUTATIONAL MODELS IN SOCIAL SCIENCE RESEARCH

KEN KOLLMAN

I do two things in this chapter. One, I provide intellectual context for computational modeling, namely the manner in which it fits into the collective enterprise of advancing modern social science theory. Given the predominance of rational choice approaches today, I devote attention to how computational modeling as it is mostly practiced today compares with analytical game theory and to some extent decision theory. Two, I evaluate claims made by critics and proponents of computational modeling in the social sciences, with a special focus on complexity models. I especially analyze claims that a range of social phenomena are well studied by computational models. My overall argument is that some justifications of computational models—that they are valuable as tools for specific kinds of scientific explanation—are valid and others not.

In social science disciplines the use of computational modeling has grown. Techniques for developing and analyzing such models are taught in social science departments and professional schools, and are increasingly used by organizational behavior specialists, business and finance analysts, and social scientists who find biological concepts and metaphors appealing. Biology is the key reference because evolutionary concepts lie at the heart of most computational models (Holland 1992a, 1992b). Social science researchers often seek to understand the consequences of simple behavioral rules (micro) for broad social systems (macro), similar to how modern biology is based on the manner in which actions of organisms driven by their needs for relative fitness (micro) cause patterns in higher-level phenomena among species and ecosystems (macro). To summarize the basic arguments that follow:

Are computational models qualitatively different tools, tools that allow us to offer explanation of things that we haven't been able to study before? Maybe, but this is not the best overall justification.

Are computational models the tools that are apt for our times, that they can capture the dynamics and complexity of the modern age? Maybe, but I am doubtful.

Are computational models tools that permit us to explain certain things similar to what we have done with other tools, only better in some circumstances, and thus we can answer some questions faster or somehow probe questions more deeply? I think, yes. What kinds of questions? Questions about social processes whereupon the goal is to explain how micro-level motivations interact with macro-level patterns, with the causal effects possibly going in both directions dynamically.

15.1. THE PURPOSES OF MODELS

At one level, good models have a flavor of "we know it when we see it." Thomas Schelling captures this when he writes that a model is "a precise and economic statement of a set of relationships that are sufficient to produce the phenomena in question" (Schelling 1978, 87). Models should fit in the useful space between obvious and impenetrable. They should be complicated enough to "produce the phenomena in question" in a way that is not so obvious or trivial that it can be explained without the model, but simple enough to be intuitive once the model's component parts and logic are described and analyzed.

In considering the role of models in the broader social scientific enterprise, they can serve different purposes, and many models serve multiple purposes. Models can be used to *predict*, such as anticipating how companies will react under a new government regulation. They can be used to gain *conceptual clarity about assumptions*, such as when a model of a relatively complicated process leads researchers to understand the importance of a particular assumption in driving theoretical conclusions. In many preference aggregation models from social choice, for instance, whether agenda-setting power matters in determining the outcome depends crucially on the dimensionality of the choice space. Closely related, models can lend *insight about patterns in the real world*, such as when models with multiple equilibria shed light on why similar social institutions can lead to entirely different outcomes. We might gain insight, for example, into why some federal systems are highly centralized while others are highly decentralized. A simple model of federated governance can show that different outcomes are possible and still be in equilibrium (that is, still held in place by the behavior of the agents who participate in the federal governance). Note that models can have insights "pop out," meaning that conclusions can emerge about things that were not the focus of attention by those constructing the models in the first place. An example is when economists generated theoretical insights about the importance of shadow prices following the development of general equilibrium models of the economy.[1]

As for the ability of models to predict, there are well-recognized trade-offs, and oftentimes prediction comes at the cost of conceptual clarity or insight. Prediction is usually enhanced to the degree that models become more complicated, and introduce more features that lend more realism (Levins 1966). At the extreme, one could try to produce a full-scale simulation of an actual experience for an agent within a particular domain. A flight simulator for pilots provides one example; within the social sciences one could build "realistic" models of how information flows through organizations, where the realism depends on the specificity of assumptions about any particular organization. The undeniable trade-off exists between generality of the conclusions drawn from simple models and the ability to predict that comes from attempts to approximate real social systems in specific circumstances.

Prediction takes a back seat for the most influential mathematical models from the social sciences. These models are typically simple but have generated insights across multiple generations of researchers: classic price and trade models from economics, the prisoner's dilemma model, and other basic 2x2 games such as the battle of the sexes or stag hunt, centipede games and chain store paradox games, the collective action problem models, Hotelling (1929) and Black (1987 [1958]) spatial voting models, social choice indeterminacy models, principle-agent models, and signaling models more generally. I cannot do justice here to describing how foundational these kinds of models are across a huge range of the work of social scientists.[2]

Most theoretical models, at least the ones that end up influencing social scientists across multiple disciplines and subdisciplines, and the ones of interest here, are much too simple to predict all that well for any specific social context. De Marchi guardedly derides "toy models," for merely lending insight and not predicting.

> Toy models are defined . . . as a class of simple models without any unique empirical referent. For example, the iterated prisoner's dilemma (IPD) is a simple game that investigates cooperation. It seems unlikely that all of human coopera-tion is a two-player contest with the exact strategy set of the IPD, and there is enormous difficulty in analogizing from the IPD to actual human behavior with enough precision to do any sort of predictive work. (De Marchi 2005, xxi).

Perhaps some of these toy models can predict an average outcome across many different social contexts, but even here, much of the action of prediction is in deter-mining which contextual condition drives a specific outcome. If this is the case, then the researchers need to be specific about where the insights from the model end and where the specific contextual details begin that drive the specific result different from the average outcome. I shall have more to say about this shortly when I discuss models with multiple equilibria.

Regardless, prediction has turned out to be a high standard for the contemporary academic researcher using formal models in the social sciences. In fact, as De Marchi claims, formal models with the desirable level of generality predict rather poorly to specific situations. For most people who create abstract social science models that get published in academic journals, and for most people who read and use models in their own work, the most immediate, and perhaps most critical, purpose of theoretical models is insight rather than prediction.

If insight is the primary goal, this begs the question of whether insight is enough, and whether we want models that are good explanations. Furthermore, what constitutes a satisfactory explanation? We can gain insight from many kinds of intellectual products—a novel or a poem, for instance—that are not intended to be explanations. But an explanation, most would say, is a stricter requirement than simply insight. Insight is person-specific, whereas explanation, at least scientific explanation, is presumably objective and person-independent. And most importantly for our purposes here, while philosophers have disagreed over the requisite ingredients for what counts as a scientific explanation, common to any philosophical approach is that explanation joins together the purposes of prediction and insight.

15.2. What Is an Explanation?

Computational models, like other formal models, can be tools for explanation. There are different philosophical conceptions of scientific explanation, and some conceptions fit the enterprise of computational models better than others. Woodward (2009) offers a helpful summary of the philosophical debates. To keep matters simple, three general approaches have traction among philosophers, all of which put quite a bit of emphasis on prediction. First, an explanation can be deductive-nomological (DN) which seeks a "sound deductive argument in which the explanandum follows as a conclusion from the premises in the explanans" (Woodward 2009). This approach, articulated by Hempel (1965) (and drawing on Hume), divorces causation from explanation. Co-ocurrence of events is the best we can hope to use toward explanation. Second, and related, explanation can be inductive-statistical (IS): "An IS explanation will be good or successful to the extent that its explanans confers high probability on its explanandum outcome" (Woodward 2009). Again, the emphasis is not on causation; in contrast to DN the IS approach acknowledges the difficulty of producing law-like predictions. Third, explanation can emphasize being causally relevant (CR), putting emphasis on the manipulability of potential causes and the assertion of causal effect with reference to a demonstrated counterfactual.

It goes without saying that across and within different social science disciplines the emphases are diverse, and thus what counts as an explanation varies. A person steeped in survey research from political science or sociology, for instance, would find useful analyzing psychological or sociological processes that influence how people make decisions over whom to vote for, or whether to participate in politics. An explanation typically involves an empirical generalization drawn from repeated demonstrations of patterns found in data from random samples. This is squarely within the IS approach and can be part of a DN approach. An economist analyzing survey data would be keen on demonstrating, not what emerges as the most important factor explaining the most variance within the survey data, but rather what, among changeable factors (such as public policy), has the largest effect on behavior at the margins (i.e., what pushes people into qualitatively different behaviors). Therein lies your explanation for a phenomenon, which some might consider the straw (factor) that broke the camel's back. This too can be an IS explanation, but blended with CR. There is a stronger emphasis on causal relevance and direct causal inference, or in some instances only on co-occurrence.

A social science researcher who relies on mathematical models, which are usually game theoretic or decision theoretic today, an explanation typically entails finding equilibrium properties of social interactions. Theory-building, of the positivist kind, would generally be following a DN approach. For game theorists or decision theorists, the outcome (equilibrium) is characterized as following logically from the interaction of the preferences and information of the agents and the choice options available to the agents. Much of the same goes for computational models— an outcome follows logically from the aggregated actions of agents—though as discussed shortly, an outcome is not necessarily an equilibrium.

Most social scientists are probably closest, when justifying their enterprise, to one of the first two approaches to explanation (IS or DN) discussed by philosophers. But of increasing status is the causal relevance (CR) approach. This includes those justifying social science research with reference to well-delineated causal relationships identified through counterfactual demonstration. In general those who put heavy weight on randomization to infer causal significance concur with this view of explanation. Experimental research is justified along these grounds, as is the recent work in matching among those analyzing data statistically.

In an attempt to introduce causal relevance into a DN-like approach, Salmon (1984) referred to explanations that were causal-mechanical (CM). The basic idea of CM is to explain something by understanding it as a mechanism, much like to explain an engine in an automobile is to characterize, for different levels of analysis, how various parts work together to produce something of interest (exhaust, heat, energy to make the car go forward). We might consider this an attempt to depict a social system, its macro properties and occasionally to connect the micro elements to those macro properties. Causation enters in the attempt under CM to characterize the way a set of interacting components produce a "mark" on the phenomena being explained. As an example, economists will explain the price of a good (a mark) as arising from the intersection of supply and demand curves among agents in a given market. Depending on the research question, much or little attention may be necessarily paid to the specific details of interactions between agents. Rather, what is of interest is the system itself and what the operation of the system affects. The elements of explanation are the appropriate assumptions made about the representative agent and the typical manner in which the agents interact in the system. While this is essentially consistent with the basic DN approach, the difference lies in the emphasis on causation and on establishing that marks occur as a result of actions occurring within the system.

For the basic DN approach the underlying goal is to understand law-like relationships between explanans and explanandum. The CM admits a broader set of goals. Under the CM approach, researchers are more open to depicting alternative possible outcomes, and so the relationships may not be law-like but more probabilistic (with "more" meaning any particular outcome might have substantially lower probability than unity). In this regard it shares features of the IS approach in linking successful explanation to matching probabilistic outcomes (perhaps) from data.

Even more important is that the CM seeks to understand how a "causal interaction involves a spatio-temporal intersection between two causal processes which modifies the structure of both—each process comes to have features it would not have had in the absence of the interaction" (Woodward 2009). In other words, the CM approach opens the way for explanations involving causal relationships flowing in more than one direction. For computational modeling, this is quite important because many such models seek to understand how, for instance, micro-level motivations affect and are affected by macro-level patterns.

Within the CM approach some promote genetic explanations. As Nagel writes, "A genetic explanation of an event is in general analyzable into a sequence of probabilistic explanations whose initial premises refer to events that happen at different times rather than concurrently, and that are at best only some of the necessary conditions rather than a full complement of sufficient ones for the occurrences which those premises help to explain" (Nagel 1961, 568). A genetic explanation pursues a description of causal links among chronological events, none of which may be necessary or sufficient but in combination produce the phenomena of interest. The combination matters—and specifically, not just the collection of elements of agents, but the patterns of their interactions can matter a great deal as well in the formulation of an explanation.

By my reading, most computational modelers implicitly adopt a causal-mechanical (CM) approach to explanation when justifying their work, with many using genetic explanations. The current trends in social science toward tight causal inference (by one variant, CR), however, are not altogether supportive of CM approaches and thus run contrary to the direction of computational models. Those who use computational models tend to justify their work as depicting structural or systemic patterns. Computational modelers are often determined to demonstrate either an existence result ("I can build a simple computational model that leads to this common real-world outcome"), or a set of results that depict a distribution of outcomes that appear to mirror the distribution of outcomes within data, or that show how systems can be time dependent. Computational models, it is argued by practitioners, are useful to describe not only how a system might come into being but also how a system evolves.

But the increasing emphasis in the social sciences on CR largely rejects these features. The key distinction here is that for CR one cannot divorce from scientific explanation the inferences drawn from analysis of controllable or alterable factors. So a genetic explanation, with prior events, none of which in isolation are necessary or sufficient for explaining an event, is much less valued than an experimental approach, for example.

To see where this matters, consider a CM model that is tested using observational data whereupon it is impossible to control for all possible confounders. A typical model in international relations tested with country-level data is an example. Researchers cannot match up countries so they are similar on all dimensions and only observe differences among the explanandum based on a single difference in an explanans. Yet models of the international system (CM models in form, with a search for some basic DN pursuing law-like regularities) are considered as part of explanations among many groups of researchers. They are content to characterize the system and test the fit of multivariate statistical models against expected patterns of the explanans and explanandum. In contrast, for proponents of the CR approach, explanation entails demonstrating the causal relevance by measuring treatment effects of variables that can actually be manipulated (impossible in this kind of research).

All of these approaches—IS, DN, CM, and CR—have both insight and prediction as elements of scientific explanation, though they vary in their emphases. Furthermore, they differ in their relative attachments to law-like versus probabilistic predictions. We can simplify the contours of social science explanation and place computational models within these contours as follows. Note that I am referring to what social scientists do in practice in what follows, not necessarily what the ideal-type research program would entail. For an IS approach, such as analysis of survey or behavioral data or cross-national data to examine correlations of variables, both insight and prediction are equally valued, with probabilistic predictions the norm. For a basic DN approach, such as simple game theoretic models, there is an emphasis on insight over prediction because the models are too simple to apply to a given situation. Nevertheless (and somewhat ironically) DN highly values law-like predictions. For CM, such as general equilibrium models or most computational models, there is a split. Some who analyze very simple computational models would emphasize insight over prediction. Others propose complicated models linked to specific settings and emphasize prediction over insight. For both cases involving computational models, probabilistic predictions are the norm. Finally, for CR, such as experiments (both laboratory and field) and evaluation using quasi-experimental methods, prediction is emphasized over insight, and law-like predictions are highly valued.

15.3. Predominant Modeling Approaches

Most modeling today in the social sciences is rational choice based and equilibrium based. Rationality means that agents are assumed to optimize their utility given their information, and agents use Bayes' rule to incorporate information into decision-making. Decision theory is the study of optimal behavior given constraints imposed by nonrational things, such as "nature" "the market," or "the electorate." Game theory, in contrast, is the study of interdependent decisions among rational agents.

Game theory is surely the dominant modeling paradigm in the social sciences. For many game theorists, an explanation is akin to a solution concept, which is really a prediction within the confines of a model. A solution concept is a set of rules for determining predictions for how players will be expected to behave (Myerson 1991, 107; Morrow 1994). Nash solutions have a primacy of place among solution concepts (Nash 1951). A Nash equilibrium is an outcome (or solution) from a game such that no rational player, given that he or she is maximizing his or her utility function, would choose another course of action given what other players are doing.

Myerson proposes an interesting distinction between solution concepts in game theory. Myerson (1991) says a solution concept is *lower* if it "excludes all unreasonable predictions but may also exclude some reasonable predictions" and a solution concept is *upper* if it "includes all reasonable predictions but may also include some unreasonable predictions" (108). He considers Nash solutions to be upper solutions, "because being a Nash equilibrium is only a necessary condition for a theory to be a good prediction of the behavior of intelligent rational players" (108). In other words, if it is not Nash, then it is not a reasonable prediction.

But are solutions to games that are actually published and widely disseminated in the social sciences actually sufficient as explanations? Surely not in most cases, largely because the models have to be much too simple to predict well. Let us take several simple examples from game theory. Suppose one wanted to explain why, when congressional pay raises are always unpopular (voters generally consider it a terrible idea), such pay raises sometimes pass into law. How do enough members of Congress, knowing they will face the wrath of voters, ever choose to vote in favor? As good a model as I can find among formal models in political science is depicted in figure 15.1. This depicts a game tree with legislator one forcing legislators two and three to vote for the raise and risking their political careers. In effect it is a large collective action problem but the utility from the pay raise is high enough to get the majority of legislators to go along with costly collective action. As an explanation, this game requires several things, among them: an assumption that at least legislators two and three value the pay raise to counterbalance the risk of losing office, sequential votes to explain why some legislators get off the hook from voting for the pay raise, and a majority voting scenario.

Most importantly, because of its simplicity, this model does not have any obvious so-called black box features and only one predicted outcome, the equilibrium of two and three voting in favor. Of course, this outcome is a consequence

Assumption 1>value of raise (r)>political cost (c)

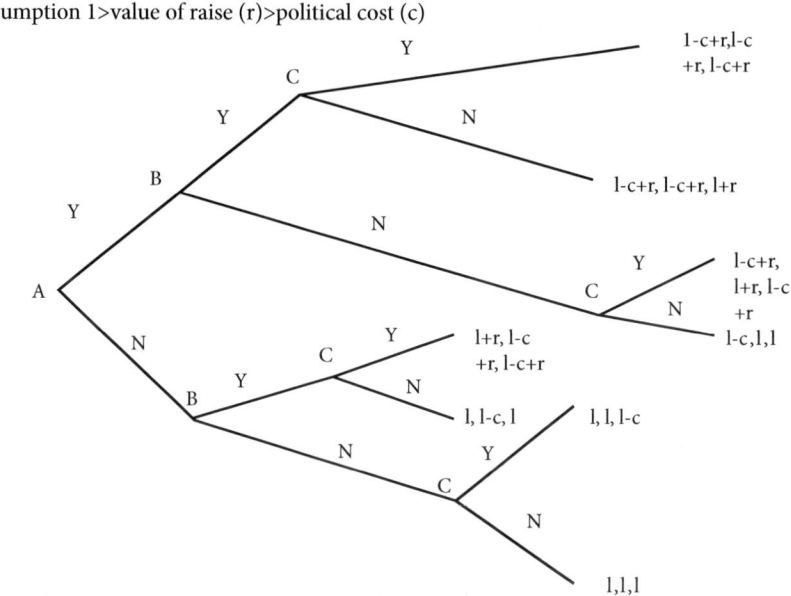

Figure 15.1 Congressional Pay-Raise Game Among Legislators A, B, and C

of the assumptions. Yet everything is here, plain as day, and the logic is both simple and compelling. It answers the question, how or why can Congress pass its own pay raises?

Squarely in the DN tradition, this model nevertheless might be best called a "potential explanation," meaning that it represents a possibility among a large set of possible constitutive relationships (Grune-Yanoff 2009). Some would consider it a narrative of an idealized situation, a template out of which causal explanations can be constructed with additional analysis of empirical data and demonstrations of versimilitude of the core assumptions (Alexandrova 2008). And it certainly is not a prediction of actual voting behavior, except in the most basic sense—that legislators will seek to avoid voting for a pay raise if voters will likely become aware of the legislators' actions.

But move, now, to a different kind of model with multiple equilibria, the well-known battle of the sexes game (see figure 15.2). There are three Nash equilibria—meaning that there is more than one outcome consistent with the assumptions of this model. This is an explanation of sorts, but it is partial in a different way. The outcome could be Chinese restaurant or it could be pizza parlor. This is not an explanation for why they chose the Chinese restaurant. It's an explanation for why the Chinese restaurant was a possible outcome where ending up at distinct places should not be an expected outcome.

Game theory models with multiple Nash equilibria require something more to be an explanation for a particular outcome. One might say that an explanation is only probabilistic, and we now know that it will be either the Chinese or the pizza parlor. Well, nothing in the model gives us any leverage over probabilities of outcomes among the equilibria. The model is only a part of an explanation, and something more is required to put any structure at all on a probabilistic account.

Pizza-Pizza	Pizza-Chinese
3,4	0,0
Chinese-Pizza	Chinese-Chinese
1,1	4,3

Figure 15.2 Battle of the Sexes

Schelling (1978) referred to the focal point effect, whereby one or another equilibrium becomes highlighted for some reason by the players. One can simply incorporate the process of creating focal points into the model and still make the model interesting, but this is both more difficult than it sounds and also quite rare among applied models. More often, focal points lie outside of the model and the model is clearly only the beginning of the explanation. The modeler has left out something important to an explanation.

When researchers propose coordination games like battle of the sexes as explanations for a given phenomenon, they then bring in historical information, or descriptions of government fiats, or tradition, or something similar to explain why one Nash outcome occurs and not the other Nash equilibria. The model is only the beginning of the explanation, and perhaps not even the most innovative from the point of view of the literature which the researchers are addressing.

Game theoretic models with multiple equilibria abound in the social sciences, some of them considered quite canonical for their subfields. (Signaling models or principle-agent models are prime examples.) These models with multiple equilibria end up being possible (or partial) explanations for how certain outcomes occur, and one must move outside of the model to hone anything close to a prediction. Furthermore, their assumptions about out-of-equilibrium beliefs were chosen for convenience, for some specific (defensible) justification such as Pareto efficiency, or to fit data.

Game theorists have wrestled with the problems of multiple equilibria and out-of-equilibrium beliefs for many decades, and they have imagined a host of philosophically interesting solutions. But it is an open question whether the most widely used of these solutions made these kinds of models more compelling as explanations for social phenomena.

The broader points, however, are (1) that nonmodeling components are often brought into research to finish the explanation for a phenomenon, and (2) moreover, that making sometimes arbitrary technical assumptions to nail down equilibria is a common move among modelers (I have done this myself with signaling models in published work.). As De Marchi notes,

> Technical assumptions end up doing a great deal of heavy lifting in many formal models. The intellectual process involved in finding a set of assumptions, choosing an equilibrium concept, and choosing an abstract game to produce an outcome desired *a priori* is not different in kind from the curve fitting of some empirical researchers. (De Marchi 2005, xix). [3]

Our foray into game theory helps to foreshadow the criticisms of computational modeling. While law-like predictions and logical consistency are the valued aspects, in fact only the latter shows up on a regular basis. Predictions are not law-like for one of two reasons, and typically both: The models are too simple, and the models have multiple equilibrium (or possible outcomes). Many of these same concerns are made about computational models, though the possible outcomes that emerge from within the model would not be imposed from things outside the model. Thus, if the overall criticisms about failure to predict or about having black box elements apply to computational models they apply as well to game theory. The difference is that some computational modelers create more complicated models, either because they can or because they want to improve prediction. In doing so they sacrifice a great deal on the insight side of the ledger, and this does cause concern and invite criticism from those wedded to the DN approach.

Let us now turn to computational models, and specifically models in the complexity tradition.

15.4. On Computational Models of Complexity

While there are various kinds of computational models and simulation techniques, today complexity models garner most of the attention and resources. In complex systems modeling, the models depict systems of interacting agents where the following hold (Miller and Page 2007):

a. Each agent's behavior is governed by a small set of simple rules, which often depend on local information and feedback from the agent's past behavior and from other agents' behavior;

b. characterizing and understanding the behavior of each of the agents does not directly lead to predicting or understanding the behavior of the entire system. The local rules produce emergent patterns—stable equilibrium cycles, unstable equilibria and long transitions to new equilibria, and randomness—and emergent properties such as robustness;

c. agents' interactions are interdependent and affect others in the system; thus removing an agent has consequences for the system beyond merely subtracting out that single agent's direct effect on other agents with which it interacts.

Researchers using complex systems methods typically rely on computer programs to simulate the interactions of artificial agents, examining the aggregate patterns that emerge from many instances of micro-level behaviors. (Some additional terminology: What is sometimes called "agent-based modeling" is the use of computation to study the links between micro behavior of agents and macro patterns in a complex system.)

But computation on an electronic machine is not required. Consider the classic Schelling model of residential segregation (Schelling 1978). It is said that Schelling proposed the first modern complex systems model in the social sciences. In research in the 1960s into the phenomenon of racial segregation in housing, he modeled a process where people (agents) decide where to live based on the racial mix of their neighborhood. Schelling randomly placed nickels and dimes on a checkerboard, with each coin resting on only one square, and with fewer coins than available squares (see figure 15.3). He then randomly picked one of the coins, say a dime, and examined its "neighborhood," meaning the squares that bordered the square upon which the dime stood. There are eight squares in the neighborhood (unless it rested on the edge of the board, which we shall ignore for this example). If the neighborhood consisted of less than five nickels, nothing happened. Otherwise, Schelling moved the dime to another place on the board where there were less than five nickels in the neighborhood. He then iteratively moved through each coin and either moved it somewhere else or kept it in place, using the 5/8 rule for tolerance of neighbors of the other type. Schelling argued that 5/8 was a pretty tolerant threshold, in that his coins (agents) would stay put even if half of their neighborhood consisted of the other type. He showed that even with this relatively tolerant threshold, the dimes and nickels segregated into homogenous zones on the checkerboard. He then started over and examined what happened with other kinds of thresholds (1/2, ¾, etc.) and how quickly, if at all, the agents segregated themselves incrementally.

Note what happens in the dynamics of the Schelling model. When a coin is moved to another area of the checkerboard, it changes its own neighborhood and the neighborhood to which it moves. A single move alters the diversity of multiple agents'

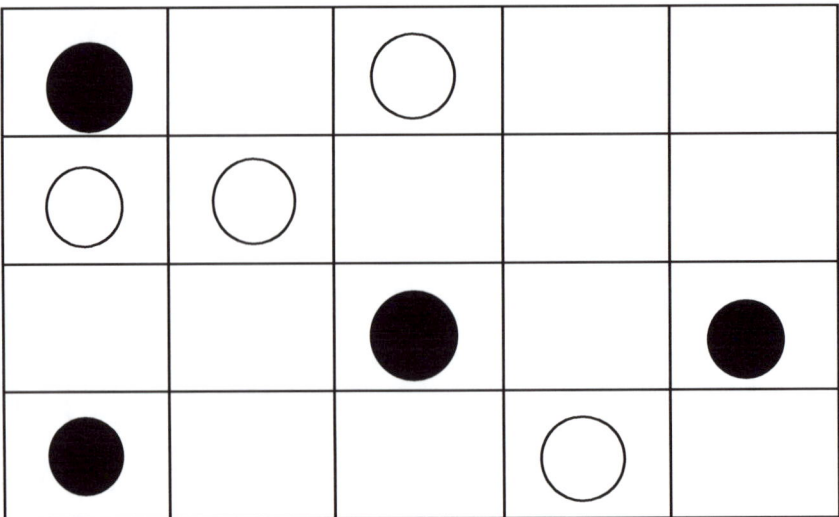

Figure 15.3 Schelling: Moving Dimes and Nickels

neighborhoods and thus potentially alters the decisions of multiple other agents. This is an example of the kind of feedback that occurs in a complex system. Furthermore, it is difficult to predict simply from the decision-rule of the agents how the system will behave. Schelling confessed that he could not predict in advance when and if the system would segregate into neighborhoods of all dimes and all nickels.

Schelling did not use a computer, at least initially, but computer programs are the main tools used since. Harrington (1998), for instance, studies a class of models that examines how diverse types of agents transcend an organizational hierarchy. The agents compete for positions based on a combination of their experience with consistent behaviors and on their abilities to adapt to a stochastic environment. Agents are diverse in the weights they give to consistent behavior versus flexibility in responding to the environment. Harrington uses computational methods to analyze the link between micromotivations (agents' types) to macro patterns (which types end up at the top of the hierarchy).

Other canonical models also include Axelrod's (1984) prisoner's dilemma tournaments, Epstein and Axtell's (1996) sugarscape platform, and the El Ferol problem (see Casti 1996). The literature on computational models in the social sciences has grown vast and has presented many varieties of models. Economists have used computational models to analyze herd behavior in markets, fashion trends, career choice, social choice, strategic price setting, and broad macro-economic patterns, both global and local. Sociologists study sorting, the emergence of social movements, cultural change, and organizational behavior both within and among organizations, and the relationships between group behavior and individual behavior. Within political science, computational models have been applied to the study of international diplomacy and war, electoral competition, voting systems, the evolution of cooperative behavior, criminal behavior and punishment, political networks, and the development of law. Social psychologists have modeled herding, habit formation, and how individual perception interacts with group behavior.

15.5. CRITICISMS AND COMPARISONS

Complexity models invite puzzlement and criticism from various corners of social science. Let us take several of the main criticisms and examine them against the requisites of explanation as defined by philosophers. It shall be useful to keep the comparisons with game theory at hand for this discussion.

What is the model and what is the prediction? One basic concern has to do with the exact status of computer programs in relationship to program output. What is exactly being produced by the computation that can be analogous to the elements of other theory-making techniques? Are the data generated by programs themselves the theory? Or is the computer program the theory, and the data generated are predictions against which to test the theory with real-world data? If the data are the theory, then what role does the computer program play? If the computer-generated data are the predictions, then well-accepted standards do not currently exist to compare those predictions to "real-world" data.

There is quite of bit of confusion on these points among computational modelers themselves and among their critics. Researchers using computational models would typically reply that the programs are logically consistent descriptions of a social process—the actors, their intentions and knowledge, their interactions— much like a set of axioms in a mathematical model. In fact, the computer program *is* a mathematical model but one that gives an output for a point in parameter space rather than theorem or proposition describing the conclusions about a swath of the parameter space.

Paul Humphreys contrasts computational models from axiomatically formulated theory (2004, S10). One major justification for computational models is their flexibility, their ability to allow modelers to relax assumptions to enable selective realism (S7). He writes that each computational model has at its core a template, which is its basic setup that may also be the setup for other models used in a variety of scientific domains. As an example, a computational model to study markets might have a genetic algorithm as a template, or perhaps a cellular automata as a template. The template is the model's underlying engine. These, Humphreys writes, "can be taken as black-box units, 'off-the-shelf' tools to be used as deemed appropriate" (S5). Then, like mathematical models, computational models, according to Humphreys, have idealized assumptions and what he calls correction sets, which are justifications for the overall model based on analogies or connections to real-world phenomena. Computational models also need to be interpreted (as do mathematical models), and the process of interpretation involves evaluating output representation. These outputs are typically computer-generated data that modelers analyze for patterns that in principle would correspond to real-world data. The patterns discerned in the computer-generated data should look something like the patterns discerned in real-world data.

If we were to draw the comparisons more directly, the defensible analogies would be as depicted in figure 15.4. One, computer code creates objects (agents,

Mathematical–equilibrium based	Computational
Axioms	Computer code
Comparative statics	Artificial data
Statistical relationship in real data	Statistical relationships between artificial data and parameter values in computer code compared to statistical relationships in real data
Assumed stochastic elements in real data	Sequences of random numbers in computer runs
Focal point effects for multiple equilibria	Sequences of random numbers in computer runs

Figure 15.4 Program vs. Output and Relationship of Math to Computer

collections of agents), describing the interactions and evolution of the agents. These are analogous to axioms in a mathematical model.

Two, computerized output, or artificial data, when analyzed to reveal statistical relationships between those artificial data and parameter values that went into the various runs of the computer model are analogous to comparative statics results from mathematical models.

Three, when it comes to the steps after modeling toward empirical analysis, comparisons can be made between statistical relationships found in artificial data with statistical relationships found in real data. To start, one can discover statistical relationships among artificial data (output) and parameter values in the simulation. Then to follow up, one can compare those relationships to statistical relationships found among (a) treatment and treatment effects in experimental or quasi-experimental empirical work, or (b) in correlations (partial or nonpartial) between independent and dependent variables in observational work. These comparisons are analogous to connections drawn between comparative statics results from mathematical models and statistical relationships between (a) treatment and treatment effects in experimental or quasi-experimental empirical work, or (b) in correlations (partial or nonpartial) between independent and dependent variables in observational work.

Four, sequences of random numbers used in the simulations are included for a variety of reasons. These reasons include generating a population of agents with diverse characteristics, determining how agents interact with each other (a randomly chosen partner, for instance), or choosing strategies of agents when it is not clear what the optimum strategies are for a given situation (i.e., the Nash strategy cannot be calculated, even by the modeler). The specific sequences of random numbers are analogous to assumed stochastic elements that shock the social system but cancel each other out over time because they have an expected mean zero effect on the equilibrium outcome.

These analogies clarify how most computational modelers consider their work to be squarely in the mainstream of theory building for any scientific discipline. But simply drawing the analogies is not entirely satisfactory in answering the questions above. Most crucially, they do not match up so easily to what rational choice modelers do, for instance, without a clarification on the status of equilibria discovered from games versus the nonequilibrium findings from computational models.

Equilibria versus nonequilibrium findings. Many computational models do not conform to the notion that a model should have an equilibrium, marking perhaps the main difference between traditional formal models and computational models. To many researchers who use formal models in the social sciences, especially from a game theoretic tradition, a model should have an equilibrium. After all, if the social system is not depicted to equilibrate, then what outcome are we comparing to the real world? The process of equilibrating? Then at what point do we assume that the real-world outcome is akin to a point along a time trajectory within the dynamics of the model?

These are not easy questions to answer without reference to specific models and drawing comparisons among them. For reasons of space I will summarize my own assessments after several decades of confronting these comparisons. First, quite a few computational models do have equilibrium outcomes. But second, defenders would say that computational models demonstrate evolutions of processes, not assumptions that describe equilibrium outcomes. The analysis of dynamics is often the main *purpose* of using computational models. Acceptable or not to critics, a main defense of these models is that the modelers see dynamics in the real world, and equilibrium models cannot do justice as explanations of those dynamics. Third, and perhaps most convincingly, models tend to derive patterns of computer-generated data that can be compared to real data because the computer-generated data exhibit enough regularities to be recognizable, either to the human eye or according to a statistical summary. (i.e., the analogy described above between patterns in output and comparative statics).

Nonclosed-form solutions. It is common to hold up having a theorem as the goal for mathematical models. Theorems are general statements describing conclusions that follow logically from a set of assumptions or axioms. What counts as a theorem (versus a proposition, for example) is largely a matter for judgment, but it is usually reserved for theoretical statements that are quite general, covering a range of parameter values, preferably the entire range of possible values of a parameter in a model. Clearly, most computational models are not developed and analyzed for the purpose of finding a theorem.

But as mentioned above, it is a mistake to argue that computational models do not place value on logical rigor. A computer program is bounded by logic, of course. The difference is that one instantiation (or "run") of the computer program produces results for a specific set of parameters, typically including random numbers generated from within the program, and not for a range of parameter values and random numbers. Large numbers of computer runs need to be analyzed to make any general claims, and even then they are just large collections of points in the parameter space. More problematic is that with theorems one can see each step in a process of deduction, whereas with some interesting computer programs it can be difficult to trace the entire process through the program. At least it is difficult to do regularly and with ease.

A related concern is the claim that models should be fully deductive, meaning that the researcher should start with general axioms assumed or known to be true, and move toward specific conclusions. Certainly this is, in principle anyway, what computational modelers consider themselves to be doing. But in practice they often do what Axelrod (1997), one of the leading proponents and practitioners of complexity modeling, argues is actually a form of induction. He says that researchers use computer simulations to generate artificial data, and like empirical researchers who discover pattern in data—induction, he says—computational modelers try to discover patterns in the artificial data and then reason to general conclusions (Axelrod 1997, 3). In other words, at the extreme anyway, the computer generates a lot of artificial data and then a large part of the scientific process is discerning what those data end up telling us *before* the development of a well-structured set of expectations (like hypotheses) guiding the search for patterns.

If the goal is explanation under any of the approaches described above, this quasi-inductive approach is not satisfactory. A high value for any theoretical model must be put on exactitude in description of the mechanisms of a model. Durlauf (2010) makes the distinction between understanding (something very close to merely insight) and explanation. The former would not permit black boxes in modeling, where one puts agents into a model and sees what comes out, while the latter may permit it. In this sense explanation includes the notion that models should connect Xs and Ys, and that it's important that every single connection between an X and a Y is well articulated and understood. Undoubtedly what are acceptable black boxes varies across disciplines and groups of social scientists within disciplines.

Start with explanations perfectly acceptable in the everyday social world, and even acceptable for some communications we do as scientists: "Explain how Jane got to the store." "She drove in her car to the store. " We do not need to know the engineering details about automobiles to be satisfied with this explanation. "Explain how Jane's car worked, the one that got her to the store." This requires a different kind of explanation. Yet another: "Explain how Jane earned the money to buy the car that got her to the store." What counts as an explanation, of course, depends on the question asked. Because different academic tribes ask different kinds of questions, they also have different standards for what counts as an acceptable black box. They have different permissible ranges of black box mechanisms that can exist and still satisfy the requirement that what is provided is an explanation.

If prediction is highly valued, then the range for acceptable black boxes increases. If we know which Xs are going in and which Ys are coming out, we are close to predicting outcomes, or at least distributions of outcomes. Certainly many computational models black box parts of the explanation, but they can provide at least decent predictions nonetheless. Computational models gain by being flexible and not requiring unrealistic assumptions merely for tractability reasons and producing good predictions, but they lose if one departs too far from exactitude, and black box more than acceptable to remain in the range of still being an explanation that includes insight. We cannot escape this trade-off.

Rationality versus boundedness. A claim can be made that models in the social world should have rational agents. After all, humans can reason and be strategic. Game theorists would argue that, contrary to the common charge, their assumptions are quite realistic.

More precisely, game theory relies on the assumptions, following the work of von Neumann and Morgenstern (1944) and Nash (1951), that agents are rational (optimize) and intelligent (they know the game they are in as well as the modeler does). Alternatively, a large portion of complexity research focuses attention on models where the agents are not fully rational in the manner defined by economists and many other social scientists. That is, agents are portrayed as adaptive and boundedly rational. To many computational modelers, Herbert Simon (1969) is a primary intellectual source to draw upon for justification, whereas Simon is not discussed in game theory textbooks. Simon, among other things, argued for introducing notions of satisficing or bounded rationality into economic models. And it has lately been more fashionable in economics to analyze bounded rationality.

Breaking it down some, boundedness means that agents display a subset of the following features:

1. They do not fully optimize their utility functions given their information.
2. They are not forward-looking in being able to predict accurately the probability of certain outcomes in the future given their behavior.
3. They are myopic in that they do not have information outside of some defined local "zone" of interaction or geography.

The third item on this list is central to the vast majority of computational models. Complexity systems models can violate both of the assumptions of rationality and intelligence, but especially the latter. It is common for agents to know only something about their immediate neighborhood, and not the entire set of possible events or agents that can influence them or be influenced by them. Note in the Schelling model described above how the agents are assumed to make decisions solely on the mix of other agents in their limited neighborhood. They do not consider the implications of their actions in the long run, nor what happens outside of their own neighborhood (either the one they leave or move to). Schelling's purpose was not finding Nash equilibria because he would consider it beside the point to draw conclusions that follow from assuming that agents were maximizing utility given what all the other agents on the checkerboard are doing. Agents look around and if unhappy move to a nearby place. They are not thinking globally, but rather quite locally. Furthermore, there are enormous numbers of Nash equilibria, and while it might be interesting to characterize classes of these equilibria, requiring that an outcome be a Nash equilibrium may miss some of the dynamics of the process that the system undergoes toward reaching a steady-state. The same can be said for the Harrington models described above.

On this score, compare the approach to the study of norms between game theory and complexity researchers. For game theorists, norms can be akin to focal points in games with multiple equilibria. Norms are the expectations about others' behavior that exist outside of the game theory model that lead people to choose one strategy or another. Or, norms could be equilibria that arise from repeated games. In contrast, norms in, say, Axelrod (1997), are often studied as something to be explained from within the models, and that emerge from repeated interactions and selection based on positive feedback.[4]

Whether or not rationality is the "right" assumption, many computational modelers see their ability to analyze boundedness as a great virtue. Insight gained from studying systems of adaptive, less-than-fully rational agents, according to many, is one of the noteworthy benefits of using complexity methods. There is nothing inherent in the methodology that requires that agents be boundedly rational or adaptive, but it is clearly a common feature of such models.

Too many parameters or too many possible models. One core criticism is stated in two ways. The criticism is that most computational models are not identified in a statistical sense. Many different theoretical models would lead to the same empirical hypotheses. Another way to say this: Computational models should, if described in a transitional matrix form with discrete values for parameters, be ergodic. Regardless of the starting point of the model and random values in the computation, the limiting distribution of outcomes should be the same. An ergodic system essentially has transition probabilities among outcomes that do not change as a result of the particular outcome reached at any point of time. Some have argued that a nonergodic system is a model with no empirical content because the transition probabilities can just wander randomly depending on what random values are generated by the computation (Bendor, Diermeier, and Ting 2003). It cannot generate a prediction. Or, in another sense, there is nothing truly exogenous in the model and therefore no way to anchor the system for purposes of identifying relational parameters in a statistical system of equations.

This is a common criticism, but it has less bite than at first appears. Let us delve into the arguments of Leombruni and Richiardi (2005). They depict an individual's state as characterized by a difference equation:

$$X_{ij+1} = f_i\left(x_{ij}, x_{-ij}; \alpha_i\right)$$

Y is some macro feature we care about:

$$Y_1 = S\left(x_1, x_2, \dots x_{\alpha i}\right)$$

We can iteratively solve for this macro variable:

$$Y_0 = S\left(x_{1,0}, x_{2,0}, \dots x_{x,0}\right)$$

$$Y_1 = S\left(x_{1,1}, x_{2,1}, \dots x_{0,1}\right)$$

$$Y_1 = S\left(f_1(x_{1,0}, x_{-x,0}; \alpha_1), \dots f_x(x_{x,0}, x_{-u,0}; \alpha_1)\right)$$

$$= g_1\left(x_{1,0}, x_{2,0}, \dots x_{n,0}; \alpha_1 \dots, \alpha_n\right)$$

$$Y_1 = g_1\left(x_{1,0}, x_{2,0}, \dots x_{x,0}; \alpha_1 \dots, \alpha_n\right)$$

Perhaps there is a time-invariant equilibrium:

$$Y^e = \lim_{t \to \infty} Yt = g\left(x_{1,0} x_{2,0}, \ldots x_{n,0}; \alpha_1, \ldots, \alpha_n\right)$$

For a typical mathematical model we assume a representative agent, or make simplifying functions mapping starting conditions onto Y. When agents are diverse as in a typical computational model, as n and t get large, the expression for g gets huge. We thus need to specify a function form fitting a set of parameter values to the artificial data generated by the simulations:

$$\hat{g}_1\left(x_{1,0}, x_{2,0}, \ldots x_{n,0}; \alpha_1, \ldots, \alpha_n, \beta\right)$$

We should then find the coefficient on g, which will give us a local functional form on a set of simulation runs. Sometimes this is called a meta-model in computer science.

All of this is a rigorous process. The problems could be that the parameter sweep is too local, or that the model is underidentified. What Leombrudi and Richiardi (2005) argue convincingly is that for computational models the parameter sweeps might be too local, but for mathematical models the set of assumptions might be too restrictive. In other words, the same identification problems occur with mathematical models. Critiques of identification problems in computational models either apply to all theoretical, formal models in the social sciences, or are false or irrelevant.

It is surely the case that for nearly every model in the social sciences, there are different ways to model the situation of interest that would lead to the same answer, or the same hypotheses about data. Rare is the model that is general enough that it covers a huge span of possible institutional mechanisms and agent preferences that lead to one single answer. Arrow's impossibility theorem has this quality, and perhaps some of the chaos theorems from social choice, but there are few others (if any). De Marchi (2005) writes of the curse of dimensionality, a problem with any set of data involving multiple factors of interest and, he argues, a problem with modeling in general. (This is the same as Leombrudi and Richiardi's point.) There is no one set of reasonable assumptions, but many, many sets of reasonable assumptions. If anything, computational modelers say, permit parameter sweeps that can test for the robustness of qualitative outcomes.

In taking stock, then, in the complexity tradition we have a modeling approach where the models do not often have equilibria, there are few analytical results like theorems, they can lead to results that depend on random values within simulations, and agents are modeled as less than rational in a way that can seem arbitrary. I have deliberately written this last sentence to sound negative. Turned around, these could all be considered positive attributes. For example, these are models that can analyze systems that do not equilibrate, and that is valuable. But standing from the point of view of those comfortable with what is currently the norm among modelers in the social sciences—in the game theoretic and decision-theoretic tradition—we can ask for more demonstration of value: What is to recommend computational models?

15.6. WHY USE COMPUTATIONAL MODELS?

Why use computational models, and specifically, complexity models? Let us turn from criticisms and concerns (last section) to summarize more directly the justifications given by those who use computational models. We can examine four (not mutually exclusive) justifications given by practitioners. The first justification is either implied or made explicitly, and is commonly what attracts graduate students to computational models in the first place. It does not end up holding water in my view if it is the primary reason for using such models.

"Look at the interesting macro-patterns we can create." Undoubtedly computational models can create macro-level patterns that we see in the real world. When justified this way, implied is that other kinds of modeling approaches (i.e., rational choice approaches) cannot generate realistic macro-level patterns without severe contortions. As an example, early generations of models of financial markets in the complexity tradition sought to produce, in artificial data, patterns of booms and busts in prices and trading volume. Such patters of occasional bursts of instability between longer periods of stability cannot be generated by models with agents under pure rational expectations assumptions. In fact, for pure rational expectations models, nothing but stability of the extreme kind should emerge: no trading of financial assets at all. To combat this kind of absurd prediction, researchers developed artificial stock markets with adaptive agents and sought to calibrate the nature of the boundedness of the agents to generate the kinds of patterns seen in real data.

It is hard to argue with moving in a new modeling direction if existing models fail to predict patterns from data. But on its own, without further elements to the justification, this kind of rationale for modeling feels cheap. At the extreme it exposes the worst features of the identification problem discussed previously. Clever computer programmers without much substantive knowledge behind them can create a model that produces familiar patterns. More directly, this sacrifices far too much insight for the sake of prediction. Unfortunately, this is how a good number of complexity models are justified.

The world is complex and closed-form solutions are too constraining. There are few constraints on computational, complexity models. One could justify computational models in the complexity tradition because of the limits of researchers. We cannot find closed-form solutions to models that incorporate feedback, adaptation, and diversity, so we should be free to rely on computer simulations to gain insight.

Consider, for instance, Bruch and Mare's (2006) reanalysis of the Schelling model. They demonstrate one of the clear benefits of computational modeling. In their models, they analyze the Schelling segregation model under different assumptions about how agents decide whether to move. They compare different response functions—step functions, smoothly monotonic functions of different convex shape, and different thresholds. What they find (the response function shape matters; Schelling's results are clearest with step functions) is less important here than for what they indicate the computer makes possible. Their comprehensive and rigorous examination of how complex social dynamics change under different assumptions about micro-level motivations would be impossible if analytical proof were required to derive a conclusion.

This kind of justification can lead to strong claims of scientific possibility. Complexity modeling, it has been argued, provides a new kind of science that will alter the ways we see the world and the kinds of social problems we can address. By one kind of justification, computational models in the complexity tradition are qualitatively different tools, tools that allow us to study things that we haven't been able to study before. They open up new vistas for viewing the social world. In short, these are tools that will take us further and faster.[5]

A related justification is that the world we live in is more complex than in the past, and these types of models are ideally suited for the contemporary era. Page (1996 and 2000) has argued that modern economies are not best studied with rational choice, general equilibrium models. When economic theorists in the early to mid-twentieth century were developing general equilibrium models of the industrialized economy, they could justifiably assume single factor production models and a representative consumer. But nowadays, the sheer scale of interactions (or better put, externalities or spillovers) across consumers, producers, traders, and investors, not to mention the diversity of conceptual frames that people bring to economic transactions, requires a methodology that can readily incorporate feedback, diversity, and nonlinear interactive effects into the modeling strategy.

I think there is something convincing about the argument that the flexibility in computational modeling allows for exploration not available from other modeling techniques. These models can capture dynamics, feedback, and disequilibrium in interesting ways that lend insight, and other approaches, especially game theory, cannot match the possibilities. Yet I am reminded of the quote by Robert Frost about free verse poetry: that it was like playing tennis without a net. Too much flexibility leaves one unsatisfied, and as always it is a combination of judgments by fellow researchers, and comparisons with data, that ultimately determine the scientific value of models and modeling techniques.

Agents are adaptive and it is better to model them this way. Some have argued that computational models are valuable mainly because they allow the analysis of bounded rationality, of adaptive agents, better than other paradigms, like game theory. And since we know that people are not fully rational in the game theoretic sense, then this is the right way to model. Thus, when studying limited agents, use computational models. This has the virtue of being a substantive justification for using these techniques.

Debates over whether rationality is the right assumption to make have been around for a long time. Some have framed it as essentially an ideological difference among people. As Brian Barry paraphrased George Orwell, "There are some people who *always* assume that the Bishop has a mistress. There are others who will go to some lengths to continue believing that the Bishops believe that pastoral care is a twenty-four hour duty" (Barry, 1978 175, emphasis Barry's).

But often rationality is convenient to assume given the tools we have. And more to the point, bounded rationality means lots of different things (i.e., there is a huge range for how someone can be less than rational) and it's not clear what difference it might make if people converge on rationality as they learn or if they are arbitrarily close to the ideal. As Durlauf writes, "To say that an individual is boundedly rational is a statement about how he makes decisions, not a statement about whether he should be modeled as doing so" (2010, 8).

One difficulty, as alluded to above, is how to model boundedness. Durlauf, again, in criticizing the complex systems literature; much of it "replaces the rationality assumptions of neoclassical economics with alternative assumptions that render the agents stupid" (2010, 3). This is probably a fair criticism for a lot of complexity work, but the criticism is certainly too broadly cast.

But the more relevant difficultly often lies in how to model the feedback between decision heuristics and aggregate outcomes. Agents themselves can be adaptive in the sense of behaving in response to stimuli without much regard for the universe of possible decisions they could make (i.e., they have limited range of vision or knowledge). Or more challenging for a modeler, they may adapt their decision-making heuristics, attempting to improve their station at a more fundamental level.

Complex systems modeling is sometimes seen as a challenge to traditional game theoretic methods of modeling precisely because of the departure from full rationality. But it must be said that most practitioners of complex systems modeling, at least within political science and economics, view it as complementary to game theoretic methods. Not only are quite a few well-known complex systems models within political science based fundamentally on game theoretic techniques, but the researchers themselves have typically published work spanning a variety of modeling tools including game theory. Well-known complexity models depict iterated prisoner's dilemma situations (Axelrod 1984). Agents in these models play repeated prisoner's dilemma games with each other and researchers seek to discover the kinds of strategies that do well in environments with agents that can alter their strategies to get ahead.

Furthermore, behavioral economics has arisen largely as a response to empirical results, especially those from laboratory settings, that cast doubt on the assumptions of rationality and intelligence common among game theoretic models (Camerer 2003). Economists have sought to model social systems with agents as adaptive, or bounded in some way. They maintain many of the same principles in modeling—the drive for defining equilibrium behavior, theorems as the standard for truth-claims, and the eventual convergence of beliefs and behavior—even when assuming boundedly rational players. And thus a lot of modern game theoretic modeling, in pursuit of realism, departs at a minimum from full rational expectations assumptions, and often from even more limited forms of Bayesian rationality.

The fact that computational models are valuable means of studying boundedness does not (1) make boundedness the right assumption and (2) make computational models the right set of tools. If boundedness is chosen on substantive grounds, and analytical solutions are extremely difficult or impossible, or if the assumptions necessary to get analytical solutions become unacceptably tight, then it seems difficult to argue against using computational models.

Useful to model each agent's cognition, behavior, and interactions. A key concept from computational models of complex systems is emergence. Emergence, or (b) above in our list of attributes of complexity models, is another way of saying that in advance of the modeling we could not predict the macro patterns from the micro-level assumptions.

Quite a few computational models are proposed with the purpose of demonstrating how a particular social phenomenon came about (i.e., a genetic kind of explanation.) The goal is to discover how an institution or behavioral trait emerges or evolves from a set or primitives. So Axelrod (1984) uses his iterated-prisoner's dilemma models to study the emergence of cooperation among egoists. Or Cederman (1997) examines the origins of empires in international politics. Emergence is perhaps the key distinctive concept in complexity modeling.

Epstein goes so far as to say, "If you didn't grow it, you didn't explain its emergence" (1999, 43). Epstein is reacting to Nash equilibrium-form explanations—a pattern exists because the agents by assumption would not choose other options—but this is likely taking it too far and limits our view of what an explanation is. If genetic-style explanation is the only form of explanation for the existence of a particular phenomenon, then much of science is far afield from explaining things in the sense of combining insight and prediction.

But a genetic motivation (emergence, really) captures one of the key (in my view commendable) attributes of these models, the ability to observe the dynamics of production, to watch processes unfold, and to study how systems that might be converging on one or another equilibrium or steady-state could have tilted into others. If we want to study paths to equilibria, game theory will not enable this, but many computational models are explicitly designed to add insight into how those paths are traversed over time.

There is a link here to rationality and boundedness. No one can settle the debate definitively about whether rationality is a realistic assumption to make to ground models in the social sciences. Certainly violations of assumed rationality occur regularly, but that's not the same as saying that any other assumption is more realistic. Evidence from numerous areas of the social sciences suggests strongly that many people, perhaps most people, make decisions using heuristics. This is especially true as their decision environments become more complicated. Decision-making in real environments can be better captured by the metaphor of adapting on a landscape rather than optimizing among the universe options (see figure 15.5).

And in fact, a core assumption of the theory of the firm in economics is that firms will change their internal organizations in response to competitive pressures. Put in everyday language, if a firm if getting beat, then it needs to reorganize so it makes better strategic decisions. How are we to model these processes of feedback, from micro to macro and back to micro? A modeling methodology that enables the analysis of these kinds of feedback processes can produce more realistic models than techniques that by assumption need preferences and calculating abilities of agents to remain fixed.

I would argue that computational models in the complexity tradition offer our best hope so far for gaining deep insights into how behaviorally relevant decision heuristics within individuals change in response to aggregate patterns of behavior. Put another way, if one wants to study the feedback between micro and macro— between how people change over time and how social systems change over time— and one wants to study these in coherent, rigorous models, then complexity modeling offers a set of valuable tools. This conclusion is mostly premised on the value of a CM approach to explanation. If one finds value in the CM approach, then computational models provide a valuable means to these styles of explanations. It also requires an acceptance of models that do not have identifiable equilibria. Computational models typically end up with paths as predictions, not equilibria as predictions. The paths will usually vary depending on parameters. We might want to know how shocks or decisions affect variations in paths, or off of paths.

Returning to Harrington's (1998) models described above, these serve as exemplary. The key move for Harrington is to have new agents coming in at the bottom of the hierarchy mimicking those at the top in terms of their emphases on experience with consistent action versus flexibility. The macro pattern feeds back to the distribution of micro motivations. He finds that organizations can tip into multiple steady-states in terms of whether their hierarchies are filled with rigid types that

Figure 15.5 Adaptation on Landscapes

behave consistently or flexible types that move with the times. Here is a research program using computational models that reveals insights and leads to probabilistic predictions based on parameter values, that can track dynamics of the system, and can capture features of common social systems (organizations) that other modeling techniques cannot.

There is little doubt that computational models permit the analysis of the aggregation of behaviors of diverse, adaptive agents that might alter their decision rules in response to aggregate patterns (i.e., feedback from macro-patterns back to micro-motivations and behavior) better than other modeling methods, especially game theoretic models. If diversity that is not best summarized with a simple statistic such as a standard error on an attribution measure is important to the insights gained from a model, then computational models will be beneficial. If feedback from an aggregate pattern to agents' behavioral rules is important to insights gained from a model, then computational models will be beneficial. If models display substantial dependence on sequences of events (loosely called path dependence among many social scientists), then computational models will be beneficial. And perhaps the concluding point from all of this, if more than one of these features is important to understanding the behavior of a system, then computational models are likely the only way to go.

ACKNOWLEDGMENTS

The first version of this chapter was prepared for presentation at the Current Issues in the Philosophy and Methodology of the Social Sciences Conference, Center for Ethics and Values in the Sciences and Department of Philosophy, University of Alabama at Birmingham, April 16–18, 2010. Other versions of this chapter were given at the annual meetings of the American Political Science Association (2010), and in the Center for Political Studies seminar at the University of Michigan. I thank participants of these meetings for helpful feedback. Special thanks to Gary Goertz, Michael Laver, Scott Page, Bill Clark, Jenna Bednar, Rick Riolo, Elisabeth Gerber, Anna Alexandrova, Keith Krehbiel, Gilles Serra, and James Woodward, who helped me considerably through interpersonal interactions on this topic or reviews of the chapter. They of course bear no responsibility for any errors, nor do they necessarily agree with its contents.

NOTES

1. Thanks to Scott Page for the discussion of things that "pop out" of models and the shadow prices example.
2. Take, for example, the subfield of comparative politics within political science. This vibrant subfield is filled with excellent work, much of which is qualitative and

historical. The repertoire of political scientists in this subfield consists of numerous concepts or models derived from analytical economics, such as transaction costs, prisoner's dilemmas, price discrimination, collective action problems, and principles-agent problems. Yet it is uncommon for works in this subfield to contain citations to the foundational works establishing or developing these concepts and models.

3. De Marchi takes issue overall with much of applied formal modeling in the social sciences. He makes a set of claims that I am generally sympathetic with, namely: (1) that rational choice formal modelers in the social sciences must acknowledge that their set of assumptions are sometimes no less arbitrary than the set of assumptions often made in empirical research; (2) and consequently, that robustness of theoretical results is as important to demonstrate as robustness of empirical results; and (3) that formal theory should be valued as much for offering new insights into mechanisms (presumably from a CM approach) as for providing prediction and testable empirical implications.

4. Thanks to Gary Goertz for making this point to me.

5. Epstein recently wrote the following in support of computational models:
"Planetary scale computational modeling is now feasible, allowing the study of coupled transitions at multiple scales. These epochal changes eclipse the turbulence of daily political affairs. Their complexity dwarfs the capacity of any individual's comprehension . . . . it is imperative that this admittedly bold step be taken: to envision how these epochal developments will interact over the next decade. The coupled socio = economic environmental dynamics will be far from linear, far from equilibrium, and far from canonically rational. But they can be understood and productively shaped." Available at http://cordis.europa.eu/fp7/ict/fet-proactive/docs/flagship-ie-jan10-05_en.pdf (accessed February 15, 2011).

REFERENCES

Alexandrova, Anna. 2008. "Making Models Count." *Philosophy of Science* 75 (3): 383–404.

Arthur, W. Brian. 1994. "Inductive Reasoning and Bounded Rationality." *American Economic Review* 84 (2): 406–11.

Arthur, W. Brian, John H. Holland, Blake LeBaron, Richard Palmer, and Paul Taylor. 1997. "Asset Pricing Under Endogenous Expectations in an Artificial Stock Market." In *The Economy as a Complex System II*, W. Brian Arthur, Steven N. Durlauf, and David A. Lane, eds., 15–44. Reading, MA: Addison-Wesley.

Axelrod, Robert. 1984. *Evolution of Cooperation*. New York: Basic Books.

Axelrod, Robert. 1997. *The Complexity of Cooperation*. Princeton, NJ: Princeton University Press.

Bak, Per. 1996. *How Nature Works*. New York: Springer-Verlag.

Barry, Brian. 1978. *Sociologists, Economists, and Democracy*. Chicago: University of Chicago Press.

Bendor, Jonathan, Daniel Diermeier, and Michael Ting. 2003. "A Behavioral Model of Turnout." *American Political Science Review* 97 (2): 261–80.

Black, Duncan. 1987 [1958]. *The Theory of Committees and Elections*. Reproduced. Dordrecht, Netherlands: Kluwer Academic.

Bruch, Elizabeth, and Robert Mare. 2006. "Neighborhood Choice and Neighborhood Change." *American Journal of Sociology* 112 (3): 667–709.

Camerer, Colin. 2003. *Behavioral Game Theory*. Princeton, NJ: Princeton University Press.

Casti, John L. 1996. "Seeing the Light at El Farol." *Complexity* 1 (5): 7–10.

Cederman, Lars-Erik. 1997. *Emergent Actors: How States and Nations Develop and Dissolve*. Princeton, NJ: Princeton University Press.

De Marchi, Scott. 2005. *Computational and Mathematical Modeling in the Social Sciences*. New York: Cambridge University Press.

Epstein, Joshua, and Robert Axtell. 1996. *Growing Artificial Societies*. Cambridge, MA: The MIT Press.

Epstein, Joshua. 1999. "Agent-Based Computational Models and Generative Social Science." *Complexity* 4 (5): 41–57.

Epstein, Joshua. 2002. "Modeling Civil Violence: An Agent-Based Computational Approach." *Proceedings of the National Academy of Sciences* 99 (10), Supplement 3: 7243–50.

Epstein, Joshua. 2005. *Generative Social Science*. Princeton, NJ: Princeton University Press.

Epstein, Joshua. 2011. Quoted in "FuturIcT—An ICT-Based 'Apollo Project' to Make Humanity Fit for Future." Available at http://cordis.europa.eu/fp7/ict/fet-proactive/docs/flagship-ie-jan10-05_en.pdf, accessed February 15, 2011.

Michael Findlay. 2008. "Agents and Conflict: Adaptation and the Dynamics of War." *Complexity* 14 (1): 22–35.

Durlauf, Steven. 2010. "Complexity, Economics, and Public Policy." Working Paper. Madison: Department of Economics, University of Wisconsin.

Grune-Yanoff, Till. 2009. "The Explanatory Potential of Artificial Societies." *Synthese* 169 (3): 539–55.

Harrington, Joseph. 1998. "The Social Selection of Flexible and Rigid Agents." *American Economic Review* 88 (1): 63–82.

Hartmann, S. 1996. "The World as a Process: Simulations in the Natural and Social Sciences." In *Modelling and Simulation in the Social Sciences from the Philosophy of Science Point of View*, R. Hegselmann, Ulrich Mueller, and Klaus Troitzsch, eds., 77–100. Dordrecht, Netherlands: Kluwer.

Hempel, Carl. 1965. *Aspects of Scientific Explanation and Other Essays in the Philosophy of Science*. New York: The Free Press.

Holland, John. 1992a. "Complex Adaptive Systems." *Daedalus* 121 (1): 17–30.

Holland, John. 1992b. "Genetic Algorithms." *Scientific American*. (July): 66–72.

Holland, John. 1998. *Emergence: From Chaos to Order*. Oxford: Oxford University Press.

Hotelling, Harold. 1929. "Stability in Competition." *The Economic Journal* 39 (153): 41–57.

Humphreys, Paul. 2004. *Extending Ourselves*. New York: Oxford University Press.

Judd, Kenneth. 1997. "Computational Economics and Economic Theory: Complements or Substitutes?" *Journal of Economic Dynamics and Control* 21 (6): 907–42.

Judd, Kenneth. 1998. *Numerical Methods in Economics*. Cambridge, MA: The MIT Press.

Kollman, Ken, John Miller, and Scott Page. 1992. "Adaptive Parties and Spatial Elections." *American Political Science Review* 86 (4): 929–37.

Kollman, Ken, John Miller, and Scott Page, eds. 2003. *Computational Models in Political Economy*. Cambridge, MA: The MIT Press.

Laver, Michael. 2005. "Policy and the Dynamics of Political Competition." *American Political Science Review* 99 (May): 263–81.

Leombruni, Roberto, and Matteo Richiardi. 2005. "Why Are Economists Sceptical About Agent-Based Simulations?" *Physica A* 355 (1): 103–9.

Levins, Richard. 1966. "The Strategy of Model Building in Population Ecology." *American Scientist* 54 (4): 421–31.

Lettau, Martin. 1997. "Explaining the Facts with Adaptive Agents." *Journal of Economic Dynamics and Control* 21 (7): 1117–48.

Lewis, David. 1973. *Counterfactuals*. Cambridge, MA: Harvard University Press.

Lustick, Ian S., Dan Miodownik, and Roy J. Eidelson. 2004. "Secessionism in Multicultural States: Does Sharing Power Prevent or Encourage It?" *American Political Science Review* 98 (2): 209–30.

Macey, Michael, and John Skvoretz. 1998. "The Evolution of Trust and Cooperation between Strangers: A Computational Model." *American Sociological Review* 63 (5): 638–60.

March, James. 1988. *Decisions and Organizations*. New York: Blackwell.

Miller, John H., and Scott E. Page. 2007. *Complex Adaptive Systems*. Princeton, NJ: Princeton University Press.

Morrow, James. 1994. *Game Theory for Political Scientists*. Princeton, NJ: Princeton University Press.

Myerson, Roger. 1991. *Game Theory*. Cambridge, MA: Harvard University Press.

Nagel, Ernest. 1961. *The Structure of Science*. New York: Harcourt, Brace and World.

Nash, John. 1951. "Noncooperative Games." *Annals of Mathematics* 54 (2): 289–95.

Padgett, John, and Christopher Ansell. 1993. "Robust Action and the Rise of the Medici, 1400–34." *American Journal of Sociology* 98 (6): 1259–319.

Page, Scott. 1996. "Two Measures of Difficulty." *Economic Theory* 8 (2): 321–46.

Page, Scott. 1997. "On Incentives and Updating in Agent Based Models." *Computational Economics* 10 (1): 67–87.

Page, Scott. 2000. "Computational Economics from A to Z." *Complexity* 5 (1): 35–40.

Pearl, Judea. 2000. *Causality: Models, Reasoning, and Inference*, Cambridge: Cambridge University Press.

Rosser, Barkley. 1999. "On the Complexities of Complex Economic Dynamics." *Journal of Economic Perspectives* 13 (4): 169–92.

Salmon, Wesley. 1984. *Scientific Explanation and the Causal Structure of the World*. Princeton, NJ: Princeton University Press.

Salmon, Wesley. 1998. *Causality and Explanation*. New York: Oxford University Press.

Schelling, Thomas. 1978. *Micromotives and Macrobehavior*. New York: Norton.

Simon, Herbert. 1969. *The Sciences of the Artificial*. Cambridge, MA: The MIT Press.

Tesfatsion, L. 2007. "Agent-Based Computational Economics: A Constructive Approach to Economic Theory." In *Handbook of Computational Economics*, Vol. 2., L. Tesfatsion and K. Judd, eds. North Holland, Netherlands: Elsevier.

Von Neumann, John, and Oskar Morgenstern. 1944. *Theory of Games and Economic Behavior*. Princeton, NJ: Princeton University Press.

Watts, Duncan J., and Steven H. Strogatz. 1998. "Collective Dynamics of 'Small-World' Networks." *Nature* 393 (6684): 440–42.

Watts, Duncan. 2003. *Six Degrees: The Science of the Connected Age*. New York: Norton.

Wolfram, Stephen. 2002. *A New Kind of Science*. Champaign, IL: Wolfram Media

Woodward, James. 2003. *Making Things Happen*. New York: Oxford University Press.

Woodward, James. 1989. "The Causal/Mechanical Model of Explanation." In *Scientific Explanation*, P. Kitcher and W. Salmon, eds. Minnesota Studies in the Philosophy of Science, Vol. 13. Minneapolis: University of Minnesota Press.

Woodward, James. 2000. "Explanation and Invariance in the Special Sciences." *British Journal for the Philosophy of Science* 51 (2): 197–254.

Woodward, James. "Scientific Explanation." *The Stanford Encyclopedia of Philosophy*. Winter 2009 Edition, Edward N. Zalta, ed., Available at http://plato.stanford.edu/entries/scientific-explanation.

PART III

Norms, Culture, and the Social-Psychological

CHAPTER 16

MODELS OF CULTURE

MARK RISJORD

16.1. INTRODUCTION

The concept of culture is one of anthropology's most significant contributions to contemporary thought. What might be now called a "classical" conception of culture developed in the mid-twentieth century. It treated cultures as homogeneous and systematic entities, something shared by individuals within a given social group. Descriptions of culture were thought to be abstracted from individual actions, and appeal to culture was taken as explanatory, both of patterns of action within social groups and of differences among groups. The culture concept influenced philosophers of language who relied on the idea that linguistic communities have relatively clear boundaries. Philosophical work on language and meaning, in turn, influenced both the anthropologists who developed the classical conception and their critics. Contemporary anthropological models of culture continue to be influenced by, and have deep relevance for, philosophical understanding of language, thought, and human nature.

While the anthropological concept of culture is little more than one hundred years old, there have been many ways of conceptualizing it. In a famous survey, Alfred Kroeber and Clyde Kluckhohn ([1952] 1963) identified 164 definitions of culture. At the risk of losing some of the texture of anthropological thought, this chapter will sort these definitions into a much smaller number of models. The earliest models treated cultures as collections of traits: a grab bag of ideas, material objects, habits, and texts. By the middle of the twentieth century, one of the dominant models came to emphasize norms, values, and beliefs as the central elements of culture, and this semiotic model is probably the notion most familiar to nonanthropologists. It emphasized the coherence of cultures, treated cultures as distinct from each other, and abstracted from the peculiarities of individual belief and behavior. The semiotic model of culture was sharply criti-cized in the 1970s and 1980s. These arguments problematized the ideas that there might be a unified set of norms that define culture and that culture might be something shared by all individuals within a group. The very idea of culture became troublesome, creating something of a crisis within the discipline. With-out culture, it is not clear whether cultural anthropology has an object of study. Anthropologists responded to these concerns by developing a variety of new models. We will examine three that have become popular in the last two decades: a neo-Boasian model that draws from the early twentieth-century trait model, the epidemiological model that allies anthropological theorizing with the results of cognitive psychology, and practice theory, which looks to integrated patterns of human response to account for norms and institutions.

These different models of culture, both historical and contemporary, speak to three philosophical issues. First, the classical conception of culture presupposed that cultures were bounded. While culture blending and change could not be denied, it made sense to think of a culture being circumscribable. In a prototypical example, any given trait was either typical of the culture or outside of its boundaries. This idea was an important part of the background to mid-twentieth-century philosophy of language. Philosophers like Quine, Wittgenstein, Austin, Gadamer, or Sellars felt no qualms about presupposing that there were identifiable and uniform linguistic com-munities. Such notions as a language game or speech community grounded ac-counts of rule-following, pragmatic force, and semantic content. In their empirical work, however, anthropologists have struggled with the problem of identifying cul-tural boundaries. While philosophers tended to treat this as a marginal, empirical problem, the history of the culture concept shows that it cuts more deeply. The idea that there are cultural boundaries makes sense only if cultures are conceived as uni-fied and coherent. As the phenomena identified as cultural are seen as a fluctuating collection of traits, representations, or practices, it becomes impossible to identify the traits that distinguish one culture from another. This puts pressure on philo-sophical views that presuppose the existence of language communities wherein dis-tinct patterns of speech and behavior can be identified. The fundamental question raised by the demise of the classical culture concept, then, is whether any of its plau-sible successors can do the same philosophical work.

A second issue, familiar in the philosophy of social science, is one form of the problem of methodological individualism: Is a culture a kind of entity distinct from the persons (and their properties) who inhabit it? The classical cultural concept man-ifested a strong anti-reductionist commitment on the part of anthropologists, and the cogency of this commitment is an important philosophical issue. The mid-century philosophical discussion of this question concerned the possibility of defining social-level concepts in terms of personal-level properties. The latter sections of this chap-ter will show how that discussion must change in the light of the new models of culture. None of the contemporary models of culture are committed to cultures as entities. At the same time, they cannot be described as individualistic in the tradi-tional sense because none dissolves cultural phenomena into the beliefs, desires, or other person-level properties. The epidemiological model looks to subpersonal, cognitive mechanisms, while practice theory seeks explanation in the properties of interpersonal interactions. There are indeed metaphysical questions here, but they are not the traditional focus of the methodological individualism debate.

Another familiar debate that must change in the light of these new models of culture is the issue about how social structures are related to agency. The question here is one of explanatory priority: Does appeal to culture explain individual behavior, or do individual choices explain cultural forms? Or is there some noncircular way of combining the two? This problem has also been discussed under the heading of methodological individualism, and is closely related to the problem discussed in the foregoing paragraph. Anthropological theories that relied on the classical conception of culture explained actions as instances of more general patterns: functions, symbolic exchanges, cultural rules, and so on. The agents were portrayed as little more than puppets or cultural dupes, moving through their lives buffeted by cultural forces. Rejecting these forms of explanation was an important factor in the critique of the classical culture concept. The alternatives that arose in anthropology and sociology, however, did not universally swing to the alternate pole by trying to explain all social phenomena in terms of individual choice. Rather, the practice theoretic models tend to place agents within a field of action where cultural norms and meanings are fair game for strategic manipulation. Matters are somewhat more complex for the epidemiological view, as we will see. The new models of culture have opened different possibilities for the explanation of action, and they present interesting challenges to our familiar ways of understanding agency.

16.2. ORIGINS OF THE CULTURE CONCEPT

The anthropological concept of culture has a number of sources in nineteenth-century thought. The canonical definition is a quotation from Edward Bennett Tylor's 1871 *Primitive Culture*:

> Culture or Civilization, taken in its wide ethnographic sense, is that complex whole which includes knowledge, belief, art, morals, law, custom, and any other capabilities and habits acquired by man as a member of society. (Tylor 1871, 1)

To understand this oft-quoted passage, it must be put into its theoretical context. Notice first that the definition is not of culture, but of "culture or civilization." In Anglophone anthropology, "culture" and "civilization" were often used interchangeably, a usage that persisted into the early twentieth century (e.g., Kroeber 1917; Sapir 1924). Tylor's project was typical of nineteenth-century anthropology. His scientific goal was to make sense of human diversity. The framework was historical and evolutionary (but not specifically Darwinian). He postulated stages though which human groups would pass. Difference among human communities was explained by the persistence of some at lower stages of culture or civilization. To compare different human groups and identify their place in the scheme, Tylor looked to shared traits and survivals. Animism, for instance, is a trait that could be identified around the globe, and Tylor assigned it to primitive forms of religion. Groups like the Australian Aborigines were placed lower on the scale partly because their religion exhibited this trait.

In Tylor's usage, culture was different from Émile Durkheim's social facts and collective consciousness. For Tylor, culture was a collection of traits that could be compared globally and historically. Appeal to diffusion and historical stages of development explained similarities and differences in the distribution of these traits. In other words, culture was the phenomenon to be explained; it was not a theoretical posit. Durkheim, by contrast, postulated the existence of patterns of thought that were distinct from the beliefs of any individual. These social facts had explanatory force in ways that Tylor's civilization did not. Society was something that might be represented in religious ritual, and social structures could explain patterns of intentional action (like suicide rates). He explicitly argued that they had an ontological status not reducible to facts about individual agents (Durkheim [1912] 1915, [1895] 1938). Because social facts are treated as things, questions about reductionism, and the relationship between social structures and intentional actions arise for Durkheim in ways that they do not for Tylor.

Franz Boas drew on Tylor's culture concept, but his challenges to Tylor's theoretical project forced important changes in the way that Boas thought about culture. Boas rejected Tylor's idea that traits could be meaningfully compared across wide geographical areas and put into historical stages (Boas 1887, [1896] 1940), which was a central methodological presupposition of Tylor's anthropology. Boas argued that a trait (e.g., a clothing decoration, a kind of snare, or a religious belief) is significant only in the context of a whole culture. Comparisons were meaningful only when there were plausible connections, either historical or contemporary, among the cultures compared. This led Boas to begin thinking about culture as holistic. He continued to conceptualize culture as a collection of traits, but the traits were integrated, coherent, and shared by a specific group of people. Traits included both material objects and ideas. Insofar as an individual's behavior is determined by his ideas, Boas thus began to hold explicitly that culture determines behavior (Boas 1901).

With Boas's modifications of Tylor's conception, as well as his adaptation of ideas from Herder, Graebner, and Virchow, the culture concept took on some (but not all) central features of its twentieth-century form. As a result, there were tensions around Boas's concept that prefigure twentieth-century philosophical debates. Insofar as cultures were treated as local, holistic collections of traits, Boas was committed to the idea of cultural boundaries. However, because Boas and his students were interested in historical questions about diffusion of traits, they recognized that there would be variability within cultures, and that boundaries might be vague or porous. While cultural identity was not an important concern, the identity of traits was. Traits are portrayed as passing among groups, hence they must be reidentifiable across space and time. But his holism entailed that the significance of a trait depends on its place in the whole culture. So, in virtue of what can it be the same trait in different cultures?

16.3. MODELS OF CULTURE IN THE EARLY TWENTIETH CENTURY

In the early twentieth century, anthropologists became increasingly committed to the idea that cultures had an ontological status of their own. Boas's students, Alfred Kroeber and Robert Lowie, each defended the idea that cultural and historical phenomena could not be reduced to biology or individual psychology (Kroeber 1917; Lowie [1917] 1929). Kroeber described cultural phenomena as "superorganic," a term he borrowed from Herbert Spencer. It is telling, however, that Kroeber continued to use "culture," "civilization," and "history" interchangeably. He was concerned to argue that there was an important difference between invention and evolution, and that this difference had ontological and epistemological consequences. Culture, civilization, and history are ontologically distinct from the nonhuman realm, and hence the social sciences are distinct from the natural sciences. However, neither Kroeber nor Lowie was inclined to treat individual cultures as distinct theoretical entities.

The ontological status of cultures was viewed somewhat differently by British anthropologists such as Bronislaw Malinowski and A. R. Radcliffe-Brown. Their functionalism was influenced by Durkheim, especially *The Elementary Forms of the Religious Life* ([1912] 1915). Durkheim argued that religious ideas represent the society, and that religious rituals fill "the need of upholding and reaffirming . . . the collective sentiments and collective ideas which make [the society's] unity and its personality" (Durkheim [1912] 1915, 427). While Durkheim's preferred term was "society," its explanatory role in his work was the same as the anthropologists' concept of culture. The society represented by religious experience was not some general form shared by all humans; it was the person's community. Functional explanations promulgated in anthropology shared the same explanatory form. The institutions within a culture were explained in terms of their capacity to fulfill social and individual needs. In addition, the British anthropologists attended to normative aspects of culture: the rules and laws that made categories of action and speech obligatory or prohibited. Since norms cannot be identified with regularities of behavior (at least, not without the philosophical gymnastics provided by a later generation of philosophers), it was natural to treat them as something distinct from the behavior.

By the 1920s, "culture" had become a theoretical entity, and anthropologists regarded the human world as populated by a large number of distinct cultures. Culture was no longer a phenomenon to be explained: It was a theoretical posit that explained a broad range of human phenomena. There remained throughout the first part of the century important differences between the Boasians and the functionalists. The differences were profound enough to justify a distinction between two early twentieth-century models of culture: the Boasian model and the functionalist model.

Boas's students, who dominated American anthropology for the first part of the twentieth century, continued to think of cultures as distinguishable bodies of traits. Again, their ontological commitment was to the irreducibility of historical processes, not to individual cultures as discrete entities. As a result, they could be relatively sanguine about how cultural boundaries were drawn. Moreover, American anthropologists were often interested in questions about the historical relationships among cultures (especially first nation peoples in the Americas). As a result, they expected traits such as mythic characters, decorative motifs, or technologies to both vary within cultures and move among them. Nonetheless, culture had explanatory power for the Boasians. It was an important part of the environment in which individuals grew up. Individuals formed their beliefs, values, and personality under the influence of the culture. Culture thus explained patterns of difference among groups of individuals. Among the Boasians, the precise role of individuals in the understanding of cultural phenomena was a point of debate. Paul Radin expressed this critique most sharply, arguing that while his colleagues recognized that there was variation within cultures, their ethnographic descriptions abstracted away from the variation. Individual agents were thus portrayed as passive receivers of culture, not agents within it. This made it impossible to properly understand the historical dimensions of cultural phenomena (Radin [1933] 1987).

The functionalist model of culture was primarily championed by British anthropologists. It treated a culture as having a framework of rules, laws, and institutions. Because of the stronger explanatory demands put on the concept of culture by the functionalists, they had deeper worries about cultural boundaries. When actions are explained as following rules, the cases of deviance become troublesome. In pure cultures, deviance should be relatively uncommon, and presumably a matter for concern or sanction. This means that culture change, cultural blending or overlap, and variation within cultures are difficult to explain. Ethnographic monographs tended to downplay variation, focusing on the pure culture. In a critique of Malinowski, Lowie argued that:

> First and foremost, a science of Culture is not limited to the study of so many integrated wholes, the single cultures. This is doubtless important, but it constitutes neither the whole nor even the preponderant part of the ethnologist's task. A science of culture must, in principle, register every item of social tradition, correlating it significantly with any other aspect of reality, *whether that lies within the same culture or outside*. In defiance of the dogma that any one culture forms a closed system, we must insist that such a culture is invariably an artificial unit segregated for purposes of expediency. Social tradition varies demonstrably from village to village, even from family to family. (Lowie 1937, 235)

If cultural boundaries are artificial and to some extent arbitrary, then the rules and norms to which the functionalists appealed in their explanations had no basis. They were identified by abstracting the rules from patterns of behavior, but those patterns were jury-rigged by the anthropologist. The whole process appears circular.

16.4. CULTURE AND MEANING

By the time the Second World War ended, the concept of culture was widely used, both within anthropology and outside of it. One of the first philosophers to turn his attention to anthropology, David Bidney, argued at this time that conceptions of culture fell into two groups, "realistic" and "idealistic" (Bidney 1944, 1942). Realists identified culture with habits, customary behaviors, and material objects. The idealist conceptions defined culture in terms of norms, ideals, and beliefs. Bidney put Tylor and Boas into the realist category, along with Boas's students, Ruth Benedict and Margaret Mead. In so doing, he highlighted an aspect of trait theories of culture: they included behaviors and material objects among the traits. Of course, they also included beliefs, values, and other elements that Bidney would label as idealist. Bidney's distinction points out an ambiguity in the early twentieth-century thinking about culture, and that ambiguity became an important bifurcation in the mid-century conceptualizations of culture.

According to Bidney, when culture is conceived in realist terms, it "is inseparable from the life of human beings in society; it is a mode of social living and has no existence independent of the actual group or groups to which it is attributed" (Bidney 1942, 449).[1] This view was perhaps best represented by theorists who continued to work in a strongly comparative and evolutionary framework, such as George Murdock (1949) and Leslie White (1949). In the fifties and sixties, this conception of culture was carried forward by those who sought the explanation of cultural phenomena in ecological or economic terms. Following Marvin Harris, this kind of work in anthropology might be called "cultural materialism" (Harris 1968). An important consequence of this approach is that it gives little or no explanatory role to culture per se. Like Tylor (and the materialist strands in Boas's thought), "culture" picks out a group of phenomena to be explained.

A wide variety of methodological and theoretical perspectives grew in mid-century anthropology that assumed an idealistic perspective, including structural functionalism, structuralism, ethnoscience, and symbolic anthropology. These views shared the assumption that culture is something *communicated*. Culture is like a code passed from one generation to another, and the aim of ethnography was to crack the code. These anthropologists harkened back to Malinowski's suggestion that ethnography capture "the natives' point of view" (Malinowski 1922, 25), but they understood that point of view to be expressed in a system of symbols or meanings. As a result, this mid-century model of culture might best be called the semiotic model. In the fifties and sixties, proponents of a semiotic model of culture were divided over the issue of methodological individualism: whether the ideas that constituted culture were individual and "in the head" of individuals, or whether they were independent of individuals and shared by them. The debate had important consequences for the structure of anthropological explanations. If culture is to figure as an explanans of human behavior, it has to be treated as independent of individuals and it must be semantic. This is the sort of appeal to culture that structural functionalists or symbolic anthropologists wanted to make. Their analyses tended to generalize strongly within a culture, treating symbolic meanings as uniform across individuals and explanatory of specific events and actions.

The individualist versions of idealism reduced culture to patterns of individual beliefs. The patterns themselves have little explanatory force, so like the materialists, individualistic versions of cultural idealism treat culture as something to be explained, as *explanandum*, not *explanans*. The ethnoscientists (an approach also known as the "new ethnography" and "componential analysis") worked with native classification schemes. By finding minimal criteria that distinguished concepts from each other, they sought the semantic rules that underlay conceptual fields. For example, among those who share my dialect, the difference between something baked and something broiled is that the latter is cooked by heat from the top only; both are cooked by hot air alone, as opposed to methods of cooking by immersion in water or oil. Using these kinds of criteria, an ethnoscientist could outline the conceptual field of my cooking terminology. They treated these conceptual rules as represented in the minds of individuals. Strongly analogous to syntactic rules, individuals within a culture had similar representations of the rules underlying their conceptual scheme. The ethnoscientists ran into several conceptual problems that pushed them toward an individualist view. Arguments reminiscent of Quine's (1960) showed that the analyses were underdetermined by the data (Burling 1964). Moreover, fieldwork showed that there was substantial individual variation in use. Some went so far as to embrace this variability and argue against the idea that culture was something shared (Goodenough 1965; Wallace 1961).

Clifford Geertz's "Thick Description: Toward an Interpretive Theory of Culture" (1973) was an important response to the problems surrounding a semiotic conception of culture. He drew on Wittgenstein and Ryle to forge a connection between meaning and behavior. Meaning is a matter of patterns of behavior in their full context. To understand a culture, the ethnographer describes and relates these patterns. "Thick description" articulates conceptual content by relating individual events to the larger patterns of which they are a part. Individual beliefs and representations get their content from the larger patterns. The meanings that constitute a culture, then, are not a kind of entity separate from the actions of individuals; yet because of the relational and contextual character, they cannot be identified with the dispositions or beliefs of individuals either. Geertz drew the conclusion that:

> Culture, this acted document, is thus public, like a burlesqued wink or a mock sheep raid. Though ideational, it does not exist in someone's head; though unphysical, it is not an occult entity. The interminable, because unterminable, debate within anthropology as to whether culture is "subjective" or "objective," together with the mutual exchange of intellectual insults ("idealist!"— "materialist!"; "mentalist!"—"behaviorist!"; "impressionist!"—"positivist!") which accompanies it, is wholly misconceived. Once human behavior is seen as (most of the time; there *are* true twitches) symbolic action—action which like phonation in speech, pigment in painting, line in writing, or sonance in music, signifies—the question as to whether culture is patterned conduct or a frame of mind, or even the two somehow mixed together, loses sense. (Geertz 1973, 10)

With Geertz's rhetorically elegant transcendence of tired dualisms, the semiotic concept of culture took a middle line on the issue of methodological individualism. Culture is not an abstract object of any kind. Metaphysically, it is nothing more than the interactions of individuals. At the same time, it does not reduce culture to the beliefs and attitudes of individuals. These are understood as requiring the cultural patterns for their significance. Thick descriptions thus have value for understanding particular events and actions. Appeal to culture retains its explanatory power without postulating new kinds of metaphysical entities.

16.5. Structure, Agency, and Emotion in Cultural Explanations

The semiotic conception of culture came under sustained attack in the 1980s, exemplified most dramatically by the essays in *Writing Culture* (Clifford and Marcus 1986). Its point of departure was a critique of the rhetoric of ethnographic writing, but it succeeded in raising deep issues about the culture concept. These critics pointed out that ethnography was monological—that is, it presented a single, unified narrative. This has two consequences for the semiotic conception of culture. First, ethnographic narratives speak of cultural phenomena as if there were a systematic, univocal set of norms, beliefs, and values: a single worldview. As Radin pointed out decades earlier, it must be created by ignoring variation within the community (or communities). The idea that there is something that might be *the* culture of a group is thus an ethnographic construct, not something discovered by anthropology. Second, because cultural phenomena were described as a monolithic system of rules and norms, appeals to culture treat individual action as empty rule-following. While neither issue was new, the arguments gained relevance from debates in the 1960s and 1970s about the way that anthropology had (or had not) been implicated in colonialism.

Geertz's assimilation of a Wittgensteinean analysis of rules with the anthropological concern for symbolic meaning left the semiotic conception with a rather pointed problem about cultural boundaries. For Geertz, the thick description synthesized a broad pattern of speech and behavior. The content of the thickly described concept thus depends on how the boundaries of the pattern are set—much in the same way as Wittgenstein's analysis of rules depends on what instances are taken to be within the proper bounds of correct or incorrect application. The semiotic conception of culture thus depends on the presupposition that there are relatively clear boundaries to the culture. The boundaries of culture presupposed by the semiotic conception of culture were problematic in many of the same ways that they were for the functionalists. As we saw above, anthropologists like Lowie already recognized that boundaries set by ethnographers were permeable and relatively arbitrary. In the 1980s, however, this critique was deepened by political concerns about anthropology's relationship to colonialism. Twentieth-century ethnographic fieldwork often followed in the wake of colonial expansion. Access to remote areas and peoples was facilitated by colonial administrations. These relationships raised the suspicion that anthropology had helped support colonial domination of indigenous peoples (Asad 1973; Hymes 1969). By presenting a single and unified view of the culture, monological ethnographies had to suppress contrarian, marginalized, or peripheral voices in favor of those who are dominant. They also obscured ways in which ideas and people from historically different communities interpenetrate, mix, and change. This means that the ethnographic representation is a *mis*representation. Within a community, there may be alternative norms, rules, and values that conflict with the dominant ones, and the interpretation of past practice may be locally disputed. Such misrepresentations are not politically neutral. The elevation of some perspectives as *the* culture and the presentation of the group as homogeneous arguably makes them better subjects of indirect rule.

The second line of critique of the semiotic conception of culture revolved around the structure-and-agency problem. We have every reason to suppose that there is wide individual variation in action, in subjective experience, in social position, and so on. Monological ethnographies papered over these differences by trying to describe general patterns that would apply to the whole group. This made it difficult to represent the relationship between the individual and the larger group. Emphasis on the normative dimensions of culture compounded the difficulty. As Renato Rosaldo argued in *Culture and Truth* (Rosaldo 1989), classical ethnographic analysis identified patterns and treated them as obligatory. As an example, Rosaldo quotes Radcliffe-Brown's ethnography of the Andaman Islanders:

> When two friends or relatives meet after having been separated, the social relation between them that has been interrupted is about to be renewed. This social relation implies or depends upon the existence of a specific bond of solidarity between them. The weeping rite (together with the subsequent exchange of presents) is the affirmation of this bond. The rite, which, it must be remembered, is obligatory, compels the two participants to act as though they felt certain emotions, and thereby does, to some extent, produce these emotions in them. (Radcliffe-Brown [1922] 1933, quoted in Rosaldo 1989, 52)

Rosaldo argued that treating such interactions as obligatory distorts social experiences and misrepresents social reality. The joy and relief of seeing one's child return from a dangerous journey is reduced to the by-product of the obligatory action of weeping. Insofar as ethnography was to capture the native's point of view, treating that experience as a kind of hollow playacting signals a failure of the project.

Not only is social experience misrepresented, treating culture as a set of shared ideas, obligatory norms, or customary behaviors prevents the ethnographer from raising questions about how individuals resist, exploit, adapt to, or reproduce the norms and practices. Pierre Bourdieu's discussion of how Kabyle men and women differently represent kin relationships provides an excellent example. According to standard ethnographic descriptions, the Kabyle practiced parallel cousin marriage, and the relationship was reckoned through the male line. This means that the preferred husband for a woman is her father's brother's son; or if the relation needed to be extended, grandsons of the woman's paternal grandfather. Bourdieu argued that in many actual cases, kin relations are also reckoned through the mother's side. Counting relationships through the male line was the official strategy, and the one used where the honor and property of the family needed to be protected or advanced. Relationships counted through the female line, while less prestigious, were used to establish appropriate family relationships in the arrangement of marriages and maintenance of practical relationships (Bourdieu 1977, 53). Given these two systems of reckoning genealogical relationships, the practice of parallel cousin marriage can bring about ambiguities. Bourdieu gives the example of a woman whose husband was both her mother's brother's son (maternal first cousin) *and* related through her paternal great-grandfather (paternal second cousin, grandson of her grandfather's brother), because of a parallel cousin marriage in the previous generation (Bourdieu 1977, 42). Bourdieu argues that both the ethnographers and their (male) informants insist on privileging the official strategy. But doing so hides the way in which individuals can strategically use such relationships. After all, the maternal first cousin relationship is much closer than the paternal second cousin relationship, and this fact may be to someone's advantage.

By endorsing the official rules or norms, ethnographers not only misrepresent the actual patterns and (perhaps unintentionally) reinforce the existing power relationships within the group. They make it impossible to see how individuals act within social structures, and how individuals instrumentally and strategically use the official rules. Rather than being programmed by culture to follow certain routines, people treat elements of their culture—explicit rules, implicit norms, all kinds of symbols and meanings—as elements of their environment. Rules and symbols are manipulated in much the same way as hammers and swords. Rules are resisted, undermined, or contravened as often as they are followed, and when they are followed, it is because doing so presents the greatest advantage in the immediate or strategic context. By emphasizing the way in which actors work within structure to achieve ends that are not socially determined, theorists like Rosaldo and Bourdieu were not falling back into a form of methodological individualism. They held that the social structures were maintained by practices that were not reproduced only by individual choice, and that the cultures informed agent's beliefs and attitudes in deep and important ways. They were arguing for a dynamic, nonreductive relationship between structure and agency, and in so doing, they moved well beyond the semiotic concept of culture that dominated mid-century anthropology.

16.6. CONTEMPORARY MODELS OF CULTURE

While the criticisms of the classical culture concept were deep and telling, anthropologists could not entirely turn away from the idea. In an often-quoted remark, James Clifford captured the discomfort of the eighties, saying that culture "is a deeply compromised idea that I cannot yet do without" (Clifford 1988, 10). After all, the difference among peoples expressed by the theoretical notion of culture was, in an important sense, a part of the phenomena ethnographers encountered. Humans recognize and name group-level differences, and such differences can be very important aspects of the way people interact. Understanding human behavior thus requires something like the culture concept. In response, many anthropologists set about retheorizing culture, and since the 1980s, a variety of suggestions have been put forward. While no single conception has come to dominate the field, there are a number of common themes. We can map the contemporary literature with three models of culture: the neo-Boasian model, the epidemiological model, and practice theory.[2]

16.6.1. The Neo-Boasian Model

The foregoing sections have shown how the problematic features of the culture concept are associated with the semiotic (Bidney's idealist) model of culture which arose mid-century. Proponents of this model tended to treat culture as strongly holistic, ontologically independent of individuals, and determinative of their behavior. A natural response to the criticism, then, would be to return to a conception of culture that predates the semiotic model. Such was the strategy of five anthropologists who published a collection of essays in a 2004 issue of *American Anthropologist*. Calling the project neo-Boasian, they sought to draw out ideas that would help cultural anthropology move beyond the critique.

Boas's conception of culture was different from the later semiotic model insofar as he did not treat cultures as theoretical posits. Because cultures were groups of traits, the issue of cultural boundaries does not arise in the way that it does for the semiotic model of culture. As we have seen, for Boas and his students, cultural boundaries were regarded as permeable and constructed by one group or another for their own purposes. Rethinking the Boasian culture concept in contemporary terms, Ira Bashkow argued that we should conceive of cultural boundaries as created to highlight differences and contrasts among groups of people (Bashkow 2004). People categorize themselves on the basis of a wide variety of criteria. While ethnographic description should recognize local distinctions, they are not bound to such categories: "The old Boasian triad of race, language, and culture ramifies today into a larger set of demarcational viewpoints that include varied constructions of society, polity, economy, geography, interactional fields, collective identities, ethnicity, cultural practice, linguistic codes, communicability and comprehension, and regional networks" (Bashkow 2004, 451). Cultural boundaries are thus interest (or observer) relative. Individuals draw on available traits to identify with, or separate from, each other. Such boundaries may be policed or enforced, but in some contexts individuals may move freely across boundaries and inhabit multiple cultures. The ethnographer should recognize local identities and understand ways that they are maintained, but ethnographic analysis is not bound to find that one demarcational viewpoint is "the" culture. The ethnographer is no more tied to any boundary than the participants;

there may be analytically useful ways of drawing boundaries that are not recognized by the subjects themselves.

The neo-Boasian view inherits a tension from its intellectual forbearers. The Boasians held that traits are both independent of particular cultural collections (hence can be reidentified across time and space) *and* depend on cultural context for their meaning. Responding to the argument that ethnographers had artificially made their subjects consistent and integrated, Bashkow (2004) and Daniel Rosenblatt (2004) argue that Ruth Benedict (one of Boas's leading students) regarded cultural integration as a historically contingent phenomenon. Under the right circumstances, cultures could become coherent and tightly integrated. Integration was not necessary, and when it did happen it was often fragile and unstable. This deflation of "integration" into a fact about some cultures at some times meets the criticism made of the semiotic model of culture, but it also weakens the neo-Boasian's position. "Culture" seems to reduce to "identity." Bashkow recognized this objection and argued against such a reduction. While a group may draw a cultural boundary around itself on the basis of some similarity, culture is more than such identities. Not only do individuals within the community differ, culture forms the background against which difference is meaningful. Bashkow goes so far as to say that "culture is not only the product of but also the precondition for meaningful action, thought, and expression" (Bashkow 2004, 452). This claim appears to conflict with the observer-relativity of cultural boundaries and the contingency of cultural integration. If culture is the precondition of meaningful thought and expression, then it does not seem like the sort of thing that individuals can adopt, shed, or strategically engage.

A second issue, concerning agency, arises for the neo-Boasians in ways that also echo earlier tensions in Boas's thought. True to the earlier Boasian position, the neo-Boasians are pluralistic about the elements that make up a culture. As Bashkow's list of "demarcational viewpoints" indicates, cultures can be identified by a wide range of objects, ideas, values, beliefs, or practices. The question is: What is the relationship between the agents who draw the cultural boundaries and the cultural forms with which they interact? By emphasizing that the agents need not recognize the cultural boundaries drawn by the theorist, the neo-Boasians risk treating the agents as relatively passive. Rosenblatt takes a different path, aligning the neo-Boasian approach with the "practice theory" of Sherry Ortner and Pierre Bourdieu (to be discussed below). The goal is to portray "cultural wholes from the point of view of the dilemmas and possibilities they presented to individual actors" (Rosenblatt 2004, 461). The actors are seen as actively shaping the culture through their action, and in turn, being shaped by it. While these remarks are more satisfactory from the point of view of the structure and agency problem, they highlight the question of cultural integration all over again. Indeed, they vividly raise the question of what such "cultural wholes" are supposed to *be*. As a version of a trait theory, the cultural wholes should be no more than a collection of traits. But what makes something a trait, an element of the culture? Once again, the neo-Boasians seem caught between the recognition of the contingency of cultural boundaries and the importance of an integrated cultural whole.

While the neo-Boasian essays of 2004 were not historically the first responses to the eighties critique of the culture concept, they do, I suggest, have a kind of logical priority. If we are to respond adequately to the critique of the eighties, then we must not think of cultures as theoretical posits with their own explanatory force. Cultural difference must be constituted by something else, and conceiving of culture as an assemblage is the natural alternative. The question is: assemblage of what? This is where the neo-Boasian view is not sufficiently articulated, and it is beholden to unresolved tensions in Boas's own thought. The two other models of culture to be discussed here, the epidemiological model and practice theory, can be viewed as attempts to further specify the traits that compose culture.

16.6.2. The Epidemiological Model

The epidemiological model of culture was proposed by Dan Sperber in his Malinowski Lecture (1985), and developed in *Explaining Culture: A Naturalistic Approach* (1996). Arguing against those who would reify culture, Sperber proposed that the field for anthropological theorizing should be conceptualized as a distribution of representations:

> Just as one can say that a human population is inhabited by a much larger population of viruses, so one can say that it is inhabited by a much larger population of mental representations. Most of these representations are found in only one individual. Some, however, get communicated: that is, first transformed by the communicator into public representations, and then re-transformed by the audience into mental representations. A very small proportion of these communicated representations get communicated repeatedly. Through communication (or, in other cases, through imitations), some representations spread out in a human population, and may end up being instantiated in every member of the population for several generations. Such widespread and enduring representations are paradigmatic cases of cultural representation. (Sperber 1996, 25)

Like the neo-Boasians, Sperber was proposing that we return to a conception of culture that treated cultures as distributions of traits. Sperber makes two apparent advances on the trait theories of the nineteenth and early twentieth centuries. First, he replaces the notion of a "trait" with the notion of a "representation." Sperber is staunchly materialist about representations. As the quotation above suggests, these may be either the mental representations of an individual, or they may be public representations. Mental representations are features of our brains that play a role in our information-processing systems (Sperber 1996, 61). Public representations are also spatio-temporal objects, such as texts, feathered sticks, or patterns of sound waves. While public in the sense of being available to many interpreters, they get their content from the individual mental representations formed from them. The second advance is made possible by the first: By conceptualizing cultural difference as patterns of distribution of representations, he can engage the resources of psychology to explain why some representations are distributed widely and endure (and hence are cultural), while others are individual or fleeting.

The choice of the word *epidemiology* to capture this new attitude toward cultural phenomena reflects both advances over older trait theories. Where the discipline of epidemiology is concerned with the conditions that explain the distribution and propagation of disease, anthropology needs to be concerned with issues of distribution and propagation of representations. And both approach their problems with an eclectic collection of middle-range theories, not by creating grand, unifying theories. Finally, an epidemiological approach is materialist in the sense that "everything that has causal powers owes these powers exclusively to its physical properties" (Sperber 1996, 10). There is no ontological commitment to cultures, norms, rules, values, beliefs, or other nonmaterial entities.

The important upshot of Sperber's epidemiology is that it changes the questions of anthropological theorizing. Anthropological work influenced by the semiotic conception of culture focused on supra-individual entities: systems of belief, social structures, power relations, or patterns of social interaction. An epidemiological approach treats all cultural phenomena as the product of individual representations. The new challenge, then, is to understand why some representations are persistent and widely distributed, for example, why a belief in supernatural beings is so common among human groups. These questions have a natural relationship to research in cognitive psychology, and the epidemiological approach has been adopted by those who seek to use the resources of psychology to explain social phenomena. This kind of work has been quite fruitful in the last two decades. Scott Atran (2002), Pascal Boyer (1994, 2001), Peter Richerson and Robert Boyd (2005), Robert McCauley and Thomas Lawson (2002), Harvey Whitehouse (1995), and others have taken up this challenge and produced very interesting and important research. For example, McCauley and Lawson and Whitehouse have used recent work on memory to explain certain features of ritual performance. Boyer and Atran appeal to cognitive dispositions to represent agency to account for the near-universal belief in supernatural beings. The empirical fecundity of the alliance between cognitive science and anthropology encouraged by an epidemiological model of culture is one of the strongest arguments in its favor.

Perhaps the most important challenge for an epidemiological approach is to account for institutions, implicit norms, and other aspects of culture or society that might be misrepresented or only partially understood by the participants. Julia Tanney points out that there is an ironic similarity between Sperber's materialism and what Bidney called idealism: culture, in Sperber's view, is nothing more than a set of ideas. In his argument for materialism, Sperber complained that marriages are not the kind of thing one can look at (Sperber 1996, 20). Tanney responds:

> But *of course* we can look at marriages: how else would we be able to gossip about them? When I remark on the fact that my friend's marriage seems to be falling apart, I am talking about her relationship, not an idea in her mind. (It is true that her belief in the sanctity of marriage might collapse too but this is logically independent of her collapsing marriage; in fact, it is obvious that my friend's marriage might be falling apart even if she—and others—believes it is sound.) If this kind of observation can be made at home there is no reason why it cannot be made during fieldwork. (Tanney 1998, 673)

Social roles and relationships can have practical consequences that are poorly understood (if understood at all) by those who occupy them. Tanney goes on to say that this is why participant observation is a useful method. By interacting in a practical way, the ethnographer puts herself in a position to make mistakes and disrupt the flow, thereby exposing patterns and implicit norms. Indeed, as Bourdieu argued, asking about beliefs will only garner the official story or dominant point of view. It is difficult, therefore, for an epidemiological model to represent the way in which agents resist, undermine, or exploit features of their social environment, and there seems to be no place for the analysis of institutions, structural constraints on action, or relationships of power and domination.

16.6.3. Practice Theory

An epidemiological model of culture refines the Boasian notion of a trait and supports it with a more robust psychology. It thereby addresses one of the tensions in a Boasian trait theory by discounting the holism and providing a clearer account of trait identity. Practice theory, on the other hand, can be seen as resolving the tension by providing an account of cultural integration that does not reify cultures and provides a more satisfactory account of agency within social structures. The neo-Boasians themselves saw their work aligned with practice theory. Writing about Benedict, Rosenblatt argued that

> her ideas have much in common with the ideas and approaches Sherry Ortner
> has gathered together under the rubric "practice theory" (1984, 1996). Like Pierre
> Bourdieu (1977), Benedict described cultural wholes from the point of view of the
> dilemmas and possibilities they presented to individual actors, and, like him, she
> saw those wholes as shaping the actors—indeed, for her, to some extent, cultural
> wholes exist through the ways they are sedimented in actors. While it is less
> obvious, Benedict also shares with "practice theorists" like Bourdieu, Sahlins
> (1985), Giddens (1979), and Ortner herself a sense that this shaping is mutual: Just
> as the culture shapes individuals, individuals can sometimes shape (and reshape)
> the culture. (Rosenblatt 2004, 461)

The essay by Ortner to which Rosenblatt refers is "Theory in Anthropology since the Sixties" (Ortner 1984), and it is often taken to be the beginning of practice theory. Ortner synthesized several strands of thought, and argued that a turn to practice was emblematic of anthropological theory in the 1980s.

Practice theory tries to split the difference between theories that treat social structures as the primary determinant of action and those that prioritize individual choices. Against the picture of action as rule-following, practice theorists viewed agents as using social norms strategically, conforming when expedient and resisting when necessary. Earlier versions of this approach tended to treat agents individualistically by analyzing motivation in terms of material and political ends. In the 1980s, practice theorists wanted to acknowledge that motivation was deeply informed by the system of norms, expectations, and institutions that make up the culture: "Action is constrained most deeply and systematically by the ways in which culture controls the definitions of the world for actors, limits their conceptual tools, and restricts their emotional repertoires. Culture becomes part of the self" (Ortner 1984, 153). Practice theory thus presented a dynamic answer to the structure and agency dilemma. Social structures and agents are mutually constituted. This perspective opens a new set of questions: "What a practice theory seeks to explain, then, is the genesis, reproduction, and change of form and meaning of a given social/cultural whole" (Ortner 1984, 149).

Ortner's essay appeared before *Writing Culture* was published, just as the concept of culture was beginning to get the scrutiny discussed in section 16.5, above. Ortner's presentation had a strong tendency to reify culture in ways that would soon make anthropologists uncomfortable: The quotations in the foregoing paragraph seem to attribute causal powers to social/cultural wholes. However, practice theory need not be beholden to such an ontology. Contemporary practice theorists have tried to split the difference on the methodological individualism issue, just as they did on the structure-and-agency issue (Schatzki 2001, 5; Rouse 2007, 645). They do so by dissolving the social/cultural whole into a set of ongoing practices, where a practice is understood as a shared set of embodied habits, cognitive capacities, abilities, and implicit (or tacit) understandings. Practices are thus embodied in individual agents and constituted by their actions, especially those patterns of behavior that are routinized or patterned. The set of practices that are found in a community will be interrelated, but they need not be coherent, or even consistent. The object of a practice theoretic analysis is to show how relationships of domination and subordination among the practices exhibited by the agents are reproduced, challenged, or changed, and contradictions in the system often play an important role in the analysis.

One way to understand a practice theoretic model of culture is as replacing the Boasian traits with patterns of behavior. This provides a way to understand the integration of traits. Since practices are embodied in the behavior of agents, the patterns of action will have to be integrated. The character of the interaction among practices, and the extent to which there are conflicts and contradictions embedded in the system, is a question for empirical study. Understanding practices as patterns of behavior, however, opens practice theory to a pair of further difficulties. In *The Social Theory of Practices* (1994), Stephen Turner pointed out that a pattern of practices requires different performances to be identified as part of the same pattern. It is not sufficient, for the purposes of a practice theoretical analysis, that the individual performances are similar in observably salient ways. Practices manifest something deeper: a norm, implicit presupposition, or tacit understanding. This must be transmitted from one individual to another if the practice is to be learned. While accounts of practice conceptualize transmission in a variety of ways, Turner argues that none of them can provide an account of transmission that will support the weight of their theories.

The second sort of problem also concerns the identity of practices. Practices are normative in the sense that individual performances may be correct or incorrect. Their normativity makes practices an attractive replacement for the norms and values that were embedded in the semiotic conception of culture. However, the normativity also creates a logical gap between the norm and any actual set of performances. Given a single set of performances, there is more than one way of expressing *the* practice they exemplify. Performances therefore underdetermine practices (Kripke 1982, Brandom 1994, Rouse 2007). This gerrymandering objection to practices is analogous to the problem of cultural boundaries that infected the semiotic model of culture, but it goes further. Treating different performances as appropriate or inappropriate will specify distinct practice norms; but the practices determine which practices are appropriate. The matter seems circular. The gerrymandering problem goes further because it argues that even if we were to stipulate which set of practices were correct, more than one (nonequivalent) rule would be exemplified. Practices seem epistemologically inscrutable.

Both Turner's argument about transmission and the gerrymandering problem arise when practices are conceived as regularities or patterns of behavior. Joseph Rouse (2002, 2007) has argued that there is an alternative way to conceive of practices, one he finds articulated in Robert Brandom's *Making It Explicit* (1994) and Donald Davidson's later work, and is to be uncovered in appropriate readings of Heidegger and Wittgenstein. In anthropology, something very like Rouse's conception of practice is at work in *The Dialogic Emergence of Culture* (Tedlock and Mannheim 1995). Rouse summarizes the position this way:

> [A] practice is not a regularity underlying its constituent performances, but a pattern of interaction among them that expresses their mutual normative accountability. On the "normative" conception of practices, a performance belongs to a practice if it is appropriate to hold it accountable as a correct or incorrect performance of that practice. Such holding to account is itself integral to the practice, and can likewise be done correctly or incorrectly. If incorrectly, then it would appropriately be accountable in turn, by responding to it as would be appropriate to a mistaken holding-accountable. And so forth. (Rouse 2007, 269–270)

The first point is that performances respond to one another, and this is what constitutes them into a practice. The performances are thus not repetitions of one another, but corrections, elaborations, inferences, or permissions. Each performance is thus already normative insofar as it is a response to a previous performance as correct or incorrect. Moreover, there is a sense in which each subsequent performance is, like taking a turn in a conversation, a reinterpretation of the previous moves. There is no attempt to capture the totality of the pattern that leads to the gerrymandering problem. Performances in the present are responsible to future performances in the sense that they may be criticized (or praised) by them, but nothing in the past determines those future performances. Practices, on this view, are importantly open-ended and indeterminate.

While Rouse's conception of practice arguably overcomes some of the difficulties that faced earlier conceptions, challenges remain. Practices have become so open and indeterminate that their stability becomes a surprising fact. Why do practices persist at all? Here, it might be helpful for practice theorists to look to some of the cognitive mechanisms to which the epidemiological theorists appeal. Such a rapprochement between practice theory and anthropological epidemiology, however, has not yet materialized.

16.7. Conclusion: Transformation of the Philosophical Problems

Throughout this chapter, we have seen various manifestations of two philosophical problems: the methodological individualism issue and the structure-and-agency issue. In their traditional guises, both philosophical debates presuppose a conception of an agent who is, in a sense, self-sufficient. The agents in question have beliefs, intentions, desires, and interests, and their intentional actions proceed from these. While the content of their propositional attitudes might depend on the local culture, the existence of such agents and their properties is independent of culture. Only with such a robust conception of agency in play can the metaphysical question of whether cultures reduce to the actions or intentional states of agents be raised. Similarly, the question of the explanatory priority of social structures or agents only arises if we presuppose that intentional action could be independent of the existence of one structure or another. The striking feature of both epidemiological models and practice theory is that they do not have a robust and traditional notion of the agent. What becomes of these traditional philosophical problems in the context of contemporary models of culture?

With respect to the methodological individualism issue, neither epidemiology nor practice theory proposes an ontological reduction. It is tempting to read Sperber's talk of populations of representations as reductionist, but this would be a mistake. Representations are relational, they are objects that represent something to someone. And not all representations are mental; public representations are a crucial part of the causal chains with which Sperber's epidemiology is concerned. Practice theory, whether it conceives of practices as regularities or the normative interaction of performances, is similarly positioned. Both models thus take some form of relationship to be a fundamental and irreducible feature of the account. At the same time, neither seems to need an ontological category over and above either the performances (for practice theory) or the material objects that constitute representations (for epidemiology). Both views seem content with a materialist ontology. Even more interesting, both views of culture depend on relating social-level phenomena (representations, practices) to something that is, so to speak, below the level of agency. This is clearest in the case of epidemiology: The fundamental explananda are cognitive mechanisms and public representations. While some older versions of practice theory juxtapose agents (as traditionally conceived) with social structures, the newer versions take agents to be created by structures. This is more striking if one adopts the kind of Brandomian account of content that Rouse uses as the basis of his account of practice. Once again, agency arises from the interaction of those capacities that make practices possible and the social practices themselves.

With respect to the structure-and-agency issue, both epidemiological models and practice theories have something analogous to structure, even if they have dispensed with a conception of culture/society as a system of rules. What corresponds to structure in an epidemiological view is the distribution of traits, but these distributions have little or no explanatory value. On the contrary, they stand in need of explanation. At the same time, epidemiological models of culture do not emphasize agency in their explanations either. For Boyd and Richerson, a notion of choice is operative in their analyses, but it is a rather thin notion that plays a minimal role. For Sperber or Atran, agent choices play no role: The explananda are subpersonal cognitive mechanisms. For an epidemiological model, then, it seems that neither structure nor agency has explanatory priority. Practice theories, on the other hand, give substantial explanatory value to practices, and these stand in for the structures of traditional theory. Their distinctive advance on these views, however, is to treat the practices and the performances as mutually constitutive. Neither has explanatory priority over the other across the board, and the direction of the explanatory relationship seems to depend on the context and what needs to be explained. This position becomes even more nuanced as we move to the kind of interactive conception of practices recommended by Rouse. The capacity to make intentional choices must be constituted by the subpersonal capacities that make performance possible, and the practices that give them content. Once again, we start to lose our grip on what would count as the agency side of the problem.

Contemporary models of culture are a fertile ground for reformulating the epistemological and metaphysical issues of the social sciences. Because they both elide robust, traditional conceptions of individual agency, the issues of methodological individualism and structure-and-agency do not arise in their classic forms. Analogous issues do arise: Both views are saddled with an ontological position analogous to non-reductive materialism in the philosophy of mind. Practice theory faces the further problem of untangling the explanatory relationship between practices and performances. These problems are new ones, not the philosophical chestnuts with which we are familiar. They are, therefore, important topics of continuing philosophical research.

NOTES

1. This quotation makes clear that, when put into contemporary philosophical jargon, Bidney's realism would be described as a form of *anti*-realism, or better, reductionism, about culture. His idealism is *realist* insofar as it takes culture to exist in addition to the individuals who inhabit it.

2. This division is not intended to be exhaustive. These three are important and widespread ideas, and they are also interesting from the point of view of the philosophy of social science.

REFERENCES

Asad, Talal, ed. 1973. *Anthropology and the Colonial Encounter*. London: Ithaca Press.

Atran, Scott. 2002. *In Gods We Trust: The Evolutionary Landscape of Religion*. Oxford: Oxford University Press.

Bashkow, Ira. 2004. "A Neo-Boasian Conception of Cultural Boundaries." *American Anthropologist* 106 (3): 443–58.

Bidney, David. 1942. "On the Philosophy of Culture in the Social Sciences." *Journal of Philosophy* 39 (17): 449–57.

Bidney, David. 1944. "On the Concept of Culture and Some Cultural Fallacies." *American Anthropologist* 46 (1): 30–44.

Boas, Franz. 1887. "Occurence of Similar Inventions in Areas Wide Apart." *Science* 9 (224): 485–86.

Boas, Franz. 1901. "The Mind of Primitive Man." *Journal of American Folklore* 14 (52): 1–11.

Boas, Franz. [1896] 1940. "The Limitations of the Comparative Method of Anthropology." In *Race, Language and Culture*, G. W. Stocking, ed. New York: Macmillan.

Bourdieu, Pierre. 1977. *Outline of a Theory of Practice*. Cambridge: Cambridge University Press.

Boyer, Pascal. 1994. *The Naturalness of Religious Ideas: A Cognitive Theory of Religion*. Berkeley: University of California Press.

Boyer, Pascal. 2001. *Religion Explained: The Evolutionary Origins of Religious Thought*. New York: Basic Books.

Brandom, Robert. 1994. *Making It Explicit*. Cambridge, MA: Harvard University Press.

Burling, Robbins. 1964. "Cognition and Componential Analysis: God's Truth or Hocus'Pocus?" *American Anthropologist* 66 (1): 20–8.

Clifford, James. 1988. *The Predicament of Culture: Twentieth-Century Ethnography, Literature, and Art*. Cambridge, MA: Harvard University Press.

Clifford, James, and George Marcus, eds. 1986. *Writing Culture: The Poetics and Politics of Ethnography*. Berkeley: University of California Press.

Durkheim, Émile. [1912] 1915. *The Elementary Forms of the Religious Life*. Trans. J. W. Swain. London: George Allen & Unwin.

Durkheim, Émile. [1895] 1938. *The Rules of the Sociological Method*. S. Solovay and J. Mueller, trans. New York: The Free Press.

Geertz, Clifford. 1973. "Thick Description: Toward and Interpretive Theory of Culture." In *The Interpretation of Cultures*. New York: Basic Books.

Giddens, Anthony. 1979. *Central Problems in Social Theory: Action, Structure, and Contradiction in Social Analysis*. Cambridge: Cambridge University Press.

Goodenough, Ward. 1965. "Yankee Kinship Terminology: A Problem in Componential Analysis." *American Anthropologist* 67 (5): 259–87.

Harris, Marvin. 1968. *The Rise of Anthropological Theory*. New York: Thomas Y. Crowell.

Hymes, Dell, ed. 1969. *Reinventing Anthropology*. New York: Pantheon Books.

Kripke, Saul A. 1982. *Wittgenstein on Rules and Private Language*. Cambridge, MA: Harvard University Press.

Kroeber, A. L., and Clyde Kluckhohn. [1952] 1963. *Culture: A Critical Review of Concepts and Definitions*. New York: Vintage.

Kroeber, Alfred Louis. 1917. "The Superorganic." *American Anthropologist* 19 (2): 163–213.

Lowie, Robert. [1917] 1929. *Culture and Ethnology*. New York: Peter Smith.

Lowie, Robert. 1937. *The History of Ethnological Theory*. New York: Holt, Rinehart and Winston.

Malinowski, Bronislaw. 1922. *Argonauts of the Western Pacific*. New York: E. P. Dutton.

McCauley, Robert N., and E. Thomas Lawson. 2002. *Bringing Ritual to Mind: Psychological Foundations of Cultural Forms*. Cambridge: Cambridge University Press.

Murdock, George Peter. 1949. *Social Structure*. New York: Macmillan.

Ortner, Sherry. 1984. "Theory in Anthropology Since the Sixties." *Comparative Studies in Society and History* 26 (1): 126–66.

Ortner, Sherry. 1996. *Making Gender*. Boston: Beacon Press.

Quine, Willard van Orman. 1960. *Word and Object*. Cambridge, MA: The MIT Press.

Radcliffe-Brown, A. R. [1922] 1933. *The Andaman Islanders*. Cambridge: Cambridge University Press.

Radin, Paul. [1933] 1987. *The Method and Theory of Ethnology*. South Hadley, MA: Bergin & Garvey.

Richerson, Peter, and Robert Boyd. 2005. *Not by Genes Alone: How Culture Transformed Human Evolution*. Chicago: University of Chicago Press.

Rosaldo, Renato. 1989. *Culture and Truth: The Remaking of Social Analysis*. Boston: Beacon Press.

Rosenblatt, Daniel. 2004. "An Anthropology Made Safe for Culture: Patterns of Practice and the Politics of Difference in Ruth Benedict." *American Anthropologist* 106 (3): 459–72.

Rouse, Joseph. 2002. *How Scientific Practices Matter*. Chicago: University of Chicago Press.

Rouse, Joseph. 2007. "Practice Theory." In *The Philosophy of Anthropology and Sociology*, S. Turner and M. Risjord, eds. Amsterdam: Elsevier.

Sahlins, Marshall. 1985. *Islands of History*. Chicago: Chicago University Press.

Sapir, Edward. 1924. "Culture, Genuine and Spurious." *The American Journal of Sociology* 29 (4): 401–29.

Schatzki, Theodore R. 2001. "Introduction: Practice Theory." In *The Practice Turn in Contemporary Theory*, T. Schatzki, K. Knorr Cetina, and E. von Savigny, eds. London: Routledge.

Sperber, Dan. 1985. "Anthropology and Psychology: Towards an Epidemiology of Representations." *Man (NS)* 20 (1): 73–89.

Sperber, Dan, and Deirdre Wilson. 1986. *Relevance: Communication and Cognition*. Cambridge, MA: Harvard University Press.

Sperber, Daniel. 1996. *Explaining Culture: A Naturalistic Approach*. Oxford: Blackwell.

Tanney, Julia. 1998. "Investigating Cultures: A Critique of Cognitive Anthropology." *The Journal of the Royal Anthropological Institute* 4 (4): 669–88.

Tedlock, Dennis, and Bruce Mannheim, eds. 1995. *The Dialogic Emergence of Culture*. Urbana: University of Illinois Press.

Turner, Stephen. 1994. *The Social Theory of Practices*. Chicago: University of Chicago Press.

Tylor, Edward B. 1871. *Primitive Culture: Researches into the Development of Mythology, Philosophy, Religion, Language, Art, and Custom*. 3d American ed., 1889 ed. 2 vols. Vol. 1. New York: Holt.

Wallace, Anthony F. C. 1961. *Culture and Personality*. New York: Random House.

White, Leslie. 1949. *The Science of Culture*. New York: Grove Press.

Whitehouse, Harvey. 1995. *Inside the Cult: Religious Innovation and Transmission in Papua New Guinea*. Oxford: Oxford University Press.

CHAPTER 17

···

NORMS

···

DAVID HENDERSON

17.1. INTRODUCTION

···

Social scientists (and their philosophical fellow travelers) have talked of norms in a number of descriptive and explanatory contexts. Their talk of norms clusters into several broad general categories.

Sometimes one talks of norms when merely describing some gross behavioral regularity within a group. (I am here using 'behavioral' broadly to include intentional actions like expressing agreement, voting, lobbying, or saving and spending, as well as more narrowly behavioral matters such as maintaining relative interpersonal distances during everyday interaction.) On this usage, a norm (common modifiers include cultural norm, or behavioral norm) characterizes some pattern in (perhaps meaningful) behavior, and perhaps in responses to deviations from that pattern. Call these *brute behavioral norms*.

There are three ways in which brute behavioral norms can figure in the social sciences. First, they can simply be of interest when characterizing certain folk—among the *P*, folk tend to *A* in circumstances *C*, and to get uncomfortable or unpleasant when one does not do so. Such can be interesting facts. However, this descriptive use is just a beginning. Second, brute behavioral norms might serve as phenomena to be explained. Some of the ways in which brute behavioral norms can feature as explananda are discussed in sections 17.2 and 17.3. Third, in a very limited fashion, brute behavioral norms can feature as explanans. But, here a caution is needed: It is *not* explanatory of some action of some agent to say that it conforms to some brute behavioral norm in that agent's population—as if characterizing that norm provided itself an explanatory generalization, so that merely subsuming the case under the brute-behavioral generalization would be explanatory. The generalization characterizing the brute behavioral norm merely characterizes a pattern of behavior and indicates that this pattern is commonly found in the agent's population. Rather than explaining individual or group behavior, this generalization leaves one with two explanation-seeking questions: (1) Why is the behavior common in the relevant population? (2) Why does the agent in particular engage in this behavior? When reflecting on how one might answer such questions, one can see that a characterization of the brute behavioral norm might have a very limited role in explanations, and then only when combined with other resources. A given agent's behavior is conditioned by the agent's expectations and preferences. So, insofar as common behaviors within a population condition the expectations and preferences of folk in that population, brute behavioral norms might feature in explanation of agents' actions. They provide the conditions for the learning, transmission, or "replication" of certain expectations and preferences, perhaps. To the extent that we understand these processes of learning, transmission, or replication, within humans, information about brute behavioral norms can provide information about the conditions in which such processes work to yield agents with the relevant expectations and preferences—and thus agents who conform to the brute behavioral norm. This in turn might afford an explanation of persistence of a brute-behavioral norm. But all this points in the direction of a more powerful way of thinking about norms.

A second broad way of thinking about norms affords richer explanatory possibilities in the social sciences. Often one talks of norms roughly as something rule-like—something that represents and prescribes (or proscribes) a way of behaving. The norm-as-rule, serving both to pick out some set of behaviors and to prescribe or proscribe behaviors of that sort, must be learned or internalized, acquired or adopted, by most (or some) in a population. In being adopted by enough of the relevant folk (and perhaps associated with expectations of sanctions for violations), such a norm has a place in the explanation for why there is some brute behavioral norm found among the relevant people. Here, brute behavioral norms are explananda, and descriptions of these norms-as-rules feature in their explanation.[1] Of course, norms-as-rule also can be the topic of an explanation. Because norms-as-rules strike me as a particularly powerful and fecund theoretical topic (both as explanans and as explananda) they will be my primary focus here. When I write simply of norms, I will be referring to norms-as-rules.

When one thinks clearly about the crude conception of norms-as-rules expressed above, one should feel a certain mix of caution and ambition—as one may wonder how seriously to take various components of that crude formulation. What kind of thing are the rules which are held by those who have learned a norm? What kind of representation are they? In what sense is one and the same representation/prescription learned and shared? How determinately does this learned or shared representation prescribe and direct some particular behaviors/actions in circumstances? How are they learned—or transmitted, or disseminated? With what psychological states do they need to be combined (within those holding them) in order for them to eventuate in the prescribed behavior? If anyone feels that their understanding of several of these matters is tenuous, and all should, then that person should feel at least some caution in freely talking about norms. This is not to say that they should stop talking about norms. Rather, one should aspire to a fuller understanding.

17.2. BICCHIERI'S ACCOUNT OF NORMS AS RULES

Among the more sophisticated discussions of this norms-as-rules approach is that of Bicchieri (2006). Her account, together with the questions above, provide the framework for my discussion here. She distinguishes three kinds of rule-like norms: social norms, descriptive norms, and conventions. In each case, the norm in question is said to be a kind of behavioral rule, one for which enough agents have a conditional preference for conformity. The conditional preferences are for following the rule, provided that sufficiently many others in the relevant population follow it (and perhaps also evaluate and sanction performances in terms of it). As Bicchieri tells the story, when individuals follow the rule, they do so in view of these conditional preferences (whose prevalence is partly constitutive of the norm) and expectations they may have indicating others (in the relevant population) generally conform to the rule (and expect conformity themselves). Thus, when sufficiently many have the conditional preferences, the known rule is a norm. When an agent holds the norm ("knows" the rule and has the associated conditional preference for conforming with it) and has the associated expectations regarding others in the population, the agent will explicably conform to the rule. When sufficiently many of the norm holders within the population have such expectations, a brute behavioral norm would result and be explicable in terms of the known rule, together with the preferences and expectations of sufficiently many of the population. That is, the brute behavioral norm would be explicable in terms of the rule-like norm.

In Bicchieri's taxonomy, the differing kinds of rule-norms each involve a rule that is fitting to a general kind of choice situation. (The choice situation itself might be understood in terms of a class of decision-theoretic games.) Here is her characterization of *social norms*, which are norms dealing with mixed-motive games. Social norms transform the mixed-motive game into a coordination game—and they serve to settle on which equilibrium (within that coordination game) folk are to coordinate (Bicchieri 2006, 33–4).

> Let R be a behavioral rule for situations of type S, where S can be represented as a mixed-motive game. We say that R is a social norm in a population P, if there exists a sufficiently large subset $P_{cf} \subseteq P$, such that for each individual $i \in P_{cf}$:
>
> 1. Contingency—i knows that R exists and applies to the situations of type S,
> 2. Conditional Preferences—i prefers to conform to R in situations of type S, given that (the empirical and normative expectations below are jointly satisfied):
>   a. Empirical Expectations—i believes that some sufficiently large subset of the population conforms to R in S
>   and either
>   b. Normative Expectations—i believes that a sufficiently large subset of the population expects i to conform in situations of type S,
>   or

b.́ Normative Expectations with sanctions—i believes that a sufficiently large subset of P expects I to conform in situations of type S, prefers S to conform, and may sanction behavior (Bicchieri 2006, 11.)[2]

On this account, there can be a social norm without it being followed—this explication of the notion of a social norm only requires that the members of P_{cf}, the sufficiently large subset of the population, have a conditional preference for following R. On the other hand, "A social norm R is followed by a population P if there exists a sufficiently large subset $P_f \subseteq P_{cf}$ such that for each individual $i \in P_f$, conditions 2(a) and either 2(b) or 2(b') are met for i" (Bicchieri 2006, 11).[3]

For a stable social norm, some of the explanatory relations are easy to trace in outline. When a given agent holding a norm thinks or expects that the conditions on the preference are satisfied, the agent conforms to the rule. When enough of the agents in a given population have such understandings, preferences and expectations, the norm is widely conformed to—thus the corresponding brute behavioral norm obtains (and is partially explained by the norm-as-rule). Initiates in a population characterized by such a brute behavioral norm then may be expected to come to know the rule, to have the corresponding preferences, and to come to expect that others will conform. Thus, the behavior of individuals may be explained with reference to the social norms in several ways. Insofar as individuals acquire the understandings and conditional preferences (the widespread prevalence of which makes for a social norm), and insofar as they acquire expectations (either on the basis of communicated commitments or observation of others' behaviors), their individual and coordinated behavior might be readily explicable. That there is a norm, and in particular, a norm widely conformed to, can presumably serve as a part of the explanation for the continued or iterated widespread learning of the relevant rule and acquisition of the relevant expectations, and thus for the stability of the coordinated behavior. (Acquisition of the conditional preferences may be the tricky part of an explanation of norms-as-rules—particularly in the case of social rules, as it will be necessary to explain how despite the payoffs associated with the relevant mixed-motive game, agents come to have conditional preferences for the cooperative solution prescribed by the norm.[4])

Explaining the stability or persistence of norms may be relatively straightforward (at least once one can readily account for the conditional preferences), but it would seem more difficult to explain how there can arise in a population widespread conformity to a new rule-like norm. For there to emerge a new norm, some behavioral rule must be widely disseminated and learned across a sufficiently large proportion of the relevant population (when such a rule was not earlier exhibited in the relevant population), and these folk must come to have a conditional preference for conforming to that rule. For it to be conformed to would then require that they also come to expect widespread conformity to the rule on the part of their cohorts, when such behavior was not hitherto widely exhibited in the population. Bicchieri (2006, chapters 4–6) explores what forms of communication (or other mechanisms) might empirically prove effective here.

17.3. INTERFIELD THEORIES

Clearly, explanation in terms of norms-as-rules is not far removed from explanation that turns on individual psychology—after all, these norms are matters of several psychological features being had by sufficiently many in the relevant population: some learned behavioral rule and some conditional preference. Further to issue in behavior, individuals must have various expectations. This is *not* to say that such an account is reductive—the rule is a norm only if these psychological features are sufficiently widespread in the population, and by its nature the rule and preferences relate to a structured choice situation, a game, that is itself social in character. The psychological features will likely be widespread only insofar as there is significant social-level phenomena in play—for example, in the payoffs that result from rule adherence in a population, and in the dissemination of the rule (and expectations) across the population. Dissemination, it seems, would best be understood in complementary social and psychological terms. Thus, rather than being reductive, Bicchieri's account of norms as rules seems to invite theorizing that integrates the economic study of norms in economics with various other fields, some of them generally psychological. Such theorizing makes for what Darden and Maull (1977) term an "interfield theory" (see also Darden 2006). This is to say that Bicchieri's approach calls for an interfield theory of norms in which one studies and understands phenomena using the resources of several fields.

It is worthwhile pausing to unpack Darden's conception of an interfield theory—and to keep it in mind as we discuss norms-as-rules, because much of the promise and fecundity of Bicchieri's exemplary norms-as-rules account turns on this: It represents a particularly plausible start on the needed interfield theory.

Fields are areas of scientific study and results. They are characterized by a central problem (or problems), a domain of items posited in characterizing a range of phenomena associated with the central problem, certain conceptions of how to solve open problems, and various techniques and methods. They are not to be identified with some one theory, and may or may not have a central theory—perhaps they have several competing theories. An interfield theory relates and integrates two (or more) fields in one theory. To illustrate, Darden and Maull (1977) discuss how theories having to do with chromosomes served to integrate work in genetics and cytology—they also discuss theories of the regulation of gene expression as instances in which "no one [antecedently existing] field had all the concepts and techniques to answer all the questions that arose concerning the phenomenon" (Darden 2006, 142). It is common for interfield theories to emerge when several fields "share an interest in explaining different aspects of the same phenomena" (Darden 2006, 133). Commonly they arise when "questions arise about [a phenomena central to] a field which cannot be answered with the technology and concepts of that field" (Darden 2006, 134). Arguably this is the case with the economic study of norms, as will become apparent as we trace some of what Bicchieri gets by pursing that theory that integrates elements from the economic study of norms with various fields in psychology (see also Guala 2007, 266–72).[5] This integrative approach should be taken as a worthwhile model for the social sciences generally.[6]

17.4. PSYCHOLOGICAL REALISM

It is one of the great strengths of this norms-as-rules approach that it invites or demands a concern for psychological realism concerning the elements involved— the rules, the preferences, the expectations, how these might be formed or conditioned, and how these might be represented in agents. In exemplary fashion, Bicchieri is attentive to psychological work regarding how local environmental factors can provide individuals with information about what people do, or about peoples' evaluations of others' actions, and can thus make salient matters on which norm adherence depends (Bicchieri 2006, 63–70, 52–175). She recognizes the significance of issues regarding just "how norms are represented in memory" and how the situational salience of competing (previously learned) normative models or rules would depend on the dynamics of memory (70–3). She is interested in the way in which situations are interpreted so as to prime the application of a rule. In such ways an interfield approach to norms-as-rules can avoid the pitfall of offering merely some convenient just-so story about coordination at the social level. It provides the promise of significant integration with work in cognitive psychology and experimental economics. As we will see, it allows one to engage in a range of informed experimental manipulations to test ideas about social and descriptive norms.

Against this background there are several issues that warrant special attention. One (the subject of the next section) is how to best understand talk of rules or behavioral rules. A second (the subject of section 17.6) turns on a point that might seem obvious, but should always be made explicit whenever talking of norms: that the norms in question need not themselves be normatively appropriate—they are not correctness-makers in any sense.

17.5. RULES?

What are behavioral rules? What is it to "know" that some rule exists? Bicchieri provides little systematic exposition of what these posits amount to. One can find some tantalizing hints scattered about her discussions, but her limited exposition regarding these matters, so pivotal to the rules-as-norms approach, is at least a little disconcerting. Apparently, one should conclude that talk of rules serves as something of a placeholder awaiting empirical investigation and elaboration—and this is to the good. Still, more can be done in framing the empirical investigation that is ultimately called for. In this section, I pursue a relatively constructive project: clarifying in outline how to understand the posits of rules and of knowledge of rules within the norms-as-rules framework.

To begin with, one should notice that talk of rules and known rules points to some matter on which one plausibly has some workable commonsensical sense for cases. Second, one can list the general theoretical demands of the norms-as-rules approach. One is not looking for an a priori account of what norms (or behavioral rules) necessarily are. And, at this juncture, one should not demand a fully fleshed out account. Instead, one seeks an orienting articulation of theoretical commitments of this approach. These are theoretical commitments that, if the theoretical approach is ultimately to prove empirically adequate, can be elaborated in related empirical work. The theoretical approach has us positing certain entities—rules—that play certain causal roles in folks' cognitive processes. What one here is looking for is, in effect, a kind of minimal characterization of the entities posited in terms of what these entities do in the production of coordinated behavior.[7] Finally, in light of one's sense for many apparent instances and noninstances of rules and of knowledge of them, and in light of this crude understanding of how these entities perform their signature causal roles in the production of coordinated social action, one could reasonably insist on an openness to letting empirical inquiry fill out our understanding of how these rules, and how folks' knowledge of them, are realized in human cognitive agents and in human society. In this way, one would look to ongoing work in psychology, cognitive science, and related disciplines to sort out more determinately what manner of psychological/cognitive things these rules are, and what knowledge of them amounts to. If the approach bears out under this empirical elaboration, one will have achieved a richer understanding of the entities or states that perform the causal role envisioned in the norms-as-rules approach.[8]

In the norms-as-rules account, one posits that one and the same thing—a rule—is shared and known by a wide portion of the relevant population. Knowledge of this one entity is then supposedly enough to shape one's behavior—at least provided the agent possesses the preferences and expectations mentioned above. (Again, the preference and expectations have to do with, and are doubtless conditioned by, social phenomena such as common evaluations—and perhaps sanctions—by others in the relevant group.) The knowledge of the rule (together with the preferences and triggering expectations) supposedly conditions behavior in way that yields a reasonable uniformity in behavior within the relevant subset of the salient population, and affords a parallel uniformity in the perception of this uniform conformity with the rule. If empirical sense cannot be made of this much, the whole approach to norms as rules seems a nonstarter.

Thus, for one's theory of norms-as-rules to warrant empirical development, it must be plausible in light of what we generally know at this point that there is some one entity, the rule so understood, that (1) is disseminated and comes to be known by some wide segment of the population, (2) is such that a wide segment of the population also have a conditional preference for actions conforming to it, and (3) is the sort of entity that can function in human cognition so as to shape behavior in a reasonably determinate and regular fashion (fitting to the sort of social regularity observed in paradigmatic commonsensical instances of norm conformity). One might imagine or entertain various stories about what these entities—these rules, functionally understood in terms of this composite causal role—will turn out to be. That is, one might entertain various ways of understanding what it is to learn, know, share, and have one's preferences and behavior informed by, these shared things. Ultimately, what we face here is an empirical issue: what cognitive psychology allows one to make sense of an entity performing these functional roles—and what, more concretely, are the dissemination, holding, preferring, and behavior guiding processes in which rules feature. To the extent that one can integrate the economic (anthropological, sociological, and related) study of norms with the relevant branches of cognitive psychology, one will have a powerful account that can feature in multiple explanatory applications.

However, in light of certain very general things that we presently know about human similarities within groups, about their differences even within groups, about their learning histories, about what they would have learned (differently and similarly), and about related largely empirical matters, one can manage to say something interesting about what rules and knowledge of them must be like if they are to conform to the minimal functional characterization just set out. There are three very general ways in which one might initially think to understand talk of rules—three kinds of things that one might think could serve the functional role envisioned—but only one is really promising on informed reflection.

First, one might suppose that rules are semantic entities—contents that prescribe or proscribe some class of actions. To do what is needed within the norms-as-rules approach, the content must be sufficient to (a) direct agents in undertaking the relevant, more or less determinate, class of actions, and (b) identify actions in others as conforming or not conforming. For there to be a norm, there then would need to be representations with such content in the minds of sufficiently many within the relevant population. Such representations of a given rule might differ across individuals in their neural, or syntactic, or physical character, and in various other respects, but these differing underlying entities each would need to have a shared content. Call this the *mental-content understanding of rules*.

Alternatively, one might imagine that a rule is the representation itself—rather than its content—the neurologically or syntactically individuated state in the mind or brain of the agents—some one syntactical or neurological state that is uniform across those in the know. Here, one distinguishes (as is common) the semantic content of one's representation from the types of physical entities or types that serve in the language-like representations having contents—one distinguishes the semantic content from the syntactical representation. This distinction is crucial to computational cognitive science, and to disciplines that draw on its theoretical framework. The distinction is important in much cognitive science that does not draw on narrowly computational models—as one there continues to distinguish between the content of representations and the diverse physical token that can have any such content. Call this the *syntactical-type understanding of rules.* The syntactical-type understanding would seem to demand implausibly much for two individuals to count as knowing the same rule. It would seem to have the consequence that individuals share remarkably few rules, and that folk should not expect others to follow the same rule.

Finally, one might understand the rule as some common expression in a natural language—"Be fair," for example, or "Don't litter." Plausibly, one counts as knowing the rule when one is able to competently apply the common action description to a significant range of clear cases and noncases. One conditionally prefers conforming one's actions to the rule when one prefers to engage in instances to which that public language description applies (provided that enough others understand that description sufficiently similarly and conform themselves). Better perhaps, folk with the conditional preference in question prefer to do *that* sort of thing (you know, "being fair") provided enough others do pretty much the same. Call this the *public-language understanding of rules.*

If one were to approach these matters from the perspective of computational cognitive science, one might suppose that rules are formal algorithms that would, if put in play, direct certain responses to particular situations. If rules were this sort of thing, then talk of shared rules would suggest that the cognitive systems of relevant folk each contain and conditionally run one and the same subroutine—the same bit of program or code. Norms then are said to involve a conditional preference for conformity. This would amount to a bit of code that initiates the system's running the rule-subroutine when the system comes to represent the social world as having enough folk who are acting as if they were running the same subroutine. The computationalist understands a behavioral rule as a particular bit of code—perhaps one determinate set of production rules—and knowing the behavioral rule amounts to having that bit of code inscribed in a knowing agent's brain.

Some readers may find this a natural presumption; I do not. Consider some examples of everyday norms. Bicchieri, for example, supposes that commonly folk in a cultural setting share a norm of fairness. But it strikes me as quite implausible that each of these folk who apparently share a rule need be endowed with a computationally identical fairness-associated subroutine. There would seem to be differences in learning histories that surely make for computational differences. If one instead thinks of the representation as a pattern of activation across a neural network, then one again confronts diversity—as the diversity of neural bases resulting from diverse learning histories is undeniable.[9] If instead one thinks in terms of representations as sets of encoded paradigms (or prototypes, or exemplars) together with an algorithm for judging similarity, the same conclusion is unavoidable. Folk can differ significantly in their paradigms or exemplars. Roughly, then, there are likely to be deep syntactical differences, or significant differences in the (computational or neural) representational states, across folk that are supposed to share a rule on any reasonable version of the norms-as-rules approach. The syntactical-type approach would seem to individuate rules in far too fine-grained a manner for our purposes. (I mention this approach for heuristic reasons: It illustrates how the demand for sharing of rules should constrain how we seek to make empirical sense of talk of rules.)

The remaining approaches seem more promising. Obviously both allow for sharing in the face of differences in underlying computational routines, realizations in neural nets, and the like. So let us focus on these. They present some parallel issues.

I would suppose that one need not share the same language to have the same norm. (For example, it is possible that some in Brazil have the same norms for gift exchanges as some in Argentina who yet speak different languages.) With a little tolerance, one adopting the public-language understanding could allow for people to know the same rule across languages, as long as the relevant action descriptions are themselves intertranslatable. However, intertranslatability is presumably a function of semantic similarity. Thus, this tolerance yields a public-language understanding of rules that is very closely related to the mental content approach: to know the same rule on the public-language understanding would turn on some facility with a bit of language expressing the same content.

This tolerant public-language approach to shared rules (keying on intertranslatability) or a parallel tolerant mental-content approach (keying on what is sometimes called wide-content) certainly would avoid the problem of individuating rules in too fine grained a manner to serve the purposes of the norms-as-rules approach. However, a little reflection will reveal that they have the opposite tendency. To see this, a little background on philosophical thinking about semantic content and intertranslatability may be helpful.

People certainly may have acquired different, sometimes very different, beliefs about some matter. For example, one person might believe (and say) that a progressive tax (and some similar policies) is unfair. Another person might believe (and say) that a progressive tax is the only fair tax. As one explored their respective beliefs about fairness, one might find extensive differences. However, it is standard to judge that their differences are over a shared subject—what is fair. When they do agree on a case (suppose they both believe and say that the division of goods in some particular case would be fair) we say that they say the same thing—that their words and thoughts there have the same content. If one is not tolerant of differences in such ways, one ends with an apparent incommensurability of what is said and thought that makes it hard to understand our disagreements as well as any agreement. To accommodate these points, it is common to distinguish the *concept* (of *fairness*, for example) and the various folks' *conceptions* (of fairness). People can share a concept even when differing significantly in their conceptions of the subject. In translating across languages, one tries to look past differences in conception to similarity or sameness of concept. When the same concepts are in play, the parallel utterances and beliefs have the same content—even when the parties have some significantly differing conceptions. Now, there certainly are tricky aspects of this story—but one should grant that it provides a good rough picture of the judgments one makes about cases, and various approaches to meaning and translation (both internalistic and externalistic) will need to make sense of roughly this much. What is more, without further details, it is enough to raise challenging questions about both the tolerant public-language and tolerant mental-content approach to rules.

This tolerant public-language approach to rules and their sharing is obscure in several respects. Consider: for some natural language terms—"fair," "just," and "morally good," are each examples—we typically allow that others can have a word in their language that is rightly translated into our language using that word, while they yet can disagree significantly over what are the clear cases to which the term applies. Indeed, even without intertranslatability across languages being at issue, even when dealing with one natural language and one term such as "fair," competent speakers of a language can disagree (even disagree violently) over what are clear cases (of fairness, or of justice). However, when agents differ in this way, it seems strained to say that they share or know one and the same rule. Such tolerance strains the commonsense grasp we have on the notion of knowing rules.

Further, were one to say that agents differing significantly in conceptions yet share one rule, then talk of rules (so understood) could contribute little to explaining either individual behavior or coordinated behavior and brute behavioral norms. For a given rule, so tolerantly understood, can issue in vastly many sets of behaviors—with the sets varying with the different conceptions that different individuals may have of the matter. Instead, what might contribute to explaining individual behavior would be something on the order of the particular individual's conception. What would contribute to the explanation of a brute behavioral norm would be the *similarity* in some set of individuals' *conceptions*. The rule, as (tolerantly understood linguistic entity), would be largely impotent. Were rules understood as conceptions (or instances of similarity classes of conceptions, perhaps) rules would not be impotent.

To make the above point less abstract, suppose that rules are encoded in sets of exemplars and similarity sensibilities. But, tolerantly understood, individuals having very different sets of exemplars and senses for similarity are thought to share the rule—say, "be fair." As a result, individuals following the same rule, tolerantly understood, would do a vast array of things. One might seek to forcibly resist the collection of "that inherently unfair progressive tax," while another might lobby against any tax that was "unfairly nonprogressive." What explains these differing behaviors are the differing conceptions individuals possess, not the tolerantly understood concept they supposedly share.

Notice also that the norms-as-rules approach requires agents to have conditional preferences for conforming to rules, provided others do similarly, but it is implausible that such preference would have to do with conformity with rules so tolerantly individuated. If I have a preference for conforming to the rule of fairness, provided enough others do so, it seems reasonable that my conditional preference turns on these others understanding fairness in a way *relatively similar to* the way I understand it. If their expected behavior does not seem largely fair to me (although it might seem fair to them), then the conditions on my preference do not seem satisfied.

It should be obvious that these problems for a simple tolerant public-language conception of rules also are challenges for the mental-content approach to rules. As long as conceptions can vary significantly while agents are using the same concepts and holding the same content, the mental-content approach will not provide rules with the functional profile posited in the norms-as-rules account. The tolerantly individuated rules will not issue in sufficiently similar behavior to make for coordination, or to specify the conditions on agents' preferences. Again, it would be the more finely individuated things—something like conceptions—that would have the fitting functional profile. What might contribute to explaining an individual's behavior would be something on the order of that individual's *conception* of what would count as conformity on the matter. At the same time, in those cases in which one would commonsensically judge that folk shared a norm, and where the rules-as-norms approach makes plausible empirical sense, one would also judge that the folk in question possessed at least reasonably similar conceptions (allowing that their conceptions varied only somewhat). What then would contribute to the explanation of a brute behavioral norm would be the *similarity* across individuals' *conceptions*. Of course conceptions can also be understood as semantic things—just semantic things that are more cognitively more faceted and less tolerantly individuated than contents commonly are.

The public-language understanding is obscure in a further respect—one that need not trouble the mental-content understanding of rules. It is often remarked that different cultures develop different conventions for maintaining comfortable interpersonal distances while interacting. Most, including Bicchieri, count such conventions as norms—and thus posit shared rules. However, in the matter of interpersonal differences, there may well be no standard linguistic expression for the rule among those who conform to the convention. Here is a further reason to favor the mental-content approach to the public-language approach. One might insist that in such matters, the various agents have learned something, or at least some similar things. They certainly have acquired a sense for comfortable distances, and there may be significant similarity across folk in their respective senses for comfortable distance—and one might plausibly suppose that there is content here.

One can say at least this: While the public-language understanding of rules has some clear problems that the mental-content approach does not face, or does not clearly face, they do face parallel challenges. In general the above considerations favor the mental-content approach to rules, while demanding one emendation. One needs to think of rules as families of similar conceptions possessed by the agents. Recognizing that this is likely a somewhat messy matter, it calls for investigators to study conceptions to understand how they are disseminated, learned, how they figure in preference, and condition behavior.

Passages in Bicchieri's (2006) seem to counsel something along the lines of the mental-content approach focused on conceptions. One interesting discussion talks of local norms. A norm or concept is *local* when its "interpretation" and the "expectations and prescriptions that surround them vary with the objects, people, and situations to which they apply" (Bicchieri 2006, 83). Folk are said to have a local norm of fairness. Thus, some cultures would allow one to take family ties into account in awarding jobs, while others would account that unfair. Thus, it is the interpretation of the norm or rule—the local norm—that directs behavior (such as admission and hiring decisions). This is very much the sort of thing that I have just termed a "conception"—supposing that folk might have similar conceptions.

Furthermore, the suggestion that a rule is subject to interpretation suggests an important role for cognitive processes in applying rules to particular cases in a way that yields specific and determinate recommendations. Both the character of learned conceptions and the processes of their (further?) interpretation-in-application thus become subjects of empirical study. Bicchieri (2006) clearly aspires to the integration of a cognitive science of concepts and conceptualization within an account of rules and norms. Thus, she draws on a psychology of concepts that understands concepts as being encoded in a set of prototypes and in a sense for similarity of instances to these prototypes. This clearly reflects a mental-content approach to rules. It is tolerant of some variation—as folk might have different prototypes and similarity senses without necessarily having a different rule of fairness—just as folk might have different exemplars or prototypes of birds, and different associated senses for similarity, and yet share the semantic concept of bird. At the same time, if what must be shared in a given norm are really similar conceptions, then in order to share the relevant local norm of fairness, there would need to be some significant similarity in the prototypes and senses for similarity disseminated and learned within the relevant population.

I would not myself insist that norms, or local norms, clearly are best understood in terms of prototypes and similarity senses. The psychological study of concepts and conceptualization continues to evolve. (Clearly the data that supported prototype theory must be accommodated.) What I would insist on is that Bicchieri is right in thinking that the theory of norms ultimately must have as a component an account of content, conceptualization, and application. To succeed here it will need to be an interfield theory. As Mendelian genetics became a richer theory, one with more empirical anchors, and one subject to greater refinement, and one consequently with greater explanatory power, when an integrated interfield account was given of its central posits (genes), so talk of rules becomes a richer theory, one with more empirical anchors and one subject to more empirical elaboration, when its posits (rules) come to be understood in part in terms of more or less determinate cognitive phenomena.

I am inclined to draw three central lessons from this section:

First, much of what is commonsensically said about folk knowing a rule, and about folk conforming to one and the same rule, seems to call for something along the lines of a content approach to rules. This approach allows for sharing because it is tolerant of individual variation in conceptions, of variation in what has been learned, and of variation in underlying program or cognitive bases.

Second, a tolerant content approach to rules and norms seems too tolerant of individual differences to do much work in a norms-as-rules account of individual behaviors or of social coordination. *What is done by an individual turns on something more like that individual's conception rather than a shared concept.* Of course, for these to play a role in coordinating behavior, there must be some significant similarity in conceptions across the various agents' various conceptions—and thus some reasonable expectation for behavior that counts as cases of "doing pretty much the same thing" on the part of the various agents. Put simply, promising understandings of behavioral rules within the norms-as-rules approach will need to understand rules as semantic things that are (a) individuated tolerantly enough to allow significant sharing of rules across agents with somewhat diverse learning histories, (b) not too tolerantly individuated to be the sort of thing for which agents reasonably might have conditional preferences of the sort needed, (c) not too tolerantly individuated to significantly direct agents in their (coordinated) behavior, and (d) the sort of thing that might be subject to empirical investigation across a range of disciplines or fields.

Third (for emphasis), if something like the norms-as-rules approach is to work, rules must be understood in a way that is intermediate between (on the one hand) the tolerant semantic approach to rules and (on the other) the approach that focuses narrowly and strictly on what may be individuals' varying conceptions or understandings. Certainly anything close to the computational approach is too narrow. Similarly, an approach to understood rules in terms of just some one individual's paradigms or exemplars and associated similarity metric would be too narrow—as too few people would share a rule. I think that a basis for splitting the difference is suggested at junctures above. Crudely put, agents are said to know the rule and have a conditional preference for conforming to it provided that enough others conform to it. It is plausible that individuals have some sense for what conformity (across a range of situations) would amount to on their own part, and on the part of others. As noted, this sense and preference is likely more restrictive than tolerant semantic approaches suggest. One wants to be fair, provided enough others are largely pretty fair—and it is not enough that they merely adhere to some (perhaps very different) conception of what it is to be fair. At the same time, one is reasonably tolerant of others who may have different paradigms and similarity spaces, provided that their somewhat different paradigms and similarity spaces lead them to do (well, pretty much) what one counts as conforming.

The issues of tolerance of difference, sharing across difference, and yet sufficient similarity to constrain of behavior are closely related to issues that concerned Wittgenstein. They also remind one of Quine's (1960, 8) figures of topiary that resemble each other despite their underlying diversity of detail. These concerns are closely related to arguments developed by Stephen Turner (1994, 2002, 2010). Clearly, talk of behavioral rules should be approached with caution, a healthy grain of salt, and a skepticism about a simple or easy story about one psychological thing shared across many members of the relevant population. Compatible with such caution, it is open to empirical investigation. Indeed, the above suggests an important matter for empirical investigation within the norms-as-rules approach: In what ways are conditional preferences associated with norms sensitive to or tolerant of differences in associated rule-conceptions within populations?

One final note is needed: Bicchieri's talk of rules being known to exist is probably an infelicitously glorified formulation. On its face, it suggests that the agents must have some meta-representation. On the mental-content understanding, this would be some representation of some content—a meta-representation of some proscription or prescription of action. It would be represented as existing in whatever sense contents can be said to exist.[10] This seems too fancy, as it seems to overly intellectualize the range of phenomena in question. Before I had any fancy meta-representational capacity regarding semantic entities, I had norms of the sort one would want to recognize using the rule-as-norms approach. Arguably, before I had the fancy capacity suggested by talk of knowing that a rule existed, I appreciated that one should share, that one should not hit your classmates, and so on. Commonly one knows this much by age three, typically before one has the capacity for fancy meta-representations of content. My own sense is that Bicchieri's formulation, in terms of "knowing [a given] rule exists," is really intended to (a) mark out a roughly recognizable grasp of what would count as cases of doing (or forbearing from doing) the relevant sort of thing, and (b) provide a way of indicating that for there to be a norm regarding such actions agents must have some conditional preference for such behavior.

In effect, what I have suggested here is an initial minimalist understanding of behavioral rules. This is meant as a friendly clarification of the norms-as-rules approach. It has the great virtue of building into the account no more than is functionally required on the part of individuals in order for that account to get traction and be developed scientifically. If there is more to such sharing than here suggested, let that be a scientific discovery. Further, let it be a scientific project to understand how folk generally do encode or possess their understanding of rules or cases, and how conceptions are activated in cases. Let it also be a matter of scientific inquiry how the associated expectations are conditioned by environmental factors. Ultimately, Bicchieri would want to understand her own talk of shared rules in the minimalist way suggested—and to leave room for the range of scientific inquiries just called for. Doing so is in keeping with her own openness to "a theoretical understanding about the individual cognitive mechanisms underlying the activation of expectations and preferences that result in norm-congruent behavior" (Bicchieri 2006, 58).

17.6. Divorcing Norms from the Normatively Correct

Philosophers (and economists) have long been too quick to suppose that certain of their own normative principles (which of course they take to represent objectively correct or appropriate practice) are explanatory—and explanatory in a way that requires one to ask no empirical questions regarding whether the folk or individuals (whose actions or thoughts are supposedly explained) grasp the principle in question, or have conditional preferences for conforming to it. Rules of rationality have been the most tempting normative principles to cast in this supposedly explanatory role—as it has commonly been insisted that one explains by demonstrating rationality.

I have repeatedly resisted this tendency to look for a transmutation of one's own normative rules and sensibilities into putatively explanatory principles. Of course, information to the effect that certain folk have learned, come to hold, and have embraced, particular normative principles (whether these are objectively correct or incorrect) is information that can inform one's explanations (Henderson 1993, 2002, 2005). But this is only to acknowledge an explanatory role for information regarding whatever it is in agents that constitute their (perhaps coordinated) normative sensibilities. More precisely, it is such information, together with information about their rudimentary or learned psychological processes that are explanatory—and such cognitive processes are matter for empirical study—not being subject to a priori determination, and not necessarily normatively appropriate.

The rules-as-norms framework allows one to perspicuously register this caution. On the present approach, norms are rules that sufficiently many in the relevant population (a) know or grasp and (b) have a conditional preference for conforming to. Such rules may be good or fitting, or they may be bad or inappropriate. What matters is the range of rules people can and do learn and embrace. What limits there are on what they can learn and embrace is a matter of human cognitive architecture. What they do embrace is a matter of that same basis and the conditions in which folk find themselves. Once one embraces a norm, behavior—conformity—yet turns on individuals having expectations for behavior and evaluation in enough of the relevant population. On this account, the rules—the sensibilities or normative conceptions in question—prescribes or proscribe a class of behaviors. Conforming to the rule may be conditionally preferred by the agents—but this does not imply that such conformity (or the rule itself) is in any significant respect a good thing. Nothing about the ultimate correctness of the rules/conceptions—their being good or fitting—is explanatory. All that matters is that, as a psychological matter, enough folk grasp the rule and conditionally prefer to act accordingly. As Bicchieri (2006, chapter 5) makes clear, rules with bad consequences and even unpopular consequences can feature in norms. Whatever the rules (good or bad, correct or incorrect) featured in a norm, the norm can be explanatory.

In *Making It Explicit*, Brandom (1998) argues that in order for there to be correct and incorrect things to do and say, there must be norms that are not to be identified with the understandings and tendencies of any actual individual or set of individuals. Real normativity, he insists, requires that there be a difference between being correct and any set of people thinking it correct. Insofar as one thinks that there are or must be such correctness-constituting norms, these cannot be the norms of any actual set of folk. Thus, for Brandom, correctness-constituting norms must be a rather different thing from the norms I have been discussing—norms that turn on individuals' conceptions of, and conditional preference for, some course of action. Brandom may be right about what it would take for there to be correctness-constituting norms. In any case, one should draw the obvious conclusion: that it would be a mistake to think that correctness-constituting norms explain any action, pattern of action, behavioral norms, or the like.[11] Brandomian norms, it seems, are not had by any flesh and blood agent at any given time—they are not properties of peoples or of any collection of people at a time. In contrast, the sort of norm that I have been discussing in this chapter—the sort of social and descriptive norms Bicchieri discusses—are held by particular people at a time. They can serve in explanations of what is done by flesh and blood people. When they do, it is not the rule itself—the content prescribing or proscribing some action (as conceived)—rather it is the norm, which again is the fact of people cognitively relating to that rule in a certain way. For there to be a norm, people must conceive of, and conditionally embrace, the rule. When one appeals to a norm in an explanation, one is noting the fact that sufficiently many in the relevant population do this—and that is the core of what is explanatory.

17.7. Norms, Invariance, and Explanation

When one characterizes a norm-as-rule, one does not merely characterize the content of some behavioral rule. Instead, one characterizes the population as having a significant subset of folk who both know (or understand or grasp) the rule and have conditional preferences for conforming to it. In the section to follow, I will sketch how characterizations of norms can be explanatory. My account there will draw on an account of causal explanations in the special sciences advanced by James Woodward (2000). Woodward's account, which I believe is the best presently on offer, allows us to see how characterizations of norms are closely related to generalizations about a system, generalizations with a moderate but significant degree of invariance that can afford explanations. One may notice a degree of indirection in the preceding sentence. I must acknowledge that I am not altogether comfortable in flatly saying that the characterization of a norm in a population is itself an explanatory generalization. It does say something general about a population. But a more cautious formulation is preferable: Characterizing a norm in a population amounts to a characterization of conditions in a population. That information about a (more or less local) social system, together with understandings of the cognitive psychology of decision-making, of how the rule conceptions are encoded, primed, or activated and deployed, of how expectations are formed, enhanced, diminished, or extinguished (and related matters), amounts to a body of information that can do the cognitive work of a moderately invariant generalization: It can allow one to appreciate patterns of counterfactual dependencies obtaining in the population as special system, and can thus be used to answer what-if-things-had-been-different questions.

In this section I set out what I take from Woodward. For our purposes here, the essentials are as follows:

First, certain generalizations support an important class of explanations by allowing one to answer a range of "what-if-things-had-been-different" questions.

This is to say that, not only can an appropriate generalization be used in connection with information about initial conditions to show the explanandum was to be expected (as the traditional D-N model would demand),[12] but it can also provide an understanding of how the explanandum-variable would be different were the explanan-variables to take a range of different values. Thinking in terms of the logic of why-questions, the point is that appropriately explanatory generalizations allow one to place the explanandum, *and its various contrasts*, within a pattern of counterfactual dependencies.

Second, whether or not a generalization can be used to explain has to do with whether it is *invariant rather than with whether it is lawful* (as nomicity is judged using traditional measures). A *generalization* describing a relationship between two or more variables *is invariant if it would continue to hold—would remain stable or unchanged—as various other conditions change* as the result of interventions. The set or range of changes over which a relationship is invariant is its *domain of invariance.*

The idea of an invariant generalization turns on the idea of an intervention. The idea of an intervention involves an idealization of an experimental situation—but one that need not be contrived and undertaken by humans: "An intervention on some variable X with respect to some second variable Y is a causal process that changes X in some appropriately exogenous way, so that if a change in Y occurs, it occurs only in virtue of the change in X, and not as a result of some other set of causal factors" (Woodward 2000, 200).

One can distinguish two sorts of changes that are relevant when thinking of invariance:

1. Changes "that we would intuitively regard as the background conditions to some generalization—changes that affect other variables besides those that figure in the generalization itself" (Woodward 2000, 205). (The gravitational inverse square law is untouched by the Dow-Jones average, or by the temperature of objects, for example. Economic generalizations, as economic systems, do depend on background conditions remaining in some range—for example, they hold for some ranges of atmospheric CO_2, but would cease to hold were human or other interventions to change CO_2 levels beyond their domain of invariance.)

2. Changes in those variables that figure explicitly in the generalization itself. "For a generalization to count as invariant, there must be some interventions . . . for variables figuring in the relationship for which it is invariant" (Woodward 2000, 206). This does not require that it is invariant across all such changes in such featured variables. The ideal gas law, $PV = nRT$, is famously invariant only under some range of interventions on temperature, for example. Invariance is a matter of degree—as a generalization may hold under a more or less wide range of interventions.

Special sciences commonly study organized systems that result from historical contingencies—for example, a biologist might focus on mammalian physiology, studying the functional organization shared by a class of organisms resulting from the notoriously contingent course of evolution. Anthropologists may study the conventional, descriptive, or social norms of some group. Economists may study the relations between variables such as unemployment, money supply, and inflation, within classes of historically contingent social systems. Each subject has to do with regularities—physiological or sociological—that are (in some important and recognizable sense) the result of historical (or prehistorical) contingencies. Such regularities are dependent on background conditions, as certain changes in those conditions would destroy or markedly modify the systems and make for violations in the regularities uncovered in the special sciences. However, some ranges of changes in background conditions would not lead to such breakdowns—and thus, within limits, the interesting systems and regularities have a degree of stability. As a result, we have an interesting and stable subject for study. Various special sciences, including social scientific disciplines and subdisciplines, grow up to study such systems—systematizing and deepening understandings that we commonly possess in some limited fashion.

17.8. Norms as Explanans—Descriptions of Norms as Generalizations with Some Invariance

Descriptions of norms in a population are, in effect, characterizations of a system—the relevant population, with attention to a significant subset having conditional preferences with respect to some rule—some family of similar conceptions, conceptions that are learned and adjusted within that population. To so characterize the population amounts to a moderately invariant generalization, or implies such. More precisely, it takes its place as a part of what should ultimately be an interfield theory—that itself provides something on the order of a sprawling invariant generalization. The description of the norm in the population, together with such interfield components as (a) an account of processes of dissemination and learning of rules, (b) an account of the cognitive dynamic of the representation and activiation of rule-conceptions, (c) an account of expectation-formation and salience, and (d) an account of the psychology of decision-making, implies a range of counterfactual dependencies. It implies that a range of interventions would make for systematic differences in the rate of conformity to the rule in the population, specifically on the part of those on whom the intervention is directed. One class of interventions would prime or make salient the relevant rule-conception, for example. Another class of intervention would provide or make salient information suggesting common or uncommon conformity within the relevant population—adjusting expectations within some members of the population.

To say that there is a social or descriptive norm in a population is to say that significantly many in the population:

   a. have some (similar) sense for what actions in situation would constitute conforming (doing the relevant action in the relevant situations) and what would constitute violations (failing to do the relevant actions in the relevant situations), and
   b. have a conditional preference for conforming, where
   c. that preference is conditioned on expectations regarding others conforming and regarding the normative stances of others within the population concerning conformity and violations by others. (Included here are expectations for various behaviors punishing violations.)

It says that a significant portion of the population have a set of standing psychological states (conditional preferences or something on the order of desires from which they consistently generate such preferences). Given the character of the preferences attributed, were the agents to have expectations about enough others in that population acting and evaluating in parallel ways, they then would act on those preferences.[13] In effect, such information specifies a number of points at which one could intervene in that system with projectable results. It thus allows one to address and answer a range of what-if-things-had-been different questions. Of course, as we further develop an interfield theory of such norms, our understanding of how rules are represented, how such representations are made active in human cognition, how elements of the representation may be made salient (or not), and related matters will add to our understanding of the points at which one can intervene, and thus to our understanding of what would have happened were things different.

Suppose then that one were to intervene in various ways to raise or lower expectations on the part of certain norm holders within the population. One might intervene so as to raise or lower what Bicchieri terms their "empirical expectations"—expectations for conforming behavior on the part of many others. Alternatively, one might intervene so as to lower or raise what Bicchieri terms their "normative expectations"—expectations for evaluations on the part of others regarding conforming or nonconforming actions. In the case of social norms, either intervention should occasion parallel changes in observed conformity with the norm among those whose expectations are effected by the intervention.

Bicchieri discusses certain studies in which investigators subtly intervened on folks' empirical expectations. Cialdini, Kallgren, and Reno (1990) investigated adherence to a norm of not littering. In their various treatment groups, they provided their subjects with what they termed "informational influences"—in effect, they manipulated the empirical expectations of subjects in various treatment groups. Subjects were presented with behavior on the part of others (notably, experimental collaborators) or were presented with clean or littered settings (strongly suggestive of rates of littering—or forbearing from littering). Subjects were also subjected to "normative influences"—in effect, manipulating their normative expectations.

Cialdini arranged to have collaborators put flyers in the hands of subjects. This could be done in a relatively pristine setting or in a relatively trashy setting. Exposing agents to a trashy setting plausibly lowers their expectations for widespread conformity with the rule of not littering, at least in that environment. If there is a social norm against littering, then diminishing individuals' expectations for widespread conformity should diminish their conformity with the norm. This is what was observed. Exposing agents to a pristine setting plausibly raises their expectations for widespread conformity, and should then lead to greater conformity with the norm against littering. Again observed. One might also intervene on individuals' expectations by presenting them with salient instances of rule violation or conformity. Thus, one might have a collaborator first receive the same flyer, then, in plain sight of the subject, deposit it in the trash or drop it to the ground. In a trashy environment, the in-your-face littering would likely provide reinforcing information about widespread norm violation. Alternatively, the collaborator might also be positioned to pick up a flyer that had been thrown down—and presumably this makes both the norm and conformity to it salient. One can then imagine various combinations of treatments; several are investigated by Cialdini and collaborators.

The central point is this: The characterization of a social or descriptive norm characterizes both an understanding of a rule possessed by many in a population and a preference that is conditioned on expectations—so that one can answer various what-if-things-had-been different questions having to do with possible interventions that would raise or lower agents' expectations for norm conformity. The characterization of the norm thus allows us to understand the pattern of counterfactual dependencies obtaining in the population in question. Interventions that effect folks' expectations for norm conformity (whether under the control of investigators in controlled experiments, or naturally occurring in the form of news stories or documentaries in wide circulation), will make a difference in patterns of behavior by making a difference in relevant expectations triggering action in accordance with preferences.

One can readily imagine various possible interventions on the normative expectations as well. One might present subjects with tapes from (perhaps staged, perhaps unstaged) interview sessions in which a diversity of folk evaluate episodes. Those interviewed might respond to descriptions or records of nonconforming acts with surprise and indignation (augmenting or supporting the normative expectations associated with the norm) or respond as if the violations were par for the course and of no concern (undermining normative expectations). One might present subjects with polling data to the effect that some percentage of folk report being (or not being) bothered by the behavior in question. When this indicates that others expect others to conform, and evaluate performances accordingly, it enhances the normative expectations on which conformity (with social norms) is supposedly conditioned. When it indicates that others do not expect folk to conform and that they do not negatively evaluate norm violations, then it diminishes the pivotal normative expectations. Again, the description of the social or descriptive norm in question would indicate a pattern of counterfactual dependencies.[14]

Recent psychological experiments suggest that interventions that make norms or evaluative expectations active can be very subtle and can work at the level of automatic processes that may not even involve consciously reflecting on the rule itself. Thus, Bargh, Chen, and Burrows (1996) primed attention to norms associated with politeness/impoliteness by having subjects undertake an ostensibly unrelated linguistic task: Subjects were instructed to quickly construct short sentences by selecting words from scrambled lists of words. Subjects were given thirty sets of five words from which they were to quickly construct thirty four-word sentences. Those in one treatment group were presented with lists including words like *aggressive, bold, and rude* in fifteen of the thirty-word sets—so that constructing those sentences would "prime the stereotype" or "construct" of rudeness. Other subjects were presented lists including words like *respect, honor, considerate,* and *patiently*—priming the stereotype or construct of politeness. Yet another treatment group was given neutral lists. At the conclusion of the task, subjects were instructed to proceed to a second room for what was said to be a second small experiment. At that room they would encounter two experimental confederates who were apparently engaged in a discussion of some task. These confederates would ignore the subject and continue their discussion. The variable of experimental concern was how quickly the subject would interrupt that conversation to request instructions. It was found that those primed for the rudeness stereotype were relatively quick to interrupt, those exposed to the neutral lists were intermediate, and those primed to think about politeness were strikingly patient. It seems reasonable to think that the priming of stereotypes enhanced the activation of various norm-associated representations. This is reasonably connected with Bicchieri's (2006, 94) suggestion that "social norms are embedded into scripts," which are "stylized, stereotyped sequences of action that are appropriate to in this [or that] context." Such scripts would be activated once a context is categorized, and that priming of normative categories can affect the categorization of contexts. It seems that something like such scripts are primed for activation in subtle ways.

I mention these empirically informed suggestions here because they provide further illustration of some ways in which a theory of norms-as-rules can become an integrated interfield theory. In particular, they illustrate how a cognitive theory of rule representation and of the associated cognitive dynamics of representation activation would reveal nuances in the causal dependencies associated with norms. In a parallel fashion, theories of learning and theories of social dissemination may constrain and be constrained by one's understanding of what are the items to be learned—the representations. And much may depend on what variation in conception (or the representation of rule) is found to characterize perceived similarity of action. Such constraints and connections make vivid the opportunities for interfield theorizing. The nuances in causal dependencies that would be posited or revealed would augment both the testability of one's theory and its explanatory power. To the extent that the norm description is augmented by related cognitive scientific information about the character of rule representations and those processes in which these representations are put to work, one will be able to envision further interventions (experimental or natural) and to look for whether the behavior that results is that predicted. The integrated interfield theory would itself entail rich patterns of counterfactual dependencies.

Finally, there is the matter of social norms as explananda. To explain norm formation on the norms-as-rules approach, (a) one would need to account for the dissemination and acquisition of the relevant class of rule representations and (b) one would need to account for the formation of preferences for conforming, a preference conditioned on enough others conforming. To explain individual conformity to the norm, (c) one would also need to account for the formation of the associated expectations. To explain widespread conformity, (d) one would then need to account for such phenomena being widespread within the population. While there are plenty of open questions associated with each of these matters, the formation of social preferences, (b), provides the biggest platter of open questions— and it is the topic of most distinctive concern for the theory of norms. Obviously, accounting for the social preferences is most daunting in the case of social norms— those that must somehow transform mixed-motive games into coordination games. Related to these questions are issues having to do with how much must be done by such social preference, or expectations of punishment, in transforming mixed-motive games to coordination games. A related question is the importance of punishment and expectations of punishment in an array of social norms. At least one prominent line of thought is that social learning in the form of "conformist transmission," affords a form of replicator dynamic that could leave punishment and related matters with relatively minimal work to do (Henrich and Boyd, 2001). However, one can certainly look for a clearer empirical understanding of the relative importance of various processes and parameters (for example, see Guala 2007). In any case, I conveniently insist that these complex issues are beyond the scope of the present chapter.

NOTES

1. Notice: The rule itself—the proscriptive/prescriptive representation (the "do such-and-such")—does of itself not feature in the explanation. Rather, it is a representation of it as a norm in a population (as being held by folk who prefer to behave accordingly) that feature in the explanation. The point is important in section 17.5.

2. While Bicchieri does not number the clauses (1) and (2) in her text, she subsequently refers to them as if they were so numbered.

3. *Descriptive norms*, in Bicchieri's taxonomy, have to do with situations that can be characterized as coordination games (rather than mixed-motive games).

Let R be a behavioral rule for situations of type S, where S is a coordination game. We say that R is a descriptive norm in a population P, if there exists a sufficiently large subset $P_{cf} \subseteq P$, such that for each individual $i \in P_{cf}$:

1. Contingency—i knows that R exists and applies to the situations of type S,

2. Conditional Preferences—i prefers to conform to R in situations of type S, given that [the empirical and normative expectations below are jointly satisfied]:

    a. Empirical Expectations—i believes that some sufficiently large subset of the population conforms to R in S (Bicchieri 2006, 31–2)

On Bicchieri's account, conventions are a special class of descriptive norms (Bicchieri 2006, 38).

4. Cooperation games have multiple equilibria, and norms solve the problem of coordination by prescribing one solution. When the norm treats of a choice situation that amounts to a mixed-motive game, agents must have some conditional preference that transforms the game into a coordination game—so that the payoffs characterizing the mixed-motive game do not exhaust the utilities of the agents in that choice situation. See also Camerer and Fehr (2004). Obviously there are important empirical issues here. In attempts to address these issues, investigators have pursued several general approaches. Some have looked for an account in which the preferences are explicable in terms of the payoffs to self-interested individuals, or expected payoffs over time in iterated episodes. Others have looked for preferences that are colored by altruistic or benevolent sentiments—and such is the approach suggested by Bicchieri (2006, 17–21). See also Camerer and Fehr (2004). In the case of mixed-motive games such as ultimatum games and public goods games different writers have explored the idea that the preferences might turn on "inequality aversion" (Fehr and Schmidt, 1999), or a tendency to reciprocity (Rabin, 1993). Bicchieri and Zhang (2012) pursue an account of a preference for rule conformity that has similarities to a reciprocity preference. Which general sort of account ultimately makes the most empirical sense will depend on observed social phenomena and upon results in social and moral psychology. In related work (for example, Henrich and Boyd 2001), it is suggested that what in effect are the rule and preferences might be transmitted by a replicator dynamic in which agents either copy common behavior (conformist transmission) or copy the behavior of relatively successful others (payoff-biased transmission) within the population. (See also Guala 2007.)

5. Such interfield theorizing would have the desirable effect of forcing investigators away from aprioristic models of norms—ones that deploy mathematical models with only an armchair grasp on the various processes that must be involved in the phenomena of concern. Guala (2007) criticizes such aprioristic theorizing.

6. The work found in Henrich et al. (2004) represents a related exemplary flowering of interfield theorizing and investigation—one treating of social norms and preferences in the array of anthropological field settings.

7. Cummins (1983) elaborates an understanding of functional analysis in which functions are causal roles in a system. One can analyze the relatively sophisticated capacity of a complex system—a computer, a radio receiver, a cognitive agent—into the organized workings of a set of simpler capacities. These simpler capacities are functions or causal roles performed by system components. The norms-as-rules approach posits entities—(representations of) behavioral rules—that have characteristic causal roles in the cognitive systems (agents) that manage to coordinate their actions in ways that allow for social life (which otherwise might succumb to narrowly selfish free riding). In articulating one's theoretical commitments in terms of such functions or causal roles, one is engaged in a midstream theoretical engagement that ultimately looks toward an empirically refinable interfield theory in which one would have a refined or elaborated

understanding of the causal roles performed and of the entities performing these roles in human cognitive systems. Cummins (1975) discusses how functions as causal roles in a system have a place in the explanation of the sophisticated capacity of the system. The resulting explanatory understanding is distinct from an explanation of why there is a system (or a component) with such capacities—analysis of how a system works is distinct from an explanation of why there are such systems, although it can often contribute to such explanations.

8. I am encouraged in recommending this constructive approach by a line of argument in Graham and Horgan (1991, 1994), developed in Henderson and Horgan (2003) to the effect that one's reflective analysis of concepts such as *belief* and *desire* ought not be "opulent," but ought to be "austere." Because one has a prima facie workable sense for cases, at least many clear cases, one should not adopt, a priori, strong commitments regarding what would make for beliefs and desires—or what would make for rules and known rules. Instead, one should be open to empirical determination of what the crudely understood entities or states amount to.

9. Turner (1994, 2002, 2010) has pressed the point. I think that one should think of the matter in these terms. In a neural net, information may be learned and contained in the weights or the strength of the connections between various neurons. This information may be accommodated automatically, without ever taking the form of articulate or paradigmatic representations in the cognitive system. Horgan and Tienson (1996) call this *morphological content*—as it is information possessed by the system, in the structured connections, and largely implicit in the structure of the system (considered as a dynamical system), yet nowhere paradigmatically represented in even a fleeting occurrent representation within the system. (See also Henderson and Horgan, 2011, chapter 7.) In light of different learning histories, the ways in which cognitive systems may contain the information may be extremely varied. It is plausible that in coming to know a rule, agents may come to possess much information in the form of morphological content. If so, there is little reason to expect that a neurological or syntactic sameness underlies their knowledge of the rules. The way connectionist systems learn some information is subject to massive multiple realization across differing neural nets with differing learning histories.

10. Or, if knowing is understood as requiring only a standing belief, rather than an occurrent doxastic state, it might require only the capacity and disposition to produce such a doxastic representation were the question to arise. What question? The question of whether some prescription or proscription made sense? Even this seems a little too fancy.

11. See Henderson (2002). Turner (2010) develops parallel misgivings.

12. To accommodate the explanation of improbable events, one would ultimately need to weaken this formulation insofar as it reflects the traditional idea that explanations need show that the explanandum is to be expected. One must mention features of antecedent events or states that made the explanandum event more probable than it would have been otherwise, and which did not also favor the members of the contrast class. (See Henderson 1993, and Humphreys 1989.)

13. To say this much calls to mind the venerable idea that norms are dispositions to certain forms of coordinated action, perhaps together with the disposition to evaluate actions that accord or fail to accord with those dispositions. It also refines that venerable approach in several ways. First, in treating of preferences, it suggests that one might measure the preferences in well-known ways, and add some precision to one's understanding of the norms in a given population. By conditioning the preferences on certain expectations, it indicates pivotal variables that are significant for understanding when conformity with the rule is to be expected. By virtue of its general psychological character,

it is readily informed by a wide range of psychological results—regarding categorization, for example, and thus the categorization of situations.

14. Bicchieri has recently partnered in several empirical investigations intended to refine our understanding of how various empirical and normative expectations are important to norm conformity. Bicchieri and Xiao (2009) investigate the relative importance of empirical and normative expectations in dictator games. Bicchieri and Chavez (2009) investigate the significance of behavioral asymmetries for norms and norm conformity in ultimatum games.

REFERENCES

Bargh, J. A., M. Chen, and L. Burrows. 1996. "Automaticity of Social Behavior: Direct Effects of Trait Construct and Stereotype Activation on Action." *Journal of Personality and Social Psychology* 71 (2): 230–44

Bicchieri, C. 2006. *The Grammar of Society*. New York: Cambridge University Press.

Bicchieri, C., and A. Chavez. 2009. "Behaving as Expected: Public Information and the Fairness Norm." *Journal of Behavioral Decision Making* 23 (2): 161–78.

Bicchieri, C., and E. Xiao. 2009. "Do the Right Thing: But Only If Others Do So." *Journal of Behavioral Decision Making* 22 (2): 191–208.

Bicchieri, C., and J. Zhang. J. 2012. "An Embarrassment of Riches: Modeling Social Preferences in Ultimatum Games." In *Handbook of the Philosophy of Economics*, U. Maki, ed. Amsterdam: Elsevier.

Brandom, R. 1998. *Making It Explicit*. Cambridge, MA: Harvard University Press.

Camerer C., and E. Fehr. 2004. "Measuring Social Norms and Preferences Using Experimental Games: A Guide for Social Scientists." In *Foundations of Human Sociality: Economic Experiments and Ethnographic Evidence from Fifteen Small-Scale Societies*, J. Henrich, R. Boyd, S. Bowles, C. Camerer, E. Fehr, and H. Gentis, eds., 55–95. Oxford: Oxford University Press.

Cialdini, R., C. Kallgren, and R. Reno. 1990. "A Focus Theory of Normative Conduct: A Theoretical Refinement and Reevaluation of the Role of Norms in Human Behavior." *Advances in Experimental Social Psychology* 24: 201–34.

Cummins, R. 1983. *The Nature of Psychological Explanation*. Cambridge, MA: The MIT Press.

Cummins, R. 1975. "Functional Analysis." *Journal of Philosophy* 72 (Nov.): 741–60.

Darden, L. 2006. *Reasoning in Biological Discoveries*. Cambridge: Cambridge University Press.

Darden, L., and N. Maull. 1997. "Interfield Theories." *Philosophy of Science* 44 (March): 43–64. Reprinted in Darden (2006).

Fehr, E., and K. Schmidt. 1999. "A Theory of Fairness, Competition, and Co-operation." *Quarterly Journal of Economics* 114 (3): 817–68.

Graham, G., and T. Horgan. 1991. "In Defense of Southern Fundamentalism." *Philosophical Studies* 62 (2): 107–34.

Graham, G., and T. Horgan. 1994. "Southern Fundamentalism and the End of Philosophy." *Philosophical Issues* 5: 219–47.

Guala, F. 2007. "Philosophy of Social Science: Metaphysical and Empirical." *Philosophy Compass* 2/6: 954–80.

Henderson, D. 1993. *Interpretation and Explanation in the Human Science*. Albany: State University of New York Press.

Henderson, D. 2002. "Norms, Normative Principles, and Explanation." *Philosophy of the Social Sciences* 32 (3): 329–64.

Henderson, D. 2005. "Norms, Invariance, and Explanatory Relevance." *Philosophy of the Social Sciences* 35 (3): 324–38.

Henderson, D., and T. Horgan. 2003. "What Does It Take to Be a True Believer? Against the Opulent Ideology of Folk Psychology." In *Mind as a Scientific Object: Between Brain and Culture*, C. Erneling and D. Johnson, eds., 211–24. Oxford: Oxford University Press.

Henderson, D., and T. Horgan. 2011. *The Epistemological Spectrum*. Oxford: Oxford University Press.

Hebrucg, J., and R. Boyd. 2001. "Why People Punish Defectors: Weak Conformist Transmission Can Stabilize Costly Enforcement of Norms in Cooperative Dilemmas." *Journal of Theoretical Biology* 208 (1): 79–89.

Henrich, J., R. Boyde, S. Bowles, C. Camerer, E. Fehr, and H. Gentis, eds. 2004. *Foundations of Human Sociality: Economic Experiments and Ethnographic Evidence from Fifteen Small-Scale Societies*. Oxford: Oxford University Press.

Horgan T., and J. Tienson. 1996. *Connectionism and the Philosophy of Psychology*. Cambridge, MA: The MIT Press.

Humphreys, P. 1989. *Chances of Explanation*. Princeton, NJ: Princeton University Press.

Lewis, D. 1969. *Convention: A Philosophical Study*. Cambridge, MA: Harvard University Press.

Quine, W. 1960. *Word and Object*. Cambridge, MA: The MIT Press.

Rabin, M. 1993. "Incorporating Fairness into Game-Theory and Economics." *American Economics Review* 83 (5): 1281–302.

Turner, S. 1994. *The Social Theory of Practices*. Chicago: University of Chicago Press.

Turner, S. 2002. *Brains/Practices/Representations*. Chicago: University of Chicago Press.

Turner, S. 2010. *Explaining the Normative*. Oxford: Polity Press.

Woodward, J. 2000. "Explanation and Invariance in the Special Sciences." *British Journal for Philosophy of Science* 51 (2): 197–354

CHAPTER 18

THE EVOLUTIONARY PROGRAM IN SOCIAL PHILOSOPHY

FRANCESCO GUALA

18.1. INTRODUCTION

The merging of economics with psychology and biology is one of the most significant trends in contemporary social science. The increasing integration between
these disciplines is taking place mainly at the level of theory and methodology, but
unsurprisingly is also influencing those areas of philosophy that are closest to the
social sciences, like social ontology, political philosophy, and ethics.

There are many ways to combine biology with social science, and inevitably one
has to make some arbitrary choices. This chapter is devoted to a specific version of
evolutionary social theory, which has recently produced a remarkable body of
research, and has attracted the attention of scholars working in different fields.[1] The
evolutionary program—as the term will be used from now on—is a descendant of
the human ethology of Lorentz and Tinbergen of the 1960s, and of the sociobiology
of E. O. Wilson of the 1970s. It partly overlaps with evolutionary psychology, evolutionary anthropology, and evolutionary game theory—three major research programs that have extended the legacy of sociobiology in the 1980s and the 1990s (cf.
Griffiths 2008). Last, but not least, the evolutionary program aims to shed light on
the origins of "fair" social contracts of the sort philosophers have theorized from the
time of Hobbes, Locke, and Rousseau, to contemporary theorists like John Rawls.

The unifying trait of evolutionary social theory is the use of biological models
of transmission and selection in heterogeneous populations. A major difference

between the models that I discuss in this chapter and those of sociobiologists or evolutionary psychologists is that contemporary theorists do not attempt to provide explanations of human behavior based exclusively on *genetic* mechanisms of transmission and selection. The commitment to genetic explanation nowadays is considered unnecessary—indeed a liability that has caused more harm than good to the evolutionary program. The work of Cavalli Sforza and Feldman (1981) and Boyd and Richerson (1985) in the 1980s convinced many scholars that learning and imitation govern the diffusion of many cultural traits that do not have a plausible genetic explanation (see also Dawkins 1976). As a consequence, most contemporary evolutionary social theorists take a pluralist or agnostic stance concerning transmission mechanisms, while retaining the Darwinian emphasis on population thinking.[2]

This agnosticism of course can be challenged and has been challenged by some critics (cf. e.g., Sober 1992, Sperber 1996, Wimsatt 1999). In this chapter, however, I shall deal mainly with disagreements that are internal to the evolutionary program. I shall also skip the most intricate technical issues and devote more space to the practical and political implications of the evolutionary approach to social philosophy. Evolutionary social theorists follow in the footsteps of Hobbes and Hume, and attempt to explain the emergence of social contracts from the interaction of individuals facing dilemmas of social cooperation. However, they have not been content to highlight the explanatory potential of their models, but have also stressed repeatedly the relevance of their work for political and social philosophy. They have claimed, in particular, that understanding the origins of social institutions will help us to avoid advocating utopian reforms with little chance to succeed (but much potential for disaster):

> Political philosophy is the study of how society might be organized. If possibility is construed generously we have utopian theory. Those who would deal with "men as they are" need to work with a more restrictive sense of possibility. Concern with the interactive dynamics of biological evolution, cultural evolution, and learning provides some interesting constraints. (Skyrms 1996,109)
>
> The most important consideration is the necessity of separating the question of what is feasible from what is optimal. To make a decision sensibly, first decide what alternatives will work, and then choose whichever of the workable alternatives you like most. (Binmore 2005,199) [3]

Utopian policymaking is the primary target of evolutionary social philosophy. Call it the realism principle: Social institutions should be designed keeping the inclinations of real human beings in mind. Rational choice theorists have often supplemented the realism principle with the claim that such inclinations are mainly selfish. Like Hume's knavery principle, of which it is a direct descendant, this approach is compatible with the recognition that there is a certain amount of nonselfish behavior in society.[4] But by taking knavery—the worst-case scenario—as the general case, at least one can make sure that our institutions cannot be exploited by self-interested players.

The knavery principle is vulnerable to a simple critique though: Institutional designs tailored on the worst-case scenario are almost certainly going to be suboptimal in some range of circumstances. If real citizens are actually a mix of knaves and knights, we are going to miss (some, or many) valuable opportunities for policy interventions that exploit the moral inclinations of (some) human beings.[5] In a separate chapter of this volume, Jim Woodward discusses in depth the implications of agents' heterogeneity for the design of optimal institutions. Here I focus on a preliminary and more fundamental issue: Nonselfish motives are certainly part of our folk understanding of the social world; but are there solid *scientific* grounds to depart from the assumption of universal knavery?

Many theoretical biologists and economists are skeptical. Moral inclinations are evolutionarily suspect, to begin with: Over time self-interested individuals should do better—and reproduce faster—than unselfish ones. Only moral behavior that is able to survive such pressure should be taken seriously for institutional design and policymaking. The realism principle hence takes the following form in evolutionary social theory: Whatever behavior policymakers intend to induce, it must be *evolutionarily stable*—it must be robust to invasion by so-called mutant strategies in the repeated games that citizens play among themselves and with their rulers. Most of the chapter will be devoted to assess this principle and its implications for social philosophy.

Since the normative relevance and philosophical success of the evolutionary program depends crucially on its scientific credentials, it will be necessary to review theories and evidence at some length. We shall see that different game-theoretic models and experiments support different accounts of human sociality, which in turn have different normative implications at the level of policymaking. Sections 18.2 and 18.3 introduce some theoretical concepts from the theory of games and evolutionary biology, focusing in particular on dilemmas of cooperation. Sections 18.4 and 18.5 discuss coordination and bargaining games. Sections 18.6 and 18.7 review the experimental evidence on coordination and cooperation. Sections 18.8 and 18.9 are devoted to Strong Reciprocity theory and the controversy it has generated. Section 18.10 concludes with some general remarks.

18.2. THE PROBLEM OF COOPERATION

Social cooperation increases fitness. Successful societies enhance the rate of survival of their members facilitating coordination and division of labor, for example, and increasing the production of resources that are collectively available for consumption. But institutions may also facilitate the distribution of these resources, creating for instance forms of insurance that smooth the cycles of production. (When food in excess cannot be stored, we are all better off if I give you what I cannot consume today, under the expectation that you will do the same tomorrow.)

Given the amazing variety of institutions that fulfill these functions in different societies, evolutionary theorists have devised simple models that try to capture the essential mechanisms of collective production and distribution. A problem of social coordination can be represented for example as a simple game like hi-lo, in figure 18.1a.

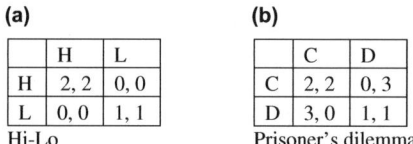

Figure 18.1 Problems of coordination and cooperation

There are two players, represented as row and column. Each letter stands for a strategy, and outcomes are represented as payoff numbers in the matrix (the first number for the row player, the second one for the column).

A social contract is a system of rules, each prescribing a certain action (for example, "Do H") in a given range of circumstances. A successful social contract (which is long-lasting and is transmitted to the next generation) must be *stable*, in the sense that players should not have a strong incentive to transgress its rules. Game-theoretic concepts of equilibrium are particularly useful to capture this idea of stability. A *Nash equilibrium* is a set of strategies (one for each player in a game) such that no one can do better by changing her strategy unilaterally. Nash equilibria are self-sustaining, or self-policing, in the sense that they are robust to individual attempts to gain by deviating from the current strategies (because, quite simply, no such gains are possible). There are two Nash equilibria in hi-lo (HH and LL), and the players must decide which one they should endorse as their social contract.

Not all social contracts are equally attractive, for efficiency gains vary depending on the specific roles and rules we adopt to regulate our conduct. "I hunt and you pick vegetables," for example, may be a relatively inefficient arrangement if you run faster and shoot more accurately than I do. This idea is captured by assigning different payoffs to HH and LL. Although some contracts are better than others, in general it is also true that *any* social contract is better than no contract at all. Homo sapiens, as far as we know, is incapable to live like a Robinson Crusoe, and life in a Hobbesian state of nature is notoriously "solitary, poor, nasty, brutish, and short." That's why HL and LH (the two symmetric coordination failures) are assigned the lowest relative payoffs in the matrix.

Coordination models are relatively favorable environments for the survival of social contracts, for they presuppose that all individuals have an incentive to abide by the rules that govern their societies. But is this always the case? Consider the famous prisoner's dilemma game in figure 18.1b. Following a tradition that goes back to Hobbes, political theorists have used the prisoner's dilemma to represent the problem of social cooperation in a situation where each individual has an incentive to defect from the social contract and free ride on the fruits of others' labor. This is the "state of nature" of classic political philosophy, where no one can trust the other players to behave pro-socially. Mutual defection (DD) is the only Nash equilibrium in the one-shot prisoner's dilemma game. Although mutual cooperation (CC) is more efficient than mutual defection, it is strictly dominated and will not be played by rational selfish individuals.

So if the social contract game were a one-shot prisoner's dilemma, a population of rational players would never be able to pull themselves out of the state of nature. Since social contracts do exist, however, we need some way to solve the puzzle of cooperation. The variety of solutions that have been proposed over the years is truly staggering, and I will not attempt a survey here.[6] I will narrow my focus on the contributions made by *evolutionary* approaches to the problem of cooperation. Four of them—based on evolutionarily stable strategies, kin selection, assortativity, and reciprocity—have dominated the theoretical literature for the last three decades, and constitute the main topic of the next section.

18.3. How Evolution May (or May Not) Solve the Problem of Cooperation

Solutions to the puzzle of cooperation can be classified in two broad categories: those that change the structure of the game and those that change the way the game is played. Approaches of the latter kind are particularly popular among those who find the classic description of economic agents (based on rationality and self-interest) implausible or distasteful: Surely only selfish economic agents defect in dilemma games, while the rest of us—"the folk"—can do much better than that. But this view is simplistic. Far from being an arbitrary assumption, the self-interest principle is well-rooted in evolutionary theorizing. Indeed, cooperation is in many ways more puzzling from a *biological* than from an economic point of view.

Biological altruism denotes any behavior that increases the chance of survival and reproduction of another organism, at the expense of the altruist's direct fitness. Biologists have known for decades that the problem of biological altruism is structurally similar to a social dilemma game in economists' sense (Trivers 1971, Dawkins 1976, Axelrod and Hamilton 1981). An organism that does not help but receives help from others will produce on average more offspring, spreading its "selfish" genes more efficiently than its altruistic fellows. Altruists (i.e., organisms playing C-strategies) in theory should be washed out by the forces of natural selection, leaving only self-interested players behind. This idea can be made more precise in the formal framework of evolutionary game theory, relying in particular on the notion of evolutionarily stable strategy.

18.3.1. Evolutionarily Stable Strategies

Evolutionary game theory is the product of two controversies—on biological altruism and on equilibrium selection—that in the 1970s simultaneously transformed the landscapes of theoretical biology and economics. Evolutionary game theory focuses on the analysis of repeated encounters—it looks at what happens when the same game is played over and over by a large number of individuals that interact in pairs with re-matching at every round. Furthermore, it abandons the requirement of perfect rationality that is central in classic game theory, and models players as relatively "dumb" automata that do not engage in chains of interactive reasoning ("I prefer D to C, he knows that I prefer D to C, I know that he knows . . ." and so forth) but instead tend to play those strategies that have been more productive in the past.[7]

The standard solution concept in evolutionary game theory is the evolutionarily stable strategy introduced by Maynard Smith and Price (1973). Informally, a strategy S is evolutionarily stable when a homogeneous population of S-type players cannot be invaded by a "mutant" playing a different strategy S'≠ S. The concept of evolutionary stability is logically stronger than the Nash equilibrium of standard game theory. Stability implies equilibrium but not the other way around.[8]

However, there is only one equilibrium in the one-shot prisoner's dilemma. Introducing an evolutionary dimension cannot change the story significantly, for a population of cooperators is always vulnerable to invasion by defecting mutants. In a repeated dilemma game with random re-matching, each new round is just another one-shot game. Since every evolutionarily stable strategy must also be a Nash equilibrium, cooperation is not even a contender in a prisoner's dilemma with random re-matching. If cooperation evolves, it must do so in a class of different games.[9]

18.3.2. Kin Selection

An altruistic gene, in biologists' jargon, encodes a trait that lowers the fitness of its carrier while raising the fitness of other organisms. Cooperation in prisoner's dilemma-like situations is altruistic in this sense, since a cooperative individual pays a cost in material terms (i.e., lowers her fitness) to benefit another individual with whom she is interacting. For this reason, she should be disadvantaged vis-à-vis an opportunistic free rider, and should not be able to spread her genes in the population unless some particularly favorable conditions obtain. W. D. Hamilton (1964) noticed that an altruistic gene can survive and multiply via natural selection, if the other organisms that benefit from altruism also carry the same gene. The condition that makes altruism evolutionarily viable is a simple formula relating the cost (c) of altruism with its benefit (b):

$$c < rb$$

The parameter r in Hamilton's rule is the *relatedness* coefficient, a measure of the probability that the altruistic gene is carried by the organism(s) with which one is interacting. This probability is highest during interactions with close relatives (parents, children, brothers) but quickly declines with cousins, grandchildren, and so forth. As a consequence, Hamilton's rule predicts that altruism and cooperation should be observed more frequently among family members than during interactions with unrelated co-specifics. This is known as the theory of *kin selection* in evolutionary biology.[10]

18.3.3. Assortativity

The implications of Hamilton's rule extend beyond the theory of kin selection and the evolution of altruistic genes. Let us interpret the variables c and b more generally as the expected cost/benefit of a cooperative act (strategy C) in a dilemma game. What makes cooperation profitable is a high probability of meeting a cooperator, rather than genetic relatedness per se. Hamilton's rule therefore can be rewritten in generalized form as $c < \pi b$, where the coefficient π represents the probability that the other player will cooperate.

A statistical correlation that biases encounters so that each player has a higher chance of meeting a similar partner than a player of a different kind is called *assortativity*. Assortativity plays a central role in so-called structural evolutionary models, and simulations have shown that in some cases even a slight statistical bias can enhance the probability that a cooperative strategy will spread in the population by making it less vulnerable to invasion by free riders (Skyrms 1996, 2004; Alexander 2007). Structural models give a slightly more optimistic message than kin selection: Cooperation may thrive not only within the family, but also in the small community of neighbors that we encounter frequently in our everyday dealings.

18.3.4. Reciprocity

Research on human cooperation over the last three decades has explored various mechanisms that in different circumstances may affect the parameter π. Assortativity can result from mere geographical factors, when a spatial barrier prevents encounters with individuals located in nearby territories. But it can also result from the decision to avoid or ostracize free riders, once these have been reliably identified. A simple device to avoid benefiting free riders is *reciprocity* in repeated encounters. Robert Axelrod's (1984) tournaments are perhaps the best-known setting of this kind. Axelrod experimented with artificial players competing in a series of repeated dilemma games. Famously, a strategy called "tit-for-tat" emerged as the winner in his tournaments. Tit-for-tat is a rudimentary rule of reciprocity, offering cooperation at the outset and then copying whatever move one's partner has made in the previous round. In the first encounter, there is no guarantee that the other player will cooperate. But from the second round onward, tit-for-tatters play C more often with cooperators than with free riders, raising the value of π in Hamilton's formula and thus making the evolution of cooperation possible.[11]

Axelrod's results had a precursor in the biological concept of "reciprocal altruism" (Trivers 1971), the idea that what seems altruistic in the short run might actually be self-serving in the long run. Organisms displaying other-regarding behavior may be indirectly maximizing their own fitness, if their help is going to be reciprocated in the future. A partner who does not reciprocate can be punished by withdrawing cooperation, a mechanism known as "trigger strategy" in game theory. Reciprocal strategies change the structure of the game that is being played, by reducing incentives to free-ride in repeated games. Repetition is crucial, so the value of π

in Hamilton's formula can also be interpreted as the probability that the interaction between two players will continue in the next round. The *shadow of the future* is a crucial ingredient to promote cooperation, for it can make the size of the (future) cake of cooperation indefinitely large.

18.4. THE FOLK THEOREM AND EQUILIBRIUM SELECTION

When biologists' ideas entered the economics literature in the 1980s, game theorists immediately recognized the analogy with a result known since the 1950s as *the folk theorem of repeated games* (Fudenberg and Maskin 1986, Fudenberg, Levin, and Maskin 1994). Informally, the folk theorem says that any strategy guaranteeing more than the worst payoff that can be inflicted by the other player is a Nash equilibrium in an infinitely repeated game. The intuition is simple: The threat of retaliation (by withdrawing cooperation) makes mutual cooperation advantageous, if the shadow of the future is long enough.

The folk theorem carries both good and bad news for evolutionary social theory. The good news is that in an indefinitely repeated game, cooperation is sustainable using trigger strategies that punish deviations from cooperative behavior and cancel the advantages of defection. The bad news is that *infinitely* many strategies are Nash equilibria of this sort. "We both cooperate all the time" is only one among many possible equilibria in the indefinitely repeated prisoner's dilemma. Consider a strategy profile such as "I cooperate on Monday, Wednesday, and Friday, and you cooperate on Tuesday, Thursday, Saturday, and Sunday." Such a profile delivers an average daily payoff of 1.71 to me, and 1.28 to you. Because it is better than the worst penalty I can inflict (by withdrawing cooperation) if you don't follow it, it is a Nash equilibrium in the indefinitely repeated game. But like infinitely many other strategy profiles, it is not equitable (it is intuitively unfair, in fact).

How do we select, among all the possible equilibria, the one that will be actually played? Evolutionary game theory, again, may come to the rescue. Some evolutionary philosophers—notably Allan Gibbard (1990), Ken Binmore (1998) and Brian Skyrms (2004)—have argued that the indefinitely repeated prisoner's dilemma game is, at roots, nothing but a coordination game. The argument goes as follows: If many strategies are equilibria in the indefinitely repeated prisoner's dilemma, the problem the agents are facing is conceptually similar to a coordination game in which the allocation of the fruits of cooperation is at stake. If they coordinate on "always defect," the fruits will be meager; if they coordinate on "always cooperate" the players will produce more. But there are going to be intermediate solutions as well.

These options can be represented as the outcomes of a *Nash bargaining problem*. A bargaining problem is an abstract coordination game defined by two coordinates: a set of "agreement outcomes," corresponding to possible divisions of the fruits of cooperation (or social contracts); and a "disagreement point" that is achieved whenever bargaining breaks down. In figure 18.1, all points in the interior of *S* are possible social contracts between players 1 and 2. The disagreement point (*d*) is set at (0, 0), where the x and y axes intersect.

Which one of the many possible agreements in *S* will be selected? That depends in part on how the coordination game is played. In a *Nash demand game*, the two players claim simultaneously their share of the fruits of cooperation. If the sum of their claims does not exceed the total size of the cake, they take whatever they have asked; otherwise, they earn nothing. Let us define a fair player as someone who always demands half of the cake. Notice that this demand includes an implicit trigger strategy: [12] Whenever a fair player is matched with a bold player who asks more than her fair share, they both get the disagreement payoff. (Fair may be a reciprocator in the repeated prisoner's dilemma, in other words, while Bold may be a free rider.)

As in the prisoner's dilemma, universal fairness is just one of many possible equilibria. The issue of equilibrium selection is particularly severe here, because every efficient pair of demands (every point on the contour of *S*) is a Nash equilibrium of the game. In a game with perfectly symmetric players, however, there seems to be no reason to claim less than an equal share. John Nash's (1950) seminal analysis of the bargaining problem was meant to capture this powerful intuition. The *Nash bargaining solution* is the combination of strategies that maximizes the product of the gains that the two players make with respect to the status quo.[13] Consider the simplified Nash demand game in figure 18.3. The game has only three possible efficient distributions of the surplus: (4, 6), (5, 5), and (6, 4); the status quo is (0, 0). The product of the gains of the two players is maximized choosing $5 \times 5 = 25$, which is therefore the Nash bargaining solution of this game. But (5, 5) is, of course, also the egalitarian solution, and the one that fits our pretheoretical intuitions about fairness.

Nash defended his solution by axiomatic method, that is, by demonstrating that it is the only allocation that satisfies four reasonable requirements.[14] But it can also be shown that the Nash bargaining solution is an evolutionarily stable strategy, and

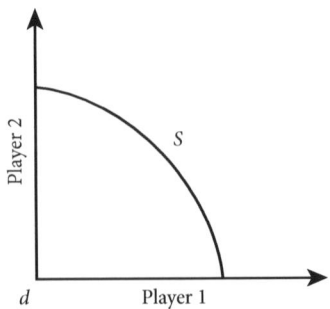

Figure 18.2 The Nash bargaining problem

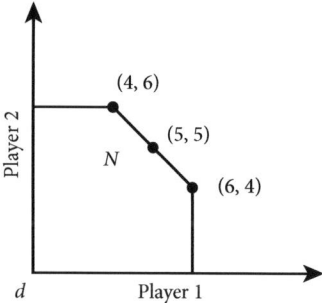

Figure 18.3 A symmetric Nash demand game

moreover that it is the stable strategy with the largest basin of attraction. In the Nash demand game a player who asks six (Bold) will make a gain only when meeting a partner asking four or less (Timid). But Timid will make gains when meeting Bold, Timid, as well as a player asking five (Fair). Thus Bold will tend to go extinct rather quickly; at that point Timid will be driven out by Fair. The unequal split (6, 4) is not evolutionarily stable in the demand game. The existence of polymorphic equilibria makes the analysis of this game somewhat complicated, but by adding just a moderate amount of correlation between strategies (assortativity), one can obtain convergence to the Nash bargaining solution.[15] It is tempting to claim that "this is, perhaps, the beginning of an explanation of the origin of our concept of justice" (Skyrms 1996,21).

18.5. POWER ASYMMETRIES

The simplified demand game analyzed in the previous section has a special, but very important feature: The position of the two players is completely symmetric with respect to their payoff structure. In such circumstances the players have equal power of bargaining, since they would lose exactly the same payoffs by not reaching an agreement. So it is not surprising that the Nash bargaining solution is also in some sense an egalitarian outcome (5, 5).[16] And yet, most cases of *real* bargaining involve asymmetries of some sort. To derive the evolution of fairness in such a special setting therefore can only be a preliminary step along the way to explaining real social contracts (Binmore 1998, Ernst 2005).

Games with asymmetric power give rise to asymmetric distributions of resources. Consider the game in figure 18.4 (we shall call it *Master and Servant*). In the state of nature—the war of all against all—Master enjoys a technological or physical advantage that allows the extermination of Servant and the appropriation of his resources. This outcome corresponds to the disagreement point (*d*) in figure 18.4. In the short term Master would benefit moderately from genocide (while Servant, of course, would go extinct). Both, however, would rather settle on a form of long-term

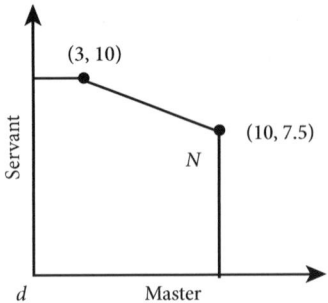

Figure 18.4 Master and Servant

cooperation that would produce greater wealth. In principle, Master would prefer Servant to work for him as a slave. This way, Master would be able to sell the product of Servant's work on the market and accumulate a fortune. Servant would get little reward and lead a miserable life but at least would be kept alive (10, 7.5). Alternatively, Master and Servant could strike a more equitable deal, where they share the fruits of Servant's labor on Master's land, and both enjoy a moderately wealthy lifestyle (3, 10).

The payoffs in figure 18.4 are normalized on a scale that goes from zero to ten. The combination that maximizes the product of players' utilities is Slavery (7.5 × 10 = 75), indicated by N in figure 18.4. Intuitively, the Nash bargaining solution captures the balance of power that is built into this game. Servant has much more to lose by not reaching an agreement: The difference between Slavery and the disagreement payoff (7.5–0) is larger, in Servant's subjective utility points, than the difference between Partnership and the disagreement point in Master's scale (3–0). Master gets a better deal, according to Nash, because he cares less about the social contract.

18.6. Fairness in the Lab

The Nash bargaining solution can be very unjust in asymmetric games, so evolutionary game theory loses some of its appeal in these contexts. But do people play the Nash bargaining solution in reality? Much of what we know about bargaining and coordination nowadays comes from experiments, and empirical data suggest that fairness and power are *both* important in real-life bargaining. In a seminal study Roth and Malouf (1979) observed that agreements in asymmetric demand games tend to fall on average between the egalitarian split and the Nash bargaining solution. This result was achieved in conditions of perfect information, but the egalitarian solution tends to become more predictive when the payoffs are not common knowledge among players.[17]

In other bargaining experiments power asymmetries are offset by fairness considerations even when players are fully informed about their own and their opponent's payoffs. A paradigmatic and much discussed case is the ultimatum game

(Güth, Schmittberger, and Schwarz 1982). The ultimatum game is the simplest sequential bargaining setting that one can think of: As in the Nash demand game, two players have the opportunity to share a sum of money, x. The disagreement point (or status quo) is zero for both players, but player 1 makes the first offer. This introduces an important power asymmetry: player 2 at this point can only accept or reject. The rational equilibrium of the ultimatum game is for player 1 to offer $(x-e, e)$, where e is the smallest positive unit of surplus division. [18] Player 2 then must accept because e is better than nothing—the ultimatum game in theory should give rise to highly inequitable distributions of the surplus.

When the ultimatum game is played for real, however, fair allocations figure prominently. Experiments in North America and Western Europe result in average offers between 30 and 40 percent of the cake, and a mode at the 50–50 split. Rejections are in the region of 20–30 percent, usually in response to unfair offers. In Japan and Israel the mode of player 1's offers goes down to 40 percent (Roth et al. 1991). Among the Au people of Papua New Guinea, the modal offer is in the region of 30 percent, and among the Hadza of West Africa it is as low as 20 percent. The Machiguenga in Peru make the lowest offers observed in the ultimatum game so far (15 percent) (Henrich et al. 2004). So it seems that while fairness norms play *some* role in these contexts, no single offer rate reflects a universal feature of human sociality. On the one hand, bargaining seems to reflect the balance of power; on the other, it seems to be influenced by local norms of fairness.

18.7. COOPERATION IN THE LAB

The ultimatum game is only one of several experimental designs delivering results that are inconsistent with game-theoretic concepts of rational play. Another important anomalous case is the class of experimental variations on the prisoner's dilemma game. A *public goods game* is a prisoner's dilemma with $n>2$ players and $s>2$ strategies. The strategies are typically framed as discrete individual contributions or transfers from a private endowment to a central "pot," which is then multiplied by a fixed factor and distributed equally among the group members regardless of their individual contributions. As in the prisoner's dilemma, the efficient solution is to put everything in the central pot (cooperate), but the Nash equilibrium is to give nothing (defect) and enjoy whatever the other players have contributed.

In spite of the theory, in one-shot public goods experiments about 50 percent of the total endowment is contributed by subjects incentivized with real money. This average hides a remarkable heterogeneity of behavior, ranging from full donations (100 percent of the endowment), to complete free-riding (0 percent), with many intermediate contributions. When the game is repeated for a finite number of rounds, the average contribution tends to decay, but it never goes to zero even after as many as 60 rounds of play.[19]

This behavior is intriguing, for a number of reasons. According to models of cooperation built on Hamilton's formula, cooperative or fair strategies should evolve only in relatively narrow circumstances. Robust cooperation should be possible within the family and in the small circle of people with whom we tend to interact frequently in our daily lives. The cooperation observed by anthropologists in small societies of hunter-gatherers and horticulturalists, which are strongly based on extended family networks and on repeated interactions with known individuals, are nicely explained by these evolutionary models. In large modern societies, however, where encounters with strangers are common and information is scant, spontaneous cooperation should break down entirely. So how do we explain the nontrivial amount of cooperation observed in experimental public goods games?

According to the friends of Hamilton's rule, the decay of cooperation lends support to their pessimistic views. Outside the boundaries of the family, the local community or the long-term relationships we cultivate with business partners, we need *other* incentives (like those provided by the police and judiciary courts) to prevent exploitation, free riding, and abuse of power (e.g., Binmore 2005, 82). The enemies of Hamilton's rule, in contrast, emphasize that a substantial amount of cooperation takes place even in adverse experimental circumstances. The typical design of public goods experiments includes random matching and strict anonymity. Moreover, people contribute to the public good even when the membership of the group changes at every round (Andreoni 1988). The conditions highlighted in classic evolutionary models—such as indefinite repetition, assortativity, perfect information, or genetic relatedness—clearly are not necessary for spontaneous cooperation to take place.

18.8. STRONG RECIPROCITY

The anomalies of public goods and ultimatum experiments have prompted many economists and social theorists to seek alternative explanations of the experimental evidence. In the remaining part of this chapter I discuss the most popular (and controversial) alternative to the classic models based on Hamilton's rule: *strong reciprocity* theory. Strong reciprocity theory stands on three legs: (1) a critique of classic accounts of cooperation; (2) a body of experimental evidence demonstrating the possibility of out-of-equilibrium behavior in games of cooperation; and (3) theoretical models simulating the evolution of reciprocal behavior in large groups.[20]

Strong reciprocity, unlike the weak form of reciprocity implicit in the folk theorem, is not driven by the maximization of future gains. A strong reciprocator does not cooperate because it is materially optimal for her to do so, either immediately or in the long run. Rather, she cooperates when others do it because she feels it is the right thing to do, and is ready to punish free riding in spite of the cost of doing so.[21] In a widely cited series of experiments, a group of economists led by Ernst Fehr have studied the effect of punishment on cooperation in public goods and other social dilemma games. The classic dilemma situation is modified adding a second stage, in which cooperators can punish free riders and destroy what they have illicitly gained. The parameter π in Hamilton's formula (the probability of meeting a cooperator) is kept high by disciplining free riders, rather than avoiding them as in assortativity, folk-theorem, and tit-for-tat approaches to cooperation. Punishment comes at a cost, however, in the form of a fee paid by the subjects who voluntarily engage in this sort of policing.[22]

In spite of the fee, many people are willing to sanction, and their threat is credible enough to raise cooperation significantly (Fehr and Gächter 2000, 2002). This result holds both when the game is played repeatedly by the same players (for a finite number of rounds), and when the membership of the group changes at every round. Costly punishment is effective even when it is administered by bystanders or third parties—that is, when the potential punishers are not themselves the victims but have merely witnessed exploitative behavior (Fehr and Fischbacher 2004).

Recent studies with brain imaging have provided further insights in the cognitive mechanisms implicated in such behavior. Costly punishment seems to be partly triggered by an impulsive negative reaction against injustice (Sanfey et al. 2003) and partly motivated by the sheer pleasure of punishing social deviants (de Quervein et al. 2004).[23] Building on this evidence, strong reciprocity theorists have argued that reciprocal motives are robust enough to be represented as social preferences governing individual behavior across a variety of decision tasks (see Falk and Fischbacher 2005).

18.9. Adaptation or Error?

Simulations and evolutionary models based on group selection suggest that strong reciprocity may evolve in favorable conditions (Boyd and Richerson 1992, Gintis 2000b, Henrich and Boyd 2001, Boyd et al. 2003, Bowles and Gintis 2003). Most of the empirical evidence in favor of the theory comes from economic experiments, however, so unsurprisingly the current debate revolves mainly about the interpretation of these results. The crucial issue is whether the behavioral patterns observed in the laboratory are robust enough to warrant the construction of models that depart substantially from the self-interest principle of classic economic theory and evolutionary biology.

Part of the problem is that evolutionary models describe behavior on an evolutionary timescale, and are not primarily intended to capture choices in experimental games that last only for a short time (Binmore 1999, 2005; Ross 2006). Of course there is no reason to expect that what evolves in the long run is similar to what we observe in the short run of experimental games. When people play public goods games in the laboratory, for example, they may bring with them norms and heuristic rules that help coordination in their everyday dealings. Such dealings are often in the form of indefinitely repeated games, where cooperation can be sustained by weak reciprocity mechanisms. The behavior observed in the laboratory thus may be just temporary error: the misapplication, in an unfamiliar setting, of a heuristic rule that works well (and is selected for) in the larger but more familiar games that we play in real life (cf. Binmore 1998, 1999, 2006; Trivers 2004; Burnham and Johnson 2005; Hagen and Hammerstein 2006). If these games were repeated long enough, out-of-equilibrium strategies would be eliminated by selection and learning, until behavior approaches the rational equilibria of the experimental games.

What is the advantage of the error account, compared to the strong reciprocity story? The key issue is whether learning takes place at such a pace that the experimental evidence of cooperation can be dismissed as mere statistical noise—temporary deviations from the robust long-term equilibria of the game of life. The critics of strong reciprocity often appeal to the decay of cooperation that is observed in repeated public goods experiments. With repetition subjects' "behavior changes as they are gaining experience," and "one can disrupt the march towards free riding in various ways, but when active intervention ceases, the march resumes" (Binmore 2010, 144). So in the repeated public goods game subjects eventually learn what is in their real interest, how to play the game correctly, or indeed what kind of game they are really playing.

Unfortunately this story is almost certainly wrong. There is extensive evidence that what subjects learn when they repeat the public goods game is *who their opponents are*. A group of 4–5 subjects (the typical size in most public goods experiments) is likely to include at least a free rider, and reciprocators who start by cooperating tend to switch to defection when they realize that another player is making an illicit profit by contributing below the group average. This move depresses the average rate of cooperation, triggering a spiral that quickly leads to the Nash equilibrium of the game. But several independent experiments show that reciprocating players who have withdrawn cooperation when matched with free riders, quickly revert to cooperation when matched with fellow reciprocators (Burlando and Guala 2005; Page, Putterman, and Unel 2005; Gächter and Thoni 2005). If they have learned what is in their true interest or what the game really is, these subjects seem to forget it very quickly as soon as their partners change.

Another weakness of the error story lies in the very idea that subjects must learn to defect in the public goods game. In fact, most reciprocators do not need to meet a free rider to learn what the appropriate response is. They know it in advance perfectly well: When asked what they would do if they met a free rider, about 50 percent of the sample declare that they would like to defect (Fischbacher et al. 2001, Burlando and Guala 2005). The decay of cooperation in finitely repeated public goods experiments is driven by conditional cooperators who learn who their partners are, not by dumb players who learn what the game is like.

One can insist of course that if the game was repeated long enough, in the *very* long run subjects would eventually learn to defect on other cooperators as well. The problem, however, is that what happens in the very long run is not empirically testable.

It is difficult to figure out what one could learn from repeating an experiment for hundreds or thousands of rounds (subjects would get bored, and what would such an experiment represent anyway? We never play the *same* game over and over for thousands of rounds in real life). Although we cannot logically rule out that convergence to rational equilibria would take place if the game was played longer, this challenge in itself does not lead to any new testable proposition: It belongs to the class of skeptical challenges that bring the discussion to a halt unless new evidence is offered in support.

18.10. Theory, Experiments, and Applications

The diffusion of experimental designs such as the public goods game and the ultimatum game in anthropology and biology is the most significant innovation of the last decade of human evolution studies. Nevertheless, there is disagreement about the implications of these experiments. Scientists with different theoretical commitments see different things through the lenses of public goods and ultimatum experiments, which is neither surprising nor disturbing given that all empirical science is theory-laden to some extent. It is more disturbing that so far supporters of different interpretations of ultimatum and public goods experiments have made little progress in reducing their disagreements by empirically informed argument. In fact, if anything they seem to have polarized on opposite positions that can hardly be reconciled (Gintis 2006, Binmore 2006).

The reciprocity debate revolves around at least two issues, which should be kept separate. One issue is *theoretical*, and concerns the use of models that depart from the standard assumptions of rationality and self-interest. The friends of Hamilton's rule argue that nonstandard models are unnecessary and sometimes misleading, while strong reciprocity theorists endorse the opposite view and claim that assuming optimizing behavior prevents full understanding of the human capacity to cooperate in complex large societies of genetically unrelated individuals.

The second issue is *practical*, and concerns the policy implications of weak and strong reciprocity models of cooperation. While supporters of the traditional approach hold a relatively pessimistic view concerning the domain of spontaneous cooperation, the friends of strong reciprocity argue that cooperation can be sustained in a decentralized manner across a much wider range of circumstances, and that the Leviathan can play a more limited role than implied by the pessimists (Fong, Bowles, and Gintis 2005).

These two issues are often conflated in the current debates. Laboratory data that are appropriate to test theoretical models are also used to draw conclusions on matters of policy and institutional design that would require a careful analysis of the conditions of application of these models. As I have argued elsewhere (Guala 2005,

2012) successful application requires the combination of laboratory *and* field data, so as to make the most of each source of evidence.

In the reciprocity controversy unfortunately the evidence pulls in opposite directions depending on which source (and which issue) one focuses on. There is no doubt that strong reciprocity theorists have scored a number of points on the theoretical front. The experimental evidence refuting standard models of cooperation is overwhelming, and the error argument largely misses the target. Yet the implications of this theoretical success are far from clear on the policy front. Elinor Ostrom—winner of the 2009 Nobel Prize for economics—has led the most sustained attempt to understand the functioning of public good institutions so far, using both experimental and field data. While her experimental evidence confirms that agents' motives are heterogeneous and depart substantially from those modeled on standard biological and economic theories, her study of naturally evolved institutions has provided insights that are largely consistent with those of the standard theories (Ostrom 1990, 2010; Poteete, Jaansen, and Ostrom 2010). The same message comes from the field data gathered by economic historians and anthropologists who have studied the emergence of spontaneous cooperation in a variety of different cultures and epochs (see Guala 2012, for an opinionated survey).

Hopefully the study of cooperation will soon address the problem of integrating field data with theoretical models and laboratory evidence. Philosophers incidentally may have something useful to say on the principles that should guide theory-choice and the use of data for policymaking, since using science to inform the design of institutions is a complicated activity that calls for special criteria of appraisal. [24] David Hume found it odd that "a maxim should be true in *politics* which is false in *fact*" (1978 [1741], 42). Accounts of cooperation based on Hamilton's rule may be a case in point: Three decades of experimentation have convinced most scholars that these models are strictly speaking false. Nevertheless, they warn us (correctly) that individual costs are crucial obstacles in the way toward cooperation and must be kept low as much as possible; that uncoordinated policing is dangerous and fragile; that the shadow of the future and the circulation of information matter enormously. Strong reciprocity models in contrast suggest that cooperation may survive even when some of these constraints are relaxed. But we currently know little about the range of situations across which spontaneous uninformed cooperation based on costly punishment may thrive, and the social engineer who decides to ignore Hume's principle will do so at her own peril.

NOTES

1. An incomplete list of monographs includes Ullmann-Margalit (1977), Schotter (1981), Sugden (1986), Binmore (1994, 1998, 2005), Skyrms (1996, 2004), Young (1998), Gintis (2000a, 2009), Vanderschraaf (2001), and Alexander (2007). Many more journal articles have been published in the same period.

2. "Gene-culture co-evolution" has become a background assumption of much contemporary research (cf. Feldman and Zhivotovsky 1992).

3. Similar claims can be found in Sugden (1986, 180–82) and Binmore (2005, 18–19).

4. "It is . . . a just *political* maxim, *that every man must be supposed a knave*; though, at the same time, it appears somewhat strange, that a maxim should be true in *politics* which is false in *fact*" (Hume 1978 [1741], 40–42).

5. See, e.g., Hausman (1998) and Fong, Bowles, and Gintis (2005). An influential contemporary defense of the knavery principle can be found in Brennan and Buchanan (1985).

6. But see Binmore (1994, chapter 2) for an opinionated critical overview.

7. Accessible introductions to evolutionary game theory can be found, e.g., in Skyrms (1996), Bergstrom (2002), Hargreaves-Heap and Varoufakis (2004, chapter 6), and Alexander (2009). For a critical perspective, cf. Sugden (2001).

8. Intuitively, a group of individuals playing a dominated strategy can always be invaded by mutants playing a dominating strategy, but not all equilibria are stable in the evolutionary sense. This is important, for the development of evolutionary game theory (especially in economics) was driven by the hope that the concept of stability would allow social scientists to make more precise predictions in games with multiple Nash equilibria (see, e.g., Samuelson 1997).

9. By assuming that a viable equilibrium must be evolutionarily stable I am applying here a particularly demanding requirement. One may argue, for example, that immunity from invasion by a large number of mutant strategies will suffice, without requiring complete immunity. This distinction, however, is not crucial for many of the arguments that follow.

10. Hamilton's formula can be derived from the so-called Price equation (Price 1970), a general description of the rate of change in a population of individuals with different traits, driven by the forces of selection and transmission.

11. Although Axelrod's results lack generality, his insights have been shown to hold in some classes of models. Interested readers are referred to Bendor and Swistak (1995, 1997) and Binmore (1998, chapter 3).

12. More generally, every demand m on the contour of S includes an implicit trigger strategy against those who ask more than $1-m$ (but not against those who ask less).

13. Or "disagreement point"—the payoffs that they would receive if their total claims exceeded the available resources.

14. The requirements are: (1) invariance to affine transformations of the payoffs, (2) Pareto optimality, (3) independence of irrelevant alternatives, and (4) symmetry. Notice that none of these properties is directly related with fairness, so the derivation of the latter is all the more remarkable.

15. Skyrms (1996, chapter 1) provides an introductory discussion of the Nash demand game. See also Young (1998) for a more technical analysis.

16. More precisely: It is "egalitarian" in the sense that it equalizes utility increments with respect to the status quo (d).

17. Other experiments tend to confirm this observation. See Kagel and Roth (1995, chapters 1 and 4), for a detailed discussion and survey of experimental results.

18. The ultimatum game has many Nash equilibria but only one *subgame perfect equilibrium*. The notion of subgame perfection formalizes the intuition that some Nash equilibria of a sequential game are to be discarded because it is not in the interest of a rational player to play them at that point of the game (they are "incredible threats"). In analyzing a dynamic game one should focus only on the paths that would be followed by a

rational player and ignore everything else. An equilibrium at the end of a path followed by a rational player is a subgame perfect equilibrium.

19. The classic survey of public goods experiments up to the early nineties is Ledyard (1995). For an update, see Chaudhuri (2011).

20. See, e.g., the papers in Henrich et al. (2004), Gintis et al. (2005).

21. This does not mean that strong reciprocators are cost-insensitive—in fact, a concern for one's own gain is always included in strong reciprocity models; it only means that reciprocity motives combined with self-interest result in individually suboptimal outcomes in a certain range of circumstances.

22. The behavior of costly punishers in public goods games, then, is analogous to the behavior of responders who reject unfair offers in ultimatum games.

23. This evidence confirms the old insight that emotions sometimes come to the rescue in situations where rational deliberation delivers suboptimal outcomes (Hirshleifer 1987, Frank 1988).

24. Unfortunately this is a neglected topic in philosophy of science, but see Alexandrova (2008) for a notable exception.

REFERENCES

Alexander, J. M. 2007. *The Structural Evolution of Morality*. Cambridge: Cambridge University Press.

Alexander, J. M. 2009. "Evolutionary Game Theory." In *The Stanford Encyclopedia of Philosophy*, Edward N. Zalta, ed., http://plato.stanford.edu/archives/fall2009/entries/game-evolutionary/.

Alexandrova, A. 2008. "Making Models Count." *Philosophy of Science* 75: 383–404.

Andreoni, J. 1988. "Why Free Ride? Strategies and Learning in Public Goods Experiments." *Journal of Public Economics* 37: 291–304.

Axelrod, R. 1984. *The Evolution of Cooperation*. London: Penguin.

Axelrod, R., and W. D. Hamilton. 1981. "The Evolution of Cooperation." *Science* 211: 1390–96.

Bendor, J., and P. Swistak. 1995. "Types of Evolutionary Stability and the Problem of Cooperation." *Proceedings of the National Academy of Science* 92: 3596–600.

Bendor, J., and P. Swistak. 1997. "The Evolutionary Stability of Cooperation." *American Political Science Review* 91: 290–307.

Bergstrom, T. C. 2002. "Evolution of Social Behavior: Individual and Group Selection." *Journal of Economic Perspectives* 16: 67–88.

Binmore, K. 1994. *Game Theory and the Social Contract I: Playing Fair*. Cambridge, MA: The MIT Press.

Binmore, K. 1998. *Game Theory and the Social Contract II: Just Playing*. Cambridge, MA: The MIT Press.

Binmore, K. 1999. "Why Experiment in Economics?" *Economic Journal* 109: F16–24.

Binmore, K. 2005. *Natural Justice*. Oxford: Oxford University Press.

Binmore, K. 2006. "Why Do People Cooperate?" *Politics, Philosophy and Economics* 5: 81–96.

Binmore, K. 2010. "Social Norms or Social Preferences?" *Mind & Society* 9: 139–57.

Binmore, K., J. Gale, and L. Samuelson. 1995. "Learning to Be Imperfect: The Ultimatum Game." *Games and Economic Behavior* 8: 56–90.

Boyd, R., and P. Richerson. 1985. *Culture and the Evolutionary Process*. Chicago: University of Chicago Press.

Boyd, R., and P. Richerson. 1992. "Punishment Allows the Evolution of Cooperation (or Anything Else) in Sizable Groups." *Ethology and Sociobiology* 13: 1–195.

Boyd, R., H. Gintis, S. Bowles, and P. Richerson. 2003. "The Evolution of Altruistic Punishment." *Proceedings of the National Academy of Sciences* 100: 3531–35.

Bowles, S., and H. Gintis. 2003. "The Evolution of Strong Reciprocity: Cooperation in Heterogeneous Populations." *Theoretical Population Biology* 65: 17–28.

Brennan, G., and J. Buchanan. 1985. *The Reason of Rules*. Cambridge: Cambridge University Press.

Burlando, R. M., and F. Guala. 2005. "Heterogeneous Agents in Public Goods Experiments." *Experimental Economics* 8: 35–54.

Burnham, T. C., and D. P. Johnson. 2005. "The Biological and Evolutionary Logic of Human Cooperation." *Analyse & Kritik* 27: 113–35.

Cavalli Sforza, L. L., and M. W. Feldman. 1981. *Cultural Transmission and Evolution: A Quantitative Approach*. Princeton, NJ: Princeton University Press.

Chaudhuri, A. 2011. "Sustaining Cooperation in Laboratory Public Goods Experiments: A Selective Survey of the Literature." *Experimental Economics* 14: 47–83.

Dawkins, R. 1976. *The Selfish Gene*. New York: Oxford University Press.

De Quervain D. J. F., U. Fischbacher, V. Treyer, M. Schellhammer, U. Schnyder, A. Buck, and E. Fehr. 2004. "The Neural Basis of Altruistic Punishment." *Science* 305: 1254–58.

Ernst, Z. 2005. "A Plea for Asymmetric Games." *Journal of Philosophy* 102: 109–25.

Falk, A., and U. Fischbacher. 2005. "Modeling Strong Reciprocity." In *Moral Sentiments and Material Interests*, Gintis et al., eds., 193–214. Cambridge, MA: The MIT Press.

Fehr, E., and U. Fischbacher. 2004. "Third-Party Punishment and Social Norms." *Evolution and Human Behavior* 25: 63–87.

Fehr, E., and S. Gächter. 2000. "Cooperation and Punishment in Public Goods Experiments." *American Economic Review* 90: 980–94.

Fehr, E., and S. Gachter. 2002. "Altruistic Punishment in Humans." *Nature* 415: 137–40.

Feldman, M. W., and L. A. Zhivotovsky. 1992. "Gene-Culture Coevolution: Toward a General Theory of Vertical Transmission." *Proceedings of the National Academy of Science* 89: 11935–38.

Fischbacher, U., S. Gächter, and E. Fehr. 2001. "Are People Conditionally Cooperative? Evidence from a Public Goods Experiment." *Economics Letters* 71: 397–404.

Fong, C. M., S. Bowles, and H. Gintis. 2005. "Reciprocity and the Welfare State." In *Moral Sentiments and Material Interests*, Gintis et al., eds., 277–302. Cambridge, MA: The MIT Press.

Frank, R. H. 1988. *Passions within Reason: The Strategic Role of Emotions*. New York: Norton.

Fudenberg, D., D. K. Levin, and E. Maskin. 1994. "The Folk Theorem with Imperfect Public Information." *Econometrica* 62: 997–1039.

Fudenberg, D., and E. Maskin. 1986. "The Folk Theorem in Repeated Games with Discounting or with Incomplete Information." *Econometrica* 54: 533–54.

Gächter, S., and C. Thoni. 2005. "Social Learning and Voluntary Cooperation among Like-minded People." *Journal of the European Economic Association* 3: 303–14.

Gibbard, A. 1990. *Wise Choices, Apt Feelings*. Oxford: Oxford University Press.

Gintis, H. 2000a. *Game Theory Evolving*. Princeton, NJ: Princeton University Press.

Gintis, H. 2000b. "Strong Reciprocity and Human Sociality." *Journal of Theoretical Biology* 206: 169–79.

Gintis, H. 2006. "Behavioral Ethics Meets Natural Justice." *Politics, Philosophy and Economics* 5: 5–32.

Gintis, H. 2009. *The Bounds of Reason: Game Theory and the Unification of the Behavioral Sciences*. Princeton. NJ: Princeton University Press.

Gintis, H., R. Boyd, S. Bowles, and E. Fehr, eds. *Moral Sentiments and Material Interests: The Foundations of Cooperation in Economic Life*. Cambridge, MA: The MIT Press.

Griffiths, P. E. 2008. "Ethology, Sociobiology, Evolutionary Psychology." In *A Companion to the Philosophy of Biology*, S. Sarkar and Plutyinski, eds., 393–414. Oxford: Blackwell's.

Guala, F. 2005. *The Methodology of Experimental Economics*. New York: Cambridge University Press.

Guala, F. 2012. "Reciprocity: Weak or Strong? What Punishment Experiments Do (and Do Not) Demonstrate." *Behavioral and Brain Sciences*. Forthcoming.

Güth, W., R. Schmittberger, and B. Schwarz. 1982. "An Experimental Analysis of Ultimatum Bargaining." *Journal of Economic Behavior and Organization* 3: 367–88.

Hagen, E. H., and P. Hammerstein. 2006. "Game Theory and Human Evolution: A Critique of Some Recent Interpretations of Experimental Games." *Theoretical Population Biology* 69: 339–48.

Hamilton, W. D. 1964. "The Genetical Evolution of Social Behavior. I." *Journal of Theoretical Biology* 7: 1–16.

Hargreaves-Heap, S., and Y. Varoufakis. 2004. *Game Theory: A Critical Text*. London: Routledge.

Hausman, D. M. 1998. "Rationality and Knavery." In *Game Theory, Experience, Rationality; Foundations of Social Sciences, Economics and Ethics: In Honor of John C. Harsanyi*, Werner Leinfellner and Eckehart Köhler, eds., 67–79. Dordrecht: Kluwer.

Henrich, J., and R. Boyd. 2001. "Why People Punish Defectors: Weak Conformist Transmission Can Stabilize Costly Enforcement of Norms in Cooperative Dilemmas." *Journal of Theoretical Biology* 208: 79–89.

Henrich, J., R. Boyd, S. Bowles, C. Camerer, E. Fehr, and H. Gintis, eds. 2004. *Foundations of Human Sociality: Economic Experiments and Ethnographic Evidence from Fifteen Small-Scale Societies*. Oxford: Oxford University Press.

Hirshleifer, J. 1987. "On the Emotions as Guarantors of Threats and Promises." In *The Latest on the Best*, J. Dupré, ed. Cambridge, MA: Harvard University Press.

Hume, D. 1978 [1741]. *A Treatise of Human Nature*. Oxford: Clarendon Press.

Kagel, J. H., and A. E. Roth, eds. 1995. *The Handbook of Experimental Economics*. Princeton, NJ: Princeton University Press.

Ledyard, J. 1995. "Public Goods: A Survey of Experimental Research." In *The Handbook of Experimental Economics*, J. H. Kagel and A. E. Roth, eds., 111–94. Princeton, NJ: Princeton University Press.

Maynard Smith, J., and G. R. Price. 1973. "The Logic of Animal Conflict." *Nature* 246: 15–18.

Nash, J. F. 1950. "The Bargaining Problem." *Econometrica* 18: 155–62.

Ostrom, E. 1990. *Governing the Commons: The Evolution of Institutions for Collective Action*. New York: Cambridge University Press.

Ostrom, E. 2010. "Beyond Markets and States: Polycentric Governance of Complex Economic Systems." *American Economic Review* 100: 1–33.

Page, T., L. Putterman, and B. Unel. 2005. "Voluntary Association in Public Goods Experiments: Reciprocity, Mimicry, and Efficiency." *Economic Journal* 115: 1032–53.

Poteete, A. R., M. A. Jaansen, and E. Ostrom. 2010. *Working Together: Collective Action, the Commons, and Multiple Methods in Practice*. Princeton, NJ: Princeton University Press.

Price, G. R. 1970. "Selection and Covariance." *Nature* 227: 520–1.

Ross, D. 2006. "Evolutionary Game Theory and the Normative Theory of Institutional Design: Binmore and Behavioral Economics." *Politics, Philosophy and Economics* 5: 51–79.

Roth, A. E., and M. W. K. Malouf. 1979. "Game-Theoretic Models and the Role of Information in Bargaining." *Psychological Review* 86: 574–94.

Roth, A., V. Prasnikar, M. Okuno-Fujiwara, and S. Zamir. 1991. "Bargaining and Market Behavior in Jerusalem, Lubljana, Pittsburgh and Tokyo: An Experimental Study." *American Economic Review* 81: 1068–95.

Samuelson, L. 1997. *Evolutionary Games and Equilibrium Selection*. Cambridge, MA: The MIT Press.

Sanfey, A. G., J. K. Rilling, J. A. Aaronson, L. E. Nystrom, and J. D. Cohen. 2003. "The Neural Basis of Economic Decision-making in the Ultimatum Game." *Science* 300: 1755–58.

Schotter, A. 1981. *The Economic Theory of Social Institutions*. Cambridge: Cambridge University Press.

Skyrms, B. 1996. *Evolution of the Social Contract*. Cambridge: Cambridge University Press.

Skyrms, B. 2004. *The Stag Hunt and the Evolution of Social Structure*. Cambridge: Cambridge University Press.

Sober, E. 1992 "Models of Cultural Evolution." In *Trees of Life*, P. Griffiths, ed., 17–39. Dordrecht: Kluwer.

Sperber, D. 1996. *Explaining Culture*. London: Blackwell.

Sugden, R. 1986. *The Economics of Rights, Cooperation and Welfare*, 2d ed. London: Macmillan.

Sugden, R. 2001. "The Evolutionary Turn in Game Theory." *Journal of Economic Methodology* 8: 113–30.

Trivers, R. L. 1971. "The Evolution of Reciprocal Altruism." *Quarterly Review of Biology* 46: 35–57.

Trivers, R. L. 2004. "Behavioural Evolution: Mutual Benefits at All Levels of Life." *Science* 304: 964–65.

Ullmann-Margalit, E. 1977. *The Emergence of Norms*. Oxford: Clarendon Press.

Vanderschraaf, P. 2001. *Learning and Coordination*. London: Routledge.

Wimsatt, W. C. 1999. "Genes, Memes and Cultural Heredity." *Biology and Philosophy* 14: 279–310.

Young, P. 1998. *Individual Strategy and Social Structure: An Evolutionary Theory of Institutions*. Princeton, NJ: Princeton University Press.

CHAPTER 19

CULTURAL EVOLUTION: INTEGRATION AND SKEPTICISM

TIM LEWENS

19.1. What Is Cultural Evolutionary Theory?

There are two rather different perspectives from which one might characterize what an evolutionary theory of culture is. The first begins from an entirely abstract standpoint. Evolution is change, and a theory of cultural evolution, one might argue, is any theory that explains cultural change, cultural stability, cultural divergence, or cultural homogenization over time. Such a usage is defensible, but it renders any diachronic theorist of culture an evolutionary theorist, whether they would willingly accept the appellation or not. Since plenty of theorists of culture—most obviously social and cultural anthropologists—have resisted the evolutionary label, we need to find another perspective from which to make sense of this resistance.

We can do this by understanding cultural evolutionary theories as reactions from within the community of evolutionary biologists to mainstream presentations of evolutionary theory itself. Textbook presentations often assume that evolutionary processes must work on genetically inherited variation (Mameli 2004). Researchers steeped in the traditions of evolutionary biology, and familiar with its explanatory tools, may then point out that genes are not the only things passed from parents to offspring (Avital and Jablonka 2000, Jablonka and Lamb 1998, Jablonka and Lamb 2005, Griffiths and Gray 1994, Richerson and Boyd 2005). In the human species (for example) skills, values, folk knowledge, technical scientific knowledge, linguistic expressions, and so forth can also be passed from parent to offspring by various forms of learning. If learned skills, or moral values, make a difference to survival and reproduction, then natural selection can promote the spread of skills or moral values, regardless of whether it is genetic inheritance or learning which explains their transmission. What's more, skills and moral values are not only transmitted vertically from parents to offspring: They can be passed from children to their friends, from teachers to children, from role models to adults, and so forth. Such forms of transmission further complexify the ways in which a population's makeup can change over time, forcing us to take into account more than vertical transmission. Those who explicitly describe themselves as cultural evolutionary theorists typically use these sorts of insights to argue that a complete account of human evolution needs modification if it is to encompass all the forces which have shaped our own species—and perhaps some cognitively sophisticated animal species—over time (Richerson and Boyd 2005).

This means that cultural evolutionary theorists tend to offer correctives to the dominant school of evolutionary psychology, the school exemplified by the work of Cosmides and Tooby (Barkow, Cosmides, and Tooby 1992; Tooby and Cosmides 1992). What is often called the Santa Barbara School of evolutionary psychology is committed to the view that human nature consists of a universal and innate set of adaptations, formed by natural selection acting on genetic variation, which has remained largely unchanged since the Pleistocene (Laland and Brown 2002). A consequence of this is that although the Santa Barbara School acknowledges that cultural change is causally significant, its impact is usually understood in terms of an altered cultural environment interacting with an unchanging set of cognitive adaptations. A good example of this sort of explanation accounts for modern levels of obesity by appealing to an ancient, adaptive preference for fatty foods interacting with far more widely available junk foods.

Cultural evolutionists typically argue for significant modifications to the general Santa Barbara view. First, they will claim that since natural selection can also act on learned traits, adaptations need not be innate. Second, they are likely to claim that cultural change can produce significant changes to our cognitive adaptations themselves, not merely to the cultural environments with which those adaptations interact.

Cultural evolutionary theory is itself a broad church. It is opposed to the most straightforward ways of applying Darwinian thinking to human culture, as exemplified by the Santa Barbara School. And yet it remains a recognizably biological way of thinking about human culture, not because it thinks of cultural phenomena as simple products or analogues of biological processes, but instead because it typically recommends that explanatory tools of a kind that have been successful in the biological sciences can be used to good effect when one confronts human culture. These include mathematical models similar to those used within population genetics, as well as various techniques for reconstructing the branching histories of biological species (Boyd and Richerson 1988; Cavalli-Sforza and Feldman 1981; Gray, Greenhill, and Ross 2007; Mace and Holden 2005).

Our two perspectives on the nature of cultural evolutionary theories allow us to make sense of what might otherwise be a puzzling tension (Lewens 2008). On the one hand, a theory of cultural evolution seems nonnegotiable: If we are to understand cultural change, there must be some way of explaining it, and whatever explains it will be a cultural evolutionary theory. On the other hand, theories of cultural evolution are up for grabs. Opposition to cultural evolutionary theories comes not from those who are opposed to understanding culture, but rather from those who doubt that tools adapted from evolutionary biology provide us with the best way of achieving that understanding (Kuper 2000b). Some even go so far as to deny that any strictly scientific account of culture is possible, while acknowledging that a more piecemeal form of interpretative explanation is appropriate (Geertz 1973). The remainder of this chapter seeks to explain and evaluate these sources of opposition, and in so doing to sharpen our understanding of the promises of cultural evolutionary theories.

19.2. Misunderstanding Evolution

Cultural evolutionary theorists themselves often suspect that hostility to their views is best explained by ignorance on the part of the objectors (see Perry and Mace 2010 for empirical evidence that this is indeed the case). Consider the example of Roger Smith, a historian much influenced by social anthropological accounts of the human species. He complains that "modern evolutionary accounts of human origins continue to reflect belief that there is an essential human nature, the nature all people share through their common root" (Smith 2007, 27). It is indeed true that the Santa Barbara School tends to assert the existence of a single shared human nature, although whether this makes human nature "essential" is far from clear. But Smith's comments don't do justice to the very broad range of conceptions of human nature, and of the sorts of forces that can affect it, that can be found in modern evolutionary thinking (Laland and Brown 2002). Cultural evolutionary theorists are likely to take issue with the Santa Barbara School on precisely the question of whether human nature is universal and unchanging.

Other instances of hostility to cultural evolution are harder to diagnose. Social anthropologists sometimes begin their attacks on cultural evolutionary theories by pointing to the worryingly progressive connotations of the term "evolution." An evolutionary account evokes images of higher and lower civilizations, and of a general tendency for societies to pass in sequence through these progressively more elaborate stages. Darwin himself tended to regard natural selection as a process with a fairly reliable tendency (albeit not a guaranteed one) to produce increasingly complex forms of organization (Lewens 2007). Early anthropologists who explicitly identified themselves as "evolutionary" also shared a commitment to this view of progress (Layton 1997, 2010). Attacks of this sort tend to rile modern evolutionary theorists, and for understandable reasons. The modern conception of natural selection has no intrinsic link to notions of progress. The fitter form will tend to replace the less fit in a given population, but there is no sense in which fitness can be equated with moral or technical superiority, and even when the fitter form replaces the less fit, mean fitness can still decrease (Sober 2000). Since the "fitter than" relation is not transitive, there is no guarantee that iterated cycles of selection will result in a population whose members would outcompete the organisms which made up the population at the beginning of the process (Lewens 2007). What is more, many cultural evolutionists are primarily interested in finding ways of explaining how learning can produce results that, from the perspective of biological fitness, do not lead to progress at all.

It remains difficult to characterize social anthropologists' hostility to evolutionary models as driven wholly by ignorance of the nonprogressive nature of modern evolutionary theory. Adam Kuper, for example, is fully aware that the modern conception of evolution has no intrinsic connotation of progress (Kuper 2000b). Kuper even claims that most modern social anthropologists probably believe that in general cultural change has been progressive (Kuper 2000a). He is emphatic that "Darwinism is, of course, utterly opposed in principle to any teleological way of thinking," and yet he immediately adds that "faith in progress is probably one of the subliminal attractions of any 'evolutionary' theory of culture" (Kuper 2000b, 179). This would amount to intolerable speculation if Kuper means to suggest that progressive notions are lurking in the minds of all cultural evolutionary theorists. Quite what Kuper does mean is not clear from his brief remark, but perhaps he is expressing concern about the ability of theorists to cleanse terms such as "evolution" of their progressive connotations, once these terms are released into the wilds of public reception.

19.3. A New Synthesis?

It is time to look in detail at some of the virtues claimed for evolutionary approaches to culture. In a special issue of *Journal of Evolutionary Psychology*, Alex Mesoudi and collaborators have recently asked, "Why Aren't the Social Sciences Darwinian?" (Mesoudi, Veldhuis, and Foley 2010). The special issue builds on earlier work by Mesoudi and others, who have made a case for thinking that the social sciences are not Darwinian, that they should be, and that one of the principle promises of taking an evolutionary approach lies in the possibility of an extended evolutionary "synthesis" (Mesoudi, Whiten, and Laland 2006). They note an apparent lack of progress in the social sciences compared with the biological sciences. They tentatively diagnose this as due to the presence of an evolutionary synthesis in the biological sciences and its absence in the social sciences. Were the social sciences to "go evolutionary," then significant progress would follow.

It is perhaps unsurprising that some anthropologists have reacted badly to these suggestions (Ingold 2007). Some prominent social anthropologists have agreed with

Mesoudi et al. (2006, 2010) regarding the lack of progress in their field, but it is hard to imagine how one could devise a measure of progress that allows the biological and social sciences to be compared. Even if lack of progress is acknowledged, it is not clear that the lack of attention to evolutionary processes is to blame. Social anthropologists, confronted with the problem of explaining cultural change and cultural diversity, are presented with the question of how to offer an account of one culture to readers from what is usually a different one. Necessarily this requires that one grapple with questions of the adequacy of translation, of the tools one has for making one group's perspective available to another, and of the nature of explanation in this domain—whether, for example, one should seek to evoke how things look to them, whether instead one should give a neutral account based on objective principles, and whether an opposition of these two approaches makes sense. This reflection also requires fieldworkers to think about the likely practical impacts of their writings on the people they study. In sum, anthropologists have found it difficult not to run headlong into complex philosophical and political questions, in ways which biologists have often been able to evade. Lack of progress is partly explained by the very difficult conceptual subject matter which confronts social anthropology; and when biological anthropologists wonder with exasperation if their social anthropological colleagues are even trying to do science, the answer is that perhaps they aren't, and with good reason (Risjord 2007). What's more, calls to render the social sciences evolutionary are hardly new: If decades of attempts to do so haven't resulted in significant progress it isn't clear if the diagnosis rests on a failure to perform that integration properly, or a simple lack of cogency of evolutionary approaches (Kuper 2000b).

Let us set these skirmishes aside. They concern the question of whether, and why, the social sciences have made less progress than the biological sciences. Instead, we can look directly at what an evolutionary synthesis would be like, and what it can be expected to achieve, within the social sciences. We can begin by asking how Mesoudi et al. understand what an evolutionary synthesis is. In a paper looking back to Darwin, they claim that:

> The synthetic framework provided by evolutionary theory . . . has successfully integrated several disparate disciplines into a coherent research program, evolutionary biology, and has the potential to do the same for the study of culture. Just as Darwin drew upon evidence from zoology, botany, geology, palaeontology, and physiology, this paper has incorporated findings from anthropology, psychology, sociology, linguistics, and history, with the hope of integrating these traditionally separate disciplines. (Mesoudi, Whiten, and Laland 2004, 9)

They are quite right to say that Darwin's theorizing drew on an extraordinary range of disciplines. The question is whether the moral for the social sciences is simply that they should also draw on insights from a wide range of disciplines, including (say) economics, sociology, biology, psychology, linguistics, history, literary studies, and so forth. That would amount to an eclectic theory, and a synthetic theory, but in what sense would that theory be distinctively evolutionary?

It is notable that even in Darwin's own thinking on (for example) the evolution of the moral sense in man, natural selection is at times in the forefront, and at times gives way to discussion of learning, the dissemination of public rules of conduct, the rational revision of moral teachings based on observed consequences, and so forth. Darwin proposes an evolutionary synthesis in the sense that he draws together numerous disciplines to provide a historical account of change in species. Darwin's synthesis does not, however, always place natural selection in the foreground, and natural selection is not always used to stitch together diverse disciplines, especially not when Darwin is discussing what we would now think of as human cultural history. One cannot use Darwin's own works to argue that the social sciences should become Darwinian, if what one means by this is that a social scientific synthesis must have natural selection at its core.

Indeed, one cannot even use the successes of biology to argue that the social sciences should become Darwinian. It has often been noted that molecular biologists frequently proceed thorough ignorance of evolutionary theory. Perhaps there are insights that they have missed because of this, and perhaps evolutionary considerations are becoming more prominent within molecular biology (Morange 2010). But one can hardly accuse their field of a lack of progress, and it exaggerates the unity of biology itself to suggest that all biologists are guided by evolutionary considerations.

There are plenty of social or cultural anthropologists who recognize the importance of an eclectic, interdisciplinary approach to their subject, which draws constructively on results from the natural sciences. Cognitive anthropologists—and here I have in mind thinkers such as Maurice Bloch (1998)—are a case in point. A modest synthesis might recognize the value of evolutionary ideas within an eclectic anthropology. But many anthropologists seem to think that cultural evolutionary concepts have nothing much to contribute, even to an eclectic synthesis (Bloch 2000). Why is that?

19.4. MEMES

One very specific source of skepticism is directed at the use some cultural evolutionists make of the *meme* concept. Meme theorists seek to understand cultural change using models which make the analogy between biological and cultural evolution very close indeed, and which draw on one rather specific account of biological evolution (Blackmore 2000, Dawkins 1989, Dennett 1996). Genes, so the story goes, are *replicators*. Roughly speaking, that means they have the ability to make copies of themselves. Replicators, the story continues, are required for evolutionary processes to occur, because evolution requires some entity that can explain resemblance across generations. The effects of genes on the "vehicles" which house them make a difference to the rate at which they are copied, and evolution is a matter of the differential survival of replicators in virtue of these effects.

Meme theorists begin by endorsing the view that evolution requires replicators, and they then expand the stock of replicators beyond genes to include cultural ones.

In a famous list, Dawkins (1989, 192) tries to illustrate the sorts of things that are memes. They are "tunes, ideas, catch-phrases, clothes fashions, ways of making pots or of building arches." What all of these things are supposed to have in common is that they are "contagious." The gist of the meme theory is easiest to appreciate if we focus on ideas. Here the story goes that different ideas—they might be scientific theories, moral values, or conceptions of the supernatural—spread from mind to mind. Alternative views about the nature of physical reality, the proper treatment of animals, or the character of God appear at moments in human history in the minds of just a few individuals, and can increase their representation in a population. They do so at different rates, and their abilities to make copies of themselves depend on their adaptive "fit" with their local environments. These environments are cultural, and are partly constituted by the successes and failures of preexisting memes: For example, the question of how likely it is that a given scientific hypothesis will take hold in a community of investigators will depend, in part, on how it integrates with what they already believe.

One might object that scientific hypotheses, say, don't make copies of themselves autonomously. If I come to believe that the theory of evolution by natural selection is true, that is in large part because of my own efforts to read biological works, or to grasp what my teachers tell me, to understand the concepts involved, and to balance evidence in favor of the view. Quite how much of a problem this is for memetics is unclear. Sensible memeticists are likely to endorse the active role of the thinking organism in the copying of memes: Even in the case of genes, replication is not literally autonomous in the sense of being independent of background conditions, and it is not a problem for memetics if humans also have very active roles in enabling the copying of ideas. But we shouldn't take seriously occasional claims by memetics' more zealous enthusiasts about the "disappearance" of the self in the light of meme theory (Dennett 2001); nor should we come to the view that it is memes, rather than thinking, deliberating agents, who are in control of cultural change.

Opponents of the meme concept have gone further than this, and pointed out a sleight of hand in the examples laid out above. It is one thing to claim, in a rather general sort of way, that different ideas may spread at different rates through a population. It is another thing to say that they do so in virtue of a copying process. In characterizing some idea as a meme, one claims that it spreads through replication. Strands of DNA count as replicators because the structure of a given DNA strand is causally responsible for the resembling structure of a daughter strand (Godfrey-Smith 2000b). Can we say the same thing about ideas? Is the structure of a given idea causally responsible for the structure of a resembling daughter idea? In some cases it may be. Sometimes individuals struggle to figure out precisely what someone else thinks, and they form similar views in virtue of that process. But this certainly isn't how ideas always spread. In some cases, large numbers of people may come to believe the same thing because they all witness similar events, not because their ideas are copied from each other. In hybrid cases one group, sharing a given set of ideas, may structure a cultural environment such that other individuals are highly likely to learn ideas of the same type from that environment. Dan Sperber and Scott Atran have complained that in many cases when ideas are reproduced, a given idea triggers the formation of a similar one in the mind of another in virtue of a commonly shared background conceptual repertoire and constraining psychological biases, not because of a strict copying process (Atran 2001, Sperber 2000). Here, again, we can document the rates of spread of different ideas through a population, but it is a mistake to think that talk of ideas as replicators is interchangeable with talk of rates of spread of those ideas.

It is important to note that theories of cultural evolution need not, and often do not, endorse the meme concept: Skepticism about memes does not amount to skepticism about cultural evolution (Lewens 2008). The most respected writers in cultural evolutionary theory tend to begin from the observation that evolutionary models need to be expanded to take account of the ways in which various forms of learning can modify the effects of natural selection (Richerson and Boyd 2005). This need not be achieved by positing cultural replicators that are analogous in their role to genes. Many cultural evolutionists have been keen to stress that they use their models to explore the ways in which cultural processes can differ from the processes of biological evolution. To give a concrete example (also used in Lewens 2008), Cavalli-Sforza and Feldman studied decreasing birth rates in Italy in the late nineteenth century (Cavalli-Sforza and Feldman 1981). Italian women went from having around five children on average to just two. Does natural selection explain this phenomenon? Surely not, or at least not as natural selection is usually conceived (Sober 1992). Sometimes one's long-run reproductive output is maximized by having just a few healthy offspring, who are likely to produce healthy grandchildren, rather than by having a great many sickly offspring, who may not survive until reproductive age. But it is hard to believe that this is what explains the reduction in birth rates in the period in question. Birth rates did not decline because birth rates are inherited, and women with low birth rates had more offspring in the long run. Instead, birth rates declined because Italian women acquired the desire for smaller numbers of children from their peers, and from women in their mothers' generation. The cultural evolutionist takes the moral of this story to be that birth rates can be modified independently of natural selection, via learning from nonfamily members. The first thing this example demonstrates about models of cultural evolution is that they need not proceed by thinking of the desire for a smaller family, say, as a cultural replicator similar to a gene.

The example also helps to illustrate a puzzling feature of models of cultural evolution. It is obvious that there are plenty of changes to human populations that are not explained by natural selection, and are instead explained by the things we learn from each other. What, then, do Cavalli-Sforza and Feldman take themselves to have achieved? Part of the answer lies in the detailed consequences of their efforts to model this change in a mathematical manner. We can ask what needs to be the case for birth rates to decline, on the assumption that natural selection favors higher birth rates. That such a thing is possible is obvious, but the precise circumstances under which it is possible are not. Cavalli-Sforza and Feldman claim that if women simply acquired whichever preference for family size was the most widely adopted in their local cultural environment, then cultural inheritance would not have enough of an effect to overcome natural selection. Women must be disposed to acquire the preference for small family size even when it is present in only a small proportion of their cultural circle if small family size is to replace large family size in the population as a whole. This sort of claim is not at all obvious.

Cultural evolutionists frequently begin their theorizing from a starting point that does not invite use of the meme concept, and may therefore appear neutral regarding its propriety. Their project is to integrate various forms of learning into evolutionary theory, in a way that leaves open the degree to which learning has anything in common with genetic inheritance. In some cases, this sort of project has the end result of undermining the meme concept. Boyd and Henrich, for example, argue that cultural evolution needs no replicators (Henrich and Boyd 2002). Even in cases where cultural evolution is cumulative—that is, where the scientific or technical achievements of one moment in time can be built upon and improved—all that is required is stability at the level of the population as a whole. They claim that this can be achieved with highly error-prone copying when individuals learn from each other, so long as the nature of the errors can be compensated for in some other way. This, they say, is achieved through "conformist bias"—a tendency individuals have to adopt whatever the most prevalent view happens to be in a given population.

19.5. Passivity

A casual reading of the meme concept might lead one to think that cultural evolutionary theories cast humans in a passive role. As noted before, this kind of thinking is encouraged by the likes of Blackmore, Dawkins, and Dennett, who occasionally talk of "viruses of the mind," of the self as a "pack of memes," and so forth. All this generates an image of humans as inadvertently colonized by memes, which they control no more than they control the bacteria in their guts. Tim Ingold complains about this in his attack on Mesoudi et al. (2006):

> There is, first of all, the question of how an approach to evolution couched in terms of the replication, transmission and distribution of "cultural traits" can accommodate historical agency. Recall that cultural traits are supposed to adapt to their environment by means of humans, rather than humans adapting by means of their cultural knowledge and skills. In this topsy-turvy world, it seems, human beings are but the means by which traits propagate themselves in an environment. (Ingold 2007, 16)

We will come to Ingold's worry about the phrase "cultural trait" later in this chapter. Let us concentrate for the moment on the alleged passivity of humans as they are cast by cultural evolutionary theorists. Evolutionary models typically aim to track the incidence of various beliefs, practices, and so forth in a population. But in itself this kind of analysis is wholly compatible with the thought that humans are active choosers, evaluators, and users of beliefs, practices, or whatever. It is ironic that Ingold attacks Mesoudi et al. (2006) on these grounds, for Mesoudi and collaborators are in the vanguard of the theory of *niche-construction*, which stresses the mistakes of thinking that adaptation is always produced by environments shaping passive organisms via natural selection, which offers as a corrective the thought that adaptation is often achieved through the alteration of environments by active organisms, and which explicitly endorses the role of choice in the construction of environments (Laland, Odling-Smee, and Feldman 2001; Mesoudi, Whiten, and Laland 2007).

As mentioned before, the historian Roger Smith (2007) has also drawn on anthropological thinking to justify his skepticism of evolutionary models. He seems to think that humans, as reflective, language-using creatures, cannot be investigated using the evolutionary tools one uses to investigate other animals. Smith cites Clifford Geertz with approval:

> Believing, with Max Weber, that man is an animal suspended in webs of significance he himself has spun, I take culture to be those webs, and the analysis of it to be therefore not an experimental science in search of law but an interpretive one in search of meaning. (Geertz 1973, 5)

Man is "an animal suspended in webs of significance he himself has spun." What is Geertz saying here? In part he is pointing out that groups of humans communicate, they formulate public rules of conduct, they develop expectations, and these acts of communication have various complex feedback relationships resulting in the formulation of new rules of conduct, new expectations, and new forms of communication. This is all undeniable, but how, if at all, does it cast doubt on the propriety of applying evolutionary thinking to humans? Perhaps one might replace Geertz's "webs of significance [man] himself has spun" with Laland, Odling-Smee, and Feldman's language of "niche-construction." The cultural environment is sustained by the niche-constructing action of humans; these cultural niches have impact on subsequent evolutionary and developmental trajectories of human populations; and different human populations occupy different cultural niches. Theories of niche-construction stress the reflexive nature of the relationship between organisms and their environments. The development of organisms is guided by stimuli from environments, but those environments are themselves produced by the earlier actions of organisms. The evolution of organisms is affected by selection pressures imposed by environments, but those environments, and the selection pressures they bring to bear, are shaped by the nature of organic activity, including active choice.

19.6. ENLIGHTENMENT

Up to this point, we have defended cultural evolutionary thinking against a variety of attacks. Cultural evolution is not committed to the existence of cultural replicators, it does not truly require that memes (as opposed to deliberating agents) are in control of cultural change, it does not deny the reciprocal interactions between humans and the cultural niches which their activities sustain. If cultural evolutionary theories can encompass so much, is there a danger that in fact they have nothing novel to offer the investigator of cultural phenomena? This criticism has also been popular among cultural evolution's critics: the taunt is not that there is no sense in which culture evolves; the taunt, rather, is that knowing that this is the case doesn't give us any insights that aren't available in a more traditional vocabulary (Lewens 2009a).

It isn't hard to see why one might have this worry. As mentioned before, the question of how likely some cultural item—an idea, a technique, a tool—might be to spread through a population will depend on a whole range of factors, such as (in the case of techniques) the ease with which it can be learnt, the perceived and actual utility it has, its integration with existing sets of techniques, its reliance on easy-to-acquire economic resources, and so forth. All of these factors can be combined to yield a single "fitness" value for the technique, and if we know which of a set of competing techniques has the higher fitness, we thereby know which is most likely to proliferate. But the evolutionary model hasn't told us anything surprising about what makes techniques likely to spread; it has simply parasitized our existing knowledge of these matters (Sober 1992, Lewens 2009a, Lewens 2008).

A poor response to this challenge, which sometimes comes from memeticists, is to argue that the evolutionary view reminds us that the adoption of a given idea, practice, or whatever need not be in the interests of its users; it need only be in the interests of the proliferating meme (Dennett 1996). We should not explain the proliferation of suicide, say, by asking how suicide benefits those who kill themselves. If the suicide meme is able to find some means of spreading swiftly through a population of thinkers it will do so, whether it benefits its hosts or not. This is a weak response because there are plenty of mainstream views about cognition that remind us that people make decisions all the time that are not in their best interests. We don't need memetics to expose the widespread existence of various forms of irrationality, weakness of will, self-deception, false consciousness, subconsciously motivated action, and so forth. We do need to understand these diverse forms of thinking better, and it isn't clear that memetics will help us to do this. The weakness of the memeticists' response is further compounded by the vacuity of the claim that the interests we should track are those of memes themselves. What this means, simply, is that the likely proliferation of an idea through some society can be represented as the "fitness" of that idea; to ask "what's in it for the meme?" is just another way of asking "what might make a given meme fit in this population?" But once again, any enlightenment to be had from this insight is parasitic on a vast range of more specific, local, and contextually sensitive concerns about why some ideas are more likely to proliferate than others. Taking the meme's-eye perspective on scientific theory change, for example, is just another way of setting out on a familiar investigation of the sorts of factors that determine which theories get accepted in a given research community.

A much better response to these charges of vacuity can be found in Sterelny's cautious defense of the meme concept (Sterelny 2006). He concedes that in many cases anything that can be explained by citing a meme's fitness can also be explained in terms of the features of human psychology which make some cultural items more memorable, learnable, or valuable than others. But Sterelny also makes a plausible case for thinking that at least in some instances the features that make technologies, say, especially easy to copy are not contingent on the precise features that human psychology happens to take in local contexts. He suggests that spears, for example, are the sorts of things whose intrinsic constitution makes them easy to reverse-engineer (that is to say, it is easy for a user or observer to figure out how they were made), valuable even when one fails to copy a spear perfectly, easy to make small improvements to, and useful to almost anyone even in their rudimentary versions. This all means that spears are the sorts of things that would be likely to be taken up and improved upon even if the fine-grained details of human needs and learning abilities had been different. For that reason, it is appropriate to focus on the properties of spears themselves, over the precise details of human psychology, when explaining the proliferation of spear technology. And that, in turn, establishes a strong explanatory role for the spear meme.

Sterelny's argument is a good one; even so, it is worth noting its significance. Sterelny advises restricting the meme concept to material artifacts, and he succeeds in showing that some artifacts have features that make it likely that they will be adopted given a broad range of plausible psychologies. This is a good response to anyone who attacks the meme concept on the grounds that it is the fine-grained features of human psychology, *rather than* features of the objects taken up and adapted by human users, which always explain cultural change. But Sterelny's response acknowledges that the question of what makes some cultural item apt for spread and refinement is a matter of interaction between features of cultural items and aspects of human psychology, even when the relevant psychological features (and hence the fitnesses of the memes in question) may sometimes be preserved across fairly broad counterfactual variation. Sterelny's argument encourages attention to the explanatory roles of features of artifacts themselves; this is something which has been underlined by a variety of theorists (including social and cognitive anthropologists) who have drawn attention to artifacts as repositories of cultural tradition and knowledge even when they have not made specific use of the meme concept (Clark and Chalmers 1998; Henare, Holbraad, and Wastell 2007; Mithen 2000).

Another good response to critics of cultural evolution draws attention to the diversity of questions one might ask about cultural change. Cultural evolutionary theorists are often interested in very broad contrastive questions. Why, for example, is our own species able to acquire increasingly detailed folk knowledge regarding local flora and fauna, in a cumulative manner, while the ability of other species (including reasonably cognitively sophisticated species) to engage in this sort of cumulative cultural evolution seems so much more limited? An answer to this sort of question needs to examine the ways in which various different forms of learning and other forms of inheritance need to be structured if skills and items of knowledge are to be preserved and refined across populations. Such a theory may tell us what it is about the human species which explains our uniquely developed capacity for constructing scientific theories. It does not follow from this that evolutionary insights will have much to say to sociologists of knowledge, intent on investigating the local factors that might explain the uptake of Darwinism in France; but the fact that many students of cultural change have little to learn from evolutionary theory does not show that the theory has nothing informative to offer to anyone.

Perhaps the most developed response to critics of cultural evolutionary theory, and one which we have already endorsed implicitly, comes from Boyd and Richerson's assertion that the key to an evolutionary theory of culture lies in "population thinking" (Richerson and Boyd 2005). They are no fans of memetics (Boyd and Richerson 2000). Their approach seeks to understand the changing constitution of groups of people over time, as they are affected by genetic inheritance, natural selection, and also by various forms of learning. Their approach is populational in the sense that instead of investigating the nature of specific episodes of learning in detail ("How, precisely, did Hank become a proficient car mechanic?"), they are interested in looking at whole populations. But they do so by examining the consequences of individual instances of learning at the population level. This demands a rather abstracted, rough-and-ready characterization of individual psychologies, albeit one informed by psychological research. Boyd and Richerson's work can provide novel insights because it is not at all obvious how the combined interaction of individual learning psychologies might yield patterns of change or stasis at the populational level. Mathematical models, sometimes reasonably complex ones, are needed to explore these phenomena. It is a surprising result to learn of the circumstances under which populations can be stable enough to enable cumulative evolution, in spite of error-prone learning. Or, to return to Cavalli-Sforza and Feldman's work, it is surprising to discover what form learning must take if it is to overwhelm natural selection.

Boyd and Richerson have articulated a good response to those who claim that models of cultural evolution have nothing to teach that we don't already know. But their argument does not provide a potent resource for those who wish to argue that an evolutionary approach might revolutionize and reinvigorate a moribund set of social sciences. First, there are costs as well as benefits to be had from abstract modeling of the sort Boyd and Richerson engage in. They point to a model by Henrich that suggests that a population of a certain size is required to sustain the know-how needed for reasonably complex technologies (Henrich 2004). This has a novel result: If we wish to explain why technological complexity decreases in given societies, it may be enough to cite dwindling population size. This is how Henrich explains declining technological complexity on Tasmania. Now while Henrich does indeed produce an abstract model whose assumptions yield the result that small populations cannot sustain complex tools, the assumptions of this model can be questioned—especially if the model has a questionable fit with what is known about technological complexity and population size. Henrich's models have been questioned on precisely these grounds (Read 2006, Kline and Boyd 2010). My point here is not to argue one way or the other for Henrich's model. My point, simply, is to keep in mind that healthy interplay between abstract populational modeling and the nitty-gritty of archaeological and anthropological fieldwork will be required to keep both sides honest.

This brings us to the question of whether population thinking is distinctively evolutionary. It is evolutionary in the very broad sense that it allows us to understand change over time. Population thinking is obviously a far broader way of approaching the phenomena of change than natural selection, and only some of the abstract models of cultural evolutionists make use of analogues of natural selection (Lewens 2009a, Godfrey-Smith 2009). Any form of inquiry that models the collective impact on a whole of the aggregated interactions of its parts seems to qualify as populational: In this sense, one might think of statistical mechanics as a form of population thinking. Partly for this reason it is hard to claim population thinking for evolutionary biology alone. Darwin was a population thinker in the minimal sense that he aimed to explain the alteration of species in terms of processes acting on individual organisms, but he did not make progress in modeling such changes mathematically (Lewens 2009b). This reinforces the verdict tentatively arrived at earlier. The tools of population thinking are perhaps the most valuable contributions that cultural evolutionary theorists bring to the study of cultural change. But population thinking is not distinctively Darwinian, nor will population thinking displace traditional forms of historical inquiry, ethnographic investigation, and so forth. Once again, the best modern synthesis we can hope for in the study of culture is an eclectic synthesis in which evolutionary tools add to, but do not dominate, the range of tools already available.

Before closing this section, let us consider a final response from cultural evolutionary theorists. In addition to studying the mechanisms underlying various forms of cultural inheritance and their impact on populational change, we can also attempt to reconstruct the pattern of cultural change. Here, again, many evolutionists have argued that biological tools might have considerable impact (Gray, Greenhill, and Ross 2007; Mace and Holden 2005). There are well-developed methods for uncovering the structure of evolutionary trees: that is, for understanding which species split from which others and when. It seems clear that cultural items of many kinds—most obviously languages, but also tools and techniques—also stand in recognizable genealogical relationships, and this has led many biological anthropologists to use phylogenetic methods from the biological sciences to reconstruct the history of borrowings in the cultural realm. A long-standing objection to the use of phylogenetic methods rests on the thought that cultural genealogies are not tree-like at all; they instead take the form of networks (Gould 1988). It is quite true that cultural change is often highly reticulated. A complex object like a car does not evolve independently of other technologies: It constantly lends to, and borrows from, other technological lineages. Any understanding of the technical genealogy of the car would have to recognize its incorporation of elements of the technical makeup of airplanes, hi-fi systems, horse-drawn carriages, and so forth.

A full examination of disputes regarding cultural phylogenies could easily occupy a book in its own right. In lieu of such a full examination, let us simply note, first, that cultural evolutionists are often happy to acknowledge the frequently reticulated nature of cultural phylogenies. They point out that we are beginning to discover the extent to which much of biological evolution is also reticulated. Bacteria, for example, do not form genealogically isolated lineages, hybridization is rife among plants, and there is also considerable borrowing of elements of the genome between apparently isolated mammalian species. Of course this might show simply that phylogenetic modes of inference are doubly imperiled: They don't work for much of the biological world either. But cultural evolutionists are further heartened by developments within biology itself, which aim to reconstruct partially reticulated trees by proposing so-called reconciliations of the conflicting trees that traditional methods often propose for species and genes (Gray, Greenhill, and Ross 2007). (To see why this is the case, consider how horizontal transfer of some genetic sequence across distantly related species will typically mean that a genealogical tree for the sequence in question will not coincide with the tree proposed for the species.)

These phylogenetic methods may be helpful to the social sciences, but they are unlikely to wholly replace more traditional genealogical techniques. Methods of phylogenetic reconstruction need to be calibrated, and this involves comparison with known histories of cultural items. So, for example, Tëmkin and Eldredge used the known history of change in the cornet (a wind instrument) to argue that most phylogenetic methods give misleading results about the instrument's true history (Tëmkin and Eldredge 2007). Gray, Greenhill, and Ross think that Tëmkin and Eldredge's work is in fact a cause for optimism: They suspect the history of the cornet may not be typical of artifact histories in general, and they point out that by refining the deliveries of phylogenetic methods in the light of known histories, we might construct better and better trees. The debate reminds us of two things. First, in many cases anthropologists have access to historical evidence, often in the shape of written documents, which gives a reasonably clear and reliable picture of the historical evolution of a given artifact lineage. They have no need of phylogenetic tools. Second, if, as Gray et al. contend, we need to withhold judgment on the extent to which cultural evolution shows general patterns of reticulation, then it seems that reliance on traditional anthropological methods of determining historical borrowings will continue to be valuable as phylogenetic methods establish their strengths and limitations.

19.7. PARTICULARITY

All theories of cultural evolution will tend to regard the cultural entities they treat—beliefs, values, techniques, and so forth—as particles. It is worth spending a little time clarifying in what sense this is the case. The population thinking which typically characterizes cultural evolutionary theories demands that we can characterize cultural entities in the abstract, in ways that allow them to be counted. These theories require, for example, that we can discuss having a small family, believing in God, or making a traditional basket in such a way that we can determine, in the population under study, how many instances of these entities may be present. If we cannot do this, then we cannot characterize a human population in terms of the differential representation in that population of one technique compared with another, we cannot characterize the individuals in the population as having cognitive dispositions making it easier for them to learn one technique over another, and so forth.

This is a minimal sense of "particle." As we have already seen, it does not entail that the cultural entities in question are understood as replicators, nor that their adoption need be understood as a passive matter. One's mind is not infested with ideas in the way that a kitchen is infested with flies. There is also a difference between thinking of beliefs as particles in this qualified sense, and thinking of cultural inheritance as particulate in the sense that genetic inheritance is particulate. Boyd and Richerson have a minimally particulate view of cultural entities, and yet they explicitly acknowledge that a given individual's beliefs are not typically copies from single sources, but are instead the blended product of exposure to several sources. If I believe that stealing is wrong, this is probably not because I have inherited this belief from one person; rather, it is because of exposure to many members of society.

Some criticisms of cultural evolutionary theory exaggerate the commitments of minimal particularity. A cultural evolutionist can acknowledge, for example, that the explanation of the spread of some belief through a given culture may not be a matter of transmission from one individual to another, but may instead be produced by the interactions of similarly structured learning dispositions with commonly encountered elements of the natural and social environments. A cultural evolutionist can also acknowledge that one cannot understand the meaning of some cultural entity in isolation. This point can be expressed in both a logical and a functional manner. On the one hand, belief in God may have quite different content, depending on the other beliefs with which it interacts (Kuper 2000b). It may involve commitment to the supernatural, to a personality of a certain kind, to intervening agency, and so forth. What's more, that belief has the potential to serve quite different functions, also depending on context. Unraveling the extent to which the content and functions of such a belief may vary from one society to another is a complex matter.

Modern cultural evolutionary theories have less in common with late nineteenth- and early twentieth-century evolutionary schools, which, as noted previously, tended to endorse a progressive model whereby cultures advance through recognizable stages, and more in common with so-called diffusionist models. The latter group argued, among other things, that direct diffusion of elements of culture from one culture to another could allow the supposed stages of the evolutionist to be jumped. The diffusionist school in turn was criticized, on much the same grounds as theories of cultural evolution have been criticized: beliefs or practices, so the story goes, are in part constituted by the elements with which they interact. There is no consistently identifiable cultural particle that can survive movement from one culture to another.

As Maurice Bloch puts it, "The fact that the habit of making noodles came to Italy from China does not explain why the Italians make noodles. . . . What noodles mean to Italians is therefore quite different from what it means to the Chinese" (Bloch 2000, 198).

A minimal conception of cultural particles can survive criticism from those who rightly point to the importance of cultural context in determining the identity of the particles in question; however, the demise of diffusionism reminds the cultural evolutionist of two very important themes that significantly complexify cultural evolutionary analysis. First, while electrons are the same sorts of particles wherever they are studied, one should not assume that a belief in God is logically or functionally the same sort of thing wherever it is studied. Second, there is little reason to think that the distinctive tools of cultural evolutionary theories—by which I mean the modeling resources of population thinking—are likely to replace traditional tools of cognitive investigation, historical understanding, and interpretive engagement, when one attempts to understand these logical and functional relations (Tehrani 2006). Having said all this, so long as cultural evolutionists are sensitive to the potentially misleading implications of particulate thinking, no impediment remains to using population thinking to understand stasis, change, and interaction once analysis is restricted to a well-demarcated cultural group. Indeed, even some of the more exotic philosophical debates about the nature of belief and interpretation, which have themselves pervaded social anthropology, can be ducked by the population thinker. Population thinking itself does not require that beliefs are inherently private, internal entities, rather than public and observable entities. Population thinking does not require mental representations to be exclusively in the head, as opposed to their being partially constituted by the materials of extended cognition, for them to be countable. This is not to say, of course, that all views about the nature of representation and interpretation are compatible with population thinking. If one thinks that individual persons simply do not hold beliefs or values, and instead one insists that beliefs and values are properties of social groups as a whole, then beliefs and values are no longer the sorts of things that can be counted in the way that population thinking tends to demand. Some of the disputes between social anthropology and cultural evolution perhaps rest on a deep clash of underlying philosophical commitments; here, though, it is worth noting the comparatively minimal, and largely intuitive, position to which the population thinker is committed.

19.8. THE CULTURE CONCEPT

Social anthropologists tend to welcome reflection on the nature of the concepts and explanations they deal in (Kuper 2000a). Suitable targets for such reflection include the culture concept itself, the nature of interpretation, the likely potential for law-like scientific anthropological insights as opposed to piecemeal local illumination, and so forth. Such reflection is typically historically and politically informed. Social anthropologists sometimes go on to accuse cultural evolutionary theorists of paying insufficient attention to what they might mean by terms like "cultural variant" or even by "culture" itself; the result is that evolutionists do not appreciate the extent to which they have assumed contentious stances, which have been held by others before them, in complex debates that are decades old. Meanwhile, cultural evolutionists shrug, and say that the only way to make progress in science is to get one's hand dirty, construct highly simplified models, and not fret too much over unproductive navel gazing (Mesoudi, Whiten, and Laland 2006).

Consider our understanding of culture itself. Mesoudi, Whiten, and Laland endorse Boyd and Richerson's definition of culture as "information capable of affecting individuals' behavior that they acquire from other members of their species through teaching, imitation, and other forms of social transmission" (Mesoudi, Whiten, and Laland 2006, 331). One problem with this definition is that it appears to exclude too much. It implies that culture consists in the sorts of elements that can be passed from one individual to another. But entities such as legal systems, even though they are sustained by large constellations of individuals, are not the sorts of things that are passed from one individual to another. These sorts of collectively maintained social institutions are surely parts of culture.

This brings us to a second problem. Boyd and Richerson's key term "information" is not given any explicit definition; instead we are told of the sorts of things it is meant to cover. It is, Mesoudi et al. say, "employed as a broad term incorporating ideas, knowledge, beliefs, values, skills, and attitudes" (Mesoudi, Whiten, and Laland 2006, 331) Note, once again, that these sorts of things are sometimes transmitted from one individual to another. They do not mention artifacts here, and yet anthropologists, as well as cognitive scientists who focus on so-called extended cognition, have drawn attention to the ways in which artifacts, too, are parts of culture, and the ways in which they might be said to store transmissible information regarding cultural traditions, status, folk knowledge, or technical knowledge (Clark and Chalmers 1998, Mithen 2000).

In general to say that something constitutes information is ambiguous. We can begin by outlining a first, broad sense of the term. Fingerprints constitute information about the perpetrator of a crime: They do so in the sense that if one knows about fingerprint patterns, one can make inferences about likely suspects. In a second and quite different sense, we can think of information as something that is intentionally encoded: In this sense, a recipe book contains information about how to make cakes, a spoken testimony contains information about a crime. If information, on Mesoudi et al.'s (2006) account, is supposed to incorporate skills and attitudes, such that the ability to kick a football (rather than a list of instructions about how to kick a football) literally *is* information, then presumably information is being used in something like the first, broad sense. But now it becomes unclear how far we should stretch Mesoudi et al.'s definition of culture. If their account is elastic enough to encompass skills, then it seems it must include artifacts, too. Artifacts (i) contain information in our first broad sense, (ii) the information contained in them can affect behavior, and (iii) they can be acquired from other species members by social transmission, for example when someone makes a pot by observing someone else do the same. If technical artifacts—pots, spears, and the like—are parts of culture, why should we now exclude social artifacts, such as legal codes or governmental systems? We have already seen that they do not seem to fit Mesoudi et al.'s (2006) definition, but it now appears arbitrary to exclude entities that clearly constrain and guide cultural change, merely on the grounds that they are not passed from one individual to another. Why not go even further, and include aspects of natural and built environments? These, too, are involved in constraining and explaining patterns of human action, and they are typically sustained (like social institutions) by the collective activities of groups of humans acting across generations. None of this is meant to constitute an assault on Mesoudi et al.'s (2006) definition: It is simply a demonstration of the complexities of saying what culture is, and of the pitfalls of assuming that culture is the sort of thing stored in people's brains.

Defining culture, then, is tricky. So is understanding how to reconcile traditional biological concerns relating to genetic inheritance with more recent cultural evolutionary concerns regarding inheritance via learning. One popular way of doing this is via so-called dual inheritance theories, which conceive of genetic and cultural inheritance as alternative inheritance channels. It can make sense to ask whether cultural variation, rather than genetic variation, explains some aspect of phenotypic variation in a population. In a group of genetic clones, in which some learn one set of moral values from their parents, and others learn different moral values from their parents, it is obviously not genetic variation that explains variation in the population. But this insight does not legitimate talk of inheritance channels (Gray 1992). In talking of "channels" one seems to imply that some aspects of phenotypic resemblance are controlled by the genetic channel, others by the cultural channel. Here there are grounds for suspicion. If one wishes to explain why offspring resemble their parents in terms of (let us say) their moral values, we need to show how it is that like comes to produce like. Without the passing on of genes, there would be no such resemblance. The same goes for the passing on of cultural resources: Unless offspring are exposed to the teaching of their parents, they will not acquire their values. But the cultural environment is itself produced by genes interacting with each other and with a diverse array of developmental resources, including preexisting social resources, to produce adults capable of communication and offspring capable of understanding. It isn't clear how we can demarcate distinct channels of inheritance within the web of developmental relations by which inheritance comes to be realized.

Both of these criticisms—of the use of the information concept and of talk of distinct inheritance channels—have been laid at the door of cultural evolutionists by social anthropologists. But again, they have also been put forward by a subset of cultural evolutionists. So-called developmental systems theory (DST), developed by Griffiths, Gray, and Oyama, places stress on the interaction of many different forms of developmental resource—anything from genetic transmission to the passing on of symbionts or the stability of the environmental niche in which parents and offspring develop—in the production of parent-offspring similarity (Gray 1992; Griffiths and Gray 1994, 1997, 2001; Oyama 2000). DST's advocates have been suspicious of the propriety of information talk (Griffiths 2001), and of the prospects for locating distinct inheritance channels within this network of interactions. And yet, some DST theorists—most obviously Russell Gray—have been among the most enthusiastic advocates of cultural evolutionary theory.

All of this suggests that developmental systems theory may provide the most likely site for a full reconciliation between social anthropology and cultural evolutionary theory. DST's insistence on the complexity of inheritance makes it a suitable venue for the eclectic synthesis I have advocated in this chapter. Indeed, Ingold's attack on cultural evolutionary theory reserves significant praise for DST (Ingold 2007). Yet there is reason to think prospects for a constructive synthesis may not be so rosy. This is not the place for a full evaluation of DST. But we can note that its critics have sometimes remarked not that DST is a distortion of biological reality, but that its insistence on complexity fails to provide the sorts of simplifications that make a biological theory workable (Godfrey-Smith 2000a). Although Mesoudi et al. insist that "it is important first to define 'culture' explicitly and to specify the precise theory of cultural evolution that we are advocating," in truth they devote rather little time to clarifying and assessing the definition they put forward (Mesoudi, Whiten, and Laland 2006, 331). This need be no bad thing. Scientific progress is often made by ignoring difficulties in defining one's terms, by deliberately distorting the complexities of real phenomena to make them tractable, and so forth. So even if some practicing biologists acknowledge that at some fundamental level DST is an appropriate view of the organic world, it is not clear that this is likely to dissuade them from what they regard as practical talk of information, inheritance channels, and so forth. As Ingold points out, social anthropologists make simplifying assumptions, too. Ethnographic fieldwork will be heavily edited before it arrives in an anthropological monograph. But here the simplifications are rarely for the sake of general explanatory models, and more usually for the sake of local explanatory narratives. Simplification is not itself a distinguishing feature of cultural evolutionary approaches; even so, we should not expect DST to provide a resolution of what are deep disputes about the proper nature of simplification. Perhaps we need no resolution. Instead, we can endorse a form of methodological pluralism, whereby cultural evolutionary theory aims for a simplifying grand theory, at the same time as social anthropology aims for detailed local narrative. In any genuine synthesis both traditions should inform each other.

ACKNOWLEDGMENTS

I am grateful to Philippe Huneman, Harold Kincaid, and Catherine Wilson for their extremely helpful comments on earlier drafts. Sections of this chapter were presented in August 2010 at the Darwin in Communication conference in Beijing, and in January 2011 at the Institut d'Histoire et de Philosophie des Sciences et des Techniques, Paris. I am also grateful to Beth Hannon for help with preparing the final manuscript. The final stages of research leading to these results received funding from the European Research Council under the European Union's Seventh Framework Programme (FP7/2007–2013)/ERC Grant agreement no. 284123.

REFERENCES

Atran, S. 2001. "The Trouble with Memes." *Human Nature* 12 (4): 351–81.

Avital, E., and E. Jablonka. 2000. *Animal Traditions: Behavioural Inheritance in Evolution.* Cambridge: Cambridge University Press.

Barkow, J. H., L. Cosmides, and J. Tooby. 1992. *The Adapted Mind: Evolutionary Psychology and the Generation of Culture.* Oxford: Oxford University Press.

Blackmore, S. J. 2000. *The Meme Machine.* Oxford: Oxford University Press.

Bloch, M. 1998. *How We Think They Think: Anthropological Approaches to Cognition, Memory, and Literacy.* Boulder, CO: Westview Press.

Bloch, M. 2000. "A Well-Disposed Social Anthropologist's Problems with Memes." In *Darwinizing Culture: The Status of Memetics as a Science,* Robert Aunger, ed., 189–204. Oxford: Oxford University Press.

Boyd, R., and P. J. Richerson. 1988. *Culture and the Evolutionary Process.* Chicago: University of Chicago Press.

Boyd, R., and P. J. Richerson. 2000. "Memes: Universal Acid or a Better Mousetrap?" In *Darwinizing Culture: The Status of Memetics as a Science,* Robert Aunger, ed., 143–62. Oxford: Oxford University Press.

Buller, D. J. 2005. *Adapting Minds: Evolutionary Psychology and the Persistent Quest for Human Nature.* Cambridge, MA: The MIT Press.

Cavalli-Sforza, L. L., and M. W. Feldman. 1981. *Cultural Transmission and Evolution: A Quantitative Approach.* Princeton, NJ: Princeton University Press.

Clark, A., and D. Chalmers. 1998. "The Extended Mind." *Analysis* 58 (1): /.

Darwin, C. 2004 [1879]. *The Descent of Man.* 2d ed. James Moore and Adrian Desmond, eds. London: Penguin.

Darwin, C. 1964 [1859]. *On the Origin of Species.* Facsimile of the 1st edition. Ernst Mayr, ed. Cambridge, MA: Harvard University Press.

Dawkins, R. 1989. *The Selfish Gene.* 2d ed. Oxford: Oxford University Press.

Dennett, D. C. 1996. *Darwin's Dangerous Idea: Evolution and the Meanings of Life.* London: Penguin.

Dennett, D. C. 2001. "In Darwin's Wake, Where Am I?" *Proceedings and Addresses of the American Philosophical Association* 75 (2): 11–30.

Geertz, C. 1973. "Thick Description: Toward an Interpretive Theory of Culture." In *The Interpretation of Cultures,* Clifford Geertz, ed., 3–30. New York: Basic Books.

Godfrey-Smith, P. 2009. *Darwinian Populations and Natural Selection.* Oxford: Oxford University Press.

Godfrey-Smith, P. 2000a. "On the Status and Explanatory Structure of Developmental Systems Theory." In *Cycles of Contingency: Developmental Systems and Evolution,* Russell Gray, Paul Griffiths, and Susan Oyama, eds., 283–98. Cambridge, MA: The MIT Press.

Godfrey-Smith, P. 2000b. "The Replicator in Retrospect." *Biology and Philosophy* 15 (3): 403–23.

Gould, S. J. 1988. *An Urchin in the Storm.* New York: Norton.

Gray, R. D. 1992. "Death of the Gene: Developmental Systems Strike Back." In *Trees of Life: Essays on the Philosophy of Biology*, Paul Griffiths, ed., 165–209. Dordrecht: Kluwer.

Gray, R. D., S. J. Greenhill, and R. M. Ross. 2007. "The Pleasures and Perils of Darwinizing Culture (with Phylogenies)." *Biological Theory* 2 (4): 360–75.

Griffiths, P. E. 2001. "Genetic Information: A Metaphor in Search of a Theory." *Philosophy of Science* 68 (3): 394–412.

Griffiths, P. E., and R. D. Gray. 2001. "Darwinism and Developmental Systems." In *Cycles of Contingency: Developmental Systems and Evolution*, Russell Gray, Paul Griffiths, and Susan Oyama, eds., 195–218. Cambridge, MA: The MIT Press.

Griffiths, P. E., and R. D. Gray. 1994. "Developmental Systems and Evolutionary Explanation." *The Journal of Philosophy* 91 (6): 277–304.

Griffiths, P. E., and R. D. Gray. 1997. "Replicator II–Judgement Day." *Biology and Philosophy* 12 (4): 471–92.

Henare, A. J. M., M. Holbraad, and S. Wastell. 2007. *Thinking through Things: Theorising Artefacts Ethnographically*. London: Routledge.

Henrich, J. 2004. "Demography and Cultural Evolution: How Adaptive Cultural Processes Can Produce Maladaptive Losses: The Tasmanian Case." *American Antiquity* 69 (2): 197–214.

Henrich, J., and R. Boyd. 2002. "Culture and Cognition: Why Cultural Evolution Does Not Require Replication of Representations." *Culture and Cognition* 2 (2): 87–112.

Ingold, T. 2007. "The Trouble with 'Evolutionary Biology.'" *Anthropology Today*: 23 (2): 13–17.

Jablonka, E., and M. J. Lamb. 1998. "Epigenetic Inheritance in Evolution." *Journal of Evolutionary Biology* 11 (2): 159–83.

Jablonka, E., and M. J. Lamb. 2005. *Evolution in Four Dimensions: Genetic, Epigenetic, Behavioral, and Symbolic Variation in the History of Life*. Cambridge, MA: The MIT Press.

Kline, M. A., and R. Boyd. 2010. "Population Size Predicts Technological Complexity in Oceania." *Proceedings of the Royal Society B* 277 (1693): 2559–64.

Kuper, A. 2000a. *Culture: The Anthropologists' Account*. Cambridge, MA: Harvard University Press.

Kuper, A. 2000b. "If Memes Are the Answer, What Is the Question?" In *Darwinizing Culture: The Status of Memetics as a Science*, Robert Aunger, ed., 175–88. Oxford: Oxford University Press.

Laland, K. N., and G. R. Brown. 2002. *Sense and Nonsense: Evolutionary Perspectives on Human Behaviour*. Oxford: Oxford University Press.

Laland, K. N., J. Odling-Smee, and M. W. Feldman. 2001. "Niche Construction, Biological Evolution, and Cultural Change." *Behavioral and Brain Sciences* 23 (01): 131–46.

Layton, R. 1997. *An Introduction to Theory in Anthropology*. Cambridge: Cambridge University Press.

Layton, R. 2010. "Why Social Scientists Don't Like Darwin and What Can Be Done About It." *Journal of Evolutionary Psychology* 8 (2): 139–52.

Lewens, T. 2007. *Darwin*. London: Routledge.

Lewens, T. 2008. "Cultural Evolution." In *The Stanford Encyclopedia of Philosophy*, Edward N. Zalta, ed. Available at http://plato.stanford.edu/archives/fall2008/entries/evolution-cultural/.

Lewens, T. 2009a. "Innovation and Population." In *Functions in Biological and Artificial Worlds: Comparative Philosophical Perspectives*, Ulrich Krohs and Peter Kroes, eds., 243–58. Cambridge, MA: KLI/The MIT Press.

Lewens, T. 2009b. "The Origin and Philosophy." In *The Cambridge Companion to the Origin of Species*, Michael Ruse and Robert Richards, eds., 314–32. Cambridge: Cambridge University Press.

Mace, R., and C. J. Holden. 2005. "A Phylogenetic Approach to Cultural Evolution." *Trends in Ecology & Evolution* 20 (3): 116–21.

Mameli, M. 2004. "Nongenetic Selection and Nongenetic Inheritance." *The British Journal for the Philosophy of Science* 55 (1): 35.

Mayr, E. 1982. *The Growth of Biological Thought: Diversity, Evolution, and Inheritance.* Cambridge, MA: Harvard University Press.

Mesoudi, A., A. Whiten, and K. N. Laland. 2004. "Perspective: Is Human Cultural Evolution Darwinian? Evidence Reviewed from the Perspective of *The Origin of Species.*" *Evolution* 58 (1): 1–11.

Mesoudi, A., A. Whiten, and K. N. Laland. 2006. "Towards a Unified Science of Cultural Evolution." *Behavioral and Brain Sciences* 29 (04): 329–47.

Mesoudi, A., A. Whiten, and K. N. Laland. 2007. "Science, Evolution and Cultural Anthropology: A Response to Ingold." *Anthropology Today* 23 (2): 18.

Mesoudi, A., D. Veldhuis, and R. A. Foley. 2010. "Why Aren't the Social Sciences Darwinian?" *Journal of Evolutionary Psychology* 8 (2): 93–104.

Mithen, S., 2000. "Mind, Brain, and Material Culture: An Archaeological Perspective." In *Evolution and the Human Mind: Modularity, Language and Meta-Cognition*, Peter Carruthers and Andrew Chamberlain, eds., 207–17. Cambridge: Cambridge University Press.

Morange, M. 2010. "How Evolutionary Biology Presently Pervades Cell and Molecular Biology." *Journal for General Philosophy of Science* 41 (1): 113–20.

Oyama, S. 2000. *The Ontogeny of Information: Developmental Systems and Evolution.* Durham, NC: Duke University Press.

Perry, G., and R. Mace. 2010. "The Lack of Acceptance of Evolutionary Approaches to Human Behaviour." *Journal of Evolutionary Psychology* 8 (2): 105–25.

Read, D. 2006. "Tasmanian Knowledge and Skill: Maladaptive Imitation or Adequate Technology?" *American Antiquity* 71 (1): 164–84.

Richerson, P. J., and R. Boyd. 2005. *Not By Genes Alone: How Culture Transformed Human Evolution.* Chicago: University of Chicago Press.

Risjord, M. 2007. "Ethnography and Culture." In *Philosophy of Anthropology and Sociology*, Stephen Turner and Mark Risjord, eds., 399–428. Amsterdam: Elsevier.

Smith, R. 2007. *Being Human: Historical Knowledge and the Creation of Human Nature* New York: Columbia University Press.

Sober, E. 1992. "Models of Cultural Evolution." In *Trees of Life: Essays on the Philosophy of Biology*, Paul Griffiths, ed., 17–40. Dordrecht: Kluwer.

Sober, E. 2000. *Philosophy of Biology.* 2d ed. Boulder, CO: Westview Press.

Sperber, D. 2000. "An Objection to the Memetic Approach to Culture." In *Darwinizing Culture: The Status of Memetics as a Science*, Robert Aunger, ed., 163–74. Oxford: Oxford University Press.

Sterelny, K. 2006. "Memes Revisited." *The British Journal for the Philosophy of Science* 57 (1): 145.

Tëmkin, I., and N. Eldredge. 2007. "Phylogenetics and Material Cultural Evolution." *Current Anthropology* 48 (1): 146–53.

Tehrani, J. 2006. "The Uses of Ethnography in the Science of Cultural Evolution." *Behavioral and Brain Sciences* 29 (4): 363–64.

Tooby, J., and L. Cosmides. 1992. "The Psychological Foundations of Culture." In *The Adapted Mind: Evolutionary Psychology and the Generation of Culture*, Jerome Barkow, Leda Cosmides, and John Tooby, eds., 19–136. Oxford: Oxford University Press.

CHAPTER 20

COORDINATION AND THE FOUNDATIONS OF SOCIAL INTELLIGENCE

DON ROSS

20.1. Introduction: The Problem of Coordinated Agency

The institutionalized arrangement of the behavioral sciences is based on a strong distinction between the study of individuals and the study of societies. Notwithstanding the sometime popularity of reductionism and methodological individualism, the autonomy of the social sciences from psychology and of macroeconomics from microeconomics reflects general awareness of something deeper than the fact that people behave differently in groups than they do when alone or with intimates. However, it is only recently, by comparison with the vintage of the main disciplinary distinctions, that a rough consensus has evolved over what the something in question is. Summarizing drastically, the following assumptions have become widely accepted: Social behavior involves coordination, and coordination is such a complicated set of processes that wherever one cannot abstract away from it, one enters into a distinct domain of modeling problems.

The rise of game theory, and of philosophical thinking informed by it, is historically crucial to the new preeminence of this understanding. Game theory makes explicit, to an extent grasped only fitfully before its development, that outcomes of social interaction tend to be radically unlike outcomes of individual cognition. People embedded in games with one another find themselves doing things they could not understand or predict through rationalization by exclusive reference to their own beliefs and desires—that is, through the mere assumption of the intentional stance toward themselves. Social scientists, especially economists, had long appreciated that competitive pressures interfere systematically with individual optimization. However, game theory has given precision and detail to a key point that Adam Smith broadly grasped: Except in the unusual case of zero-sum games competition is not the opposite of coordination, but is mediated by it. Businesses selling similar products in the same market typically want to coordinate on strategies for competing with one another that do not drag them into price wars. People seeking social power aim to recruit at least some useful followers from among those they succeed in outcompeting, so political success does not best consist in the incapacitation of all rivals. And so on.

The thinker who contributed more than any other to carrying the message of the centrality of coordination from the precincts of formal game theory out into the broader community of social scientists was Thomas Schelling (1960). A key insight of Schelling's was that players' knowledge of one another's strategy sets and utility functions, no matter how complete, is insufficient for efficient coordination in many games that have multiple equilibria. Players should also model one another's recursive belief structures, using whatever knowledge they happen to possess about one another's behavioral track records and exposure to data, in search of information bases for coordination of expectations. Harsanyi (1967) launched the ongoing project of formalizing such phenomena. It is sometimes complained, especially by philosophers who seek rational foundations for all choice, that the use of exogenous focal points—recursively structured networks of players' beliefs about what other players are most likely to cognitively attend to or behaviorally respond to—has resisted such formalization. This is confused if understood in one sense. Focal points are products of shared psychology and cultural convergence. There is no reason to expect that a theory of rationality will have anything to say about their provenance, though it has much to say about their exploitation.

When modeled explicitly, the reasoning processes needed to support equilibria in beliefs seem highly cognitively demanding, even in simple two-person cases. Consider, for example, the common game structure that came to be known as battle of the sexes. Preserving the gender stereotypes that inspired that name, suppose that, in a lost age before mobile telephones, a couple who have faithfully imprinted their culture's preferred models of men and women go their separate ways in the morning, agreeing to meet to see a film in the evening. Suppose that their tendencies to thoughtlessness extend into the very practical domain, so that before parting they neglect to jointly decide which movie to see. Back when there were no cell phones there were a lot of cinemas, so as the evening approaches the members of the couple have a problem: At which cinema does each expect to find the other?

If they were a new couple who didn't yet know much about one another's preferences or histories, they might both be well advised to choose a cinema that has some distinguishing property that makes it publicly salient. For example, they might go to the largest cinema in town, or the most central. Another possible principle would be to focus on a property that is specially salient to their two-person subsociety, such as closeness to their home. These are alternative focal points. Our couple will see a film together only if they each focus on the same principle of salience.

The example so far closely recapitulates Schelling's original thought experiments. Such instances lead immediately to reflection on conventions.[1] Treatments of the standard battle of the sexes game in introductory game theory texts typically fail to note that the sexism of the classic toy case is not gratuitous. Culturally promoted stereotypes might lead the woman to expect that the man will prefer the most violent of the available film choices. The same culture might instruct him that she will favor a romantic option. This yields the familiar matrix shown in figure 20.1.[2] In this case, if the structure of the game captures everything the players know, then the Nash equilibrium strategy is for each to randomize, while attaching a higher weighting to their own preferred alternative. Depending on the cardinality (in the von Neumann-Morgenstern sense) of their preferences, they will coordinate on the same film less than 50 percent of the time. Once again, however, sexist culture might help them to do better. If men suffer less social disapproval for selfish behavior than women, then our couple might effortlessly converge on the violent option with high or even complete reliability. (Of course, such gains in efficiency should not generally be expected to be larger than the welfare losses suffered by women as a result of sexist norms; this relationship will vary with economic circumstances.)

Two general principles for the foundations of social science have been widely absorbed from considerations of stylized problems such as battle of the sexes. First, coordination is intrinsically difficult due to multiplicity of equilibria in most interactions. Second, many features of social organization evolve and stabilize because they ease this difficulty. These principles have been widely put to work at both local and general levels of explanation. On the local level, they are often applied to explain specific social phenomena. For example, Young (1998) uses them to explain the evolution of traffic rules and norms governing contracts between landlords and sharecroppers. More broadly, they have been used to explain the general phenomenon of co-evolved sociality and extreme cognitive-behavioral plasticity—that is, intelligence—in humans.

| | Woman | |
	Violence	Romance
Man Violence	3, 2	1, 0
Man Romance	0, 1	2, 3

2 pure strategy NE: (V, V) and (R, R); many mixed strategy NE

Figure 20.1 Battle of the sexes

The two principles as stated above are broadly correct, but they are crude. First, they do not distinguish between different ways in which coordination problems might be thought to be difficult, which may in turn imply different solution mechanisms that interact with one another in human social structures and evolution. Second, they are silent on the different possible dynamic trajectories by which coordination problems and socialization might drive one another. Did socialization come first in hominid evolution, giving rise to complex coordination problems that higher intelligence then evolved to solve? Or, in light of the importance of social norms and conventions for selecting focal points in coordination games, did intelligence generate coordination problems to which increasingly complex social structures are adaptations?

Several authors (Ross 2005, 2008, 2011; Thalos and Andreou 2009) have recently drawn attention to a philosophical blind spot in the tradition that borrows decision theory and game theory to model problems in the foundations of social science. It is standard practice to hold the identities of agents playing games as fixed throughout all stages of analysis. In classical applications players are assumed to correspond to biological organisms that persist in their agency through their lifetimes. In evolutionary games, players are lineages of linked genes—approximately, species, or frequency-dependent equilibrium strategies in within-species evolutionary games that have polymorphic equilibria. The latter approach is entirely appropriate, though, as Thalos and Andreou (2009) note, it lacks a general technique for modeling ways in which intelligent individuals or coalitions of them can subvert the strategies they have genetically inherited. The classical assumption, that individual agents are coextensional with individual organisms, is simply atomistic dogma.

A recently developed theme in some methodological and philosophical literature on applications of game theory to social science has been the human disposition to engage in *team reasoning* (Hollis 1998, Bacharach 2006). People, it is suggested, can under some circumstances at least partially fuse their agency, and evaluate alternative strategies with respect to their value to "us" or "our current project" instead of to "me." This suggestion makes many economists uneasy, because the relevant framing calls upon individuals to mysteriously forget their own interests. It is true that team-reasoning models risk being untestable unless we have empirically motivated and rigorously formulated constraints on changes in players' frames while games evolve. Ross (2005, 2007, 2008) labels this "the game determination problem" and discusses constraints on its solution. A problem with Ross's examples is that they involve complex shifts in cultural identities, which may make the phenomenon of endogenous game determination seem exotic and of marginal importance, encouraging economists to set it aside as not generally worth its cost in model tractability. Thalos and Andreou (2009) bring the point down to earth by drawing attention to a basic instance hiding in plain view: bonding between animal mothers and their offspring. Of course one *can* treat a mother bear and her cub as separate players in a game, with distinct utility functions and strategy sets. Insofar as the cub selfishly exploits its mother in certain respects, one must so treat them to capture the respects in question. But these issues truly *are* marginal for purposes of behavioral ecology and ethology. Within those settings, modeling parsimony dictates treating the mother and her cub as a single agent, whereas insistence on methodological individualism entails pointless modeling complications and risks obscuring available generalizations. If, for some modeling purposes, it is best to represent two bears as coordinated to the point of agent-fusion, why should the same device not be available where humans are concerned?

This rhetorical question, it will be pointed out, has answers. People, but perhaps not mother bears, can always *remember* that the relevance of their distinct identities lurks in the background when they are cooperating; so the game theorist modeling their interactions should remember it too, by including the necessary variables and parameters in her model. Thalos and Andreou respond to this in a way that is not quite satisfactory. Natural selection, they say, should force humans to sometimes forget themselves for the same reason it forces mother bears to do so. Of course, they recognize—indeed emphasize—that in more cognitively sophisticated organisms the mechanisms of bonding must be and are more complex than the relatively mechanical imprinting and control by oxytocin that seems to characterize many animal parent-offspring bonds. But this recognition undermines their simple resort to natural selection in the face of the hypothetical economist's objection that unless people can forget their individuality as thoroughly as mother bears do, then modelers should not forget it either.

I will not attempt to resolve this problem in the pragmatics of game theoretic modeling here. Suppose we agree only that groups of human individuals can and often do come to have very closely aligned utility functions, and strategy sets that depend on this alignment (i.e., moves they can each make in games only by acting together). This *mere* recognition assumes away questions about whether and when coordination is difficult by treating it as accomplished from the start. The problem for the couple trying to select cinemas in our previous example was not that they lacked commonality of interests or strategy sets, but that they might lack important information needed to exploit these commonalities. We can generalize this point by distinguishing between two potential problems:

1. coordination is often or sometimes difficult because agents are selfish and tempted by opportunities to free ride;
2. coordination is often or sometimes difficult because agents have limited access to information they need in order to operate effectively as teams.

In what follows, I will set (1) aside, taking Thalos and Andreou's main conclusion as read. Notwithstanding the fact that free riding regularly disrupts or blocks coordination on particular occasions, it is an observational datum that people regularly bond with one another using a variety of mechanisms, including *identifying* their own agency with patterns of performance necessary to achieve team objectives. This leaves problem (2). As we will see, it can be especially acute when efficiency involves division and specialization of labor, that is, when successful accomplishment of team objectives requires each team member to adopt a unique strategy.

I will survey recent progress on problem (2) with regard to the following question in the foundations of social science: To what extent is the evolution of social intelligence explained by appeal to the difficulty of coordination? Thalos and Andreou reject some popular approaches in the study of the foundations of social intelligence on the basis of their view that the difficulty of coordination, in sense (1), has been exaggerated due to the influence of individualistic assumptions. I believe they are right about this. However, their diagnosis of the issue is incomplete until it is complemented by consideration of problem (2).[3]

20.2. Game Theory and the Social Intelligence Hypothesis

Among the most salient correlations in population-level animal biology is that holding between noneusocial sociality and intelligence. Consider a partial list of animal types that are highly social, not eusocial, and highly intelligent: primates, canines, hyenas, toothed whales, elephants, raccoons, pigs, corvids, and parrots. It is easy to consider for comparison a *complete* list of organism types that are highly intelligent and not highly social, because this list contains no or almost no members.[4] Finally, a complete list of organism types that are highly social and not highly intelligent includes all and only the eusocial types (termites, some hymenoptera, naked mole rats). Most types on both the first and third lists are more closely related to some types not on their lists than they are to some types with whom they share their list membership. Thus the co-occurrence involves convergent evolution and is not an accident of genetic history.

This is the observational basis for the widely accepted social intelligence hypo thesis, first articulated by Humphrey (1976). According to this hypothesis, non-euscial sociality and intelligence coevolve because the main selection pressure that gives rise to advanced cognitive facility in various species is the value to individuals of remembering particular social colleagues' identities, along with their varying track records of reciprocal cooperation and tendencies to engage in conflict over mates, food, status, and other resources. A later, somewhat more specific version of the proposal is the so-called Machiavellian hypothesis, which emphasizes the importance of keeping track of who is in whose collation of alliances for the sake of political success in maintaining status and rank (Byrne and Whiten 1988, Whiten and Byrne 1997). Dunbar (1998) constructs a more precise subsidiary generalization, the social brain hypothesis. According to this hypothesis, the need for intelligence to manage larger numbers of social relationships explains observed correlation between average sizes of social groups in species and order-relative encephalization quotients (EQs), which measure the extent to which actual brain sizes differ from expected brain sizes when other relevant influences are controlled for. More specifically, according to Dunbar, EQ sets upper limits on group sizes. Surveys of recent empirical investigations based on all of the variants of social intelligence theory are provided in Emery, Clayton, and Frith (2007).

A key commitment of social intelligence theory is that sociality and intelligence *co*evolve. This is encapsulated in the relevant idea of sociality at play in the first place. Many relatively unintelligent animals cluster together in herds for protection from predators, but do not enter into complex relationships with specific individuals as defined by properties other than consanguinity relationships (Ross 2010). A group of organisms constitutes a *society*, as opposed to a herd, when (i) the expected individual fitness of each organism is partly a function of the differential fitness of the group, (ii) individuals are to some extent restricted, by factors going beyond geographical proximity or physical barriers, in their ability to switch groups, (iii) most group members are associated with some other members, aside from mates, direct ancestors, and direct descendants, in ways that influence their expected fitness, and (iv) random re-permutations of the individuals figuring in these within-group associations would produce wide variations in fitness distributions after sex and age differences are controlled for. These properties give rise to complex interdependence that implies need for coordination.

Within social intelligence theory, the Machiavellian and social brain hypotheses attach particular emphasis to properties (iii) and (iv). What cognitive challenges are specifically implied by these properties? Authors discussing the Machiavellian and social brain hypotheses often write as if the main pressure arises simply from the need to remember the identities and dispositions of many individuals. However, the extent to which this taxes neural functioning is not obvious, and cannot validly be inferred from the large experimental literature showing that people have difficulty holding significant numbers of unrelated objects in simultaneous conscious attention. Mammal brains have prodigious capacity for unconsciously remembering lexical associations, thanks to parallel distributed processing and massive neuronal and synaptic capacity (Deacon 1997). For example, squirrels, which are not especially intelligent mammals, store impressive lists of food cache sites in memory (though not without errors).

From the game-theoretic perspective, we can identify two approaches to cognitively representing coordination dynamics in sets of interacting individuals with distinctive strategic dispositions. One approach simply stores and updates lists of condition-action pairs. Thus, for example, an animal might tag each conspecific with which it has a strategic relationship with labels such as "reciprocated cooperation last time" or "failed to reciprocate cooperation last time." Updating of such tags on each episode of interaction could readily facilitate use of simple but relatively robust strategies such as tit for tat in coordination games with competitive aspects. Again, however, it is not clear that storing and using lists requires unusual intelligence.

The alternative approach to cognitively controlling one's own interactive dynamics with specific individuals is to compute representations of, and solutions to, extensive-form games. This might be done using heuristics that are less reliably accurate and powerful than a game theorist's trees or sets of equations, but on any implementation it is likely to require considerable neural processing resources.

However, for the analyst, fleshing out the Machiavellian or social brain hypotheses using this cognitive conjecture faces two serious empirical problems. First, observed instances of so-called reciprocal altruism among nonhuman animals are largely limited to interactions most naturally characterized using binary strategy sets (e.g., regurgitate blood for another vampire bat or don't; guard another's offspring or ignore them) and repeated iterations of identical stage games. It is unclear in such cases why representation of extensive-form games would have any advantages over, or be behaviorally distinguishable from, simple condition-action list storage. Second, numerous experiments show that *people* do not, except after substantial situational training (Kagel and Levin 1999; List and Lucking-Reiley 2002; Levitt, List, and Sadoff 2011), choose strategies using the kind of backward-induction logic that game theorists rely upon for solving extensive-form games. A particularly persuasive demonstration of this, using MOUSELAB, is given by Camerer et al. (1993). And it is unlikely that any nonhuman animals are better *theoretical* strategists than humans.

Thus *one kind* of coordination that seems to be difficult for untrained humans, and by implication for animals in general, is coordination on *socially efficient* equilibria *in pure strategies* while playing *one-shot* games with *new partners*. This should not be assumed to simply be the limiting case of a more general fact that all coordination is difficult. A background contributor to the difficulty that untutored natural agents encounter in finding subgame perfect and sequential equilibria[5] may be precisely that they usually find it *easy* to locate many equilibria involving mixed strategies, especially where these make allowance for quantal responses[6] (McKelvey and Palfrey 1995) by statistical tuning. This can lead groups of players to be captured by such equilibria. Game theorists, by contrast, identify the hard-to-find pure-strategy equilibria by deduction.

How might natural agents find it easy to implement mixed-strategy equilibrium play? A research program initiated by Paul Glimcher and collaborators (see Glimcher 2003a), based on single-cell recordings in monkeys, strongly suggests that, at least in primate brains, individual neurons in the circuit that estimates comparative reward values directly compute statistical variations in choice that track Nash equilibrium (NE) mixtures.

In Glimcher's basic paradigm, monkeys are trained to implement choices by directing their gaze to one member of a set of colored flashes on a computer screen. While the monkeys do this, activity in single neurons in the lateral intraparietal area (area LIP) is recorded. Neurons in this area encode salience of visual targets, and thereby direct attention to them. They deliver output to parts of the visuomotor system that plan and execute eye saccades. Thus it is hypothesized that area LIP neurons do not compute, but are closely correlated with, the monkeys' decisions about where to look. One of Glimcher's early breakthrough experiments (Glimcher 2003b) found that when monkeys played a game involving competitive coordination against a computer (the so-called inspection game shown in figure 20.2), firing rates of LIP neurons were equal for each pure strategy that was mixed in NE. If the neurons were tracking probabilities of movement instead of expected utility, this should not have been observed. This interpretation of the observations was greatly strengthened and enlarged in importance by a subsequent experiment (Dorris and Glimcher 2004) in which monkeys learned changing reward values in the same game. Trial-by-trial fluctuations in LIP activity correlated with trial-by-trial behavioral estimates of expected utility.

Work by Lee et al. (2004) has extended the implications of this result where coordination in games is concerned. Lee's group investigated the performance of nonhuman primates in the matching pennies game (figure 20.3) played against a computer. In the figure, H and T simply denote heads and tails in a coin-flipping task.

In this game, one player is incentivized to coordinate and the other player is symmetrically incentivized to avoid coordination. Of course, the anticoordinator

	Computer	
	Inspect	Don't inspect
Monkey Work	2, 2	2, 4
Shirk	-2, -2	4, -4

NE = (randomize, randomize)

Figure 20.2 The inspection game

	H	T
H	-2, 2	2, -2
T	2, -2	-2, 2

NE = (randomize, randomize)

Figure 20.3 Matching pennies

must identify coordination, at least implicitly, in order to avoid the other player's effort to achieve it. The game's unique NE is mutual randomization. This may make it appear unpromising as a test-bed for an experiment on equilibrium selection. However, by locking the computer into non-NE strategies, or depriving the computer of the ability to punish non-NE play by its opponent, Lee's team could present monkeys with alternative best-reply strategies.

Monkeys were divided into three groups, each of which played a computer implementing a different algorithmic strategy. Algorithm 0 played the mixed NE strategy unilaterally, without looking for patterns to be exploited in the monkeys' responses. In such cases monkeys show strong biases toward one or another of the pure strategies. (The source of these biases in the experiments is unknown and was not investigated.) Algorithm 1 detects such biases and counteracts them by driving the computer toward the opposite bias. Monkeys respond by dynamically conditioning switches between pure strategies on specific wins and losses. This win-stay, lose-switch (WSLS) strategy is an implementation of matching behavior, which has long been identified by animal learning theorists as the default strategy adapted by most learners confronted with uncertainty in alternative reward streams (Herrnstein 1961, 1982). It is as good a strategy as any other against Algorithm 1. Finally, Algorithm 2 looks for patterns in recent histories of monkey play compared with the monkey's gains and losses and exploits any such patterns. The only NE response to Algorithm 2 is randomization between pure strategies. Monkeys learn this.

A follow-up experiment (Lee et al. 2005) applied the same protocol to the familiar rock-paper-scissors (R-P-S) game, which exactly reverses the logic of coordination. In response to Algorithm 0, monkeys again tended to settle on a preferred pure strategy. In response to Algorithm 1, they played the so-called Cournot best response, biasing their choices in each round n by reference to the pure strategy that would have won or did win in round $n-1$. In response to Algorithm 2, monkeys approximated but didn't quite achieve randomization. In particular, they came as close to randomization as implementation of a classical Rescorla-Wagner conditioning rule can get. This is highly suggestive and should mitigate initial surprise at the monkeys' demonstrated skill with statistical induction. Game strategy choice that is not based on backward induction or conjectures respecting Bayes' rule can very closely mimic optimal play simply through standard conditioning. Outside of some rigorously monitored asset markets and game theorists' experimental labs, it is unlikely that humans, let alone monkeys, often face opponents that can detect and exploit the difference between true NE play and NE-mimicry.

These results motivate search for a neural mechanism that will adjust stochastic response frequencies toward WSLS when the environment strategically adapts to it but doesn't model it, and implements reinforcement learning when the environment strategically models it. Direct recording has identified individual neurons in dorsolateral prefrontal cortex (dlPFC) that modulate their activity in ways that allow for trial-by-trial comparison of two alternatives, as in matching pennies (Barraclough, Conroy, and Lee 2004; Seo, Barraclough, and Lee 2007). Crucially, some dlPFC neurons store "eligibility traces," that is, modulate their response probabilities in light of results of previous responses. This would be necessary in a neural system able to learn best (or near-best) replies to Algorithm 2.

Lee and Wang (2009) review models of processes by which some individual DLPFC neurons might adjust their stochastic response probabilities in such a way as to implement WSLS when randomization doesn't improve on it, and randomize when the environment responds as if strategically modeling the organism's behavior. The first is a specific type of "ramping-to-threshold" model based on drift diffusion. Suppose we have two alternatives X_1 and X_2 for comparison, where $X = X_1-X_2$. Then the dynamics of X are modeled by drift diffusion if

$$dX/dt = \mu + \omega(t)$$

where μ is the drift rate and $\omega(t)$ is a white noise of zero mean and standard deviation σ. μ represents a bias in favor of one alternative X_1 or X_2. The system is a perfect integrator of the input

$$X(t) = \mu t +^t \int \omega(t')dt'$$

and terminates whenever $X(t)$ reaches a positive threshold θ (choice 1) or $-\theta$ (choice 2). If μ is positive then choice 1 is correct, while choice 2 is an error; otherwise the opposite. If μ is 0 the system is "set" to randomize.

Can neural circuits implement this model? Lee and Wang point out that they can't perfectly integrate inputs, because they "leak"—that is, drift with time independently of μ. (That is to say: They forget.) However, Wang (2001, 2002) and others have demonstrated that this can be corrected by recurrent activation. So as long as input meets some persistence threshold, and the neuron is embedded in a network that receives stabilizing feedback from elsewhere in the brain (i.e., there is recurrence), then a neuron's stochastic response rate can systematically adjust in the way approximately described by the drift diffusion model. If neurons ramp to threshold, then learning must involve adjustments to the thresholds (e.g., to θ in the model). Lee and Wang suggest that this is what the dopamine signal in the midbrain reward circuit does.

We can shift to a less abstract level of modeling—but constrained by the higher-level models—in search of greater biophysical accuracy. A *spiking network* model takes account of the specific rise-times and decay-times of synapses. Lee and Wang point out that "synaptic dynamics turn out to be a crucial factor in determining the integration time of a neural circuit dedicated to decision making, as well as controlling the stability of a strongly recurrent network" (2009, 499).

In general, what hold stochastic neural firing frequencies within stable but adjustable bands are presumed to be network properties that create complex dynamics with multiple attractors. Pairs of neural networks linked to one another by both excitatory and inhibitory connections decide between two alternatives A and B, with C_A and C_B denoting recurrence of input favoring A and B respectively, according to the softmax function

$$P_A(C_A - C_B) = 1/(1 + \exp(-(C_A - C_B))/\sigma$$

where σ denotes the "extent of" stochasticity in the network. Such a system will decide between A and B even when absolute magnitudes of C_A and C_B are small, and when $C_A = C_B$. Lee and Wang claim that the function performs well in describing monkey behavior in the matching pennies game, but hasn't yet been tested on single neuron responses in DLPFC during game play. They report that it has produced good fits in estimating firing rates in area LIP when monkeys learned to anticipate stochastic changes in visual displays. However, it should be noted that this claim is too imprecise as it stands to be empirically evaluated. Lee and Wang do not discuss possible ways of generalizing the softmax function to describe dynamic attraction that would incorporate choices among more than two alternatives, as in their R-P-S experiment. Nor do they mention any test of a relationship between their model and the reported pattern of monkey play in R-P-S.

Lee and Wang introduce an additional methodological strategy by using their model to generate a simulation of neural learning of the monkeys' task in the matching pennies experiment. It captures the broad characteristics of the observed behavior, though it underpredicts the monkeys' frequency of use of WSLS against Algorithm 1. To reproduce this, Lee and Wang adjust the model by using "a different learning rule, according to which synapses onto both neural populations (selective for the chosen and unchosen targets) are modified in each trial. This is akin to a 'belief-dependent learning rule'" (2009, 498). They report that the model used for the simulation required different parameters for play against each of the three algorithms, and that they "incorporated a meta-learning rule proposed by Schweighofer and Doya (2003) that maximizes long-term rewards" (Lee and Wang 2009, 498). Thus the simulation really tests a *joint* hypothesis: that some neurons in the reward system tune their response probabilities by ramping to thresholds via strongly recurrent dynamics, thereby learning strategically superior stochastic behaviors, *and* parameters that govern applications of this learning model are themselves learned by some so far unspecified neural process somewhere else in the brain that implements the Schweighofer-Doya meta-learning rule.

The evidence to this point thus suggests that individual neurons in the primate reward system, possibly supplemented by more distributed encoding of some learned parameters, steer the organism as a whole to approximate NE behavior in basic coordination games. This hypothesis incorporates a significant element of speculation, due to its partial reliance on simulation. And one naturally wonders whether significant differences would be observed if the experiments with monkeys were replicated in less social or less intelligent animals. On the other hand, the part of the hypothesis that is on firmest empirical ground has portentous implications for social intelligence theory. This is that solutions, or at least behaviorally similar near-solutions, to basic coordination problems are computible as statistical exercises by primate brains and do not need to rely on culturally evolved focal points. Furthermore, the kind of coordination that even people find very difficult, collectively identifying equilibria by backward induction in novel, extensive-form games that depend on modeling specific, idiosyncratic partners, seems *too* difficult to have pushed hominids up the ramp to highly social intelligence, because even modern people's untutored and unscaffolded cognitive dispositions are not up to the job.

Thalos and Andreou (2009) are skeptical about social intelligence hypotheses on the grounds that such hypotheses begin from the assumption that coordination arises when utility-maximizing *individuals* are confronted with political challenges. They maintain instead that the foundation of the extreme social integration found in humans lies in the fact that the evolution of coordination describes processes by which people evolved to face their most complicated social situations not as individuals but as members of teams. They therefore reject accounts that depend too heavily on internal cognitive representation of coordination dynamics by individuals. Human coordination plausibly arises, they argue, from emergent dynamics without need for sophisticated cognitive representation; to this extent, humans more closely resemble eusocial animals than most of the literature supposes. One obvious objection to this thesis is that whereas we know roughly how ants and bees chemically transmit the information to one another that is necessary to support the coordination they noncognitively achieve, it is implausible that humans could informationally support their much more complex coordination dynamics using only low resolution subcognitive signaling such as odors and posture.[7] The findings in monkeys as reviewed above go some way toward answering this objection. All primate—and, for that, mammalian—midbrain reward systems are anatomically alike, and most evidence to date at least weakly supports functional similarity. Thus the single-cell work with monkeys is evidence that people's brains contain neuronal groups that are, in effect, automatic mixed-strategy equilibrium calculators. In one respect this motivates moderating Thalos and Andreou's hypothesis. If human brains calculate NE of games amongst individuals, then this implies that in some sense brains do represent their social situations in terms of such games after all. On the other hand, the representation in question could be—in the case of the monkeys, surely is—subcognitive and distributed. Since the reward system appears to be encapsulated from conscious representation and deliberation, allowing that it solves games among individuals as input to further frontal processing, where reframing in social context might occur, seems to be consistent with Thalos and Andreou's intended main emphasis. This concession would begin to address the serious problem with their hypothesis that its informational basis is completely unspecified.

This does not see off the whole of the skeptic's objection, however. We noted earlier that an economist might defend a strongly cognitivist model of game representation and solution in a way that resembles the standard defense of rational expectations in macroeconomics. Ants and bees probably *cannot* represent themselves as independent agents, whereas humans evidently can and do so conceive of themselves. Therefore, we should be at least uneasy with the suggestion that they forget to so conceive of themselves precisely in the sorts of situations, social exchanges, where members of our species typically invest their largest personal stakes. This is the sort of objection, however, to which the evidence about people's failures to use extensive-form representation and the backward induction it supports is precisely relevant. To the extent that coordination dynamics among people rely on reframing of agency buttressed by subcognitive prediction of outcomes based on conditioned Rescorla-Wagner learning and drift diffusion, we should predict that people would find everyday coordination in relatively structurally simple games easier than defenders of social intelligence hypotheses generally assume, but that efficient coordination in games with relatively more complex informational dynamics might often or usually fail to be achieved. We will consider further evidence for this in the next section.

A further respect in which the neuroscientific experiments with monkey strategic choice may be taken to support Thalos and Andreou's thesis is that the mechanism, in representing and solving games as statistical rather than logical problems, is more naturally adapted to coordinating the individual's behavior with that of a group, rather than to supporting idiosyncratic models of specific individuals. This theme will also loom large in the next section of the chapter.

Merlin Donald's (1991) theory of the evolution of the modern human mind, based on interpretation of physical and cultural anthropological evidence, can be retrospectively interpreted as providing further support to Thalos and Andreou's thesis. Donald argues that the career of *Homo erectus* involved a major transition from the *episodic* representations of social situations upon which contemporary great apes rely to *mimetically* structured representations. The latter are presented as a necessary platform for the later transition to the fully semiotic, abstract representations characteristic of the modern human mind and expressed in modern humans' distinctive use of languages with structured grammars. The core difference between an episodic and a mimetic representation is that the latter, but not the former, involves perceiving and storing memories of specific behaviors of others by reference to general stylistic features that allow them to be subsequently reenacted. This in turn provides a basis for limited cross-generational learning and cultural accumulation. Donald argues that this significantly increased the selection advantage of greater memory capacity, and that the flowering of mimesis in *H. erectus* thus predicts and partially explains the major advance in encephalization that make this species the pivotal anatomical transition figure between apelike hominids and modern humans. We cannot here devote space to reviewing the rich mix of evidence that Donald's theory integrates. The important point for present purposes is that, according to his well-received account, imitation, though it rested on prior increases in cognitive capacity in the hominid line, was a necessary precursor to the runaway evolution of intelligence that radically distinguishes late *H. erectus* and his descendents from all other primates. Imitation, especially of the fully mimetic variety that does not require the immediate presence of the imitated party's behavior, is the simplest and most direct possible vehicle for coordination.

Donald of course does not imagine that mimesis could have evolved in a species that was not social, or not highly socially intelligent. His account of the sociality-intelligence dynamic is therefore, like almost all competing stories currently taken seriously, a coevolutionary one. However, we can say that it presents sophisticated coordination as an enabler of (rather than a consequence of) distinctively *human* intelligence, since according to Donald it was a qualitatively novel form of coordination that provided the platform for a qualitatively novel level of niche transformation, opportunity conception, and problem solving, rather than the other way around. It is for this reason that I interpret his theory and the evidence he assembles for it as supportive of Thalos and Andreou's main conjecture.

However, introducing Donald's theory into the picture directs attention to complicating considerations. Thalos and Andreou cite with approval Haim Ofek's (2001) account of the role of specialization of labor and of markets in the evolution of *both* human sociality and human intelligence. Unfortunately, instead of acknowledging complexities that Ofek's thesis raises for theirs, they attempt to brusquely expropriate it by first raising a specious objection to details of Ofek's historical conjecture,[8] and then answering their own objection by simply shoehorning Ofek's thesis into theirs despite the fact that his text provides no support for their doing so.

Ofek's main contribution is to offer evidence for introducing market exchange as a third element in the coevolutionary matrix that produced *H. sapiens*'s remarkable ecology. Reasoning carefully from the range of economic problems that faced prehuman and early human hunter-gatherers, Ofek builds a case that development of the metabolically expensive brain required dietary shifts that could only be supported by the development of specialization of labor and exchange across bands. The earliest tradables produced by specialist producers, Ofek suggests, were fire-maintenance services[9] and sheep and goat herding. Cross-band exchange in turn required the partial displacement of natural xenophobic violence by diplomacy, thus promoting social intelligence and the enhanced strategic competence in which it partly consists.

Specialization and market participation are forms of coordination that cannot be based on imitation alone, since they crucially depend on polymorphic strategy selection in the population. At the very least, they also require equilibrium learning; families should have imitated successful fire-keepers only up to the point where the opening of one more competing fire service station equalized the expected utility of the next fire-keeping family and the expected utility of remaining hunter-gatherers. Now, it has already been suggested that Thalos and Andreou's thesis is strengthened, although in a more complicated version, if we take account of the evidence for subcognitive computation of equilibria by primate neuronal groups. However, the Glimcher and Lee and Wang experiments test only for computation of equilibria in games involving two players where information is perfect and all moves are directly observed. *Homo erectus* families might have found labor market equilibrium much harder to track. And this was the very dawn of labor market formation; as Seabright (2010) discusses, the complexity of such problems swiftly exploded for people, and still continues to accelerate.

The point here is that the evolution of human coordination capacities was not simply a single ascent up one complexity gradient. Social intelligence hypotheses are intended as accounts of the early coevolution of sociality and intelligence that facilitated team reasoning in small family bands. In my view, the considerations surveyed in the present section provide persuasive motivation for suspecting that

Machievellian arms races were at best a small part of this story. Coordination, including coordinated competition, was simply not as difficult for our ancestors, even our relatively small-brained ones, as tellers of social intelligence tales often suggest. However, to confine attention to the period before small bands of hunter-gatherers began to coalesce into large, settled societies is to avert our gaze from the most dramatic and biologically revolutionary episodes in the distinctively *human* career of socialization. The specialized division of labor became a globally transformative force once it was applied beyond simple barter exchange between kin groups. The basic dynamic of coordination, and its relationship with socialization, changed equally profoundly. The logical basis of this has already been identified above: As market pressures and opportunities begin to dominate social organization, people must abandon coordination based on simple imitation, lest everyone be trapped in buying high and selling low. In the concluding section of the chapter, I will suggest reasons for thinking that the more complicated demands of market coordination provided the impetus for a novel twist in the evolutionary dynamics of coordination capacities, one that turned in the opposite direction from that emphasized by Thalos and Andreou: People learned to construct themselves as distinctive individuals who could participate in multiple teams at the same time.

20.3. GLOBAL GAMES, OVERCOORDINATION AND THE VALUE OF INDIVIDUALITY

The previous section surveyed responses to a bias in intellectual history, mainly derived from the extension of game theoretic reasoning into the foundations of social science. The bias in question exaggerates the difficulty of equilibrium selection in normal-form games of complete information among small numbers of players.[10] The reader might reasonably feel some surprise at this. Since when did economists, of all people, get stuck in cul-de-sacs by *underestimating* human capacities for tracking statistical regularities? Economists, after all, are the people who have given us such virtuosos of instantaneous complex computation as participants in Walrasian auctions, holders of rational expectations, and infinitely lived participants in efficient markets.

The answer, already hinted at, is that economists and game theorists didn't underestimate pre and early humans' computational abilities. (Few have directed their attention to these agents at all.) Rather, they encouraged relatively thoughtless projection, by other behavioral scientists, of the more complicated coordination problems that preoccupy current policy engineers to the early stages of hominid social formation. In the kinds of coordination games that most interest economists, agents' choices, at least collectively, exert more power over available outcome spaces than do the choices of monkeys playing matching pennies against preprogrammed opponents. This power destabilizes agency itself, by making utility functions dynamic and by embedding games within meta-games. The evolution of modern societies is characterized by dizzying acceleration in the special human capacity for niche construction; by their behavior traders don't merely adapt to markets, but change their structures. This raises the following problem for the game modeler. If, as we should expect to be typical, people approach their strategic interactions with both asymmetric information and the ability to exploit this information to dynamically influence outcome spaces, why and how should we imagine that agents converge on a shared model of outcomes? Such convergence is a necessary condition on our being able to say anything about players' levels of knowledge of the structure of their games.

Morris and Shin (2003) note a particular path by which economists have introduced indeterminacy in outcome identification into many—indeed, most—models of coordination around investment and saving behavior. We begin by supposing that all agents deduce correct beliefs about the distributions of beliefs, and of beliefs about beliefs, and so on, among all agents involved in a game. Now imagine that, as is common in market interactions, some beliefs are self-fulfilling: Agents choose actions on the basis of their beliefs about beliefs, others correctly believe they will take the actions in question (because their belief assignments are also correct), and then the actions in question, when taken, confirm the beliefs. Finally, suppose that all exogenous aspects of the state of the economy are common knowledge. This set of standard assumptions, made partly for the sake of tractability, but also because alternative assumptions are arbitrary in the absence of special considerations, produces perfectly coordinated beliefs and actions. In that case we have no means of discriminating different probabilities associated with different equilibria unless we know how the agents arrived at their initial beliefs before they computed the solution to the game. These beliefs drive everything, and so do *all* of the work in selecting an equilibrium. But of course we generally do not, and cannot, have empirical access to processes by which agents arrived at their initial beliefs.

This problem doesn't rest on the assumption that coordination per se is unrealistically difficult. Rather, it makes outcome prediction based on the assumption that coordination will be achieved unrealistically difficult.

A technology that tries to break out of this kind of cul-de-sac, developed by Carlsson and van Damme (1993), is known as global game theory. In a global game, players receive slightly noisy, nonpublic, signals about uncertain states of the economy. If players have correct beliefs about the sources of noise, when each one observes his own signal he can estimate the distributions of signal values received by other players. Not knowing their background beliefs, he assumes that these are randomly distributed about the unit interval, because in his ignorance this is the least arbitrary prior. (Morris and Shin say that it resembles Laplace's principle of insufficient reason: When no consideration favors one possibility, assume equiprobability.) On this basis the player estimates the probable distribution of actions by others and chooses his best reply. Carlsson and van Damme show that given some plausible technical restrictions, this setup mimics the solution space of standard, pre-epistemic game theory, while nevertheless taking into account that players choose actions in light of their beliefs about the beliefs of others. Put less impres-sionistically, and following Morris and Shin's (2003, 86) exposition, suppose we have the game shown as figure 20.4. Each player I observes a signal $x_i = \theta + \sigma\epsilon_i$, where the ϵ_i are eight-dimensional noise terms. So σ parameterizes an incomplete information game. If the payoff vector $\theta \in R^8$ is drawn according to a strictly posi-tive, continuously differentiable, bounded density on R^8, and the noise terms for each player are drawn according to a continuous density with bounded support, independently of θ, then as $\sigma \to 0$ any sequence of strategy profiles that survives it-erated elimination of strictly dominated strategies converges to a unique limit, independent of the noise distribution, which includes the unique NE of the under-lying complete information game if it exists, and the risk-dominant NE if there is more than one strict NE.

A major application of global game theory has been to speculative crises in financial markets, which in the standard game-theoretic models are unpredictable because of multiple equilibria. Morris and Shin (1998) develop a global game in which a bank run becomes a unique equilibrium if a parameter driving expected rate of return for longer-term depositors falls below a specifiable threshold. Critics (beginning with Atkeson 2001) have raised doubts that global games are actually up to the task of predicting banking crises in real markets, but we may pass over this problem when our interest, as here, is merely in qualitative representation of infor-mational dynamics. The key points for present purposes are as follows. First, global game theory provides a formal framework for representing the way in which agents with imperfect information can converge on a common model of their games. To this extent it mitigates the apparent difficulties raised for coordination by informa-tion asymmetries. However, global game theory is also useful in helping us to describe the basis for a different problem that may beset populations that are driven to coordinate by group selection dynamics (i.e., property [1] among our previously identified conditions for sociality) and which are therefore also under pressure to coordinate on relatively *efficient* equilibria. This is that global game play, by elimi-nating indeterminacy, helps to show how coordinators can converge on inferior equilibria, or traps—for example, bank runs that can only be stopped by exogenous interventions.

The difficulty associated with coordination can thus be reframed. Much of the social intelligence literature imagines agents with given, relatively selfish utility

	1	0
1	θ_1, θ_2	θ_3, θ_4
0	θ_5, θ_6	θ_7, θ_8

Figure 20.4 Incomplete information game with payoff vector $\theta \in R^8$

functions struggling to compute coordinated strategies. By contrast, our attention is now focused on agents who find coordination relatively straightforward, but who partly for that reason may overcoordinate—that is, converge on an inefficient game structure and eliminate strategic variance within the population that might otherwise have provided the basis for discovery of paths to sets of equilibria containing superior outcomes.

Note that this problem is related but not identical to the less abstract herding problem that has been studied by an extensive experimental literature descended from a classic 1992 paper of Banerjee. The herding problem is that agents who are unsure about the distribution of private information in a market can, under certain plausible conditions, rationally choose to imitate strategies of other participants when they have misidentified others' herding behavior as revealing private information, and thereby be led to ignore their own genuine private information. This implies that their information is lost to the market's available information set, which implies inefficiency and can amplify through its effects on other participants' actions, creating cascades of inefficient information management. Furthermore, if initial observers happen to be unlucky, the result can be a "reverse cascade" in which everyone converges on an incorrect model.

Experimental tests of herding have generated equivocal but interesting results. Anderson and Holt (1997) found significant cascading and reverse cascading even when participants knew that they were at no disadvantage with respect to the quality of their private signals. Sgroi (2003) replicated this result with endogenous timing, that is, where subjects could decide to wait to choose until they had observed choices of others. Sgroi also tested the effect of correcting errors incorporated in reverse cascades. In these instances, participants tended to move further away from Bayesian rationality, suggesting failure to fully recognize that rational choice can produce suboptimal outcomes. On the other hand, Huck and Oechssler (2000), Noeth et al. (1999), and Spiwoks, Bizer, and Hein (2008) found general failures of Bayesian rationality, overweighting of private signals, and therefore fewer cascades.

Two experimental reports are especially interesting in the present context. Hung and Plott (2001) found prevailing near-rationality, and broad confirmation of Anderson and Holt's findings, when subjects were encouraged to frame their decisions as individuals. (Near-rationality refers to the fact that subjects produced fewer cascades than fully rational agents would be predicted to do.) However, when they understood that the majority decision would bind all participants, and were thus incentivized to reframe the choice problem as one confronting a team, subjects paid more attention to their private signals. This contrarian behavior will tend to improve social efficiency in a very noisy environment, while lowering it in a highly transparent one. However, as a further complication, when Corazzini and Greiner (2007) encouraged subjects to frame their choices in the familiar context of independent choices over lotteries, herding collapsed and individually irrational but socially efficient contrarian behavior abounded.

The logic of the herding problem applies to market efficiency *after* agents have estimated the structure of their game through global game play. This is why it is a more interesting problem for application to markets governed by actually institutionalized rules. The problem of inefficient convergence in global games is relevant to potential selection of inefficient institutions in the first place. Now recall, from section 20.2, the conditions that govern the evolution of sociality, where the inclusive fitness of individual agents is conditioned by correlation between strategies and genetic relatedness of interactors. Thalos and Andreou follow current fashion in using the phrase "group selection" here, though this invites many common confusions (West, El Mouden, and Gardner 2010). People who structure their environments using more efficient market institutions will tend to outcompete people who rely on nonmarket institutions or, more realistically, less efficient market rules.

This hierarchy of global and local games, based on different scales of analysis where both time and agency are concerned, allows for qualitative dynamics in which agents disposed to contrarian behavior give other agents incentive to favor them because they thereby reduce the relative size of the basin of attraction of overconvergence in the space of evolutionary global games. Put in plainer terms, where the dynamic of socialization leads to evolutionary competition among groups that have developed market exchange and specialization of labor, pressure can arise that favors the cultivation of a form of *socialized* individuality that is distinct from genetic individuality. The individuality in question is socialized because it is a set of dispositions to favor certain strategies over others in global games; thus it presupposes and arises from complex sociality.

Since contrarian behavior can lead to inefficiency as markets become more transparent, the evolution of socialized individuality does not counterfactually predict the triumph of efficient markets. Indeed, models can be written in which the market volatility caused by contrarian behavior—which Thalos and Andreou might characterize as the disintegration of teams—serves as a limiting factor on the evolutionary pressure, at a coarser scale, for wider dispersion of types of individuals at the population level, with the richer space for specialization and market complexity that such dispersion implies (Richerson and Boyd 2005).

Socialized individuals are not merely genetic individuals who can refer to themselves, as fantasized by thinkers in the venerable Western philosophical tradition of social atomism. Normal human individuals are adaptations to social pressures to conform to prevailing norms but, within those limits, to cultivate patterns of distinctive, re-recognizable (and therefore relatively predictable) self-models that govern their own behavior. Such selves can perform the unique trick, valuable only in the context of the unusual human ecological strategy, of facilitating division of labor within *novel* and *creative* group enterprises. It was likely our ancestors' capacity for such joint creativity that allowed us to survive the concertina of glacial advances and retreats during our species' early career—and, by standard Darwinian logic, those same pressures that made us the unique virtuosos of coordination that we are.

One among several prerequisites for such enterprises are signaling systems—languages—that stabilize ranges of possible signal meanings by digitalizing reference. That is, human language enables one to communicatively refer to "Napoleon" exactly, not just to an indefinite range of things sharing to various degrees Napoleon's analog blend of properties (i.e., "napoleonishness"). Thus humans can coordinate on plans involving hypothetical objects picked out by digital contrast with other members of classes into which the grammars of public languages permit them to be sorted (Ross 2007). Some philosophers (e.g., Searle 1995), in their abiding preoccupation with reference, have been overimpressed by this, suggesting that language plus shared perceptual saliences are sufficient to account for people's ethologically unique capacity to coordinate. But this is yet another aspect of the intellectual legacy that makes *basic* coordination seem harder than people actually find it to be, imagining them to begin as isolated in interior worlds that they must struggle to render commensurable. (Consider, for example, Wittgenstein's [1953, 100] famous beetle in the box thought experiment, which draws upon a theme central to Western philosophy since Locke.) The evolution of fully symbolic representation in people was enormously important to *intergenerational* coordination that, by conserving cultural and technological discoveries, accelerated human niche construction. But this is not the sort of basic coordination on which philosophers inspired by game theory—for example, Lewis (1969) and Skyrms (1996, 2010)—have so far concentrated.

As argued by a range of theorists including Bruner (1992, 2002), Dennett (1991), Turner (1998), and Ross (2005, 2007), a crucial evolved basis for guiding socialized individuality, and consequent approximate equilibria in networks of behavioral expectations, are common perceptions of narrative coherence. People insist that others with whom they enter into coordination exercises tell dramatically structured, publicly ratifiable stories about themselves and conform their behavior to these stories. This enables not only public predictability, but, for organisms with enormous information-processing devices that are largely opaque to their direct inspection, *self*-predictability (Dennett 1991).

People mutually ease the imposed burden of consistent self-construction by assisting each other as coauthors of narratives, recording expectations, rewarding enrichments of each other's subplots, and punishing overly abrupt attempts to revise important character dispositions. Parents initially impose this regime of self-construction on their children, later handing over primary control (often with much resistance) to their offspring's peer groups. Thus people become and remain distinct while simultaneously remaining comprehensible and predictable.

The fact that self-creation and self-maintenance are *achievements* requiring effort is what explains prevailing *normative* individualism. Socialized individuals are centrally important to people partly *because* they don't just drop out of the womb. A person's own social self is of particular importance to her because if its integrity is cast into doubt her capacity to enter into mutually beneficial exchanges—the fundamental survival strategy of *Homo sapiens*—is threatened. The integrity of other people's selves is valuable to each individual because this is the basis for convergence in global game play, and then for coordinating without sacrificing specialization and all private information to imitation.

What neither theory nor experimental evidence yet support, however, are general theorems on the social welfare properties of varying levels of entrenchment of socialized individuality. Self-construction necessarily reduces the strategy sets available in coordination dynamics, since the predictability of the socialized individual depends on foreclosing some possibilities for action that would otherwise be available. At the same time, it reduces the loss of private information in imitation cascades by facilitating adoption of contrarian behavior in the sense of the herding literature. Socially optimal trade-offs between these effects are almost certainly highly sensitive to specific levels of risk, environmental change, and transparency of information about contingent relationships between present states and possible outcomes.

20.4. CONCLUSION

Methodological individualism is currently a minority position in the philosophy of social science. The majority of economists likely still pay lip service to it, though modeling and explanatory practice in the discipline regularly, and increasingly, ignores it (Ross 2011). However, residues of methodological individualism, and the more general ontological atomism from which it derives, persist in influencing foundational assumptions. One of these is that coordination is sufficiently difficult in principle that it might furnish the basic challenge that was overcome by the evolution of humans' runaway evolution of cognitive plasticity.

No considerations reviewed in this chapter undermine, or are intended to undermine, the tight coevolutionary relationship between sociality and intelligence. However, the picture of initially isolated individuals under pressure to develop ingenious strategies for achieving coordination appears to be almost exactly backward. Primates and other social animals are equipped by basic and nonmysterious biological devices and behavioral dispositions to coordinate, at least in the statistical sense relevant to selection of mixed strategies without backward induction. But capacities for easy coordination are potential barriers to specialization of labor and to efficient exploitation of private information. The social evolution of norms that encourage and maintain individual variation among human selves is best understood in light of this.

NOTES

1. Lewis (1969) is usually cited in this connection. Lewis's account involved some significant distractions because he imposed the strong and unnatural constraint that a convention solves a coordination problem only in cases where all players are indifferent among the set of equilibria from which the convention picks a member. This restriction has its origins in the problems in the philosophy of language and the philosophy of science that

motivated Lewis's study, but it has no basis in either game theory (Ross 2008) or social theory (Gilbert 1989).

2. The standard normal-form version allows that the payoffs in each of the outcomes (Violence, Romance) and (Romance, Violence) might be (0,0). This is useful for ease of solution, and to illustrate a general logical point about randomization, but less intuitively natural than the payoffs given here.

3. From the very origins of game theory, modelers have attended to the strategic dynamics of players who can make binding promises to one another under the rubric of cooperative game theory (von Neumann and Morgenstern 1944). However, the main focus in cooperative game theory has been on coalition formation and has presupposed complete information.

4. Orangutans, which are among the most intelligent of mammals, were once thought to be solitary. This has turned out to be inaccurate as a generalization; and such solitude as is observed in some orangutans now appears to be a recent adaptation to habitat changes. See Dunbar (1988).

5. Subgame-perfect equilibria are those identified by backward induction in extensive-form games where all players have perfect information. In extensive-form games where some players are uncertain about the game structure, reasoning deductively from conjectures, and applying Bayes' rule to ensure consistent conditional probability assignments to such conjectures, identifies so-called sequential equilibria (Kreps and Wilson 1982).

6. Quantal response equilibria allow for varying indifference bands in agents' ordinal rankings of outcomes, and /or inability among players to discriminate among outcomes as finely as the analyst.

7. It can rightly be pointed out, following Deacon (1997), that human subcognitive coordination is not informationally restricted in this way because symbolic representation and linguistic processing structure representational dynamics throughout the brain. However, the point at issue here is that Thalos and Andreou's hypothesis can be defended without *needing* recourse to Deacon's.

8. Ofek argues that fire keeping was the first specialized occupation in human evolution. This rests on an economic argument that, for *H. erectus* and his immediate successors, it was much more efficient for specialists to maintain fires from which bands of local hunter-gatherers could draw in exchange for food and pelts than for each small band of hunter-gatherers to search for suitable kindling each day—which would have severely restricted their foraging ranges—and then endure the high-risk, failure-prone ordeal of starting a nightly fire without modern ignition technology. Thalos and Andreou object that Ofek fails to demonstrate that early humans could not have become trapped in the less efficient of these two production equilibria. This point is valid but irrelevant, since the internal logic of Ofek's argument merely requires him to show that the first equilibrium could have been arrived at by a sequence of behavioral adjustments that were all Pareto-improvements. This he does. Thalos and Andreou, in reconstructing Ofek's story, also ignore the importance in it of the scarcity of kindling. Leaving out this aspect makes the path to discovery of the first equilibrium seem much less likely to have been stumbled across than on Ofek's fully specified account.

9. Caves, Ofek argues, were not primarily used as homes by early humans, as popular imagination supposes, but as fire service stations. This naturally leads one to speculate, though he does not, that cave art might have had the intended function of attracting customers.

10. Bacharach (2006) is particularly clear and insistent in identifying this cause of intellectual frustration.

REFERENCES

Anderson, L., and C. Holt. 1997. "Information Cascades in the Laboratory." *American Economic Review* 87: 847–62.

Atkeson, A. 2001. "Rethinking Multiple Equilibria in Macroeconomic Modeling: Comment." In *NBER Macroeconomics Annual 2000*, B. Bernanke and K. Rogoff, eds., 162–71. Cambridge, MA: The MIT Press.

Bacharach, M. 2006. *Beyond Individual Choice*. Princeton, NJ: Princeton University Press.

Banerjee, A. 1992. "A Simple Model of Herd Behavior." *Quarterly Journal of Economics* 107: 797–817.

Barraclough, D., M. Conroy, and D. Lee. 2004. "Prefrontal Cortex and Decision-Making in a Mixed Strategy Game." *Nature Neuroscience* 7: 404–10.

Bruner, J. 1992. *Acts of Meaning*. Cambridge, MA: Harvard University Press.

Bruner, J. 2002. *Making Stories: Law, Literature, Life*. New York: Farrar, Strauss and Giroux.

Byrne, R., and A. Whiten, eds. 1988. *Machiavellian Intelligence: Social Expertise and the Evolution of Intellect in Monkeys, Apes and Humans*. Oxford: Oxford University Press.

Camerer, C., E. Johnson, T. Rymon, and S. Sen. 1993. "Cognition and Framing in Sequential Bargaining for Gains and Losses." In *Frontiers of Game Theory*, K. Binmore, A. Kirman, and P. Tani, eds., 27–47. Cambridge, MA: The MIT Press.

Carlsson, H., and E. van Damme. 1993. "Global Games and Equilibrium Selection." *Econometrica* 61: 989–1018.

Corazzini, L., and B. Greiner. 2007. "Herding, Social Preferences and (Non-)conformity." *Economics Letters* 97: 74–80.

Deacon, T. 1997. *The Symbolic Species*. New York: Norton.

Dennett, D. 1991. *Consciousness Explained*. Boston: Little, Brown.

Donald, M. 1991. *Origins of the Modern Mind*. Cambridge, MA: Harvard University Press.

Dorris, M., and P. Glimcher. 2004. "Activity in Posterior Parietal Cortex Is Correlated with the Relative Selective Desirability of Action." *Neuron* 44: 365–78.

Dunbar, R. 1988. *Primate Social Systems*. London: Croom Helm.

Dunbar, R. 1998. "The Social Brain Hypothesis." *Evolutionary Anthropology* 6: 178–90.

Emery, N., N. Clayton, and C. Frith. 2007. *Social Intelligence: From Brain to Culture*. Oxford: Oxford University Press.

Gilbert, M. 1989. *On Social Facts*. Princeton, NJ: Princeton University Press.

Glimcher, P. 2003a. *Decisions, Uncertainty and the Brain*. Cambridge, MA: The MIT Press.

Glimcher 2003b. "The Neurobiology of Visual-Saccadic Decision Making." *Annual Review of Neuroscience* 26: 133–79.

Harsanyi, J. 1967. "Games with Incomplete Information Played by 'Bayesian' Players, Parts I–III." *Management Science* 14:159–82.

Herrnstein, R. 1961. "Relative and Absolute Strength of Response as a Function of Frequency of Reinforcement." *Journal of the Experimental Analysis of Behavior* 4: 267–72.

Herrnstein, R. 1982. "Melioration as Behavioral Dynamism." In *Quantitative Analyses of Behavior, Volume II: Matching and Maximizing Accounts*, M. Commons, R. Herrnstein, and H. Rachlin, eds., 433–58. Cambridge, MA: Ballinger.

Hollis, M. 1998. *Trust Within Reason*. Cambridge: Cambridge University Press.

Huck, S., and J. Oechssler. 2000. "Informational Cascades in the Laboratory: Do They Occur for the Right Reasons?" *Journal of Economic Psychology* 21: 661–71.

Humphrey, N. 1976. "The Social Function of Intellect." In *Growing Points in Ethology*, P. Bateson and R. Hinde, eds., 303–17. Cambridge: Cambridge University Press.

Hung, A., and C. Plott. 2001. "Information Cascades: Replication and an Extension to Majority Rule and Conformity-Rewarding Institutions." *American Economic Review* 91: 1508–20.

Kagel, J., and D. Levin. 1999. "Common Value Auctions with Insider Information." *Econometrica* 67: 1219–38.

Kreps, D., and R. Wilson. 1982. "Sequential Equilibria." *Econometrica* 50: 863–94.

Lee, D., M. Conroy, B. McGreevy, and D. Barraclough. 2004. "Reinforcement Learning and Decision-Making in Monkeys During a Competitive Game." *Cognition and Brain Research* 22: 45–48.

Lee, D., B. McGreevy, and D. Barraclough. 2005. "Learning and Decision-Making in Monkeys During a Rock-Paper-Scissors Game." *Cognition and Brain Research* 25: 416–30.

Lee, D., and X.-J. Wang. 2009. "Mechanisms for Stochastic Decision Making in the Primate Frontal Cortex: Single-Neuron Recording and Circuit Modeling." In *Neuroeconomics: Decision Making and the Brain*, P. Glimcher, C. Camerer, E. Fehr, and R. Poldrack, eds., 481–501. London: Elsevier.

Levitt, S., J. List, and S. Sadoff. 2011. "Checkmate: Exploring Backward Induction Among Chess Players." *American Economic Review* 101: 975–90.

Lewis, D. 1969. *Convention*. Cambridge, MA: Harvard University Press.

List, J., and D. Lucking-Reiley. 2002. "Bidding Behavior and Decision Costs in Field Experiments." *Economic Inquiry* 40: 611–19.

McKelvey, R., and T. Palfrey. 1995. "Quantal Response Equilibria for Normal Form Games." *Games and Economic Behavior* 10: 6–38.

Morris, S., and H.-S. Shin. 1998. "Unique Equilibrium in a Model of Self-Fulfilling Currency Attacks." *American Economic Review* 88: 587–97.

Morris, S., and H.-S. Shin. 2003. "Global Games: Theory and Applications." In *Advances in Economics and Econometrics, Theory and Applications, Eighth World Congress, Volume 1*, M. Dewatripont, L. Hansen, and S. Turnovsky, eds., 56–114. Cambridge: Cambridge University Press.

Noeth, M., C. Camerer, C. Plott, and C. Weber. 1999. "Information Aggregation in Experimental Asset Markets: Traps and Misaligned Beliefs." Working Paper: 1–50. Available at http://ideas.repec.org/p/clt/sswopa/1060.html.

Ofek, H. 2001. *Second Nature*. Cambridge: Cambridge University Press.

Richerson, P., and R. Boyd. 2005. *Not by Genes Alone*. Chicago: University of Chicago Press.

Ross, D. 2005. *Economic Theory and Cognitive Science: Microexplanation*. Cambridge, MA: The MIT Press.

Ross, D. 2007. "*H. sapiens* as Ecologically Special: What Does Language Contribute?" *Language Sciences* 29: 710–31.

Ross, D. 2008. "Classical Game Theory, Socialization and the Rationalization of Conventions." *Topoi* 27: 57–72.

Ross, D. 2010. "Naturalism: The Place of Society in Nature." In *The Sage Handbook of Philosophy of Social Science*, I. Jarvie and J. Zamorra-Bonilla, eds. Thousand Oaks, CA: Sage.

Ross, D. 2012. "The Economic Agent: Not Human, But Important." In *Handbook of the Philosophy of Science, v. 13: Economics*, U. Mäki, ed. London: Elsevier. Forthcoming.

Schelling, T. 1960. *The Strategy of Conflict*. Cambridge, MA: Harvard University Press.

Schweighofer, N., and K. Doya. 2003. "Meta-Learning in Reinforcement Learning." *Neural Networks* 16: 5–9.

Seabright, P. 2010. *The Company of Strangers*. 2d rev. ed. Princeton, NJ: Princeton University Press.

Searle, J. 1995. *The Construction of Social Reality*. New York: The Free Press.

Seo, H., D. Barraclough, and D. Lee. 2007. "Dynamic Signals Related to Choices and Outcomes in the Dorsolateral Prefrontal Cortex." *Cerebral Cortex* 17: 110–17.

Sgroi, D. 2003. "The Right Choice at the Right Time: A Herding Experiment in Endogenous Time." *Experimental Economics* 6: 159–80.

Skyrms, B. 1996. *Evolution of the Social Contract*. Cambridge: Cambridge University Press.

Skyrms, B. 2010. *Signals*. Oxford: Oxford University Press.

Spiwoks, M., K. Bizer, and O. Hein. 2008. "Informational Cascades: A Mirage?" *Journal of Economic Behavior and Organization* 67: 193–99.

Thalos, M., and C. Andreou. 2009. "Of Human Bonding: An Essay on the Natural History of Agency." *Public Reason* 1: 46–73

Turner, M. 1998. *The Literary Mind*. Oxford: Oxford University Press.

Von Neumann, J., and O. Morgenstern. 1944. *Theory of Games and Economic Behavior*. Princeton, NJ: Princeton University Press.

Wang, X.-J. 2001. "Synaptic Reverberation Underlying Mnemonic Persistent Activity." *Trends in Neuroscience* 24: 455–63.

Wang, X.-J. 2002. "Probabilistic Decision Making by Slow Reverberation in Cortical Circuits." *Neuron* 36: 955–68.

West, S., C. El Mouden, and A. Gardner. 2010. "Sixteen Common Misconceptions About the Evolution of Cooperation in Humans." *Evolution and Human Behavior* 32: 231–62.

Whiten, A., and R. Byrne, eds. 1997. *Machiavellian Intelligence II*. Cambridge: Cambridge University Press.

Wittgenstein, L. 1953. *Philosophical Investigations*. Oxford: Blackwell.

Young, H. P. 1998. *Individual Strategy and Social Structure*. Princeton, NJ: Princeton University Press.

CHAPTER 21

MAKING RACE OUT OF NOTHING: PSYCHOLOGICALLY CONSTRAINED SOCIAL ROLES

RON MALLON AND DANIEL KELLY

21.1. INTRODUCTION

Race is one of the most common variables in the social sciences, used to draw correlations between racial groups and numerous other important variables such as education, health care outcomes, aptitude tests, wealth, employment, and so forth. But where concern with race once reflected the view that races were biologically real, many, if not most, contemporary social scientists have abandoned the idea that racial categories demarcate substantial, intrinsic biological differences between people. This, in turn, raises an important question about the significance of race in those social sciences: If there is no biological basis of race, why are racial categories useful to social scientists? More specifically, in virtue of what are racial categories a successful basis of informative, important social scientific generalizations?[1] We'll call this social science's *race puzzle*.

A main aim of this chapter is to set out the sort of solution that has typically been given to this race puzzle, and suggest some ways in which such a solution might be extended and improved. We begin by developing what we will call the *standard answer*: Racial categories are not biological groupings, but are rather social roles of some sort. These social roles are produced and sustained by cultural understandings, social conventions, institutions, and common practices of classification. Those social roles, in turn, causally influence the individual persons that occupy them. Generalizations involving races are about individuals occupying the same type of (racial) social role, and the regularities those generalizations capture exist because those individuals are subject to the same types of socially mediated causal influences.

While we believe the standard answer explanation of racial difference is basically correct, we hold that development of the standard answer's explanation of racial difference is hampered by an *antipsychological bias* that manifests itself in the dearth of discussion of the underlying psychological mechanisms that support and shape racial social roles. We argue that appreciation of these mechanisms leaves us better equipped to explain a range of phenomena of importance to social scientists of race, including:

1. The particular patterns of racial categorization and inference characteristic of racial categories.
2. The stability of racial categories over time and the reappearance of similar categories across cultures and history.
3. The nature and character of racism, and the sources and persistence of certain racial disparities.

In short, we argue that understanding the way racial social roles are *psychologically constrained* allows us to develop a more complete and satisfactory solution to the social sciences' race puzzle.

Here, then, is how we do this. In section 21.2, we set out a more detailed account of the standard answer. Then, in sections 21.3 and 21.4, we go on to illustrate how the kind of recent work in evolutionary, cognitive, and social psychology that can be used to develop a hybrid social constructionism about race. In section 21.3, we discuss recent developments in the evolutionary cognitive approach to racial categorization that suggest certain features of racial classification and generalization emerge from the nature of the particular cognitive mechanisms subserving those capacities. Then, in section 21.4, we go on to discuss recent work in the social psychology of racism, suggesting that many racial evaluations emerge as the result of implicit and automatic evaluation, and that the relevant mechanisms can contribute to different kinds of racial inequalities. Finally, in section 21.5, we pull strands of these previous discussions together to formulate the idea of a psychologically constrained social role. We briefly situate this idea with respect to other work in the social sciences that explores how what seem to be small factors operating at the level of individuals— what have been called micro-affirmations and micro-inequalities—can scale up to influence or create regularities at the level of groups and societies.

21.2. THE STANDARD ANSWER

The orthodox view of race and racial phenomena is that regularities expressed by generalizations using racial terminology exist as a consequence of current or past social conventions, practices of racial classification of persons, and the differential treatment of those persons. We will unpack the two main components of this view: the denial of the biological reality of race, and an account of racial phenomena spelled out in terms of social roles, representations, and practices of racial classification.

21.2.1. Denying the Biological Reality of Race

Denials of the biological reality of race rest on a combination of conceptual and empirical arguments. The most widespread conceptual argument involves characterizing "folk racialism," a term used to capture the classificatory and inferential principles that implicitly govern folk conceptions of race, as committed to essentialism about racial categories. Essentialism here is the idea that categories like *black* or *white* pick out some inner, defining essence of those people they apply to. Such essentialism about race, however, is now widely recognized to be implausible on biological grounds. This is based both on the general considerations that lead contemporary biological thought to the abandonment of essentialist thinking about types (Mayr 1976, Sober 1980), and also on the specific consideration that intragroup variation in biological races is nearly as great as intragroup variation (Lewontin 1995), leaving candidate essences thin or nonexistent.

This consensus has not been complete. Some biologically oriented philosophers have suggested that the resulting antiracialist view is both quite weak (Mallon 2007) and one that biologically sophisticated racialists would be unlikely to hold (Edwards 2003; Kitcher 1999; Mallon 2007; Sesardic 2003, 2010). Moreover, it has long been known that human populations—even ones that are geographically and ethnically closely related—are characterized by biological differences, including genetic differences, even if these differences are not essences (e.g., Ward and Neel 1970). More recently, the availability of ancestry identifying genetic tests and the public discussion over race-specific medicine have seemed to lend plausibility to the idea that racial categories have at least some biological correlates.

On the other hand, a host of additional arguments against the biological reality of race have also been advanced in recent decades. These include the claims that:

1. Genes are independently assorted, and so unlikely to cluster with racial membership (Lewontin 1972, 1974; but see Edwards 2003).
2. Human natural history is such that evolution is unlikely to have continued (Root 2000, but see Cochran et al. 2006; Hawks et al. 2007).
3. Human variability is continuous (e.g., Diamond 1994).
4. The kinds or populations identified by such a view would be unlikely to match up with folk racial divisions (Appiah 1996, 73; Glasgow 2003, 458ff; Zack 2002, 76).

Some take such arguments to undermine the existence of race outright (Appiah 1996; Blum 2002; Zack 2002) while others argue for skepticism about race on broadly pragmatic grounds (Kitcher 2007). Still others remain unconvinced that there is no acceptable biological grounding for race (Edwards 2003, Sesardic 2010).

Our goal here is not to adjudicate this debate, but to explore and develop the possibilities for the standard answer as an account of racial difference. Despite ongoing debate about the biological or psychological (e.g., Rushton and Jenson 2005) reality of race, and some evidence from what may be special cases (e.g., Cochran et al. 2006), many of the social sciences and humanities proceed on the assumption that biological races do not, in general, exist. It is this state of affairs that gives rise to what we're calling the race puzzle. Denying the biological reality or significance of race, or denying the explanatory relevance of whatever differences might exist, creates the need for an alternative, nonbiological account of those racial differences that *do* figure so prominently in the investigations and discoveries of contemporary social sciences.[2]

21.2.2. In Place of Biology, Step 1: Enlightened Realism about Social Practices

The standard answer explains many differential features of race by reference to our historical and contemporary classifications. In this regard, the standard answer is an instance of a more general strategy, common throughout the social sciences, of understanding certain regularities as being themselves produced by other social practices. Michael Root invokes the strategy clearly for the case of race:

> Race is like marital status; no one would be married or single had we not invented matrimony; however, given that we did, we now divide ourselves along discernible boundaries, into categories like "husband" and "wife" or "single" and "divorced" and treat each other differently depending on which of these categories we belong to. So too with race; we assign each other a race and treat each other differently depending on that race. As a result, epidemiologists can discover that the rates of mortality or morbidity are different for one race than another even though race is not biological just as they can discover that health risks vary with marital status even though marital status is not in our genes. In other words, race can be a biologically salient category even though there are no biological races, and race can mark the risk of a biological condition like diabetes or heart disease even though race is not itself a biological condition but a social status. (2003, 1175)

This strategy may raise eyebrows of those concerned to defend a realist interpretation of the phenomena studied by social sciences, or of those who think that science is or should be in the business of describing what is *real*. It might seem that, according to the standard answer, race is real only because we treat it as being real. Such worries, though understandable, are misplaced here; we need only recall that our social practices are real things, with real causal effects, and that any social science that left out these practices and their effects would surely provide an incomplete picture of the various social phenomena they seek to understand (Taylor 2000, Sundstrom 2002).

As it happens, racial classifications are used to express and explain numerous phenomena—for example, differential tuberculosis rates among American blacks (but not those in the United Kingdom) (Root 2000); differential test performances resulting from so-called stereotype threats (Steele 2010); different rates of drug use (Bachmann et al. 1991); or effects of race in jury selection (Haney-Lopez 2000).

21.2.3. In Place of Biology, Step 2: Racial Social Roles

From the recognition that social practices—conventions, patterns of classification and evaluation, and so forth—have real and systematic effects on individuals and social groups, one can begin to develop the notion of a social role. The fundamental idea of a social role is that the differential properties of individuals who fall in a human category are to be explained (at least in part) by the set of (stable) understandings, policies, and practices concerning proper classification and differential treatment that a community holds about those persons. We can characterize this idea more precisely as follows:

i. There is a term, label, or mental representation that picks out a category of persons *P*, and a set of beliefs and evaluations—or a *conception*—of the persons so picked out.

ii. Many or all of the beliefs and evaluations in the conception of the role are widely shared by members of a community, as is the knowledge that they are widely shared, and so forth. That is, the conception of the category is *common knowledge*.[3]

iii. Many of the beliefs and evaluations are action guiding, specifying appropriate behavior by and toward members of *P*.

Because communities use classifications of persons as a basis for identifications, predictions, explanations, and coordination, a conventionally secured social role creates a social context in which individuals in the category develop, live, and act. To the extent the representations and conventions constituting the role are stable, the actions and evaluations they motivate will be stable too. This illuminates how social roles can give rise to stable, socially produced regularities (cf. Mallon 2003).

Note, for now, that this way of unpacking the idea of a social role appeals to a variety of psychological entities: representations, beliefs, evaluations, knowledge, and the like. At this level of generality, we do not take ourselves to be saying anything controversial—any plausible spelling out of the idea of a social role must acknowledge that the causal pressures that shape social roles are psychologically mediated. Below we make our case for a stronger claim; roughly, that the character of the mediating psychology helps explain the character of the resultant social roles, and ultimately the character of the associated regularities and differences.

This is the burden we take up in the next two sections, where we consider two types of psychological systems that are implicated in racial cognition. First, in section 21.3, we explore the possibility that racial conceptions are shaped by innate, domain-specific, and species-typical proclivities of the sort described in recent evolutionary and cognitive psychology. If those conceptions are thus influenced, then their associated social roles are as well, and it follows that understanding the relevant psychological proclivities can illuminate the explanation of racial difference. In section 21.4, we explore another sort of proclivity: implicit biases. We argue that specifically racial biases (which may well be learned) are another kind of individual-level psychological mechanisms that ought to figure in standard answer explanations of racial difference. Finally, in section 21.5 we discuss more generally how appreciation of such psychological proclivities can help shed light on the nature of the social roles that they shape, and hence help explain the types of regularities that many of the social sciences investigate.

21.3. AN EVOLUTIONARY COGNITIVE APPROACH TO RACIAL REPRESENTATIONS

21.3.1. Social Construction and the Race Puzzle

"Social constructionists," as we use the term here, explain things as products of human culture and human decision. The standard answer is a sort of social constructionism about racial difference (and one we endorse) because it explains racial difference by appeal to human culture and the beliefs and practices that such culture structures.

However, social constructionism about racial difference is traditionally paired with another sort of social constructionism: social constructionism about the *representations* that in part constitute the culture and social roles that figure in the standard answer. The claim is, in effect, that our individual or collective racial representations have the content that they do, rather than some other content (or no content at all), because of the content of transmitted human culture and human decision. Call this *parallel constructionism*, for it holds that the social construction of racial representations proceeds in parallel with the construction of racial difference among those represented.

In contrast, in this section, we pair social constructionism about racial difference with a partially nonconstructionist account of racial representations. We argue that the available empirical evidence better supports this view, which we call *hybrid constructionism*. Recent work in evolutionary and cognitive psychology has suggested that important features of racial representations are explained by appeal to mental mechanisms that are species-typical, domain-specific, and innate (Astuti et al. 2004; Hirschfeld 1996; Gil-White 2001a, 2001b; Gelman 2003; Machery and Faucher 2005a, 2005b; Jones 2009; cf. Mallon 2010). But we also note that traditional social constructionist explanations are ill equipped to explain the stability and distinctiveness of racial representations, and this compromises their ability to fully address social science's race puzzle. In effect, we are arguing that relaxing one's commitment to the social construction of racial representations strengthens one's hand with respect to the social construction of race.

Social constructionist explanations of racial representations and recent evolutionary cognitive explanations of racial representations are different empirical hypotheses about why racial representations have the content they do. They also make different predictions: evolutionary cognitive accounts suggest that at least some significant aspects of our racial representations are constrained by psychological mechanisms that are innate, domain-specific, and species-typical—in effect that racial representations are stabilized by features of human nature. In contrast, in insisting that racial representations are supported by human culture and decision alone, social constructionist explanations in effect suggest that such representations should vary considerably over historical time and across cultures as the content of culture itself shifts.

And this is, in fact, what constructionists say. For example, a frequent claim of humanists and many humanistically oriented social scientists is that the idea or concept of race was itself invented, perhaps at the end of the eighteenth or the beginning of the nineteenth century, but at least sometime since the Renaissance (e.g., Fredrickson 2002, Guillaumin 1980, Banton 1978). Racial thinking, according to this line of thought, is a socio-historically local product of the West, produced in a crucible of disparate forces that include the declining influence of the Roman Catholic church and of religion more generally, the rising influence of science, and the need for Europeans and Americans to justify their colonial adventures and slaveholding in a political environment in which democratic equality was an emerging norm (Fredrickson 2002). Not only are racial representations supposed to be historically local, but they are often said to be unstable, as in this much-quoted passage from Michael Omi and Howard Winant's *Racial Formation in the United States*, wherein they urge "effort must be made to understand race as *an unstable and 'decentered' complex of social meanings constantly being transformed by political struggle*" (1986, 68; italics in original). These claims express exactly what we should expect if social constructionism about racial representations were true, for without a culturally independent reality to track (for race is not biologically real) *and* in the absence of psychological proclivities stabilizing the content of racial representations, racial representations would be relatively unconstrained, exhibiting a lack of stability over time.

21.3.2. Evolutionary Cognitive Accounts of Racial Essentialism

Recent evolutionary cognitive work suggests the possibility of a more stable core of racial representations that, despite numerous changes in cultural understanding over time, is organized by the theoretical assumption of *racial essentialism*. While essentialism is a fixture of social theoretical discussions of race and many other kinds (e.g., Putnam 1975, Appiah 1996, Mallon 2007), recent psychological work suggests its role in categorization judgments, inductions, and inferences involving inheritance in the biological and racial domains (Hirschfeld 1996, Astuti et al. 2004, Kanovsky 2007, Jones 2009, Mallon 2010). In the biological and racial domains, such essentialism amounts to the assumption that kind-membership is underwritten by an underlying explanatory property that both explains kind-typical properties and is passed on in biological inheritance. For example, knowing that an individual baby animal or plant seed is of a certain kind causes children to judge that it will develop the typical properties associated with that kind, even when its developmental environment is characteristic of another kind. And Susan Gelman and Henry Wellman (1991, experiments 3, 4 and 5)) showed that four-year-old children judge that a baby cow, raised by pigs, will nonetheless say "moo" rather than "oink." The work suggests such patterns emerge early (Hirschfeld 1996) and cross-culturally (Astuti et al. 2004; Atran 1990, 1998; Atran and Medin 2008; Gil-White 2001a, 2001b; Kanovsky 2007; Jones 2009; cf. Mallon 2010) in the biological and racial domains, and because of the parallels, suggests a common psychological mechanism at work in both domains. While the specific content of, for example, American racial categories is tied to the American racial context, human groupings organized by similar, essentialist assumptions are relatively easy to find across a range of cultures. For instance, while Indian castes have many differences among themselves and with American racial classifications, they nonetheless exhibit the idea that "to be of high or low caste is a matter of innate quality or essence" (Bayly 1999, 10).

Many evolutionary cognitive theorists hypothesize that racial cognition shares a common structure with biological cognition, and some view this structure as an evolutionary *adaptation*. However, in part because they do not believe in biological race, evolutionary cognitive theorists do not believe this mechanism is adapted *for* thinking *about race*. Rather, they believe it is adapted for some other domain—for example, for thinking about important social kinds (Hirschfeld 1996) or about human ethnic groups (Gil-White 2001a).

21.3.3. The Explanatory Relevance of Evolutionary Cognitive Accounts

These features of the mechanism thought to underlie racial categorization, together with the assumption made by most theorists that the mechanism in question is a part of an innate, species-typical psychological endowment of humankind, can explain features of racial representations that are important and relevant to a wide range of investigations of racial thought and racial difference in the contemporary humanities and social sciences. Here we focus upon three examples: category stability, patterns of cultural commonality and variation, and the distinctiveness of the causal effects of racial categories.

21.3.3.1. Category Stability

We have already noted social constructionists' emphasis on the malleability and instability of racial representations. But the suggestion that categories are so unstable raises the question of how they could be the basis for successful generalizations in the social sciences—the suggestion, in effect, threatens to undermine the standard answer's social role strategy for answering the race puzzle.

Consider Signithia Fordham and John Uzo Ogbu's controversial and influential claim that American blacks' lower performance in schools than white peers was the result of a black culture that devalues excelling at school as "acting white" (Fordham and Ogbu 1986). This hypothesis suggests that students manage their behavior in ways that attempt to balance the needs of successful self-presentation to one's peers against other values, and it fits nicely as an example of social role explanation of differential behavior. However, subsequent research has cast doubt on the explanation. In 2003, Karolyn Tyson and William Darity Jr. directed a North Carolina study that found no difference in school attitudes between white and black students. However, more recent work by Roland Fryer and Paul Torelli (2010) suggests there may still be something to the idea. Crucially, for our purposes, is the question of if and how such findings might generalize. If racial representations are so unstable, it is unclear how claims about, for example, black North Carolinian attitudes toward education in North Carolina in the twenty-first century could generalize to or have any bearing at all on claims about black Californian attitudes toward education in the late twentieth century. Unless we take the predicate "black" to have a common meaning purporting to pick out a single sort of person, it is unclear how a social role structured by such meaning could perform explanatory work stably across time and space.

Elsewhere, one of us has argued that some stability can be achieved in a social milieu in which conventions of classification are at some sort of equilibrium with the social regularities they produce (Mallon 2003; also see Hacking 1995, 1999). Appeal to equilibria is less and less plausible over further and further stretches of time and cultural distance. However, once we recognize that folk racial conceptions are structured by underlying assumptions of racial essentialism, we can see that variation in beliefs about race over time often overlie (and leave untouched) an essentialist theoretical core that explains the stability of racial classifications over broader expanses of time and space.

21.3.3.2. *Patterns of Cultural Variation*

Of course, to say that evolutionary cognitive explanations of racial essentialism explain some aspects of racial representations is not to say that all aspects of those representations are fixed by innate, domain-specific, species-typical mechanisms. This leads to a prediction: There should be less variation across time and cultures in features of the representation that reflect underlying essentialist assumptions and more variation in those beliefs that escape such assumptions.

A case in point is mixed-race categories. If folk racial essentialism is the product of applying a mechanism to human groups that is adapted to producing judgments about certain sorts of biological populations, then it makes sense to think that it would have little to say in cases where human populations are unlike biological species. For while (many sorts of) biological species exhibit considerable reproductive isolation, human populations readily interbreed. So the anthropologist Doug Jones (2009) and one of us (Mallon 2010) have each predicted that principles for the categorization of mixed race individuals should vary more widely across cultures than principles for the categorization of individuals with biological or cultural groups, and Jones (2009) has argued that this is indeed the case.

If borne out, this prediction looks to have practical consequences. For it suggests that a certain strand of racial skepticism born of attention to the ubiquity of mixed-race individuals in the modern world (Zack 1992) has a foundation in our cognitive architecture. When we attend to the complexity of mixed biological parenthood, we may dumbfound the essentialist assumptions by which our minds attempt to organize our social world. Something like this is almost certainly at work in the widely remarked upon diminished role of race in Latin American life. The historian George Fredrickson (2002) writes:

> [In Latin America] an attempt to order society on the basis of *castas* defined in terms of color and ethnicity eventually broke down because the extent and variety of *mestizaje* (interracial marriage and concubinage) created such an abundance of types that the system collapsed into the three basic categories of white, *mestizo*, and Indian. Those categories lacked the rigidity of true racial divisions, because aspirants to higher status who possessed certain cultural and economic qualifications could often transcend them. (39–40)

21.3.3.3. *The Causal Effects of Racial Categories*

An ongoing feature of theoretical conversation about racial categories is how such categories related to other categories like class, sex, gender, ethnicity, and so forth. One distinctive feature of racial classification that looks to be an outgrowth of the kind of essentialism that orders the biological domain is the inheritance of racial membership. In this way, racial membership looks unlike other categories that have been social bases of oppression. This difference also looks to have systematic effects. Consider, for example, that contemporary blacks typically have a greater percentage of black ancestors than contemporary whites do (while they don't differ in the same way in the percentage of, for example, women ancestors). This, in turn, means that past oppression of blacks exerts causal effects differentially on current generations of blacks in a way that past oppression of women does not. Consider that according to the Federal Reserve, white Americans possessed *ten times* the wealth of black Americans in 2007 (Lui 2009). Because wealth is typically passed on by descent in parallel with race, past racial oppression cascades down to current generations, differentially influencing members of different races. If the evolutionary cognitive program is right, the distinctive way that racial membership is inherited may be in part a product of the cognitive proclivities underwriting folk racial categories—mechanisms that tie racial membership with racial inheritance (Mallon 2010).

21.4. IMPLICIT BIASES AND RACE

In this section we shift gears to focus on a different research program, one that investigates what social psychologists call implicit biases. While the evolutionary cognitive program discussed in the last section held that specific aspects of racial representations might be the product of innate, domain-specific, and species-typical proclivities to essentialize human groups, we make no similar nativist claim about implicit racial biases. Implicit racial biases appear to be members of a family of more general biases that can be directed at a range of different types of people; research has revealed implicit race biases, but also implicit gender biases, implicit age biases, and so forth. Moreover, the ontogenetic origin of such biases remains unclear, and they may be acquired via individual or social learning. Our main focus here is on the evaluative component of racial cognition, and its connection to features like the sources and persistence of racial disparities found at population levels. We begin by describing a prominent approach to understanding such disparities—one that emphasizes *institutional racism*—and we discuss its connection to the race puzzle and the standard answer. We go on to describe in more detail some psychological findings about implicit racial biases, and then illustrate their explanatory value for addressing social science's race puzzle.

21.4.1. Social Construction, the Institutional Approach to Racism and the Race Puzzle

Although there is no single canonical statement of *institutional*—or, alternatively, *structural*—approaches to racism, accounts that go under that name have a common orientation. Here is a typical description:

> A "structural racism" approach considers the ways in which the networked operations between historical legacies, individuals, and institutional arrangements produce unequal and hierarchical racial outcomes. Thus, rather than understanding racism as an isolated or individual phenomenon, a structural racism approach understands it as an outcome and suggests that different societal institutions work together to distribute or limit opportunity along racial lines.[4]

Several features of this statement deserved to be unpacked. First, this approach uses a conception of racism that is *outcome* focused. Intuitively, discrete actions, attitudes, and individual people can be racist, but this approach focuses primarily on unequal social-level outcomes. In addition to this distinctive way of conceiving racism itself, institutional approaches typically favor a distinctive, anti-individualist kind of explanation of those disparate outcomes as well. The sources and persistence of such inequalities are best explained not by appeal to the characteristics of individual people (including their psychological characteristics), but mainly by appeal to the institutions, social structures, and policies of the society in which individual people live and the policies that govern them. For many advocates of the institutional approach, the details about individuals and their psychological makeup are of minor explanatory value, if of any at all. Because racism (in the form of unequal outcomes) can exist and thrive even in the absence of racists (individual people who evaluatively rank racial groups), institutional approaches to racism countenance the possibility of racism without racists (for discussion, see Arthur 2007, Berard 2008, Brown et al. 2003).

Like our own approach, institutional approaches provide a version of the standard answer to explaining racial difference. They disavow biological explanations, and instead explain, for example, racial inequality by appeal to features of cultures, policies, conventions, and institutions—an approach we have unpacked in terms of social roles (section 21.1). However, institutional approaches also exhibit a resistance to psychological explanation with which we disagree. In this case, the reluctance to engage with psychological research appears to stem from the anti-individualist strand. Indeed, some who favor institutional approaches to racism explicitly argue that understanding racial cognition is irrelevant to a proper understanding of racism, and to the most promising strategies for dealing with it (Wellman 2007).[5] This sort of institutional approach also suggests rather straightforward predictions about how to correct or ameliorate the forms of outcome-based racism it focuses on: Rather than directly targeting individual behaviors or attitudes, the institutional orientation suggests making higher-level changes to the structure of the institutions and the governing policies themselves.

In what follows, we will make our case that standard answer approaches focusing on institutions need not be hostile to psychological research, and that relaxing one's commitment to anti-individualism, and taking account of the types of psychological proclivities that influence racial evaluations, allows for a more complete and explanatorily powerful application of the standard answer to racial difference.

21.4.2. Brief Overview of Implicit Racial Bias

For roughly the last twenty years, social psychologists have been developing more sophisticated, indirect ways of measuring individuals' attitudes, biases, and other mental states (Devine 1989, Greenwald and Banaji 1995, Fazio et al. 1995.) To say these methods are indirect is to say that they do not simply use introspection and self-report, but instead rely on performance on tests or tasks relevant to the types of mental states under investigation. Many of the most well-known and widely used indirect tests, such as the implicit attitude test, or IAT, are sorting tasks, in which subjects must classify stimuli like words or faces as quickly as possible, and under a variety of conditions. Such methods, designed to bypass the difficulties associated with self-deception, lack of sincerity, or problematic introspective access, are often used in conjunction with more direct measures, such as surveys in which participants simply answer questions or rate the degree to which they agree or disagree with a relevant statement.[6] These methods have been used to gather an enormous amount of data, and shed light on the workings of implicit and automatic cognition in a number of different domains. Of the mental states investigated using such indirect techniques, some of the most well known have come to be called implicit biases. As noted above, social psychologists have found evidence of a variety of implicit biases. These include biases against the elderly (Levy and Banaji 2002) biases associated with gender (Lemm and Banaji 1999) biases associated with sexuality (Banse, Seise, and Zerbes 2001), biases associated with weight (Schwartz et al. 2006), biases against the disabled, as well as biases against religious groups (see Lane et al. 2007 for a review). Some of the earliest discovered, and most well confirmed, are implicit racial biases.

The literature on implicit biases is large and growing, so instead of attempting to give a comprehensive review, we will confine our discussion to some the most relevant and stable lessons that can be drawn from this research project. Perhaps the most striking thing about implicit biases, including racial biases, is that they can coexist within a single individual, with explicit attitudes that are prima facie incompatible with them. A single person can explicitly embrace antiracist doctrines and can loudly and sincerely profess to hold egalitarian and tolerant racial views, on the one hand, while still harboring implicit biases against members of certain races, on the other. Though they are about the same groups of people (in this case, races), racial evaluation appears to involve two distinct types of mental states, each processed by its own distinct kind of cognitive mechanism.

In addition to being distinct from their explicit counterparts, implicit biases have a number of surprising features (much of this, and the evidence in support of it, is reviewed in greater detail in Kelly, Machery, and Mallon 2010). Implicit biases appear to be easy to acquire, and are difficult to get rid of once acquired. As revealed by a number of studies, some utilizing several indirect techniques, these biases are unconscious and difficult to detect via introspection. Despite this, however, implicit biases are far from causally inert. Indeed, they have been found to influence evaluations of people who are classified as belonging to a particular race, and, in turn, have been found to influence interactions with members of that same race. Even for those who become aware of implicit racial biases, and the fact that they themselves harbor them, those implicit biases do not appear to be easily or straightforwardly manageable. Indeed, a wide range of strategies for mitigating the influence of implicit racial biases have and continue to be investigated, and while it is not yet clear what separates out those that have some degree of success from those that do not— or those that outright backfire—it appears that consciously attempting to suppress their influence on thought and behavior provides an incomplete and only sometimes effective solution (also see Kelly, Faucher, and Machery 2010 for discussion).

21.4.3. Explanatory Benefits

Implicit racial biases can be thought of as features of individual psychologies that, as such, exert influence on individuals occupying the racial social roles that are in part constituted by racial representations. We maintain that, collectively, the influence of implicit biases can scale up to shape the types of population regularities that social sciences attempt to capture with generalizations about race in particular societies, cultures, and institutions. In what follows we will go over a specific example in some detail in an attempt to illustrate how this might work.

We may first note that what we will be proposing there is not completely without precedent. For example, Haney-Lopez (2000) advocates a form of institutional explanation of racism that he calls the "New Institutional" approach. His concern is with racial outcomes at the level of prosecution and conviction of certain crimes.

He finds that for the trials he is looking at, the defendants were Mexican Americans, but the juries contained little or no Mexican Americans. He argues that the outcome of those trials is in part explained by appeal to the racial composition of the juries. He further argues that the racial composition of those juries, in turn, is in part explained by appeal to a form of racism, more specifically racial discrimination on the part of the judges who selected the relevant juries.

Haney-Lopez's discussion is particularly useful from our point of view for a pair of reasons. First, it represents an attempt to expand the institutional approach to racism so that it can take into account characteristics of individual actors—particularly actors who occupy important "gatekeeper" roles within the context of their institutions, and who are therefore in a position to exert more amplified influence over institutional outcomes. Perhaps more importantly, however, is his sensitivity to the psychological subtleties involved. The judges relevant to his explanation explicitly claim, under oath, to not harbor any conscious or intentional discriminatory intent. He sees this as compatible with his favored explanation, which appeals to discrimination on the part of the judges who selected the juries. Indeed, his stated goal is to

> elaborate a theory of racism capable of reconciling the statistical evidence of judicial discrimination with the judges' insistence that they never intended to discriminate. More generally, it sets out to build a theory of racism that explains organizational activity that systematically harms minority groups even though the decision-making individuals lack any conscious discriminatory intent. (Haney-Lopez 2000, 1717)

We need only to point out that the research on implicit biases provides a wealth of empirical support for the kind of psychological possibility required by Haney-Lopez's explanation—that actors can be explicitly unbiased but implicitly biased. Thus, incorporating the findings of empirical work on racial cognition is not only compatible with institutional approaches to racism, but can substantially enrich the associated explanations of racial regularities and outcomes.

Finally, however, it is worth reflecting on how appreciation of the nature of implicit biases might help understand certain components of racial representations themselves. More specifically, appeal to implicit biases may help explain some of the evaluative, rather than purely descriptive, content that racial representations can take on.[7] If this line of thought is on target, then it supplies one more way in which a parallel constructionist account of race and racism is at best incomplete; important elements of the evaluative components of racial representations are a product of psychological proclivities—in this case, the implicit biases—of the classifiers.

Racial disparities in employment provide another area in which social scientific explanations can be usefully enriched by appeal to implicit racial biases. Consider the study performed by Bertrand and Mullainathan (2003), who sent out over 5,000 resumes in response to help wanted ads in Boston and Chicago for a range of different types of jobs. Each of the resumes was made up. Some resumes were designed to be highly qualified for the position they were sent in response to, while others were not. Finally, each resume was given either a very black sounding name or a very white sounding name.

The results were eye-opening. First, the resumes with white sounding names got roughly 50 percent more callbacks in general. Second, within the set of resumes with white sounding names, those that were highly qualified for the respective position received 30 percent more callbacks than others, but no similar effect was found for resumes with black sounding names. Being more qualified did not increase the chance that a resume with a black sounding name would get an interview. Third, the relative levels of discrimination were similar across occupations and industries. Finally, just less than one third of those companies explicitly described themselves as "Equal Opportunity Employers" in their help wanted ads. Despite this assertion, these companies showed similar patterns and levels of discrimination against resumes with black sounding names.

Bertrand and Mullainathan are at pains to show that the discrimination revealed by this study is a result of race and not some other factor. They show that the patterns cannot be explained by appeal to the address listed on the resume (whether the applicant lives in a good or bad neighborhood) or facts about the different types of job requirements or industries associated with the positions being applied to.

Before discussing this in terms of the social science's race puzzle, we need to make the case that these patterns of discrimination are caused, in part, by the implicit racial biases of people making decisions about individual resumes. This, of course, requires some speculation, but we believe the claim is plausible. Bertrand and Mullainathan show that the discriminatory patterns are linked to race, as indicated by the names on the resumes. This leaves two possibilities: Either the people deciding which resumes did or did not deserve a callback are explicitly racist, or they harbor implicit racial biases that influence their decisions. We believe the latter explanation is more plausible. First, implicit racial biases are relatively widespread, and research has demonstrated that implicit biases can influence the judgments and behaviors of individuals in a number of ways, and in a number of conditions (Lane et al. 2007). So they are able to do the explanatory work being asked for them. Second, it seems to us that implicit rather than explicit biases are more likely to be the culprits in this case. In general explicit racial biases have been on the decline in the population for some time (Schuman et al. 1997). Furthermore, Bertrand and Mullainathan found similar patterns of discrimination in those businesses that went out of their way to describe themselves as equal opportunity Employers. This means that, collectively, those individuals making decisions about resumes in Equal Opportunity businesses produced patterns of racial discrimination despite having instructions and incentives to assess resumes impartially.

Now, let us recall the race puzzle: If biological races offer no explanatory purchase, then what explains the success of racial categories in expressing the types of true generalizations studied by the social sciences? If there are no biological races of the sort once thought, then why are there robust population-level statistical regularities that are captured using racial terminology? What we called the standard answer claims that racial categories are social roles that are invented but then take on a life of their own once they become involved in the looping effects of human classificatory dynamics. Our discussion here accepts this as far as it goes, but we think that it leaves out an important piece of the puzzle: namely, the influence of specific features of individual psychologies on those classificatory dynamics, and the types of patterns those features can generate and sustain.

We think Bertrand and Mullainathan's resume study finds a pattern that illustrates just this phenomenon: Resumes with white sounding names are 50 percent more likely to get interviews than resumes with black sounding names. Explaining this, we claim, involves not just appeal to explicit beliefs about race, but also appeal to the fact that, at the individual level, many people have implicit racial biases that tacitly influence their judgments about those categories and the people that fall under them. The effects of these biases, in turn, scale up to help produce the types of population-level patterns discovered by social scientists, such as the disparity in interviews offered to resumes bearing black versus white sounding names. In general, such biases can contribute to the types of disparities in employment documented by social scientists and others working on race (for instance, see Horton 1995; Bendick and Egan 2009; Bendick, Rodriguez, and Jayaraman 2009).

Race may not be biologically real, but it remains important because people think and act as if it is, thus keeping racial categories and social roles in high currency. Racism remains very real, in part because the cognitive machinery that underpins how people think about and act on racial social roles involves implicit biases, and the influence of those biases scales up to systematically shape population-levels patterns concerning race and discrimination.

21.5. PSYCHOLOGICALLY CONSTRAINED SOCIAL ROLES AND THE POWER OF SMALL CAUSES

Social sciences' race puzzle arises from the assumption that there is no or little biological basis of race, which leaves it unclear why racial categories can serve as a successful basis of informative, important social scientific generalizations. As we have argued, the standard answer to this puzzle is a social constructionist explanation of racial difference, invoking something like racial social roles. While we agree with this answer, we have argued that the exploration and development of more sophisticated forms of the standard answer have been hindered by anti-psychological bias manifested in two related strands of thought, which we have called *parallel constructionist* and *anti-individualist*, respectively. Instead, we have argued that versions of the standard answer can be supplemented and improved by taking account of the types of psychological findings we have discussed in the last two sections.

Let us sum up the argument we have been offering. Standard answer explanations of category difference appeal (tacitly or otherwise) to the way representations structure our social lives, an idea we have sketched in terms of social roles. Any plausible account of these representations and the ways they structure our social lives will appeal to psychological entities and processes that can guide practices of classification, influence social conventions, and shape formal and informal policies concerning membership in a social role.

Parallel constructionists see these representations as themselves being socially constructed, and thus exclusively the product of human decision and culture. As such, parallel constructionists see the social roles they structure as primarily a result of historical circumstances, social conventions, and common practices of classification. Anti-individualists see social regularities and outcomes as best explained by appeal to features of institutions and social policies, rather than individuals. Both explanations exhibit antipsychological bias.

Another way to think of this is that both parallel constructionist and anti-individualist explanations deal in what might be called *purely conventional* social roles. Some social roles, such as *divorcee* or *licensed chihuahua owner*, may very well be purely conventional, in this sense. We have offered reason to believe, however, that others are what we can call *psychologically constrained* social roles. To say that a social role is psychologically constrained is to say more than the (fairly trivial claim that) relevant representations are, at some point, operated on or mediated by individual human psychologies. It is rather to claim that social roles are strongly influenced, in some way or another, by the specific character of the psychological mechanisms in play.

Understood in these terms, the case we have been making in the last couple of sections is that the behavior of the racial social roles invoked by the standard answer is best understood as psychologically constrained in a number of ways. To make this case, we have tried to show that explaining the stability and distinctiveness of racial social roles, and explaining the evaluations associated with and the causal effects of those social roles requires a better appreciation of the specific character of the psychological mechanisms that contribute to and constrain them.[8,9]

One might suspect that the types of psychological influences that we claim can constrain social roles are too small to actually shape population-level regularities. However, intuition is not always the best guide to understanding how factors that are slight, even at the level of the individual, will aggregate upward to affect the character of a population, especially when those factors are widespread. Indeed, the power of micro-affirmations and micro-inequalities is beginning to be discussed and better appreciated by those attempting to understand the sources of persistent population-level disparities associated with gender (Rowe 2008; also see Saul forthcoming). Theorists of culture, attempting to understand the engines and dynamics of cultural change and stability more generally, make a similar point: "Small, dull effects at the individual level are the stuff of powerful forces of evolution at the level of populations" (Richerson and Boyd 2005, 123). In the types of (psychologically constrained social role) cases we're talking about, some of those small, dull effects are generated by features of individual psychologies and the psychological mechanisms they contain. That said, we see no reason that their being *psychological* would make them an exception to the rule that when such effects are slight but many, they can aggregate upward to have powerful effects at the level of populations, either as forces of change or as forces that help maintain certain aspects of the status quo. The best explanations of many population-level generalities, outcomes, and disparities, then, may very well be found in psychologically constrained social roles.

ACKNOWLEDGMENTS

Our thanks go out to Luc Faucher, Jennifer Saul, Emma Gilby, Harold Kincaid, and the participants in the Current Issues in the Philosophy and Methodology of the Social Sciences conference at the University of Alabama at Birmingham for providing useful feedback on previous versions of this material.

NOTES

1. We are indebted to Root's (2000) articulation of this problem.

2. In the philosophy of race, widespread endorsement of the failure of biological race as a referent for racial thought and talk has given rise to a debate over whether we should retain or eliminate racial categories like "black," "white," "Asian," and "race" from our ordinary, expert, and policy discourse. While much of this discourse has been, at least on the surface, guided by semantic assumptions—for example, assumptions about the conditions under which terms like "race" would refer—there are substantial practical questions about the relative value and costs of racial classification also in play (Mallon 2006, 2007).

3. David Lewis (1969) introduced the idea of common knowledge. See Vanderschraaf and Sillari (2009) for an extensive discussion of a range of ways of specifying the idea.

4. Available online from the Ohio State University's Kirwan Institute for the Study of Race and Ethnicity at www.structuralracism.org/publications/documents/SRC%20 SR%20Bibliography_No%20annotations.pdf.

5. Wellman even goes a step further, arguing that certain psychological explanations of racism actually inhibit efforts to deal with it. See Machery, Faucher, and Kelly (2010) for discussion and rebuttal of those arguments.

6. Descriptions of indirect testing methods, and the statistical techniques used to interpret data gathered using them, can get quite technical (see citations in main text, and also Lane et al. 2007 and Greenwald et al. 2009). One can get a visceral feel for such tests by taking an IAT online at https://implicit.harvard.edu/implicit/demo/.

7. One useful way of thinking about this is in terms of the philosopher Bernard Williams's (1985) distinction between *thick* and *thin* ethical concepts. Thin concepts are purely evaluative, and often quite abstract; examples include *good, justice, wrong*, etc. Thick concepts, on the other hand, are hybrid concepts, in that they contain both descriptive and evaluative elements; examples here include *courageous, compassionate, brutal,* and *untrustworthy*. Certainly in some cultures, racial terms seem to operate like "thick" concepts; they not only purport to pick out a group of people based on some description, but also carry an attendant evaluation of that group of people as well.

8. Compare with the notion of "multidisciplinary explanations" of racism discussed in Machery, Faucher, and Kelly (2010).

9. Psychologically constrained social roles could be appealing in areas of philosophy and social science beyond discussions of race though the burden of this chapter has been to make the case that *racial* social roles in particular are constrained in a number of interesting and perhaps unexpected ways.

REFERENCES

Appiah, K. A. 1995. "The Uncompleted Argument: Du Bois and the Illusion of Race." In *Overcoming Racism and Sexism*, L. A. Bell and D. Blumenfeld, eds., 59–77. Lanham, MD: Rowman and Littlefield.

Appiah, K. A. 1996. "Race, Culture, Identity: Misunderstood Connections." In *Color Conscious: The Political Morality of Race*, K. A. Appiah and A. Guttmann, eds. Princeton, NJ: Princeton University Press.

Arthur, John. 2007 *Race, Equality, and the Burdens of History*, Cambridge: Cambridge University Press.

Astuti, R., G. E. A. Solomon, and S. Carey. 2004. "Constraints on Cognitive Development: A Case Study of the Acquisition of Folkbiological and Folksociological Knowledge in Madagascar." *Monographs of the Society for Research in Child Development* 69 (3): I, v, vii, viii, 1–161.

Atran, S. 1998. "Folk Biology and the Anthropology of Science: Cognitive Universals and Cultural Particulars." *Behavioral and Brain Sciences* 21 (4): 547–609.

Atran, Scott. 1990. *Cognitive Foundations of Natural History*. New York: Cambridge University Press.

Atran, Scott, and Douglas L. Medin. 2008. *The Native Mind and the Cultural Construction of Nature*. Cambridge, MA: The MIT Press.

Bachmann, J. G., J. M. Wallace Jr., P. M. O'Malley, L. D. Johnston, C. L. Kluth, and H. W. Neighbors. 1991. "Racial/Ethnic Differences in Smoking, Drinking, and Illicit Drug Use Among American High School Seniors, 1976–89." *American Journal of Public Health* 81 (3): 372–77.

Banse, R., J. Seise, and N. Zerbes. 2001. "Implicit Attitudes Toward Homosexuality: Reliability, Validity, and Controllability of the IAT." *Zeitschrift für Experimentelle Psychologie* 48 (2): 145–60.

Banton, M. 1978. *The Idea of Race*. Boulder, CO: Westview Press.

Bayly, Susan. 1999. *Caste, Society, and Politics in India*. New York: Cambridge University Press.

Bendick, M., and M. L. Egan. 2009. *Research Perspectives on Race and Employment in the Advertising Industry*. Washington, DC: Bendick and Egan Economic Consultants, Inc., for the Madison Avenue Project. Available at http://bendickegan.com/pdf/2009/ Bendick%20Egan%20Advertising%20Industry%20Report%20Jan%2009.pdf.

Bendick, M., R. Rodriquez, and S. Jayaraman. 2009. *Race-Ethnic Employment Discrimination in Upscale Restaurants: Evidence from Paired Comparison Testing*. Washington, DC: Bendick and Egan Economic Consultants, Inc., for the Madison Avenue Project. Available at http://bendickegan.com/pdf/2009/Testing_article_%20Feb_2009.pdf.

Berard, Tim J. 2008 "The Neglected Social Psychology of Institutional Racism." *Sociology Compass* 2 (2): 734–64.

Bertrand, M., and S. Mullainathan. 2003. "Are Emily and Greg More Employable Than Lakisha and Jamal?: A Field Experiment on Labor Market and Discrimination." Poverty Action Lab Paper No. 3. Cambridge, MA: Abdul Latif Jameel Poverty Action Lab. Available at http://povertyactionlab.org/papers/bertrand_mullainathan.pdf.

Blum, L. 1999. "Race, Community and Moral Education: Kohlberg and Spielberg as Civic Educators." *Journal of Moral Education* 28 (2): 125–43.

Blum, Lawrence. 2002. "*I'm not a Racist But . . .*" Ithaca, NY: Cornell University Press.

Blum, L. 2009. "Prejudice." In *Oxford Handbook of Philosophy of Education*, H. Siegel, ed., 451–68. Oxford: Oxford University Press.

Brown, Michael, Martin Conroy, Elliott Currie, Troy Duster, David B. Oppenheimer, Marjorie Shultz, and David Wellman. 2003. *Whitewashing Race: The Myth of a Color-Blind Society*. Berkeley: University of California Press.

Cochran, G., J. Hardy, and H. Harpending. 2006. "Natural History of Ashkenazi Intelligence." *Journal of Biosocial Science* 38 (5): 659–93.

Devine, P. 1989. "Stereotypes and Prejudice: Their Automatic and Controlled Components." *Journal of Personality and Social Psychology* 56 (1): 5–18.

Diamond, Jared. 1994. "Race Without Color." *Discover* (Nov.): 82–89.

Edwards, A. W. F. 2003. "Human Genetic Diversity: Lewontin's Fallacy." *BioEssays* 25: 298–801.

Fazio, R., J. Jackson, B. Dunton, and C. Williams. 1995. "Variability in Automatic Activation as an Unobtrusive Measure of Racial Attitudes: A Bona Fide Pipeline?" *Journal of Personality and Social Psychology* 69 (6): 1013–27.

Fordham, S., and Ogbu, J. 1986. "Black Students School Success: Coping with the Burden of Acting White." *Urban Review* 18 (3): 176–206.

Fredrickson, G. M. 2002. *Racism: A Short History*. Princeton, NJ: Princeton University Press.

Fryer, R., and Paul, Torelli. 2010. "An Empirical Analysis of Acting White." *Journal of Public Economics* 94 (5–6): 380–96.

Gelman, S. A. 2003. *The Essential Child: Origins of Essentialism in Everyday Thought*. New York: Oxford University Press.

Gelman, S. A., and H. M. Wellman. 1991. "Insides and Essences: Early Understandings of the Non-Obvious." *Cognition* 38: 213 44.

Gil-White, F. 2001a. "Are Ethnic Groups Biological 'Species' to the Human Brain?" *Current Anthropology* 42 (4): 515–54.

Gil-White, F. 2001b. "Sorting Is Not Categorization: A Critique of the Claim that Brazilians Have Fuzzy Racial Categories." *Cognition and Culture* 1 (3): 219–49.

Gil-White, F. 2006. "The Study of Ethnicity and Nationalism Needs Better Categories: Clearing Up the Confusions That Result from Blurring Analytic and Lay Concepts." *Journal of Bioeconomics* 7 (3): 239–70.

Glasgow, Joshua. 2003. "On the New Biology of Race." *The Journal of Philosophy* (September): 456–74.

Greenwald, A., and Banaji, M. 1995. "Implicit Social Cognition: Attitudes, Self-Esteem, and Stereotypes." *Psychological Review* 102 (1): 4–27.

Greenwald, A., D. McGhee, and J. Schwartz. 1998. "Measuring Individual Differences in Implicit Cognition: The Implicit Association Test." *Journal of Personality and Social Psychology* 74 (6): 1464–80.

Greenwald, A. G., T. A. Poehlman, E. Uhlmann, and M. R. Banaji. 2009. "Understanding and Using the Implicit Association Test: III. Meta-Analysis of Predictive Validity." *Journal of Personality and Social Psychology* 97 (1): 17–41.

Guillaumin, Colette. 1980. *The Idea of Race and Its Elevation to Autonomous Scientific and Legal Status. Sociological Theories: Race and Colonialism*. United Nations Educational, Scientific and Cultural Organization (UNESCO). Paris: UNESCO.

Hacking, I. 1995. "The Looping Effects of Human Kinds." In *Causal Cognition*, D. Sperber et al., eds., 351–94. New York: Clarendon Press.

Hacking, I. 1999. *The Social Construction of What?* Cambridge, MA: Harvard University Press.

Haney-Lopez, I. 2000. "Institutional Racism: Judicial Conduct and a New Theory of Racial Discrimination." *The Yale Law Journal* 109 (8): 1717–885.

Hawks, J., E. T. Wang, G. M. Cochran, Henry C. Harpending, and R. K. Moyziz. 2007. "Recent Acceleration of Human Adaptive Evolution." *Proceedings of the National Academy of Sciences* 104 (52): 20753–58.

Hirschfeld, L. W. 1996. *Race in Making: Cognition, Culture, and the Child's Construction of Human Kinds*. Cambridge, MA: The MIT Press.

Horton, Hayward Derrick. 1995. "The Impact of Population and Structural Change on Racial Inequality in the United States: An Examination of Employment Toward the 21st Century." In *Race and Ethnicity in America: Meeting the Challenge in the 21st Century*, G. E. Thomas, ed., 227–37. Washington, DC: Taylor and Francis.

Jones, Doug. 2009. "Looks and Living Kinds: Varieties of Racial Cognition in Bahia, Brazil." *Journal of Cognition and Culture* 9 (3): 247–69.

Kanovsky, Martin. 2007. "Essentialism and Folksociology: Ethnicity Again." *Journal of Cognition and Culture* 7 (3–4): 241–81.

Kelly, D., L. Faucher, and E. Machery. 2010. "Getting Rid of Racism: Assessing Three Proposals in Light of Psychological Evidence." *Journal of Social Philosophy* 41 (3): 293–322.

Kelly, D., E. Machery, and R. Mallon. 2010. "Race and Racial Cognition." In *The Oxford Handbook of Moral Psychology*, J. Doris et al., eds., 433–72. New York: Oxford University Press.

Kirwan Institute for the Study of Race and Ethnicity, "Bibliographical Guide to Structural Racism." Available at www.structuralracism.org/publications/documents/SRC%20 SR%20Bibliography_No%20annotations.pdf.

Kitcher, Philip. 1999. "Race, Ethnicity, Biology, Culture." In *Racism*, L. Harris, ed., 87–120. New York, Humanity Books.

Kitcher, Philip. 2007. "Does 'Race' Have a Future?" *Philosophy and Public Affairs* 35 (4): 293–317.

Kurzban, R., J. Tooby, and L. Cosmides. 2001. "Can Race Be Erased? Coalitional Computation and Social Categorization." *Proceedings of the National Academy of Science* 98 (26): 15387–92.

Lane, K. A., M. R. Banaji, B. A. Nosek, and A. G. Greenwald. 2007. "Understanding and Using the Implicit Association Test: IV: Procedures and Validity." In *Implicit Measures of Attitudes: Procedures and Controversies*, B. Wittenbrink and N. Schwarz, eds., 59–102. New York: Guilford Press.

Lemm, K., and M. R. Banaji. 1999. "Unconscious Attitudes and Beliefs About Women and Men." In *Wahrnehmung und Herstellung von Geschlecht (Perceiving and performing gender)*, U. Pasero and F. Braun, eds., 215–33. Opladen: Westdutscher Verlag.

Levy, B., and M. R. Banaji. 2002. "Implicit Ageism." In *Ageism: Stereotyping and Prejudice Against Older Persons*, T. Nelson, ed., 49–75. Cambridge, MA: The MIT Press.

Lewis, D. 1969. *Convention: A Philosophical Study*. Cambridge, MA: Harvard University Press.

Lewontin, R. 1972. "The Apportionment of Human Diversity." *Evolutionary Biology*, T. Dobzhansky, M. Hecht, and W. Steer, eds., 381–98. New York: Appleton Century Crofts.

Lewontin, R. 1974. *The Genetic Basis of Evolutionary Change*. New York: Columbia University Press.

Lewontin. R. C. 1995. *Human Diversity*. New York: Scientific American Library.

Lui, Meizhu. "The Wealth Gap Gets Wider." *Washington Post*. March 23, 2009.

Machery, E., and L. Faucher. 2005a. "Why Do We Think Racially?" In *Handbook of Categorization in Cognitive Science*, H. Cohen and C. Lefebvre, eds., 1009–33. Orlando, FL: Elsevier.

Machery, E., and L. Faucher. 2005b. "Social Construction and the Concept of Race." *Philosophy of Science* 72 (5): 1208–19.

Machery, E., L. Faucher, and D. Kelly. 2010. "On the Alleged Inadequacies of Psychological Explanations of Racism." *The Monist* 93 (2): 228–55.

Mallon, Ron. 2003. "Social Construction, Social Roles and Stability." In *Socializing Metaphysics*, F. Schmitt, ed., 327–53. Lanham, MD: Rowman & Littlefield.

Mallon, Ron. 2006. " 'Race': Normative, Not Metaphysical or Semantic." *Ethics* 116 (3): 525–51.

Mallon, Ron. 2007. "Human Categories Beyond Non-Essentialism." *Journal of Political Philosophy* 15 (2): 146–68.

Mallon, Ron. 2010. "Sources of Racialism." *Journal of Social Philosophy* 41 (3): 272–92.

Mayr, E. 1976. "Typological versus Population Thinking." *Evolution and the Diversity of Life*, 26–29. Cambridge, MA: Harvard University Press.

Omi, Michael, and Howard Winant. 1986. *Racial Formation in the United States: From the 1960s to the 1980s*. New York: Routledge.

Putnam, Hilary. 1975. "The Meaning of 'Meaning.' " *Mind, Language and Reality: Philosophical Papers*, Vol. 2., 215–71. New York: Cambridge University Press.

Richerson, P., and R. Boyd. 2005. *Not by Genes Alone*. Chicago: University of Chicago Press.

Root, M. 2000. "How We Divide the World." *Philosophy of Science* 67 (Proceedings): 628–39.

Root, Michael. 2003. "The Use of Race in Medicine as a Proxy for Genetic Differences." *Philosophy of Science* 70 (5): 1173–83.

Root, M. 2005. "The Number of Black Widows in the National Academy of Sciences." *Philosophy of Science* 72 (5): 1197–207.

Rowe, M. 2008. "Micro-Affirmations and Micro-Inequities." *Journal of the International Ombudsman Association* 1: 1.

Rushton, J. Philippe, and Arthur R. Jensen. 2005. "Thirty Years of Research on Race Differences in Cognitive Ability." *Psychology, Public Policy, and Law* 11 (2): 235–94.

Saul, J. "Implicit Bias, Stereotype Threat and Women in Philosophy." In *Women in Philosophy: What Needs to Change?*, F. Jenkins and K. Hutchinson, eds. Forthcoming.

Schwartz, M. B., L. R. Vartanian, B. A. Nosek, and K. D. Brownell. 2006. "The Influence of One's Own Body Weight on Implicit and Explicit Anti-Fat Bias." *Obesity* 14 (3): 440–47.

Sesardic, Neven. 2003. "Book Review of N. Zack, Philosophy of Science and Race." *Philosophy of Science* 70 (2): 447–49.

Sesardic, N. 2010. "A Social Destruction of a Biological Concept." *Biology and Philosophy* 25 (2): 143–62.

Schuman, H., C. Steeh, L. Bobo, and M. Kryson. 1997. *Racial Attitudes in America: Trends and Interpretations*. Cambridge, MA: Harvard University Press.

Sober, E. 1980. "Evolution, Population Thinking, and Essentialism." *Journal of Philosophy* 47: 350–83.

Steele, C. 2010. *Whistling Vivaldi: And Other Clues to How Stereotypes Affect Us*. New York: Norton.

Sundstrom, R. 2002. "Racial Nominalism." *Journal of Social Philosophy* 33 (2): 193–210.

Taylor, P. 2000. "Appiah's Uncompleted Argument: Du Bois and the Reality of Race." *Social Theory and Practice* 26 (1): 103–28.

Tyson, Karolyn, William Darity Jr., and Domini Castellino. 2004. "Breeding Animosity: The 'Burden of Acting White' and Other Problems of Status Group Hierarchies in Schools." Working Paper. Chapel Hill: Department of Sociology, University of North Carolina.

Vanderschraaf, Peter, and Giacomo Sillari. Spring 2009. "Common Knowledge." *The Stanford Encyclopedia of Philosophy*. Available at http://plato.stanford.edu/archives/spr2009/entries/common-knowledge/, accessed December 2009.

Ward, R. H., and J. V. Neel. 1970. "Gene Frequencies and Microdifferentiation Among the Makiritare Indians IV. A Comparison of a Genetic Network with Ethnohistory and Migration Matrices: A New Index of Genitic Isolation." *American Journal of Human Genetics* 22 (5): 538–61.

Wellman, David. 2007. "Unconscious Racism, Social Cognition Theory, and the Legal Intent Doctrine: The Neuron Fires Next Time." In *Handbook of Racial and Ethnic Relations*, H. Vera and J. Feagin, eds., 39–65. New York: Springer.

Williams, B. 1985. *Ethics and the Limits of Philosophy*. London: Fontana.

Zack, N. 1993. *Race and Mixed Race*. Philadelphia: Temple University Press.

Zack, N. 1998. *Thinking about Race*. Belmont, CA: Wadsworth.

Zack, N. 1999. "Philosophy and Racial Paradigms." *Journal of Value Inquiry* 33 (3): 299–317.

Zack, N. 2001. "Race and Philosophical Meaning." In *Race and Racism*, B. Boxill, ed., 43–57. New York: Oxford University Press.

Zack, N. 2002. *Philosophy of Science and Race*. New York: Routledge.

Zack, N. 2003a. "Race and Racial Discrimination." In *The Oxford Handbook of Practical Ethic*, H. Lafollette, ed., 245–71. New York: Oxford University Press.

Zack, N. 2003b. "Reparations and Rectification of Race." *The Journal of Ethics* 7 (1): 139–51.

Zack, N. 2004. "American Mixed Race." In *Mixing It Up: Multiracial Subjects*, S. Kwan and K. Speirs, eds., 13–30. Austin: University of Texas Press.

PART IV

Sociology of Knowledge

A FEMINIST EMPIRICAL AND INTEGRATIVE APPROACH IN POLITICAL SCIENCE: BREAKING DOWN THE GLASS WALL?

AMY G. MAZUR

THERE is arguably much misunderstanding over feminist knowledge production among social scientists who do not take an explicitly feminist approach. Far too often, the conventional wisdom about feminist analysis is that it is imbued by postmodern agendas and is antiscientific, seeking to deconstruct established knowledge cumulation and theory development through politicized research that focuses on women's experiences, outside of standard social science practice. Often, these views of feminist research are based on caricatures of what the full range of feminist scholarly activity is actually undertaking. Such stereotypes, which are rarely articulated officially, may very well be a major key to understanding why much nonfeminist analysis throughout the social sciences has ignored feminist scholarship on gender or only marginally addresses its empirical, methodological, and theoretical contributions, a trend which appears to be fully operative in 2010 (e.g., Beckwith 2010 and Grasswick 2011).

As a consequence, the potential of newer feminist scholarship to improve knowledge and theory building in the mainstream[1] is at best mitigated, if not altogether thwarted, by an opaque glass wall. The wall blurs the true nature of feminist approaches and prevents constructive cross-fertilization between feminist and nonfeminist scholars, even when feminist scholars seek to directly contribute to research and theory-building that is not explicitly feminist.

The goal of this chapter is to contribute to breaking down this glass wall by examining in detail how one feminist area of study located in political science, feminist comparative policy (FCP), takes an empirical and integrative approach to feminist analysis, rather than one that is uniquely grounded in standpoint and/or postmodern feminist epistemologies.[2] Reflecting trends in gender and politics scholarship more broadly speaking in political science, FCP has become a highly institutionalized and active area of comparative scholarship that brings together over one hundred researchers in Europe and the United States to assess the dynamics and determinants of gender, policy, and the state. As this chapter shows, this international feminist "epistemic community" (Haas 1992) places feminist empiricism to the fore with a focus on scientific method and empirical observation. This scientific community also brings in other feminist approaches, to a certain degree, in the spirit of methodological pluralism and problem-driven research. FCP scholars actively seek to contribute to—rather than ignore or reject—nonfeminist theory development, methodological debates, and the cumulation of knowledge; thus they are often the loudest critics of the glass wall between nonfeminist and empirical feminist knowledge creation. At the same time that this area has developed and consolidated achieving quite high rates of scientific success, its contributions have been largely ignored by nonfeminist scholarship in adjacent areas. Thus, examining the case of FCP allows for a deeper understanding of the empirical integrative approach as well as the mechanisms that maintain the glass wall between feminist and nonfeminist scholarly communities even when they share similar epistemological and methodological principles and values.

To understand the context for FCP's empirical integrative approach, the analysis first provides an overview of the different feminist epistemological approaches and traditions in social science. Next, the trend toward integration and empiricism is mapped out in the discipline of political science as a whole in both the United States and Europe and across the different established subfields of political science. In the last part of the chapter, the case of FCP is first presented in terms of its emergence from the 1980s to 2000 and then of more recent developments in the past ten years across nine large-scale international research projects. Next, the chapter reflects upon what this body of work brings to the table for nonfeminist research and theory-building and how and why adjacent nonfeminist scholarship tends to overlook findings in one of the nine research projects, the Research Network on Gender, Politics and State (RNGS).

22.1. Approaches to Feminist Epistemology in the Social Sciences

22.1.1. What's Feminist about Feminist Epistemology?

First and foremost, to understand the range of feminist approaches to knowing and knowledge cumulation, an operational definition of this oft-contested concept needs to be presented. While for many feminist analysts it is not crucial, or even desirable, to develop a core definition of feminism, for empirically inclined feminist scholars it is of fundamental importance to identify the operational definition of feminism in order to advance research agendas. Pinpointing a core definition of feminism does not negate the fact that there are different families of feminism that share certain central characteristics, depending on the context in which the concept is used (McBride and Mazur 2008). In this perspective, feminism is seen as a "family resemblance" (Goertz 2006) concept, rather than a classical one based on hierarchically defined categories. Feminism is defined here using the approach of recent work that recognizes the core ideas of Western feminism from which academics, activists, and policy practitioners choose.[3] These core ideas include

1. a certain understanding of women as a group within the context of the social, economic, and cultural diversity of women;
2. the goal of advancing women's rights, status, or condition as a group in both the public and private spheres; and
3. the desire to reduce or eliminate gender-based hierarchy or patriarchy that underpins basic inequalities between men and women in the public and private spheres.

Any feminist epistemological approach in the social sciences takes into consideration, on some level, this threefold definition with regards to ontology, methodology, and methods, theory-building, and the production of knowledge and its relation to nonfeminist knowledge building. More concretely, there is a common understanding across all feminist approaches that established knowledge creation is biased, due in some way to gender-based hierarchies within the established scientific community that produces male domination. This bias excludes the serious consideration of issues related to the complex processes of gender as they are intertwined with sex, and in more recent years with race/ethnicity, age, sexuality, disability, and so on—referred to as "intersectionality"[4]—in analysis and/or theory. This patriarchal/gender-biased/androcentric nature of social science,[5] so the analysis goes, means that scholars tend to be predominantly men, and women are excluded from the process of knowing and studying. To do gender analysis from a feminist perspective, therefore, is to first develop a critique of established epistemological and methodological norms and then bring women, and for some feminists, men with feminist goals, into the research process as well as gender as an object of analysis and theorizing. Ultimately, the inclusion of feminist actors and ideas stands to improve established knowledge cumulation and the scientific process. As the next section shows, the degree to which women need to be in control of the entire research process as well as the extent to which feminist analysis needs to challenge existing modes of study and develop separately, outside of conventional scientific realms, to create a new feminist approach varies across different feminist epistemological approaches.

22.1.2. Stances on Nonfeminist Scholarship: Transformative and Integrative

Two general stances with regard to established social science practice have been identified in the feminist literature: transformative/revolutionary and integrative (Squires 2004, Tripp 2010, Staudt and Weaver 1997). Rather than a dichotomous concept where individuals take either a transformative or integrative approach, these two stances should be seen as ideal types each at the end of a continuum where individuals and approaches can be placed.

Transformative————————————————————Integrative

A *transformative stance* seeks to pursue feminist change separately outside of the existing system to radically reshape knowledge cumulation to incorporate feminist goals. The claim is that this can only happen through a woman-only process that occurs outside of established scientific channels in a new space. In this perspective, the scientific dialogue about gender needs to happen in gender-specific journals and publication venues with a new epistemic community of analysts who share feminist values. The development of women's/gender/feminist studies outside of the established academic disciplines is a key part of achieving this agenda for change and improving knowledge creation generally speaking.

An *integrative approach* asserts that meaningful feminist change can only occur through dialogue with existing knowledge cumulation and that bringing a feminist perspective into nonfeminist work will produce a more accurate pursuit of knowledge. Put simply, feminist integration will make science more scientific. The integrative agenda is pursued in both gender-specific and mainstream outlets and individual scholars seek to participate in larger nonfeminist projects to bring gender considerations in. While a feminist epistemic community emerges, its members are quite often active in other nonfeminist communities with the aim of bringing their work and research questions about gender to bear on the research of the nonfeminist epistemic community. Integration can also take place across different feminist approaches through collaboration between empirical, standpoint, and postmodern feminists, or combining different methodological feminist approaches that come out of each epistemology within a single project. Reflecting current developments, the feminist communities that follow these approaches have become less adversarial, incorporating different takes on doing feminist research and knowledge production.

22.1.3. Three Feminist Epistemologies: Postmodern, Standpoint, and Empirical

Beyond these stances, three feminist epistemologies are generally identified within feminist studies. Many attribute the threefold taxonomy to philosopher of science Sandra Harding, who first wrote about feminist ways of knowing across all of the sciences in her groundbreaking book *The Science Question in Feminism* in 1986. Her goal was to show the biased nature of existing scientific knowledge cumulation across the social and physical sciences and the potential for feminism to address those gender-based biases to make for a more just and equitable scientific process. She also sought to critique existing feminist approaches. Thus, in some ways these three approaches are rhetorical constructs, but they have remained important touchstones in any treatment of feminist epistemology (Hawkesworth 2006; Squires 2004, 2007; Hesse-Biber, Nagy, and Yaiser 2004; Fonow and Cook 1991; Grasswick 2011). Taken together, the taxonomy shows how ideas from the second wave feminist movements of the 1960s and 1970s were transported into the scholarly realm of research and analysis by academics first through the newly created women's studies departments in universities. More prevalent in the United States than in Europe, these departments were a major by-product of women's movement mobilization and some would say a part of the women's movement itself. Later, feminist researchers trained and grounded in established disciplines as well as feminist studies entered into discipline-based departments alongside the women/gender /feminist studies programs.

These three approaches must be seen as separate strands rather than a single unified feminist approach. To be sure, all three approaches share a feminist core, but there are essential differences that distinguish each epistemology and at times put them at odds with each other in terms of the best feminist route to science and the cumulation of knowledge. Furthermore, for many feminist scholars, the three-part taxonomy has an evolutionary element. Harding and others originally asserted that the first stage of this process was empirical feminism, what she referred to as "spontaneous feminist empiricism" (2004, 41). Other feminists then "advanced" (*sic*) the agenda through postmodern and standpoint approaches, which more directly challenged the highly androcentric scientific establishment.[6] These early empiricists or prefeminists, so the story goes, did not look for the causes of the androcentric nature of the scientific establishment or seriously treat gender as a complex analytical category. Rather, they simply added women and stirred: they brought sex or gender in as a variable or a simplistic element. It is interesting to note that many feminist analysts' bias against feminist empiricism is based on this interpretation of the early feminist empiricists.

Thus, underpinning this taxonomy for many feminists is the notion that feminist empiricism is not as feminist as postmodern or standpoint feminism. More recently, feminist philosophers have shown that feminist empiricism can be an equally acceptable and effective avenue for social science change, in large part due to the extent to which feminist empiricism has taken some of the lessons of other feminist approaches, referred to by Longino (1990) and Hankinson-Nelson (1990) as "contextual feminist empiricism." Feminist empiricists still find themselves having to justify their approach to standpoint and postmodern feminists. For example, Saltzman Chaftez's chapter in an edited volume on feminist epistemology from 2004 was titled "Some Thoughts by an Unrepentant 'Positivist' Who Considers Herself a Feminist Nonetheless."

Unlike using a continuum to map out the two feminist stances, it is better to think of the three feminist approaches as three circles with some areas of overlap in

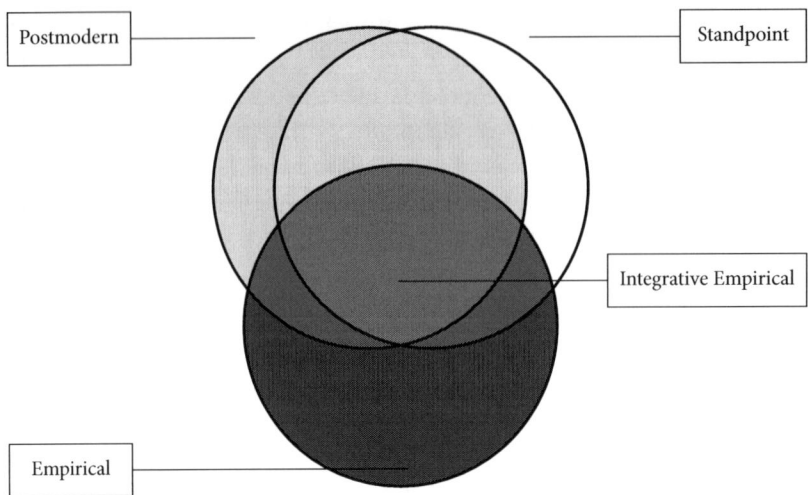

Figure 22.1 Mapping Feminist Epistemologies in 2010

figure 22.1 particularly given the extent to which in recent years there has been a certain sharing and blending of the different epistemological underpinnings of the three approaches in the interest of advancing a common feminist scholarly/ scientific agenda and not only developing a critique of existing social science practices.[7]

Postmodern feminist epistemology is based on the principles that truth is unknowable and that how one sees power depends on where the "knower" is situated; patriarchy determines that universal concepts about men and women maintain established gender roles and the ensuing systems of gender discrimination. As a result, these universal categories should be deconstructed and put into question, including feminism itself. Established scientific practice and any pursuit of theory is rejected as well as the notion that women can actually make a difference in the existing system. As Julia Kristeva (1980, 166) famously asserted, "If women have a role to play ... it is only in assuming a negative function: reject everything finite, definitive, structural, loaded with meaning, in the existing state of society" (cited in Squires 2004, 61).

Standpoint feminism, in contrast, emphasizes the key role of women and their experiences as analysts and as objects of analysis and asserts that women need to identify the patriarchal nature of scientific production as well as the methods and concepts that are used and then create a new way of conducting research to produce new "gynocentric theory" (Ferguson 1993), concepts, theory, and knowledge. For Squires (2004, 60), "the aim is not to break the link between experience and knowledge, but to enable a different set of experiences to provide a basis for new knowledge claims." Some standpoint feminists, but not all, assert that women as well as men can do feminist research since research is grounded in "the epsitemic advantage of the margins," and knowledge creation is "situated" within the researcher's position of marginality with regards to the mainstream/dominant (*sic*) scientific process (Wylie 2011, 157).

In the beginning of the development of women's studies, postmodern and standpoint approaches were quite separate, with the emphasis on eschewing the development of new theories by postmodern feminists and embracing that development by
standpoint theorists. Later analysis has shown that the dividing lines between the
two have blurred (Squires 2004 and Hawkesworth 2006). Both share a transformative approach for the most part with an emphasis on the importance of understanding the power-biased nature of existing categories and theories, the need to
develop new categories and theories based on women's experiences in the context of
class, race, ethnic, and other important sociocultural differences among women, and
by women themselves. The underlying assumption is that this process should take
place outside of established patriarchal scientific arenas—for example, in separate
women's studies departments—so as to bring out the contributions of the marginalized that comes from their structural position in society as well as the established
scholarly order.

Figure 22.1 shows the recent overlap between postmodern and standpoint approaches, which is not as pronounced, with regards to these two approaches and
empirical feminism with its distinctly different ontological foundation, inspired by
"positivism" or "naturalism" (Moses and Knudsen 2007).[8] Here, unlike constructivism, which sees all knowledge as being socially constructed and embedded in
established power relations and hence not objectively knowable, knowledge can be
established through the observation of reality that exists outside any power relations. But the feminist assumptions about gender bias are still part and parcel of the
approach, albeit with a softer, less structural connotation than the other feminist
approaches, which emphasize the patriarchal nature of established science—where
male domination marginalizes and minimizes women's contribution. In this view,
the "androcentric" and "masculinist" (Harding 1984, 134–35) nature of the scientific
process prevent research questions and design from going beyond cultural biases
against women and gender-specific objects of study which downplay their analytical salience; the outcome is bad science. To change this, women and men, infused
with feminist ideas from the women's movement, need to follow the established
norms of science—replication, falsifiablity, and the scientific method of hypotheses
testing and empirical theory building—to address the biases in the definitions of
research, concepts, methods, theory generation, and outcomes.[9]

Thus, conducting empirical feminist research is a two-part process that is sometimes contradictory: promoting a critique of existing scientific practices based on a
set of normative ideas coming out of feminism in order to do better, more objective
science. In the social sciences this has meant bringing gender processes into studies
as the object of analysis, generating new empirically based theories that operationalize feminist propositions, but also putting established nonfeminist theories to the
test of gender. In other words, empirical feminism inherently takes a more integrative approach to social science research, which is not necessarily the case for postmodern and standpoint feminist epistemologies. Newer forms of empirical
feminism have been called "contextual empirical feminism" (Longino 1980 and
Hankinson-Nelson 1990) to reflect the importance of understanding women's

experiences and position in the androcentric system as objects and subjects: direct lessons from standpoint and postmodern feminism. As figure 22.1 shows, there are soft and hard forms of empirical feminism—the newer contextual empirical feminism that this chapter calls *empirical and integrative feminism* overlaps with postmodern and standpoint feminism, integrating certain aspects of these approaches and dialoguing with scholarship from that area. It is this softer form of empirical feminist epistemology that drives much but not all gender research in political science.

22.2. Feminist Approaches in Political Science: A Trend Toward Empiricism and Integration

22.2.1. The Larger Disciplinary Context in the United States and Western Europe

While the standpoint and postmodern approaches have been foundational for many women's/gender studies programs and departments, empirical feminism has been an important influence in the development of gender and politics as an area of study within political science in the United States and Europe, arguably more than in other social sciences. In the United States, this is in part due to the heavy influence of behavioralism with its strict naturalist approach to political science and the assumption that methodology and methods should be based on quantitative principles of statistics and large "n" analysis and that science should be value-free. This mono methodological approach was put into question by the Perestroika movement, which developed around the critique of the main disciplinary journal, the *American Political Science Review*, in the late 1990s.

The claim, articulated by over one hundred political scientists, was that the APSR represented the dominant behavioralist trend in political science and did not seek to publish research that was less methods-driven. Submissions were rejected that used a multiplicity of approaches to answer the particular question being studied, including quantitative, but also qualitative, interpretivist, or constructivist and/ or explicitly took a problem-driven approach, where research was to examine real-world problems and provide solutions for them while still developing theory. The Perestroika group also asserted that this type of work was not valued by the dominant core of American political science either.[10] The movement achieved its immediate goal of creating a new disciplinary journal—*Perspectives in Politics*—that could serve as an explicit platform for this problem-driven and methodologically pluralistic work. The discipline as a whole became more open and pluralistic, albeit for many members of the original movement only to a limited degree.

Feminist scholars were a part of the Perestroika movement. They showed the parallels between feminist epistemological approaches that identified the normative nature of what was seen as value-free political science and the need to analyze gender in a meaningful way and not just to "add women and stir." Thus, this notion was not just associated with early empirical feminists, but also in political science, with nonfeminist analysts who treated sex or gender as a simplistic variable or an add-on rather than rethinking research design, methodologies, and theories in terms of feminism and gender (Carroll and Zerilli 1993). Methodological pluralism and problem-driven research are often associated with a focus on the analysis of discourse. Interpretivism and constructivism is more pronounced in European political science than in the United States, where the interpretivist/discursive turn in political analysis is quite pervasive. Thus, European feminist analysts have integrated social constructivism and a focus on discourse analysis more than in the United States (Lombardo, Meierm, and Verloo 2009; Kantola 2006; Verloo 2007).

The Empirical and Integrative Feminist Approach

Despite the differences between the disciplinary context in Europe and the United States, the empirical and integrative feminist approach in political science followed by a highly international feminist epistemic community shares common features that both contributed to and came out of the larger movements toward problem-driven and multi-methods research that eschews classic distinctions between positivism and constructivism: that is, where research is still based on the assumption that reality exists and can be studied, but that a part of reality is the construction of meaning/gender relations in particular. The goal of scholars who take this approach is to operate within a cumulative, yet critical, dialogue between feminist and nonfeminist research—through hypothesis testing and development and the scientific method as well other epistemological systems that may not emphasize hypothesis testing, like constructivist/interpretivist approaches. While, to be sure, it is important to acknowledge the androcentric nature of established political science, it is of fundamental importance to bring gender research and gender researchers into nonfeminist political science for promoting better science. It is also important to remember the position of researchers and their experiences within the research process as well as the diverse contexts of gender and women's experiences as objects of study.

As Siim (2004, 97) describes, "There is a conversation between an empirically grounded political research, cross-national analysis sensitive to context, and discourse analysis inspired poststructuralism." This focus on integration *and* empiricism can be seen in the classic foundational writings of feminist political science.[11] In particular, Randall (1991) clearly calls for a study of politics that is oriented toward cumulation and hypothesis testing. Thus, feminist political scientists clearly distinguish themselves from feminist scholars more aligned with postmodern and/or standpoint approaches at the intersection, as figure 22.1 above shows, of the three feminist epistemologies.

Gender and politics as a subarea in political science is necessarily cross-cutting. Gender scholars in political science focus on different ways in which gender is processed by the political system in both public and private spheres and with regard to objects of analysis, like social movements, that have not been typically examined by mainstream political science. As early feminist political scientists pointed out, "gendering" political science is a highly complex process that aims to locate gender and gender processes in all aspects of politics broadly defined, from a feminist perspective to incorporate both the public and private spheres (Lovenduski 1998 and Sapiro 1991). Feminist political scientists, first in Australia, sought to dissaggregate the state to look at its different parts as potential arenas for social change, rather than just dismiss the entire state as a monolithic patriarchal entity, as many post-modern feminists did (Pringle and Watson 1992 and Franzway, Court, and Connell 1989). The subsections of a recent reader on gender and politics scholarship show the major loci for analyzing gender in political science: social movements; women and political parties; women, gender, and elections; women, gender, and political representation; women, gender, and social policies; and women, gender, and the state (Krook and Childs 2010). There is also a strong emphasis on analyzing gender at different levels—local, subnational, national, and supranational.

The European Political Consortium for Research (ECPR) and the American Political Science Association (APSA) have active and large subgroups on the study of gender. While the ECPR Women and Politics standing group holds an semiannual meeting that attracts over three hundred scholars, the APSA Women and Politics division organizes more than twenty-five panels at the annual APSA meetings. It also publishes the journal *Politics and Gender*. There are also three other journals that publish gender and politics research—*International Feminist Journal of Politics*, *Journal of Women, Politics & Policy*, and *Social Politics*. *Politics and Gender* and *Journal of Women, Politics & Policy* both US-based journals, tend to emphasize the more empirical side of feminist research, with some representation of standpoint and postmodern work. *International Feminist Journal of Politics*, a European-based journal, publishes more standpoint and postmodern feminist work. *Social Politics* blends all three feminist approaches, in part due to its highly international editorial board. The four journals play an important institutionalizing role in solidifying the new international feminist empirical epistemic community within political science that has increasingly become "contextual and comparative."[12]

22.2.2. Variations Across the Subfields

At the same time feminist political scientists operate within a separate subarea of gender and politics they also dialogue and choose to work within the established sub-areas of political science as a part of the feminist empirical and integrative agenda. There, they try to interface with nonfeminist scholars to show the importance of gender analysis to nonfeminist theories, methodological approaches, and knowledge creation. It is also in these subdisciplinary sites where the glass wall between feminist and non-feminist scholars and scholarship is most evident with clear resistance to integrating the major findings of these studies on the part of nonfeminist analysts, although some subfields are more resistant than others. There is also variation across the subfields as to the extent the integrative empirical approach is taken by feminist scholars.

Feminist theory is arguably the most oriented toward more transformative perspectives (Mackinnon 1989 and Butler 1990), although there are many feminist theorists that dialogue with nonfeminist democratic theory as well (Phillips 1995 and Mansbridge 2003).[13] Moreover, unlike other areas of study, there is an overlap between theoretical and empirical work in gender and politics; empirically oriented analysts often seek to operationalize and test propositions from feminist theory.[14] Feminist international relations (IR) scholars for the most part take a more empirical and integrative approach as well as tend to "rejoice in the contradictions and tensions of adopting and exploring all [feminist approaches]" (Squires 2004, 62). Some of these feminist IR scholars have separated to pursue a nonfeminist focus on gender and international relations which examines gender outside of a feminist perspective (Tripp 2010, 191).[15]

In comparative politics, feminist scholars have developed a quite unified empirical and integrative research agenda, called the comparative politics of gender (CPG). A recent symposium in *Perspectives* contains ten articles on this analytical take on gender and politics (Beckwith 2010). As Tripp (2010) points out, this sub-area has been less critical than other feminist approaches and has sought to make contributions with other work in comparative politics. Caraway (2010) presents a figure that shows how CPG has the potential to intersect substantively with five other areas of comparative politics research (172). At the same time, much nonfeminist work in comparative politics ignores this new feminist work. One of the main comparative journals, however, *Comparative Political Studies*, has made an effort to publish work in this area, thanks to editor-in-chief, James Caporaso's, interest in feminist work. A central concern of CPG is to conduct good research based on valid and reliable conceptualizations and measurements as well as to retain a problem-driven focus. The recent movement from studies based in a single region or on a single country to more cross-regional studies indicates efforts to make more macro-level grand theory from empirically based studies (Htun and Weldon 2010).

Gender work in American politics is perhaps the most empirical and the least integrative with other areas of feminist analysis. It tends to focus on sex rather than complex notions of gender as socially constructed category, comparing women's and men's political behavior with little reference to other adjacent feminist literature that does not take a purely empirical approach (e. g., Burns 2002).

22.3. Putting the Empirical Integrative Approach into Action: Feminist Comparative Policy

Feminist comparative policy resonates the most with scholarship on the comparative politics of gender. Scholars of FCP follow a "scientifically realist approach" (Moses and Knudsen 2007)—problem-driven research, methodological pluralism replete with "creative tensions" (Siim 2004) found in much feminist political science work. They combine both constructivist, through the discursive turn in analysis, and naturalist approaches. In this final section of the chapter, the features of the FCP approach and its four areas of research up to the year 2000 are first discussed based on a large-scale assessment of the field (Mazur 2002). The findings of an analysis of nine FCP research projects carried out since 2000 in Mazur (2009) are presented in the next part to show how the contours of the integrative feminist approach have recently evolved in FCP. The last part of this section takes a closer look at one of these nine projects, the Research Network on Gender, Politics, and the State (RNGS), to better map out the specific contributions this feminist research makes to nonfeminist scholarship and to better understand the mechanisms of the glass wall that continue to block feminist empirical scholars from making lasting contributions outside of their own feminist epistemic community.

22.3.1. FCP up to 2000

Feminist policy scholars in Western Europe first acknowledged the empirical gaps and gender biases in theory and methodology used in the study of the state and public policy in the early 1980s. By the early 1990s, researchers in North America and Australia joined their Western European counterparts in the new feminist academic enterprise that sought to systematically study the interface between gender and the state. In the mid-1990s, a loose consensus in this transnational community around conventions for conducting research, developing theory, and reporting findings moved the field into a new stage of vitality and institutionalization. In 2000, with over four hundred published pieces, of which one quarter has been published in the previous five years, an estimated 20 million euros in research funding since the mid 1980s, and four journals that served as major outlets for FCP work—*Social Politics, International Journal of Feminist Politics, Politics and Gender,* and *Women and Politics*—FCP scholars and their work constituted a formidable presence in political science. The following features drove (and continues to drive) the work of the scholars in this growing feminist area of study.

Feature 1: An Applied Feminist Empirical Approach. FCP scholars fully embrace empirical feminism. Often, they design their studies so that findings may be used to help policy practitioners and activists in women's policy agencies, political parties, movements, and organizations learn more about the causes of gender-based inequities and the complex range of solutions, including different ways of designing good practices. Since the early 1980s, FCP scholars have been consulted regularly in their expert capacity by the European Union—in particular, in the context of the action plans on gender equality—the Council of Europe, the Nordic Council, and the United Nations, as well as numerous country-based commissions at national and subnational levels.

The applied feminist empirical approach underpins FCP scholar attitudes about identifying with specific feminist currents of thought and about adhering to a single fixed definition of what constitutes feminist policy, feminist states, and feminist political action more generally. FCP scholars tend to avoid articulating a specific political stance on feminism in their research and teaching. The definitions of feminism FCP researchers use in their analyses, therefore, are related to broader principles of women's inclusion, representation, democracy, and gender equality. FCP scholars tend to be leery of pinning down a single narrow definition of feminism connected to a specific current of Western political thought. In recent years, many agree that there is a growing consensus around broad definitions of feminism, like the one proposed above, that take into consideration the diversity of feminist ideas in Europe and travel across national boundaries.

Feature 2: Operationalizing Normative Feminist Theory on Democracy. Normative political theory has been an integral part of the development of feminist studies in general. A major question asked by the large literature on feminist theory is whether Western democracies are as democratic as observers think, particularly given the degree to which women and women's issues have been excluded from politics, in the context of the formal articulation of universal and gender-blind values of equality, freedom, and representation (Squires 1999). Feminist theorists who write on democracy argue for a better inclusion of women and ideas that favor women's rights in the political process through "descriptive" representation, women representatives speaking for women as a group and "substantive" representation, and women's interests being included in a meaningful manner in public discussions and policy (Pitkin 1967). These themes of representation and democracy are at the center of FCP studies insofar as they ask the empirical question of whether, how, and why democratic states can be feminist. The question is less about the specific form and design of democracy than its capacity to incorporate women's interests and women themselves into the political process and, in doing so, to promote gender equality and a more complete democratic system.

Feature 3: Bringing the Patriarchal State Back in as a Research Question. As most political scientists agree, particularly since the state was "brought back in" in the 1980s (Skocpol 1985), the concept of the state—government structures as opposed to country—is not a simple idea. For many feminist theorists, the state is highly problematic given that it is a product of systems of power based on male domination or patriarchy. From the assumption of the patriarchal nature of the state, where state actions, structures, and actors seek to perpetuate systems of gender domination that keep women in their inferior positions in the public and private spheres, many feminist analysts dismiss or are highly critical of the state as an arena for positive social change. Other feminist theorists provide a more malleable view of state patriarchy and argue that certain state arenas may be appropriate sites for feminist action. FCP analysts do not entirely dismiss the possibility of a patriarchal state; they see the issue of state patriarchy as a question for empirical research. Some parts of the state may be patriarchal while other parts may have the potential to be quite woman friendly. FCP places the state and its institutions at its analytical core; the four major areas of FCP research, outlined in the next section, all focus on some aspect of the state or state action.

Feature 4: Using Gender as a Category of Analysis. Since the mid-1980s, feminist research across different disciplines has shifted its focus from sex, a more-or-less dichotomous variable based on biological differences between men and women, to gender, the social construction of sexual difference between men and women.[16] As Joan Scott first asserted in 1986, the relational concept of gender should be the prime category of analysis in theoretical frameworks and research designs. This holistic approach to the use of gender is intended to push analyses beyond the add women and stir phase, where sex or women is added as an analytical afterthought. Since the mid-1990s, FCP scholars have incorporated gender into their research designs in a variety of ways.

Feature 5: Comparative Theory-Building in Western Postindustrial Democracies. FCP scholars seek to develop theory through culturally sensitive, comparative, and cross-national analysis. They often employ principles of research design and methods developed outside of a feminist perspective. Up until 2000, with a few exceptions, FCP work utilized small "n" analysis—case studies and the comparative method. In recent years many studies include a large number of observations and, hence, use the statistical tools of large "n" analysis; other studies take a bridging approach, incorporating both qualitative and quantitative analysis. FCP studies take a most similar systems approach, where economic and political development in Western postindustrial democracies are the control variables and variations in nation-based culture, state-society relations, women's movement mobilization, government design, and so on are examined as they influence gender, state, and policy issues. Most FCP work assumes that postindustrial countries from the West, unlike other countries of the world, share certain environments and institutions, with notable cross-national variations. A part of the common heritage is that women's movements have developed strategies aimed, at least in part, to influence the democratic policy process and the development of large welfare states. Designing and using concepts like feminism that are able, as Giovanni Sartori first elaborated, to travel across national boundaries without stretching the core meaning is also a key part of the comparative agenda of FCP (1970).

Feature 6: One-Way Intersections with Nonfeminist Political Science. Many FCP scholars since the mid-1990s have actively sought to intersect their work with nonfeminist literature. Instead of completely rejecting traditional political studies or uncritically using feminist studies, FCP work purposefully develops the strengths and shores up the weaknesses of each to advance knowledge in both areas. In general, efforts to intersect work with nonfeminist political science tend to be one-way, confronting the glass wall that is at the center of this chapter's analysis. FCP scholars seek to contribute to nonfeminist work and nonfeminist policy analysts ignore FCP theory-building that speaks directly to central analytical issues. Even within the context of the increasing methodological pluralism of political science, few studies outside of the purview of feminist analysis use the findings or concepts of FCP research or even focus specifically on gender policy dynamics. This trend may be in the process of being reversed with the growing academic influence and reputation of FCP scholars and their work; however, as will be shown below, the obstacles to complete intersection persist.

22.3.2. Epistemic Community and Infrastructure

Following this unified approach, FCP scholars examine four different substantive areas related to the state and its institutions in a large and growing literature.[17] *Feminist policy formation* work scrutinizes the ways in which public policy promotes women's status and strikes down gender hierarchies through studying the obstacles, actors, content, and processes of policy that is purposefully feminist. *Feminist movements and policy* research is concerned with the interplay between women's movements, the state, and policy. A major issue of interest here is to evaluate the success of women's movements in influencing public policy and the structures of the state. *State feminism* scholarship considers whether state structures and actors can promote feminism through focusing on the relations between women's movement actors and the activities of women's and gender equality policy machineries and the bureaucrats, or femocrats, that staff them, in a wide variety of government agencies and branches. *Gender and welfare state* literature examines the welfare state as a prime obstacle and/or promoter of gender discrimination and equality. Much of this scholarship looks at the impacts of social policy in terms of women's social conditions in comparison to men's in the public and private spheres.

In 2001, there were roughly one hundred scholars who worked regularly on FCP research. To be counted as a part of the FCP community, individuals needed to have two or more publications on an FCP topic. The list of active FCP scholars used for this analysis is available on request. Members of the FCP scientific community are mostly women. More than a result of any collective decision to exclude men, their absence is a result of the realities of graduate education; women tend to be more interested in the study of feminist politics and male students tend to be channeled away from what is often perceived as a less prestigious area of study. Less than one quarter of FCP scholars are from the United States, and nearly three quarters from Europe. One half of FCP scholars is based in English-speaking countries—Ireland, the United Kingdom, Canada, Australia, and the United States. The other half is based in continental Europe—the Netherlands, Germany, Austria, Italy, Spain, Denmark, Norway, Sweden, Finland, France, Belgium, and Greece. Controlling for national population and size of university infrastructure, this community is quite evenly spread among the different countries. Many FCP researchers are trained in one country and then work and live in others.

FCP practitioners began to develop research networks in the early 1980s. The networks often meet at the conferences of the European Consortium of Political Research (ECPR), the American Political Science Association, the International Political Science Association, or the International Studies Association. At least fifteen FCP books have come out of ECPR workshops. In the 1990s, FCP scholars increasingly developed multinational research projects. Once in place, the network convenors secure funds from a combination of supranational, national, university, private funding agencies, and other institutionalized venues that are not overtly feminist. These projects implement a complex, long-term, gendered research program, produce a series of publications, and often create more permanent infrastructure like newsletters, journals, home pages, graduate funding, and permanent teaching programs.

22.3.3. Developments Since 2000: An Analysis of Nine FCP Projects

The nine FCP projects that were analyzed are presented in table 22.1.

While by no means a systematic assessment of all recent work in feminist comparative policy, this analysis provides an opportunity to reflect upon the state of current comparative gender and policy scholarship, particularly given that over 160 scholars in twenty-seven countries have actively participated in these studies. In some ways gender and comparative policy scholarship has not changed since 2000. Gender remains a fundamental category for analysis; issues of patriarchy, gender-biased norms, and the state are at the center of study designs; feminist and nonfeminist theory continues to be operationalized in studies, and comparative theory building based on qualitative analysis is an important part of analysis. At the same time, there have also been significant new developments reflected in these projects, also identified by other feminist policy scholars (Beckwith 2005 and Squires 2007), to which the analysis in this section now turns.

While not a prerequisite, the creation of a large international research group is becoming more of the norm, as a reflection of shifting priorities of major government funding agencies and efforts to include a broader range of countries into comparative studies. Given that research funding is often provided for by women's policy agencies also with feminist agendas, the goals of the researchers tend to be quite compatible with the funders. The inclusion of East Central and South Eastern European countries into the analytical purview of many of the newer FCP projects opens the door for the consideration of countries from outside of the West with different levels of economic and political development and cultural

Table 22.1 List of FCP Research Projects

Women's Movements and Reconfigured States (1997–2003) Banaszak et al. (2003)

Gendering Europeanisation (1999–2003) Liebert (2003)

RNGS (1995–2009). Research Network on Gender, Politics and the State http://libarts.wsu.edu/polisci/rngs (e.g., McBride and Mazur 2010)

EGG (2002–2005). Enlargement, Gender and Governance: The Civic and Political Participation and Representation of Women in Central and Eastern Europe http://www.qub.ac.uk/egg/ (e.g., Galligan et al. 2007)

MAGEEQ (2003–2007). Policy Frames and Implementation Problems: The Case of Gender Mainstreaming http://www.mageeq.net/ (e.g., Verloo 2007)

QUING (2006–2011). Quality in Gender Equality + Policies http://www.quing.eu/ (e.g., Lombardo et al. 2009)

FEMCIT (2006 2010). Gendered Citizenship in Multicultural Europe: The Impact of Contemporary Women's Movements http://www.femcit.org

VEIL (2006–2009). Values Equality and Differences in Liberal Democracies http://www.univie.ac.at/veil/

Governing Difference (2006–2009). A Challenge for New Democracies in Central and South Eastern European Countries contexts. As a result, FCP is faced with a new level of cultural diversity and the need to rethink core analytical concepts to make them better travel across cultural boundaries. This new development may allow FCP analyses of Western countries to bridge the gap with a growing and rich body of comparative work on non-Western countries and research that analyzes trends across a broad range of regions of the world (Rai 2003, Howell and Mulligan 2005, Htun and Weldon 2010). This push to go beyond the West clearly resonates with the calls for systematic cross-national research made by the advocates of a comparative politics of gender as well.

The analytical perspective of FCP has clearly gone beyond the nation-state to include a multilevel approach where the subnational and extranational levels are just as, if not more, important than the national level. Also, cultural differences must be placed in an intersectional perspective where race, ethnicity, class, religion, and sexual orientation become important and fundamental considerations alongside gender. Time period and policy issue areas have also become salient analytical dimensions when understanding the dynamics and determinants of gender and policy processes, perhaps even more important than national-level trends and dynamics.

Normative and empirical questions of democracy have increasingly become a focal point of FCP studies in terms of placing women's movements at the center of making the democratic process more democratic, and for the newer democracies in terms of effective transitions to democracies. An increasing emphasis on representation as a means to link issues of women's presence to policy outcomes in the FCP scholarship dovetails with comparative scholarship on women in politics, which is also taking a more systematic look at substantive representation and policy outcomes (Celis and Childs 2008). Thus, whereas in 2002 the work on women's political representation was identified as an adjacent area of research, today policy and representation research are becoming one and the same. Here too intersectional approaches are becoming essential; women's interests, movements, and representation must be disaggregated and understood in terms of differences among women by religion, race, ethnicity, class, and so on.

Methodological pluralism is also a more pronounced attribute of recent feminist comparative policy work. Much work is qualitative, emphasizing the importance of expert analyses of country cases and process tracing. Studies are also increasingly bringing in quantitative large "n" analysis out of necessity, due to the tendency to include more countries in study designs. In addition, the tools of moderate "n" analysis outside of any feminist purview, qualitative comparative analysis (QCA, e.g., Rihoux and Ragin 2008) are also being increasingly used in FCP studies (McBride and Mazur 2010a, Krook 2009). An emerging part of the feminist approach is to more formally conceptualize and to develop specific data collection and analysis techniques, drawing from both feminist and nonfeminist work. While earlier FCP studies tended to take a more purely empirical feminist approach where studies were designed to test hypotheses through empirical analysis without putting into question the scientific method, some of the more recent feminist research has embraced the European "discursive turn" (Kantola 2006). The studies have brought in approaches based on feminist standpoint theory and social constructivism with a focus on framing, discourse, and policy content and often a rejection of the scientific method.

This shift is not necessarily positive. On one hand, the key issues of whether formal polices are effectively implemented to actually change gender relations in society is left relatively unexamined due to the focus on discourse and policy content; on the other, an absence of clearly articulated hypotheses, formal concepts, and findings may limit the broader empirical and applied messages of the studies. Without this systematic consideration of policy implementation and impact, the feminist scholarship that focuses on discourse, frames, and the positionality of researchers in the process and the power system risks to miss the central questions of FCP—whether all of this new state activity actually matters. Also, the tendency of the more critical discourse analysis to not directly dialogue with the full range of feminist and nonfeminist scholarship on policy and the state limits the overall contribution of this work to wider discussions of democracy, policy, and the state.[18] At the same time, the increased emphasis on bringing research to public officials and citizens through public meetings, conferences, and training, an emphasis brought in by a standpoint approach, potentially outweighs these empirical gaps.

Identifying common trends in findings is still an open-ended question, awaiting a systematic meta-analysis of all current FCP work to try to develop propositions about gender, policy, and the state that can be fine-tuned in future studies.[19] Indeed, the FCP projects reviewed here do not directly build from each other and have little direct intragroup communication except through a few individuals who are in several projects. Analyzing the results and common conclusions of all current FCP research has the potential to build a bridge among all of the studies and in so doing to allow FCP scholarship to more systematically contribute to theory-building and the cumulation of knowledge.

One characteristic of FCP that has remained quite similar is the degree to which nonfeminist policy studies and political science continue to ignore gender and policy research. Mainstream comparative politics and policy studies still do not integrate the findings of feminist scholarship in a meaningful way or bring gender, women's movements, or women's representation in as an important aspect to be analyzed in comparative studies of democratic politics.[20] To be sure, there has been an increase in publications of gender research in nonfeminist journals, but few nonfeminist scholars have seriously gendered their own analysis beyond isolated cases or the more expedient approach of add women and stir.

Research Network on Gender, Politics and State (RNGS) Contributions and the Glass Wall. Similar to FCP work more broadly speaking, it is puzzling why nonfeminist analysts have tended to ignore this large-scale study of women's policy agencies conducted by forty-three researchers in seventeen countries across five policy areas from the late 1970s to 2000, particularly given that it is firmly located in the integrative and empirical feminist camp.[21] The study design is based on standard principles of replication, sample selection, conceptualization, and measurement; is informed by feminist and nonfeminist literature on social movements, institutions, policy, and democracy; and uses a mixed methods design that integrates established qualitative and quantitative analysis. It has produced seven books with major publishers, a publicly accessible dataset, and numerous articles in feminist and nonfeminist refereed publications. The project was funded by some of the top scientific agencies at the national and supranational levels.

To date, a handful of nonfeminist scholars have formally recognized the RNGS project—mostly in terms of its methodological approach; some have shown interest in using the dataset, with no publications yet.[22] The RNGS dataset was nominated twice for the comparative politics division of the American Political Science Association award for the best dataset; both times it was not selected. The newest nonfeminist work on institutions, social movements, public policy, and democracy makes little mention of the core finding of the project that women's policy agencies have significantly changed the contemporary state to bring in women's movement demands and women's movement actors. Under certain conditions and in certain policy areas these agencies play crucial roles in helping women's movement ideas and actors enter the state and hence make democracies more democratic.[23] Social movement scholars still make little mention of the importance of the women's movements or how RNGS has measured them; institutionalists never mention women's policy agencies and their discursive presence in the state; comparative scholars of democracy ignore the impact of state feminism on democracy; and public policy scholars have not recognized the importance of women's policy agencies or women's movements in the policy process. More broadly speaking, the comparative lessons about the importance of policy sector over national styles of policymaking, a theme that runs through all of the RNGS books, has only been taken up by FCP scholars.

It is interesting that where RNGS work has been acknowledged is in qualitative methods circles more than comparative politics circles, where there is more support of methodological pluralism and keen interest in examples of good practice in multi methods research.[24] The focus on good conceptualization is another shared area of concern between the researchers in the RNGS project and qualitative methodologists. Also, many of the leaders of the qualitative methods movement, who are men, are very knowledgeable and interested in gender research for methodological reasons; thus the feminist argument of androcentricism seems not to work where there is a shared scholarly interest between feminist and nonfeminist epistemic communities.

Still, this begs the question of why the other scholars who work on social movements, institutions, and policy have not made connections between the RNGS study and findings and their own works. Here too these fields tend to be dominated by male scholars. Recently, Myra Marx Ferree, one of the leading scholars of comparative gender and politics, asserted at a public lecture at the University of Leiden that the apathy toward comparative feminist research was simply due to sexism—male political scientists are not interested in work conducted by women and about women. Moreover, in many continental European countries, certain male political scientists have been seen to make public statements about how gender research is not legitimate.

It is important to recognize timing as a factor as well. Up until this year, the major publications coming out of the RNGS project have been the issue-specific edited books. This year the group produced a mixed methods analysis of all of the RNGS findings in a final book (McBride and Mazur 2010a) and a presentation of its methodology in a qualitative methods publication (McBride and Mazur 2010b). One could argue that these books have not received the same attention that an overview of the findings across all five policy sectors would. At the same time, there seems very little uptake of the RNGS issues books published from 2001 to 2006 in the nonfeminist circles in comparative politics. Thus, what the RNGS case shows is that the persistence of the glass wall is a result of a complex combination of factors- shared scholarly agendas, androcentrism, publication strategies, and timing even when a great deal of resources, time, and effort are marshaled behind the scientific endeavor and it meets the conventional disciplinary standards of excellence.

22.4. CONCLUSIONS

The feminist empirical and integrative approach is appearing to become increasingly the norm in the study of gender within political science and reflects a broader trend in social science toward "scientific realism" (Moses and Knutsen 2007), and in political science in methodological pluralism and problem-driven research. The emergence, consolidation, and institutionalization of FCP more specifically represents the development of an internationally based, epistemic feminist community that seeks to dialogue and contribute to the general cumulation of knowledge on gender, politics, and the state, whether it takes an explicitly feminist approach or not. While, to be sure, the shared values of the community are integrative and feminist, there is no consensus about the use of a uniquely empirical approach; in fact, combining constructivist and empirically oriented approaches can be seen to bring more analytical leverage to a question. Thus integration involves interfacing with other nonfeminist areas of study, but also between different feminist approaches, something that is relatively new.

Hopefully, the conventional wisdom about feminist approaches can now be laid to rest both on the part of feminist and nonfeminist analysts and more constructive and productive dialogues can occur to systematically incorporate gender and gender findings into theories, research designs, and research questions. Indeed, this chapter is an illustration of this feminist empirical and integrative effort in itself, to better engage the mainstream, to contribute to the cumulation of knowledge, and ultimately to do better science.

As the case of FCP and more specifically the RNGS project show, breaking down the persistent barriers between feminist and nonfeminist research is a slow process, one that takes considerable resources on the part of feminist scholars, the presence of male allies on the nonfeminist side who see the importance of gender research, and also the persistence and power of female feminist scholars to pursue the integrative agenda in nonfeminist publication and scholarly outlets. In the final analysis, similar to many feminist struggles throughout history, the glass wall between feminist and nonfeminist research is slowly being broken; time will tell if ultimate scientific integration can be achieved.

ACKNOWLEDGMENTS

I would like to thank Harold Kincaid for organizing this ambitious project, which included a conference at University of Alabama at Birmingham on the book. It provided a priceless venue for contributors to present their in-progress research and pursue a highly stimulating exchange of ideas. I also appreciate his feedback on this chapter. Special thanks also go to Gary Goertz, David Henderson, Mark Risjord, and Andreas Schedler for their suggestions.

NOTES

1. The term "mainstream" is often used by feminist scholars to describe work that neither includes gender as an object of analysis nor takes account of feminist critiques of established and dominant epistemologies and research traditions. It usually carries negative connotations that feminist work is marginal to mainstream work and implies that feminists need to work outside of the more established areas of scholarship. Other feminist analysis uses the label "nonfeminist" to denote a more neutral relationship between feminist and nonfeminist scholarship and a possibility for dialogue. In this chapter, the feminist/nonfeminist distinction is used.

2. In the tradition of feminist research, it is important to note my position in the scientific process to be clear about my own knowledge gaps and biases. I am not a philosopher of science, but a political scientist who has spent over twenty years conducting and coordinating research. I am a part of the FCP community; coconvener of the Research Network in Gender, Politics and the State; and coeditor of *Political Research Quarterly*, a nonfeminist political science journal. I take an empirical and integrative feminist approach in all of my work.

3. Whether this notion of Western-based feminism can travel outside of the West is a question for research. Some argue that feminist ideas can be found outside of the Western context with modifications that take into consideration the particular context—i.e., Islamic feminism, developmental feminism. Others argue that it is not a useful concept in settings outside of the Western postindustrial world. For more on defining feminism, see McBride and Mazur (2008), and on concept traveling, see Goertz (2006) and Sartori (1970).

4. For more on intersectionality as an empirical concept and research agenda in political science, see the Weldon (2008) and the recent mini symposium in *Political Research Quarterly* edited by Hancock and Simien (2011).

5. These three concepts represent variations on the same theme of male domination with patriarchy being used to address the underlying gendered power relations and institutional outcomes within cultural, social, and political systems. The terms "androcentric" and "gender-biased" indicate that a given system is male dominated and based on notions of masculinity. For some, using the term "gender-biased" or "gender hierarchy" is a softer concept than patriarchy—a strategic choice made even to avoid alienating nonfeminist audiences. The concept androcentrism, rather than patriarchy, is used in feminist epistemological discussions of how established scientific communities have been male dominated and defined in terms of masculine/sexist notions of research questions, knowledge cumulation, methodologies, etc. (Harding 1986,1987, 2004; Hawkesworth 2006; Hesse-Biber and Yaiser 2004; Fonow and Cook 1991).

6. This story of feminist epistemology is recounted in work on feminist epistemology generally speaking, for example, Hesse-Biber, Leavy, and Yaiser (2004) or Fonow and Cook (1991) and more discipline-based analysis. In political science, see, for example, Squires (2004), Hawkesworth (2006), or Tripp (2010).

7. The summaries of the three feminist approaches are thumbnail sketches presented to better contextualize FCP as an empirical integrative approach and develop the chapter's argument. They draw upon a rich wealth of literature on feminist epistemology, some of which is cited here.

8. Moses and Knutsen (2007) opt for the label "naturalist" over "positivist" given the extensive critiques of positivism and its often politicized implications.

9. In the feminist empirical approach it is important that men as well as women pursue the feminist agenda. At the same time, it is important to note that women scientists tend to be the motor for the epistemological shift and hence their presence in positions of power are key to doing more objective science.

10. For more on Perestroika and its implications for political science, see, for example, Monroe (2005) and Schram and Caterino (2006) For more on problem-driven or "use-inspired" research, see Schramm and Caterino (2006) and Stokes (1997). For an excellent treatment of the interpretivist approach in political science, see Yanow and Schwartz-Shea (2006).

11. To name some of the most notable, Githens (1983), Carroll and Zerilli (1993), Lovenduski (1998), Sapiro (1991), and Randall (1991).

12. The *Oxford Political Handbook on Gender and Politics*, edited by Karen Celis from Belgium, Johanna Kantola from Finland, Georgina Waylen from the United Kingdom, and Laurel Weldon from the United States is an important source of current scholarship in this area and touchstone for the international gender and politics community. The four editors represent the national as well as epistemological diversity of this scientific community.

13. For an excellent review of feminist political theory, see Squires (1999).

14. Feminist theories on representation and democracy have been at the center of much empirical scholarship on representation. See, for example, Celis and Childs (2008).

15. For more on feminist approaches in IR, see Ackerly, Stern, and True (2006).

16. For more on research on gender and the state, see Htun (2005).

17. See the bibliography in Mazur (2002) for a complete presentation of the FCP literature in 2000.

18. See my review of Lombardo, Meier, and Verloo (2009) in the *Journal of Women, Politics & Policy* (2010), where I further develop this critique in the case of this book's study, which comes out of MAGEEQ and QUING, two of the FCP projects covered in this section.

19. Poteete and Ostrom's (2005) development of a large "n" database from small "n" studies on water collective action to manage natural resources in the United States provides a potential roadmap for the construction of a database on FCP scholarship.

20. A theme that cuts across all of the articles in the *Perspectives* symposium on the comparative politics of gender (Beckwith 2010).

21. For the RNGS project design, detailed project information, and the SPSS dataset suite, see http://libarts.wsu.edu/polisci/rngs/index.html.

22. The dataset was publicly released at the APSA meetings and on the RNGS website in 2007.

23. The articles in Beckwith (2010) also draw attention to the serious gaps in the nonfeminist literatures in these areas with regard to feminist scholarship.

24. The following nonfeminist qualitative scholars have integrated aspects of the RNGS project into their published work: Charles Ragin, Benoît Rihoux, Gary Goertz, David Collier, Evan Lieberman, Andreas Schedler, and Cas Mudde. Many of these scholars do comparative work as well, but their treatment of RNGS findings is in the context of methodological issues.

REFERENCES

Ackerly, Brooke A., Maria Stern, and Jacqui True, eds. 2006. *Feminist Methodolgies for International Relations*. Cambridge: Cambridge University Press.

Banaszak, K. Beckwith, and D. Rucht, ed. 2003. *Women's Movements Facing Reconfigured State*. Cambridge: Cambridge University Press.

Beckwith, K. 2005. "The Comparative Politics of Women's Movements." *Perspective in Politics* 3 (3): 583–96.

Beckwith, K., ed. 2010. "Symposium: A Comparative Politics of Gender." *Perspectives on Politics*. 8 (1): 159–240.

Burns, Nancy. 2002. "Gender: Public Opinion and Political Action." In *Political Science: The State of the Discipline*, Ira Katnelson and Helen V. Milner, eds., 466–87. New York: Norton. 466–87.

Butler, Judith, 1990. *Gender Trouble: Feminism and the Subversion of Identity*. New York: Routledge.

Caraway, Teri. 2010. "Gendering Comparative Politics." *Perspectives on Politics*. 8 (1): 169–76.

Carroll, Susan and L.M.G. Zerilli. 1993. "Feminist Challenges to Political Science." In *The State of the Discipline*, Ada Finifter, ed., 55–76. Washington, DC: The American Political Science Association.

Celis, K., and S. Childs, eds. 2008. "Special Issue: The Substantive Representation of Women." *Representation* 44 (2) July: 5–155.

Chaftez, Janet Salzman. 2004. "Some Thoughts by an Unrepentant 'Positivist' Who Considers Herself a Feminist Nonetheless." In *Feminist Perspectives on Social Research*, Sharlene Hesse-Biber and M. Yaiser, eds., 320–29. Oxford: Oxford University Press.

Ferguson, Katherine. 1993. *The Man Question: Visions of Subjectivity in Feminist Theory*. Berkeley: University of California Press.

Fonow, Margaret, and Judith A. Cook, eds. 1991. *Beyond Methodologies: Feminist Scholars as Lived Research*. Bloomington: Indiana University Press.

Franzway, S., D. Court, and R. W. Connell. 1989. *Staking a Claim: Feminism, Bureaucracy and the State*. Sydney: Allen & Unwin.

Galligan, Y., S. Clavero, and M. Calloni. 2007. *Gender, Politics and Democracy*. Farmington Hills, MI: Barbara Budrich Publishers.

Githens, Marianne. 1983. "The Elusive Paradigm: Gender, Politics and Political Behavior." In *Political Science: The State of the Discipline*, Ada Finifter, ed., 471–501. Washington, DC: The American Politcal Science Association.

Goertz, G., and A. G. Mazur, eds. 2008. *Politics, Gender and Concepts*. Cambridge: Cambridge University Press.

Grasswick, Heidi, ed. 2011. *Feminist Epistemology and Philosophy of Science: Power in Knowledge*. Berlin: Springer.

Goertz, Gary. 2006. *Social Science Concepts: A User's Guide*. Princeton, NJ: Princeton University Press.

Haas, P. 1992. "Introduction: Epistemic Communities and Internationl Policy Coordination." *International Organization* 46 (1): 1–35.

Hancock, Marie Ange, and Evelyn Simien. 2011. "Mini Symposium: Intersectionality Research." *Political Research Quarterly* 64 (1): 185–243.

Hankinson Nelson, Lynn. 1990. *Who Knows. From Quine to a Feminist Empiricism*. Philadelphia: Temple University Press.

Harding, Sandra 2004. "Rethinking Standpoint Epistemology: 'What Is Strong Objectivity'?" In *Feminist Perspectives on Social Research*, Sharlene Hesse-Biber and M. Yaiser, eds., 39–64. Oxford: Oxford University Press.

Harding, Sandra. 1986. *The Science Question in Feminism*. Ithaca, NY: Cornell University Press.

Harding, Sandra. 1987. "Conclusion: Epistemological Questions." In *Feminism and Methodology*, S. Harding, ed., 39–64. Bloomington: Indiana University Press.

Hawkesworth, M. 2006. *Feminist Inquiry: From Political Conviction to Methodological Innovation*. Piscataway, NJ: Rutgers University Press.

Hesse-Biber, Sharelene Nagy, Patricia Leavy, and Michelle L. Yaiser. 2004. "Feminist Approaches to Research as Process: Reconceptualizing Epistemology, Methodology, and Method." In *Feminist Perspectives on Social Research*, Sharlene Hesse-Biber and M. Yaiser, eds., 3–26. Oxford: Oxford University Press.

Hesse-Biber, Sharlene Nagy, and Michelle Yaiser, eds. 2004. *Feminist Perspectives on Social Research*. Oxford: Oxford University Press.

Howell J., and D. Mulligan, eds. 2005. *Gender and Civil Society: Transcending Boundaries*. London: Routledge.

Htun, Mala. 2005. "What It Means to Study Gender and the State." *Politics and Gender* 1 (1): 157–66.

Htun, Mala, and Laurel Weldon. 2010."When Do Governments Promote Women's Rights? A Framework for a Comparative Analysis of Sexual Equality." *Perspectives on Politics* 8 (1): 207–16.

Kantola, Johanna. 2006. *Feminists Theorize the State*. New York: Palgrave Macmillan.

Kristeva, Julia. 1980. "Oscillation Between Power and Denial." In *New French Feminisms*, Elaine Marks and I. de Courtivron, eds., 185–223. Amherst: University of Massachusetts Press.

Krook, Mona Lena. 2009. *Quotas for Women in Politics: Gender and Candidate Selection Reform Worldwide*. New York: Oxford University Press.

Krook, Mona Lena, and Sarah Childs, eds. 2010. *Women, Gender, and Politics: A Reader*. New York: Oxford University Press.

Liebert, U., ed. 2003. *Europeanisation and Gender Equality. Reframing Public Policy in EU Member States*. Bruxelles: Peter Lang.

Lombardo, Emanuela, Petra Meier, and Mike Verloo, eds. 2009. *The Discursive Politcs of Gender Equality. Stretching, Bending and Policymaking*. New York: Taylor and Francis.

Longino, Helen. 1990. *The Science Questions in Feminism*. Ithaca, NY: Cornell University Press.

Lovenduski, Joni. 1998. "Gendering Research in Political Science." *Annual Review of Political Science* 1 (1): 333–56.

MacKinnon, Catharine. 1989. *Toward a Feminist Theory of the State*. Cambridge, MA: Harvard University Press.

Mansbridge, J. 2003. "Rethinking Representation." *The American Political Science Review* 97 (4): 515–28.

Mazur, Amy G. 2002. *Theorizing Feminist Policy*. Oxford: Oxford University Press.

Mazur, Amy G. 2009. "Comparative Gender and Policy Projects in Europe: Current Trends in Theory, Method and Research." *Comparative European Politics* 9 (1): 12–36.

McBride, Dorothy, and Amy Mazur. 2008. "Women's Movements, Feminism and Feminist Movements." In *Politics, Gender and Concepts: Theory and Methodology*, C. Goertz and A. Mazur, eds., 219–43. Cambridge: Cambridge University Press.

McBride, Dorothy E., and Amy G. Mazur. 2010a. *The Politics of State Feminism: Innovation in Comparative Research*. With participation of Joni Lovenduski, Joyce Outshoorn, Birgit Sauer, and Marila Guadagnini. Philaldelphia: Temple University Press.

McBride, Dorothy E., and Amy G. Mazur. 2010b. "Integrating Two Cultures in Mixed Methods Research: A Tale of the State Feminism Project." *Qualitative and Multi-Method Research: Newsletter of the APSA Organized Section for Qualitative and Multi-Method Research* 8 (1): 35–40.

Monroe, Kristen Renwick, ed. 2005. *Perestroika!: The Raucous Rebellion in Political Science*. New Haven: Yale University Press.

Moses, Jonathon W., and Torbjørn Knutsen. 2007. *Ways of Knowing: Competing Methodologies in Social and Political Research*. London: Palgrave Macmillan.

Phillips, Anne. 1995. *The Politics of Presence*. Oxford: Oxford University Press.

Pitkin, Hannah. F. 1967. *The Concept of Representation*. Berkeley: University of California Press.

Poteete, R., and Ostrom, E. 2005. "Bridging the Qualitative-Quantitative Divide: Strategies for Building Large-N Databases Based on Qualitative Research." Presented at the American Political Science Association Meetings, Washington, DC. September 1–4.

Pringle, Rosemary, and S. Watson. 1992. "Women's Interests and the Post Structuralist State." In *Destabilizing Theory: Contemporary Feminist Debates*, M. Barrett and A. Phillips, eds., 53–73. Cambridge: Polity Press.

Rai, S., ed. 2003. *Mainstreaming Gender, Democratizing the State? Institutional Mechanisms for the Advancement of Women*. Manchester: Manchester University Press.

Randall, Vicky. 1991. "Feminism and Political Analysis." *Political Studies* 39 (3): 513–32.

Rihoux, B., and C. C. Ragin, eds. 2008. *Configurational Comparative Methods. Qualitative Comparative Analysis (QCA) and Related Techniques*. Applied Social Research Methods Series. Thousand Oaks, CA: Sage.

Sapiro, Virginia 1991. "Gender Politics, Gendered Politics: The State of the Field." In *Political Science: Looking to the Future*, William Crotty, ed., 165–88. Evanston: Northwestern University Press.

Sartori, Giovanni. 1970. "Concept Misformation in Comparative Politics." *American
    Political Science Review* 64 (3): 1033–53.
Skocpol, Theda. 1985. "Bringing the State Back In: Strategies of Analysis in Current
    Research." In *Bringing the State Back In*, Peter B. Evans, Dietrich Rueschemeyer, and
    Theda Skocpol, eds., 3–37. Cambridge: Cambridge University Press.
Schram, Sanford F., and Brian Caterino, eds. 2006. *Making Political Science Matter:
    Debating Knowledge, Research, and Method.* New York: New York University Press.
Scott, Joan. 1986. "Gender: A Useful Category of Historical Analysis." *American Historical
    Review* 91 (4): 1053–75.
Siim, Birte. 2004. "Towards a Contextual and Gender Sensitive European Political Science.
    European Political Science 3 (2) 97–101.
Squires, J. 2007. *The New Politics of Gender Equality*. Hampshire: Palgrave.
Squires, Judith. 1999. *Gender in Political Theory*. Cambridge: Polity Press.
Squires, Judith. 2004. "Introduction to Symposium on Feminist Methodologies." *ECPR
    European Political Science* 3 (2): 59–66.
Staudt, Kathleen A., and William G. Weaver. 1997. *Political Science & Feminisms: Integra-
    tion or Transformation?* Woodbridge, CT: Twayne Publishers.
Stokes, Donald. E. 1997. *Pasteur's Quadrant Basic Science and Technological Innovation.*
    Washington, DC: Brookings Institution Press.
Tripp, Aili Mari. 2010. "Toward a Comparative Politics of Gender Research in Which
    Women Matter." *Perspectives on Politics* 8 (1): 191–98.
Verloo, M. 2007. *Multiple Meanings of Gender Equality: A Critical Frame Analysis of Gender
    Policies in Europe* Budapest: Central European University Press.
Weldon, Laurel. 2008. "Intersectionality." In *Politics, Gender and Concepts: Theory and
    Methodology*, C. Goertz and A. Mazur, eds., 193–218. Cambridge: Cambridge Univer-
    sity Press.
Wylie, Alison. 2011. "What Knowers Know Well: Women, Work and the Academy." In
    Feminist Epistemology and Philosophy of Science: Power in Knowledge, Heidi Grass-
    wick, ed., 157–59. Berlin: Springer.
Yanow, Dvora, and Peregrine Schwartz-Shea, eds. 2006. *Interpretation and Method:
    Empirical Research Methods and the Interpretivist Turn.* Armonk, NY: M. E. Sharpe.

CHAPTER 23

....

SOCIAL CONSTRUCTIONS
OF MENTAL ILLNESS

....

ALLAN HORWITZ

23.1. INTRODUCTION

....

Both professionals and laypeople view mental illnesses as qualities of individual minds, personalities, and brains. This assumption provides the basis for the official classification of psychiatric disorders—the *Diagnostic and Statistical Manual of Mental Disorders (DSM)* of the American Psychiatric Association (2000). This manual assumes that its various diagnostic entities both have a natural underlying reality and are universal so that the symptoms defining each diagnosis are comparable wherever and whenever they appear. These individualistic and naturalistic conceptions are entrenched in the major mental health professions that define, study, and treat mental illness as well as in common sense. Sociologists who study conceptions of mental disorder thus confront deeply rooted and socially legitimated asociological models.

In contrast to commonsensical and psychiatric views of mental illness, the sociology of knowledge studies the social meanings attached to mental symptoms and categories. The sociology of knowledge focuses on collective, intersubjective social worlds that are distinct from both the subjective inner worlds of individuals and the objective, universal worlds of natural objects (Zerubavel 1997). This perspective traces these meanings to their roots in cultural assumptions and interest group practices (Mannheim 1936). It grounds all knowledge, including scientific knowledge, in its historical and social settings. Social processes influence classifications of knowledge as well as the institutions, practices, and behaviors in which this knowledge is embedded.

A critical, but unresolved, question in the sociology of psychiatric knowledge is the sorts of articulations that exist between culturally embedded assumptions about mental illnesses and any natural reality that underlies these illnesses. The pure, interactive, and harmful dysfunction views provide three different perspectives about how cultural and natural factors shape conceptions of mental illnesses.

23.2. THREE STYLES OF SOCIAL CONSTRUCTION

23.2.1. Pure Constructionism

One branch of social construction, which I call "pure" social construction, assumes that mental illnesses are culturally constituted. This perspective views concepts of mental illness as reflections of social values; people who are considered to be mentally ill have violated particular kinds of norms (Scheff 1966). These norms are not part of the natural world but arise from social rules that power structures reinforce. Because norms are social products, mental illnesses have no universal foundation and display substantial variation across different times and places.

Pure constructionism in the study of mental illness grew out of attempts to show how current Western categories of disorder are actually culturally relative. Philosopher Michel Foucault (1965) famously viewed mental illness as a social and historical rather than as a medical problem. He asserted that Western notions of reason and rationality, which claim to have universal validity, actually reflect historically contingent processes of understanding. Madness, for Foucault, is a disorder of modernity. Psychiatry embodied a new code of knowledge that used medical discourse to classify, contain, and control those who it called "mad." Before the seventeenth century the mad were viewed as possessing special insight into fundamental aspects of existence. After that time, however, the psychiatric profession emerged to manage and discipline the mad—who were not economically productive citizens— and to segregate them from normals. Its diagnostic systems demonstrated the fundamental irrationality of mental illness and provided experts with the power to define fundamental aspects of the identities of those that it categorized. Psychiatric classification schemes used seemingly objective scientific language to stigmatize and exclude the mentally ill.

A long anthropological tradition preceding Foucault also focused on how the presumably natural phenomenon of mental illness in fact reflected cultural values and practices. In her classic essay "Anthropology and the Abnormal," Ruth Benedict (1934) questioned the universal nature of Western definitions of normality and pathology. Using a variety of examples such as paranoia, seizures, and trances, she asserted that virtually every behavior that Western psychiatry defined as abnormal was seen as normal in some other culture. For example, the native peoples of Siberia viewed seizures as signs of special connections to supernatural powers rather than as dreaded illnesses. Likewise, the Dobuans of Melanesia typically have paranoid personality styles marked by constant suspicions and fears. Modern Americans, in contrast, would view comparable styles as indicators of paranoid disorders. For Benedict (1934, 79), "all our local conventions of moral behavior and of immoral are without absolute validity." Normality resides in culturally approved conventions, not in universal standards of appropriate psychological functioning.

Many contemporary anthropologists follow the pure constructionist tradition that Benedict established. For them, emotions are not natural kinds that refer to the biological things that are being classified but to culturally determined classification schemes that humans use to interpret their own and others' experiences (Barrett 2006). The huge variety of emotional expressions across cultures and history is a particularly important indicator of the thoroughly psychosocial nature of emotional norms and deviations from these norms (Gross 2006). Cultures provide norms that indicate what emotions people should show in given situations, the idioms through which they are supposed to show them, and the feelings connected to the emotion that they ought to experience. For example, anthropologists and historians suggest that there are as many types of sadness as there are cultures (Barr-Zisowitz 2000). Likewise, anger stems from inequitable social relationships, not from any biological grounding (Gross 2006).

Because mental illnesses—no less than customs, values, and norms—are social artifacts, they cannot be universal. Instead, definitions of mental disorder stem from culturally specific learning. "These cultural schemas," notes anthropologist Richard Castillo, "can cognitively construct a particular behavior as an episode of mental illness, whereas a different set of cultural schemas can cognitively construct a similar behavior as something normal and normative" (1997, 16). Conceptions of mental disorder are—in all important respects—social constructions.

Psychologist and philosopher Derek Bolton provides a variant of the pure constructionist view. Like it, he regards definitions of mental disorder as aspects of social norms. Psychiatric symptoms are not intrinsically pathological but are deviations from evaluative norms of appropriate behavior: " 'Normal' carries the implication *like us*, and 'abnormal' *not like us*" (2008, xiv). For Bolton, the boundaries between normality and disorder are inherently fluid and subject to negotiation, rendering the quest to define "real" mental disorder as meaningless. No objective standards can indicate when the concept of mental disorder is used legitimately or illegitimately: Success in this enterprise is simply a matter of who has the power to negotiate a broader definition. What makes conditions "disorders" are their harmful social and psychological consequences, which stem from value-laden decisions.

Bolton, however, deviates from most pure constructionists who typically critique the expansion of psychiatric control. Unlike them, he believes that the current *DSM* classifications pragmatically capture the harmful conditions that the mental health professions ought to be treating. He urges psychiatry and allied professions to give up fruitless attempts to define genuine disorders but instead to treat all conditions that lead to suffering, impairment, and adverse outcomes. "What matters is," according to Bolton, "consequences in terms of distress, disability and risk" (2008, 200).

Pure constructionist views have several inherent deficiencies, which have more or less importance depending on the particular variant of this perspective that is in question. The first lies in equating mental disorder with violations of social norms. The claim that "mental disorder" is solely an evaluative concept fails to distinguish what is distinctive about mental illness vis-à-vis many disvalued conditions, ranging from ignorance and ugliness to adultery and crime, which also violate social norms (Wakefield 1992). A pure constructionist perspective has no factual criterion it can use to distinguish mental disorders from other negatively evaluated states that are not considered to be disordered.

A second problem of pure constructionist views lies in their conflation of the expression of symptoms, which culture profoundly influences, with the underlying conditions themselves, which can have biological foundations. Emotional displays can be overt, culturally influenced, manifestations of covert, brain-based processes (Turner 1999). For example, constructionists often contrast physiological displays of depression in non-Western cultures with its psychological manifestations in the West, arguing that the two distinct idioms have little in common (Kleinman 1988). Yet some underlying condition must be present to even allow for a comparison of different forms of the same state. Comparison is only possible if something constant serves as a point of reference to observe meaningful variation. Contrasting different symptomatic presentations simply makes no sense if they are not variants of a more basic phenomenon.

A third problem of pure social constructionism lies in its inability to consider any natural effects of diseases that arise independently of their social classifications. The distorted thought processes of schizophrenia, massive and continual use of alcohol, or extravagant behaviors of bipolar disorders can have real consequences regardless of the social definitions placed upon them. These effects are not comparable to phenomena such as money that are pure social constructions and that would lose significance if people stopped believing in their value. While social classifications of mental illness have undoubted importance, they do not exhaust or constitute the phenomena of mental disorders.

Fourth, pure constructionist views inherently lack any objective concept that can serve as the basis to critique particular views of mental disorder. Only some standard of judgment that stands outside of particular cultural categories can show that one model is more or less adequate than any other model. Paradoxically, because constructionists (Bolton notwithstanding) are often among the most strident critics of the psychiatric profession, their premise that mental illness is whatever is defined as such in a particular cultural context provides no logical grounds for claiming that any view of mental illness is either better or worse than any other. For example, psychiatrists in the Victorian era generally considered masturbation to be a serious mental disorder: A pure constructionist has no grounds for saying that their views were simply *wrong*. Because they lack any standards that can transcend particular cultures, pure constructionism cannot provide coherent critiques of concepts of mental disorder.

Finally, perhaps the major failing of pure constructionist views is that they consider nature and culture to be two opposing forces. For them, social values and cultural processes are distinct from, not complementary to, natural phenomena. To the extent that mental disorder is socially constructed, it ceases to be grounded in biological forces. Natural and cultural processes, however, are often complementary: Humans are hard-wired to respond to collective cultural symbols and social dynamics (Horwitz 2007). The question should not be whether nature or culture influences pathology; instead, we want to know the particular ways that natural and cultural forces interact to produce mental illnesses.

23.2.2. Interactive Social Construction

A second style of social construction does not take as its target the existence of a universal conception of mental disorder. Instead, it brackets the question of whether mental illnesses have a natural reality, focusing instead on how cultural categories and individual responses to these categories interact to produce historically specific biographies of mental disorder. The interactive view emphasizes how cultural conceptions of mental disorder shape the behaviors of people to whom these notions are applied and how their reactions to being categorized in turn change the original stereotypes. Interactive social construction sets aside the extent to which fluctuations in types of mental illness reflect or deviate from any natural kind as irrelevant to its intellectual project.

The philosopher Ian Hacking provides the most prominent and incisive interactive social constructionist view (Hacking 1995, 1998, 1999). Hacking assumes a fundamental difference, albeit more in degree than in kind, between mental and physical illnesses. Physical diseases are indifferent to their classifications: Cultural assumptions about bodies have little or no impact in changing the underlying nature of disease. In contrast, classification of mental illnesses can profoundly change how people think about themselves and respond to the way they are classified. Both interactive and indifferent forms of classification are important: "We need to make room, especially in the case of our most serious psychopathologies, for both the constructionist and the biologist" (Hacking 1999, 109).

Hacking uses case studies of particular mental illnesses to illustrate how people are aware of the ways they are classified and how they actively modify their behavior to conform to—as well as struggle against—the ways that others categorize them. He describes a looping effect whereby labeling people in one way rather than another causes them to change their behavior in light of professional classifications. For example, multiple personality disorder (MPD) is a condition in which patients see themselves as having many mutually exclusive personalities that presumably develop as a result of repressed memories of abuse in early childhood (Hacking 1995). Once professionals developed this stereotype they applied it to patients, who themselves came to view their past childhood experiences differently and genuinely came to believe that they had been abused. Their acceptance, in turn, confirmed the validity of the initial stereotype.

Psychiatry forged, rather than discovered, the connection between early child abuse and the later development of multiple personalities. It provided a culturally acceptable mode of expressing distress that became widely adopted (and then quickly repudiated). For Hacking, the truth or falsity of conceptions of MPD and other mental disorders is beside the point: The importance of social constructions lies in the ways in which categorizations change the way that people think about themselves, describe their behavior, and act according to the assumptions embodied in them. People construct their pasts based on which cultural narratives provide them with coherent and satisfying accounts of their distressing conditions, not those that conform more or less closely to some presumably objective disease condition. Mental illnesses thus are likely to develop when ecological niches that exist in specific times and places provide them with fertile grounds in which to grow and flourish (Hacking 1998).

Hacking's notion of the interactive nature of conceptions of mental illness heightens the complexity of distinguishing what is natural from what is social. For example, we might ask if some natural reality underlies social conceptions of attention deficit hyperactivity disorder (Hacking 1999, 102–103). Yet pure forms of attention deficit hyperactivity disorder (ADHD) cannot be isolated from the ways in which this construction is institutionalized and used, and changes the behaviors, explanations, and experiences of those who are classified. Not just children themselves but also their parents, teachers, and physicians use classifications of ADHD to interpret behaviors and their interpretations shape the resulting behaviors and experiences of the diagnosed people. Moreover, as the term "interactive" suggests, the influences between classifications and individual behaviors goes in both directions. Social classifications profoundly affect individual behaviors but the interpretations and responses of the subjects of classification also can change the initial labels.

The works of philosopher Mikkel Borch-Jacobsen also illustrate the interactive social constructionist perspective. Like Hacking, Borch-Jacobsen considers the question of whether any mental illness is "real" or "constructed" a false one. Instead, he asks: "How is it made? Out of what elements? How does it work? What purpose does it serve?" (2009, 71). Borch-Jacobsen's studies illuminate the social biographies of mental illnesses such as hysteria, depression, and PTSD. For him, the fact that mental illnesses have particular histories and cultures that are constructed, negotiated, and renegotiated through the efforts of professionals, drug companies, and patients has no bearing on the question of whether they are also natural facts.

Other interactive constructionists emphasize that—although mental illnesses are social constructions—they have genuine effects. Lennard Davis (2008), for example, analogizes mental illness to money, which is a totally human-made invention that lacks any grounding in the natural world but nonetheless has tremendously important consequences. Mental disorders, like money, only exist to the extent that people recognize them. Once they are embodied through social processes of categorization, however, labels take on a genuinely causal power that influence the behavior of those who are classified (Davis, 2008, 7).

Interactive conceptions of mental disorder show the influences of social classification through situating them within institutional practices, social meanings, and interactions. They avoid the problems of the pure constructionist perspective because they do not set relativistic social conceptions against universalistic natural conceptions. Instead, they usefully circumvent the dichotomy of nature and culture by bracketing the reality of the former. One of their shortcomings is that they don't differentiate the extent to which different sorts of conditions are more or less interactive: Schizophrenia, for example, might be less responsive to social labeling than anorexia or MPD. Another drawback is that—lacking a conception of what is natural—they cannot evaluate and critique the adequacy or inadequacy of various concepts of mental illness. The harmful dysfunction perspective seeks to fill this gap.

23.2.3. Harmful Dysfunction

The harmful dysfunction (HD) conception developed in the prolific writings of Jerome Wakefield (1992, 1999, 2007) is the major conception of mental disorder that joins social to natural considerations. Its use of an evolutionarily grounded concept of mental disorder, which serves as a universalistic base for analyzing social variation, distinguishes it from both the pure and interactive versions of social construction. It diverges from these two perspectives because it assumes that the natural biological functioning of psychological mechanisms, as well as social values, must be incorporated into adequate explanations of mental disorders. Only psychological conditions that are caused by dysfunctions—failures of psychological mechanisms to perform the functions that evolution designed them to serve—are mental disorders. The HD conception uses this universalistic standard as a basis to show how much cultural deviation exists around biologically grounded psychological dysfunctions (Wakefield 2002).

The HD analysis views psychological dysfunctions as conceptually equivalent to physical dysfunctions. Just as the heart is designed to pump blood, the lungs to breath, or the kidneys to process waste, evolution designed psychological processes of cognition, motivation, emotion, and the like to operate in certain ways: Fear emerges in response to danger, sadness to loss, anger to inequity, and so forth. A mental disorder exists when some psychological mechanism is unable to perform its natural function, that is, the function that evolution designed it to do. Dysfunctions, which can lie in the hardware of the brain or the software of the mind, exist when psychological processes either arise in contexts they are not designed for (e.g., fear in the absence of danger or sadness without loss) or fail to emerge in contexts when they ought to arise (serious danger or loss).

There is a major difference, however, between mental and physical dysfunctions. Mental dysfunctions are inherently *contextual*. In contrast to physical organs, which do not turn off and on but which operate continuously, psychological mechanisms are designed to be triggered in certain contexts and not to emerge in the absence of appropriate triggers. Both cultural and subjective systems of meaning influence what contexts are and therefore what normal responses to them should be. This means that the determination of what an appropriate or inappropriate context for the emergence of an emotion is much more difficult to detect for psychological than for physical functioning. For example, witches and ghosts might be appropriate sources of fear in cultures with meaning systems that emphasize the reality of these phenomena but are inappropriate in the absence of such meaning systems.

Several bodies of evidence indicate the universality of some psychological dysfunctions. Horwitz and Wakefield (2007) use loss response mechanisms as an example. Even though the evolutionary functions of loss response mechanisms are not fully known, findings from studies of primates, infants, and a wide range of cultures indicate that humans are biologically designed to become sad in situations that involve losses of valued close attachments, social statuses, and meaning systems. Nonhuman primates show a clear resemblance to humans in observable features of expression, behavior, and brain functioning in the ways they respond to loss. Loss responses thus appear to be an inherited aspect of the human genome. Moreover, human tendencies to become sad in response to loss appear very early in life before infants have learned culturally appropriate ways of expressing sadness. Further, cross-cultural and historical studies show distinct continuities in the expression of loss across widely different cultural contexts, presumably because these stem from the evolution of humans as a species. The biological roots of normal sadness in no way preclude important social influences in the particular types of situations that trigger loss responses, the sorts of symptoms that arise in response to loss, and the norms regarding the appropriate expression of sadness. While cultural and individual meanings play essential roles in shaping the final expression of emotions, what they shape is biologically embedded.

The harmful component of the HD analysis stipulates that only conditions that are harmful can be mental disorders. When dysfunctions are also socially disvalued, and therefore harmful, they are mental disorders. Because social values always at least partially determine what conditions are harmful, concepts of mental disorders are to some degree intrinsically relative to particular times and places. For example, dyslexia is a disorder in literate societies where it is seriously handicapping but is not harmful, and therefore not disordered, in preliterate ones that neither teach nor value reading (Wakefield 2007). Likewise, social phobias only emerge in groups where anxiety over interacting with strangers leads to social disabilities. Identical conditions can thus be disordered in one group but not in another.

The HD analysis, however, differs from the pure constructionist view because negative social evaluations are never sufficient conditions for the presence of disorders. Many conditions, whether ignorance, ugliness, lack of willpower, or criminality, are also socially disapproved and impairing, but are not disordered because they do not result from psychological dysfunctions. An adequate concept of mental disorder thus requires a factual component that distinguishes disorders from other negative conditions. Only harmful conditions that also stem from psychological dysfunctions are mental disorders.

The HD concept has a number of strong points. Its central notion of dysfunction is compatible with commonsense intuitions that have underlain conceptions of disorder for millennia. Aristotle, for example, associated depressive disorders with internal dysfunctions when he defined them as "groundless despondency" and "beyond due measure" (in Jackson 1986, 32). He thus distinguished disorders from natural emotions that are grounded in and proportionate to external circumstances. It also usefully distinguishes mental disorders, which arise when some internal psychological mechanism is not performing its naturally selected function, from other sorts of deviations such as ignorance, nonconformity, and normal—but socially disvalued—emotions. Only violations of social norms that stem from an inability of a psychological mechanism to perform its natural function are mental disorders.

The HD perspective is also useful because it distinguishes underlying mental dysfunctions, which are universal, from idiomatic expressions of symptoms, which are culturally influenced. It recognizes that phenotypical expressions of mental illnesses can be social expressions of an underlying natural genotype. For example, panic attacks in the United States, *ataques de nervios* in Puerto Rico, or *koro* in Melanesia might be differing cultural expressions of a similar core anxiety condition. The HD conception is compatible with the critical role of social factors in shaping the variety of expressions of mental disorders as well as with differing definitions of what behaviors are defined as disordered in particular times and places.

In addition, the HD view provides the grounds for critiquing mental health practices. The failure to perform an evolutionarily designed function is a necessary condition that sets limits on the legitimate use of the concept of mental disorder. A condition that is not a dysfunction is not a disorder. For example, the current *DSM* definition of major depression conflates normal sadness that arises after loss and that naturally dissipates over time with true depressive disorders that are not proportionately grounded in social contexts (Horwitz and Wakefield 2007). This definition not only medicalizes normal emotions but hampers the search for the causes, prognoses, and treatments of true disorders that are dysfunctions.

Finally, the HD concept usefully distinguishes clear poles of disordered and nondisordered conditions but at the same time is compatible with vague, fuzzy, and ambiguous boundaries between disordered and nondisordered states. Cultural values and social interests, not nature, set the borders between definitions of normality and pathology that are found in any particular time and place. The HD perspective accepts the underlying reality of natural mental disorders while at the same time recognizes that culture has profound influences on the expressions, definitions, and responses to mental illness. Nature and culture do not provide opposing explanations but are complementary parts of a single conception of mental disorder.

The HD conception, however, remains underdeveloped. Knowledge about the natural functions of most emotions, and thus of their dysfunctions, often relies on speculation and awaits further development. The "harm" element, in particular, has not been adequately specified. When wide social variation exists in definitions of harm, designations of mental disorder correspondingly become highly varied across cultures. This feature seemingly invalidates the HD claim to universality. A more coherent natural concept of mental disorder might solely rely on the "dysfunction" component of the HD definition. Harm would then become one of a number of social dimensions that indicate social variation around a universal conception of psychological dysfunction.

23.3. SOCIAL CONSTRUCTIONS OF CONTEMPORARY PSYCHIATRIC KNOWLEDGE

This section illustrates how social constructionist views can shed light on several issues surrounding current psychiatric classifications. The many psychiatric diagnostic entities in the current official manual, the fourth edition of the *Diagnostic and Statistical Manual* (APA 2000) are now taken-for-granted reflections of genuine natural pathologies. The origin of this manual lies in the *DSM-III*, which the profession established in 1980. The *DSM-III* is viewed as a turning point in psychiatric history because it provided a better and more objective portrayal of natural reality than the psychodynamically oriented *DSM-II* that it replaced. A president of the American Psychiatric Association, Melvin Sabshin (1990, 1272), called it a triumph of "science over ideology." Another prominent psychiatrist explained that "the old psychiatry derives from theory, the new psychiatry from fact" (Maxmen 1985, 31). An eminent psychiatric researcher, Kenneth Kendler (1990), proclaimed that "scientific evidence" rather than the charismatic authority of "great professors" stands behind the classificatory systems of the recent *DSMs*. The *DSM* diagnostic entities presumably provide evidence-based categories that are based upon underlying natural entities.

The various psychiatric classificatory manuals since the *DSM-III* enumerate precise definitions of each of several hundred conditions that rely on the presence of given numbers of presenting symptoms. These symptoms can be isolated from the personal histories and social contexts in which they arise and thus can be compared across different individuals who display the same symptoms. Such disorders as major depression, bipolar disorder, posttraumatic stress disorder, attention deficit disorder, and many others are now widely recognized both within the mental health community and the culture at large. How do the various social constructionist perspectives illuminate the development and institutionalization of the *DSMs* since 1980?

23.3.1. Pure Constructionism

Before the *DSM-III* was published in 1980, specific diagnoses had a limited role in psychiatry. The earlier manuals, the *DSM-I* (APA 1952) and *DSM-II* (APA 1968), used a psychodynamic framework that viewed overt symptoms as disguising a far more complex underlying reality. Unconscious mechanisms could produce a variety of outward manifestations such as anxiety, hysteria, sexual perversions, and character disorders. The same symptoms might stem from different causal mechanisms or distinct symptoms might develop from the same underlying mechanism. For example, depending on complex developmental dynamics, the repression of deviant sexual urges might lead to hysterical symptoms in one person but to obsessive-compulsive disorder in another. Therefore, the manuals that preceded the *DSM-III* did not place much stake in particular diagnoses because manifest symptoms were no more than clues that often hid the fundamental causes of various disorders.

The *DSM-III* revolutionized psychiatric diagnosis by providing the profession with numerous conditions that were sharply differentiated from each other, easy to measure, and thought to reflect underlying diseases. The entities of the *DSM* are so widely accepted that it is difficult to realize how arbitrary many of them initially were. Depression provides an example. In 1976, the prominent British psychiatric diagnostician R. E. Kendell published an article whose subtitle accurately conveyed the classificatory situation at the time: "The Classification of Depressions: A Review of Contemporary Confusion." Kendell reviewed twelve different systems of classification of depression, none of which had priority over the others. No consensus existed regarding many issues including whether psychotic and neurotic depressions were distinct or variants on a continuum; whether endogenous and exogenous depressions were similar or different; how many variants of depression existed; whether depressive symptoms were continuous or discrete; the relationship of depressive illness to depressive temperament; and how depressive disease was related to normal sadness. In 1979, just a year before the publication of the *DSM-III*, prominent psychiatrists Nancy Andreasen and George Winokur (1979) concluded that research on depression consisted of "a hodgepodge of competing and overlapping systems."

Yet the *DSM-III* definitions almost immediately gained virtually unchallenged acceptance. It is now the authoritative manual used in all settings that require diagnoses, including general medical and specialty mental health practices, research studies, epidemiological investigations, and clinical trials of all forms of treatment. How did a confused hodgepodge of distinct classifications become transformed into such a widely acknowledged, scientific reflection of natural reality in such a brief period of time?

A pure constructionist view emphasizes how the *DSM-III* arose to help psychiatry resolve the legitimacy crisis it underwent in the 1970s, raise professional prestige, and protect the financial interests of the profession. By the 1970s, the classification system of dynamic psychiatry that was embodied in the *DSM-I* and *DSM-II* created serious credibility problems for the profession. In particular, the field lacked discrete disease entities that were foundational for any respectable medical specialty (Rosenberg 2008). The emphasis on understanding underlying unconscious mechanisms and resulting neglect of overt symptoms meant that psychiatrists had trouble defining and measuring the disease conditions that purportedly gave legitimacy to the profession. Psychiatry was mocked within the broader culture for not even being able to recognize what mental illness was (Rosenhan 1973, Szasz 1974). Other medical specialists also looked down on psychiatrists for practicing what they regarded as more of an art than a science. Moreover, competing mental health professionals, including clinical psychologists and psychiatric social workers, could assert that they possessed comparable expertise in treating psychosocial problems. In addition, the growth of third-party funding of payment meant that psychiatrists feared they would have trouble getting reimbursed for treating the often unmeasurable entities of psychodynamic thought. The growing importance and regulation of psychoactive drugs also required a model that assumed that specific disease conditions were the targets of treatment.

The diagnostic paradigm embodied in the *DSM-III* helped solve many aspects of the crisis of psychiatric legitimacy. It divided the many developmental difficulties, life problems, and distressing conditions in the psychodynamic model into suitable disease entities, in the process providing the psychiatric categories that a medical paradigm demanded. These categories not only justified psychiatry's place as a legitimate medical specialty but also warded off competition from nonmedical psychotherapeutic professionals who could legitimately claim to provide therapy to people with psychosocial problems in living but had no warrant to treat diseases. Its system of disease categories also fit the demands of third-party payers, which required greater accountability in the results of treatment, and of pharmaceutical researchers and manufacturers, which required specific illnesses as targets for drug treatments. Although the manual rejected etiology as a basis for its definitions of disorders, their formulation as "diseases" could easily elide into the brain-based conditions that biologically oriented psychiatrists and, later, family advocacy groups promoted.

The *DSM-III* categories gained their acceptance and became "real" through the political, professional, and institutional advantages they had, not from an accumulation of new scientific knowledge. No empirical research had shown that they were superior to alternative diagnostic systems. Their "scientific" nature consisted solely of the fact that they were easy to measure, not that they helped elucidate the etiology, prognoses, or treatments for the various entities they classified. Their adaptation and acceptance had little to do with science but resulted from their usefulness, convenience, and rhetorical value to powerful interest groups. In this sense, they were purely social constructions.

23.3.2. Interactive Constructionism

The pure constructionist view elucidates many aspects of the development and institutionalization of the *DSM-III*. It also has several limitations. One is that it provides a strictly top-down view of mental illness categories. It neglects the study of how official diagnostic classifications influence the self-conceptions and behaviors of people to whom they are applied and how patients in turn shape these labels to achieve their own ends. In contrast, an interactive constructionist view shows how patients often aggressively seek out and apply disease labels to themselves for such purposes as obtaining drugs to relieve suffering or to enhance performance (Borch-Jacobsen 2009, chapter 13; Conrad 2007). Disease labels also sometimes help to explain otherwise inexplicable symptoms or even to provide valued identities (Hadler 1996, Grinker 2008). In other cases, lay resistance to the *DSM* categories led to alterations in the diagnostic criteria (Hacking 1995).

The interactive view shows how transformations in psychiatric knowledge can also have wide-ranging consequences that extend beyond the *DSM* to influence theories of motivation and interpersonal behavior in the broader culture. For example, "chemical imbalance" is the most popular current explanation of mental disorders in the population at large (Carlat 2010). This notion is relentlessly promoted through drug advertisements that emphasize how correctable chemical imbalances cause mental disorders, public service messages that stress how these disorders stem from flaws in brain chemistry rather than in character, and mental health advocacy groups that advance the message that mental disorders are physical, brain-based illnesses, just like diabetes or asthma.

Paradoxically, the growing public acceptance of neurochemical theories of behavior has been accompanied by growing scientific skepticism that chemical imbalances can account for the development of mental disorders (Lacasse and Leo 2005). It is difficult to isolate levels of neurochemicals and, to the extent that this is possible, there is little evidence that, for example, depressed patients have lower serotonin levels than others. Similarly evidence is weak that the most popular class of drugs, the selective serotonin reuptake inhibitors (SSRIs), which elevate serotonin levels, produce better results than treatments that work through other mechanisms. The wide range of conditions that the SSRIs affect, including anxiety, eating, attention deficit, substance abuse, personality, and a host of other conditions, suggests that the drugs are not correcting a specific neurochemical abnormality but are instead acting on very general brain functions that influence many emotional and behavioral systems.

Nevertheless, the notion that levels of various neurochemicals affect a variety of behaviors has permeated into not just popular discourse about mental disorders but also into lay theories of the foundations of self-conceptions and social behavior. For example, some dating sites match couples on the basis of their presumed levels of various neurochemicals. Helen Fisher (2008), the developer of one such site, explains the basic philosophy behind it: "I think we fall in love with someone who has a different chemical profile for dopamine, serotonin, estrogen and testosterone that complements our own. This is the basic premise behind my work with Chemistry.com."

People also have come to attribute their own behaviors to their levels of these neurochemicals. For example, Paul and Patricia Churchland are two prominent philosophers of neuroscience. A *New Yorker* profile describes a typical interaction between them:

> One afternoon recently, Paul says, he was home making dinner when Pat burst in the door, having come straight from a frustrating faculty meeting. She said: "Paul, don't speak to me, my serotonin levels have hit bottom, my brain is awash in glutocortocoids, my blood vessels are full of adrenalin, and if it weren't for my endogenous opiates, I'd have driven the car into a tree on the way home. My dopamine levels need lifting. Pour me a Chardonnay and I'll be down in a minute." Paul and Pat have noticed that it is not just they who talk this way—their students now talk of psychopharmacology as comfortably as they talk of food. (MacFarquhar 2007, 69)

The growing public acceptance of neurochemical theories illustrates the interactive nature of explanations of human conduct. A stereotype emerges that chemical deficiencies are responsible for behavior and is relentlessly promoted through ubiquitous advertisements, news stories, Internet sites, and public service messages. People come to use it to explain their own experiences, despite the fact that there is no way that they could know what levels of neurochemicals actually accompany their own behaviors. The increasing penetration of neurochemical theories of behavior into personal and cultural explanations reinforces the power of the original conception.

Interactive social constructionist perspectives illustrate the dynamic relationship between systems of categorization and resulting behaviors. Explanations that attribute mental illnesses to levels of neurochemicals do not stem from the actual locus of symptoms in the brain but from the high degree of credence that the current culture places on brain-based accounts of behavior. Attributing symptoms to depleted levels of serotonin has no more inherent validity as a cultural explanation than attributing them to witchcraft, phrenology, or the unconscious. Once such reasons are given credence, they become grounds to contest notions of responsibility, liability, and stigma. Whether or not they succeed or fail lies less in their correspondence to a presumed reality than in their power as cultural accounts and rationales for particular interest groups.

Neither the pure nor the interactive perspectives can address the relationship between socially created classification schemes and the underlying reality that is presumably being classified. Strict constructionist views deny that such a reality exists because any classificatory system is inherently culturally constituted. Likewise, the interactive view brackets but does not address this issue. Therefore, neither view has a place to stand that would provide a principled critique that can suggest how the *DSM* and biologically oriented theories of mental disorder could provide a more accurate portrayal of the entities that they classify and study.

23.3.3. Harmful Dysfunction

The grounding of mental disorders in dysfunctional psychological mechanisms provides a basis for distinguishing mental disorders from other sorts of socially disvalued experiences and thus to suggest revisions when the *DSM* fails to apply this distinction. Two current controversies illustrate the value of the HD perspective for critiquing the current *DSM* diagnoses.

The first controversy is over whether or not bereavement should be considered a mental disorder. Voluminous evidence indicates that people naturally grieve after the death of an intimate (Archer 1999; Horwitz and Wakefield 2007, 30–33). For example, the earliest known literary portrayals of human experience such as *Gilgamesh* and *The Iliad* focus on grief as a basic human emotion. Likewise, while different cultures have varying expressions of grief, sadness and accompanying psychological and somatic symptoms after the loss of a loved one is a universal experience. Even many primates show demonstrable signs of depression-like symptoms after the death of a close relation. In most cases, the universal symptoms of grief dissipate with the passage of time and only a minority of the bereaved remains highly symptomatic after several months (Bonanno 2009).

Current *DSM* criteria recognize the normality of intense sadness among bereaved people. Criteria for major depressive disorder (MDD) require five or more out of nine symptoms that include sadness or lack of interest or pleasure, last for at least two weeks, and create clinically significant impairment or distress. However, MDD criteria also contain an exclusion criterion for people who meet these criteria as a result of bereavement: "The symptoms are not better accounted for by Bereavement" (APA 2000 , 356). That is, people who develop enough symptoms to meet the MDD criteria after the death of an intimate are nevertheless not defined as disordered but instead as suffering from a natural, nondisordered response to loss unless their symptoms are especially severe or long-lasting. Yet many losses in addition to bereavement—the sudden ending of a romantic relationship, the loss of a valued job, the discovery of a life-threatening illness in a loved one—can also trigger symptoms of MDD. The *DSM*, however, makes no comparable exception for any kind of loss other than bereavement.

Wakefield and colleagues (2007) use the HD conception to demonstrate that bereavement and other kinds of losses have virtually identical consequences in terms of such factors as the number, severity, and persistence of symptoms and the degree of interference with life. There are, therefore, good reasons to believe that bereavement is a model for other types of loss responses rather than a categorically unique stressor. They conclude that intense sadness is a biologically designed response to a broad range of losses, from separation from a love-object to a decline in social status. They thus recommend that, parallel to the bereavement exclusion, depressive symptoms that appear as a response to major losses should not be classified as disorders even when they satisfy *DSM* symptom criteria.

Despite the great similarities between bereavement and depressive conditions that emerge after other losses, it is unlikely that the *DSM-5* will expand the bereavement exclusion. Indeed, the initial recommendation of the *DSM-5* task force on mood disorders is to *eliminate* the bereavement exclusion on the grounds that "evidence does not support separation of loss of loved one from other stressors" (APA 2010). Given the two-week required duration of a major depressive episode, abandoning the bereavement exclusion could result in the massive pathologization of a normal, ubiquitous behavior. Almost everyone experiences the loss of an intimate at some point in their lives. Many, possibly even most, of these grief reactions meet MDD criteria after a two-week period. The proposed change could, at a stroke, define a majority of the population as suffering from a mental disorder. The HD perspective provides powerful criteria that, at minimum, justify maintaining the current bereavement exclusion and perhaps the grounds for extending it to cover other major losses.

While the controversy over the bereavement exclusion shows the value of the HD perspective to critique psychiatric criteria, it also indicates that who is "right" about the nature of the reality underlying psychiatric classifications will not determine the status of the bereavement exclusion or any other controversy over *DSM* criteria. Instead, factors such as the persuasiveness of arguments for treating as wide a range of people as possible for impairing conditions, the composition of the membership of diagnoses-defining committees, and the interests of pharmaceutical companies and mental health professionals in having the largest potential markets will determine if the bereavement exclusion disappears, remains, or broadens. While the concept of a natural distinction between normal sadness and depressive disorder provides a powerful rhetorical tool, cultural values and social power rather than the accurate portrayal of nature will determine the outcome of this debate.

A second example of the HD critique of the application of psychiatric knowledge lies in debates over the value of screening for depression and other mental disorders. Although mental health practice is far less coercive than in the past, new forms of control continue to arise. One is the establishment of screening programs that attempt to identify people who are not in mental health treatment but who have or who are at risk for developing mental illnesses (Horwitz and Wakefield 2007, chapter 7). For example, New Jersey now requires health care providers to screen all new mothers for signs of postpartum depression. Likewise, many programs have emerged that encourage primary care physicians to screen all their patients for conditions such as depression, anxiety, and PTSD. Adolescents attending schools are an especially common target of screening programs. A presidential commission has proposed that "every child should be screened for mental illness once in their youth in order to identify mental illness and prevent suicide among youth" (New Freedom Commission 2003).

Screening efforts among adolescents arose after studies identified large proportions of adolescents—sometimes the majority—as suffering from depression, anxiety, substance abuse, and other mental disorders. Moreover, these studies found that most of these conditions went unidentified and untreated. Screening advocates view the early identification of such conditions as a means of facilitating appropriate treatments and preventing the subsequent onset of more serious conditions. In addition, they see programs that screen for and subsequently identify mental health problems as a way of thwarting the development of associated impairments such as poor school performance, interpersonal problems, and teenage pregnancies.

Typical screening instruments ask students questions such as the following: Have you often felt sad or depressed? Have you slept more during the day than you usually do? Do you feel tense and nervous when you're around other people? Youth who affirm a number of these questions—usually a third or more of all students who take these tests—are then given a more intensive, second-stage interview using *DSM* diagnostic criteria. Those who are confirmed as disordered in these interviews are then referred to mental health treatment. Depending on the instrument used, around 5 to 10 percent of school populations are identified as requiring treatment at any particular time.

The HD perspective provides the grounds for showing how screening programs that aim to detect untreated mental illness are instead more likely to mislabel normal and widespread adolescent distress and emotional angst as mental disorders (Horwitz and Wakefield 2009). It shows how screening instruments pervasively confuse ubiquitous feelings of sadness, irritability, oversleeping, nervousness, embarrassment, restlessness, and the like with mental disorders. These so-called symptoms are common results of normal responses to life stressors, family and school problems, and the natural intensity and lability of adolescent emotions. Most such distressing states will be short-lived and highly situational and so are not signs of mental disorders.

The use of second-stage instruments based on *DSM* diagnostic categories is presumed to insure that only true cases of disorder are identified. Yet many *DSM* diagnoses—especially major depressive disorder (MDD)—themselves do not separate normal sadness and other distressing emotions from mental disorders. Because they do not require clinicians to place symptoms in the context of events in adolescents' lives, they do not distinguish symptoms that are signs of underlying disorders from those that arise from the turmoil and stressfulness of adolescence. Moreover, the two-week required duration requirement for MDD symptoms insures that diagnostic interviews fail to separate the transitory nature of normal emotions from the enduring and often chronic nature of most mental disorders. Yet once adolescents are wrongly identified as disordered they often become the object of surveillance and subsequent drug and psychotherapeutic treatment.

The HD analysis indicates that current *DSM* definitions pervasively confuse problematic but natural human emotions that develop as responses to stress with mental disorders. It thus provides the grounds for critiquing control efforts such as screening because they misidentify large proportions of adolescents who display normal levels of negative affect in response to stressful events as suffering from disorders that warrant professional treatment. As with efforts to change the bereavement exclusion, conceptual tools can only provide the intellectual foundation for critiquing mental health practice. Interest group politics and the relative success of rhetorical claims that mental health screening programs help identify and treat needy populations vis-à-vis that they mislabel normal distress as mental disorders will determine whether these programs will succeed or fail.

23.4. CONCLUSION

This chapter has focused on one aspect of the social nature of mental disorder: the different ways that cultural and natural aspects of mental illnesses are formulated. It outlined three ways of examining the relationship between psychiatric knowledge and social reality: the pure constructionist, interactive, and harmful dysfunction approaches. These styles provide useful accounts of such issues as the emergence of general systems of psychiatric classification, the adaptation of brain-based idioms for explaining behavior, and controversies over the application of psychiatric knowledge.

The profound social influences on constructions of mental disorder suggest the value of sociological approaches for the study of phenomena that are typically viewed as aspects of individual personalities and brains. Social perspectives can also provide valuable insight on other aspects of psychiatric knowledge such as the structuring of the symptoms of mental illness into culturally appropriate idioms, social influences on the development of mental disorders, the political economy of mental illness, and the contextual reasons for how people come to define themselves and others as having a mental illness and to seek various forms of treatment once these definitions are made, among many others.

REFERENCES

American Psychiatric Association (APA). 1952. *Diagnostic and Statistical Manual of Mental Disorders*. Washington, DC: American Psychiatric Association.

APA. 1968 *Diagnostic and Statistical Manual of Mental Disorders*, 2d ed. Washington, DC: American Psychiatric Association.

APA. 1980. *Diagnostic and Statistical Manual of Mental Disorders*, 3d ed. Washington, DC: American Psychiatric Association.

APA. 2000. *Diagnostic and Statistical Manual of Mental Disorders*, 4th ed., text rev. Washington, DC: American Psychiatric Association.

APA. 2010. DSM-5 Development. Online. Available at www.dsm5.org/ProposedRevisions/Pages/proposedrevision.aspx?rid=427#. December 3, 2010.

Andreasen, Nancy C., and George Winokur. 1979. "Newer Experimental Methods for Classifying Depression." *Archives of General Psychiatry* 36 (4): 447–52.

Archer, John. 1999. *The Nature of Grief: The Evolution and Psychology of Reactions to Loss*. New York: Routledge.

Barr-Zisowitz, Carol. 2000. "'Sadness'—Is There Such a Thing?" In *Handbook of Emotions*, Michael Lewis and Jeanette M. Haviland-Jones eds., 607–22. New York: Guilford Press.

Barrett, Lisa F. 2006. "Are Emotions Natural Kinds?" *Perspectives on Psychological Science* 1 (1): 28–58.

Benedict, Ruth. 1934. "Anthropology and the Abnormal." *Journal of General Psychology* 10 (1) : 59–80.

Bolton, Derek. 2008. *What Is Mental Disorder? An Essay in Philosophy, Science and Values*. New York: Oxford University Press.

Bonanno, George A. 2009. *The Other Side of Sadness: What the New Science of Bereavement Tells Us About Life After Loss*. New York: Basic Books.

Borch-Jacobsen, Mikkel. 2009. *Making Minds and Madness: From Hysteria to Depression*. New York: Cambridge University Press.

Carlat, Daniel J. 2010. *Unhinged: The Trouble with Psychiatry*. New York: The Free Press.

Castillo, Richard J. 1997. *Culture & Mental Illness*. Pacific Grove, CA: Brooks/Cole.

Conrad, P. 2007. *The Medicalization of Society: On the Transformation of Human Conditions into Treatable Disorders*. Baltimore: Johns Hopkins University Press.

Davis, Lennard J. 2008. *Obsession: A History*. Chicago: University of Chicago Press.

Fisher, Helen. 2008. Available at www.chemistry.com/drhelenfisher/interviewdrfisher.aspx, accessed August 22, 2010.

Foucault, Michel. 1965. *Madness and Civilization: A History of Insanity in the Age of Reason*. New York: Pantheon.

Grinker, Roy R. 2008. *Unstrange Minds: Remapping the World of Autism*. New York: Basic Books.

Gross, Daniel M. 2006. *The Secret History of Emotion: From Aristotle's Rhetoric to Modern Brain Science*. Chicago: University of Chicago Press.

Hacking, Ian. 1995. *Rewriting the Soul: Multiple Personality and the Sciences of Memory*. Princeton, NJ: Princeton University Press.

Hacking, Ian. 1998. *Mad Travelers: Reflections on the Reality of Transient Mental Illnesses*. Charlottesville: University Press of Virginia.

Hacking, Ian. 1999. *The Social Construction of What?* Cambridge, MA: Harvard University Press.

Hadler, Norton M. 1996. "If You Have to Prove You Are Ill, You Can't Get Well. The Object Lesson of Fibromyalgia." *Spine* 21 (20): 2397–400.

Horwitz, Allan V. 2007. "Classical Sociological Theory, Evolutionary Theory, and Mental Health." In *Mental Health/Social Mirror*, Bernice Pescosolido, William Avison, and Jane McLeod, eds., 67–94. New York: Springer.

Horwitz, Allan V., and Jerome C. Wakefield. 2007. *The Loss of Sadness: How Psychiatry Transformed Normal Sorrow into Depressive Disorder*. New York: Oxford University Press.

Horwitz, Allan V., and Jerome C. Wakefield. 2009. "Should Screening for Depression Among Children and Adolescents be Demedicalized? Placing Screening in the Context of Normal Intense Adolescent Emotion." *Journal of the American Academy of Child and Adolescent Psychiatry* 48 (7): 683–87.

Jackson, Stanley W. 1986. *Melancholia and Depression: From Hippocratic Times to Modern Times*. New Haven: Yale University Press.

Kendell, R. E. 1976. "The Classification of Depressions: A Review of Contemporary Confusion." *British Journal of Psychiatry* 129 (1): 15–28.

Kendler, Kenneth S. 1990. "Toward a Scientific Psychiatric Nosology: Strengths and Limitations." *Archives of General Psychiatry* 47 (10): 969–73.

Kleinman, Arthur. 1988. *Rethinking Psychiatry: From Cultural Category to Personal Experience*. New York: The Free Press.

Lacasse, Jeffrey R., and Jonathan Leo. 2005. "Serotonin and Depression: A Disconnect between the Advertisements and the Scientific Literature." *PLoS Medicine* 2 (12): e292.

MacFarquhar, Larissa. "Two Heads: A Marriage Devoted to the Mind-Body Problem." *The New Yorker*, February 12, 2007. 58–69.

Mannheim, Karl. 1936. *Ideology and Utopia*. New York: Harcourt, Brace & World.

Maxmen, Jerrold. 1985. *The New Psychiatrists*. New York: New American Library.

New Freedom Commission on Mental Health. 2003. *Achieving the Promise: Transforming Mental Health Care in America (DHHS Publication No. SMA-03-3832)*. Rockville, MD: US Department of Health and Human Services.

Rosenberg, Charles. 2008. *Our Present Complaint*. Baltimore: Johns Hopkins University Press.

Rosenhan, David L. 1973. "On Being Sane in Insane Places." *Science* 179 (4070): 250–58.

Sabshin, Melvin. 1990. "Turning Points in Twentieth-Century American Psychiatry." *American Journal of Psychiatry* 147 (10): 1267–74.

Scheff, Thomas J. 1966. *Being Mentally Ill: A Sociological Theory*. Chicago: Aldine.

Szasz, Thomas S. 1974. *The Myth of Mental Illness*. New York: Harper & Row.

Turner, Jonathan H. 1999. "Toward a General Sociological Theory of Emotions." *Journal for the Theory of Social Behavior* 29 (2): 133–62.

Wakefield, Jerome C. 1992. "The Concept of Mental Disorder: On the Boundary Between Biological Facts and Social Values." *American Psychologist* 47 (3): 73–88.

Wakefield, Jerome C. 1999. "Evolutionary Versus Prototype Analyses of the Concept of Disorder." *Journal of Abnormal Psychology* 108 (3): 465–72.

Wakefield, Jerome C. 2002. "Fixing a Foucault Sandwich: Cognitive Universals and
     Cultural Particulars in the Concept of Mental Disorders." In *Culture in Mind: Toward
     a Sociology of Culture and Cognition*, Karen A. Cerulo, ed., 245–66. New York:
     Routledge.
Wakefield, Jerome C. 2007. "The Concept of Mental Disorder: Diagnostic Implications of
     the Harmful Dysfunction Analysis." *World Psychiatry* 6 (3): 149–56.
Wakefield, Jerome C., Mark F. Schmitz, Michael B. First, and Allan V. Horwitz. 2007.
     "Extending the Bereavement Exclusion for Major Depression to Other Losses."
     Archives of General Psychiatry 64 (4): 433–40.
Zerubavel, Eviatar. 1997. *Social Mindscapes: An Invitation to Cognitive Sociology.*
     Cambridge, MA: Harvard University Press.

PART V

Normative
Connections

CHAPTER 24

COOPERATION AND RECIPROCITY: EMPIRICAL EVIDENCE AND NORMATIVE IMPLICATIONS

JAMES WOODWARD

24.1. INTRODUCTION

There is now a rich empirical literature in economics and other disciplines concerning the conditions under which humans cooperate (or do not) and the motivations that underlie cooperation. To a very large extent, however, there has been little work to date by philosophers directed at exploring the philosophical implications of this literature—which include both potential normative consequences for social and political philosophy and methodological implications for how cooperative behavior is best explained. My aim in this chapter is to explore, in a preliminary way, some of these implications. I will be particularly interested in trying to forge connections with issues in normative political philosophy concerning the role of reciprocity in cooperative behavior and in our sense of justice. One of my main themes will be that the empirical literature supports a picture according to which humans are often motivated in cooperative endeavors by a particular conception of just or fair behavior—a conception of justice as reciprocity. However, this conception differs in some important respects from what many philosophers have had in mind when they have talked about justice as reciprocity.

I should say at the outset that I intend my discussion as merely a first-pass investigation of the very difficult and underexplored question of the ways in which empirical results of the sort I describe might be relevant to normative theory. I write mainly in the hope that my discussion will stimulate others to consider these issues—there is philosophical gold in them, regardless of whether one agrees with the particular conclusions I reach.

24.2. BARRY AND GIBBARD ON JUSTICE AS RECIPROCITY

To set up the problems with which I will be concerned, I begin by recalling a disagreement between Brian Barry and Allan Gibbard about the relationship between different theories of justice and the motivations underlying them.

Barry claims that

> a theory of justice may be characterised by its answers to three questions. First, what is the motive (are the motives) for behaving justly? Secondly, what is the criterion (are the criteria) for a just set of rules? And thirdly, how are the answers to the first two questions connected? We want to know exactly how somebody with the stipulated motive(s) for behaving justly would be led to comply with rules that are just according to the stipulated criterion or criteria. A theory of justice that cannot answer the third question satisfactorily fails on the ground of internal inconsistency. (1989, 46)

In this connection, Barry distinguishes two different theories: justice as mutual advantage (JMA) and justice as impartiality (JI). For our purposes, we may think of JMA as claiming that just behavior is whatever is in our self-interest in contexts in which we are interacting with others who are similarly self-interested and that just rules or institutions for some group are whatever patterns emerge from interactions of the people making up this group when they act in ways that best advance their self-interests. Just rules or institutions will thus be those that emerge as an equilibrium in some appropriately specified game among self-interested players. By contrast, in Barry's characterization, the motive for behaving justly according to JI is the desire "to act in accordance with principles that could not reasonably be rejected by people seeking an agreement with others under conditions free from morally irrelevant bargaining advantages and disadvantages." As understood by Barry (and many others), JI sometimes mandates cooperation when such behavior does not best advance a subject's self-interest and sometimes requires unconditional altruism in the sense of benefiting another, independently of whether, for example, the beneficiary has behaved cooperatively.

Barry goes on to claim that these are the only two coherent conceptions of justice. In particular, he denies that there is a coherent and normatively attractive conception of justice as reciprocity (JR) that is distinct from both JMA and JI. According to Barry, under careful examination JR collapses into either JMA or JI.

In a well-known discussion of Barry's claims, Alan Gibbard (1991) claims, contrary to Barry, that there is a distinct conception of justice as reciprocity (Gibbard frequently writes "fair reciprocity") which is normatively important. He writes:

> If I return favor for favor, I may be doing so in pursuit of my own advantage, as a means to keep the favors rolling. My motivation might, though, be more intrinsically reciprocal. I might be decent to him because he has been decent to me. I might prefer treating another well who has treated me well, even if he has no further power to affect me. We tip for good service in strange restaurants. (266)

He adds:

> Is Justice as Fair Reciprocity a distinct alternative to Barry's two? Is it different in any way from Justice as Mutual Advantage and Justice as Impartiality? The case that it is, in a nutshell, is this: On the one hand, it is distinct from Justice as Mutual Advantage because it draws on non-egoistic motives. On the other, it is distinct from Justice as Impartiality because it says that a person cannot reasonably be asked to support a social order unless he gains from it. (266)

One might put Gibbard's claim this way: On the one hand, I might regard my returning favor for favor as simply a means for inducing you to keep providing favors, assuming that such exchanges best advance my self-interest. In this case, we may think of my behavior as motivated by a conception of justice as mutual advantage. On the other hand, my motivation might be intrinsically reciprocal—I might want to return a favor to you because you have benefited me, even if it is not in my self-interest to do so. According to Gibbard, this motivation is distinct not just from JMA but also from the motivation that underlies JI because it is prompted by (or is conditional on) the fact that you have previously benefited me.

Some questions raised by these claims are straightforwardly empirical: Is there evidence for a motive to reciprocate, in the sense envisioned by Gibbard, that is distinct from the motives underlying JMA and JI? How should this motive be characterized? How strong or pervasive is the motive in human interaction and in what circumstances does it operate? What is the detailed structure or structures of this motive? I will explore these questions below.

In addition to these empirical questions, there are related normative questions—most obviously the question of whether and in what circumstances JR embodies a morally appealing conception of justice. There is also the question of how (if at all) the empirical issues described in the previous paragraph might bear on these normative issues. Since this last issue is central to what follows, I turn first to it.

24.3. The Descriptive and the Normative

A standard line of argument emphasizes the logical gulf between "is" and "ought." For the purposes of this chapter, I will accept that this gulf exists: Normative claims can't be deduced from descriptive claims alone; hence to bring the latter to bear on the former we require connecting principles of some kind, relating the two. In my view, one plausible candidate for such a connecting principle appeals to considerations of *stability*: We want schemes of cooperation (or more broadly rules of justice) to be stable in the sense that given the motivations that people actually have (or may come to have), they will not act in ways that seriously undermine these schemes.[1] Forms of this idea are endorsed by many writers including, most famously, Rawls (1971), who argues against utilitarianism partly on the grounds that rules and institutions based on it will be unstable, given facts about human motivation and behavior. Similarly, if very few people possess the motives to reciprocate described by Gibbard or rarely act on such motives, this suggests that schemes of cooperation based on this motive are unlikely to be stable. Those of us who regard stability as a desideratum in a theory of justice will in turn judge that such schemes are prima-facie normatively defective. More generally, we can say that whether a set of rules or institutions is stable will depend in large part on descriptive facts about the motivations and beliefs people actually have and what happens when people with those beliefs and motivations interact in various settings. This yields one important way in which descriptive facts can be brought to bear on normative conclusions.

A second set of considerations potentially linking the descriptive and the normative is the following: It is frequently claimed that one of the tasks of a theory of justice is to capture "our" conception of justice—or at least a conception that bears some relation (perhaps after being put through some process of reflective equilibrium) to a conception that is recognizably ours. Presumably, it is an empirical matter what conception of justice we or any other group of people hold. Moreover, although what people say and think is certainly relevant to their conception of justice, so too are their nonverbal choices and behavior—what they actually choose to do in contexts in which questions of justice arise, how they respond behaviorally to the choices of others (which tells us something about whether these are perceived as just or unjust), and so on. More broadly, it seems plausible (indeed inevitable) that there should be some connection between normative rules and "what we care about"—normatively appealing rules should implement, further, protect, and respect what we care about and reflect moral conceptions and values that we accept or can come to accept on reflection. (In part because only such rules are likely to be stable, but also because it is hard to see on what other basis normative justification might proceed except via *some* connection to what we value.) Again, what we care about is, if not a purely empirical matter, a matter to which empirical evidence about people's actual behavior (including their nonverbal behavior) is relevant. For example, it is an empirical question whether large numbers of people care about whether others behave reciprocally toward them, or about responding reciprocally when others have benefited them. As we shall see, the evidence suggests that people do care about such things and this, I suggest, has some bearing on the form that a normatively appealing conception of justice should take.

Although this consideration gives us another potential connection between the descriptive and the normative, the connection is not straightforward. One complication, which will emerge more clearly below, is that there seems (again as an empirical matter) to be considerable heterogeneity in people's preferences, motivations, values, and behavior in cooperative interactions—both in the sense that different people have different preferences and in the sense that single people are influenced by different motivations and preferences. For example, many people in the contemporary United States (roughly 40 percent in the experiments considered below) behave in many cooperative interactions as though they are guided by a conception of appropriate behavior that roughly corresponds to JMA—they free ride or defect when others cooperate if they think that it is in their self-interest to do so. But many others (another 40–60 percent) behave more reciprocally and show, when given the opportunity, that they strongly disapprove of nonreciprocal behavior. (For example, they are willing to sanction such behavior at a cost to themselves.) Such subjects behave as though they are motivated by something that looks more like JR. Moreover, those who behave reciprocally, when the appropriate occasions arise, also often exhibit unconditionally altruistic preferences in other situations, especially when those benefited are incapable of reciprocation. (Unsurprisingly, such altruistic preferences are far weaker when potential beneficiaries are capable of reciprocation but fail to reciprocate.) Unconditional altruistic preferences themselves take a variety of different forms—some, to the extent their preferences are altruistic, seem to behave like utilitarians, others as though they are guided by a maximin rule, still others as though they are guided by a weighted average of these two, and so on.

These observations create difficulties for the assumption that there is some single, mono-criterial ur-conception of justice that "at bottom" all of us share and which it is the task of normative theory to articulate. However, I believe they do not undermine the more modest claim that facts about what large numbers of people value form, so to speak, one source of raw material for the construction of normative arguments— raw material in the sense that the valuations in question can be thought of as reasonable starting points in normative argument which then need to be critically assessed in terms of coherence with other values and consistency with empirical facts. If, say, large numbers of people care about reciprocity, their doing so is not based on mistaken factual assumptions, and we can see how reciprocity connects up with and supports other things we value, then this constitutes a prima-facie case for taking reciprocity seriously as a normative value. Or so I will assume in what follows.

24.4. Empirical Results Concerning Reciprocity and Cooperation: General Themes

With these metaethical remarks as background, I turn to some general themes from the empirical literature on cooperation, which I then illustrate in more detail.

1. Many features of observed patterns of human cooperation (both in experiments and in the field) seem best explained by the assumption that participants are heterogeneous in their motivations and behavior. In particular, it will be useful to

distinguish three different possible behavioral/motivational patterns or profiles. First, subjects may sometimes act in ways that are self-interested in the sense that the goal of their action is to maximize the subject's own advantage, understood in material terms. To the extent subjects exhibit such behavior, let us call them SIs. Second some subjects (As) may act in ways that are relatively unconditionally altruistic. Third, some subjects may act as conditional cooperators or reciprocators (Rs). In speaking of motivational and behavioral heterogeneity, I want to leave open which of two possible forms this takes. One possibility is that the very same individuals may act differently or be differently motivated on different occasions, sometimes acting in a purely self-interested way, and sometimes acting altruistically or as a reciprocator. The second possibility is that people exhibit some substantial stability of type, with the same individual regularly behaving as an SI, an A, or an R across some range of different contexts. On the one hand, there is some evidence for stability of type when subjects play the same game repeatedly. On the other hand, there is also little doubt that previous experience and many other contextual and environmental factors can alter the extent to which subjects behave as SIs, Rs, and As. For example, subjects who begin a series of interactions by behaving cooperatively may "learn" to behave in more self-interested ways (even with new partners) if they are subject to a lot of uncooperative behavior. In the discussion that follows, what will matter most is not the precise degree of stability of type people exhibit but rather the fact of heterogeneity—people (either different people or the same person on different occasions) exhibit (s) the different behavioral profiles described above when opportunities for cooperation present themselves.

2. Returning now to the reciprocators described under (1), we may think of their motivation and behavior as including (although not necessarily limited to) the profile described by Gibbard: As a preliminary characterization, Rs are motivated to act so as to benefit others who they believe have intentionally benefited them even if this choice does not maximize their self-interested payoffs and they are so motivated *because* they wish to benefit those who have benefited them. As an illustration, consider a one-shot sequential prisoner's dilemma in which player one chooses first whether to cooperate and her move is made known to player two who then chooses whether to cooperate. If player one cooperates, a second mover who is a reciprocator will also cooperate (and cooperate because player one has cooperated), even though defection is the self-interested choice. My reading of the empirical evidence is that it is also plausible to assume that reciprocators are not merely motivated to benefit others who have benefited them but are sometimes willing to behave cooperatively in order to encourage cooperation among others who they regard as potential reciprocators, as when a first mover cooperates in a sequential PD in the hope that this will induce the second mover to cooperate. Finally, I assume that part of what it means to be a reciprocator is that reciprocators exhibit a differential response to cooperative and noncooperative behavior, although response to the latter my take many different forms, from withdrawal of future cooperation to active punishment or sanctioning ("negative reciprocity"), even when this is costly for the subject.[2]

3. The notion of a reciprocator employed in (2) is closely related to the notion of "strong reciprocity" employed in the experimental economics literature. According to Fehr et al. (2002), "[a] person is a strong reciprocator if she is willing (i) to sacrifice resources to be kind to those who are being kind (= strong positive reciprocity) and (ii) to sacrifice resources to punish those who are being unkind (= strong negative reciprocity)." My understanding of reciprocity is similar, although I would also emphasize that reciprocators may be motivated by the *prospect* of reciprocation as described under (2) above, rather than just by a desire to respond to kindness with kindness.

4. The general category of Rs covers many more specific possibilities. One dimension of variation has to do with how cautious a reciprocating subject is, and what circumstances (or threshold) will prompt cooperation or its withdrawal. For example, many reciprocators may behave cooperatively or extend benefits to others who have not yet behaved cooperatively toward them as long as they believe that those others will reciprocate—they extend benefits as a way of inducing trust and cooperation. Other reciprocators may be more cautious, extending benefits or cooperation only toward those others who have already provided benefits to them.

Another dimension of variation is this: Although reciprocators respond to behavior that benefits them by returning benefits, this leaves open the question of what counts for the subjects as a benefit, an appropriate return of benefit, what costs it may be reasonable to expect that one incurs in the course of reciprocating a benefit, and so on. As we shall see, all of this is likely to be very context-specific; in many cases it is not fixed by the general dispositions to reciprocate that subjects may have, but rather by contextually established reference points and norms.

Parallel remarks apply to reciprocators' responses to noncooperative behavior.

5. Many readers will be familiar with the idea that in some classes of repeated games (a repeated prisoner's dilemma furnishing perhaps the best-known example) "reciprocal" or cooperative strategies (like "tit for tat") can be sustained among self-interested players, given certain further assumptions (such as that the players have a sufficiently low discount rate and have knowledge of one another's previous choices)—with these assumptions, the mutual choice of such strategies is a Nash equilibrium of the repeated game, given self-interested players. (That these are *among* the Nash equilibria of the repeated game is a consequence of the so-called folk theorem for repeated games—see Binmore [1992].). This may seem to suggest that an appeal to self-interested motives in repeated interactions is sufficient to explain whatever reciprocal behavior exists, and that there is no need to appeal to distinct motives to reciprocate. For both theoretical and empirical reasons I believe this view is mistaken. It is a consequence of the folk theorem that there are many, many Nash equilibria in many two-person repeated games. While some of these may be cooperative, many others will not be. For example, in a repeated prisoner's dilemma, the Nash equilibria include such choices as continual mutual defection. So even in this case, while standard game theoretical analyses may explain how it is possible for cooperative interactions to occur, assuming self-interested players (since these are among the possible equilibria in repeated games), they do not really explain under what conditions cooperative rather than noncooperative solutions emerge or

why cooperation is as common as it appears to be (since relatively uncooperative equilibria are generic). When one moves to settings in which more than two players interact (e.g., public goods games for n > 2, discussed in more detail below, and/or in which the assumptions of the folk theorem are relaxed), theoretical considerations suggest that there should be little or no cooperation, which is contrary to what is observed. In addition, the assumption that players are purely self-interested cannot explain why people behave reciprocally (as in fact many do) in one-shot games such as the sequential prisoner's dilemma. Finally, as discussed below, there are many other features of the behavior exhibited in repeated games (such as the positive cor-relation between whether players contribute in public goods games and their beliefs that others are contributing) that are difficult to explain on the assumption that players are purely self-interested.

These considerations suggest that many examples of behavior that involve returning benefit for benefit cannot be explained purely in terms of self-interest; instead distinct motives to reciprocate not based purely on self-interest are required in at least some subjects.

6. Although the presence of Rs (or As) in a population is often or typically necessary for cooperation to occur it is usually not sufficient when, as virtually always the case, SIs are also present. Instead, whether cooperation can be sustained in a group that consists of SIs, Rs, and As depends on how these different types inter-act and the particular incentives that they face. This in turn depends on the rules or institutions that are present that influence such interactions and incentives. A par-ticularly important issue is whether these institutions provide adequate control of the potentially exploitive (free-riding) behavior of SIs toward Rs and As. More gen-erally, to the extent that people are reciprocators (and especially when reciprocators are mixed in with nonreciprocators), institutions matter in sustaining cooperation. A shared general disposition to reciprocate is usually not sufficient for successful cooperation in the absence of the right sort of rules and institutions.

7. Another crucial feature of Rs is that (as an empirical matter) they are sensitive to the motives or intentions of those they interact with and not just to the material payoffs they receive as a result of others' behavior. This is one way in which considerations often considered "nonconsequentialist" (or "deontological") enter into the behavior of Rs.

8. The dependence of the cooperative preferences of Rs on the behavior and in-tentions of others provides another reason why these preferences are often very complex and context sensitive. We cannot adequately predict the behavior of Rs across different contexts simply by supposing that they have, in addition to self-interested preferences, stable "other regarding" preferences regarding payoffs to others (whether "utilitarian," "maximin," or "inequity averse") that are independent of their beliefs about the behavior and intentions of those others. One role for rules and institutions is that they allow subjects who wish to reciprocate to successfully predict and coordinate their behavior. This points to another reason why appropriate rules or institutions are generally necessary for Rs to achieve successful cooperation.

9. The remarks above focus on what might be called dyadic reciprocity in which A both benefits B and receives a benefit from B. It is an important fact about

human reciprocity that it can take other, more indirect or generalized forms. One example is the empirically well-supported willingness of third parties (Cs) to benefit those As who have benefited Bs that are distinct from Cs. Another example is the ability of human societies to sustain chains of reciprocity in which A benefits B who in turn benefits C and so on. Reciprocal motives of this sort play an important role in systems of intergenerational transfer, such as the food-sharing schemes described in section 6 below, as well as pension and social security schemes in more modern welfare states.

I will suggest below that these features of reciprocators, taken together, point to a normative possibility—a conception of justice based on reciprocity—that is distinct both from what emerges from the interactions of purely self-interested players (JMA) and conceptions that rely on ideals of unconditional altruism and impartiality (JI).

24.5. EMPIRICAL EVIDENCE

I turn now to a very selective look at some evidence for the above claims.

24.5.1. Prisoner's Dilemmas

In their 2003 study Ahn, Ostrom, and Walker asked subjects to state preferences regarding outcomes in one-shot double-blind prisoner's dilemmas (that is, games that were prisoner's dilemmas when evaluated in terms of monetary payoffs), both involving simultaneous and sequential moves. In the simultaneous move version of the game, 10 percent of subjects ranked (C, C) > (D, C). Another 19 percent ranked (C, C) = (D, C) despite the fact that (D, C) provides a higher payoff to self than (C, C). In the sequential move game, 40 percent ranked (C, C) > (D, C) and another 27 percent were indifferent. Assuming the self-interested choice in both the simultaneous and sequential version of the game is to defect, these preferences, if taken at face value, suggest the existence of a substantial proportion of subjects that are not purely self-interested. Lest these be dismissed as mere verbal reports, Ahn et al. also reported results from behavioral experiments that are broadly consistent with these expressed preferences: 36 percent of subjects cooperated in the simultaneous move game, and in the sequential game, 56 percent of first movers cooperated and 61 percent of second movers cooperated when first movers cooperated. By contrast, virtually no second movers cooperated when first movers defected, suggesting that subjects were not unconditional altruists but rather reciprocators or conditional cooperators. Commenting on these results elsewhere, Ostrom (2005) writes that these results "confirm that not all subjects enter a collective action situation as pure forward looking rational egoists" and that "some bring with them a set of norms and values that can support cooperation" (129). However, she also adds that

> Preferences based in these [cooperative] norms can be altered by bad experiences. One set of 72 subjects played 12 rounds of a finitely repeated Prisoner's Dilemma game where we randomly matched partners before each round. Rates of cooperation were very low. Many players experienced multiple instances where partners declined to cooperate (Ahn, Ostrom, and Walker 2003). In light of these unfortunate experiences, only 19 percent of the respondents now ranked (C, C) above (D, C) while 17 percent were indifferent (ibid.). In this uncooperative setting, the norms supporting cooperation and reciprocity were diminished by experience, but not eliminated. (Ostrom 2005, 129)

Thus there is evidence that the preferences of subjects for reciprocation are not fixed and immutable, but rather change in response to experience and learning.

24.5.2. Linear Public Goods Games

In a linear public goods game, each of N players can contribute an amount c_i of their choosing from an initial endowment w_i which is the same for each player. The total amount Σc_i contributed by all players is multiplied by some factor m where $1/N < m < 1$ with each player receiving $m\Sigma c_i$. (m is the marginal per capita return or MPCR) The net amount held by each player is thus $e_i - c_i + m\Sigma c_i$ where e_i is the player's initial endowment. The game may be either played once or repeated, with total contributions announced after each round. If a player is purely self-interested in the sense of wishing only to maximize his return, he will contribute nothing (free-ride), since what he receives from others is independent of his contribution.

Here are three relevant stylized facts about contributions in repeated public goods games:

1. Average contributions begin, in the opening round, at about 50 percent of the total endowment. The contribution level is similar in a one-shot public goods game.
2. There is considerable variation in individual contributions, with some contributing a substantial portion of their endowment and others contributing nothing.
3. Average contributions typically decline sharply over time, although not necessarily to zero.

Why do contributions decline over time? Two possible explanations have been considered in the literature:

4. All or virtually all of the subjects are self-interested but some are initially confused about what will best promote their self-interest—that is, they don't initially understand the structure of the game and/or mistakenly assimilate it to some game in which contribution is the self-interested strategy. They then gradually "learn" from the results of repeated play that the self-interested strategy is to contribute nothing.
5. A number of the subjects are purely self-interested (presumably those who contribute nothing right from the outset). However, a substantial number of

subjects are not entirely self-interested; the majority of these are Rs rather than As. The decline in contributions over time may be partly due to learning of the sort described under (1) but it also is due in substantial part because the reciprocators who are present in the population gradually withdraw their cooperation in response to free-riding by self-interested types.

There are several different kinds of evidence that support the claim that hypothesis (5) is an important part of the explanation for the decline in contributions under repetition.

Heterogeneous Grouping Effects

Page, Putterman, and Unel (2005) gave subjects information every three rounds about the contributions of other subjects in previous rounds and also the opportunity to express preferences about future partners. Subjects whose mutual rankings were the lowest (= partner is most preferred for cooperation) were organized into a first group; those with intermediate rankings were organized into a second group and so on. The result was that the average level of contribution across all groups was much higher than the average level of contribution in a baseline treatment in which there is no regrouping (70 percent versus 38 percent). Moreover, the average levels of contribution varied greatly across the groups, with this following the order of group formation. That is, participants in the first group (consisting of the most cooperative participants classified on the basis of previous behavior) contributed the most and their level of contribution declined very little under repetition. By contrast those in the last group contributed little or nothing throughout the experiment. This may be contrasted with another study of grouping in a repeated public goods game by Ehrhart and Keser (1999) in which, unlike the Page et al. experiment, subjects were allowed to move unilaterally from one group to another without the agreement of those in the group being joined. Unsurprisingly, those inclined to free-riding joined groups containing the highest contributors, with the result that those contributors (behaving like reciprocators) contributed less and less over time. Other grouping experiments such as Gunnthorsdottir, McCabe, and Houser (2007) have obtained similar results. These results suggest that subjects are heterogeneous in their dispositions to cooperate. They are also difficult to explain in a non–ad hoc way on the assumption that cooperation is just the result of "confusion."

Restart Effects

In a repeated public goods game with restarting, play is stopped after ten rounds, for example, and subjects are told that a new ten-round repeated game will begin (with the same partners) (cf. Andreoni 1988). Contributions follow the usual pattern of decline over the first ten rounds, but the effect of the restart is to temporarily boost contributions—the average level is much higher in the eleventh round. Again this is prima facie inconsistent with an interpretation according to which subjects are gradually learning, through repeated play, that zero contribution is their best strategy, since there is no obvious reason why they should suddenly "forget" what they have learned in the eleventh round. A more natural alternative interpretation is that there is some substantial group of subjects who contribute more when the restart begins as part of an attempt to signal anew their willingness to contribute if others are willing to do so as well; their increased level of contribution is an attempt to get others to change their behavior and no longer free ride.

Comparative Statics

If a significant portion of subjects are reciprocators, one would expect the contributions of this group to be positively correlated with their beliefs about the extent to which others are contributing, since reciprocators contribute more to the extent that they believe others are contributing more or may be expected to do so. This prediction contrasts with the predictions that follow from other hypotheses about the motivations of subjects who contribute. For example, if subjects are purely self-interested and contribute (to the extent that they do) only out of confusion, there is no obvious reason for expecting that their level of contribution should vary with their beliefs about the extent to which others are contributing. Similarly, a simple model according to which subjects are unconditional altruists who care, in addition to their own self-interest, only about the aggregate amount contributed by all, predicts that individual subjects will contribute less if they believe that others will contribute more. In an experimental study of this issue employing a repeated public goods game, Croson (2007) found, in accordance with the hypothesis that a large portion of subjects are reciprocators, a strong positive correlation between a subject's beliefs about how much others would contribute and that subject's actual contributions, as well as a correlation between individual contributions and the actual level of others' contributions across different periods of the game. Many field studies show a similar pattern—for example, people's willingness to fully pay taxes is highly correlated with their beliefs about whether others are similarly complying.

Punishment

A number of recent experiments have explored the effects of introducing a costly punishment option into a repeated public goods game (cf. Fehr and Gächter 2000). This allows subjects, at a cost to themselves, to punish specific noncontributors by imposing a fine that reduces their earnings. Under this condition, a number of subjects punish noncontributors, even in the final round of the game, in which punishment cannot influence future behavior, so that punishment is clearly not a strategy that increases the punisher's expected payoff. Introduction of this option prevents the decline in contributions with repeated play that is otherwise observed. An obvious interpretation is that the punishers are reciprocators who are willing to engage in negative reciprocation, even when it is not in their self-interest to do so. In the absence of an explicit punishment option, reciprocators have no way of responding negatively to free riding except by withdrawing their contributions; when a punishment option is provided, they make use of this instead and do not reduce their contributions.

The Role of Intentions (and Available Alternatives)

I claimed above that reciprocators care, not just about the benefits they receive or expect to receive from those with whom they interact, but also care about and respond to (what they believe to be) the intentions or motivations with which others act.

As a simple illustration, consider a so-called mini-ultimatum game with the following structure: A chooses between two divisions of a ten-dollar stake between himself and B: (8, 2) and (2, 8). B then chooses between accepting this division or rejecting it, in which case both players get nothing. In this case, most As choose (8, 2) and most Bs accept this division. Now contrast this with a second mini-ultimatum game in which A chooses between (8, 2) and (5, 5). In this case, B is much more likely to reject if A chooses (8, 2). A natural interpretation is that A's choice of (8, 2) over (5, 5) is taken by B to represent a more selfish or hostile intention/motivation than a choice of (8, 2) over (2, 8) even though the payoff to B, in material terms, is the same in each case. Put slightly differently, B may think that it is unreasonable to expect that A should sacrifice his own welfare to the extent of choosing (2, 8) over (8, 2) (reciprocity doesn't demand this) but may think that it is reasonable to expect A to sacrifice to the extent of choosing (5, 5) over (8, 2)—failure to do this shows a lack of concern for B's interests and invites a negatively reciprocal response.

As another illustration, consider the following two versions of a trust game. (cf. McCabe, Rigdon, and Smith 2003).

In figure 24.1, player 1's choice of "down" is "trusting" in the sense that she foregoes a certain payoff of 20 in order to give player 2 an opportunity to choose an alternative that is better for both, but also trusting that 2 will not choose down. If 2 is a reciprocator she may choose to repay this trust by choosing 25, 25. By contrast, in figure 24.2, player 1's only choice is to move down. Thus her choice of "down" cannot communicate to 2 an intention to trust 2. As a result, in the second game, one of 2's motives to move across is removed: the motive of reciprocating the benefit or trust bestowed by player 1 in choosing "down." As the attached numbers (giving the proportion of subjects who make each choice in the two games) show, the choice of down is much more frequent in the second game. Again this makes sense if many subjects in the position of player 2 are reciprocators—they are motivated to reciprocate 1's trust or kindness in the upper game but since 1 makes no choice that exhibits a benevolent intention in the second game, in this case no such reciprocal motive becomes operative on the part of 2. Similarly, by choosing "down" in the first game, player 1 indicates that she anticipates of expects that player 2 will behave as a reciprocator or that she hopes to induce this behavior in player 2.

It is worth noting that these observed differences in behavior across the two games are not predicted by any model of the preferences of the subjects that attributes their behavior to unconditional dispositions to cooperate or benefit others,

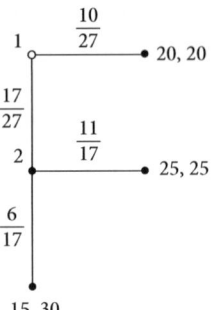

Figure 24.1

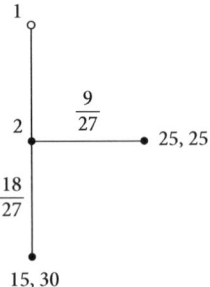

Figure 24.2

independently of their choices and behavior or their expected choice and behavior. A similar point holds for models that take subjects to care only about the outcomes (understood just in terms of material benefits) they and others receive, such as "utilitarian" models that take subjects to have preferences for maximizing the sum of benefits received for all affected. All such models predict there should be no difference in the proportion of player 2's choosing across versus down across the two games since the outcomes for both players under these two choices are the same across both games. Models that take subjects to care about reciprocity and to expect that others will wish to reciprocate when benefited do a better job of explaining behavior in these games.

24.6. Possible Forms of Reciprocity

I said above that positive reciprocity involves returning a benefit for a benefit or providing a benefit in expectation of a benefit. In order to avoid vacuity, I take it to be a necessary condition for a person to be "benefited" in a reciprocal exchange that the person receive a material benefit he or she values from a purely self-interested point of view and that this benefit results from the action of another person.[3] Even with this assumption, we still face issues both about what counts as a benefit for purposes of understanding of reciprocation and about the detailed structure of reciprocation. To illustrate the first set of issues, return to the ultimatum game in which A chooses between (8, 2) and (5, 5). If A chooses (8, 2) he provides, in one obvious sense, a benefit for B, in the sense that B (if she accepts) is better off materially than if the interaction with A had never occurred (or if B rejects). Nonetheless, B is unlikely to think that A has acted toward her in a spirit of positive reciprocity or out of an *intention* to benefit her. (From B's perspective, her receipt of 2 is an unintended side effect of a self-interested choice by A.) This assessment is reflected in the decision of many Bs to reject when offered an (8, 2) split under these circumstances.

This example and many others suggest that for the purposes of understanding reciprocity what counts as a benefit (or a "cost" or "loss") must be assessed relative to a contextually determined reference or status quo point of some kind such that changes that are favorable with respect to that reference point count as gains and unfavorable changes count as losses.[4] This reference point shifts with context, available alternatives, and other considerations in such a way that the same material outcome may or may not count as provision of a benefit or imposition of a loss.

Focusing for the sake of simplicity just on one-shot two-party interactions, suppose that 1 is considering providing a benefit $B_{12} > 0$ to 2 (where B_{12} is assessed relative to some appropriate reference point) and that it costs 1 C_1 to provide this benefit (where C_1 is also is assessed relative to some appropriate reference point). If the benefit is provided, 2 considers responding by providing benefit B_{21} to 1 at cost C_2 to 2. Suppose these are the only relevant benefits and costs from the point of view of 1 and 2.

If 2 is purely self-interested and $C_2 > 0$, she will not provide B_{21}. If 1 can anticipate this and is self-interested or a reciprocator, she will not provide B_{12}.

Putting this possibility aside, we can consider several possible models of reciprocal behavior. First (1), it might be that 1 and 2 have the following preferences: 1 wishes to provide B_{12} as long as 2 will provide B_{21} in response and 2 wishes to provide this response as long as B_{12} is provided. In this case, both 1 and 2 ignore their costs and also ignore the relative sizes of B_{12} and B_{21}. All that matters is whether there has been some mutual exchange of benefits or the expectation of this.

An alternative possibility (2) is that in addition to preferences for mutual exchange of benefits in the sense of (1), both 1 and 2 require that they "come out ahead" or "gain," taking into account both their benefits and costs, before they engage in the interaction. (Or at least they don't think of the interaction as reciprocal or motivated by preferences for reciprocation unless this condition is met.) In other words, for reciprocation, 1 requires that $B_{21} - C_1 > 0$ and 2 requires $B_{12} - C_2 > 0$, evaluated with respect to some suitable reference point. Note that is *not* the same as assuming that 1 and 2 are purely self-interested or that they act so as to maximize their self-interested payoffs. Suppose that in a sequential prisoner's dilemma, the reference point is no interaction or mutual defection. Then a second mover who cooperates when a first mover has cooperated gains with respect to this reference point, as does the first mover, although the second mover does not maximize his material payoff, which would require defection. Similarly, in the first version of the mini-trust game above, if 1 moves down, 2 "gains" by moving across, in comparison with what she would have received if 1 had moved across, although 2's move across is not a payoff-maximizing move for 2.

Yet another possibility (3) is that for reciprocal interaction not only must both parties gain in the sense of (2) but the overall gains of both must be related in some appropriate way: perhaps they must be equal $(B_{12} - C_2) = (B_{21} - C_1)$ or "proportional": $(B_{12} - C_2) = k(B_{21} - C_1)$ (a number of writers talk of reciprocators gaining "proportionately" from their interaction). Or perhaps some other requirement concerning how the gains from the reciprocal interaction are to be divided must be satisfied. For example, many Rawlsians claim that considerations of reciprocity, as applied to the basic structure, require that interactions be such that the least well off among the reciprocators be made as well off as possible.

I take (1) to be an uncontroversial requirement for positive reciprocation. The various requirements mentioned under (3) may characterize particular kinds of reciprocal interaction but it seems dubious that any of these is a requirement that must be satisfied by all cases of reciprocation. (2) strikes many as a natural assumption, as the remark from Gibbard about fair reciprocity involving the idea of "gaining" from supporting a social order perhaps illustrates, assuming that "gain" means "come out ahead overall when all of the costs and benefits of such support are considered."

I believe that while socially important instances of reciprocity that clearly violate (2) may be uncommon, there are many cases in which it is unclear whether (2) holds, at least if we employ nonquestion begging systems of accounting. In such cases, I think that we have some tendency to assume, as a default, that (2) is satisfied or at least we tend not to closely monitor whether or not it is violated. (That is, we tend to behave in this way as long as there is some exchange of benefits and no clear evidence that [2] is violated.) In other words, we tend to treat in cases in which it is unclear whether (2) holds, as cases in which it does hold (or perhaps as cases in which it does not matter whether it holds exactly) and hence as cases in which requirements of reciprocity come into play. Unequivocally determining whether (2) holds requires, among other things, a common "currency" or metric for adding up benefits and costs as well as information about the magnitudes of these, and unambiguous reference points from these may be measured and often it may be very unclear how to assess these. Suppose I help clean out your garage and you reciprocate by providing me with dinner. You benefit from my help and incur costs in producing dinner, I may incur costs in helping and receive the benefit of dinner. But how exactly do we assess the magnitudes of these? Are my "costs" in helping my opportunity costs in foregoing some alternative way of spending my afternoon? The energetic cost of working instead of loafing? Suppose that I enjoy helping you and that while working together, we have a very stimulating conversation. How do we factor this in? Your costs for dinner presumably include the costs of the raw materials, but do they also include your labor costs and if so, how are these evaluated? How do we evaluate such diffuse benefits as the mutual goodwill engendered by our interaction and its contribution to sustaining a relationship that may benefit each of us in the future in unanticipated ways? The fact that reciprocators care not only about material benefits and costs but also the intentions and attitudes that underlie these makes the notion of exact cost/benefit analysis even more problematic in this sort of case. Of course we might, in the spirit of revealed preference theory, take the very fact that we voluntarily engage in the activities described above to show that both of us gain on balance from them, since otherwise we would not engage in them. However, this obviously trivializes the requirement that for reciprocation both parties must gain from the interaction.

In light of these considerations, it is not surprising that empirical studies of reciprocal interactions involving friends and acquaintances in real-life contexts tend not to find the kinds of precise quid pro quos (or expectations of quid pro quos) that are suggested by models of reciprocity as mutual gain or equal exchange. Instead, what empirical studies (as well as ordinary experience) suggest is a much looser and vaguer pattern of accounting: Often (and particularly when there is some degree of closeness between the parties) those involved in reciprocal interactions don't even try to keep track of the precise balance of costs and benefits (both because this is difficult or impossible and because it seems contrary to the character of the relationship the reciprocating parties would like to maintain between themselves) but nonetheless are sensitive in the long run and in the aggregate to large imbalances of costs over benefits, especially insofar as these result from failures to reciprocate in situations in which reciprocation is possible. In other words, while reciprocators are typically not completely cost-insensitive in the spirit of (1), in many cases they do not closely monitor whether (2) is satisfied, withdrawing reciprocation only when violations are large and obvious. This is what I meant above in saying that the "default" is often to assume that the conditions for reciprocation are satisfied, in the absence of clear evidence for the violation of (2).

Can something similar hold for more impersonal interactions involving larger numbers of people? One relevant example is provided by anthropological studies of food distribution in groups that are a few hundred people in size. Such studies show strikingly large imbalances in food "flow" among both individuals and subgroups (cf. Kaplan et al. 2000). In particular, young and middle-aged males generate many more calories from hunting and other activities than they consume, with the surplus going to women, children, and the elderly. Moreover, there are large differences in hunting and food gathering skill among men in this age group, so that they generate differing amounts of food resources. In addition, there is considerable variation in food consumption across families, with some having more dependents than others.

Do successful hunters gain from this arrangement, despite the caloric transfer? One possibility is that they receive other benefits besides food such as increased mating opportunities and a consequent overall gain in fitness. However, it has been difficult to establish that such benefits are present in sufficient magnitude to offset the fitness costs associated with hunting and food sharing—another illustration of the difficulties facing treatments of reciprocity that demand precise systems of accounting of costs and benefits. Of course, one might postulate still more diffuse benefits such as increased prestige and goodwill for successful hunters, and contend that when these are taken into account the sharer's benefits will exceed his costs, but in the absence of any way of quantifying the benefits the claim that they outweigh the costs seems ad hoc.[5]

In the remainder of this chapter, I focus mainly on the form of reciprocity represented by (2) (and to a lesser extent [3]), bearing in mind that exact assessments of gain may be very difficult. On either understanding of reciprocity, the empirical evidence outlined above supports the claim that a substantial number of people have preferences for reciprocity that are distinct both from purely self-interested preferences and from unconditionally altruistic preferences. Moreover, this evidence also supports the claim that we need to take account of these preferences in order to design stable rules and institutions governing cooperation. If, for example, the rules and institutions allow self-interested people to free ride on the cooperative behavior of reciprocators, the latter will withdraw cooperation, with the result that cooperative schemes will unravel.

24.7. SOME NORMATIVE CONSEQUENCES

I turn next to an exploration of some of the normative implications of the empirical results described above.

24.7.1. The Scope of Reciprocity

My first observation concerns the *scope* of the notion of reciprocity. One of the most common objections to accounts of justice based on reciprocity is that these are unable to account for the obligations of the able-bodied to provide aid to those who are unable to reciprocate. For example, Alan Buchanan characterizes justice as reciprocity as the view that "an individual has a right to a share of social resources (or moral rights of any kind) only if that individual contributes or at least can contribute to the cooperative surplus" (1990, 228).

On this interpretation, reciprocity-based considerations constitute the whole of justice: There are no requirements of justice (or perhaps of morality more generally) except those based on reciprocity.[6] Of course, normative theorists are free to stipulate what they mean by justice as reciprocity, and Buchanan is simply describing an account of justice that he takes to be influential and which he wishes to criticize. However, despite what some normative theorists may suppose, I doubt many actual reciprocators hold this view of reciprocity. What the empirical results surveyed above show is that considerations of reciprocity play a role in motivating behavior that is independent of considerations of self-interest and unconditional altruism. However, it is not true that people are willing to provide benefits (even at a cost to themselves) only to people who have benefited them or are capable of doing so. For example, in the trust game described in figure 24.2, one third of players in the second mover position choose across, benefiting player 1 at a cost to themselves, although in doing so they are not motivated by reciprocation. Empirical results from many other games as well as casual observation support the claim that many people will choose to confer benefits on others, even when there is no prospect of reciprocity. Thus, when we consider how people think about the significance of reciprocity, it seems, as an empirical matter, unlikely that most suppose that considerations internal to the notion of reciprocity mandate not helping others whenever those others are unable to reciprocate. Someone who fails to save a drowning child when he could easily do so, on the grounds that the child is unlikely to reciprocate his help, is not likely to be regarded as someone who shows a proper regard for the significance of reciprocity in moral decision-making. A more empirically plausible picture of how many people (including reciprocators) actually think is that in such situations considerations of reciprocity provide no reason for help but that other motives and considerations, not based on reciprocity, come into play. We may add that presumably most reciprocators will distinguish cases in which someone is in need of aid and reciprocity is not possible from cases in which aid is needed and the needy person is able to reciprocate but does not do so. Nonreciprocity-based motives for helping are likely to be stronger in the former case.

24.7.2. JI and JR Compared

One of the most salient consequences of justice as impartiality (as this is understood by Barry and many others) is that we may have obligations of justice to aid in circumstances in which aid is not only not in our interest but in which we are not and will not be involved in any ongoing scheme of reciprocation with those aided.

Consider an example, originally due to Nozick (1974), and also discussed by Barry (1989) and Gibbard (1991). Two groups of people exist on two separate islands, one group being wealthy and the other needy (or at least considerably poorer). There is no prior interaction or pattern of reciprocation between the two groups until the wealthy group one day discovers the existence of the poorer group. Suppose that the wealthy group can aid the poorer group but, for whatever reason (perhaps because of technological difficulties or because they lack the resources), the poorer group can do nothing to reciprocate this help. With Barry, I interpret JI as generating at least a prima facie reason to aid. By contrast, JMA generates no reason to aid. According to JR (as I interpret it) there is also no reciprocity-based reason to aid. This is not to say, as emphasized above, that there are no reasons grounded in justice to aid, but rather that to the extent these reasons exist, they must be based on some other set of considerations besides reciprocity. From the point of view of JR, this case is thus importantly different from a case in which the wealthier group is engaged in an ongoing scheme of cooperation/reciprocation with the poorer group. In this second case, the wealthier group has a motive to help that is not present in the original case. A similar point holds if there are people on the wealthier island who are in need of aid and who are part of an ongoing scheme of reciprocation with the others living on that island—JR generates a reason to aid them which does not apply to those living on the poorer island (again, assuming the absence of any on-going scheme of reciprocation between the two islands), even if they are worse off than the poor on the wealthier island. (This bears on the different implications of JR and JI in international contexts; see section 24.7.4.)

In the case considered above, those on the poorer island are not capable of re-ciprocation. Contrast this with a case in which there are ongoing interactions between two groups: those in the second group are in need of aid, those in the first group are able to help, and those in the second group are able to reciprocate in some relevant fashion but fail to do so and instead act (or previously have acted) in ways contrary to ideals of reciprocation—perhaps in the past they have failed to share resources with the first group when the latter were needy, perhaps when aided they continue to treat the first group in ways that are damaging to its interests, perhaps they squander the aid and then ask for more, or perhaps they simply say to the first group, "We welcome your aid, but understand that if the tables were turned, we would never help you." As I interpret JR, such nonreciprocal behavior by the second group removes or at least greatly diminishes one set of reasons (those grounded in reciprocity) for helping them. By contrast (on one natural interpretation), JI provides reasons to aid those in need, even if they behave nonreciprocally.

24.7.3. Contributions When Others Behave Nonideally

We can explore this feature of JR in more detail by comparing its recommendations about contributions in public goods games with the recommendations of other nor-mative theories. Murphy (1993) claims, roughly, that one has a duty to maximize well-being but subject to constraint that one is required to do no more than what one's fair (proportionate) share would be if all others were complying with this duty. Thus, "in situations of partial compliance . . . the sacrifice each agent is required to make is limited to the level of sacrifice that would be optimal if the situation were one of full compliance" (280). Applied to a repeated public goods game, this pre-sumably implies that one should determine what one's share of the total contribu-tion would be if all were contributing such that total contributions were optimal and then contribute that amount. One's contribution thus should be *independent* of what others are in fact contributing.

Arneson (2004) objects to Murphy on utilitarian grounds—given utilitarianism and other assumptions Arneson finds plausible, one should contribute more if others are contributing less since the less others contribute, the greater the shortfall from what is ideal from a utilitarian point of view. Thus, in contrast to Murphy's view, Arneson holds that in such circumstances, justice requires that your contribu-tions should be *negatively correlated* with total contributions by others.

As I interpret JR, it suggests instead that in a repeated public goods game your contribution should be *positively correlated* with the contributions of others (insofar of course as additional contributions add more than they cost to the value of the public good, as will be the case in a linear public goods game in which there are constant returns to scale, and perhaps insofar as certain other conditions are met).[7]

In other words, you should contribute more as others are also willing to contribute more. As noted above, this, rather than the behavior recommended by Murphy or Arneson, is the pattern that is seen empirically in many interactions involving the provision of public goods. JR is also naturally interpreted as making additional recommendations. These are that in cases in which the level of contribution to public goods is low, rules and institutions should be introduced that make it easier for positive reciprocity to flourish: these may include the introduction of sanctions against noncontributors, institutional changes that allow those who are willing to reciprocate to interact preferentially with one another and exclude free riders, and so on. Those who take JR seriously as a normative theory are likely to think that changes of this sort are likely to be more effective in providing public goods than exhortations to contribute more as others contribute less.[8]

24.7.4. The Welfare State

Both philosophers and nonphilosophers frequently claim that the modern welfare state is based (largely or entirely) on reciprocity. One finds this idea, for example, both in Rawls and in many commentators who make use of Rawlsian ideas, particularly in the context of issues about obligations of justice that extend across national borders. In particular, a number of writers (e.g., Sangiovani 2007) appeal to the following complex of ideas: (i) people living in a single nation state may be involved in relationships of reciprocity with one another that they do not have with at least some people living outside their national borders, (ii) considerations of reciprocity can generate demands of justice that are distinct from the demands generated by other kinds of moral considerations—distinct, for example, from whatever obligations we may have to aid others in need independently of whether we have relationships of reciprocity with them, (iii) because of (i) and (ii) there may be more stringent requirements of distributive justice governing relations among people within a country than those governing relations among people in different countries. In particular, it is suggested that (iv) considerations of reciprocity may support application of the Rawlsian difference principle within countries but this principle may not apply between countries.

Provided that a suitable set of grounds can be provided for (i), the inference to (iii) seems fully in keeping with the conception of justice as reciprocity explored in this chapter. Or, to turn the matter around, to the extent that (iii) strikes many people as intuitively plausible (as it apparently does), this probably reflects, at least in part, a commitment to the idea that considerations of reciprocity can generate requirements of justice that are distinct from those generated by JI and JMA. However, in connection with (iv), although the matter deserves more discussion than I can give it here, it seems unlikely that the bare notion of reciprocity (or the general idea that relationships should be governed by norms of reciprocity) in itself can generate anything as specific as the difference principle. This is because, as we have seen, what specifically counts as appropriate reciprocation in a given situation depends on contextually established reference points, which rules and institutions are in place, a choice of metrics for comparing benefits, and so on. The difference principle perhaps implements *one* particular version of reciprocity, but as an empirical matter, it seems implausible that all interactions that reasonably can be regarded as reciprocal must conform to this principle. Of course this doesn't rule out the possibility that there may be some *other* nonreciprocity-based argument that uniquely singles out the difference principle as the correct principle governing certain distributive justice problems.[9]

Finally, on what bases might one argue for (i)? It is clear enough how those aided by various state programs benefit from these arrangements, but what about those who are well off and who may seem to pay more in taxes than they receive in benefits? The usual responses appeal to several considerations. First, the well off benefit from institutions and infrastructure that makes possible their success and these are either directly state-supported or else maintained and regulated by substantial state activity: they include a functioning legal and financial system, an educational system, a military that provides for external defense, physical infrastructure like roads and bridges, and so on. Fellow countrymen contribute to these through taxes and other forms of direct participation—they provide police, teachers, employees, and so on, and this is enough to establish an obligation to reciprocate on the part of the better off. Second, it is sometimes suggested (e.g., Gibbard 1991) that the well off also benefit from the willingness of others to not appropriate their goods or to harm them. Of these two sets of considerations, the first strikes me as more a more plausible basis for claims that the better off owe (or are likely to be motivated by) obligations of reciprocity. Here (as in the food-sharing example discussed earlier) the flexibility of the notion of "benefit" works to the advantage of such claims as does the difficulty, particularly in cases of interactions with diffuse benefits, of ruling out the possibility that all participants have gained, in some way relevant to establishing relations of reciprocity. The second set of considerations may also play an important role in the willingness of the well off to support welfare schemes, but it seems to appeal to the self-interest of the well off rather than to their motivations to reciprocate. "Give me your food or I will take it (or hurt you)" can be a perfectly justifiable threat in the right circumstances but if someone complies only because it seems too costly to resist, it is hard to see him as moved by considerations of reciprocity.

24.8. FURTHER DEFENSE AND CONCLUSION

I expect that the response of many normative to the ideas presented above will be this: Although significant numbers of people may behave as though they are guided by JR, *they shouldn't be*. It will be said that JR concedes too much to human frailty; people may be more inclined to help those to whom they stand in reciprocal relationships than those to whom they are not so related, but they should overcome this inclination; they should contribute to those in need just because they are in need, independently of whether they reciprocate.

Fully evaluating these claims would require discussion of foundational issues in moral and political philosophy that are far beyond the scope of this chapter. So in response I will confine myself to just a few observations.

The first thing to say is that JR embodies a recognizable and apparently coherent ideal of justice that is fairly widely shared (although, as we have also emphasized, not everyone holds this view and, even among those who hold it, it is not regarded as the whole of justice). People do care (in a noninstrumental way and not because of obvious mistakes about matters of fact) about reciprocity and it is unclear that there are any nonquestion-begging grounds on which it might be shown that they are mistaken in doing so. Of course it is might be contended in response that JR is a second best concession to human motivational limitations, with something more like JI capturing the "correct" underlying foundation for all truly fundamental considerations bearing on justice. However, we do live in a world in which large numbers of people seem to behave either in a self-interested way or as reciprocators—this fact has probably played a large role in shaping "our" conception of justice, insofar as there is such a thing, leading us to accord considerable importance to the considerations associated with JR. That we might have had a very different way of thinking about justice, centered only on JI, if human beings behaved quite differently (and human frailty wasn't such a problem) does not by itself undermine the claim that in our actual circumstances JR captures important elements of what people care about when they think about justice. To this we may also add the considerations having to do with stability introduced at the beginning of this chapter: someone who makes normative recommendations based just on JI and who regards it as morally irrelevant that in many circumstances many people are conditional cooperators is likely to produce recommendations (and rules and institutions) that are unstable and lead to undesirable outcomes, by any reasonable metric of evaluation.

To flesh out this last point, consider a feature of JR that is implicit in my discussion above but which so far has received relatively little emphasis. This is that JR (and people motivated by JR) are relatively less exploitable (by self-interested types among others) than JI (and people motivated by it)—this is presumably one reason why, at least in many circumstances, many more people seem to have preferences corresponding to JR than to JI. As an illustration, suppose that someone follows Arneson's recommendation to contribute more as others contribute less. The result will be that that the resources of those who free ride increase and those who contribute diminish. To the extent that the resources of those inclined to contribute are depleted, this will often be undesirable. In addition, to the extent that people's motivations are malleable and change with experience, and that people can learn to become more self-interested, this recommendation is likely to lead to more free riding, as undecided types observe free riders prospering at the expense of altruists. More generally, although a disposition to unconditional altruism may seem morally admirable in the abstract, we should realize that it can encourage the flourishing of selfish or exploitive behavior on the part of others—in effect it subsidizes such behavior. By contrast, because reciprocators condition their behavior on the behavior of those that they interact with, they automatically provide incentives to others not to engage in exploitive behavior. Indeed, under the right conditions, their presence can provide incentives for selfish types to behave in reciprocal ways, so that they can earn the benefits of interaction with reciprocators. Of course in a world characterized by ideal theory in which there is full or near full compliance with whatever morality requires none of this would matter, since we in effect assume away the existence of exploitive types. But in the real world, as it is, such types are present (in fact, common) and moral and political rules need to be designed with this fact in mind. As I see it, one of the larger normative lessons of the empirical observations in this chapter about the heterogeneity of human motivation, and the presence of both self-interested types and reciprocators in real human population, is that it indicates the need to move away from the current emphasis in political theory on what happens in ideal circumstances in which there is full compliance with normative recommendations. Instead, we need to think about which rules and institutions work best for human beings as they are or (realistically) might become.

NOTES

1. Obviously this formulation is indeterminate in important ways. At one extreme, perhaps most people will agree that it is a deficiency in a normative theory if it requires people to act or be motivated in ways that are literally impossible for them ("ought" implies "can"). At the other extreme, any plausible normative theory will require that people sometimes have obligations to do things that they don't want to do or find it difficult to do. Those who take stability seriously as a normative constraint want to avoid assuming, unrealistically, that people will always act as angels, but they should also avoid setting their sights too low, never requiring that people act any differently than they are presently inclined to act. Unfortunately, I have nothing general to say about where the happy medium between these two extremes lies or about (so to speak) exactly how much stability requires us to concede to human frailty. This will depend (somehow) on the details of specific cases. But our inability to say much that is both general and precise about this is not a good reason for simply ignoring the relevance of motivational considerations in normative theorizing.

2. Of course it is an empirical question to what extent subjects who are positive reciprocators are also like to behave as negative reciprocators, in the sense of being willing to incur costs to impose costs on noncooperators. Fehr and Gächter (2000) report evidence that many of the same subjects who are positive reciprocators in their experiments are also negative reciprocators. Charles Plott (2005) claims that in many experiments these two groups are largely distinct.

3. If it is assumed that whenever I provide a material benefit to someone that person provides me with a nonmaterial benefit in the form of a warm glow or some other psychological good that I derive from acting altruistically, all actions benefiting others threaten to become cases of reciprocity.

4. The role played by reference points in measuring gains and losses is emphasized in a number of theories of individual decision-making including prospect theory (cf. Kahneman and Tversky 1979). It is also emphasized by Matthew Rabin, among others, in connection with the structure of social preferences and preferences concerning "fairness" (see Rabin 1993).

5. Another consideration, also illustrating the unclarity of the notion of mutual gain in this sort of context, concerns the choice of reference point and assumptions about feasible alternatives. If the status quo from which the food-sharing hunter's gains are measured is nonparticipation in his group (the group will oust him if he does not share) then he clearly gains from sharing. If the relevant reference point is that he keeps more calories for himself and his immediate offspring, the calculation may come out differently.

6. The interpretation also seems to assume the "net gain" conception of reciprocity (2). It is also worth noting that, quite apart from the question of whether reciprocity constitutes the whole of justice, Buchanan's formulation does not closely track the notion of reciprocity discussed in this chapter. According to that conception, relations of reciprocity are in place among those who do in fact contribute when others contribute. If others "can" contribute but don't, then, as far as reciprocity goes, they are not owed anything. Being able to contribute does not in itself generate rights to resources.

7. The anonymous referee points out that many public goods exhibit diminishing returns to scale beyond some point. One might think that well before the point at which additional contributions are wealth-destroying, people who are motivated by considerations of reciprocation may reasonably decide that they have contributed enough (and enough of the public good has been created), regardless of what others are doing. If, to use the referee's example, a total of $10 million is enough to build a safe, sturdy bridge and an additional $10 million would turn it into an architectural masterpiece, then even if this additional amount adds value to the bridge, one might think that one is not required to continue to contribute once the $10 million threshold is reached, even if some others continue to contribute.

8. Rule utilitarianism is often formulated as an ideal theory that builds in assumptions about universal compliance: The best rules are those that if followed by everyone would produce optimal consequences. Obviously such rules may not be best in more realistic circumstances in which there is far from universal compliance: Even if it is true that following the requirements of JI would produce optimal results if everyone were to do so, following these requirements may not produce optimal results in circumstances in which many people are SIs. One might imagine, however, a more tempered or realistic formulation of rule utilitarianism: The best rules are those whose promulgation and enforcement would produce optimal consequences, given the actual motivations and behavior of those subject to the rules (which may involve significant noncompliance, attempted noncompliance, responses to noncompliance, etc.). It is arguable that JR performs better than JI when assessed according to this criterion for the reasons given above in the text. As the anonymous referee has pointed out to me, JR also does well when assessed according to a publicity criterion. If everyone knew the actual distribution of motivations to comply with various conceptions of justice (how many people are SIs, Rs, and compliers with JI), more might favor JR than favor JI.

9. I will add, though, that there seems to be some tension between the use of reciprocity-based considerations to delimit the populations to which the difference principle applies and the principle itself, which seems largely motivated by luck egalitarian ideals rather than anything specifically having to do with reciprocity.

REFERENCES

Ahn, T., E. Ostrom, and J. Walker. 2003. "Heterogeneous Preferences and Collective Action." *Public Choice* 117: 295–315.

Andreoni, J. 1988. "Why Free Ride? Strategies and Learning in Public Goods Experiments." *Journal of Public Economics* 37: 291–304.

Arneson, R. 2004. "Moral Limits on the Demands of Beneficence?" In *The Ethics of Assistance: Morality, Affluence, and the Distant Needy*, D. Chatterjee, ed., 33–58. Cambridge: Cambridge University Press.

Barry, B. 1989. *Theories of Justice: A Treatise on Social Justice*, Volume 1. Berkeley: University of California Press.

Binmore, K. *Fun and Games.* 1992. Lexington, MA: D. C. Heath.

Buchanan, A. 1990. "Justice as Reciprocity Versus Subject-Centered Justice." *Philosophy & Public Affairs* 19 (3):227–25.

Croson, R. 2007. "Theories of Altruism and Reciprocity: Evidence from Linear Public Goods Games." *Economic Inquiry* 45: 199–216.

Ehrhart, K.-M., and C. Keser. 1999. "Mobility and Cooperation: On the Run." Working Paper 99s-24. Montreal: Centre Interuniversitaire de Recherche en Analyse des Organisations.

Fehr, E., and S. Gachter. 2000. "Cooperation and Punishment in Public Goods Experiments." *American Economic Review* 90: 980–94.

Fehr, E., U. Fischbacher, and S. Gachter. 2002. "Strong Reciprocity, Human Cooperation, and the Enforcement of Social Norms." *Human Nature* 13: 1–25.

Gibbard, A. 1991. "Constructing Justice." *Philosophy and Public Affairs* 20: 264–79.

Gunnthorsdottir, A., K. McCabe, and D. Houser. 2007. "Disposition, History, and Public Goods Experiments." *Journal of Economic Behavior & Organization* 62: 304–15.

Kahneman, D., and A. Tversky. 1979. "Prospect Theory: An Analysis of Decision under Risk." *Econometrica* 47: 263–91.

Kaplan, H., J. Hill, J. Lancaster, and A. Hurtado. 2000. "A Theory of Human Life History Evolution: Diet, Intelligence, and Longevity." *Evolutionary Anthropology* 9: 156–85

McCabe, K., M. Rigdon, and V. Smith. 2003. "Positive Reciprocity and Intentions in Trust Games." *Journal of Economic Behavior and Organizations* 52: 267–75.

Murphy L. 1993 "The Demands of Beneficence." *Philosophy and Public Affairs* 22: 267–92.

Nozick, R. 1974. *Anarchy, State, and Utopia.* New York: Basic Books.

Ostrom, E. 2005. *Understanding Institutional Diversity.* Princeton, NJ: Princeton University Press.

Page, T., L. Putterman, and B. Unel. 2005 "Voluntary Association in Public Goods Experiments: Reciprocity, Mimicry and Efficiency." *The Economic Journal* 115: 1032–53.

Plott, C. 2005. Personal communication.

Rabin, M. 1993. "Incorporating Fairness into Game Theory and Economics." *The American Economic Review* 83: 1281–302.

Rawls, J. 1971. *A Theory of Justice.* Cambridge, MA: Harvard University Press

Sangiovani, A. 2007. "Global Justice, Reciprocity, and the State." *Philosophy & Public Affairs* 35: 2–39.

CHAPTER 25

....

EVALUATING
SOCIAL POLICY

....

DANIEL M. HAUSMAN

PUBLIC policies serve many objectives. They aim to protect people's rights and to enhance their freedoms and opportunities. They aim to relieve suffering and to promote the general welfare. They seek to preserve natural resources and historical monuments. They aim to secure just terms of cooperation, constrained by requirements of equality before the law and protections for minorities. They aim to promote health, culture, education, and human excellence. This partial list is heterogeneous, and it difficult to see what principles should govern trade-offs between these different objectives. One way to simplify the task would be to prioritize a single objective. So, for example, some libertarians would maintain that the protection of liberties is the sole ultimate aim of government. The other concerns are instrumental toward protecting freedom or are not important as social objectives, or they are better secured by individual action than via public policy. Another way to simplify the task is consequentialist: One needs to find some common currency in which the value of competing policies can be measured. A third, less systematic alternative makes do with a variety of priority principles of limited scope with deliberative processes responsible for shaping the principles and adjudicating conflicts among the principles.

A good deal of consequentialist assessment can, of course, find a place within less systematic approaches that employ a variety of principles. Such is, I take it, the actual state of affairs. A further feature of actual policymaking is that it is segmented into different departments, such as health policy, educational policy, environmental policy, transportation policy, criminal law, and so forth. This segmenting has serious drawbacks, since the effects of policies do not respect the boundaries between government departments. Health policies affect educational outcomes, and education policies, like environmental policies, transportation policies, and criminal law, affect population health. But dividing up the monitoring and execution of policies into departments is unavoidable. This division of policy creates a division in the evaluation of policy. One needs to determine both how to evaluate policies and distribute resources within some department of government and how to distribute resources across departments of government. In this chapter I shall be concerned with the role of quantitative and consequentialist considerations in the evaluation of policies *within* departments of government.

Consequentialist appraisals of policies of some particular kind, whether they are transportation or education policies, are typically constrained by nonconsequentialist commitments, often concerning fairness or justice. In addition, these consequentialist appraisals are typically *narrow*—that is, devoted to promoting some one among an array of goods which are not all compatible. Let us call consequentialism of this sort— narrow and constrained consequentialism—*restricted consequentialism*. Restricted consequentialism sits uneasily within a pluralist approach to policy evaluation, always threatening to enlarge its role and swamp competing considerations. How does one adjudicate between, on the one hand, net benefits estimated by economists in dollars and cents and, on the other hand, an increase in inequality, a loss of freedom, or the curtailment of a right? Numbers seem to be hard facts, unlike unquantifiable benefits and losses, and for this reason they may have an exaggerated influence. Yet regardless of one's attitude toward utilitarianism or cost-benefit analysis, quantitative considerations are of obvious importance. It matters to policy how many people are affected and the magnitudes of the effects.

This chapter focuses on the difficulties of within-department consequentialist policy evaluation itself, in the realistic case in which it is subsumed in a pluralist method of evaluation. Studying these difficulties seems to me a valuable task regardless of one's philosophical predilections, because a great deal of policy evaluation relies in fact on restricted consequentialism, and it is hard to envision any alternative.

Restricted consequentialism specifies only a *structure* of policy evaluation. It says that a policy is acceptable (other things being equal) if and only if no alternative results in better consequences and that a policy is required (other things being equal) if and only if its consequences are better than any alternatives. To put some flesh on this structural skeleton, one needs to specify what it is for consequences to be better or worse. Ideally, there is a single quantifiable value so that in principle it is possible to compare the consequences of policies both within and across departments and perhaps even to drop the other things being equal qualification. Even if one were committed to evaluating consequences in terms of some single quantifiable variable, comparisons of policies themselves would still be limited by uncertainty about what the consequences of policies will be. So, for example, classical utilitarianism combines a consequentialist structure with the view that the sole good is happiness, which most utilitarians (unlike Mill) took to be measurable on a single scale. Classical utilitarian policy aims to maximize happiness. Uncertainty makes this difficult to do, and utilitarians such as Mill urged reliance on intermediate principles, such as his principle of liberty, to operationalize the task.

If there are multiple values that cannot be located on a single scale, then the values of consequences will not always be comparable, and, even if there were no uncertainty, restricted consequentialism might not be able to compare some policies. If one were, like Bentham, Mill, and Sidgwick, attempting to defend a general theory of what is right and wrong, then such failures of comparability would be intolerable, but if one is instead seeking practical assistance in evaluating policies, all help is appreciated. Being able to make some comparisons is better than being able to make none at all. For example, if personal security is a good thing—as it surely is—and two policies differ only in the extent to which they enhance personal security, then one can compare those policies, whether or not one is able to evaluate or compare any other policies.

So for the purposes of guiding policy, consequentialists need not be committed to a unitary theory of what is intrinsically or ultimately good. Though an account of value that renders all consequences quantitatively comparable would be extremely convenient, much less can be useful. When one turns to practice, there is, however, a further requirement. To make restricted consequentialism not only contentful but also applicable, one needs to specify both what counts as better or worse and how one can find out whether consequences of policies are better or worse. If one is comparing policies on the basis of their consequences with respect to some value, one needs some way of measuring that value. Without some way to measure the value of the results of policies, consequentialism, whether restricted or not, is of no practical use.

25.1. RESTRICTED CONSEQUENTIALIST HEALTH POLICY

An extended example will help clarify the issues I am concerned with. One important good is health. Unless one holds a view like the libertarians, whereby only some specific good such as freedom bears on government policy, it would appear that promoting and protecting health is a legitimate concern of government. Every modern government has a department of health. Health obviously contributes to well-being, so welfarists will be concerned with health. But, as Norman Daniels in particular has argued (1985, 2007), health also bears crucially on opportunity. So liberals, who believe that individuals are responsible for their own welfare and that government is responsible only for creating an environment in which individuals can successfully pursue what matters to them, should also defend a role for government in securing individual health.

From a policy perspective, it does not matter whether health is an intrinsic as well as an instrumental good. All that matters is that health is a sufficiently significant good that some division of government is charged with the task of protecting and promoting it. Although the details concerning the provision of health care and the implementation of public health policies may vary greatly, the achievements of modern medicine oblige all governments to take steps to protect public health through policies concerning nutrition, sanitation, control of infectious diseases, lifestyle choices, and, to the extent that it is affordable, individual health care. Within a set of financial and ethical constraints, which are often binding, the health sector has the job of protecting and promoting health.

Although I shall devote a good deal of this chapter to the example of health policy, analogous claims can be made about other areas of government responsibility such as education, security, or transportation. In each case there is a sufficiently important and general good at stake to justify establishing a separate division in government devoted to its protection and promotion. In each case policy is heavily influenced by restricted consequentialist considerations concerning how to maximize the goods with which the particular division of government is concerned, but other ethical concerns always constrain consequentialist maximizing ambitions. None of the goods with which these branches of government are concerned is purely intrinsic, and it is questionable whether any is ultimate.

In order for restricted consequentialist calculations concerning how to maximize some particular good to help guide policy, the particular good or goods with which a branch of government is concerned must be measurable. To charge the health sector with the task of protecting and promoting health is meaningless if there is no way to measure health. Some very imperfect measures are readily available. Infant mortality and longevity tell us a good deal about maternal health and the incidence of fatal ailments and accidents. But many health conditions, such as migraine headaches or schizophrenia, clearly diminish health, despite having little effect on longevity. In nations that have conquered destitution and infectious diseases, the most important controllable influences on health may bear more heavily on morbidity than on mortality. So a measure of population health that is not based exclusively on mortality data is needed.

It is possible to do health policy without a measure of population health, though it is not possible to do it well. One can address specific health problems such as flu pandemics. One can promote vaccinations that prevent serious and widespread diseases. One can combat health threats such as obesity. But there are always opportunity costs—that is, other things that the resources could have been used for. If one wants guidance on how to prioritize interventions with respect to different health problems, one needs some measure of the comparative health benefits the different health interventions provide. In order for restricted consequentialism to guide the allocation of health-related resources, one needs some measure of health.

25.2. Measuring and Valuing Population Health

Let us assume that population health is the sum or average of the health of the individuals in the population. Consequently, though there may be aggregate indicators, it seems that to measure population health, one needs measures of overall individual

health. Moreover, to make measurement feasible, one will need some common measuring rod that applies to everyone in a specified population or subpopulation. One
common way to simplify the task of generating a *generic* health measure (that is, a
measure of overall health, as opposed to a specific health measure, such as a measure
of kidney function or emotional stability) is to suppose that health is a time integral of
instantaneous health states. If two individuals are in full health during some year, apart
from an episode of back pain, the healthier individual is the one whose back pain is
milder or briefer. So, for example, the measure of Ann's health in the decade between
2000 and 2009 consists of the sum of the measures of the health states she has been in
during the decade, each multiplied by the length of time she occupied those health
states. If $h_1, h_2, \ldots, h_n$ are quantities measuring the health of the n health states that
Ann occupied during the decade, and $t_1, t_2, \ldots, t_n$ are the quantities of time she spent
in each of the n health states she occupied during the decade, then Ann's health in the
decade 2000–2009 would be $h_1 t_1 + h_2 t_2 + \ldots + h_n t_n$. If h_i is the "quality adjustment" for
health state *i*, with full health having a quality "adjustment" of one and death counting
as zero, and time is expressed in years, then $h_1 t_1 + h_2 t_2 + \ldots + h_n t_n$ consists of the
number of quality-adjusted life years (QALYs) Ann enjoyed in that decade. If Ann
were fully healthy during the whole period, she would have had ten quality-adjusted
life years. Depending on what sort of diminished health states Ann occupied and how
long she occupied them, the number of QALYs might be appreciably less than ten. On
this way of thinking about health, diseases imply trajectories through health states.
Though this way of understanding health implies that someone with a fatal disease
who currently has no symptoms is in an excellent health state (which sounds absurd),
their dire condition can be expressed by the expected trajectory of their health states.

One well-known problem with this way of proceeding is that it assumes, falsely,
that the severity of a health state is independent of how long someone is in it. On
this view, a migraine headache that lasts for one minute is exactly one-sixtieth as
bad as a migraine headache that lasts for an hour. Clearly the interactions between
time and diminished health are more complicated, but one has to start somewhere,
and one might hope that this false assumption will not seriously bias the resulting
measures of health states.

In this way, the problem of measuring health is reduced to the problem of
measuring *health states*, where health states are individuated symptomatically or
phenomenologically in terms of features such as pain and functional limitations.
Serious difficulties remain. Since health states differ across many different dimensions, it is questionable whether any scalar (that is, one-dimensional) measure of
overall health is well defined. Does it make sense to say that someone who has
chronic moderate back pain is healthier (or less healthy) than someone who is
pain free but has difficulty walking? What most commentators have concluded
(although there are some prominent dissenters[1]) is that the comparison of health
states is a comparison of the *value* of health states—of what *matters* about health
states—not a comparison of the quantity of health itself.

Let us retrace our steps. Health, like education or transportation, is an important good, the possession of which depends on social policy. From both a welfarist

and a liberal perspective, government has an obligation to protect and to promote the health of citizens. To employ a restricted consequentialist health policy, it is necessary to measure health and hence to quantify health states. But because health is multidimensional,[2] health states cannot in general be compared in terms of the quantity of health they contain. To compare health states requires instead that they be valued. So it will not do to say simply that health is a good and that the promotion of health requires a measure of health. On the contrary, it is necessary to say what kind of a good health is so that its value can be measured.

The utilitarian, or the quasi-utilitarian economist is waiting in the wings. One tempting thought is that what really matters about health is its bearing on individual well-being. The right way to compare health states that differ across different health dimensions is thus to compare how well off individuals are who occupy those diminished health states. Moderate back pain is worse than needing a cane to walk if and only if individuals with moderate back pain are on average worse off than individuals who need a cane to walk. As John Broome has argued, health states should be evaluated so as "to measure how good a person's health is for the person, or how bad her ill-health. . . . That is to say, it aims to measure the contribution of health to well-being" (2002, 94). Even if one has no sympathy for utilitarianism, this proposal seems sensible. Why should policy be concerned about health apart from its consequences for an individual's well-being?

Yet the proposal has a serious technical problem, which reflects the general difficulty of preventing restricted consequentialist appraisals from collapsing into utilitarianism. The problem is that the effects of diminished health on well-being are not separable from the effects of other factors. Though moderate back pain may diminish well-being by much the same amount regardless of wealth or family situation, this is not the case for health deficiencies such as partial paralysis, whose consequences will vary considerably depending on whether one can afford a car or servants or whether one has family to help one with everyday chores. One could pick as a reference point from which to measure the effects of health states on well-being some average set of values for the other variables that interact with health in producing well-being, but the choice would appear to be largely arbitrary, and any choice would bias the measure for or against particular health deficiencies whose effects on well-being are variably sensitive to different nonhealth variables.

Broome concludes that this problem of separability undermines the whole idea of assessing health policies with respect to their bearing on well-being due to health. In his view, the only defensible alternative is to assess policies directly in terms of their consequences for overall well-being. Although this approach need not suffer a complete collapse into utilitarianism, if it continues to register a separate concern for fairness, we're clearly on our way toward utilitarianism.

Another alternative endorsed by Dan Brock among others (2002) is just to live with the imperfections in measurements of the value of health (in terms of the consequences of health for well-being). These will be significant, but policy evaluation is not an exact science. It is an empirical question whether inseparability is such a large problem in practice that sensible rough-and-ready evaluations of health states in terms of their consequences for well-being are not possible. Most health economists have in effect bet that the errors will be not be unacceptably large, because almost all of the prevailing methods of health state evaluation are arguably implicitly committed to evaluating health states by their consequences for well-being.

This claim might be questioned, since most health-state evaluations depend on the elicitation of *preferences* among health states rather than an explicit consideration of the relations between health states and well-being. But most economists identify well-being and preference satisfaction or take preference satisfaction as conclusive evidence of well-being. Although, in fact, satisfying my preferences need not enhance my well-being, when my preferences are not self-interested or are based on false beliefs, these issues are of little salience to economists (Hausman and McPherson 2006, chapter 8, 2009). In measuring preferences among health states, health economists take themselves to be measuring the bearing of health states on well-being.

25.3. WHY EVALUATE CONSEQUENCES BY MEASURING PREFERENCES?

Since virtually all health-state evaluation rests on preferences, one would assume that there must be strong reasons for proceeding in this way. I shall consider and criticize five arguments in defense of evaluating health states by measuring people's preferences among health states.[3] None of these arguments relies on anything peculiar to health, and all can be adapted to argue for relying on preferences in other applications of restricted consequentialism.

1. (*Well-being proxy*) Preferences constitute or provide evidence concerning well-being, and what matters about consequences is their bearing on well-being.
2. (*Legitimacy*) Deriving values ("quality adjustments") from preferences gives those quantities legitimacy.
3. (*Popular sovereignty*) Evaluating outcomes by measuring preferences permits these values to depend on the views of the target population.
4. (*Feasibility*) The only nonarbitrary and feasible way of determining the value of outcomes is to measure preferences.
5. (*Preference determination*) In measuring preferences among outcomes or states of affairs, economists are measuring what determines their value.

We've already considered the first argument, that what matters about health is its bearing on well-being, and that preference satisfaction either constitutes well-being or provides good evidence concerning well-being.

The second argument points out that evaluating health states or any other outcomes by measuring preferences legitimizes those evaluations. When asked why some health states are assigned lower numbers (quality weights) than others, the health economist can reply, "That's how the members of the population who provide the resources and are affected by health policy on average compare those health states." Instead of having to defend the evaluation on its merits or to defend the credentials of the so-called experts who assign the values, aggregating preferences guarantees that the evaluation respects, at least on average, the values held by members of the target population and in that way helps to secure the legitimacy of the evaluation. The same argument can be used in defense of relying on preferences in evaluating other outcomes such as bridges or educational programs.

The legitimacy argument, which is sensible, should be distinguished from the third argument in terms of popular sovereignty, which is mistaken. The popular sovereignty argument maintains that health states should be evaluated by measuring preferences, because doing so respects democratic ideals. The thought is that since the distribution of health-related resources should be up to the population that provides the resources and whose health is at stake, the values that population attaches to health states should determine how health-related resources will be distributed. So health states should be evaluated by individual preferences. But popular sovereignty implies only that the target population should decide how to allocate health-related resources. It does not imply any particular way of making the allocation, let alone of measuring what is to be allocated.[4] Similarly, popular sovereignty implies that the target population should decide on the procedure to be used in determining where to locate a highway, not that the location should be subject to a vote, nor that the benefits be determined by a survey.

A fourth and very influential argument in defense of evaluating health states or consequences in general by measuring preferences is that it is the only feasible method. Psychometricians have a good deal of experience and knowledge concerning preference measurement, and economists have a significant body of knowledge concerning the validity of inferences concerning preferences drawn from choice behavior and concerning the conditions under which preferences can be numerically represented. There is really no other game in town. Joining the first argument (that preference satisfaction constitutes or is evidence for well-being) with the last argument, many economists regard the evaluation of health states by measuring preferences as inevitable, self-evident, and unavoidable. For example, in *Methods for the Economic Evaluation of Health Care Programmes*, Drummond and his coauthors simply *define* value as preferences over alternatives involving no risk or uncertainty (1997, 146–49), while Patrick and Erickson write, "Measures of health-related quality of life that incorporate explicit values in the ordering of health states are referred to as utility-weighted or preference-weighted measures" (1993, 65).

But, one might object, there must, in fact, be some other game in town, or else the project of evaluating health states (or anything else) in terms of preferences could never get started. Unless individuals are able to evaluate health states and to generate preferences among them, there will be no individual preferences among health states to be measured. But individual evaluations of health states do not derive from preferences among health states. What determines a survey respondent's comparative evaluation of back pain versus difficulty walking is not his preference for one or the other. He doesn't think that it would be worse for him (or for people in general) to have problems walking than to suffer moderate back pain *because* he prefers moderate back pain. On the contrary, if he prefers moderate back pain, he does so because he judges that or feels that it is not as bad as having difficulty walking. Whether or not this judgment or reaction is based on other preferences, it is not based on a preference between moderate back pain and difficulties in walking. Insofar as the comparison is rational (and it need not be), respondents must somehow use their knowledge of what these health states feel like and what their consequences are to evaluate them. And if survey respondents can carry out such evaluations, then health analysts ought to be able to do so, too. Indeed, knowing more about how health states affect individuals and about the consequences of diminished health states for careers, socializing, recreation, and so forth, health analysts ought to be able to evaluate health states more accurately than survey respondents.

25.4. Evaluation

This objection to the argument that there is no alternative to measuring preferences brings us to the last argument in defense of preference-based evaluation and to some very tricky issues, which deserve a section of their own. The last argument maintains that health states should be evaluated by people's preferences among them on the grounds that the value of health states is a subjective matter concerning which an individual's preferences are decisive. Evaluating health states by measuring preferences allegedly respects this insight. Indeed it is the right way to evaluate health states (and other states of affairs and consequences) because it measures precisely what *determines* the value of states of affairs, including health states.

There appear to be two major problems with this preference determination argument. First, as already mentioned in the objection to the feasibility argument, to claim that preferences determine values appears to get things backward. An individual's preferences among health states are not a basis on which an individual relies in evaluating health states. On the contrary, an individual does not have preferences among health states until the individual has evaluated them. Preferences among alternatives are either caused or constituted by evaluations of those alternatives.

Everyday talk about preferences is ambiguous. There are two main meanings of the claim "A prefers x to y." First, one might mean that A *enjoys* x more than y. A takes more pleasure in x than in y, looks forward more eagerly to experiencing x than y, or looks back with more satisfaction on experiencing x than y. Even though Ann would never think of eating chocolate ice cream because of the ravages it inflicts upon her complexion, Ann might, in this sense of preference, still enjoy chocolate ice cream more than raspberry sorbet and in this sense prefer it. But the main meaning of "A prefers x to y" is that A ranks x above y, when A takes into consideration almost everything A deems to be relevant to the appraisal of x and y.

In this sense of "prefer," Ann prefers the sorbet, despite loving the taste and creamy texture of chocolate ice cream. If x and y are objects of choice, ranking x above y is judging x to be more choiceworthy than y and being disposed, other things being equal, to choose x rather than y when one knows one faces such a choice. If x and y are not objects of choice, but consequences of choices, then ranking x above y implies (other things being equal) a ranking of those objects of choice that make x more likely above those objects of choice that make y more likely. Another way of expressing this meaning of a preference is that it is a *comparative overall evaluation*, a judgment that x is better than y, taking almost everything into account.

I speak of an overall evaluation rather than a total evaluation—of an evaluation that takes into account *almost* everything the agent takes to be relevant, but may leave out some things—because in everyday life, people regard some factors that influence choice as competing with preference rather than as determining preference. Depending on the context, we might count Ann's moral obligation to keep a promise as leading her to attend a meeting despite preferring to spend the afternoon with a friend, rather than taking her obligation as among the factors leading her to prefer to attend the meeting.

Usage in economics is more precise. Rather than taking preferences sometimes as expressions of liking and sometimes as comparative evaluations, economists always take preferences to be comparative evaluations. And in place of the overall evaluations of everyday language, which leave a place for factors that compete with preferences in influencing choices, preferences in economics are *total* comparative evaluations—evaluations of alternatives in terms of *all* considerations that the agent takes to influence his or her choices.[5]

So the first problem with the preference determination argument for evaluating health states by measuring preferences is that an individual's evaluations of health states could not possibly depend on their preferences among health states. If prefer ences are comparative evaluations, then comparative evaluations obviously cannot depend on preferences. What responds to this first problem and saves the general idea of evaluating health states by measuring preferences from incoherence is that health economists are deriving a *social* or *public* evaluation of health states from individual or private preferences among health states. Evaluating health states by measuring preferences in this regard resembles social choice theory: It aims to derive a social evaluation of health states from individual evaluations of health states.

This way of defending the coherence of the project of evaluating health states by measuring preferences among health states creates a second problem for the preference determination argument. Rather than respecting the decisiveness of an individual's own judgment of the severity of a health state, the point of evaluating health states in order to implement a restricted consequentialist assessment of health policy is to derive social or public values for health states, which will differ from individual values. If half the population feels that, on a scale that assigns a value of 0 to death and 1 to full health, blindness has a value of 0.9 while the other half assigns a value of 0.7 to blindness, any assignment of a social value to blindness will have to conflict with the judgment of at least half the population. Averaging and assigning a social value of 0.8 to blindness lessens the magnitude of the disagreement between the social value and the individual values but increases its scope. Nobody assigns to blindness the value of 0.8. Instead of respecting the judgments of individuals and taking them to be decisive concerning the severity of their own health states, averaging in this case overrules everybody's preference. This is true, whether or not averaging in some sense respects preferences better than alternatives. Deferring to individual preferences or to individual judgments argues against any social evaluation of health states.

Furthermore, as argued especially by Thomas Scanlon (1975), there are good reasons to deny that social evaluation should defer to individual evaluations. From a broadly liberal perspective, health policy, education policy, transportation policy, and so forth should be directed toward ends that are public and political, in the sense that they result from public debate and do not rely upon a commitment to any one among the competing conceptions citizens hold of what is truly valuable. So private preferences will not be decisive. For example, there may be a social obligation to provide nutrition, shelter, and medical care to some group of people, even if they would prefer to use the resources to build a temple to their deity (Scanlon 1975, 659–60).

Rather than favoring measuring preferences on the grounds that the evaluation of health states should defer to preferences, one might interpret the argument as favoring measuring preferences, because individual preferences in fact determine the value of health states. Putting the argument this way apparently runs afoul of the objection that has already been discussed, that preferences depend on or are constituted by evaluations, rather than vice versa. If evaluations are judgments that are correct or incorrect and that can be carried out more or less rationally, then it would seem that one should study how these judgments are made to see what determines values. Preferences among the alternatives would be action-guiding rankings that express the outcomes of evaluations but which are irrelevant to the process of evaluation.

But is it true that evaluations are judgments that are correct or incorrect? Many philosophers would be inclined to deny this claim, and in doing so they shore up this last argument in favor of evaluating health states by measuring preferences. Following Hume, many would maintain that rather than judging correctly or incorrectly the values of alternatives, an individual's evaluations express the individual's attitudes or emotional reactions to the alternatives and thereby *determine* their value. This value determination can be done badly when the individual has false beliefs concerning the properties and consequences of the alternatives to be evaluated, but such evaluative mistakes are misapprehensions concerning what it is one is reacting to, not a mistake how one reacts. As Hume put it,

> Reason is, and ought only to be the slave of the passions, and can never pretend to any other office than to serve and obey them: . . .
>   A passion is an original existence, or, if you will, modification of existence, and contains not any representative quality, which renders it a copy of any other existence or modification. When I am angry, I am actually possest with the passion, and in that emotion have no more a reference to any other object, than when I am thirsty, or sick, or more than five foot high. 'Tis impossible, therefore,

that this passion can be opposed by, or be contradictory to truth and reason; since this contradiction consists in the disagreement of ideas, consider'd as copies, with those objects, which they represent. (Hume 1978 [1738], bk. 2, pt. 3, sec. 3)

One can easily interpret Hume's remarks as depending on the untenable premise that emotions have no objects, as maintaining, for example, that anger is just a feeling, like vertigo, with no connection to an object, except possibly as a cause. But of course people are typically angry *at* other people, and they are angry *about* what other people have done. Hume recognizes this fact and speaks about passions "accompany'd with" judgments. If one takes passions not to be simply feelings, but feelings accompanied with judgments, one can reinterpret Hume as espousing a view that cannot be rejected out of hand. Judgments concerning what has happened or will happen and concerning what people have done or will do are partly constitutive of emotions such as anger, grief, admiration, or gratitude.[6] The Humean will argue that these are not, however, judgments concerning the *value* of actions or state of affairs. They are instead judgments concerning the nonevaluative properties of actions or states of affairs. Values then arise from the feelings people have while making these factual judgments. A Humean can allow that people can mistakenly evaluate states of affairs, when they are mistaken about the characteristics and consequences of states of affairs. But if they correctly understand the characteristics and consequences of the state of affairs they are evaluating, and they are not ill or under the influence of drugs or physical conditions that provoke distorted emotional responses, then their responses cannot be faulted, and neither can the evaluations their responses determine.

Like survey respondents, health analysts will have reactions to health states, and those reactions are less likely to be misleading, because the health analyst's understanding of what she is reacting to is superior to the understanding of respondents. But the health analyst's evaluation is just her emotional reaction, and there is no sense in speaking of its accuracy or correctness. The point of surveying many individuals from different walks of life and with different experiences is to get a more representative evaluation, not a more accurate one. The health economist's reactions are no worse than anybody else's, and they are more likely to be reactions to the properties and consequences of the health state to be evaluated rather than reactions to something else. But the health economist's reactions are also no more accurate than anybody else's and unlikely to be representative of the target population. So the right way to evaluate health states is to measure the preferences among health states of members of the target population who are knowledgeable concerning the characteristics and consequences of the health states to be evaluated and then to aggregate or average them.

This Humean response to the objection that there must be some other way to evaluate health states apart from measuring preferences thus grounds this final argument in favor of evaluating health states by measuring preferences. Individuals evaluate health states by their emotional reaction to them. The reason one should measure individuals' preferences among health states is that individuals' evaluative attitudes toward health states, which are expressed in their preferences, *constitute* the value of health states. Individuals' preferences are not evidence as to the true value of health states. There is no true value. There are only people's emotional and appetitive reactions, which their preferences summarize. In measuring individual preferences among health states, one is measuring what determines the value of health states.

Since the value of health states is not separable from other determinants of well-being or other objects of desire—that is, since reactions to health states differ depending on what the other circumstances of a person's life may be—either one needs to follow Broome and move away from restricted consequentialism, or one has to live with the mess and hope that the results of one's efforts to evaluate health states separately are nevertheless of some value.

Although I have developed the challenges to implementing restricted consequentialism with respect to the specific example of evaluating health, analogous issues arise in other applications of restricted consequentialism. For example, education is clearly a good, and a division of government is charged with promoting education. But how does one measure the quantity of education an individual has? Does George, the English major who can quote long speeches from Shakespeare but whose mathematical abilities are scarcely up to the challenge of balancing his checkbook, possess more or less education than Michael the mathematician, whose idea of a good book is a Hardy Boys adventure? Just as the relation "is healthier than" is incomplete, so is the relation "has more education than." So rather than attempting literally to measure education, one might attempt to value it. But the value of education appears so intertwined with a person's mode of life that ranking the education of individuals as better or worse along some single scale seems to be an infeasible and indeed foolish task. This undermines restrictive consequentialism directed toward promoting education. There is no single value to be promoted. Unlike the case of health, where it seems sensible to direct policy toward maximizing health, subject to constraints of fairness and competing uses of resources, education policy is more likely focused on a certain minimum education coupled with expanding individuals' opportunities to become educated in the ways that they choose. Quantitative assessment will depend on a hodgepodge of measurements of variables such as class sizes, dropout rates, and scores on standardized tests.

25.5. AGAINST PREFERENCE-BASED EVALUATION

The Humean view that values are constituted by reactions that are not themselves subject to any normative evidential or rational standards is not, of course, obviously correct; and Hume himself backed away from it when discussing aesthetic judgments (1963 [1741]). One serious problem with its application to restricted consequentialism is that the values that are at stake with respect to health, education, environmental amenities, or transportation do not all reduce to some overall notion of betterness.

They are more specific. Preferences are concerned with *all* evaluative features of alternatives, whether these have anything to do with well-being or with the value of health (Hausman 2011). So Michael might, for example, prefer health state *x* to health state *y*, even though Michael believes that he would be better off in health state *y*, on the grounds that being in health state *x* would enable him to accomplish some non-self-interested goal, such as taking care of his frail mother or saving the Siberian tiger from extinction. Furthermore, neither Michael's preferences among health states nor his ranking of health states in terms of his own well-being need match his judgment of which health states are better or worse. People can distinguish how bad a health state is from how badly off an individual in a health state is (Nord 2001); and neither of these coincides with a comparative evaluation of heath states with respect to all relevant considerations.

The most dramatic demonstration of possible divergence between, on the one hand, preference or well-being and, on the other hand, judgments of the value of health states comes from people's reactions to certain disabilities such as deafness and paraplegia. Few people want to lose their hearing or the ability to walk, and an accident that costs people their hearing or ability to walk almost always makes them worse off, at least initially. So it might appear that preferences among health states or appraisals of the consequences of health states for well-being correctly evaluate health states. But people are adaptable, and those who are disabled are typically able to build good lives for themselves. Indeed some individuals can construct what they judge to be better lives than they had when not disabled. For example, many of those who are deaf maintain that they prefer to be deaf (Lane 2002). These judgments and expressions of preference may express self-deception, but there is no justification for dismissing them. There is absolutely no reason why *life* must be worse if one's health is *worse* or why, all things considered, a worse health state must be worse overall. Being unable to hear, which is obviously a significant health deficit, might help someone to concentrate and to accomplish some task that gives her life greater meaning and value than it could have had if she had not lost her hearing. It is false to maintain that health state S is better than health state S' for some person P if and only if P prefers S to S',[7] and it is false to maintain that P judges health state S to be better than health state S' if and only if P is better off in S than in S'. The value in terms of which health states differ and are to be compared is not well-being, nor is it the totality of evaluative considerations embodied in preferences.

Elsewhere I have argued that there are two crucial dimensions along which health states differ in value: subjective experience (feeling) and activity limitations (Hausman 2010). What makes deafness a diminished health state is the fact that it makes many valuable human activities impossible. What makes vertigo a diminished health state is how miserable those who are dizzy feel.[8] Few prefer pain to pleasure or anxiety to calm; and few prefer to be unable to listen to music or to go for a walk, so preferences will be correlated with judgments of the value of health states. Unpleasant feelings and activity limitations typically lower well-being, so assessments of health states in terms of their bearing on well-being also roughly correspond to judgments of their value. But, as exemplified by the possibility of having an excellent life despite one's disabilities, what is relevant to the evaluation of health are feelings and activity limitations, not preferences or consequences for well-being.

To accept this point does not require that one abandon a subjective view of value (and this chapter is, in any case, not the place to challenge subjectivism), but a plausible subjective view of value will have to be less simple than the Humean view sketched above. Evaluations can be partial or aspectual. Our rankings are not limited to preference rankings. A prettier house can be less comfortable than an uglier one. People rank alternatives in hundreds of different ways. Some of these rankings are not evaluative, such as rankings in terms of size, financial cost, or weight—though size, cost, and weight may sometimes significantly influence the value of alternatives. Others are evaluative, such as rankings in terms of taste, smell, beauty, or virtue. A ranking of the badness or severity of health states is not a preference ranking or a ranking in terms of well-being. Not everything that is relevant to preferences among health states or to well-being is relevant to the ranking of health states in terms of their severity. Michael may prefer a manic episode because it permits him to complete some project, without judging that bipolar disease is not a disease. Peter may judge that he is better off having lost a toe, because it exempts him from the draft, without asserting that it improves his health.

Recognizing the importance of aspectual evaluation narrows the gap between judgment and evaluation. If what I care about is how large a piece of pie is, I can evaluate the five pieces in the cafeteria line by weighing them. My passions still play a role ("I want lots of pie"), and in conformity with a Humean perspective, one can describe my evaluation as divided into a factual exercise of determining the properties of the five slices and then reacting to each alternative. But it is more plausible for the subjectivist to allow that we have emotional reactions to *properties* or *attributes* of states of affairs. Given those reactions, our ranking of objects with respect to those properties or attributes can then be an entirely cognitive matter. So the subjectivist can insist that our reactions to unpleasant feelings and to activity limitations that result from diminished health are what make these bad things and determine the extent of their badness. But given these reactions to unpleasant feelings and activity limitations, the appraisal of health states depends on judgments concerning where the health state falls in the spectrum of unpleasant experiences and activity limitations rather than directly on subjective reactions to health states. The determination of the value of health states could then be a largely cognitive matter of quantifying feelings and activity limitations. Describing exactly how to carry out such a quantification is a task for another occasion. It will not be a matter of measuring preferences among activity limitation and feeling pairs, nor will it be a matter of determining their effects on well-being.

Another possibility, which is theoretically less satisfying but possibly all that is possible, is to give up on the attempt to generate a single measure of health and rely instead on a variety of imperfect indicators of population health, ranging from infant mortality and longevity to sales of antidepressants. With the help of such indicators, one can to some extent identify health needs and monitor the success of policies in meeting them.

Appraisals of other sorts of policies face similar challenges. When those working in the department of education are appraising educational opportunities, they are not asking which are better with respect to every relevant evaluative consideration. Nor (though this is more controversial and requires the sort of argument that I have elsewhere made with respect to health) are they asking which lead people to be better off. What matters with respect to educational opportunities, like what matters with respect to health, is more specific. It is partly a quantitative matter—how large is the space of educational possibilities open to the population? But there are obviously evaluative questions, too, about the worth of specific opportunities. Like the value of health, the value of the range of educational opportunities available in a particular society cannot be measured directly in terms of either preferences or well-being. And it may be that all we can measure are features that are roughly correlated with educational opportunity such as class size, scores on standardized tests, graduation rates, and so forth.

25.6. Conclusions

Consequentialist considerations play an important role in policy evaluation. Regardless of how unsympathetic one may be to utilitarianism, quantitative considerations concerning how large an effect policies have on how many people should have an important influence on policymaking. Since the only feasible way to organize policies and gather data on what is needed and what is working is to divide policies into different categories, such as health, education, transportation, security, defense, environmental protection, and so forth, consequentialist policy evaluation is typically narrow—that is, focused on only some of the consequences and goods affected by policies. Since many ethical principles affect our assessment of policies, consequentialist evaluation is also heavily constrained. As both narrow and constrained, consequentialist policy evaluation is what I have called *restricted.*

This chapter has argued that it is very difficult to implement restricted consequentialist policy assessment, because it is hard to identify and measure some specific value that (other things being equal and subject to constraints) a particular department of government policy should aim to maximize. Either the value is something general, such as preference satisfaction or well-being, which undermines the pluralist framework, or the value is hard to measure on a single scale. As a practical matter, evaluation often relies on a messy ad hoc set of measures.

ACKNOWLEDGMENTS

This chapter draws from previous work on health measurement (Hausman 2006, 2010) and from *Preference, Value, Choice, and Welfare* (2011), and all those who helped me with this previous work deserve thanks here as well. I am also grateful to two anonymous referees for a number of helpful suggestions.

NOTES

1. Salomon et al. write, "We may avoid these difficulties if we seek health state valuations that provide cardinal index values for the overall levels of health associated with multidimensional health states. . . . Almost everybody can agree that a person with one amputated leg is healthier than a person with two amputated legs, all else being equal, without resorting either to the language of choice or to statements about the overall well-being of either person. . . . Indeed, this common-sense notion extends beyond ordinal comparisons, for example, allowing us to say that going from good health to having a sore throat is a smaller change in health than going from a sore throat to quadriplegia. In all of these cases, we submit that there is an intuitive understanding of the meaning of health that is not based on the concept of choice. People may usually (but not always) prefer to be in a better state of health, but levels of health may be understood as distinct from these individual preferences" (2003, 410–11).

2. I shall not explore the difficult questions concerning the definition of health, but shall take for granted both that health is at least a matter of being free of pathology and that pathologies are diverse.

3. For extended critiques of relying on preferences or well-being to evaluate health states, see Hausman (2006 and 2010).

4. Indeed, one fascinating survey found that survey respondents did not think that surveys of their preferences should guide health resources allocation decisions. See Richardson and Olsen (2005).

5. I argue for this claim in chapters 2–4 of *Preference, Value, Choice, and Welfare*. Given what many economists, particularly defenders of revealed preference, say, this claim might appear to be both contentious and dubious. But no other interpretation of preference—and certainly not any definition of preference in terms of choice—conforms to the basic axioms governing preferences or to the ways in which economists use preferences to predict and explain choices.

6. Nussbaum argues that judgments concerning how what has happened bear on one's goals constitute emotions (2001a, 2004).

7. Paul Dolan and Daniel Kahneman (2007) also criticize equating the value of health with the extent to which people prefer health states, though on very different hedonistic grounds. What disqualifies preferences is their inaccuracy as indicators of subjective experience. Although I agree with Dolan and Kahneman that subjective experience is relevant to the evaluation of health states, I do not agree that the value of health states is simply the value of the subjective experience of health states.

8. In emphasizing activity limitations, this proposal has some affinities with the proposal to rely on capabilities and functionings in evaluating states of affairs (Sen 1993, Nussbaum 2001b). But the evaluative task here remains a narrow one focused on the value of health states.

REFERENCES

Broome, John. 2002. "Measuring the Burden of Disease by Aggregating Well-Being." In *Summary Measures of Population Health: Concepts, Ethics, Measurement and Applications,* Christopher Murray, Joshua Saloman, Colin Mathers, and Alan Lopez, eds., 91–113. Geneva: World Health Organization.

Brock, Dan, 2002. "The Separability of Health and Well-Being." In *Summary Measures of Population Heath*, Christopher Murray et al., eds., 115–20. Geneva: World Health Organization.

Daniels, N. 1985. *Just Health Care*. Cambridge: Cambridge University Press.

Daniels, N. 2007. *Just Health*. Cambridge: Cambridge University Press.

Dolan, Paul, and Daniel Kahneman. 2007. "Interpretations of Utility and Their Implications for the Valuation of Health." *Economic Journal* 118: 215–34.

Drummond, Michael, Bernie O'Brien, Greg Stoddart, and George Torrance. 1997. *Methods for the Economic Evaluation of Health Care Programmes*. 2d ed. Oxford: Oxford University Press.

Hausman, Daniel. 2006. "Valuing Health." *Philosophy and Public Affairs* 34: 246–74.

Hausman, Daniel. 2010. "Valuing Health: A New Proposal," *Health Economics* 19: 280–96.

Hausman, Daniel. 2011. *Preference, Value, Choice, and Welfare*. Cambridge: Cambridge University Press.

Hausman, Daniel, and Michael McPherson. 2006. *Economic Analysis, Moral Philosophy, and Public Policy*. New York: Cambridge University Press.

Hausman, Daniel, and Michael McPherson. 2009. "Preference Satisfaction and Welfare Economics," *Economics and Philosophy* 25: 1–25.

Hume, David. 1978 [1738]. *Treatise of Human Nature*. Rpt. and ed. L. S. Selby-Bigge and P. H. Nidditch. Oxford: Oxford University Press.

Hume, David. 1963 [1741]. "Of the standard of taste." In *Essays Moral, Political and Literary*. Rpt., 231–55. Oxford: Oxford University Press.

Lane H. 2002. "Do Deaf People Have a Disability?" *Sign Language Studies* 2: 356–79.

Murray, Christopher, Joshua Salomon, Colin Mathers, and Alan Lopez, eds. 2002. *Summary Measures of Population Health: Concepts, Ethics, Measurement and Applications*. Geneva: World Health Organization.

Nord, Erik. 2001. "The Desirability of a Condition Versus the Well Being and Worth of a Person." *Health Economics* 10: 579–81.

Nussbaum, Martha. 2001a. *Upheavals of Thought: The Intelligence of Emotions*. Cambridge: Cambridge University Press.

Nussbaum, Martha. 2001b. *Women and Human Development* Cambridge: Cambridge University Press.

Nussbaum, Martha. 2004. *Hiding from Humanity: Disgust, Shame, and the Law*. Princeton, NJ: Princeton University Press.

Patrick, Donald, and Pennifer Erickson 1993. *Health Status and Health Policy: Quality of Life in Health Care Evaluation and Resource Allocation*. New York: Oxford University Press.

Richardson, J., and J. Olsen 2005. "Welfarism or Nonwelfarism? Public Preferences for Willingness to Pay Versus Health Maximisation." Monash: Monash University, Centre for Health Economics Research Paper 2005(10). Available from www.buseco.monash. edu.au/centres/che/publications.php.

Salomon, Joshua, Christopher Murray, T., Bedirhan Üstün, and Somnath Chatterji. 2003. "Health State Valuations in Summary Measures of Population Health." In *Health Systems Performance Assessment: Debates, Methods and Empiricism*, Christopher Murray and David Evans, eds., 409–36. Geneva: World Health Organization.

Scanlon T. 1975. "Preference and Urgency." *Journal of Philosophy* 72: 655–69.

Sen, Amartya. 1993. "Capability and Well-Being." In *The Quality of Life*, Martha Nussbaum and Amartya Sen, eds., 30–53. Oxford: Clarendon Press.

CHAPTER 26

VALUES AND THE SCIENCE OF WELL-BEING: A RECIPE FOR MIXING

ANNA ALEXANDROVA

26.1. INTRODUCTION

More than ever before, human well-being is currently a subject of extensive research all across the social and medical sciences, from psychology and psychiatry to economics and epidemiology. For the findings of this science to be relevant and applicable in practice, we need reasons to believe that whatever the scientists are calling "well-being" in their studies is indeed worth pursuing for individuals, communities, and nations. This is a question of prudential value, which is supposed to be addressed in the venerable philosophical tradition of theorizing about well-being. However, as I will argue, the state of the art in philosophy is of limited help for the task at hand. Not because there is no agreement on what the correct theory of well-being is—but rather, because the assumptions behind the existing philosophical project are fundamentally at odds with the assumptions behind the scientific project.

There is a discrepancy in the way the notion of well-being functions in philosophy on the one hand, and in the sciences (and the everyday life, for that matter) on the other. In philosophy, well-being is a concept that applies in a precisely defined narrow context—evaluation of a person's life as a whole, or *in general*; and potential theories of well-being are evaluated on their ability to fulfill this role. In the sciences, the notion of well-being behaves very differently: Many different practical contexts are thought to require a notion of well-being, even those that do not involve evaluation of life as a whole. Most studies in social and medical sciences that are purportedly about well-being do not make general but only *context-specific* evaluations. As a result, a great variety of constructs of well-being are used in the various scientific projects. *Which of the many things called* well-being *in the scientific literature is the correct notion to use and for which purpose?* To answer this question, we need a framework that makes philosophical analysis of well-being more responsive to the needs and realities of social science and policy. My goal here is to explore the basics of such a framework.

In part I of this chapter, I explain the discrepancy between well-being in philosophy and well-being in science, illustrating it with examples from development economics, gerontology, and the study of child well-being. This discrepancy is harmful for all concerned. It robs science and public policy of the expertise of philosophers that could be employed to evaluate empirical claims about well-being promotion. And it robs philosophy of a chance to play this important role in a meaningful way. The culprit, I claim, is the prevalent status quo in philosophy—a view I call *well-being invariantism* (WBI), which takes the scope of the concept of well-being to be narrow (i.e., only the general evaluation of individual life) and works on the assumption that a single substantive theory of well-being is applicable in all cases.

In part II, I consider a way out. I articulate a view called *well-being variantism* (WBV), which denies both of these claims: that is, it claims that the concept of well-being has a broader application than WBI assumes, and that no single substantive theory is likely to be enough to tell us what well-being amounts to in the various contexts in which the concept applies. I also argue that WBV is naturally understood in terms of *contextualism* about the content of well-being assertions. Finally, I claim that WBV fits scientific practice better than WBI, and carries no danger of relativism or eliminativism about well-being. Instead it is a first step toward explaining and evaluating construct pluralism in the sciences and for judging policy relevance of scientific findings about well-being. When a scientist claims that a given intervention would improve well-being, we can use WBV to make an informed judgment about whether this is indeed well-being relevant in a given situation.

26.2. PART I

26.2.1. Well-Being in Philosophy

In philosophy well-being is identified with prudential good, a technical term which denotes the value to a person, as opposed to a nonpersonal moral or aesthetic value, in the broadest sense; the sort of value that makes this person's life go well. The focus of the concept of well-being is taken to be *general*—whatever is good for a person, in the sense of being her prudential good, is good for her in general, not in some specific practical context.

There are several well-developed substantive theories of this value. Convention divides them into those emphasizing subjective or objective elements as constituting well-being, where the former require that an agent endorse a value, perhaps under idealized conditions, while the latter does not (Parfit 1984). For example, most desire fulfillment views (Railton 1986, Brandt 1979), some versions of hedonism (especially those that take pleasure to require a positive attitude to a mental state [Feldman 2002]) and theories identifying well-being with happiness (Sumner 1996) are subjective theories. Theories that make some pleasure to be good for a person irrespective of her attitude (Crisp 2006), and objective list theories that maintain that something can be good for a person whether or not she endorses it and whether or not it is pleasurable (Griffin 1986, Darwall 2002, Arneson 1999, Haybron 2008, and many others) are objective. Each of these theories has opponents who, using intuitive counterexamples, argue that it misses something fundamental about well-being that the other theory captures successfully. As the debate continues these theories become more and more intricate and detailed. Although philosophers agree on some substantive claims about the nature of well-being (for example, that mere satisfaction of actual desires is insufficient for it), there is no agreement on what well-being is. Not on the nature of goods that constitute it (for instance, whether they are certain mental states or states of lives), nor on the necessary level of these goods (how much pleasure, how many desires satisfied, or how much of some other objective good constitutes well-being). Of course, in itself this fact does not show that the debate is unfruitful. But it is an indication of the potential trouble for using philosophical accounts of well-being for regulating the scientific and policy issues.

More importantly for our purposes, the philosophical debate proceeds on the assumption that the concept of well-being is the concept used for evaluating a person's state or life only as a whole, taking into account all of its constituents. When we are asking how well a person is doing, philosophers have assumed we are asking how well his life is going in general, all things considered. It is for this special context that philosophers are seeking a correct substantive theory of well-being. This is also why it makes sense to speak of a correct or an incorrect theory of well-being *simpliciter*, rather than a theory of well-being that applies or does not apply in a given context. I refer to these presuppositions as *well-being invariantism* (hereafter WBI). WBI encompasses two claims:

1. The concept of well-being concerns the most general evaluation of the prudential value of a person's life and not anything else. I call this assumption the *deathbed assumption* because it identifies the focus of the concept of well-being with the sort of evaluation we might undertake at a person's deathbed:[1] How has she done in life, all things considered?
2. The substantive theory of well-being specifies the unique set of conditions that apply in all and only cases of well-being.[2] Whenever the concept of well-being applies, the substantive theory of well-being is supposed to tell us what it is. Let us call this assumption the *uniqueness assumption*.

Together the deathbed and the uniqueness assumptions imply that a single substantive theory of well-being should yield the conditions under which a person's life is going well in general. I contend that this is a very narrow and impoverished goal for theorizing about well-being. In social sciences especially, we need much more than that.

Indeed outside philosophy, the concept of well-being behaves very differently. I argue that it violates WBI. Instead its behavior is best explained by well-being variantism[3]—the view that rejects both the deathbed and the uniqueness assumptions. Well-being variantism (hereafter WBV) is thus characterized by the following commitments:

1. The term "well-being" (and its cognates) can invoke many different kinds of evaluations depending on context, of which the general deathbed sort is only one kind. Though a general notion of well-being exists and is useful in some contexts, it is not *uniquely* useful. Context is constituted by the relevant characteristics of the subjects of evaluation (whether they are a toddler, a country, or a caretaker of a demented patient) and the specific features of the situation in which this evaluation takes place (whether well-being is invoked in a doctor's office, by an international aid organization, in a heart-to-heart conversation with a friend, etc.).

2. Depending on context, a different substantive theory of well-being can be appropriate for specifying the conditions constituting well-being in each particular case. Thus in different contexts well-being may amount to the subject's hedonic profile, or their objective quality of life, or certain aspects of their health, and so on.

I shall articulate this view more fully in part II. For now, a few details will suffice. WBV is called such because it takes the diversity of notions and standards of well-being to be fundamental to the way we use this notion in everyday life and in the sciences; by the same token it should be fundamental to philosophical theorizing about well-being. Still, a weaker and a stronger version of WBV are available. The stronger version takes WBV to be a philosophical thesis about the nature of prudential value, squarely in the province of metaethics. It is an attack on the very idea of a unified theory of well-being. On the weaker version, we put aside the deep questions of metaethics and treat WBV as only a methodological thesis about how best to approach the social and medical sciences that employ the notions of well-being. In this chapter, I will be concentrating on the methodological thesis.

In principle, the weaker version of WBV could even be compatible with some kind of invariantism about well-being—for example, a kind that admits that any general theory of well-being, though it may be uniquely correct, is not well suited for addressing the concerns arising in the sciences of well-being. This general theory may fail to be useful because, for instance, it is too abstract and too thin to yield context-specific notions of well-being necessary for science and policy. Whatever general theory of well-being is correct, justifying local constructs of well-being is a context-specific affair in which the general theory plays little role. But even this weaker thesis is strong enough to undermine the current status quo in which the bulk of normative theorizing about well-being is done in separation and often in ignorance of the specific concerns of the sciences.

The view I am exploring here can be understood on the analogy with other pluralist views in philosophy of science. Concepts of species, innateness, gene, and others, it has been suggested, do not admit of a stable meaning; nor is a single substantive theory of these, both informative and true, possible (Ereshefsky 1998, Griffith 2002, Griffith and Stotz 2006, among others). And yet these concepts remain useful, notwithstanding various calls for their elimination. Mark Wilson recently went as far as arguing that this is indeed the normal behavior of scientific concepts. If we take seriously the practical minutiae of use and application of scientific concepts for specific purposes and projects, we see that even familiar notions such as color, weight, hardness, etc. only show stable content and orderly behavior in patches here and there, not universally, and only when they are anchored by reliable measurement and inference procedures (Wilson 2006). Well-being might be a concept that functions similarly, and is able to regulate production, interpretation, and the use of scientific knowledge without being part of a stable and unified theory.

What evidence is there for such a view?

26.2.2. Well-Being in Everyday Life

In everyday talk outside academia well-being is rarely referred to by this name. If it is used at all, usually in the cosmetics or the self-help industry, it means something like the subjective *sense* of well-being, or the psychological state of happiness.[4] But that is not a crucial difference.

More often, the concept of well-being is invoked in questions such as "How are you doing?," "How is it going?," "How's life?." This is where the difference with philosophy is stark.

First of all, well-being is discussed in many more contexts than just the general deathbed context privileged by philosophers, the one in which life is evaluated as a whole. A professor posing one of these questions to a student in office hours is really inquiring about how the student is doing in his class, not in life in general. A therapist posing this question to her patient slowly emerging from depression means "Have you been able to control your depression?" A stranger on the street addressing a pedestrian in apparent distress means "Do you need immediate help?" At least in some of these cases, it is plausible to treat these questions as their language indicates, as questions about well-being. However, the notions and standards of well-being here are different from those used by philosophers.

Secondly, verdicts about whether one is doing well and assumptions about what it takes to do well vary with context. Thus depending on context a different threshold may be used to mark well-being from ill-being, and a different substantive theory can be called to evaluate it. The professor in the example above takes the well-being of a student in her office hours to consist of reasonable progress in the course, the therapist—in the patient's ability to survive without anxiety and sadness, the stranger on the street—in her fellow pedestrian's ability to walk normally, and so on. Of course, a shift in context might prompt each of these evaluators to adopt a different notion of well-being. (In part II, I give a contextualist interpretation of these shifts.)

These examples do not invalidate WBI on their own. Indeed the project here is not a conceptual analysis of the concept of well-being, whether in everyday life or in the sciences. Rather than capturing the usage of the term under one common banner, my goal is a framework that ensures that the notion of well-being can play the role that we need it to play in scientific research and its application.[5] To do so effectively, this framework needs to help us direct our efforts—in particular, it needs to tell us which notion of well-being is appropriate in which context and why. I believe that some version of variantism is better able to do so than invariantism. (Though I won't be defending this claim explicitly here, the motivation for it will become clear when I review the state of art in the sciences of well-being.) But even if one does not aim at conceptual analysis, the role that a concept plays in everyday discourse is a useful indication of where a philosopher should look. These linguistic data-points, along with the examples discussed in section 26.3, plausibly provide prima facie empirical evidence against WBI. They show that this philosophical ideal diverges substantially from the way the term "well-being" functions in the sciences and the everyday life. But the main evidence against WBI is theoretical—there is simply no good reason for this divergence.

In order to reject these intuitions as irrelevant to the truth of WBI, its proponent must claim that the professor, the psychiatrist, and the stranger on the street are not talking about well-being, but rather about something else. For example, the professor is talking about the student's progress in the class, the therapist about the patient's recovery. These may be components or aspects, or causes of well-being but they are not well-being proper. If this is correct, then the question "How are you doing?" may on some occasion be a question about well-being proper, but most of the time it is not. In what contexts does this question concern well-being proper? An earnest conversation between two philosophers well versed in what "well-being" means in the professional literature is one obvious context. Outside philosophy there are few such contexts. The deathbed context is one. Another is a serious intimate conversation, say, between friends, in which the question "So, how are you?" is asked in that special significant tone of voice and invokes an all-things-considered examination of a life. Then and only then, the argument goes, are we properly talking about well-being rather than parts or components or aspects of it.

The problem with this response is that it arbitrarily postulates the scope of the notion of well-being as narrowly circumscribed. This is why I shall call this response a *circumscription strategy*. The cost of adopting this strategy is the necessity to provide and to motivate a boundary within which "How are you doing?" is a question about well-being, while beyond it, a question about something else. Philosophers have already observed that specifying the scope of well-being—that is, where quality of life, happiness, welfare, etc. end and well-being proper begins—is a tall order (Scanlon 1998, Raz 2004). At what point precisely and why "How are you doing?"

ceases to be a question about well-being appears to be a hopeless question. Simple postulation that all and only deathbed contexts are the contexts in which well-being proper is in question is simply unmotivated. No justification for it is on offer at the moment.

As I will argue in section 4, the circumscriptionist's case is even harder to make once we see how the concept of well-being functions in the sciences.

26.2.3. Well-Being in the Social and Medical Sciences

In the social and medical sciences, the term "well-being" is referred to by this name and is used even more diversely than in the everyday context (and now more widely than ever). What gets called well-being depends on the discipline, the purposes and constraints of the research project, the potential application, and so on.

I will discuss three particularly striking examples: development economics, gerontology, and the study of child well-being.

26.2.3.1. Development Economics

In development economics, the goal is often to evaluate large-scale public policy in poor countries, the sort of policy that gets undertaken by governments, international banks, and large aid organizations. Such evaluation often takes form of the question "How well is this country doing?." Economist Partha Dasgupta proposes a construct for this purpose in his book *Human Well-Being and the Natural Environment* (Dasgupta 2001). He argues that this class of evaluations requires that we focus *not* on economists' favorite welfare (i.e., satisfaction of preferences as revealed by choices) but on *aggregate quality of life*. It has to be aggregate in two senses: firstly, the construct needs to represent the state of many people and, secondly, their quality of life must be constituted by several elements. The focus has to be on quality of life rather than happiness or preference satisfaction. The construct also needs to allow comparisons across time and nations and hence must be capable of ordering the states of well-being on some sort of a scale. This way of conceptualizing well-being is not unusual and indeed well established in development economics. The emphasis on multidimensional measures that focus on key elements of human functioning is central to the capabilities approach that gave rise to the now twenty-year-old Human Development Index (Sen and Anand 1994).

What is quality of life for a development economist? Dasgupta argues that "a minimal set of indices for spanning a reasonable conception of current well-being in a poor country includes private consumption per head, life expectancy at birth, literacy, and civil and political liberties"(54). Private consumption per head encompasses food, shelter, clothing, and basic legal aid. Life expectancy at birth is the best indicator of health, while literacy is a proxy for basic primary education. Civil and political rights allow people to function independently of the state and their communities. Each of these are necessary because they comprise human capital. They cannot be reduced to some one item, in particular their market value, because they may be undervalued by the marketplace or by the subjects themselves. Dasgupta then goes on to painstakingly explore what measures would best capture this construct.

Of course, the existence of a variety of measures of a country's well-being is not necessarily evidence of the existence of a variety of notions of well-being. A good measure of X does not need to measure X directly, but can proceed via good enough statistical proxies. Indeed, Dasgupta claims that well-being of a country is often best measured by its determinants rather than constituents (Dasgupta 2001, chapter 3). But even keeping separate the problem of identification of well-being from the problem of its measurement, it is plausible that development economics operates with its own construct of well-being, distinct from either happiness or pleasure or satisfaction of desires or an Aristotelian exercise of virtues. Dasgupta does not claim that his is the uniquely correct account of well-being, but that it is the correct one for some purposes of development economics. Nor does he claim, as the circumscription theorist would have it, that his is an account of quality of life *rather* than well-being. His calls his construct well-being even though aggregate quality of life shares little content with fulfillment of agent's goals, happiness, flourishing, and other elements that dominate philosophical theories well-being.

26.2.3.2. *Gerontology*

Gerontology, the study of health and well-being of the elderly, also operates with its own set of notions referred to by the name "well-being." The prevalent conceptualizations of well-being can be garnered from the articles in the main journals of the discipline (*Archives of Gerontology and Geriatrics, Gerontologist*, etc.). For the most part, well-being is identified with a combination of subjective satisfaction and objective functioning, where the latter is understood as the ability to go through one's day independently and the standard of functioning is adjusted specifically for the elderly. More often than not, the construct is adjusted even further to the more specific purposes of the study.

Thus we find some very specialized notions of well-being developed by researchers for specific problems that arise in connection with the elderly. Some studies of the elderly identify quality of life as general healthy functioning, using measurement instruments such as the Nottingham Health Profile and the Sickness Impact Profile (Hunt, McEwen, and McKenna 1985; Bergner et al. 1981). The World Health Organization Quality of Life questionnaire is also a mixture of questions about general physical ableness, subjective health, negative emotions, pain, and environmental stressors. It is quite distinct from the eponymous quality of life measure proposed by Dasgupta for development economics, but that does not stop gerontologists from referring to the construct that it measures as "quality of life" or "well-being" (Takai et al. 2009).

Along with these generic instruments researchers also use constructs and measures designed to gauge well-being of people with a specific illness. It is thought that these specific instruments "may be more valid, in the sense that they measure quality of life more accurately in that particular disease than generic instruments" (Lips et al. 1999, 151; see also Fitzpatrick et al. 1992 and Fletcher et al. 1992). For example, the European Foundation for Osteoporosis has recently developed a quality of life measure specially for people with vertebral fractures and osteoporosis (Lips et al. 1997).[6]

Further constructs are developed to fit social circumstances that often arise in connection with the elderly, for example, caring for their spouses with heavy chronic illnesses. The notion of caregiver strain was proposed specifically to mark the hardship of the caregiver. Well-being of caregivers is then conceptualized as subjective satisfaction with one's life and also freedom from caregiver strain (Visser-Meily et al. 2005). The latter is measured by a Caregiver Strain Index, a questionnaire with thirteen yes/no questions that gauge the caregiver's sleep disturbance due to the illness of the care recipient, loneliness, lack of control over personal and social plans, family adjustments and arguments, upsetting behavior of the care recipient, his or her loss of the former self, worry, fatigue, and financial strain (Gerritsen and Van Der Ende 1994). Caregiver's burden is not reducible to more generic ill-being, at least on the existing measures, and is thought to capture the unique outcomes related to caregiving. It will thus likely remain a key construct of this field of study (Stull, Kosloski, and Kercher 1994).

A variantist interprets these proposals as a claim that the special circumstances that aging people tend to face necessitate specialized notions of well-being. Some of these notions are built around health; others, more specifically around the social circumstances in which the elderly are more likely to find themselves. On the contrary, an invariantist, instead of attributing to gerontologists a different notion of well-being, may argue that gerontologists are only committed to the view that each of the many constructs of well-being describes causes or components of general well-being, which are particularly important for the elderly. Gerontologists are thus proposing *measures* of well-being rather than new constructs, and these measures are justified by a causal or a statistical connection between their elements and well-being.

Is the invariantist response plausible? It can be. But it depends on showing the clear and tight connection between a general theory of well-being and the constructs of gerontology. The theory (along with assumptions about what causes well-being in particular contexts) should deductively imply the constructs. But there are two problems with this proposal. Firstly, looking at contemporary theories of well-being, it is hard to see this relation of implication. Each of the main candidates—desire fulfillment, hedonism, eudaimonism—are too abstract, too general to serve as genuine justifications of the many specific constructs in the social and medical sciences. A variantist does not need to deny that there is some connection between a general and the context-specific notions of well-being; she just insists that this connection isn't as tight as the invariantist needs. Secondly, the assumptions about causes of well-being needed to derive the specialized constructs are often not known, and indeed are precisely what the science of well-being is trying to study.

Variantism's other advantage is that it takes sciences on their own terms. The researchers in gerontology do not hesitate to call whatever it is they are measuring well-being or quality of life. They do so despite the fact that in other contexts it would be inappropriate to call freedom from Caregiver Strain, or from verterbral fractures, or just general healthiness, well-being. And they do so in full awareness of the difference between measures and constructs. Objective and subjective health, freedom from vertebral fractures, or from Caregiver Strain are all, on occasion, taken to be *not* merely causes or statistical correlates of well-being, but rather its constituents.

26.2.3.3. *Child Well-Being*

Our final example is the study of child well-being. Here again we find constructs representing general well-being of children and some more specialized constructs for specific contexts arising for children. In the past decade various agencies around the globe (UNICEF, the Annie E. Casey Foundation, etc.) have produced "state of the child" reports focused on children of various geographic areas and nationalities. The goal of such reports is to evaluate how well a given group of children is doing. The early reports defined well-being using a minimal list of objective indicators such as mortality, school enrollment, and vaccination. Now the constructs are broader. They include an objective state of the children and also their feelings and subjective evaluations (Ben-Arieh 2006). Their objective state is defined by the level of fulfillment of their current needs and their participation in activities thought to be crucial to a good childhood (for example, schooling and play as opposed to strenuous work or truancy or deviance). Children's subjective judgments, though increasingly taken into account, are never taken to be the sole constituents of child well-being.

Several features of these well-being constructs are of particular interest to us. Firstly, the objective indicators, along with the traditional ones such as health, consumption and education, include children-specific items, for instance, play. Secondly, these indicators are adjusted to the age and circumstances of the children. Thus the quality of life of adolescents is thought to encompass their drug, tobacco, and alcohol use and their sexual behavior. Former child soldiers and victims of bullying each get their own constructs of well-being (Benbenishty and Astor 2007, Pedersen and Sommerfelt 2007). Thirdly, researchers developed a concept called "well-becoming"—that is, the children's ability and potential for transition into well-functioning adults (Ben-Arieh 2000, 2005).

Of course, the examples can be multiplied. Crucially, the study of well-being across social and medical sciences *does not* present a unified front with similar definitions of constructs and measurement instruments. On the variantist view of well-being to be defended shortly, some such diversity makes good sense. But before articulating this view, I must address a seemingly invariantist strain in the current scientific practice.

26.2.4. Subjective Well-Being, Hedonic Psychology, and Happiness Studies

There exists a different strand of well-being research. This stand originates in psychology and is now gaining more visibility outside its discipline than any other approach. The apparent consensus among psychologists about what well-being is might raise doubts about my contention that scientific practice favors a variantist view of well-being. But that, as we shall see, would be premature.

Perhaps unsurprisingly given their focus on mental states and mental processes, psychologists by and large adopt a subjective view of well-being, though there are some differences in the precise nature of the subjective states claimed to constitute well-being. There are several constructs one regularly encounters in the psychological literature. Here are the most common ones:

1. Hedonic balance, that is, the ratio of positive to negative affect (Kahneman 1999, Kahneman et al. 2004, Frederickson and Losada 2005, Gilbert 2006, and many other researchers on social cognition).
2. Life satisfaction, that is, whether the subject approves of how her life is going (Diener et al. 1985, 2008; Lever 2000; and researchers in social and personality psychology and sociology).
3. Positive functioning, that is sense of autonomy, mastery, purpose, connectedness to people, and so on (Ryff 1989; Keyes 2002; Kendler, Myers, and Neale 2000; and many psychiatrists and clinical psychologists).

The existence of several constructs of well-being in psychology does not imply a corresponding number of different phenomena. All three constructs have fairly good correlations between each other, so much so that researchers talk of a single construct called *subjective well-being*, or SWB (Diener 1984).

SWB is not a monolithic phenomenon. Rather, three fairly independent factors have been discovered to inform subjects' responses to various SWB scales and questionnaires: positive affect, absence of negative affect and a cognitive judgment of life satisfaction. That these phenomena can, to some extent, exist independently of each other was suspected already in the 1970s. More recent statistical analyses of questionnaire responses confirmed their discriminant validity (Diener and Emmons 1985, Arthaud-Day et al. 2005). It seems reasonable that all three of these phenomena form part of the overall SWB (though this argument is rarely made explicitly[7]). So it is now thought that a proper measure of SWB must include the proportion of positive to negative emotions and a considered judgment as to the state of one's life (Diener and Seligman 2004). However, there is a decent correlation between affect and life satisfaction, at least by the standards of psychology.[8] It is thus common practice to administer only the Satisfaction With Life Scale (the best current measure of life satisfaction) and to claim that one has measured SWB as a whole (Diener et al. 1985, Diener and Seligman 2004).

Exceptions to this rule are the researchers who stick to a more monolithic hedonistic understanding of well-being, focusing only on the subject's raw experience of life, not on their judgment about whether their life is going well (Kahneman et al. 2004, Gilbert 2006, Layard 2005, etc.). This restriction is often motivated by the instability of the judgments of life satisfaction, that is, their sensitivity to various features of context in which this judgment is made (Schwarz and Strack 1991, 1999). But even those researchers who focus on the hedonic quality of life agree that life satisfaction represents an important dimension of well-being (Kahneman and Riis 2005).

When psychologists studying SWB discuss the relevance of their work to policy, they almost always say or assume that SWB constitutes well-being proper, and that policy discussions should take into account, among other things, the impact of new policies on SWB (Diener and Seligman 2004, Layard 2005, Diener et al. 2008, Dolan and White 2007, Kahneman et al. 2004). There is some concern about whether SWB and well-being proper are coextensive, but even if they are not, SWB is better at tracking well-being proper than the standard economic indicators, and hence should be used (Dolan and Peasgood 2008). Since on any conception of SWB individuals suffer acutely the effects of unemployment and social isolation, these areas are often proposed as crucial for policy interventions (Kahneman and Krueger 2006, Diener et al. 2008). This picture, I submit, is not an endorsement, explicit or implicit, of WBI.

First of all, well-being variantism allows that there exist contexts in which SWB is the correct (or more or less correct) construct of well-being. Perhaps one such context is the evaluation of policy measures designed to improve well-being of a large group of middle-class Westerners, whose basic needs are satisfied and who are not likely to be strongly deceived about their objective situation.

Secondly, SWB is useful as a construct even if one does not take it to constitute well-being in all, nor even in *any*, contexts. It may constitute the subjective aspect of the various local notions of well-being. As such SWB can be embedded into the more context-specific constructs. This is indeed the current practice as I described it in the sections on gerontology and the study of child well-being. People suffering from mental health problem, caregivers, commuters, and so on can all be helped enormously if their SWB is improved, but, judging by the constructs currently used, SWB is not the only indicator or constituent of how well they are doing (Dolan and White 2007, 80).

Finally, even if some rhetoric in this field is invariantist, many practices of construct choice and measurement are variantist. Ken Kendler, an eminent psychiatrist at Virginia Commonwealth University, studies genetic influences on mental health and well-being. When I asked him why he does not use subjective measures of well-being in his twin studies he explained that these measures might conceal the use of mood-altering medications, which, if present, indicate ill-being instead. Thus subjective constructs can fail to be valid (Kendler 2007). In the context Kendler is working in, a more objective notion of positive functioning, similar to number 3 on the list above, is better than SWB (Kendler, Myers, and Neale 2000). Recent proposals to identify mental health with psychological and social flourishing, a notion far richer and more objective than SWB, follows the same reasoning: In contexts studied in psychiatry and clinical psychology we need more than SWB to pin down well-being (Keyes 2002).

26.3. PART II

26.3.1. Can Well-Being Invariantism Be Salvaged? Should It Be?

Worries and skepticism about the possibility of one grand theory of well-being are not new in philosophy. Recently, both Thomas Scanlon and James Griffin expressed doubts about the possibility of one general theory of well-being. Scanlon worries that this one notion cannot play the three roles it has been assigned: to help individual deliberation, to regulate third-person beneficence, and to be a consideration in political theory. It is likely that we shall have to develop separate notions for each of these purposes (Scanlon 1998, 118). Griffin questioned the very existence of a single notion of well-being, hypothesizing that instead philosophers have been speaking "of quite different things" (happiness, quality of life, etc.) without disagreeing with each other (Griffin 2007).[9]

We can now see that the common practice in the social and medical sciences raises similar doubts. The current practice of adjusting the construct of well-being to the specific characteristics of the subjects and the situation implicitly rejects WBI. It does so in two ways: first, by defining well-being as many different context-specific rather than exclusively general evaluations, and, second, by using different substantive theories to identify its constituents, sometimes one and at other times another.

But, of course, actual scientific practice is only some evidence for or against a philosophical position. To mount an argument in favor of WBV, we need reasons to think that the current scientific practice is indeed generally successful at identifying well-being. This is precisely the claim that an invariantist will contest. So let us see why the invariantist's response will not do.

The response invokes what I have called a circumscription strategy. According to this strategy the focus of well-being proper is distinct from happiness, quality of life, good functioning, welfare, and so forth. Well-being overlaps with these concepts, because quality of life, happiness, etc., are arguably necessary for well-being, but it is not coextensive with them (see Scanlon 1998, among many others, for such an argument). Well-being is a concept applicable only in a very specific context, when an individual's life is evaluated as a whole, all things considered. In all other contexts, such as when we are talking about how well a country, a depressed caregiver, or a child is doing, we should be using other concepts, for example, quality of life or mental health.

There are several problems with the circumscription strategy. The biggest problem is that in restricting the concept to such narrow confines this response makes well-being much less useful and relevant in practice. Sure, it is important to consider one's life as a whole, but most of the time we don't do that. In the great majority of circumstances, a locally appropriate notion of well-being helps us to deliberate about where we stand and what we should do. Knowing that my grandfather is doing well or badly for an eighty-year-old with Parkinson's disease helps me decide on the course of action. This judgment takes into account his health (using a fairly low threshold given the circumstances) and emotional well-being, *not* whether his life as a whole instantiates the ideal that he would wholeheartedly endorse given full information (or whatever else the true well-being is according to our best philosophical theory). It is not clear what resources a circumscription strategist would have me use for this purpose.

The second problem is to explain the apparent divergence between the way regular folk and social scientists use the language of well-being and the way circumscriptionists say we should. The circumscriptionist is clearly in the minority. Certainly, the majority usage is not a trumping consideration for evaluating any philosophical view, but a consideration nonetheless. If, as I have argued, the concept of well-being is used in ways radically different from those assumed by a philosophical view, then it is incumbent upon philosophers to justify their ways. Specifically they are committed to an error theory that claims that speakers routinely fail to appreciate the true scope of the notion of well-being. The vast majority of uses of well-being in everyday and scientific contexts are mistaken.

Justifying this error theory is a tall order. It requires an appeal to special authority of philosophers over social scientists and the folk. Questions such as "How are you doing?," "How is life going for Somalis?," "What is the state of our children?" are, as far as the latter are concerned, questions about well-being, in places where, according to the invariantist, other notions should be used.

On top of the error theory, the invariantist also has to motivate the restriction of the function of well-being in accordance with the circumscription strategy. What is the boundary where well-being ends and quality of life, happiness, good functioning, etc. begin? Why can't this boundary depend on context? Until we have plausible answers to these questions, we should give variantism a chance.

My prima facie case against well-being invariantism is based not on the fact that this view is at odds with scientific and everyday practice, but rather on the fact that this discrepancy is arbitrary, unmotivated, and offers no help with practical tasks that require an appeal to a notion of well-being.

These worries are not just theoretical. The discrepancy between the notions of well-being in philosophy, on the one hand, and in the sciences and everyday life, on the other, has very real consequences. It erects a wall of incommensurability between philosophy and other disciplines. With this wall in place it is hard to see how philosophers can participate in the debates happening right now about the relevance of well-being research for social policy. One might argue that so much the worse for philosophers. But they are not the only losers, since scientists themselves have no framework for understanding how the great variety of well-being constructs does or does not fit together. What is the alternative?

26.3.2. What Is Well-Being Variantism?

The time has come to articulate WBV in more detail. In section 26.1 I identified WBV with two proposals: first, the broadening of the concept of well-being to include context-specific as well as general evaluations and, second, the denial that one single substantive theory of well-being is able to yield the correct account of well-being in each case in which this concept applies. Both claims are motivated by the prevailing practices in the social and medical sciences. The first claim takes seriously the widespread and liberal use of well-being in contexts other than an all-things-considered general evaluation of a life as a whole. The second claim, though it has not received full attention in this chapter, reflects the fact that there does not appear to be one grand theory of well-being that motivates all the discipline-specific constructs, and that serves as the basis for deriving these constructs. It is indeed possible that such a theory does exist, but the existing scientific practices certainly do not manifest a reliance on or presupposition of such a theory. For all we know now, different fields operate with their own rough sketches of what constitutes well-being. There may be some substantive similarities between them, but whether or not these similarities amount to a full substantive theory of well-being remains to be shown.

I propose to flesh out the commitments of WBV using, in part, the tools of contextualism. Familiar from recent debates in epistemology and philosophy of language, contextualism is a view that the semantic content of propositions that attribute knowledge, and hence their truth conditions, vary with context. The context is defined not just by what evidence there is about the truth and justification of a belief but also by practical circumstances, for example, how much rides on the proposition being false. When not much rides on it, the standards are lower than otherwise and hence it takes less for the same knowledge sentence to come out true than when the stakes are higher.[10]

Contextualism about well-being extends this picture to the term "well-being" and its cognates, maintaining that the semantic content of sentences in which these occur depends on the context in which it is uttered. Thus "Subject X is doing well" (or "Subject X is not doing well") may express different propositions in the mouths of a developmental economist, clinical psychologist, or gerontolotist. Perhaps the most important consequence of this view is the impossibility of fully specifying the semantic content of well-being assertions *simpliciter*. Rather, their content needs to be specified by reference to certain specific practical circumstances (annual doctor's visit, extreme poverty relief on country-wide scale, heart-to-heart conversation with a friend, etc.). Since these circumstances will inevitably differ from situation to situation, so will the semantic content of well-being. In one situation, this content is minimal quality of life, in another healthiness, in another freedom from depression, and so on. The context of an all-things-considered evaluation of life as a whole privileged by philosophers is just that: *one* of the *many* contexts in which well-being is in question.

Propositions involving well-being may differ in what counts as the threshold that separates well-being from ill-being, as well as in the substantive definition of what well-being is. Thus in the context of development economics, the content of well-being expressions might essentially involve quality of life and a certain level of it, whereas in a different context, it might not. Constructs of well-being in the social and medical sciences pick out this variable semantic content. This explains why the notion of well-being may at times involve a general and at other times a context-relative evaluation.[11]

26.3.3. WBV: Rules for Proper Use

The goal of WBV is to eliminate or at least to narrow the gulf between the philosophical project and the scientific investigations of well-being, thus making it possible that the much needed normative analysis that philosophers can supply is brought to bear on the policy relevance of scientific findings about well-being. Of course, there is much more to be said about how this will actually be achieved. So I want to end with some details, promissory notes, and warnings:

1. **A mapping from constructs to contexts**: WBV promises to provide a proper way of marrying the empirical study of well-being with value judgments that are necessary for using this knowledge for policy. To make good on this promise, we need to supplement WBV with a mapping from constructs of well-being to contexts in which these constructs are appropriate. The exact nature of this mapping deserves a chapter unto itself, but some principles that should govern it are relatively clear. What standard of well-being is appropriate to what circumstances must depend, among other things, on the relationship between the subject(s) and the potential benefactor. Some relationships call for greater obligations than others. Plausibly, the closer the relationship between the subject and the benefactor, the richer and more demanding the appropriate notion of well-being is. Another relevant factor is the practical feasibility for a benefactor of a given course of action in a given situation. The less the benefactor can do for the subject of beneficence, the lower is the standard of well-being that the benefactor can set.[12]

2. **No relativism about well-being**. WBV does not imply that what well-being amounts to in a given situation is solely a matter of taste, opinion, or the psychological makeup, whether of the judge or the subject. Nothing in the contextualist articulation of WBV precludes us from setting objective constraints on the correctness of a given well-being standard. WBV advocates should allow that the subject of a well-being attribution, or the attributor for that matter, can be wrong about this attribution. She can do

so by appealing to objective features of a situation that make it the case that a certain notion and standard of well-being applies or does not apply to a given situation. The fact that these features may vary from case to case does not jeopardize their objectivity. However, WBV advocate insists that these objective constraints do not amount to a general all-purpose theory of well-being.

3. **Neither eliminativism, nor promiscuous pluralism.** WBV does not mean that every theory of well-being is correct in some context, nor necessarily that there is no such thing as well-being at all. Eliminativism can be precluded by specifying the common core features shared by all context-specific notions of well-being. A variantist is committed to denying that this common core constitutes a full theory of well-being, but not to the existence of some structural similarities between all well-being standards. The question is what these similarities are actually able to do in practice when it comes to evaluating construct pluralism. According to WBV, not much. Promiscuous pluralism can be stopped in its tracks too. WBV need not maintain that for every existing notion of well-being, there is a context in which it applies. Whether or not this is true depends on the precise nature of the mapping from constructs of well-being to contexts. It is perfectly conceivable that this mapping will leave some constructs without a context, or some contexts with several equally applicable constructs, and so forth.

4. **General evaluation of well-being still has a place**. Finally, WBV need not deny that sometimes we need to combine several context-specific constructs of well-being into a more general notion. There are situations, and not just on the deathbed, in which we need to aggregate the judgments of the development economist, the gerontologist, the psychologist, etc. In cases such as these, a good old philosophical all-things-considered analysis is still useful and indeed unavoidable. WBV need not be opposed to this goal. Rather it is opposed to treating this as a model for all uses of the notion of well-being.

ACKNOWLEDGMENTS

Many people helped me to develop and improve the ideas in this paper. I would like to thanks Dan Haybron, Valerie Tiberius, Mark Weber, Dan Hausman, Don Ross, Harold Kincaid, Irem Kurtsal Steen, Gualtiero Piccinini, Brit Brogaard, Tyler Paytas, John Doris, Simine Vazire, Robert Northcott, and audiences at the Saint Louis University Philosophy Department Colloquium in September 2008, Washington University in St. Louis Philosophy-Neuroscience-Psychology Colloquium in January 2010, the Central Division of the American Philosophical Association meeting in February 2010, the Boulder Conference in

History and Philosophy of Science in October 2009, University of Missouri-St. Louis Works in Progress Series February 2009, and the Methods of Social Science conference in Birmingham, Alabama April 2010.

NOTES

1. Of course, deathbed is not the only context in which we evaluate a life as a whole.

2. Naturally, this theory does so at a very general level without implying that only a certain specific kind of life can be good for a person.

3. I owe the term "variantism" to Doris, Knobe, and Woolfolk 2007.

4. See Raz 2004 for a similar observation.

5. See Haybron 2008 for an articulation of this methodology.

6. This questionnaire consists of forty-eight questions about five areas: pain, physical function (activities of daily living such as sleep, bath and toilet, dressing, jobs around the house, mobility), social function, general health perception, and mental function.

7. Though see Kim-Prieto et al. 2005.

8. The cognitive and the affective portions of SWB are distinct phenomena. That people can score high on life satisfaction and low on positive affect (and the other way around) is not just intuitive, but actual. Studies find that the correlations between these two aspects of SWB range from 0.3 to 0.7 (Arthaud-Day et al. 2005; Lucas, Diener, and Suh 1996). In some groups the correlations are weaker than in others; Asians appear to take less notice of their affect when judging their life satisfaction than people from Western cultures (Suh et al. 1998). So it takes a philosophical judgment to unify the two phenomena into one construct.

9. For more doubts along these lines, see Kagan (1992) and for an anticipation of WBV, see Tiberius (2007).

10. See Rysiew (2007) for an overview of epistemic contextualism.

11. For reasons I discuss elsewhere, I believe contextualism is the best option for articulating WBV (Alexandrova Forthcoming). In particular, it is better than a version of subject-sensitive invariantism (Hawthorne 2004, Stanley 2005).

12. Often this feasibility will affect who the subject's state should be compared to, and depending on the contrast class—for example, Monaco or Port-au-Prince residents—a different standard will be appropriate.

REFERENCES

Anand. S., and A. Sen. 1994. "Human Development Index: Methodology and Measurement." Occasional Papers. Human Development Report Office. HDOCPA-1994-02 (1992–2007). United Nations Development Programme (UNDP).

Alexandrova, A. "Doing Well in the Circumstances". *The Journal of Moral Philosophy.* Forthcoming.

Arneson, R. 1999. "Human Flourishing Versus Desire Satisfaction." *Social Philosophy and Policy* 16 (1): 113–42.

Arthaud-Day, M. L., J. C. Rode, C. H. Mooney, and J. P. Near. 2005. "The Subjective Well-Being Construct: A Test of Its Convergent, Discriminant, and Factorial Validity." *Social Indicators Research* 74 (3): 445–76.

Ben-Arieh, A. 2000. "Beyond Welfare: Measuring and Monitoring the State of Children." *Social Indicators Research* 52 (3): 235–57.

Ben-Arieh, A. 2005. "Where are the Children? Children's Role in Measuring and Monitoring Their Well-Being." *Social Indicators Research* 74 (3): 573–96.

Ben-Arieh, A. 2006. "Is the Study of the 'State of our children' Changing? Re-Visiting After 5 Years." *Children and Youth Services Review* 28 (7): 799–811.

Benbenishty, R., and R. A. Astor. 2007. "Monitoring Indicators of Children's Victimization in School: Linking National-, Regional-, and Site-Level Indicators." *Social Indicators Research* 84 (3): 333–48.

Bergner, M., R. A. Bobbitt, W. B. Carter, and B. S. Gilson. 1981. "The Sickness Impact Profile: Development and Final Revision of a Health Status Measure." *Medical Care* 19 (8): 787–805.

Brandt, R. 1979. *A Theory of the Good and the Right*. Oxford: Clarendon Press.

Crisp, R. 2006. "Hedonism Reconsidered." *Philosophy and Phenomenological Research* 73 (3): 619–45.

Darwall, S. 2002. *Welfare and Rational Care*. Princeton, NJ: Princeton University Press.

Dasgupta, P. 2001. *Human Well-Being and the Natural Environment*. Oxford: Oxford University Press.

Diener, E. 1984. "Subjective Well-Being." *Psychological Bulletin* 95 (3): 542–75.

Diener, E., R. Lucas, U. Schimmack, and J. Helliwell. 2008. *Well-Being for Public Policy*. New York: Oxford University Press.

Diener, E., and R. A. Emmons. 1985. "The Independence of Positive and Negative Affect." *Journal of Personality and Social Psychology* 47 (5): 1105–17.

Diener, E., R. A. Emmons, R. J. Larsen, and S. Griffin. 1985. "The Satisfaction with Life Scale." *Journal of Personality Assessment* 49 (1): 71–75.

Diener, E., and M. Seligman. 2004. "Beyond Money: Toward an Economy of Well-Being." *Psychological Science in the Public Interest* 5 (1): 1–31.

Dolan, P., and T. Peasgood. 2008. "Measuring Well-Being for Public Policy: Preferences or Experiences?" *Journal of Legal Studies* 37 (June): S5–S31.

Dolan, P., and M. White. 2007. "How Can Measures of Subjective Well-Being Be Used to Inform Public Policy?" *Perspectives on Psychological Science* 2 (1): 71–85.

Doris, J. M., J. Knobe, and R. Woolfolk. 2007. "Variantism About Responsibility." *Philosophical Perspectives: Philosophy of Mind* 21 (1): 183–214.

Ereshefsky, M. 1998. "Species Pluralism and Anti-Realism." *Philosophy of Science* 65 (Mar.): 103–20.

Feldman, F. 2002. "The Good Life: A Defense of Attitudinal Hedonism." *Philosophy and Phenomenological Research* 65 (3): 604–28.

Fitzpatrick, R., A. Fletcher, S. Gore, D. Jones, D. Spiegelhalter, and D. Cox. 1992. "Quality of Life Measures in Health Care I. Applications and Issues in Assessment." *British Medical Journal* 305 (Oct.): 1074–7.

Fletcher, A., S. Gore, D. Jones, R. Fitzpatrick, D. Spiegelhalter, and D. Cox. 1992. "Quality of Life Measures in Health Care. II. Design, Analysis and Interpretation." *British Medical Journal* 305 (Nov.): 1145–8.

Fredrickson, B. L., and M. F. Losada. 2005. "Positive Affect and the Complex Dynamics of Human Flourishing." *American Psychologist* 60 (7): 678–86.

Gerritsen, P., and P. Van Der Ende. 1994. "The Development of a Care-Giving Burden Scale." *Age and Ageing* 23 (6): 483–91.

Gilbert, D. T. 2006. *Stumbling on Happiness*. New York: Knopf.

Griffin, J. 1986. *Well-Being: Its Meaning, Measurement and Moral Importance*. Oxford: Clarendon Press.

Griffin, J. 2007. "What Do Happiness Studies Study?" *Journal of Happiness Studies* 8 (1): 139–48.

Griffiths, P. E. 2002. "What Is Innateness?" *The Monist* 85 (1): 70–85.

Griffiths, P. E., and K. Stotz. 2006. "Genes in the Postgenomic Era?" *Theoretical Medicine and Bioethics* 27 (6): 499–521.

Hawthorne, J. 2004. *Knowledge and Lotteries*. New York: Oxford University Press.

Haybron, D. 2008. *The Pursuit of Unhappiness*. New York: Oxford University Press.

Hunt, S., J. McEwen, and S. P. McKenna. 1985. "Measuring Health Status: A New Tool for Clinicians and Epidemiologists." *The Journal of the Royal College of General Practitioners* 35 (273): 185–8.

Kagan, S. 1992. "The Limits of Well-Being." *Social Philosophy and Policy* 9 (2): 180–98.

Kahneman D., and J. Riis. 2005. "Living, and Thinking About It: Two Perspectives on Life." In *The Science of Well-Being*, F. A. Huppert, N. Baylis, and B. Keverne, eds., 285–304. Oxford: Oxford University Press.

Kahneman, D., and A. B. Krueger. 2006. "Developments in the Measurement of Subjective Well-Being." *Journal of Economic Perspectives* 20 (1): 3–24.

Kahneman, D., A. Krueger, D. Schkade, N. Schwartz, and A. Stone. 2004. "Toward National Well-Being Accounts." *American Economic Review* (May): 429–34.

Kahneman, D. 1999. "Objective Happiness." In *Well-Being: The Foundations of Hedonic Psychology*, D. Kahneman, E. Diener, and N. Schwarz, eds., 3–25. New York: Russell Sage.

Kendler, Ken. 2007. Personal conversation. February.

Kendler K. S., J. M. Myers, and M. C. Neale. 2000. "A Multidimensional Twin Study of Mental Health in Women." *American Journal of Psychiatry* 157 (4): 506–13.

Keyes, C. L. M. 2002. "The Mental Health Continuum: From Languishing to Flourishing in Life." *Journal of Health and Social Behavior* 43 (June): 207–22.

Kim-Prieto, C., E. Diener, M. Tamir, C. N. Scollon, and M. Diener. 2005. "Integrating the Diverse Definitions of Happiness: A Time-Sequential Framework of Subjective Well-Being." *Journal of Happiness Studies* 6 (3): 261–300.

Layard, R. 2005. *Happiness: Lessons from a New Science*. London: Penguin.

Lever, J. 2000. "The Development of an Instrument to Measure Quality of Life in Mexico City." *Social Indicators Research* 50 (2): 187–208.

Lips, P., C. Cooper, D. Agnusdei, F. Caulin, P. Egger, O. Johnell, J. A. Kanis, U. Liberman, H. Minne, J. Reeve, J.-Y. Reginster, M. C. de Vernejoul, and I. Wiklund 1997. "Quality of Life as Outcome in the Treatment of Osteoporosis: The Development of a Questionnaire for Quality of Life by the European Foundation for Osteoporosis." *Osteoporos International* 7 (1): 36–38.

Lips, P., and C. Cooper, D. Agnusdei, F. Caulin, P. Egger, O. Johnell, J.A. Kanis, S. Kellingray, A. Leplege, U.A. Liberman, E. McCloskey, H. Minne, J. Reeve, J.-Y. Reginster, M. Scholz, C. Todd, M.C. de Vernejoul, and I. Wiklund for the Working Party for Quality of Life of the European Foundation for Osteoporosis. 1999. "Quality of Life in Patients with Vertebral Fractures: Validation of the Quality of Life Questionnaire of the European Foundation for Osteoporosis (QUALEFFO)." *Osteoporos International* 10 (2): 150–60.

Lucas, R. E., E. Diener, and E. Suh. 1996. "Discriminant Validity of Well-Being Measures." *Journal of Personality and Social Psychology* 71 (3): 616–28.

Parfit, D. 1984. *Reasons and Persons*. Oxford: Oxford University Press.

Pedersen, J., and T. Sommerfelt. 2007. "Studying Children in Armed Conflict: Data Production, Social Indicators and Analysis." *Social Indicators Research* 84 (3): 251–69.

Railton, P. 1986. "Facts and Values." *Philosophical Topics* 14 (2): 5–31.

Raz, J. 2004. "The Role of Well-Being." *Philosophical Perspectives* 18 (1): 269–94.

Ryff, C. 1989. "Happiness Is Everything, Or Is It?: Explorations on the Meaning of Psychological Well-Being." *Journal of Personality and Social Psychology* 57 (6): 1069–81.

Rysiew, Patrick. "Epistemic Contextualism." *The Stanford Encyclopedia of Philosophy (Winter 2011 Edition)*, Edward N. Zalta, ed. Available at <http://plato.stanford.edu/archives/win2011/entries/contextualism-epistemology/>, accessed on January 3, 2011.

Scanlon, T. M. 1998. *What We Owe to Each Other*. Cambridge, MA: Harvard University Press.

Schwarz, N., and F. Strack. 1991. "Evaluating One's Life: A Judgment Model of Subjective Well-Being." In *Subjective Well-Being*, F. Strack, M. Argyle, and N. Schwarz, eds., 27–47. Elmsford, NY: Pergamon Press.

Schwarz, N., and F. Strack. 1999. "Reports of Subjective Well-Being: Judgmental Processes and Their Methodological Implications." In *Well-Being: The Foundations of Hedonic Psychology*, D. Kahneman, E. Diener, and N. Schwarz, eds., 61–84. New York: Russell Sage.

Stanley, J. 2005. *Knowledge and Practical Interests*. New York: Oxford University Press.

Stull, D. E., K. Kosloski, and K. Kercher. 1994. "Caregiver Burden and Generic Well-Being: Opposite Sides of the Same Coin?" *The Gerontologist* 34 (1): 88–94.

Suh, E., E. Diener, S. Oishi, and H. Triandis. 1998. "The Shifting Basis of Life Satisfaction Judgments Across Cultures: Emotions Versus Norms." *Journal of Personality and Social Psychology* 74 (2): 482–93.

Sumner, L. W. 1996. *Welfare, Happiness, and Ethics*. Oxford: Clarendon Press.

Takai, M., M. Takahashi, Y. Iwamitsu, N. Ando, S. Okazaki, K. Nakajima, S. Oishi, and H. Miyaoka. 2009. "The Experience of Burnout Among Home Caregivers of Patients with Dementia: Relations to Depression and Quality of Life." *Archives of Gerontology and Geriatrics* 49 (1): e1–e5.

Tiberius, V. 2007. "Substance and Procedure in Theories of Prudential Value." *Australasian Journal of Philosophy* 85 (3): 373–91.

Visser-Meily, A., M. Post, V. Schepers, and E. Linderman. 2005. "Spouses' Quality of Life 1 Year after Stroke: Prediction at the Start of Clinical Rehabilitation." *Cerebrovascular Diseases* 20 (6): 443–48.

Wilson, M. 2006. *Wandering Significance: An Essay on Conceptual Behavior*. Oxford University Press.

INDEX

....

Printed and bound by CPI Group (UK) Ltd, Croydon, CR0 4YY